IF BOOK DAMAGED
PLEASE TELL STAFF

Continuing Canadian Constitutional Dilemmas

Wapiti regional library

Continuing Canadian Constitutional Dilemmas

Essays on the Constitutional History,
Public Law and Federal System
of Canada

W. R. Lederman,
Q.C., B.A., LL.B., B.C.L., LL.D., F.R.S.C.
Professor of Law
Queen's University
Kingston.

8514745

PAPL
DISCARDED

Butterworths
Toronto

Continuing Canadian Constitutional Dilemmas

© 1981 Butterworth & Co. (Canada) Ltd.

All rights reserved. No part of this publication may be reproduced, stored in a retrieval system, or transmitted, in any form or by any means, photocopying, electronic, mechanical, recording, or otherwise, without the prior written permission of the copyright holder.

Printed and bound in Canada

The Butterworth Group of Companies

Canada:
Butterworth & Co. (Canada) Ltd., Toronto
Butterworth & Co. (Western Canada) Ltd., Vancouver

United Kingdom:
Butterworth & Co. (Publishers) Ltd., London, Borough Green

Australia:
Butterworths Pty. Ltd., Sydney, Melbourne, Brisbane, Perth, Norwood

New Zealand:
Butterworths of New Zealand Ltd., Wellington

South Africa:
Butterworth & Co. (South Africa) Ltd., Durban

United States:
Butterworth (Publishers) Inc., Boston
Butterworth (Legal Publishers) Inc., Seattle
Butterworth & Co. Ltd., Ann Arbor
Mason Publishing Company, St. Paul

Canadian Cataloguing in Publication Data

Lederman, William R., 1916-
   Continuing Canadian constitutional dilemmas

ISBN 0-409-84460-8 pa ISBN 0-409-84461-6 bd

1. Canada—Constitutional law—Addresses, essays, lectures. I. Title.

KE4219.5.L43   342.71   C80-094843-2

Printed by John Deyell Company

Foreword*

The emergence of this volume of Professor Lederman's "Essays on The Constitutional History, Public Law and Federal System of Canada" is an event of great significance for Canadian constitutional law. It contains most of Lederman's seminal essays on constitutional law in the broadest sense over a period of 25 years (1953-79), which hitherto were scattered in legal journals and in a dozen other volumes of essays contributed by a variety of authors.

Bringing them within the covers of a single volume is an important event because Lederman is a leading constitutional authority. I think I might say that he is the leading constitutional lawyer in Canada today who is giving nearly all his time and effort to thinking and writing about the constitution. We have not yet reached the point in Canada where a practising lawyer can build a rewarding practice on constitutional law alone, however able and knowledgeable he is: he needs other strings to his bow as well, and cannot focus all his attention on constitutional law alone. The academic lawyer teaching constitutional law in a law school therefore has the advantage if he is disposed to concentrate on deep thought and concentrated effort in that field.

At any rate, Lederman is the leading academic constitutional lawyer. This is testified to by the high value put on his opinion by governments, governmental agencies and leading corporations. More than one senior judge has told me that judges, faced with a difficult constitutional case, always want to know what Lederman has said on the matter.

The principal point supporting my judgment, however, is this volume of essays. In them, Lederman ranges over the whole field of our constitutional history, the clauses of the B.N.A. Act, and the leading judicial decisions interpreting those clauses.

In an essay on *Mr. Justice Rand and the Constitution* in this volume, he describes with favour, Rand's way with *stare decisis* which clearly is his own. Rand, he says (p. 389), was impatient with narrow and rigid doctrines of *stare decisis,* but remained loyal to, and respectful of them. At the same time, "he tended to look through and beyond the literal reasoning of previous cases to discover the broader principles of which these cases were but examples, and then to base his reasoning on those broader principles". This is Lederman's way too.

---

*By Dr. J. A. Corry, Principal Emeritus, Queen's University, Kingston.

He knòws it is a *constitution* that is to be interpreted, designed to guide and govern the polity over a long period of time and through changing circumstances, and *not* to be read in a narrow, niggling literal sense like an ordinary statute which the appropriate legislature can readily amend if the judges go off the rails. (Judges have too often asserted that the B.N.A. Act, being a statute, is to be interpreted in full obedience to well-known canons of statutory interpretation.) Without being cavalier about the canons, Lederman is as concerned with the spirit of the constitution as he is with the words in which it is phrased.

So, he is always mindful of the history of the efforts at Union and keeps searching for the "broader principles" on which the settlement of 1866-67 can be discerned to be based. His method for the search, he says, is philosophical-juristic, and painstaking analysis by this method in the 28 chapters gives a remarkable coherence and unity to the whole. This could only have been attained by a high level intelligence and prodigious energy. In addition, Lederman was extremely fortunate in his education.

I have often said that an able, industrious person cannot be ruined by any kind of education. But an education suited to one's temperament can fire enthusiasm and give direction and guidance to the work. Knowing, as I do, a good deal about his education, a few words about it may be illuminating. He took both an Arts degree and a Law degree at the University of Saskatchewan. He took History with George Simpson who knew how to make it live. He studied Political Science, and particularly Canadian Constitutional History, with R. MacGregor Dawson who lifted students out of their seats by his enthusiasm—and his stentorian voice: it was physically impossible to go to sleep in his class!

Lederman's arousal to philosophical-juristic considerations awaited his entry into the Saskatchewan Law School. The then Dean, Fred Cronkite was one of the early accomplished teachers of law in Canada with a marked philosophical bent. Among his favourite subjects were Jurisprudence and Canadian Constitutional Law which he taught for many years. Of an enquiring and skeptical mind, his teaching of Constitutional Law was permeated by juristic considerations. It was here that Lederman found a focus for his interests and energies.

Serving throughout the war in the Armed Forces, he was not able to take up his Rhodes Scholarship till 1946. But here again he was fortunate in coming under the influence of A. L. Goodhart, then Professor of Jurisprudence, in a course of lectures he gave in Jurisprudence. Also, he was in a small seminar Goodhart led in the same subject and this was supplemented by an extensive reading list covering the leading theoretical jurists. Here Lederman became familiar with the thinkers who appear often in the footnotes and quotations to these essays: Roscoe Pound, Morris Cohen, Hohfeld, John Dickinson, the Austrian analytic jurist Hans Kelsen, Olivecrona, the Swede, and others. His sustained application to these studies brought recognition: in 1948, he was awarded the Vinerian Scholarship, the blue ribbon prize in legal studies at Oxford.

From these sources, he learned how to avoid the traps into which budding jurists are likely to fall. He also learned to be extremely systematic. The original writing of these essays was spread over the last 25 years. Whenever intervening events have put a different face on the topic just discussed, or where he has changed his mind somewhat, the reader is told of it in an appendage to the essay: "Further Thoughts" or "Further Developments". We are not left in doubt where the author stands now.

Perhaps the leading example of his use of juristic method appears in Chapter 12, *Classification of Laws and the B.N.A. Act*. The light this piece of close reasoning throws on the problem of interpreting any law, and so on many of the puzzles dealt with in other essays, clears the fog that often envelops interpretation. It dispels the illusion that general words and phrases have a clear literal and exclusive meaning in relation to all the complex and varied sets of facts and circumstances which arise to be dealt with. Grammatical logic alone will often fail to give an answer. It shows us that the dream of distributing legislative power between provinces and a national federal government so clearly that no possible doubt can arise as to which legislature has the power is a chimera. In relation to particular facts and circumstances, genuine doubts will often arise, with equally able and honest judges taking different views.

To come right down to the specific, it shows that there will always be cases to which the most scrupulous logic does not give an answer. Arguments based on analogy to other clauses and facts or on some presumed intention of the founders will at times bring the judges out to different views.

Critics with strong views therefore, on occasion will feel driven to conclude that the judges, or at least some of them, are immune to logic, lack integrity, or are generally incompetent. Careful attention to Lederman's analysis in this essay and his use of it in many of these essays, particularly Chapters 14 and 15, will dispel most of these suspicions. But it still leaves an important question to be settled in these instances of genuine doubt: What is the individual judge to do when so confronted? The one thing he cannot do is refuse to give an answer; he must render a decision.

Lederman throughout these essays tells us what the judge's choices are. If the *constitution* does not tell him what to do, he must decide on some view of *policy*. But what view of policy?; *his own* preference for national or provincial power in the particular case before him? Or does he reflect on the likely consequences of preferring national power or provincial power: which would likely be the best for the country? Or on his estimate of which decision would be most likely to draw the support, or at least, resigned acceptance by the publics most deeply concerned? He must make value decisions. In the author's own words, on pp. 280-81, "the classification process joins logic with social fact, value decisions and the authority of precedents, to define the distribution of law-making powers. The reasoning involved is not automatic or mechanical; rather it makes the highest demands on learning, intellect, and conscience. It permits expression to the real issues of public policy. . . . [It] is the inevitable operating jurisprudence of the federal form of social order".

There are some clues in the essays to his own preferences in this kind of situation. In the two chapters in Part I, he goes into the fundamentals of the constitution: who has the supreme power—always a vexed question in a federal state like ours? He faults John Austin, a highly influential English jurist of the nine-teenth century for trying to find it in a specific group of persons, the persons who have supreme law-making power at the moment. Lederman's argument is more realistic: certain deep-rooted widely held beliefs have more enduring power than any ruling clique. Particularly in an effective democracy, such beliefs as no man is above the law, freedom of speech and assembly and the independence of the judges, even though rarely articulated, are bred in the bones of the people. They are very likely to be more powerful in the long-run. These particular ideas inci-dentally, as is seen in Chapter 1, were among those vital to Goodhart's analysis. These and other strongly held ideas are part of the Common Law, basically rooted in custom, drawing their power from the respect of the judges for them and their adherence to long-standing precedent.

In all this he is close to a pithy comment of David Hume: opinion is King. And here he disagrees profoundly with the American school of realist jurispru-dence which flourished in the 1920s and 1930s, holding that so called rules of law cannot bind the judges because the rules have no genuine existence. They held with Bentham that so-called rules labelled as duty, right, obligation, are nothing but metaphysical nonsense. So it was concluded that judges had to de-cide by gut-feeling. While asserting firmly that from time to time judicial deci-sions on the B.N.A. Act must rest on a view of policy, Lederman has great re-spect for the rules of the Common Law and the binding authority of precedent which he elaborates in Chapter 2 on the *Common Law System in Canada*. And he affirms that, while the Common Law and the Civil Law of Quebec are markedly different in content, the reasoning used by judges in both systems in applying their rules to particular cases is very similar.

Lederman is much more than a philosophical jurist. In Chapters 3, 4, and a long Chapter 7 he shows a thorough grasp and deep understanding of the varying fortunes of British legal and parliamentary systems in North America, culminat-ing in a federal system and a congressional governmental structure in the United States, a federal system married to a Parliamentary system in Canada, and broadly speaking, a remarkable copying of the essentials of the Common Law and its judicial institutions in both. He is thoroughly at home on the development of Canadian independence; and particularly on the detail of the safeguards that buttress the independence of the judiciary in Britain and here.

A topic very much on everybody's minds nowadays is the process of consti-tutional amendment, and the desirable changes which agreement on a method would facilitate. In the broadest sense, nearly all these essays bear more or less heavily on this topic. (See especially Chapter 4.)

This analysis highlights the critical role of the Supreme Court of Canada as the final authority on the meaning of the constitution and on the distribution of legislative authority between provincial legislatures and Parliament. Hence the current concern about the method of appointing its judges and the exact scope of its jurisdiction (seeing that there are inescapable human limits to what a single final court of appeal can digest and decide responsibly). Also, there have been mounting provincial anxieties about the regional distribution of appointments to it. Admittedly, it is important that the judges of the Court should be aware of, and sensitive to, provincial and regional concerns and aspirations within the larger framework of Canadian unity.

Lederman acknowledges this but thinks that provincial anxieties are exaggerated: the judges are not voting as provincial delegates but deciding according to a law which they have solemnly sworn to uphold. No doubt, at times strictly constitutional logic fails to provide them with an inevitable answer, and leaves them with a measure of discretion. They could retort with Abraham Lincoln's answer to charges of bias in his high office: ''the things I deal with are too vast for malice''!

Several essays in this collection deal with the various aspects of concern over the Supreme Court: (see particularly Chapters 6, 8, 10, 11, 14, 15, and 16). Some indication of the respect in which Professor Lederman is held by the judges can be gleaned from his arguments in Chapters 6 and 15 as certified to in Further Developments and References. At stake in these chapters just identified were two recent references by the Government of Canada to the Supreme Court on the validity of the federal Anti-inflation Act of 1975, and of a portion of the federal Bill C-60, 1978, raising the power of Parliament to modify the powers and composition of the Senate by Act of Parliament alone. In both cases, a majority of the Supreme Court preferred Lederman's views to those of the law officers of the Crown.

The fact that cases arise in which the Supreme Court rejects the views and arguments pressed by the Government of Canada should be reassuring rather than disturbing: at least it shakes the views of those who hold that the Supreme Court is in the Federal Government's pocket! Yet it is disquieting when the Federal Government can insist, as it did in the Senate Reference Case, that the powers of Parliament under the B.N.A. Act extend to matters on which the provincial governments are united in dissent. It shows that there are still obscurities in the Act over which reasonable men may differ and gives continuing relevance to the uncomfortable fact that we have never been able to agree on a method of amending the Act for the purposes of clearing up obscurities which Canadians can exercise without getting formal approval from Westminster.

One of the themes of these essays is the present way of amending the Act and the desirable changes in that method if we are to bring the Constitution home. Lederman thinks that, strictly speaking, the consent of all provinces as well as of the Federal Government is a necessary requirement for any change which affects the constitutional powers, rights and privileges of the provinces. He hopes for an agreement on a method along the lines of the Victoria Charter of 1971. At the very least, all the consents mentioned above would have to be secured for one last time if we are to get an acceptable formula for all future amendments.

Chapters 5 and 6 present a thoughtful, thorough and systematic discussion of this vexed question. Then, in the *Addendum,* Chapters 27 and 28, carry on with the topic into suggestions for the minimum content of the constitutional amendments needed now to deal with our present discontents.

Whatever the content of the amendments needed now, they cannot be expected to provide us with the ideal constitution many still dream of, one which sets up separate, water-tight, and utterly clear enumerations of federal and provincial powers which enable the federal Parliament and the provincial legislatures each to go its own sweet way, relying on its own taxing powers to meet its needs, without obtruding on one another and avoiding all collisions. If there ever was such a possibility, it is now gone forever!

Our affairs have become much more complex. The whole country is now locked in interdependence. The roles of governments, both federal and provincial, have increased enormously, and all have parts to play in keeping this interlocked and interdependent socio-economic structure in running order. We learned fifty years ago that there is no way in which each of these eleven units of government can separately of its own efforts and resources raise the revenues to match its responsibilities: so, looked at from one point of view, Canada now has only one public finance structure made to work by the Federal Government transferring public funds of varying amounts to several provinces in the form of equalization and stabilization payments.

In more recent years some of the entanglements of federal and provincial governments have become much more intricate and severe, due to proliferating and ever more complex technology which threatens to outrun our control, to rapid and dislocating social and economic change, and to changing social values to which governments must respond. Instances are consumer protection, disorderly urban growth and decay, and environmental pollution. The last of these is the most revealing of these problems. To endow any single government with the great range of powers needed to cope with the manifold aspects of pollution would make a mockery of the federal system and distributed legislative powers.

In 1867 the Fathers of Confederation found only two areas where legislative power over the same subject-matter seemed to need to be shared: agriculture and immigration. They dealt with these in s.95 of the B.N.A. Act, giving concurrent powers over these two areas and providing that where provincial legislation was repugnant to an existing act of Parliament the federal power should override the provincial. We tried to reduce the danger of such clashes (not always successfully) by understandings reached between federal and provincial governments.

For some time now, and with increasing frequency, the judges have been finding that sections 91 and 92 are not wholly separate compartments fully insulated from one another. Again and again, a subject-matter expressly reserved to one legislature or the other is found to have important aspects which fall also within the subject-matter conferred on the other level.

In such cases, there are only two choices. In one particular instance, the judges may be convinced that either the provincial or national aspect is the more important and therefore should be dominant. Or, failing such a conviction, the judges must imply some measure of concurrent power and stake out areas for concurrent operation. Attempts by the judges to sort out these puzzles are described in full detail in Chapter 13.

Such parcelling out is often delicate and difficult. And then to make it workable with a minimum of friction, there has to be close and continuous cooperation between federal and provincial governments. These areas of concurrent operation of federal and provincial laws have been one of the main sources of what has been called cooperative federalism for the last forty years.

The comparatively new constitutional issues raised by cooperative federalism are carefully explored and lucidly analyzed in Chapters 13, 17, 20 and 22. Attention is given to the machinery developed for federal-provincial consultation. It consists now mainly of a host of federal-provincial committees composed of officials of the several governments, engaged in hammering out many federal-provincial agreements, frequent meetings of both federal and provincial ministers and first ministers. Decisions are reached, approved and adopted almost entirely by the executive arm of the governments with very little participation by Parliament and the other legislatures. Chapter 22 deals with the problem of reconciling all this activity with the indispensable primacy of Parliament and legislatures. This issue is considered cautiously and anxiously there, with the author uncertain whether a constitutional amendment of our federal-provincial machinery for consultation will make the restoring of Parliament and legislatures easier to achieve.

To judge of the adequacy of the processes and machinery of the constitution and of its substantive provisions, one must first of all have a conception of its purpose; what do we want to achieve by it or prevent? This is why Goodhart insisted that ideas in the long run are more powerful than the men of power: they are certain to be under the domination of some ideas, good, silly, or wicked. In the Anglo-American world, at any rate, one of these sovereign ideas has been that those who govern do so as elected representatives subject to change. Lederman pays homage to that idea in the chapter we have just discussed. Another of these ideas is freedom of expression (which he describes as a "Master Principle"), along with a considerable list of supportive rights and freedoms needed to make freedom of expression genuinely effective in the practical world.

In Part V, Chapters 24-26, *Guaranteed Human Rights and Freedoms in Canada,* Lederman turns to the protection of human rights. First, he shows that juristic analysis reveals that the guarantee of human rights is not a simple matter. It is easy to give general expression to a right or freedom in a constitution. But that alone does not define the scope of the freedom or set its limits. Freedom is illusory unless it is freedom under law; limited by the right of others to an identical freedom. Also, a multitude of statutes confer rights and reciprocal duties. Not infrequently, two statutes of the same legislature or of coordinate legislatures will be inconsistent with each other in the rights they purport to secure. So there must be a higher law which can be read as determining which has the priority, or defining a compromise between them.

Bringing them down to earth in the concrete is the task of the judiciary. It has been said of the famous Bill of Rights in the American Constitution that the Supreme Court has had to write "reasonable" into every one of its clauses giving rights or freedoms. This is how freedom under law has been imported into the Constitution. Caution should be used by constitution-makers in distributing abstract general rights with too lavish a hand.

The main discussion in these chapters focuses mostly on the Canadian debate. First, whether to entrench highly valued human rights in the constitution, and if so, how many and how much, or to continue to rely on ordinary civil law and statutory provisions to protect them. The second is the special Canadian issue of French-English language rights which has been with us from the beginning and now is hotly debated. Perhaps the hottest issue and the most intractable is the right to education in the mother tongue.

In principle, Lederman has strong sympathies with those who assert the high importance of education in the mother tongue as a central feature of the right to freedom of expression. He says French-speaking minorities in Ontario and Manitoba have been unjustly denied it in the past. And now the English speaking minority in Quebec are faced with somewhat similar treatment. He does not venture final solutions but sees clearly that the present crisis in national unity is in large part, language related, and that solutions to it will involve compromise and much goodwill. And the nearer to unanimity we can come in reaching the compromises, the stronger the message to the judges, and the Supreme Court, the message that in their interpretation of the clauses on language rights, they should be guided, wherever possible by the purpose and spirit of the settlement expressed in these clauses.

Finally, there remains another group of essays which should be noted. These are found in Chapters 18-21. They focus on particular features of the distribution of powers in sections 91 and 92 and their interpretation by the courts: the power to create corporate bodies in relation to the functional distribution of legislative power; the power to implement treaty obligations; the power to tax and the power to spend (particularly the federal spending power) and the much contested power to tax and to allot revenues raised by federal taxation of natural resources. This latter power is a hotly debated matter between the federal government and several provincial governments, and it almost certainly will have to be part of any constitutional revision.

Lederman does not undertake to say what the solution of these contested issues should be; he recognizes that they are as much—or perhaps more—political than constitutional, and therefore for decision by negotiation between governments. His function is to clarify. And this he does coolly, judiciously and systematically, bringing to bear his jurisprudential analysis and his unrivalled knowledge of the course of interpretation of sections 91 and 92. Nevertheless he gives us some warnings at various places in these essays. On p. 281, "If we understand the [interpretation] process, we will expect neither too much nor too little of the constitutional distribution of legislative powers as it stands now, or as it may be if certain changes are made. There is much more room for reasonable differences of interpretation than people realize. These differences then should not be regarded as evidence of bad faith or ignorance; rather, they should be taken as a challenge calling for support of the working of our system of interpretation at its best level."

On p. 379, he states his two basic positions on constitutional development and reform. His first is the need to establish better, more systematic and more regular practices for federal-provincial consultation. I quote his second: "the basic background division of powers is the last thing you tamper with in seeking constitutional improvement, not the first thing. . . . the essence of co-operative federalism is federal-provincial agreements about complementary uses of these basic powers and resources, and so presupposes their stability. That is, unless the definitions of them remain reasonably constant as the basis of the autonomy of the parties, subject only to a process of gradual adjustment step by step, cooperative federalism will be frustrated.''

In relation to the view often expressed about inextricably entangled matters like environmental pollution, we are often told that there must be one single authority to deal with all aspects of such matters. Lederman disagrees—''I claim that this is a dangerous fallacy. To me, it is a dangerous oversimplification that could lead to constitutional chaos or to the end of federalism.'' There are many other firm assertions like these where there is no wavering.

These last quotes reveal some characteristics of the work as a whole. There is a vision which sees the constitution as a whole, sitting more or less comfortably within the wider policy. It enables the author to put first things first and to see that there is a future to be thought of as well as a past and a present. In the light of the circumstances as we now see them, there is a cool foresight and admirable caution. At a time, when there is so much worry, tension and confusion of tongues, and thus serious danger of precipitate action or inflammatory dissension, here is a voice counselling careful thought and moderation. It is an event of great significance for the country as a whole.

J. A. Corry,
Queen's University.
August 1980.

Preface

The essays collected in this volume identify and analyse basic themes and problems of the constitutional law of Canada in a broad sense, including (but not confined to) the nature of Canadian federalism since 1867. For this reason, though the essays were written over a period of some 25 years without a master plan in mind, they are not miscellaneous. In fact they have lent themselves, without too much straining, to a systematic rather than a chronological arrangement according to the subjects, processes or institutions dealt with.

While I have appended to some of the essays, especially the older ones, notes designed to bring them up-to-date in certain essentials, I do not claim that the overall result is complete coverage as if I *had* set out to compose in one operation a systematic treatise on Canadian constitutional law. Nevertheless I do claim that the coverage afforded by the collected essays is wide-ranging, reaching to most of the essential processes and institutions of our constitution which provide us with government under the rule of law. Dr. J. A. Corry's foreword encourages me to think that this claim is valid.

At this point let me say how very much I am in debt to Dr. Corry for his generous foreword. In it he tells of my educational background, gives a synopsis of the systematic coverage of the essays, and renders a favourable judgment on their quality, for all of which I am indeed most grateful.

There are just two additional items of some interest that I might add here to what Dr. Corry has said. First, at the heart of my reasoning about the interpretation of Canada's federal distribution of legislative powers is the logical and philosophical process of the classification of laws and legal issues. Some authorities prefer to speak of "characterization" rather than "classification"—the words are synonymous. In any event this process and theory is also at the heart of choice-of-law problems in Private International Law (a subject alternatively called the Conflict of Laws). The fact is that I first became interested in classification theory in connection with the study of Private International Law, which was one of my main preoccupations at Oxford from 1946 to 1948. There I became familiar with the very extensive literature in English on classification in the Conflict of Laws, including essays on the subject by Dr. J. D. Falconbridge of the Osgoode Hall Law School, who was a distinguished international authority in these matters. In an essay on the Conflict of Laws published in 1937,[1] and also in later essays, Dr. Falconbridge commented in passing that the characterization

---

[1](1937), 53 Law Quarterly Review 235, at 253.

problems typical of the Conflict of Laws were also basic to the interpretation of Canada's federal system for the distribution of legislative powers between the central parliament and the provincial legislatures. "There is an obvious analogy", he said, "between the problem of characterization as it may present itself in the conflict of laws, and as it may present itself in connection with legislative power in Canada".[2]

Falconbridge did not himself pursue the implications of this observation for the analysis of problems of Canadian constitutional law. Rather, he stayed with his studies of the Conflict of Laws. In any event, when I came across his observation, I soon realized that he had suggested a fruitful theme for a student of Canadian federalism to explore and develop, in theory and in explanation of the constitutional cases in the courts. Shortly after I returned from Oxford to a career of legal teaching and research in Canada, I took up this line of enquiry. The first result was my essay entitled "Classification of Laws and the B.N.A. Act", published in 1953. It forms Chapter 12 in this collection. And in later essays, also reproduced in this volume, I further developed and refined the reasoning of 1953. So, as a matter of legal science and philosophy, I first discovered systematic classification theory and jurisprudence in connection with Private International Law, and then found it transferable in aid of the understanding of federal constitutional law. It was valuable indeed for me to confirm in my own experience early in my career that good general theory crosses boundaries.

The second item I would add to the foreword concerns Dr. Corry himself. Our paths never crossed as teacher and student, but I learned from him none the less. I read with great profit, as did so many others, his master treatise entitled "Democratic Government and Politics", first published in 1946. To give but one example of my scholarly benefit from this, readers of Part V of these essays, on guaranteed human rights and freedoms, will see that I owe much to Dr. Corry's wisdom concerning which are the more important political rights and civil liberties to be given special protection as the basis of a democratic constitution.

W. R. Lederman,
Queen's University.
August 1980.

---

[2]*Essays on the Conflict of Laws*, J. D. Falconbridge, 2nd ed. (Toronto: Canada Law Book Co. Ltd., 1954), p. 88.

Acknowledgements

The author is indeed grateful for the consents given, by those who first published these essays, to their re-publication in this collection. For each essay, the citation for the first publication is given.

I thank also Mrs. Netta Falder for excellent secretarial assistance over the many months required to put this collection together.

Finally, my thanks are due to the editorial staff of Butterworth & Co. (Canada) for their patience, and their untiring efforts to produce this book in good form and good time.

Table of Contents

Part I
The Nature of Constitutions and of Legal Reasoning

Chapter 1

Characteristics of Constitutional Law*

Reprinted with permission from Ontario *Royal Commission Inquiry into Civil Rights*, Part IV, Report No. 2, 1969.

Some appreciation of the broad sweep of a comprehensive document declaring the rights of individuals can be gained by reading the preamble and the thirty articles of the Universal Declaration of Human Rights of the United Nations. Here are expressed succinctly and in very general terms the qualitative standards which the modern State is expected to meet in and throughout its legal system, in discharging its responsibilities for the welfare of its citizens in a healthy economy. The Universal Declaration is recognized as a great document. It has had a far-reaching beneficial effect as a persuasive and educational document. Nevertheless, reading it leads to the realization that a comprehensive "Bill of Rights" opens up issues of fairness and justice in great detail over the whole range of the public and private law system of the country. All laws are concerned with human conduct in some form. Every law necessarily affects the rights, powers, liberties and obligations of some person or group in relation to other persons or groups. Almost every law defines someone's "right" and imposes some obligations on someone, including officeholders at all levels of government as well as private citizens.

The Federal Government has proposed "A Constitutional Bill of Rights" to bind Canada and the provinces as superior constitutional law. In order to assess this proposal, and the available alternatives properly, one must first examine the different senses in which the word "constitutional" is used. This is particularly necessary because of the potentially ubiquitous character of such general declarations or catalogues of human rights.

I. CONSTITUTIONAL LAW IN THE BROAD SENSE

As Sir Ivor Jennings has said,[1] in a sense all law is constitutional law. Even the most particular laws and legal decisions must be legitimate in the sense that their validity can be traced to the first principles of the constitution. The law

---

*As a consultant to the Royal Commission, W. R. Lederman was joint author with the Honourable J. C. McRuer, the Commissioner, of this portion of the Commission's Report.

[1]Jennings, *The Law and The Constitution* (5th ed.) Chapters II, III, Appendix IV; See also Kelsen, *General Theory of Law and State,* Chapters X, XI.

against theft and convictions under it are valid because the offence is expressed in a statute of the Parliament of Canada, the Criminal Code. The statute is valid because it is "Criminal Law" which is one of the subjects of federal power conferred on the Canadian Parliament under the British North America Act, an Act of the British Parliament, which continues to provide the basic federal law of Canada and given the first principles of the primary division of law-making powers between Canada and the Provinces. But the whole legal system cannot be regarded as superior constitutional law. So when one speaks of a "constitutional" Bill of Rights, one is using the word "constitutional" in a limited sense.

Some jurists divide all laws into two categories, public law and private law, and it is a proper sense of the term "constitutional law" to consider it as synonymous with "public law". This is a more limited, but still very broad sense of the term. It excludes the provisions of private law, the law primarily concerned with relations between private citizens, for example, the bodies of law concerned with property, contract and tort (or delict).

Normally officials in public office do not intervene in the legal relations of private citizens except to vary the content of the laws by legislation, if that is deemed necessary, or to give them authoritative interpretation when disputes arise between private parties in their relations with one another. On the other hand, public law as constitutional law defines all the offices of the State from the highest to the lowest, distinguishing all official persons (office holders) from private citizens. It tells us for instance who are for the time being the members of parliament, the cabinet ministers, the judges, the municipal councillors, the civil servants and policemen. It tells us how they attain office (by election or appointment) and how they may be removed and replaced from time to time. Public law tells us what the respective powers of office holders are and the procedures they must follow for the valid exercise of their powers—that is, how they are to exercise official discretions, entrusted to them by law. Constitutional law as total public law then is concerned with the definition of public offices and the powers and activities of all official persons as such. Students of the constitution must seek out the general principles or ideas that are implicit in and constitute guidelines for the total of valid official activity.[2]

II. CONSTITUTIONAL LAW IN THE LIMITED SENSES

There is however, a narrower use of the term "constitutional law" which is often employed and which confines the sense of the phrase to only a part of public law, the part that is at times found enshrined in some countries in a single document of great authority. Sir Ivor Jennings seems to favour this use of the term. He says:

> The word constitution . . . means the document in which are set out the rules governing the composition, powers and methods of operation of the *main* institu-

---

[2]No doubt there is a twilight zone between public and private law, for example, in the regulation of relations of labour and management in industry. Nevertheless, the distinction stands as a matter of main emphasis.

tions of government, and the *general principles* applicable to their relations to the citizens.[3]

The author cites the Constitution of Ireland and the Constitution of the United States as outstanding examples. He then goes on to point out that you cannot find any similar single document that expresses the constitutional law of Britain as a superior type of public law. Nevertheless, as he makes clear, the United Kingdom does have a system of public law covering these areas, though its different parts take various legal forms, i.e., customs, conventions, common law dependent upon judicial precedent and ordinary statutes of Parliament. As far as Britian herself is concerned, constitutional law embraces the rules governing the composition, powers and methods of operation of the *main* institutions of government, and the *general principles* applicable to their relations to the citizens, whatever the legal or documentary forms involved in the expression of these rules may be. This is a material definition of constitutional law dependent upon content and not upon form.

There are other formal or procedural definitions of the word constitutional, where, for example, certain principles or rights are said to be "constitutional" because, regardless of content, they are included in a special document, or because an extraordinary method of legal change (amendment) is applicable to them. These other meanings will be discussed later.

A very basic question now arises whether one thinks of constitutional law as the whole of public law or in the more limited sense suggested by Sir Ivor Jennings. Where does sovereignty lie in this official organization and apparatus of the State? Does it lie in a special group of persons or in a special set of concepts or ideas? John Austin's theory of sovereignty is that it lies in a special group of persons.[4] Unfortunately his theory has had a significant influence on English legal thinking and some still accept its basic premises concerning supreme power or sovereignty in the state.

(a) Austin's Theory of Sovereignty

The Austinian theory of sovereignty was that total and final legal supremacy in the modern state was both personal and fully concentrated on all matters whatsoever. His starting point was to observe the system of order in a particular country and, as a matter of observable social fact, to seek the answer to this question: upon which person or group of persons does the obedience of the bulk of society eventually and finally centre? That person or group of persons was for him the sovereign person or group. All other persons in the society were subject to the commands of the superior person or persons. Their commands were the laws. Austin recognized delegation of the commanding power and thus subordinate legislation, but nevertheless, when one traced the delegations to their source, the source was the one sovereign group of actual persons exercising sovereign authority, simply because the sovereign group were the focus

---

[3]Jennings, *The Law and The Constitution* (5th ed.) 33. (Italics added.)
[4]Austin, *Lectures on Jurisprudence,* Vol. 1, 223, 247, 261, 269 (1885).

of general social obedience. They had the power to accompany their commands with effective sanctions, to be applied against the disobedient members of society. Thus, as Austin put it, sanction is the badge of law, the characteristic mark of all laws.

Austin admitted there were moral and political limitations on the sovereign group of persons, but no legal limitations by constitutional law or any other kind of positive law. By this definition, then, the sovereign group of persons were *above the law*, for they could not be subject to that of which they were the source. The sovereign group were, for him, real and identifiable persons at any given moment in the life of the State.

The Austinian theory then means that the primary group of official persons in the state could put themselves beyond any legal controls whatever. It means, among other things, that there is no such thing as international law, but just certain rules of international positive morality that the sovereign groups of each national State respect or not as they choose and as it suits them. This concept of personification of power becomes of great importance when we come to discuss the constitutional entrenchment of a Bill of Rights.

Austin's principal subject of study was Nineteenth Century Britain, and there he found that the primary or sovereign group were the Members of the House of Commons with the Lords and the Queen, though he did recognize a sort of political trusteeship in the Members of the House of Commons for the benefit of the electorate. Indeed he falls into some confusion on this point.

(b) Dicey's Theory of Sovereignty

Professor Dicey, in his classic Nineteenth Century work, *The Law of the Constitution* stated his view of the legal supremacy of Parliament in this way:

> The principle of Parliamentary sovereignty means neither more nor less than this, namely, that Parliament [the Queen, the House of Lords, and the House of Commons] . . . has, under the English Constitution, the right to make or unmake any law whatever; and, further, that no person or body is recognized by the law of England as having a right to override or set aside the legislation of Parliament.[5]

> The one fundamental dogma of English constitutional law is the absolute legislative sovereignty or despotism of the King in Parliament.[6]

Dicey added to this Austinian view of Parliamentary sovereignty the idea that nothing was law that would not be recognized and enforced as such by the traditional courts.

(c) The Sovereignty of the Ideas of the People

Austin was wrong to consider that final power in the state at any given time must necessarily be both fully personified and fully concentrated on all conceivable subjects of law-making. In other words, he was wrong to consider that the social obedience of most of the people must centre most of the time on an

---

[5]Dicey, *The Law of the Constitution* (10th ed. 1961), 39-40.
[6]*Ibid.*, 145.

actual group of superior official persons, persons who would therefore be themselves above the law. This error of the personification of final law-making power is dangerous to the rights of ordinary citizens. The truth lies elsewhere.

It is certain organizing ideas for the relevant society and not certain official persons that are supreme or sovereign. The primary organizational ideas of a modern state are its fundamental constitutional laws. It is those primary doctrines, principles and procedures that are the focus of obedience; they are supreme, not particular persons in office at particular times. It is fundamental to "The Rule of Law" that in the end such enduring ideas are supreme and, therefore, it follows that all officeholders are under the law, none are above it. This principle was recently affirmed as part of the general public law of Canada by the Supreme Court of Canada in the case of *Roncarelli v. Duplessis*. [7]

Law is not primarily a matter of coercion and punishment, rather it is primarily a matter of setting standards for society and devising solutions for critical social problems that attract willing acceptance from most people because those standards and solutions offer some measure of the modern concept of substantial justice. [8]

It is true of course that ideas must live in the minds of people, but the basic ideas of the constitution endure through generations because they are loyally accepted over long periods of time. In this real sense they have objectivity and are not just subjective to particular persons at a particular time. This point has been made with great clarity by the Swedish jurist Olivecrona.

> The machinery of the state is run by an ever changing multitude of persons, acting as monarchs, presidents, heads and members of the government, members of parliament, and so on. In general not one of these persons has even the faintest idea that the law should consist of his commands. Everyone of them finds in existence the rules which are called the law and are on the whole enforced. He can only bring about a change in some part of the law. The bulk of it existed before him and will continue to govern the life of the country when he is gone.
>
> Further it is to be noted that the law givers in general attain their positions and exercise their power by means of the rules of law. The monarch owes his place to the rules of the constitution concerning the succession to the throne, the head of the government has been appointed by the monarch, the members of parliament have been legally elected, and so on. It makes no sense to pretend that the rules which carry these people to their position are their own commands. [9]

Fortunately, the Austinian theory of the English Constitution lived in theory only. It never has represented the working principles of English constitutional law throughout the hundreds of years of historical development leading to its present position and content. The true basis of English constitutional law was perhaps first stated by Bracton who, in the Thirteenth Century when the language of the law was still Latin, wrote the first great English legal treatise. He said:

---

[7][1959] S.C.R. 121.
[8]See Lederman, *The Nature and Problems of a Bill of Rights*, 37 C.B.R. 4, 14 (1959).
[9]Olivecrona, *Law as Fact*, 32-3.

The King himself ought not to be subject to any man, but he ought to be subject to God and the law, *since law makes the King*. Therefore let the King render to the law what the law has rendered to the King, viz., dominion and power for there is no King where will rules and not the law.[10]

If for "King" you substitute the primary group of official persons for the time being, whoever they are, the modern relevance of Bracton's words becomes clear. Sir Arthur Goodhart and Sir Ivor Jennings both take this view of the nature of law in general and of the English constitution in particular, rejecting the views of Austin and Dicey.

In his Hamlyn lectures in 1952, Sir Arthur Goodhart set out four principles that he maintains are basic and interdependent as the first principles of the English constitution.

(1) No man is above the law.
(2) Those who govern Great Britain do so in a representative capacity and are subject to change.
(3) Freedom of speech, thought and assembly.
(4) The independence of the judges.

The first is stated to be "the most fundamental one." After referring to the passage we have just quoted from Bracton, Professor Goodhart goes on to say that the essential freedom of the person prevails in England because the officers of the State are controlled by the law through the writ of *habeas corpus*.

We can do no better than to quote in full what he said as to the second, third and fourth principles.

The second fundamental principle of the British Constitution is that those who govern Great Britain do so in a representative capacity and are subject to change. The elections that are held are not a meaningless ritual. It is true that at a time of great emergency Parliament is capable of continuing its own life from year to year, but if it attempted to do so indefinitely in the time of peace we should all recognize that the Constitution had been destroyed. An immortal government tends to be an immoral government, for it deprives men of that freedom of choice on which free government is based. Professor Fuller, of Harvard, has stated this truth with admirable clarity:[11]

"The greatness of what we call democratic government does not lie in the mere fact that a numerical majority controls at election time, but at a point further removed from the ballot box, in the forces which are permitted to play upon the electorate. For in the world as it is now constituted, it is only in a democratic and constitutionally organised State that ideas have a chance to make their influence felt. By preserving a fluidity in the power structures of society, by making possible the peaceful liquidation of unsuccessful governments, democracy creates a field in which ideas may effectively compete with one another for the possession of men's minds."[12]

Here, again, it is true to say that the free election of the members of the House of

---

[10]Bracton, *De Legibus et Consuetudinibus Angliae*, quoted by Goodhart, *English Law and the Moral Law*, 56.
[11]Goodhart, *English Law and the Moral Law*, 56.
[12]Fuller, *The Law in Quest of Itself*, 123.

Commons is a basic principle of English constitutional law. Without "the peaceful liquidation of unsuccessful governments" the English system would come to an end.

The third basic principle covers the so-called freedoms of speech, of thought and of assembly. These freedoms are an essential part of any Constitution which provides that the people shall be free to govern themselves, because without them self-government becomes impossible. A totalitarian government, which claims to have absolute and unalterable authority, is acting in a logical manner if it denies to its subjects the right of criticism, because such criticism may affect the authority of those in power. To ask that a totalitarian government should recognise freedom of speech is to ask for the impossible because, by its very nature, such a government must limit the freedom of its subjects. On the other hand, such a system of government as exists under the British Constitution must recognise the necessity for freedom of speech and of association, because if public criticism is forbidden and if men are prevented from acting together in political associations, then it would be impossible to make a change in the government by the free, and more or less intelligent, choice of the people.

This does not mean that the constitutional government of a State must recognise that there is a right to advocate the overthrow of that constitution by force, because force is the negation of reason. You cannot argue safely with a man who is threatening to draw a revolver. Like all the rights which the law gives, the liberty which a man has to express his opinions is not an absolute one, but must be exercised within reasonable bounds. It is one of the virtues of the common law that it refuses to go to extremes; the argument that because the law has taken step A therefore it is logical that it should also take the further step B has never impressed the English judges. Having spent little time in the study of metaphysics, they have not been misled by this specious argument. It is because the common-law rights of the Englishman are never doctrinaire that they have such strength and vitality. Here, again, it is obvious that Parliament could not, even if it wished to do so, abolish freedom of speech in this country. It is therefore correct, both in fact and in theory, to say that this limitation is a part of constitutional law.

The fourth and final principle which is a basic part of the English constitution is the independence of the judiciary. It would be inconceivable that Parliament should today regard itself as free to abolish the principle which has been accepted as a corner-stone of freedom ever since the Act of Settlement in 1701. It has been recognised as axiomatic that if the judiciary were placed under the authority of either the legislative or the executive branches of the Government then the administration of the law might no longer have the impartiality which is essential if justice is to prevail.

It is important to point out that the doctrine establishing the independence of the judiciary does not mean that the judges themselves are absolute. They are bound to follow the law they administer. To deny that the judges are subject to the law, because there may be no effective sanction if they disregard it, is to misunderstand the nature of law itself. The judges recognise that they are bound by the law, just as the army recognise that it is bound by the law. If either group refused to obey we would, of course, have a revolution. The only difference between the two would be that the military revolution would be more likely to succeed than the judicial one.[13]

---

[13]Goodhart, *English Law and the Moral Law,* 56 ff.

III. CONSTITUTIONAL DIVISION OF LEGISLATIVE POWERS

Representative parliamentary democracy, responsible government, essential personal freedoms and an independent judiciary having crossed the ocean and become part of the public law in Canada before Confederation, were carried forward into Confederation with respect to the federal and the provincial governments with the essentials of federalism added, primarily those contained in sections 91 to 95 of the British North America Act.

The existence of viable federal constitutions makes clear that personification of primary power was not Austin's only error in his theory of sovereignty. He was also wrong to insist that all legal power on every subject whatsoever must be concentrated in some one set of persons. If the supreme authority lies in ideas and not in present persons than an *original* distribution of law-making powers by classification of subjects is possible and acceptable as the first legislative principle of the constitution. So also is an *original* withholding of ordinary legislative power in certain classes of subjects by a specially entrenched Bill of Rights. This means there is an extent to which the rights and freedoms of the citizen cannot be infringed upon by an ordinary statute passed by an ordinary majority.

In the American Constitution powers are distributed between Congress and the states and all legislative bodies are limited in the exercise of these powers by the constitutional Bill of Rights which cannot be altered except by a very difficult amending procedure that has been seldom used.

Canada has the federal distribution of powers between the central government on the one hand and the provincial governments on the other hand. With very few exceptions,[14] we do not have specially entrenched clauses in our Constitution as do the Americans in their Bill of Rights. We are urged that we should now move more in the American direction in this respect. Also, we are urged to move in the American direction in another respect. We are pressed to express all our essential constitutional law (presumably in accordance with Sir Ivor Jennings' limited sense of "constitutional") in a single document that is more elegant, coherent and inspiring in the literary sense than is the British North America Act.

At present the constitutions of Canada and the Provinces, in the quite limited sense of the Jennings' definition, are found in a great variety of legal forms, just as they are in England, and it is a serious error to think that the British North America Act either gathers them all into one document or was ever intended to do so. Some of the constitutional essentials are found in the B.N.A. Act, but many more are outside it in federal statutes, provincial statutes, judicial interpretations of the B.N.A. Act, historically received English judge-made public law, conventions of cabinet government, rules of parliamentary procedure and other sources. We do not propose to assess here the "one great document" idea for all things constitutional, but later we shall consider whether there are certain basic human rights and freedoms that should be given authoritative documentary form, and, what the options are for legal and constitutional forms for them.

---

[14]For example B.N.A. Act, s. 121 re free trade between the provinces and s. 133 re use of English and French language.

Chapter 2

The Common Law System in Canada

Reprinted with permission from *Canadian Jurisprudence The Civil Law and Common Law in Canada*, Edward McWhinney, ed. (Toronto: The Carswell Company, 1958)

I. INTRODUCTION:
THE RECEPTION OF ENGLISH LAW AND INSTITUTIONS

There are two great legal traditions in the Western World: one—the Civil-Law tradition—continues the age-old influence of the Roman Law, while the other finds its origin in the English Common Law as developed since the time of Henry II. In the field of private law Canadians inherit both traditions, the former prevailing in Quebec and the latter in the remaining provinces and territories. Comprehensive codification is associated primarily with civilian tradition, and judicial law-making from case to case with the English central royal courts of justice that moulded the Common Law, This does not involve as much contrast as many think—indeed, allowing for certain differences in emphasis, both systems share what might be called legal reason, which in its turn depends on the same principles of thought and logic that apply in all fields of human endeavour. The attempt in this essay is to develop the nature of legal reason as manifest in the Common Law system.

It was the combination of English settlement and conqest abroad that carried English law overseas, but the constitutional rules for its extension varied, depending on whether overseas territory was acquired by peaceful occupation or by conquest. Speaking of colonies acquired by settlement, Chief Justice Halliburton of Nova Scotia said:[1]

> Among the colonists themselves there has generally existed a strong disposition to draw a distinction between the common and the statute law. As a code, they have been disposed to adopt the whole of the former, with the exception of such parts only as were obviously inconsistent with their new situations, whilst far from being inclined to adopt the whole body of the statute law, they thought that such parts of them only were in force among them as were *obviously* applicable to, and necessary for them. . . . Indeed the distinction exists in the very nature of things, and is derived from the origin of the two codes. The common law has its foundations in those general and immutable principles of justice which should regulate the intercourse of men with men, wherever they may reside. The statute law emanates from the wisdom of the legislature of the day, varies with varying circumstances, and

---

[1] *Uniacke v. Dickson* (1848), 2 N.S.R. 287, 289-90.

consists of enactments which may be beneficial at one time and injurious at another. . . .

With perhaps some differences in emphasis on the doctrine of suitability to local conditions, these rules brought English private law to all parts of British North America except the old province of Quebec, the latter originally including the territory that later became Upper Canada and then Ontario. But when Upper Canada was formed, one of the first statutes of its new legislative assembly replaced French private law with the corresponding English law, so the position in Upper Canada or Ontario became essentially the same as if the territory had been originally acquired by settlement.

Obviously the date of reception is crucial respecting the automatic extension to a given colony of suitable English local statutes, but our main concern here is the Common Law for which, for reasons pertinent to this analysis, dates of reception are not significant. Chief Justice Halliburton expressed very clearly the prevailing eighteenth and nineteenth century Blackstonian concept of the Common Law. He saw it as a substantively complete and closed system of justice—a detailed natural-law system—that was progressively discovered by the judges as its various pre-existing parts were needed. If one conceives of the Common Law in this way, one simply does not date it for the purpose of colonial reception or any other purpose. Anyway, even if one permits the judges a more creative role, it would still be very difficult to date most Common Law doctrines with anything like the precision that is possible with parliamentary statutes. Finally, until as late as the end of 1949, Canadian courts were still constitutionally bound to follow pertinent decisions of the English Judicial Committee of the Privy Council and of the House of Lords, and were in the habit of paying almost as much respect to other English superior courts. This also has contributed to a continuing rather than to a dated reception of the English Common Law.

The mention of Canadian Courts reminds us that British North America also received English governmental institutions. These were provided for a colony either by prerogative decree of the Crown-in-Council or by express statute of the Imperial Parliament. Also, once local legislatures had been established, local statutes approved in London went further with the provision of colonial governmental bodies. In these ways the British North American colonies acquired superior courts on the model of the English central royal courts of justice, and, with some delays, fell heir to their status, their procedures (including the nineteenth century reforms) and their principles of precedent.[2] We turn then to the form and meaning of these rules of precedent, for this leads to the nature of the Common Law system.

II. THE FORMAL RULES OF PRECEDENT IN COMMON LAW COURTS

"From earliest times", says a famous legal historian, "the Royal Courts have always had some sort of regard for previous decisions."[3] And yet, through the

---

[2]I have traced this history in some detail in an article entitled "The Independence of the Judiciary" (1956), 34 Can. Bar Rev. 769 and 1139.
[3]Plucknett, "A Concise History of The Common Law" (5th ed., 1956), 342.

centuries, great departments of the law have been made, without benefit of parliamentary statutes, by creative judicial development of legal rules and principles to decide specific cases before the courts. The tendency to judicial loyalty—*stare decisis*—has been and is still a strong one, but it has gone side by side with judicial legislative accomplishments of great importance. How is such creative activity combined with doing what has been done before—with the following of precedent? An extended answer will be attempted in Part III of this essay, but meanwhile the following words of Lord Mansfield are suggestive:[4]

> The law of England would be a strange science if indeed it were decided upon precedents only. Precedents serve to illustrate principles and to give them a fixed certainty. But the law of England . . . depends upon principles, and these principles run through all the cases according as the particular circumstances of each have been found to fall within the one or the other of them.

It is then the rule or principle used to decide a specific case in court—the *ratio decidendi*—that embodies the significance of that case as a precedent. It is to this normative proposition that the duty of judicial loyalty is owed.

The formal rules of precedent on the English model are in the main simple to state. We start by distinguishing binding and persuasive precedents. The chief rule respecting the former is that, within any particular system of judicature, the lower courts in the heirarchy are bound to follow the rules previously used to decide sufficiently similar cases in the higher court or courts of the heirarchy. Whether any given court is bound to follow its own previous decisions in sufficiently similar cases is a matter of some variation and controversy. Superior courts of original jurisdiction are not so bound, but the English Court of Appeal and House of Lords have respectively ruled that they themselves are so bound. On the other hand, the Judicial Committee of the Privy Council has reserved a right to depart from its own previous decisions in sufficiently strong cases, though the Committee's record indicates that explicit departures are rare. The Supreme Court of Canada and certain of the provincial Courts of Appeal in Canada seem to be following the Privy Council line. Anyway, even though a court regards its own previous decisions as persuasive only, they turn out to be so highly persuasive that the distinction from a binding precedent becomes rather dim. Finally, between separate systems of courts in different Common Law jurisdictions, all precedents are at the persuasive level, and may suffer rather critical appraisal before acceptance across jurisdictional boundaries, particularly if these are national boundaries. The whole subject of precisely correct and detailed exposition of the formal rules of precedent has been much agitated in learned articles,[5] and will not be further pursued here, except to note two matters peculiar to Canada.

---

[4]*Jones v. Randall* (1774), Cowp. 37, quoted by Sir Carleton Allen, "Law in the Making" (Oxford, 6th ed., 1958), 212.

[5]See for instance:

Friedmann, "Stare Decisis at Common Law and under the Civil Code of Quebec" (1953), 31 Can. Bar Rev. 723.

Gooderson, "Ratio Decidendi and Rules of Law" (1952), 30 Can. Bar Rev. 892.

Joanes, "Stare Decisis in the Supreme Court of Canada" (1958), 36 Can. Bar Rev. 175.

The first point may be made in the words of Dean H. E. Read, who, while acknowledging the great debt of Canada to her inheritance of the English law and judicial system, nevertheless complains, citing chapter and verse, that Canadian judges have been too much inclined mechanically to follow English precedents, whether persuasive or binding. In other words, Canadian courts have too often followed English precedents uncritically and automatically when the comparative circumstances were not really sufficiently similar to necessitate this:[6]

> In 1956 there is little doubt that almost exclusive dependence on English authority led during the first half of this century to a habitually mechanical operation of legal rules by many Canadian judges which may have depreciated their capacity to meet the challenge which now confronts them. They are now required to play an effective part in a period of legal transition in the wake of the accelerated economic growth and social transformation of mid-twentieth century Canada.

The second point to be made is that any formal constitutional necessity to follow English judicial precedents in Canada has ended. Appeals to the Judicial Committee of the Privy Council were abolished by the Parliament of Canada with effect December 23rd, 1949, so that *all* English decisions since that date are now at the persuasive level. The only source of binding precedents for all the Common Law Canadian provinces is now the Supreme Court of Canada. In these circumstances, as Dean Read implies, Canadian judges ought to take a fresh look at the nature of the Common Law judicial process, and emphasize the creative and flexible elements that have always been there.

> No one would reasonably suggest that the great heritage of English-made law should be jettisoned; but it should be utilized as a fortress from which to advance, not as a place of rest.[7]

It is appropriate then to probe deeply the nature of our Common Law system.

III. NATURE OF THE COMMON LAW JUDICIAL PROCESS (The Courts and the Common Law)

(a) Competing Theories of the Common Law Judicial Process

As the preceding sections of this essay make obvious, our Common Law system assumes that decided cases use and express rules of law, and moreover confer on these rules an authoritative character. How then does one extract the rule used from the facts or the judicial opinion or the order made, or any combination of these, in a specific case? This question leads to the very heart of the Common Law system, and to suprisingly deep disagreements, depending basically on different views of the nature of laws and legal systems. The extremes may be described by saying that we find the "Blackstonians" arrayed against the modern "legal realists". The position of the first named is that certain basic self-evident

---

[6]Read, "Some Characteristics of the Judicial Process in Common Law Canada, 1906-1956" in "The Administration of Justice in Retrospect" (Harding, 1st ed., 1957), 64.
[7]Read, *op. cit.*, 73.

legal principles are given which are potentially complete in their substantive scope, so that from them detailed normative rules for every life-situation can be deduced by traditional Aristotelian logic, with a certainty comparable to the reading of results from a trigonometric table. The quotation given earlier from Chief Justice Halliburton illustrates that this was the prevalent view of the nature of the English Common Law in the eighteenth and nineteenth centuries and influenced the reception of that system in both British North America and the United States of America. It embodies the idea that the judicial process is merely to discern and apply all-sufficient pre-existing rules. But this concept of a substantively closed system gravely over-simplifies and misconceives the function and flexibility of logical principles of thought, as well as the possibility of human omniscience. It has properly earned the uncomplimentary title of "mechanical jurisprudence" from Dean Roscoe Pound[8] and of "the phonograph theory" from Professor Morris R. Cohen.[9] Nevertheless there are *some* valid elements here.

At the other extreme rest the so-called "legal realists", who seem to have reached their zenith in the twenties and thirties of the present century. The late Judge Jerome Frank is perhaps the most typical of them for our purpose. They took an extreme pragmatic position permeated with philosophic nominalism. Not only did the legal realists deny the existence of a "Blackstonian" type of a closed system, some of them at least seemed to deny the very possibility of any system whatever, for they denied the possibility of significant generalization or abstract thought in the field of law, or for that matter in other comparable fields of human endeavour. The net result here is the idea that understanding the judicial process is almost entirely a matter of predicting, with the aid of behaviourist psychology, the largely irrational conduct of judges in deciding what they have to decide.[10] Some of the realists pursued this line in supposed imitation of the methods of modern experimental natural science, and in the hope of providing legal progress comparable to that achieved in such fields as physics and chemistry. But this hope rests on misconception of the nature of modern scientific method, and also ignores certain stubborn differences between atoms and human beings. It is not difficult to see why this so-called "realism" was labelled by one critic as "the chaos school of jurisprudence".[11]

---

[8]Pound, "Mechanical Jurisprudence" (1908), 8 Columbia L. R. 605.

[9]Cohen, "Law and the Social Order" (1933), 233.

[10]Frank, "Law and the Modern Mind" (1930. Sixth printing, 1949). The following passages are typical:

"The law in the sky, above human experience, is valueless to the way-faring man. Principles, rules, conceptions, standards, and the like, may be law for lawyers, regardless of whether such law ever comes into contact with the affairs of life. But not for the rest of humanity. To mere humans, law means what the courts have decided and will decide, and not vague, 'pure' generalizations.", 55.

"The ideas and beliefs of all of us may be roughly classified as of two kinds: those that are based primarily on direct observation of objective data and those that are entirely or almost entirely a product of subjective factors—desires and aims that push and pull us about without regard to the objective situation.", 28.

"The 'facts', it must never be overlooked, are not objective. They are what the judge thinks they are, and what he thinks they are depends on what he hears and sees as the witnesses testify—which may not be, and often is not, what another judge would hear and see". (p. xvi, Preface to Sixth Printing).

[11]See generally Allen, "Law in the Making", 5th ed. (1951).

The truth lies somewhere in the middle ground between these two extreme positions, and inhabitating this area of moderation are found distinguished academic jurists like Dean Roscoe Pound and Professors John Dickinson and Morris R. Cohen. Here also are found many practicing jurists (lawyers, judges, senior governmental officers and legislators), the nature of their views of the legal system being expressed or implied in their statements and proceedings in the course of duty. For these persons the Common Law judicial process is neither completely mechanical in the one hand nor personally arbitrary and chaotic on the other. It obeys the normal laws of thought or principles of logic common to all departments of knowledge, so that understanding and progress, though often delicate, tentative and difficult, depend on constant striving to follow rational processes to the limit of human capacity. As Professor Morris Cohen points out, the judges, while avoiding extremes, must appeal both to reason and intuition:[12]

> The trained mind sees in a flash of intuition that which the untrained mind can succeed in seeing only after painfully treading many steps. They who scorn the idea of the judge as a logical automaton are apt to fall into the opposite error of exaggerating as irresistible the force of bias or prejudice. But the judge who realizes that all men are biased before listening to a case, is more likely to make a conscientious effort at impartiality than one who believes that elevation to the bench makes him at once an organ of infallible logical truth.

It will be the task of the balance of this essay to attempt a restatement and justification of this moderate view of the Common Law system, of what might be termed an enlightened orthodoxy respecting the nature of Common Law judicial process. The essence of the orthodox view is that judges do proceed by reasonable means to decide what they have to decide, and that they are to be believed, and indeed must be believed, when they expound the principles or rules of law they respectively purport to use to decide their cases. This sounds like labouring the obvious, but contrary views, as already indicated, have had and still have wide influence. In any event, since we are asking whether rules can be extracted from decided cases, and if so how, it is pertinent now to probe the nature of rules of law themselves for clues to the answer.

(b) Considerations of Metaphysics and Logic supporting the Orthodox View of the Judicial Process

Each of us must live in a world crowded with other human beings and with things and events. There is much that remains the same but also much that changes, and we must pursue our fate taking account both of the constant and the changing factors, striving to control them for the better where we can. Some success in this is possible because man has powers of reason, and so may make reasoned propositions about his world to lay the basis for some measure of understanding and control of it. Three main types of these propositions may be discerned, the descriptive, the causal and the normative. These are not mutually exclusive, for there may be mixed propositions that combine some or all of these elements, and in-

---

[12]Cohen, "The Place of Logic in the Law" (1916), 29 Harv. L. R. 622, 638.

deed causal and normative propositions necessarily have their descriptive parts. The purely descriptive statement or proposition simply points to or designates some fact or group of facts like a person, thing, relation, idea or quality. The causal statement or proposition deals in the realm of invariant or inevitable cause and effect, and is peculiarly though not exclusively the field of the natural experimental scientist. The normative statement deals in the realm of human choice in human relations, the area where there is significant freedom or power of choice about what conduct might be, and where therefore the question arises as to what it ought to be. This is the field of the jurist and of systems of laws, also of ethical and moral philosophers and their systems of value.

Certain of my starting assumptions need exposition at this point, for differences between this analysis and both "mechanical jurisprudence" and so-called "legal realism" are rooted at this primary level. First, what is the nature of the reality about which man makes reasoned propositions? Particular individual persons, things and events are real and distinct enough, but reality does not stop there. Human beings and things do not exist, nor do events occur, in particular and singular atomistic isolation. Rather they are related in time and space, in sequences of cause and effect, and by common attributes. These relationships, denoted by concepts (ideas, abstractions, universals) are necessarily just as real and true as the things related. Professor M. R. Cohen drives the point home in the following words:[13]

> It ought to be quite clear that abstractions and universals exist in every sense in which individual things can be said to exist, and by the same evidence. If any statement like "Smith is white and an honest man" is true, whiteness, honesty and manhood must exist as truly as Smith. Similarly, if it is true that one body is equal to, greater than, or less than another, the relations of equality, greater than, or less than, exist just as truly as the bodies between which they hold. If the results of logical and mathematical reasoning are observed to hold true of nature, it seems more proper to say that nature is logical and mathematical than to suppose that logical and mathematical principles are just words having no meaning in nature, or that they have a dubious existence "in the mind only" (the "mind" being conceived as outside nature) . . . In brief, it seems that the actual procedure of natural and logical science demands the doctrine that universals do exist but that they exist as universals, not as additional individual things.

So, the position here taken is that objectively true or valid abstractions (ideas, concepts, universals) are possible for the human mind, in other words that abstractions are not mere figments existing in the mind only with no hold whatever on objective reality. Hence, it is possible to do much in the way of checking the validity or truth of abstract propositions against objective reality by logical thought, experiment, observation, study and dialectical discussion. All this, as we shall see, is a denial of the basic premises of the nominalists or extreme pragmatists, who maintain that only directly perceptible particular things exist in nature and that all, or at least most, abstract thought is completely subjective and unreal in the sense of having no objective truth. The modern legal "realists" are

---

[13]Cohen, 29 Harv. L. R., 629. See also his "Law and the Social Order", 226.

either nominalists or extreme pragmatists in the juridical field, and unfortunately other influential jurists have followed their views in part. An important example for our purposes, to be examined later, is Dr. A. L. Goodhart in his well-known analysis of the determination of the *ratio decidendi* of a case.

But, to return to the assumptions of this eassy, I say that much is possible in the checking of the validity or truth of abstract propositions against objective reality, rather than that *all* is possible, because of another basic premise—that man is not omniscient. If all men had perfect reason, all would agree on just the right propositions of every kind about everything, and act in harmony accordingly. There would be no social problems. But only partial insight is given us, so our propositions describing and explaining our world and what human conduct is or ought to be are very often tentative, incomplete in scope, partial in truth or validity. Yet our abstractions remain fruitful exercises in reason—they do achieve a partial uncovering of the true order of the universe—they have made possible great advances in every field of human endeavour and will produce many more. Nevertheless we remain, and I venture to say will continue to remain, far short of omniscience. This denies one of the basic premises of "mechanical jurisprudence", which, as we shall see, did assume this very omniscience as the producer of a substantively complete and valid legal system.

Finally, in the list of assumptions, we come to questions of semantics—problems of the use of words as vehicles of meaning and tools of thought in relation to objective reality and truth. Words are indispensable to intellectual processes—all types of propositions mentioned earlier having to find formulation in appropriate words. Undeniably much useful juristic study and effort has been concentrated in the field of semantics. These are efforts to sharpen and refine the meaning of words, and to improve systematic legal terminology, efforts especially characteristic of analytical jurists like John Austin and Hans Kelsen.[14] Also I would agree that most if not all of the great issues of metaphysics and logic can at least be raised through the study of language, for, as Professor John Dickinson puts it, "thinking is almost wholly synonymous with the language process."[15] Nevertheless, semantical problems as such are not basic, for words *are* reasonably adequate vehicles of meaning and tools of thought in relation to objective reality, as this essay conceives that reality to be.[16] The extreme pragmatist and the nominalist will doubt this, *but they doubt it because of their own fundamentally different concepts of the nature of reality.* If you think, as they do, that reality is limited largely or wholly to particular directly perceptible things

---

[14] A striking example of fine writing in this respect is:
Levi, "An Introduction to Legal Reasoning" (1949). Professor Levi's essay is however subject to the limitations of studies that are primarily semantical.

[15] Dickinson, "Legal Rules: Their Function in the Process of Decision" (1931), 79 U.Pa. L.R. 833, 842.

[16] Speaking of the argument "that the meaning of a proposition is purely subjective because there is always a certain conventional element in langauge", Cohen continues: "We can, to a very limited extent, like Humpty Dumpty, make words mean what we please. But all convention presupposes communication in a form which is ultimately not conventional but grows out of the fact that the communicants live in a common world and respond in similar ways to similar symbols."
Cohen, "A Preface to Logic" (1956), 42.

and happenings, then only words specifically referential to these things will have for you objective fixity of meaning. All else will be hopelessly subjective. Then indeed words seeking to denote abstractions, relationships, qualities and ideas would seem empty sounds with meanings varying indefinitely between different individuals. It is no accident that the modern legal realists have taken a very pessimistic view (to put it midly) of the possibility of some objectivity and fixity of meaning for the abstract words so widely used in laws and legal systems. So, to repeat, this essay assumes that semantic problems are not in themselves basic and that words *are* reasonably adequate vehicles of meaning and tools of thought, even though perfection eludes us here as it does in other human affairs. Communication, thought and social organization would simply be impossible if this were not so. We proceed then on the basis of this and the other assumptions stated[17] to a detailed analysis of legal reasoning—the basic process of a living legal system.

(c) Legal Reasoning

(i) The unity of all appeals to reason

Much has been heard in legal speculation of the difference between induction and deduction, with allegations that the former is the method of the English Common Law and its claim to distinction, if not superiority, in relation to the deductive method of codified legal systems. The extremely pragmatic or nominalist jurists go further, claiming that induction is the method of the natural experimental scientists, and they attempt to apply this method, as they conceive to be, to legal problems. But this contrast between induction and deduction is a false one, and misconceives the method of natural science in any event. The latter misconception is to the effect that what the natural scientist does is to embark on a vessel named "Research" in which he sails about on a voyage of discovery over the sea of directly perceptible particular facts, whereupon, if only he will listen, the "facts" will speak to him of the secrets of the universe. Transferred to the normative sphere of the law, this misconception is found in the lawyer or judge or jurist who thinks that, if only he can accumulate a great enough number of "cases" in his brief or opinion or text-book, his mountain of particular instances will somehow by its own weight squeeze out principles of law for the purpose in hand. The falsity of this has been exposed by Professor Cohen:[18]

> It is an illusion to suppose that we can build up a legal system or science of law by simply gathering all the cases together. For the very first question, What does the case stand for?, involves a theoretical issue—namely, On what principle can the actual decision be supported, or from what principle can it be deduced?

Scientific and juristic thought both necessarily depend on and obey the same rules of sound thinking or logic, *though logic alone is not in the end all-sufficient*

---

[17]I do not pretend that these great questions can be disposed of in a few sentences, but if I am to challenge the assumptions and premises of others, I should give some account of my own, so far as I am aware of them.

[18]Cohen, "Law and the Social Order" (cited in footnote 9), 190.

for the purposes of either. It is after logical procedures have done their essential part for both the natural scientist and the jurist that differences between them appear, arising from the distinct natures of the causal and normative spheres with which they are respectively concerned. These distinctions will engage us presently, for the moment we shall explore further the logical process that scientific and juristic thinkers have in common. Both employ hypothetico-deductive reasoning procedures, what Professor Morris Cohen has called "that most wonderful discovery, or invention, of the Greeks—rational deductive system".[19] Natural scientists must formulate their general working hypotheses about cause and effect, make logical deductions from them to define particular instances consistent therewith, and then devise verifying experiments or improve and refine their observations of reality to see whether particular instances can be made to happen, or do occur, as expected on the basis of the starting hypotheses. Natural scientists attempt all ranges of abstraction from the lowest to the highest by a constant process of interaction between abstract propositions (with their detailed logical implications) on the one hand, and the results of particular observations and experiments (with their abstract implications) on the other. For example, the existence of a minute organism of the type "virus" was deduced by medical scientists before the thing was actually seen through the newly-invented electron microscope. Charles Darwin already had the general idea of evolution in his mind before he made what were for him the confirming detailed observations in the South Seas. Thus it is not the primary feature of natural science that "objective facts" speak to the natural scientist. He has to ask the right questions before he has a chance to get fruitful answers from his objective world of cause and effect.[20] And here, the scientist makes a basic assumption that he cannot finally prove—that fundamentally there is order in the universe, in other words that there is a realm of consistent inevitable cause and effect in nature. As Bertrand Russell put it:[21]

> The belief in the uniformity of nature is the belief that everything that has happened or will happen is an instance of some general law to which there are no exceptions . . . Science habitually assumes, at least as a working hypothesis, that general rules which have exceptions can be replaced with general rules which have no exceptions. "Unsupported bodies in air fall" is a general rule to which balloons and aeroplanes are exceptions. But the laws of motion and the law of gravitation, which account for the fact that most bodies fall, also account for the fact that balloons and aeroplanes can rise; thus the laws of motion and the law of gravitation are not subject to these exceptions.

Professor John Dickinson refers to the same basic scientific premise, and continues:[22]

---

[19]Cohen, "The Place of Logic in the Law" (1916), 29 Harv. L.R., 624.

[20]"The history of science shows beyond doubt that the vital factor in the growth of any science is not the Baconian passive observation but the active questioning of nature, which is further by the multiplication of hypotheses is hypotheses": Cohen, "A Preface to Logic", (cited in footnote 16) 21.

[21]Russell, "The Problems of Philosophy" (reset edition 1946) 63-4.

[22]Dickinson, "Legal Rules: Their Function in the Process of Decision" (1931), 79 U.Pa. L.R. 833, 860.

Scientific thought, therefore, concerns itself with analyzing and classifying the elements of given fact situations and determining their relations to one another for the purpose of acquiring ability to predict the relations between these elements if recurring in future situations. This procedure involves the same basic thought-processes which are also involved in the procedure of judicial thinking,—the isolation of identities, their formulation in general propositions, and the application of these propositions to specific situations. Here however, the resemblance ends.

As suggested by the closing words of this quotation, we must now attend to the differences between the natural scientist and the jurist. Both must and do employ hypothetico-deductive methods, but they do so for different ends dictated by the different natures of their respective spheres of the causal and the normative. Taking as true the basic faith of the natural scientist in an orderly realm of cause and effect, then it follows that the more often the scientist finds A and B associated in nature, the more probably true it is that they have invariant causal relation one to the other, and this probability often amounts to virtual certainty.[23] Moreover, A and B are not necessarily particular perceived facts, they may be and very often are abstractions at various levels of generalization. This principle of probability in the realm of invariant cause, according to Russell, is the inductive principle. Induction then is not some mysterious progression from the "particular" to the "general". *Neither is it a concept relevant to the purely normative sphere, except indirectly. Where the question is what human conduct ought to be in given circumstances, because there is choice between alternatives of what that conduct might be, we are simply beyond the reach of the idea of induction.* So far as indirect bearing is concerned, causal considerations may enter the normative picture as part of the circumstances that form the conditions in which a normative choice needs to be made, but that is all. For example, Jones may in certain given circumstances have the choice of doing A or B or C. Which course of conduct ought he to follow? Causal reasoning and causal concepts like induction enable us to predict what the respective consequences of doing A, B or C are likely to be, but there they leave us. If we have found that conduct A is likely to injure Brown whereas courses of conduct B and C threaten injury to no one, then the law of negligence in many such cases directs Jones that he ought to avoid A and choose to do B or C. The law here embodies and expresses a moral decision arrived at by applying a system of values to this issue of choice, so that if Jones makes the wrong choice he must take the consequences by payment of compensation to Brown. Whether definition of the right choice is easy or difficult, it is never just "a question of fact".[24] The legal injunction to the citizen to be a reasonable man is an injunction to him to be a reasonably *moral* man.

It was said earlier that the natural scientist and the jurist were both under the same necessity to use logic, but that logic was not all-sufficient for the purposes of either. This may now be further explained. The jurist must have certain start-

---

[23]Russell, "The Problems of Philosophy" (cited in footnote 21) 66-67.

[24]Where the contrast between causally dangerous conduct and a causally safe alternative is clear and great, the "right" choice would be obvious by any acceptable system of values. But every student of the law knows of cases of great difficulty. Is an ambulance on an emergency call entitled to go through a red light?

ing assumptions about what human conduct ought to be, and he must develop the logical implications of his general propositions through stages of decreasing abstraction in order to assess the detailed consequences of applying such propositions as the laws of the land for particular persons and groups of persons. Likewise, he must try to discern the general implications, in the realm of standards of conduct, of the particular facts of social life. Here again we see the necessity for constant interaction between the abstract elements of particular facts of experience, and the testing of abstract propositions by the checking of their deduced implications against facts and events of experience. To go up and down the scale of consistent implication between more or less abstract propositions is logical process, involving syllogistic reasoning and the other well-known rules of logic.

But the process of testing the correctness or validity or truth of a series of logical propositions in the light of real facts and consequences is not in the end a logical matter. At this point, the natural scientist, like a physicist or chemist, is able to put his question to the causal realm of nature itself. This he does by controlled experiment, improved observation or improved interpretation of factual data already available. Logical process has prepared the way for this by helping to determine the terms of the question to be put to nature and the manner of putting it, but logical process itself does not give the answers. And even after nature has answered, it may take the brilliant intuition of an Einstein or a Darwin to see the correct abstract causal implication of particular experimental results and other observed data.

Now the jurist, like the scientist, proceeds to the point of testing by use of logic, and likewise finds that logic will carry him no further. He finds himself with alternative propositions about what human conduct ought to be in a given type of situation, and between them he must choose if he is to settle the issue before him, as judges, legislators and lawyers must do. But nature is not now the oracle for the jurist that it is for the natural scientist. As a jurist he is concerned to separate the better from the worse where either could be chosen and made to happen. Since he is not investigating causal inevitability, this final question of the jurist cannot be put to the causal realm of nature by experiment, observation and the use of induction, in the proper sense of that word. The final question of the jurist must be put to some acceptable system of values, and this explains why difficult legal problems are finally decided by the dialectical and authoritative processes of court room or legislative chamber, rather than by experiment in the laboratory. The natural scientist then has a much easier task than the working jurist, as the necessary contrast in their final methods testifies. The contrast definitely does not mean, as is too often suggested, that the jurist is simply inferior in performing his tasks because he does not apply himself sufficiently to emulating the natural scientist.

Nevertheless, in spite of these differences, juristic thinking has benefited from the example of experimental science—specifically from the tentative attitude of the natural scientist toward his premises and his scrupulous care to test and review their accuracy in relation to relevant real facts of experience. It is at this point that we can appreciate more clearly both the errors of ''mechanical jurisprudence'' and the great contribution of moderate sociological jurists like Dean Roscoe Pound.

As stated earlier, the essence of ''mechanical jurisprudence'' is to conceive the judicial process as merely one of discovery of pre-existing rules which form a complete system—complete in the sense of already holding the solution to all problems that have required or that may require legal regulation. This assumes that all-sufficient original premises about what human conduct ought to be have been revealed to man, and that they are capable by deductive logical development of giving just the one ''right'' legal rule for each particular situation, old or new. On this view, it would be superfluous carefully to assess what the application of these rules would mean in detail in terms of the facts of social life, before confirming them as the ''right'' rules by the authority of court or legislature. If you are sure the master principles are right and complete and capable of development in detail by an automatic logical process to the one ''right'' particular ruling, then it follows that people must fit themselves and their affairs to these rules, whatever the real hardship. Thus, in England, the fellow-servant rule[25] was judicially created and maintained for over one hundred years as an inevitable implication of the principles of freedom of contracting and of the sanctity of contracts once freely made. The developing social facts of unequal bargaining power between the parties and of the new conditions of mass production and employment in industry were not permitted much influence. Similarly, in the United States, the courts at first struck down as unconstitutional the early workmen's compensation statutes because allegedly they violated the master principle of ''no liability without fault''.

> It was the confident belief of the historico-analytical common-law lawyer that he could solve any problem whatsoever on the basis of the seventeenth-century English law referred back to its simplest ideal form in the Year Books. New forms of doing business, new agencies of menace to the general security, new forms and purposes of association, new conceptions of human relations and new social habits were quite immaterial. Here were the absolute universal legal conceptions. Likewise the results in the individual cases decided were quite immaterial. It was the office of the judge to fit the case to the conception after the manner of Procrustes.[26]

What then is wrong with mechanical jurisprudence that makes it unsuitable as an explanation of what the Common Law system has been or should be? It is basically in error in two ways concerning the normative sphere of human affairs to which legal systems belong. It is erroneous to assume that the Common Law is a complete system, *i.e.* that the human mind is omniscient in the sense that it could fully conceive or observe and perfectly operate such a system. Also, it is erroneous to neglect careful investigation of the effect of existing or proposed laws as a matter of social fact, for the specific persons and circumstances contemplated by their terms. As we have seen, the modern experimental scientist does not abjure general propositions and abstract concepts in his causal realm, far

---

[25]This was to the effect that an employee impliedly agreed in his contract of employment to assume the risk of injury to himself by the carelessness of a fellow-employee, thus freeing the employer of a vicarious liability that would otherwise have obtained in these circumstances.

[26]Pound, ''The Theory of Judicial Decision'' (1923), 36 Harv. L. R. 641, 802 and 940, 817.

from it. Rather, he believes his causal generalizations only tentatively until they can be tested in terms of the objective facts. Even then, he keeps open in his mind the possibilities of new evidence from objective reality and of wider or different abstract propositions than will absorb or displace the ones he presently holds. He does not consider that his present hypotheses are certain and complete in scope beyond all questioning and checking. This amounts to saying that the scientist does not assume man to be omniscient in the realm of cause, and accordingly he is ready to revise his concepts and prepared to give continual attention to what more experience, observation and experiment can tell him.

We have already seen that juristic and scientific thinking parallel one another in some ways and diverge in others, and from this comparison certain lessons may be drawn. As I understand Dean Pound and the other moderate sociological jurists, they are in effect urging that the jurist, in his realm of the ought-to-be, should emulate the natural scientist by a corresponding humility about the validity and incomplete nature of man-made abstract propositions; for man is no more omniscient in the one realm than in the other. Also, they urge that the jurist should continually investigate the actual social effects of rules of law. The data thus gathered cannot and will not help the jurist as much as experiments and observations help the natural scientist, but nevertheless the legal process is better if judges and legislators are disposed to show constant concern for the gathering of relevant data in the realm of objective reality.

> The sociological movement in jurisprudence is a movement for pragmatism as a philosophy of law; for the adjustment of principles and doctrines to the human conditions they are to govern rather than to assumed first principles; for putting the human factor in the central place and relegating logic to its true position as an instrument.[27]

Also, the moderate group insist that logic, as an instrument, is much more flexible than the mechanical jurists have thought it to be. Logic in the law is not inexorably the servant of just one set of "assumed first principles". Rather, it is the rational procedure for developing the abstract implications of any proposed or possible legal rules as well as those actually prevailing, and the means of exposing their probable consequences in society. Logic then is equally applicable throughout the whole field of juristic possibility, and so, among other things, is the appropriate and indispensable servant of moderate sociological jurisprudence.[28] This concept of legal reasoning, with its implications for the judicial process, deserves to be designated "orthodox", for in the main it has prevailed in the English central royal courts of Common Law and Chancery through the centuries, and in the courts overseas following the English model, though of course in both the old world and the new there have been digressions and instances of verbal homage to other ideas. The point is that Common Law judges have always been confronted with real and specific facts of social life when called upon to find or make rules of law. Dean Pound puts the point with his usual clarity:[29]

---

[27]Pound, "Mechanical Jurisprudence" (1908), 8 Columbia L. R. 605, 610.
[28]Cohen, "Law and the Social Order" (cited in footnote 9) 232.
[29]Pound, "The Theory of Judicial Decision" (1923), 36 Harv. L. R., 953.

For it is no mean advantage of our doctrine of precedents and judicial finding or making of law that the Common Law is always found and made with reference to actual controversies. It is not declared in the abstract except in relatively rare cases by legislation. For the greater part it is made under the pressure of actual human claims asserted in pending litigation and to meet the needs of a satisfactory adjustment of these concrete claims. Thus, no matter how abstract and mechanical our legal theory for the time being, it can never develop that serene indifference to the facts of life that has sometimes marked the juristic speculation of the civilian.

So, the example of the modern experimental scientist, valuable though it is where relevant, really serves mainly to remind the Common Law jurist of old well-trodden paths of reasonable and realistic judicial process. Historically, great English judges were proceeding scientifically when some of their contemporaries in the natural sciences were insisting, in the face of contrary evidence, that the earth was flat. It is a nice question who has learned what from whom.

(ii) The orthodox theory of judicial decision as a reasonable process. The nature of legal propositions and the multi-relevance of facts

The general analysis of legal reasoning just given clearly implies the validity of the orthodox view of the Common Law judicial process—that judges are to be believed, and indeed as a rational matter must be believed, when they enunciate the legal propositions (rules, principles, standards, abstractions or generalizations) that move them to decide their respective cases as they do. We must now examine this process in detail, and once again words of Dean Pound set the stage.

At least if he is an appellate judge, and to some extent in any court of general jurisdiction (the Anglo-American judge) . . . must so decide that his decision will enter into the body of the law as a precedent. He must so decide that his decision or the grounds thereof will serve, first, as a measure or pattern of decision of like cases for the future, and, second, as a basis of analogical reasoning in the future for cases for which no exact precedents are at hand.[30]

One cannot understand American case law without bearing in mind the disturbing influence of the facts of particular cases upon the general rule. Nor can he understand American judicial decision without bearing in mind the disturbing effect of the exigencies of our doctrine of precedents upon the disposition of particular cases. At one moment courts are tempted to modify a general rule with reference to appealing circumstances of one case. The next moment fear of impairing a settled rule or of unsettling it by analogy will tempt them to ignore appealing circumstances of another case.[31]

As the words of Dean Pound suggest, judicial reasoning is at critical times a delicate and difficult operation, and we must now explore further these delicacies and difficulties. In general analytical terms, the formula of a rule of law or legal proposition is—if a certain type of situation happens, then the person or persons involved ought to adhere to a specified type of conduct. For instance, the law of negligence specifies that any person who drives a car upon the highway ought to

---

[30]Pound (1923), 36 Harv. L. R. 940-1.
[31]Pound (1923), 36 Harv. L. R. 942-3.

take reasonable care to avoid causing injury to other highway users. The criminal law tells us that a person whose ability is sufficiently impaired by alcohol or drugs ought not to drive a car upon the highway at all. It can readily be seen that both the typical fact-situation and the desirable conduct coupled with it are ideas or concepts expressed in terms more or less abstract. Together they make up the normative proposition. Legal results in the courts are obtained by judicial application of such rules to certain specific persons and circumstances contemplated by their terms. Or, to say the same thing the other way around, legal results are obtained by subsuming the specific facts presenting a legal issue under the rules of law containing the abstract concepts appropriate to them. The facts and the rules are thus correlative, for rules are meaningless unless there have been or may be real and specific facts relevant to their terms, and likewise facts as such cannot have legal significance except by relevance to the abstract concepts of rules of law.[32]

In this intellectual combined operation, it is fruitless to worry about which comes first, appreciation of the abstract idea or of the specific case, because (a) at some times the start of legal reasoning will be with abstract ideas, at other times with specific cases, and (b) in any event the essence of legal reasoning is the unqualified necessity for constant interaction between the two. Perhaps this interaction may start simply, but, nevertheless, as it continues it will often yield more complex results through the appreciation of further abstract features in the specific facts, matched by reciprocal appreciation of the relevance to those facts of an increased range of abstract legal propositions.[33]

What must now be understood is that logic will give us a very considerable range of possible abstract legal propositions relevant to the same single set of facts of occurrence and experience. Some relevant propositions may form the elements of an hierarchical and logically consistent system of propositions progressing from lower to higher levels of abstraction—from narrower to broader generalizations. Here the higher propositions include the lower, and more besides. By contrast, other propositions may overlap and conflict *in spite of their logical relevance to the same single set of facts*. Both these situations have profound implications for the nature of the judicial process. Well-known examples from the law of negligence may make this clear.

The following legal propositions are quoted from the opinions of the judges forming the majority in *Donoghue v. Stevenson*,[34] being the rules they respectively deemed appropriate for the single real fact-situation there in question, involving as it did the young man treating his girl friend to a bottle of ginger beer at Minchella's refreshment parlour in Paisley, Scotland.

---

[32]Legal "issues" take shape under our system of pleading by competing preliminary allegations about the facts and their legal significance, *i.e.* about the rules of law deemed to be applicable. The allegations are then reasonably and authoritatively assessed by the dialectical processes of a court trial.

[33]This is as true of the process of applying a civil code in the Roman tradition as it is of applying Common Law in the English tradition. As someone has aptly put it, if the Roman jurist Ulpian and Lord Justice Scrutton have met in the hereafter, they will have had no difficulty talking to one another about legal problems.

[34][1932] A.C. 562.

(1) You must take reasonable care to avoid acts or omissions which you can reasonably foresee would be likely to injure your neighbour. Who then in law is my neighbour? The answer seems to be—persons who are so closely and directly affected by my act that I ought reasonably to have them in contemplation as being so affected when I am directing my mind to the acts or omissions which are called in question. (Lord Atkin)[35]

(2) A manufacturer of products, which he sells in such a form as to show that he intends them to reach the ultimate consumer in the form in which they left him with no reasonable opportunity of intermediate examination, and with the knowledge that the absence of reasonable care in the preparation or putting up of the products will result in injury to the consumer's life or property, owes a duty to the consumer to take that reasonable care. (Lord Atkin)[36]

(3) In the daily contacts of social and business life human beings are thrown into, or place themselves in, an infinite variety of relations with their fellows; and the law can refer only to the standards of the reasonable man in order to determine whether any particular relation gives rise to a duty to take care as between those who stand in the relation to each other. (Lord Macmillan)[37]

(4) A person who for gain engages in the business of manufacturing articles of food and drink intended for consumption by members of the public in the form in which he issues them is under a duty to take care in the manufacture of these articles. (Lord Macmillan)[38]

(5) The respondent, in placing his manufactured article of drink upon the market, has intentionally so excluded interference with, or examination of, the article by any intermediate handler of the goods between himself and the consumer that he has, of his own accord, brought himself into direct relationship with the consumer, with the result that the consumer is entitled to rely upon the exercise of diligence by the manufacturer to secure that the article shall not be harmful to the consumer. (Lord Thankerton)[39]

Lord Atkin's proposition about neighbours (1) is indeed very general or abstract. Logically, it includes but is not exhausted by his own manufacturer-consumer proposition (2) and as well includes the second and narrower proposition of Lord Macmillan (4) and the single proposition of Lord Thankerton. Likewise, Lord Macmillan's very general proposition (3) is consistent with but not exhausted by the narrower propositions (2), (4) and (5).

As for the girl friend, Donoghue, and the Scottish ginger-beer manufacturer, Stevenson, they turn out to be neighbours by the foresight test (1), consumer and manufacturer of the thing consumed (2), persons in circumstances of relation such that a reasonable man would say one ought to take care for the other (3), consumer of an article of food or drink and the manufacturer of same who issued it in finished form for gain (4), and consumer of an article of drink and manufacturer thereof who issued it in finished form. These relations or abstract features all objectively existed in the real circumstances of the actual persons Donoghue and Stevenson, and hence logically could be made the basis of rele-

---

35[1932] A.C., 580
36[1932] A.C., 599.
37[1932] A.C., 619.
38[1932] A.C., 620.
39[1932] A.C., 603.

vant and consistent legal propositions, as indeed they were. These propositions are consistent as normative propositions because they all lead to the same result for the persons Donoghue and Stevenson in their actual circumstances. And, be it noted, there is no logical ground to prefer one over the other as the *ratio decidendi* of the case. Logical system gives us consistency of implication, but affords no test for choice between the consistent alternative propositions it displays.

In any event, one may ask, if the result is the same for the present specific parties, why try and choose between consistent alternative propositions at differing levels of generality? The answer in the words of Dean Pound already quoted, is that the Common Law judge "must so decide that his decision will enter into the body of the law as a precedent". Other parties in the future in essentially similar circumstances will expect, and are entitled to expect, the same treatment from the law. Even the present parties expect that they will be treated as others similarly circumstanced have been or would be treated. As a fundamental of justice, the demand is that the legal system strive for consistency at some understandable and acceptable level of generality or abstraction.[40]

The scope and significance of a case as a precedent then depends on the relevant abstract propositions the judge selected, expounded and used to reach his decision. This is well illustrated by the judicial treatment of *Donoghue v. Stevenson* since 1932, particularly in the later case of *Haseldine v. Daw*.[41] Here, an employee of an engineering firm, engaged to overhaul and repair the mechanism of an elevator in an apartment building, neglected to put back certain vital parts of the machinery. As a consequence, very soon the elevator crashed from the upper floors with the plaintiff on board and injured him. In his action against the firm of engineers, the plaintiff argued that *Donoghue v. Stevenson* was a precedent in his favour, and he succeeded two to one in the English Court of Appeal. But the three Lords Justices each differed on the meaning of *Donoghue v. Stevenson* as a precedent. Lord Justice Scott said he found the *ratio decidendi* in Lord Atkin's very abstract proposition about "neighbours" and that the present parties were such neighbours, hence for him the liability of the defendant followed. Lord Justice Goddard found the *ratio decidendi* in the more narrow manufacturer-consumer proposition of Lord Atkin, but said he was persuaded to extend it by analogy to repairmen and users of the thing repaired, so he also found for the plaintiff. But Lord Justice Clauson dissented. Though he accepted Lord Atkin's manufacturer-consumer proposition as the rule of *Donoghue v. Stevenson*, he considered that a repairman was not a manufacturer, that holding a manufacturer liable to a consumer was going quite far enough in this sort of situation, and he refused to include repairmen by analogy.

---

[40]". . . [I]nequalities arbitrarily created arouse the sense of injustice, because equal treatment of those similarly situated with respect to the issue before the court is a deep implicit expectation of the legal order . . . The point is that inequalities resulting from the law must make sense. If decisions differ, some discernible distinction must be found bearing an intellegible relation to the difference in result. The sense of injustice revolts, against whatever is unequal by caprice": Cahn, "The Sense of Injustice" (1949), as reprinted in "The American Jurisprudence Reader" (1956), 53.

[41][1941] 2 K.B. 343.

Thus far we have been speaking of propositions logically consistent with one another at different levels of abstraction. But there may also be contrary principles that overlap so as to be relevant to the same facts, and which therefore compete to govern these facts. For example, the Common Law knows the principle *caveat emptor*. The proposition here is that a manufacturer is only liable for harm done by a defect in the thing made if he has sold it under a contract with terms to that effect, and then of course liability is only to the other contracting party and does not run to any third person. Logically, this proposition is relevant to the circumstances of Donoghue and Stevenson, and would give the opposite result to any of the propositions quoted earlier from the majority opinions in that case. So far as a working legal system is concerned, one of these opposing rules must be chosen over the other completely, or there must be a compromise by division of the field of potential application between them. The latter has been the solution adopted in English and Canadian courts in the type of situation we are discussing, the rule of *caveat emptor* being applied to builders of houses while the foresight test of Lord Atkin is applied to manufacturers of movable things. These cases illustrate several vital points about legal reasoning in general and the Common Law judicial process in particular. First, they demonstrate the necessity to take the judge's word for it on the rule of the case—the legal proposition for which it stands. Second, they point to the significance of the degree of abstraction the rule of the case represents. It seems possible logically almost always to move to broader consistent principles at higher levels of abstraction. Where then is this broadening process to stop in the derivation of legal propositions from decided cases? This is important in relation to the nature of analogical reasoning and also respecting the persistent but quite erroneous idea that, in the Common Law, a case can only stand for the most specific (*i.e.* the least abstract) proposition that was used or could have been used to decide it as it was decided. Finally, it will be seen that the broader the generality of the rule of a given case, the greater is the reach of that case as a precedent for new fact-situations, but greater then too is the chance of conflict with another broad but quite contrary principle from another case, the latter being also logically relevant to the same new fact-situations. How are such conflicts to be resolved or compromised so far as this can be done logically?

If man was omniscient in these matters, so that everyone could fully understand and completely accept the one right and consistent system of legal propositions, ranging from multitudinous specific ones to the one great final abstraction—the finally just and comprehensive normative abstraction—then none of these problems would arise. But we are far from omniscience and must be content to strive for the best that can be done by partial insights. As we shall see, it is these exigencies of imperfection that account for the need of constitutional authority in the judicial process, or for that matter in any effective process of legal decision. These several issues now need detailed attention.

As stated earlier, the orthodox theory of the nature of the Common Law judicial process holds that the rule of the case is the rule the judge states he is using to reach his decision. Even this doctrine leaves difficulty enough when alternative rules have been stated in the several opinions of a plural bench, or even within a single judicial opinion. Nevertheless, in the vast majority of cases, one rule is clearly enough expressed, and even when alternative rules have been given, at least, on the orthodox view, one is confined to these alternatives for the significance of the case as a precedent. But, if once we disregard the deciding judge's chosen rule, we are left only with the specific facts given in evidence[42] and the specific order made for one party or the other. Under these conditions, he who would determine a rule for which the case stands now confronts hundreds if not thousands of possible rules at many levels of abstraction, any one of which could account for the order made on these facts, yet each of which would give the case different scope as a precedent. Logic, as we have seen obtains throughout the whole realm of juristic possibility and cannot be more closely confined. Professor Julius Stone has made this point about *Donoghue v. Stevenson*, demonstrating the vast number of logically relevant rules that could be conceived to account for the finding made for the plaintiff in that case.[43] So, if you do not take the deciding judge's word for it on the *ratio decidendi* of a case, whose word do you take? What then is your criterion of selection? Proponents of the orthodox theory correctly point out that disregard of the deciding judge's chosen rule leads to a sort of mysterious confusion, if not indeed to complete chaos.

Yet, no less an authority than Dr. A. L. Goodhart has categorically called for just this disregard of the deciding judge's opinion, in his well-known essay on determining the *ratio decidendi* of a case. His position may be given in his own words:[44]

> The rules for finding the principle of a case can, therefore, be summarized as follows:
> (1) The principle of a case is not found in the reasons given in the opinion.
> (2) The principle is not found in the rule of law set forth in the opinion.
> (3) The principle is not necessarily found by a consideration of all the ascertainable facts of the case, and the judge's decision.
> (4) The principle of the case is found by taking account (a) of the facts treated by the judge as material, and (b) his decision as based on them.

So, we are to disregard the judge's stated rule, and to derive instead a different rule by combining the "facts" that the judge indicated as "material" with the order he made. The rule thus conceived by some later reviewer of the case is said to be the rule for which the case stands. But, as we have seen, this actually leaves the later reviewer a free hand with the great numbers of alternative princi-

---

[42]Indeed, "the specific facts given in evidence" have not simply arrived "on the record" under their own power. They were admitted in evidence because logically relevant to rules of law alleged to be applicable. These allegations occur in the pleadings, the legal briefs and the argument of a civil case, and in the corresponding processes of a criminal prosecution. Nothing illustrates more clearly that the reciprocity between fact and proposition in legal reasoning starts up at once—just as soon as a lawyer sits down to draft the originating document for either a civil or a criminal case. But even if the way facts become relevant evidence is disregarded, the case for neglecting the deciding judge's reasons will not stand up.

[43]Stone, "The Province and Function of Law" (1946), 187-8.

[44]Goodhart, "Essays in Jurisprudence and the Common Law" (1931), 25.

ples logically available, any one of which would lead to the same order on the same facts, and each of which varies more or less in the scope it would give to the case in question as a precedent.

Dr. Goodhart first published these views in 1930, and they show him to have been strongly under the influence of the contemporary American legal realism. For instance, he certainly goes for toward maintaining that deciding judges proceed irrationally, as apparently only a later reviewer can "find" the rule of a case, the deciding judge cannot give it. We are not told what makes the later reviewer of a case (who will often be another judge) so rational and the deciding judge himself so irrational. It is true Dr. Goodhart says he will take the deciding judge's word for what were the "material" facts of the case, but this puts him on the horns of a dilemma. Either Dr. Goodhart is committing one of the cardinal errors characteristic of philosophic nominalism or he is conceding the validity of the orthodox theory of precedent without knowing it. On the one hand, if his idea is that the facts themselves will somehow speak of a principle to the later reviewer of them, he is accepting the misconceived version of induction already seen to be erroneous for both natural science and jurisprudence. On the other hand, if Dr. Goodhart would stress the deciding judge's choice of "material" facts, what then is this "materiality"? *If you add the deciding judge's order to his spelling out of "material" facts, you have the rule of law the judge says he is using, and moreover you have it in the judge's own words*. A "material fact" is an abstraction or concept, as Dr. Goodhart in effect concedes when, in an example taken from the law of contract, he speaks of "consideration" as a material fact in his sense.[45] And if "material here is to be considered as a synonym for "relevant", then it is a term of relation and one must ask "material" or "relevant" to what? To the legal proposition the deciding judge has chosen to use, what else! Nowhere does Dr. Goodhart explain his critical term "material", but, if it has any public meaning at all in this context, it tacitly concedes the validity of the orthodox view of precedent in the Common Law.

We turn now to problems related to the degree of abstraction or generality of the rules to be derived from judicial opinions. As the preceding analysis centred on the cases of *Donoghue v. Stevenson* and *Haseldine v. Daw* implied, here again we take the choice of the deciding judge, for, as a matter of juristic possibility, there is a wide range of consistent legal propositions running through many different levels of abstraction, all relevant to the fact-situation of the actual case. The orthodox theory holds then that *ipso facto*, the deciding judge sets the level of abstraction, be it high or low, broad or narrow, by his choice of the rule to be used. When, as in Lord Atkin's judgment in *Donoghue v. Stevenson*, two propositions are expressed, one at a much higher level of generality than the other, at least the orthodox theory reduces us to these simple alternatives for the rule of the case. And indeed, if the broader proposition is accepted, the case stands for both, as the greater includes the lesser.

But there is a persistent idea that, when two or more propositions of differ-

---

[45]*Op. cit.*, 24.

ing generality have been given, the case is to be taken to stand only for the one of lesser or least generality, Dr. Goodhart has necessarily taken this position:[46]

> If in a case there are several opinions which agree as to the result but differ as to the material facts, then the principle of the case is limited so as to fit the sum of all the facts held material by the various judges.

Professor R. N. Gooderson, though he purports to uphold an "orthodox" theory of precedent, in that he would take the rule the deciding judge expressed as the rule of the case, nevertheless agrees in the result with Dr. Goodhart. Professor Gooderson says:[47]

> (I)f the judge states his proposition of law several times, now broader, now narrower, only the narrowest is the *ratio decidendi*, and . . . in courts consisting of several judges who decide the same way on different grounds of law, only the narrowest proposition of law is the *ratio decidendi*.

But in the case of *Haseldine v. Daw*, all three judges purported to follow *Donoghue v. Stevenson*, and not one of them took the narrowest proposition in the majority opinions—that of Lord Thankerton. Both Lord Atkin's propositions have often been followed in subsequent cases. As we have seen, there is simply no logical ground for preferring the narrower to the broader of two consistent legal propositions. Indeed, as a matter of judicial intention, the deciding judge may well have intended the narrower proposition simply as an illustration of the broader one, while standing on the latter. The idea that the narrower proposition is to be preferred over the broader seems to be a deduction from the assumptions of extreme pragmatism, which, as we have seen, simply rejects the objective validity (if not indeed the possibility) of any higher levels of abstraction. As would be expected, this tendency is seen most clearly in certain of the modern American legal realists like Professor H. Oliphant and Professor W. W. Cook. Professor Oliphant has said:[48]

> There has been an asserted or tacit assumption that there exists certain general principles of inherent and abiding validity, and that, therefore, a new case can be properly decided by deducing from some general principle the particular rule applicable to the case at hand. The invalidity of the method is, of course, fundamental. It is found in the fact that all of our so-called general principles are but experimental rationalizations of our previous experiences and, therefore, they cannot contain the inevitable solution of new problems, which of necessity form no part of the experience rationalized.

These jurists do not deny the need for a very modest degree of generalization, but they do insist that legal propositions must be kept very narrow and specific if they are to have validity. Professor Oliphant's disparagement of "so-

---

[46]*Op. cit.,* 26.

[47]Gooderson, "Ratio Decidendi and Rules of Law" (1952), 30 Can. Bar Rev. 892, 904.

[48]Oliphant, "Current Economic and Social Problems" (1923), 10 Proc. Acad. of Political Science, 325-6. Quoted by Cahill, Jr., "Judicial Legislation" (1952), 117. Note the implication that "new problems" are *completely* unique. This denies the objective validity of abstractions that more orthodox jurists think can and do connect old and new situations.

called *general* principles'' has just been quoted. Likewise, Professor W. W. Cook favours what he calls the "multiplication of working concepts'',[49] by which he means dependence on many very specific and narrow concepts rather than on fewer and more general ones. This automatic and invariable preference for low levels of abstraction, then, seems to come from the extreme pragmatism which holds that abstractions or concepts must be kept very specific, for only then can they be in close connection with that which *is* real—particular things and happenings that we see, touch, or hear. If one does not accept this very restricted picture of reality, there is no ground for the preference of lower over higher abstractions in logic or metaphysics.

Once again we see that the middle position of the orthodox theory of precedent between mechanical jurisprudence and extreme pragmatism is supported by moderate sociological jurists, or moderate pragmatists, like Dean Roscoe Pound and Professor M. R. Cohen. If you recognize with them that abstract features and qualities of facts of experience and occurrence partake of reality, just as much as do those parts of such fact-situations available to direct sensory perception, then you refuse to admit any automatic interdict against ascending to higher levels of abstraction—to broader levels of generality—in determining the legal propositions for which cases are to stand. Certainly, the natural scientist, if he is to be the model, recognizes no such interdict against higher levels of abstraction in his realm of cause and effect. Indeed, the essence of the genius and achievement of men like Albert Einstein is precisely that they *have* succeeded in scaling the heights to new high levels of abstraction, for which verification has followed in experiment and further observation of nature. As Professor M. R. Cohen indicates, there seems to be a positive urge among thinkers to strive for the larger generalizations.[50]

> We try to reduce the law to the smallest number of general principles from which all possible cases can be reached, just as we try to reduce our knowledge of nature to a deductive mathematical system.

Likewise, Dean Pound believes in and positively advocates reaching for wider generalities.[51] This is the answer to those of his critics who suggest that Dean Pound's views do not differ from those of the legal realists—that the latter merely made further logical deductions from Dean Pound's premises, from which deductions Pound himself then recoiled.[52] Since a striving for broader

---

[49] Cook, ''Select Essays in the Conflict of Laws''.

[50] Cohen, ''The Place of Logic in the Law'' (1916), 29 Harv. L. R. 622, 624.

[51] ''William James tells us that 'the course of history is nothing but the story of man's struggle from generation to generation to find the more inclusive order'. Certainly such has been the course of legal doctrine. But here, too, the endeavour has been to prevent friction and eliminate waste.

''In law this means an endeavour to eliminate the arbitrary and illogical; *a conscious quest for the broad principle* that will do the work of securing the most interests with the least sacrifice of other interests, and at the same time conserve judicial effort by flowing logically from or logically according with and fitting into the legal system as a whole'': Pound, ''Juristic Science and Law'' (1918), 31 Harv. L. R. 1047, 1062-3 (The italics are the writer's). See also Pollock, ''A First Book of Jurisprudence'', 2nd ed. (1904), 81.

[52] This criticism of Pound is made by Cahill Jr., ''Judicial Legislation'' (cited in footnote 48), 80-81.

legal propositions is central to Dean Pound's philosophy of law, he necessarily rejects the extreme pragmatism or nominalism of the realists, *and this difference is basic.* Indeed, Pound's "jural postulates of the civilization of the time and place" are attempts to explain in a few propositions at a very broad level of generality what it is that citizens expect and need from their legal system. It is true that Dean Pound distinguishes between rules, principles and standards, but these are all normative propositions and there is nothing here inconsistent with the analysis being pursued in this essay. His "rules" are specific or detailed legal propositions at a low level of abstraction, whereas his "principles" and "standards" run at higher levels of abstraction.[53]

But, though Professors Pound and Cohen insist on the necessity and value of abstract thought in the law, as did certain natural-law jurists of past centuries, this does not mean that they have sold out to "mechanical jurisprudence." While Pound and Cohen agree with older natural-law theorists on the necessity to pursue abstract thought to the limit of human capacity, they differ on what that capacity is. The jurists named, and others who think like them, do not have the old natural law faith that man has uncovered and fully appreciated the one just and complete legal system, running from the highest to the lowest levels of abstraction. Nor do they think this is likely to come about in the foreseeable future. Nevertheless, they do have faith in the possibility of partially significant insights into the proper order and truth of human relations, and are convinced of the need to strive for such insights for legal purposes in terms of generalized normative propositions. Though much has been and can be accomplished, success remains partial, and the exigencies of this imperfection necessitate a moderate pragmatism. The pragmatic jurist will constantly check his abstract principles for the actual consequences they have or would have in operation for the specific persons and circumstances they contemplate by their terms, in order to help assessment of their value. Also, he regards this testing process as necessary because the real circumstances of human relations, *both specific and abstract,* exhibit changing as well as constant factors. Hence the moderate pragmatist would detect these changes as best he could and seek to adjust legal rules to them when appropriate.

So, social facts must be gathered carefully and constantly on the consequences of actual or proposed rules, that is, on the results of observing and enforcing them in the society for which they are intended. The value of the various rules is then to be judged in the light of all that can be learned by such diligent

---

[53]Pound, "Juristic Science and Law" (1918), 31 Harv. L. R., 1060-63. It is not clear in Pound's scheme of "rules", "principles" and "standards", when one moves from the lower level of abstraction (that of rules) to the higher level of abstraction (that of principles or standards). Neither am I able to distinguish principles from standards. For instance, Dean Pound speaks of the "standard of the reasonable man" and of the "principle of negotiation in good faith". "Reasonableness" and "good faith" are both abstract concepts to me, and each could be designated "standard" or "principle" interchangeably. Anyway, Dean Pound would agree that one progresses from lower to higher levels of abstraction, and that is enough for purposes of agreement with the analysis presented in this essay.

social research. The light thus shed is not perfect, but it does show the way to better legal propositions in terms of human welfare than would be possible without it. Thus, the valid parts of pragmatism may be accepted without going to extremes.

The main theme of this essay may now be explicitly affirmed—that the underlying philosophy of the orthodox Common Law system of precedent is the moderate sociological jurisprudence, or moderate pragmatism just explained. When this is coupled with a proper appreciation of the nature and flexibility of logic as an instrument, we get the Common Law system at its best. We then see relevant legal propositions for a given type of fact-situation logically developed through both their more abstract and their more specific ranges of implication, and tested against social reality by the constant interaction between fact and proposition explained earlier in the comparison of scientific and juristic processes of reasoning.

At this point a *caveat* should be entered and explained. I do not say, and I am sure Professors Pound and Cohen would not say, that a judge should always enunciate the most general or abstract principle he can possibly contrive to decide a given case. This would be as erroneous as to hold that he should never do so, or that he should always use as narrow a rule as he can contrive. Striking the correct or just level of generality is a delicate and difficult business, as *Donoghue v. Stevenson* and subsequent cases relying on it show. Lord Atkin went high up the scale of abstraction in framing his proposition about neighbours—as high as he thought he should go—but this was not the top, as he himself pointed out when he said he could not make a legal injunction out of the moral precept to *love* one's neighbour. Also, as we have seen, the principle of *caveat emptor* is in direct conflict (respecting the legal rights of third persons) with Lord Atkin's proposition about neighbours and foresight, or even with his lesser proposition about manufacturers and consumers, if understood to cover *all* things manufactured. For legal purposes, these conflicting principles must be somehow compromised or one of them rejected outright. The English and Canadian courts have resorted to compromise, achieved by narrowing both rules—by retreating down the scale of abstraction in both cases—until they no longer overlap. The rule of *caveat emptor* is limited to manufacturers and vendors of houses, and the foresight test of manufacturers' liability is limited to manufacturers of tangible movable things. This is a poor compromise at best, for why should the maker of a dangerously defective house escape liability to third persons when the maker of a dangerously defective automobile does not? In any event, this is an actual example that illustrates the logical technique of compromise. Likewise, family maintenance statutes represent a compromise between freedom of testation and the responsibility of deceased fathers and husbands to provide for dependants. This compromise is achieved by dividing the estate into two parts, one to be disposed of on one principle and one on the other. The legal system is full of these adjustments or equilibrium points, which, as illustrated, involve striking the respective degrees of generality that will effect justifiable compromises between rules or principles that overlap and conflict. This is a delicate and difficult process, *not in the least automatic as to either greater or lesser degrees of generality.*[54]

The question of greater or lesser degrees of generality is also involved in assessing the claim that the Common Law judicial process is marked by a unique system of thought called analogical reasoning or reasoning by examples. Analogy and example are certainly involved in legal reasoning, but just as certainly this is not at all peculiar. Rather, legal reasoning shares analogy and example with all other reasonable processes in other departments of knowledge and human endeavour.

Let us suppose that Judge Jones, trying case X, is faced with the allegation by the plaintiff that previous case A affords the proper precedent, whereas the defendant alleges that, on the contrary, previous case B affords the proper precedent. The rules used in A and B respectively are both logically relevant to the new fact-situation X, but conflict one with the other. How does Judge Jones choose between them, or can he reject both and turn legislator? Now in some respect or other, the facts of X are novel—there is some uniqueness to every fresh fact-situation. Yet, on the other hand, the facts of X are not completely novel, for always there are some real elements of identity with past situations. The delicate nature of the task of Judge Jones now emerges. He must compare present fact-situation X with the past fact-situation A to determine what are the elements of uniqueness or difference between them and what are their elements of identity. This is repeated between fact-situation X and fact-situation B. The process involved here is the tested hypothetico-deductive reasoning explained earlier, including assessment of various more or less abstract propositions that by their terms comprehend both X and A, or X and B. One of these logically relevant propositions has already been expressed as the rule of case A and another as that of case B. Judge Jones must balance the elements of identity between A and X against the elements of difference. If the differences are insignificant and the elements of identity numerous and important, he will conclude that case X is analogous to case A, or "on all fours" with case A. This means he had decided that, while fact-situation X is not identical with fact-situation A, it is *sufficiently similar* that the rule of law appropriate for A is also appropriate for X. The fact-situation B would be judged not sufficiently similar (analogous) to X, so that the rule of B is not appropriate for X.

---

[54]Furthermore, one may insist on this point and yet admit that at times the Common Law judges have been properly cautious about proceeding from the more specific to the more general levels of abstraction. The caution is justified when the actual social and moral implications of the more general propositions cannot be appreciated with reasonable assurance and accuracy. But this is not at all to say that there is some automatic priority for the lesser levels of generality.

Also, without impairing the points made above, one may concede that the applicable rule of law is in many cases clear enough. This is particularly true of a mass of specific rules at a low level of generality, such as characterizes the field of real property. Mr. Justice Cardozo made this point eloquently: "In countless litigations, the law is so clear that judges have no discretion. They have the right to legislate within gaps, but often there are no gaps." See: Cardozo, "The Nature of the Judicial Process" (1921), 129. Also, Pound said: "Happily, the bulk of . . . cases repeat or ring insignificant changes upon familiar states of fact" (36 Harv. L. R. 941). Nevertheless, the rarer and doubtful case is of critical importance.

If cases A and B were decided in courts constitutionally authoritative over the court of Judge Jones, he is now bound to follow the rule of A, rejecting that of B. The judicial process then is *not* just a matter of finding *any* element of identity between a present and a past fact-situation, rather it involves finding *sufficient* elements of identity that the rule of the previous case "makes sense" for the present one also. This determination of sufficiency is the critical one, and is entirely a matter for the reasoning faculty of the deciding judge. It is precisely this that Sir Carleton Allen had in mind when he said that even the humblest judicial officer places the fetters of a House of Lords precedent on his own hands. Professor Thayer had like considerations in mind when he remarked that there can be no mandamus to the logical faculty. At this point at least, the Common Law system is pure reason unalloyed by authority.

Before leaving this particular topic, we should notice an important intermediate stage in the assessing of elements of identity and difference that is also called "analogy". Suppose that Judge Jones decided that case X was not sufficiently similar to case A or case B that he was bound to follow the rule of either. In other words, suppose Judge Jones has decided that the elements of novelty in case X predominate in comparison with any previous cases in courts of authority for him. Now Judge Jones has no binding precedent, and whether he wishes it or not, a significant degree of innovation is required of him to formulate a rule for case X. He now has a degree of discretion that is said to be legislative. Likely though, he will still "reason by analogy" to previous cases that are not sufficiently similar to be "on all fours" with case X, but which are nevertheless similar in a significant though lesser degree. This is what Lord Justice Goddard did in *Haseldine v. Daw*. He said in effect: "A repairman is not a manufacturer, so I am not bound to apply Lord Atkin's manufacturer-consumer proposition; the elements of identity are not great enough for that. But the situations are similar enough that I do not think a repairman should escape a type of liability imposed on a manufacturer. They are close enough to doing the same sort of thing, that I think it right to extend the liability of the manufacturer to the repairman by analogy". Why has Lord Goddard connected the manufacturer and the repairman in this way? Because Lord Atkin's manufacturer-consumer proposition implies a somewhat broader consistent principle that would go something like this: All those who manufacture, process or repair movable things and by carelessness leave hidden and dangerous defects in such things are liable to consumers or users of them. This wider proposition does literally contemplate the facts of both *Donoghue v. Stevenson* and *Haseldine v. Daw*. This is the "same thing" of which both are examples. Reasoning by analogy from a given legal rule in this latter sense then means that, though the given rule does not itself comprehend the new facts, *it suggests a consistent broader rule that will do so*. This logically suggested use of a more inclusive principle is simply one of the features of any process of abstract thought. But, though it is not peculiar, it does represent a vital growing point of the Common Law. For example, Professor Fifoot shows that, when increased traffic on highways and in harbours seemed to require a broader doctrine of liability for harm done, the general tort of negligence was developed out of the older specific categories of liability for carelessness of bailees, professional men, and those handling fire. The process has been described with great clarity by the late Chief Justice of Canada, Sir Lyman Duff:[55]

> The circumstances of a particular case may be such that, to them, none of the rules as formulated and applied in decided cases or books of authority is strictly appropriate; and then one must have recourse to analogy, and to the principles underlying the decisions or the rules as formulated or deductible therefrom.

Reasoning by analogy, then, in any of its senses, is a matter of comparing the elements of identity and difference between various fact-situations in the light of logically relevant legal propositions. It is one of the exigencies of imperfection referred to earlier that often those propositions will overlap inconsistently for particular facts and therefore cause "competing analogies". The need to choose between them leads to the final topic, value decisions and the place of constitutional authority in the judical process.

(d) Value Decisions and Constitutional Authority in the Judicial Process

At an earlier point in this essay, it was said that the final question of the jurist in his realm of the normative must be put to some acceptable and understandable system of values, by contrast to the natural scientist who, in his realm of cause, can contrive a reference to nature for his answers. Also, it was asserted that moral or policy decisions would be better ones if the way were prepared for them and the alternative solutions defined by sound logical method in combination with diligent accumulation and assessment of relevant social facts. Nevertheless, logical method and social research only lead to the necessity of final choice beyond logic and social fact. But, for this final step, what system of values is to prevail with those who have the official duty of decision? There are of course certain broadly accepted community values that judges will share, but nevertheless we do live in a pluralistic society of many different groups holding to different and at times conflicting value preferences, and each group seeks to have its own preferences promoted or supported in some way by legal rules. In addition, over a considerable range of actual or possible situations calling for legal decisions, there are no coherent public attitudes at all, whether consensual or conflicting, on the preferences of valuation concerned.

Accordingly, when a judge is confronted with a degree of novelty that requires him to be creative (*i.e.* to exercise a legislative discretion), what is he to do when he reaches the stage of final choice between alternatives? Does he follow his own sense of right and wrong, or does he seek for and follow a community consensus, if any, or is there some other formula?

Various prescriptions have been suggested for solving this difficulty. Dean Pound says that inconsistent interests reflected in conflicting demands are to be compromised by composing legal rules that make the goods of existence go around as far as possible among the members of society with the least friction

---

[55]*The King v. National Trust Co. Ltd.*, [1933] 4 D.L.R., 468-9.

and waste. These are for him the better rules. Jeremy Bentham exhorts us to contrive legal rules that promote the maximum surplus of pleasure over pain, as he defines pleasures and pains. Jacksonian democrats make an oracle of "the people" and would have final legal choices in great number and detail continually put to the vote, or to public opinion. Extreme pragmatists make a god of what they call social fact and would judge the worth of laws by their degree of harmonious "adjustment" to such "fact".

None of these formulae is satisfactory, though they do have some valid features. Dean Pound's formula seems to call for favouring the value propositions that have the greatest volume or weight of popular demand behind them, for this would appear to hold the best promise of the least friction and waste in the social distribution of goods of existence. But it is not either desirable or possible to take votes or even Gallup polls on every sort of legal issue. The judge or legislator who would follow Dean Pound's formula can only estimate the relative weight behind conflicting demands, and in so doing he will tend to favour that principle he himself believes to be the better or more worthy one. This principle will naturally strike him as the one best calculated to attract public support by its inherent merit, and so make the goods of existence go around with the least friction and waste. In many if not most creative judicial decisions, this is the only sense in which it is possible to estimate and be guided by public opinion. The same comment can be made about Bentham's calculus of pleasures and pains. The Benthamite estimator of pleasure surpluses cannot possibly indulge in continual mass psycho-analysis on the pleasure or pain producing propensities of actual or proposed rules of law. Like Pound's social engineer, he will tend to consider that the rules he himself believes to be the better ones are those most likely to give pleasure-surpluses. Moreover, Bentham's definitions of pleasures and pains include such things as pleasures of skill or talent, pleasures of piety, pleasures of benevolence or sympathy, and pleasures of friendhip and good reputation. Here then is no mere census of sensual desires—Bentham's definitions of simple pleasures themselves acknowledge the necessity for ethical decisions by his estimators of pleasure-surpluses.

Of course it would be naive to suggest that either Dean Pound or Jeremy Bentham was calling for an actual mass census of personal desires or pleasures, but they do in effect call upon legislators and judges to estimate what the results of an actual census would be if it could be and were held on the issues confronting them. What Pound and Bentham do not frankly acknowledge is that this necessarily involves the legislator or judge in personal responsibility for an ethical choice.

A less sophisticated attempt to follow public opinion is found in the Jacksonian conception of democracy, that public opinion is an oracle that will continually give detailed decisions on final legal issues if one just keeps on consulting it by voting about nearly everything and everybody in public affairs. The fallacy here has been tersely described by the aphorism that there is no public opinion on the rule against perpetuities. The average private citizen cannot be preoccupied with and fully informed on the multitude of legal and governmental issues that arise continually for decision. There just is no pre-existing public opinion on many if not most issues that judges and legislators must decide from day to day in the course of duty.

Finally, as we have seen earlier in this essay, it is also fallacious to expect with the extreme pragmatist (the pragmatist who is also a nominalist) that social fact will somehow make the correct normative rule for the situation concerned. What social fact calls for in the way of adjustment through legal rules is assumed to be obvious or self-operating once social fact has been ascertained. Again, as in the case of the other formulae, unmentioned value premises will enter here in the would-be adjuster's judgment of what is "social fact" and what is "adjustment".

But the judge must still decide the cases that come before him by the use of acceptable and understandable normative principles, and the member of Parliament is in a like position when framing proposed laws. As humane and democratic men what are they to do when they reach these moments of final discretion and choice? The foregoing reasoning implies that in numerous cases the only thing the judge or legislator can do is to apply his own system of values, on the assumption that he is typical of his fellow-citizens. In other words, while a judge should select the rule that a reasonable and moral man in our society would say was a proper rule to apply to the situation concerned, the point is that often the only clue to these typical or objective values will be the judge's own personal standards of better or worse, right or wrong. Whenever he is in doubt about typical values (and this will be frequently) the judge must resort to his own. This is the meaning of the phrase "the agony of decision". The judge who understands what he is doing has many lonely moments of responsibility in the realm of ethics for the use of discretions that come to him by the combined action of legal reasoning and constitutional duty.[56]

Nevertheless, the judge or legislator is not entirely alone; he is not altogether without help or guidance in these high responsibilities. The processes of both court and legislature in our country are democratic and dialectical in that they seek to ensure that all interested parties are heard and that alternative principles for solution are appreciated before a decision is made. Thus, by submission and argument, in both court room and legislative chamber, attempts are made to elucidate the values that ought to attract the support of the citizens as reasonable and moral men. In some instances there will be an ascertainable community consensus on value propositions of great importance. Obviously much of this kind of agreement lies behind the criminal law, or the development of the welfare state with its forms of protective legal status for the aged, the unemployed and the incurably ill. But also, in many instances, there will be disagreement and conflict on values between large and powerful groups, and then compromises that keep

---

[56]Professor Edmond Cahn points out that this was the position taken by Professor John Chipman Gray, with whom Professor Cahn expresses agreement. See: Cahn, "The Moral Decision, Right and Wrong in the Light of American Law" (1955), 301-2, and see generally his chapter x. Further support for the view expressed above is found in: d'Entrèves, "Natural Law" (1951). Professor d'Entrèves maintains that one of the abiding truths of natural law philosophy is "that law is a part of ethics" (116); that "laws are nothing but the outcome of the quest for clear and definite standards of valuation whenever action is involved" (118).

the peace but please no one are often the best that can be done for the moment. The logical technique for effecting such compromises has already been illustrated. Certainly, present liquor laws or divorce laws in most provinces of Canada bring about an uneasy armistice between large and powerful groups sincerely holding to opposing values. Paradoxically, to have displeased everyone concerned to some extent may be the sign, in such situations, that the best compromise rules available for the time being have been made.

Also, and more happily, it may be conceded that at times, different persons or groups will for different reasons of preference accept a rather specific rule as right or proper in a given situation. The socialist, the nature-lover, the landscape artist, the highway safety officer, and the business man dependent on tourist trade—all these are likely to support a rule of law forbidding the placing of large sign-boards for commercial advertising along the fringes of country highways. So, we may say that, while some possibilities of ascertaining a moral consensus in the community do exist, the fact remains that more often than not the deciding official in a position of discretion has no alternative but to turn to his own system of values, for the reasons already given.

At this point, the need for authoritative decision becomes plain. As seen earlier, we do not have the possibility of a finally valid and substantively complete legal system which, by its obvious merit, attracts the total support of omniscient citizens. Yet there is stark social and constitutional necessity for decision on standards to govern at critical points in human relations. Hence, as a minimum, any advanced constitution must designate official persons and invest them with the authority of the organized community to speak the last word for legal purposes. This last word, when spoken, damps down debate and defines the principle for action that is to be implemented for the issue in hand. If the last word is not spoken in critical situations, the essential order of society based on law will dissolve in endless debate and procrastination, or in civil war. The characteristic Common Law judicial principles of *res judicata* and *stare decisis* express and implement this primary constitutional necessity,[57] as does also the principle of the legislative finality of parliamentary statutes. Professor Hans Kelsen gives us a sophisticated and correct picture of this constitutional necessity in his concept of the basic norm as the source of an hierarchy of consistent and progressively more specific norms of authority, defining who speaks the last word, and by what procedure he does so, at the various points where decisions are needed. This tells us nothing substantive about what is to guide these decisions, but, in the purely procedural sense of constitutional regularity we do get a complete and closed hierarchial system of propositions of authority. This is a poor but necessary substitute for the lack of full rational and moral consensus on complete substantive principles and rules of justice, a consensus that is always in considerable measure beyond human reach for the public ordering of human relations. The

---

[57]"If the judicial matters of record should be drawn in question, by partial and sinister supposals and averments of offenders, or any on their behalf, there will never be an end of a cause, but controversies will be infinite": Coke, quoted by Holdsworth, "A History of English Law" (1922), Volume VI, 237.

need to fall back on a complete system of authoritative regular deciding procedure is, then, one of the exigencies of imperfection mentioned earlier.

Yet, to win and hold the support of the people by serving human welfare, these constitutional processes need to provide for resort to the best that man can accomplish in reasonable thought, social research and moral insight as the basis for official decision, however partial these powers of reason and insight may be from time to time. In a democratic country, this requirement is a fundamental element of what we call "the rule of law".

These constitutional objects may be, and of course are, served in different ways. One way is the election of members of Parliament and parliamentary procedures for legislation, another is the appointment of superior court judges to secure tenure and independent status appropriate for the traditional processes of the royal courts of justice. The very purpose of the judge's secure and disinterested constitutional status is to free him from all other influences except those of reason and conscience.[58]

Admittedly this essay has described the Common Law system at its best, but often it has lived up to its best features, and the successes of the system as well as its shortcomings are our inheritance in Canada. Though our representative legislatures and administrative bodies are necessarily much more active than in the past, due to the increasing complexity of our civilization and legal needs, this also augments rather than diminishes the need for courts on the traditional English model and the reasonable processes whereby they created and developed the Common Law. There is a great and continuing need for judge-made rules of law, and even the statutes of a representative legislature may benefit by reasonable and creative interpretation in the courts.

FURTHER THOUGHTS AND REFERENCES

While the foregoing essay is entitled "The Common Law System in Canada", and so does concentrate on the operating jurisprudence of our inherited English judicial institutions, nevertheless it does have a broader sweep and purpose. It seeks to explore the nature of legal systems and legal reasoning generally for all persons having significant discretion for legal decision-making, including of course the judges but is not limited to them. Accordingly the essay is placed very early in this book so that two main points of importance may be made right away.

First, while the examples used are from the private law, this essay does re-

---

[58]See Dawson, "The Government of Canada", 2nd ed. (1954), 486. See also Louis L. Jaffe and Edith G. Henderson, "Judicial Review and the Rule of Law: Historical Origins" (1956), 72 L.Q. Rev. 345. In particular see the passages on pages 346-47. These authorities make it clear that an appointed superior court judiciary on the English model is not a contradiction of the democratic concept of the rule of law. Indeed, the converse is the truth, a democratic rule of law requires such a judiciary. To the same effect is Calamandrei, "Procedure and Democracy" (1956), especially Chapter III.

veal and develop more fully than any other my continuing basic premises and beliefs concerning some of the principal issues of legal science and philosophy; and
these are pertinent not only to private law problems but to those of public law as
well. Accordingly, these same premises and beliefs will be found at the basis of
much of my reasoning in essays written in later years, especially those in Parts
IV and V on constitutional interpretation in the courts.

Secondly, it will have been noted that I derived conclusions about the basic
elements of legal reasoning by study of decision-making under the common law.
Though my knowledge of the Civil Code of Quebec is very limited, nevertheless
I am convinced that, for the most part, the two systems have in common the same
methods of legal reasoning for decision-making. I suspect the differences to be
mainly lesser matters of emphasis and form rather than essentials of the process.
Indeed, as I have argued in the essay just reproduced, I think good legal reasoning to be itself simply a manifestation of sound reasoning or thinking in general. I
do not deny of course that there are at times important specific differences in the
substantive content of the Common Law and the Civil Code on various subjects.
I am referring rather to the methods of thought by which the two systems are
operated to accomplish decision-making. In the essay just reproduced on the
"Common Law System" I spoke of legal decision-making as the matching of
facts on the one hand with relevant legal rules or principles on the other. Then I
added that "In this intellectual combined operation, it is fruitless to worry about
which comes first, appreciation of the abstract idea or of the specific case, because (a) at some times the start of legal reasoning will be with abstract ideas, at
other times with specific cases, and (b) in any even the essence of legal reasoning
is the unqualified necessity for constant interaction between the two." (p. 00). It
may well be true that under the Civl Code there may be more emphasis at the
start upon abstract rules and principles, whereas under the common law there
may be more emphasis at the start on the particularity of the facts in issue. Nevertheless, in the end, I argue that the total process of thought for both systems is the
same—a full-fledged "combined operation" in which "facts", and "rules" or
"principles" interact.

Moreover, the extent of the common ground here is accentuated by the fact
that Quebec, on the public law side, has the same English-type judicial and parliamentary institutions that obtain in the other provinces and also at the level of
the central government of Canada. So, one may conclude that Quebec jurists and
common law jurists from the other provinces should have little difficulty understanding one another for purposes of working our common federal constitution,
among other things. I believe the evidence shows this to have been our Canadian
experience.

I suggest that much support for what I have just been saying may be found
in the following sources: "P. B. Mignault, "The Authority of Decided Cases"
(1925), 3 Can. Bar Rev. 1-24; W. Friedmann, "Stare Decisis at Common Law
and under the Civil Code of Quebec" (1953), 31 Can. Bar Rev. 723-51.

Part II
Constitutional History, Independence and Amendment

Chapter 3

The British Parliamentary System and Canadian Federalism

Reprinted with permission from *One Country or Two?* R. M. Burns
(ed.) (Montreal and London: McGill-Queen's University Press, 1971)

Canada's present constitution, and her system of public law generally, are the products of a long history of development following for the most part the model afforded from time to time by the British constitution, as that constitution grew and developed over the centuries for the internal government of Britain herself. This process culminated for British North America in the winning of responsible government in 1848. This was the transfer to British North America of the full-fledged British cabinet and parliamentary system as it was in the middle of the nineteenth century. Here is the root of a vitally important difference between Canada and the United States today, for the American inheritance from Britain is dated in the late eighteenth century, stopping with the British constitution as it stood in 1776. Only about seventy years intervened between 1776 and 1848, but this particular seventy years say critical changes in the British constitution; specifically they saw the development of the cabinet system in Britain, particularly after 1832, and the prompt transfer of that system to British North America. We will return later to the modern significance of this vital difference between the Canadian and American systems of government.

But the British North American colonies in the nineteenth century were also very much a part of the New World, and the example and influence of the United States in things constitutional and legal was strong. In 1867 the British North American colonies adopted the idea of federal union from the United States, though of course in the new Canadian federation parliamentary institutions on the British model were continued at the provincial level and were set up also at the national level of the central federal government.

So we may say that the two high points of Canadian constitutional development were responsible government in the 1840s and federation of the British North American colonies in the 1860s. Amid our present constitutional discontents in Canada we should pause to remember that Quebec and French Canada have been well served by Parliamentary democracy (with its concomitant cabinet system) and by federalism. These two institutions were and are important bulwarks protecting the distinctive French-Canadian way of life in Canada and

North America. Of course, there were other objectives being sought as well in the historical movements of the nineteenth century directed to winning responsible government and bringing about federation. The acquisition and development of the Northwest is an example. But none of the other objectives was more constant or more important than the objective of assuring reasonable security for the essentials of the French-Canadian way of life, as those essentials were conceived to be at the time. The leaders of English Canada entered into close and continuing partnerships with the leaders of French Canada to accomplish this end in the case of both these developments. The extent to which they succeeded in safeguarding the French-Canadian way of life was very significant and should not now be disparaged.

Moreover, responsible parliamentary government and federalism are vital cohesive factors for all the various parts of Canada today, and indeed they may have even greater importance than in the past. Even if Quebec were to separate, these cohesive influences would remain operative for the other provinces and regions of Canada. But the main thrust of my comments is to argue that both the lessons of our history and the pressures of the modern world demonstrate that the best security French Canadians can now have for their way of life lies in the continuing federal unity of Canada, including Quebec. No doubt it is true that the range of political and constitutional options, as we approach extreme solutions, may be decisively limited by the balance of overall economic costs and benefits for Quebec and other parts of Canada. The economic considerations are obviously important and at some point may become critical to what happens. Nevertheless, I argue from the conviction that political and social traditions and their expression in constitutions and laws are supreme over economics.

This has been shown in our history by the fact that Canadians have always paid, and willingly, an economic price for maintaining a national identity separate from the United States of America. If we maintain present Canadian unity, I believe that Canadians can continue so to govern themselves that the economic price of remaining separate from the United States will stay within acceptable limits on into the future. Our system of government is just as democratic as that of the Americans; moreover, the Canadian parliamentary and cabinet system is more efficient than the American congressional and presidential system. In addition, the Canadian type of federalism has turned out to be more balanced, that is, more sensitive and responsive to cultural duality and regionalism, than is the case with the modern federalism of the United States.

But if Quebec insists on separation, then these issues are shrouded in rather ominous uncertainty, with the continued distinctiveness of Quebec in the greatest peril of all. In other words, there would then be a serious question whether Quebec alone, or the other parts of Canada (separately or together), could so reorganize their life and industry through the medium of democratic governmental institutions as to keep the costs of avoiding absorption by the United States within acceptable limits, economic and otherwise. Probably Canada without Quebec could do so if the other provinces and regions stayed together in a federal parliamentary union. I am sanguine enough to believe that the will to maintain such a union would be there. But the better and much more likely alternative for all is the continuation of the present Canadian federation, with Quebec as a vital member. We must seek the political and constitutional adjustments that would facilitate this.

It is true, of course, that we cannot simply rest on past successes in accommodating the French Fact in British North America, but, nevertheless, it is still worth looking in some detail at certain highlights of the nineteenth century in this respect, because those were troubled times too and there *are* lessons for today and tomorrow in what was accomplished then. We shall look at the winning of responsible government, the achievement of federation of the British North American colonies, and at the contrasts between the Canadian and American constitutions in these and certain other matters.

We consider first the development of the cabinet system in Britain, that is, the nature of the relation between the Crown and Parliament—the executive and legislative bodies in the state. This was one thing in the late eighteenth century wherein the internal British governmental system provided the model for the new American constitution. But the relations of Crown and Parliament in Great Britain had become something quite different some seventy years later, when these relations provided the model for responsible government as granted to the British North American colonies in the period from 1841 to 1848.[1]

The nature of the eighteenth-century British constitution can be seen in the position of King George III. He was the real executive head of the nation, though it was true that parliamentary legislative power prevailed over the royal prerogative power and Parliament held the purse strings. The royal prerogatives still included control of colonial administration and policy, foreign relations, and the command of the armed forces. The executive power and initiative generally were thus very much in the hands of the king. He selected his own ministers or advisers, some from the House of Commons, some from the House of Lords, and some who were not in either House. It is true enough that he usually had a "First Minister." There were no political parties in the modern sense, and there was no prime minister in the modern sense—indeed George III, in effect, acted as his own prime minister. The chosen group of royal advisers came and went as individuals or in various combinations pretty well as the king determined they should. When meeting, they considered only matters on which the king had requested their advice. The executive primacy of the king was not affected by whether or not he attended cabinet meetings—in any event he settled the questions to be considered, and the resulting advice was reported to him, whereupon he could accept it or reject it.

It is true that the king had some need of a sympathetic House of Commons and of some ministers who sat in the House, so that on occasion he could obtain the statutes and money votes he wanted. But in the eighteenth century the king first selected his ministers and then, if necessary, constructed a sympa-

---

[1]See A. H. Birch, *Representative and Responsible Government* (Toronto: University of Toronto Press, 1965), chap. 10; and John P. Mackintosh, *The British Cabinet* (London: Stevens, 1962), chap. 2.

thetic House of Commons at the next election. The parliamentary constituencies at this time were extremely unequal in population and a great many of them could be managed, either because they were "rotten" boroughs up for sale or "nomination" boroughs where the choice of member was controlled by a local patron. By the use of patronage and preferment for various public offices, the king and his ministers could assure themselves a House of Commons that would go their way.

If there was a defeat in the House in these earlier times, the ministry did not resign but waited for the right moment to call an election and reconstruct the membership of the House. No British ministry resigned as a result of a defeat in the House between 1783 and 1830. At the time of George III then, the executive powers of the Crown and the legislative powers of Parliament were autonomous and separate. They had to seek one another's co-operation from time to time, but there was no regular or consistent system for the co-ordination of executive and legislative functions. This is one reason why George III was able to make his arbitrary American policy prevail with the eventual result that the American colonists were provoked to successful revolution. It is true that the Prime Minister, Lord North, and all his colleagues except the Lord Chancellor resigned in 1782 when confronted with a very hostile House of Commons. But this was most unusual, and in any event the American Revolutionary War had then been lost.

In constitutional terms, the chief complaint of the American colonists was that the British government in London would not export the internal British constitution of the day to the American colonies.[2] London would not give the colonial assemblies the same control over their respective local affairs that the British House of Commons possessed over the internal affairs of Britain, including legislative and financial means of imposing some control on the royal governors appointed and instructed from London. George III and his ministers resisted this solution to the bitter end, claiming that the British constitution could not be exported in full to a colony, since no royal governor could be accountable to two masters, the king and parliament in London on the one hand, and the respective colonial assemblies on the other.

When the American colonists won the revolutionary war and broke with Britain, they promptly adopted the main features of the eighteenth-century British constitution. In the American constitution of 1789, the position stipulated for the American president in relation to the American congress is essentially the same as that of George III in relation to the British parliament. There is, of course, the difference that the president is elected separately from congress for a four-year term, so that heredity was replaced by democratic electoral processes in this respect. But once elected, the American president possesses separate and independent executive power following the eighteenth-century English model.

There is a serious defect in this model, the lack of systematic co-

---

[2] L. W. Labaree, *Royal Government in America* (New Haven: Yale University Press, 1930), 394-395.

ordination between the legislative and executive functions or branches of government. This defect became fixed—indeed frozen—in the written constitution of the United States in 1789. However, the unwritten British constitution continued to develop and change through practice and custom, so that, by the time some sixty more years had passed, this defect had been remedied in Britain. As we shall see, the new and better system was passed on to the British North American colonies in the 1840s. As we shall also see, the new system served French Canada well. The main features of this later part of the story are as follows.

The development of the full-fledged cabinet system in Britain owes a great deal to William Pitt. He became Prime Minister in 1783, and with only one brief break of three years (1801-1804) he remained in office until 1806. Shortly after 1783, George III suffered permanently declining health, and his repeated illnesses left Pitt virtually in a position of primacy. Pitt had the personal qualities to take advantage of this, and he developed and consolidated the power of the office of Prime Minister. He established the principle of cabinet solidarity: that the cabinet must take a single position on matters of policy and stand together in support of that position. He also effectively asserted his own control as Prime Minister over the composition and agenda of the cabinet. These were long steps forward toward the modern cabinet system, and both the Prince Regent and William IV accepted the new custom and practice—they had no interest in re-asserting George III's earlier authority. However, Pitt continued to manipulate electoral representation in the House of Commons in the old way, to ensure himself the favourable House that was recognized as necessary. He ignored several defeats in the House of Commons.

It was not until after 1830 that the further principle was established, by practice and custom, that the prime minister must resign, or ask for dissolution and an election, if an important cabinet-sponsored measure was defeated on a vote in the House of Commons. The resignation of the Duke of Wellington as Prime Minister in 1830 was the first instance of this. The Great Reform Act of 1832 reorganized the parliamentary constituencies and widened the franchise so that Parliament became more democratic and much less subject to manipulation of membership by a prime minister. Very quickly after 1832, the precedents for resignation or dissolution on defeat in the House multiplied and the rule became firm. Thus, in Britain by the 1830s, the defect of the eighteenth-century British constitution had been cured. Effective co-ordination and harmony between the executive and legislative powers in the state had been achieved on a systematic basis which held the executive accountable to the elected chamber of the legislature as indicated.

Let us look now at relevant developments in British North America after the American Revolution.[3] At first Britain continued to govern the remaining British North American colonies along the old lines, though there were some minor administrative reforms. To make a long story short, we find that the

---

[3]In general, see Chester Martin, *Foundations of Canadian Nationhood* (Toronto: University of Toronto Press, 1955), Parts I and II.

same constitutional conflicts that had preceded the Revolution in the American colonies surfaced again in the British North American colonies during the 1820s and 1830s. The governor, appointed and instructed from London, held the whole of the executive power in a colony, along with his appointed executive council. This oligarchy came into conflict in the old way with the elected assembly of the colony. As in 1776, the British government could see no way out of this dilemma—the colonial governor still could not serve two masters. The result was rebellion in both Upper and Lower Canada in 1837. It is noteworthy that the rebel leaders, Mackenzie in Upper Canada and Papineau in Lower Canada, both advocated the American constitutional system as the solution. The rebellions quickly failed, but they did prompt the British Government to send Lord Durham to British North America as Governor General, charging him to report on the situation and propose remedies.

As explained earlier, this was the very decade in which the final steps rounding out the full modern cabinet system were taken in Britain itself. Moreover, while full collective cabinet responsibility thus became established in practice, there was little public explanation or articulation of what had happened. Indeed, many in Britain still considered cabinet accountability to the House of Commons to be what it was in the time of Pitt or even the earlier years of George III. But Lord Durham, being a Radical and a reformer in British politics, was well aware of the new position. Another person who knew of it was Robert Baldwin, one of the leaders of the ''Reform'' party in Upper Canada. His reform group, which had wide support, preferred the British to the American constitution and wished loyally to maintain the British connection. Robert Baldwin made representations to Durham, on the latter's invitation, urging that the grant of cabinet or responsible government to each of the colonies for all purposes of internal self-government was the great and necessary measure to be taken. No doubt this influenced Lord Durham greatly; in any event this was the principal recommendation of the Durham Report to the British Government in 1839. Speaking of the nature of cabinet or responsible government in the Report, Lord Durham said:

> In England, this principle has so long been considered an indisputable and essential part of our constitution, that it has really hardly ever been found necessary to inquire into the means by which its observance is enforced. When a ministry ceases to command a majority in Parliament on great questions of policy, its doom is immediately sealed; and it would appear to us as strange to attempt for any time, to carry on a government by means of ministers perpetually in a minority, as it would be to pass laws with a majority of votes against them. The ancient constitutional remedies, by impeachment and a stoppage of supplies, have never, since the reign of William III, been brought into operation for the purpose of removing a ministry. They have never been called for, because in fact, it has been the habit of ministers rather to anticipate the occurrence of an absolutely hostile vote, and to retire, when supported only by a bare and uncertain majority.[4]

Professor A. H. Birch points out that, even for Britain herself, this is the first authoritative statement in a great public document of the nature of the collective re-

---

[4]Quoted in Birch, *Representative and Responsible Government,* 132.

sponsibility of the cabinet. Commenting on the passage just quoted from Durham's Report, Professor Birch says: "This statement is worth quoting in full because it was the first clear assertion of what later became known as the convention of collective responsibility. In giving the impression that this was a long-established principle of the British constitution, Durham (who was a Radical) was rather misleading. In fact it had been established only during the previous three or four decades, and securely and irrevocably established only since the Reform Act of 1832."[5] So, the Canadian reformers and Durham himself were indeed very much up-to-date respecting the state of the British constitution on its home ground. The newness of this development at the time in Britain explains some of the misunderstandings of the period, in both Britain and Canada, about what "responsible government" did mean.

Finally, there was a vital refinement to Durham's proposal. In proposing that the colonial governor should govern under the advice of a cabinet dependent on the elected assembly of his colony, Durham reserved certain subjects, those of persisting importance being foreign relations, foreign trade, and the constitution of the colonial system of government itself. On these matters the governor would continue to take his instructions from London, but on all other matters he would act under the advice of his colonial prime minister and cabinet, according to the newly established principles of cabinet government. This federal formula for executive responsibility helped to solve the dilemma of the first British Empire; that dilemma being the old idea that a colonial governor could not respond to two masters if there was to be an Empire at all. He *could* respond to two masters *on different subjects*. Thus Lord Durham pointed the way to full colonial domestic self-government coupled with the maintenance of the British connection. There was now no need for a second American Revolution. It should be noted that Lord Durham's constitutional solution was largely made possible by the emergence in Britain herself, just a very few years before this mission to British North America, of the full-fledged cabinet system.

Nevertheless, in 1839 and 1840 the outlook for the French Canadians was dark and gloomy indeed. Unfortunately Lord Durham's Report had another principal feature. In the aftermath of armed rebellion, he advocated the anglicization of the French Canadians. To this end, he proposed the union of Upper and Lower Canada to form the United Province of Canada. In the electorate for the parliament of the United Province, the English Canadians of Upper and Lower Canada would be a majority and the French Canadians a perpetual minority. Even before receiving Durham's Report, the British Government had decided on union, and in the Imperial Act of Union of 1840 they went even further than Durham had proposed. They provided that Upper and Lower Canada (Canada West and Canada East) were to have an equal number of members in the union parliament, though the population of Lower Canada was considerably greater than that of Upper Canada at the time. Thus the English element of the combined electorate was given even greater influence than it would have enjoyed on strict principles

---

[5]*Ibid.*

of representation by population. Moreover, it was provided that English was to be the sole language of the new parliament.[6]

At this point, something of great importance happened. After Papineau fled, Louis La Fontaine, who had not taken part in the rebellion, became the most influential political leader of the French Canadians. Meanwhile, the British Government made it clear that they were not accepting Lord Durham's proposal for responsible government in Canada—they still considered the constitutional dilemma of the old Empire insoluble, and did not perceive that Durham had found a solution. The Reform party of Robert Baldwin in Upper Canada realized that they would have to organize and fight political battles in the new united parliament to win responsible government. This meant they needed allies in Lower Canada, and so they sought a reform alliance with La Fontaine and his followers. The Baldwin party in Upper Canada was concerned to get rid of the Family Compact, and the La Fontaine party in Lower Canada was just as anxious to eliminate the corresponding oligarchy there, the *château clique*.

The events of the next few years can be given briefly as follows. Baldwin and Hincks assured La Fontaine that responsible government, if it were won for Canada, would provide the French Canadians with enough real political power that they could effectively protect and preserve the French-Canadian culture and way of life. Indeed, they argued that this was the best if not the only way open to do so. La Fontaine was persuaded and managed to carry his followers with him. He and Baldwin held to the alliance with great mutual sympathy and integrity, and responsible government was achieved in a very few years, with the results for French Canada and that Baldwin and Hincks had predicted and supported. The vital historical fact, then, is that the dominant political leaders of English Canada at this time took the initiative and joined hands with the dominant political leaders of French Canada to ensure the continuance and protection of the French way of life in Lower Canada. English Canadians and French Canadians together used the winning of responsible government to frustrate the British Government's plan to anglicize the French Canadians. Professor Chester Martin's account of the formation and development of this alliance is worth quoting in full.

> Hinck's first letter to La Fontaine, dated April 12, 1839, was written without previous acquaintance. Between that date and the first session of the Canadian Assembly in June, 1841, no fewer than thirty-four of these confidential letters are to be found in the La Fontaine Papers. So discreet and secret was this intercourse that it could not be entrusted to the post office of those days. The good offices of trusted friends and a visit of La Fontaine to Toronto during the summer of 1840 enlarged the confidential circle to include Morin, Cherrier, Viger, Woodruff, and a few others. With the meeting of La Fontaine and Baldwin the alliance took on a deeper and more intimate relationship. Domestic bereavement for both charged this friendship as time went on with mutual sympathy and affection. Baldwin's incorruptible character, his uncompromising rectitude, his inflexible "principle," remained the sheet-anchor of the Canadian reform party until responsible government was won.

---

[6]See generally on this period, J. M. S. Careless, *The Union of the Canadas, 1841-1857* (Toronto: McClelland & Stewart, 1967).

But the strategy was the strategy of Francis Hincks, and the political alliance which he advocated became a landmark in Canadian politics.

The induction of a group of young French Canadians, trained in the Papineau school of uncompromising obstruction, into the Eleusinian mysteries of responsible government was no easy task. La Fontaine's long association with Papineau, his ineradicable bitterness intensified by Durham's proscription of "his people," the brutal terms of the union and the manner of its passing in Lower Canada, must have given many a rankling reflection to a young patriot of La Fontaine's sensibilities. How he responded to the crisis, how he mastered his old prepossessions and turned with his new friends to face the unpredictable prospects of the union, with smouldering faith but with a grim sense of destiny for his country, is traceable in the La Fontaine Papers. How he succeeded in purveying that faith to others, in training them to discipline and forbearance and acquiescence if not confidence in the mysteries of a new technique, remains a more baffling problem, one to which Canadian history has not yet found the answer.

The burden of Hinck's argument was threefold: that the union which outraged La Fontaine's instincts and many of his dearest interests in detail could yet, through the co-operation of trusted allies restore French Canada to an honourable and honoured place in Canadian politics; that responsible government, with all its indirection and conventions would be more effective for this purpose than uncompromising obstruction; and finally that the British connexion, exploited though it had been by the *château clique*, could be a better guarantee for the rights of "his people" at the darkest hour of their fortunes than the most logical application of the "elective principle" under a hypothetical republic. All three of these arguments were fairly won: sometimes by ingratiating candour, sometimes by the adroit indoctrination of events, and not infrequently by invoking the serene faith, the incorruptible character, of Robert Baldwin.[7]

There is no need to retrace in detail here the last few steps during the 1840s toward responsible government. A new British government adopted Durham's plan in 1846 and instructed the British North American governors accordingly. The reform parties won elections both in Nova Scotia and Canada in 1847 and 1848, whereupon the respective governors installed responsible ministries in office, first in Nova Scotia and a few weeks later in Canada, in the early months of 1848. It should be noted that this was a victory for democracy, as well as for efficiency in the co-ordination of legislature and executive. While there were property qualifications on the franchise in Canada at the time, farmers and small shopkeepers were able to meet the requirements and possessed the vote. Thus both representative assembly and cabinet came under the control of a broadly based electorate. In these circumstances the Jacksonian democracy of the United States ceased to be attractive as an alternative for British North America. The executive oligarchies of the colonies were replaced by cabinets responsible through the elected assemblies to the electorate itself.

The first Prime Minister of the United Province of Canada was Louis La Fontaine, as Canada East had elected the larger number of Reform party members. It was, however, a partnership, being the La Fontaine-Baldwin min-

---

[7]Martin, *Foundations of Canadian Nationhood*, 160-161.

istry. Specific results beneficial to French Canada were quick in coming under the new ministry. "During their administration, three legislative measures of particular significance to French Canada were given royal assent. One permitted the last of the exiled rebels of 1837-38 to return home, the second gave official recognition to the French language. The third, and most controversial, was the Rebellion Losses Act, by which Lower Canadians were permitted to put forward claims for compensation for damages sustained during the Rebellions."[8]

French Canada had come a very long way indeed in ten years. Thus we see that Baldwin and La Fontaine had made cultural duality and racial collaboration part of the pattern of Canadian life, along with democratic responsible government. This pattern of life had endured, though it has been ineffectively challenged from time to time. One challenge was immediate. The Montreal English merchants, angry at the Rebellion Losses Act and despairing because of the abrupt ending of Imperial trade preferences by the British government, proposed union with the United States in their Annexation Manifesto of 1849. They got nowhere. Professor J. M. S. Careless describes and interprets the reaction to the Annexation Manifesto as follows:

> The peak came in October, when in Montreal the Annexation Association issued a jolting manifesto. Pointing darkly to "ruin and decay" throughout Canada, the barren hope of the canals, the vital need for new markets and capital, the document called for "friendly and peaceful" separation from Britain and union with the United States. Its three hundred and twenty-five signatories included a future father of Confederation, Alexander Tilloch Galt a later conservative prime minister, J. J. C. Abbott, and two subsequent leading liberals, Antoine-Aimé Dorion and Luther Holton; but the list read chiefly like a roster of Montreal's business élite. Response was rapid. There was a clamour of anti-annexation meetings and addresses, drowning minor echoes elsewhere of the Montreal declaration. Indignant argument and agitation went on through the winter. Yet well before the year's end it was evident that the Annexation Manifesto had been scarcely more than a final bout of Montreal fever, not the herald of a new popular upheaval.
>
> It had shown, in fact, that the mass of Canadians were essentially satisfied with their political state, whatever the burdens of depression. In French Canada, the very success of responsible government, of La Fontaine's leadership, of the Rebellion Losses Act, had left small margin for Papineau and the *rouges'* annexationism. A largely cautious, conservative-minded people were in the mass but little stirred by visions of democratic and republican perfection; and they saw joining the United States as the virtual extinction, not the realization, of the national identity which they had so resolutely defended. *Survivance* within the Canadian union looked far more feasible and desirable than the radicals' dream of *nationalité* within the American union. Furthermore, the fact that *rouges* revived the old anti-clericalism of the *patriotes*, and warmly hailed the liberal, anti-papal revolution of 1848 in Rome, turned the potent influence of the church with increasing effect against them.
>
> In Upper Canada among all parties, the strength of British allegiance, the ingrained resistance to the United States, and the feeling also for a separate identity in

---

[8]Margaret Elizabeth Abbott Nish, *Racism or Responsible Government: The French Canadian Dilemma of the 1840s* (Toronto: Copp Clark, 1967), 131.

America, had brought the emphatic rejection of annexationism. Besides, now that responsible rule had so clearly been established, any former association of annexation with self-government had lost much of its meaning. Joining the republic meant, instead, associating with slavery and sectional conflict, and (as the Toronto *Globe* energetically informed the West) abandoning the free, efficient system of British cabinet and parliamentary rule for a rigid, unwieldly, even old-fashioned American written constitution.[9]

So much then for the winning of responsible government and its service to the preservation of the French-Canadian way of life. The other great landmark of our constitutional history is the achievement of federation of the British North American colonies in 1867 and the years following and this too served the same purpose in a very significant way, though of course federation had other motives and purposes as well.

The story of the achievement of confederation is better known than is that of the winning of responsible government. My present purpose, then, is simply to recount enough of the confederation story to show that, once again, there was at work a close, sympathetic, and effective partnership between the political leaders of English Canada and French Canada concerned to ensure continuing security for the French-Canadian way of life.

It would be wrong to suggest that, after the advent of responsible government, all was smooth sailing in the United Province of Canada. In fact, though much was accomplished, the successive governments, partnerships between English Upper Canadians and French Lower Canadians though they were, became increasingly unstable. For many purposes Upper and Lower Canada were still treated as separate. At times the political claim was made that there should be a majority from each section (a ''double majority'') to pass new legislation, but this never became a consistent practice. By the late 1850s, Upper Canada had quite considerably surpassed Lower Canada in population, so that now the shoe of under-representation by population was pinching the Upper Canadian foot, reversing the position of 1841. This was aggravated by some instances where the informal double-majority idea was ignored when it did seem relevant. Perhaps the most striking of these was the Taché School Act of 1855, where a big majority of Lower Canadian votes was used by John A. Macdonald to ensure the passage of legislation applying to Upper Canada alone and requiring in Upper Canada tax-supported separate schools for Roman Catholics. There was a considerable storm of protest in Upper Canada about the way this was done, but the legislation was never repealed and indeed its essential provisions were eventually guaranteed by section 93 of the British North America Act of 1867 and stand today as part of the school law of Ontario. In 1855, however, this did sharpen the campaign in Upper Canada for representation by population, led by George Brown of the *Globe* Newspaper.[10]

George Brown had succeeded Baldwin as the chief Reform Party leader in

---

[9]Careless, *Union,* 129-130.
[10]Careless, *Brown of The Globe,* 2 vols. (Toronto: Macmillan of Canada, 1959-62), 1:203-204; and *Union,* 216-217.

Upper Canada while John A. Macdonald became the principal leader of the Upper Canadian Conservatives. In Lower Canada, George Etienne Cartier had succeeded La Fontaine as the most influential leader of the French Canadians. Brown and Macdonald were bitter political rivals in Upper Canada, but nevertheless as the 1850s passed into the 1860s they both became exasperated over the frequency with which governments in the United Province were falling. At this period, both leaders on occasion publicly advocated a federal solution of some kind. In the early 1860s, also, Brown and Macdonald tentatively sounded one another out through intermediaries about reform along federal lines, but nothing came immediately of these indirect soundings. Finally, matters came to a head in May and June of 1864. Taché and Macdonald had formed a ministry on 30 March, but it was defeated on a vote in the House on 14 June. There was no prospect that another election would bring different political party groupings and more stability.

In these circumstances, George Brown took a "dramatic initiative."[11] He passed the word through friends to John A. Macdonald that he, Brown, would be interested in the possibility of a coalition government dedicated to major constitutional reform along federal lines. Macdonald responded positively and quickly, he and Galt opened negotiations with Brown and soon they were joined by Cartier. In the background Lord Monck, the Governor General, gave enthusiastic encouragement. So the Taché-Macdonald-Brown-Cartier coalition ministry was formed, with Brown and two other Upper Canadian Reformers in cabinet positions. This meant a break between Brown and former political allies in Lower Canada. The intention and mandate of the new coalition was to pursue a federal solution for the political and constitutional ills of the United Province of Canada. Brown's preference was for a federal union of Upper and Lower Canada, with the union to be widened later to the East and to the West in British North America, if possible. John A. Macdonald preferred to seek the wider union first, and to fall back, if necessary, on the federation of Upper and Lower Canada only. This was just a difference in emphasis about what was politically more practical, so the coalition government started out on Macdonald's course, which was consistent enough with Brown's basic approach. From this point on, the consummate political skill of John A. Macdonald, and his vision of a new British country from sea to sea, were the guiding factors in achieving the wider union, so that the alternative of a federal union of Upper and Lower Canada alone never had to be considered.

It is true that John A. Macdonald would have preferred legislative union of British North America, and on occasion he said so rather wistfully. The United States was in the midst of a bloody civil war and this was hardly an encouragement to Canadian federalists at the time. But both Macdonald and Brown knew all along that a federal solution designed to give very significant autonomy to Lower Canada was essential. Both accepted this. The French Canadians were to be asked to give up their very powerful position in the parliament of the United

---

[11]Careless, *Brown,* 2: chap. 4 [the phrase "dramatic initiative" is the author's]; and Donald Creighton, *John A. Macdonald: the Young Politician* (Toronto: Macmillan, 1952), chap. 12-13.

Province of Canada for a lesser influence in the new parliament of a federated British North America composed on principles of representation by population. They had to be given in return an autonomous provincial parliament for Lower Canada in which the same population principle would ensure a French-Canadian majority position with power over subjects vital to the French-Canadian way of life, like education and laws covering property and civil rights. To this extent Brown was willing to give federalism priority over the principle of representation by population, and likewise Macdonald surrendered his preference for legislative union. At this point, we must appreciate the vital part played by Cartier. Professor J. M. S. Careless pays him the following tribute.

> Without his willingness to pledge support of the French-Canadian majority—and thereby mortgage his entire political future with his people—the new government and its project would have been wholly impossible. Essentially it took two to end deadlock, the two who could swing the votes of the two opposed sectional majorities: Brown to make the offer, Cartier to receive it. In agreeing to that offer, the Bleau leader was accepting both the loss of the entrenched French position in the existing union and the establishment of rep by pop within a new federation. It was an act of highest political courage, and, one might add, of undeluded vision. Brown gained new respect and fellow-feeling for Cartier on their joining forces, for, as one sectional leader, he knew what it had cost the other to come to terms. The two of them brought the majority votes, Grits and Bleus, that made the Confederation ministry politically viable. It could not have existed or pursued its ends without them both.[12]

Once again then, as in the 1840s, the English-Canadian political leaders of Upper Canada formed a partnership with the French-Canadian political leader of Lower Canada to ensure security for the French-Canadian way of life in the new constitutional arrangements contemplated. Perhaps the geographical extent and natural regionalism of British North America from sea to sea would have required a federal solution in any event, but the duality of cultures in the United Province of Canada made federalism essential regardless of geography.

The present constitutional debate in Canada has been marked by much adversely critical reference to historical sins of omission and commission by British Canadians against their French-Canadian fellow citizens. No doubt the record is not spotless; certain valid causes of complaint have occurred and some still exist. But we have heard too much in recent years of these things and not enough of the other side of the story. There has been too much disparagement along historical lines of British Canadians—some of it coming from French Canada but some of it being undue self-disparagement by British Canadians themselves. As I have tried to show, and the two cases covered are only examples, there have been very important positive factors in the historical record to the credit of British Canadians in relation to French Canadians. I have written in the conviction that it is time to recall the establishment of responsible government and confederation with pride in the common achievements they represent for British and French Canadians alike. It is time also to appreciate the great positive potential of parlia-

---

[12]Careless, *Brown*, 2:145-146.

mentary democracy, the cabinet system, and federalism for ensuring the continuance of Canadian unity today and tomorrow.

More needs to be said, in conclusion, on this last point. Though the main outlines of the confederation plan were given in the British North America Act, much vital fleshing out of the full meaning of the division of legislative powers between the federal parliament and the provincial legislatures remained to be done. By judicial interpretation and governmental practice, before the nineteenth century had ended, we had developed in Canada a well-balanced federalism in which the full autonomy of the provinces in their allotted legislative sphere was made explicit. Sir Oliver Mowat, as Premier of Ontario, was the principal champion of a strong position for the provinces in the later years of the nineteenth century, and the powers of the Government of Quebec benefited from the successes of the Mowatt Government in some of the constitutional cases it took to court. Some think judicial interpretation went too far in favour of the provinces. Be that as it may, the rules of the game started to change anyway with growing demands from the public for greatly increased activity and responsibility by all governments. This caused a shift in the nature of Canadian federalism, a process still going on, from dual federalism to co-operative federalism, in the sense in which Professor R. L. Watts has used these terms.[13] He explains that both types of federalism are based on the principle that the country concerned has one basic constitutional system under which the central government on the one hand and the respective regional governments on the other ''are assigned co-ordinate authority such that neither level of government is legally or politically subordinate to the other.'' But the classical dual federalism assumed also that the central and regional governments could and would operate in separate spheres without any functional dependence one upon the other. This may have been accurate to a considerable degree in the Canada of one hundred years ago, but it has simply not been the truth of the relationship in recent decades. The provincial governments on the one hand and the federal government on the other, though still coordinate in constitutional status, have become dependent on one another in many ways. Federal and provincial finances, laws, and responsibilities interact and interpenetrate in numerous areas of urgent social concern, making a genuinely co-operative federalism necessary, if federalism we are to have at all. But this is a very demanding and delicately poised form of government and requires the spirit of true partnership from our political leaders, both federal and provincial, if it is to work successfully. While primary leadership must come from the federal government on the public control of many of the problem areas of modern society, nevertheless the provinces (large or small) must be treated as equals and not as subordinates. They have their own contribution to make.

We are developing in Canada sophisticated processes of intergovernmental consultation, so that there may be collaboration and agreement in providing the public control measures (both federal and provincial) for sweeping problem areas like poverty, pollution, regional economic disparities, urban reform and renewal,

---

[13]Ronald Lampman Watts, *New Federations: Experiments in the Commonwealth* (Oxford: Clarendon Press, 1966), 12-13.

privacy, the new electronic technologies of communication and information processing, and so on. In fact, co-operative federalism, Canadian style, is already emerging as the pattern of the future for a united Canada.[14] The present systematic review of constitutional issues is bringing federal and provincial ministers and principal civil servants together in many more intergovernmental consultations than ever before. This may or may not result in some formal changes in the federal constitution of the country. I strongly suspect that, in the end, we shall find the historical importance of these many meetings of ministers and officials to be elsewhere. We may find their importance to lie in the development of more regular and effective intergovernmental co-operation for the co-ordinated use of existing federal and provincial powers, or at least for the use of federal and provincial powers that are not much changed from what they are now.

This should not be viewed as an anti-democratic development, though some commentators and editors would have us believe that this is so. Because of the cabinet system, the ministers who engage in intergovernmental consultations are responsible to their respective democratic parliamentary bodies for the policies they sponsor, the concessions they make, and the agreements they sign.[15] The policies and agreements can be considered and debated under many different procedural arrangements in the legislative bodies concerned, to ensure the accountability of cabinets to their respective parliaments and so to the people themselves. I hope I am right when I think that I see emerging in Canada a more effective co-operative federalism that Quebec needs as much as, if not more than, the rest of us. A dynamic, balanced co-operative federalism of this type offers the best security now available for the French-Canadian way of life.

By contrast, the United States has really ceased to be a federal country in the Canadian "distribution-of-powers" sense. The legislative supremacy of the national congress over the state legislatures is now established to the extent that statutes of the congress almost invariably prevail over state laws on just about any subject. American writers speak of this as the demise of dual federalism.[16] This may well be a perfectly proper and desirable development for the United States, as their response to the modern demand for governments to be ever more active with social control measures of all kinds. Indeed, in the absence of a cabinet system in Washington and the state capitals, to accept the legislative supremacy of the national congress may be the only way the American constitutional system can respond to the modern need for social legislation of a sweeping nature in so many fields. The president and the state governors are often not in harmony with or in control of their respective legislative bodies, so they are unable to con-

---

[14]See W. R. Lederman, "Some Forms and Limitations of Co-operative Federalism," *Canadian Bar Review* 45 (1967): 409-436; and Queen's University at Kingston, Institute of Intergovernmental Relations, *Report: Intergovernmental Liaison on Fiscal and Economic Matters* (Ottawa: Queen's Printer, 1969).

[15]For example, Premier Lesage first agreed to the Fulton-Favreau Formula for Amendment, at Charlottetown in 1964, and then repudiated it after encountering strong opposition in his own party on his return to Quebec.

[16]See, for example, Bernard Schwartz, American Constitutional Law (Cambridge: Cambridge University Press, 1955), 167-175.

clude intergovernmental agreements as partners and make them stick, either as a matter of money or legislation. Canadian cabinets can make their agreements stick with both money and legislation.

This leads to the thought that it is highly important in Canada today to improve the procedures of our parliamentary bodies (federal and provincial) to ensure that the elected members (including the cabinet ministers) are better informed and more sensitive concerning the problems of our society and the needs of the people. We do see major improvements in parliamentary procedure being developed. Real progress has been made recently in the Parliament of Canada and changes are also under way in the Legislative Assembly of Ontario. It is most important that these reforms should continue so that, among other things, democratic controls should operate well on the processes of co-operative federalism.

If we make a success of the Canadian type of balanced co-operative federalism, this will be a useful example and prototype for the extension of the rule of law in other areas of the world—areas where local autonomy is highly prized but where there is yet critical need for wider regional authority and unity as well. American congressional supremacy within the United States does not offer such a model to the world.

If Quebec were to separate, then it might well happen that both Quebec and other parts of Canada would soon be absorbed piecemeal into the United States. There are worse fates possible in the modern world. The American constitution does provide one of the world's greatest systems of democratic government, in spite of serious defects that have been mentioned. Nevertheless, we in Canada do have a distinctive society in North America that differs in vital ways from that of the United States. Our revolutionary tradition of constitutional change and our better systems of government and law have much to do with these distinctions. The lesson of our history and present situation is that all Canadians, including those of British and French origin, should hold together in a federal Canada, separate from the United States. To borrow the words of Professor Careless, Canadians have a "feeling" for "a separate identity in America."[17]

---

[17]In this essay nothing has been said of the respective judicial systems of the United States and Canada, but here also there is the same story, lesson, and result as in the case of the cabinet system. The later nineteenth century was a period of great reform in England resulting in radical simplification of judicial procedure and organization of the courts. Both before and after Confederation, the British North American parliaments followed British example with reform statutes of their own on the British model. The United States, however, took English courts and procedure as it found them in the late eighteenth century before the great era of reform referred to. In many states of the Union, the court systems and procedure are still pretty much in the unreformed condition of overlapping powers, confusion, and complexity inherited from eighteenth-century England. See Lederman, "The Independence of the Judiciary," *Canadian Bar Review* 34 (1956): 769 and 1139.

Chapter 4

The Extension of Governmental Institutions and Legal Systems to British North America in the Colonial Period*

Reprinted from *Canadian Constitutional Law,* J. D. Whyte and
W. R. Lederman (eds) 2nd ed. (Toronto: Butterworths, 1977) 2-1

I. THE GENERAL PRINCIPLES

During the main period of British territorial expansion overseas in the 17th, 18th and 19th centuries, there was not just one simple and consistent pattern for the extension of governmental institutions and legal systems to the new territories. Moreover, there was at times considerable divergence between practice and theory, as we shall see in the case of Newfoundland. Constitutional history in full detail is beyond the scope of this book, but nevertheless a succinct review of the highlights is necessary.

By the middle of the 18th century, the main rules of constitutional law for the colonial relationship had emerged respecting the territories comprising the first British Empire. These rules postulated the supremacy overseas of the main governmental institutions of the mother country herself, namely the King in Council, and the King in Parliament. This supremacy was effective not only for the initial establishment of legitimate government and law in overseas territories, but obtained also for the continuing supervision thereafter of colonial governments and legal systems.

The initial provision of governmental institutions for an overseas colony required a legislative act of some kind, either by the King in Council in London or by the Imperial Parliament. This was true whether the overseas territory was a colony acquired by discovery and settlement, as was Nova Scotia, or by conquest and cession in a treaty of peace, as was New France.

But why was there this alternative between the British King in Council, or the British Parliament as the progenitor of governmental institutions for a new colony? The answer to this is found in the main constitutional development of the 17th century in Britain herself. The revolution of 1688 had confirmed the para-

---

*I wrote this historical account as one of my contributions to the volume "Canadian Constitutional Law", of which my colleague, John D. Whyte, is co-editor and co-author. It is reproduced here with his agreement.

mountcy of Parliament, with special emphasis on the House of Commons, in relation to the King and his long-standing original powers of government by virtue of the royal prerogative. In other words, by the end of the 17th century, the basic constitutional principle was established in Britain herself that, for all purposes, the Imperial Parliament was legislatively supreme over the King in his Privy Council, in any respect in which Parliament chose to exercise that supremacy. However, the original wide-ranging royal prerogative powers of government were not thereby abrogated; far from it, subject to the potential supremacy of Parliament, they remained intact in theory and practice. The royal prerogative powers simply continued to be used with full effect in areas where Parliament did not choose to intervene and take over by statute. Moreover, aside from such legal authority of a legislative character, the King in Council continued to be the final executive authority in government for Britain herself as well as for overseas territories. This meant that, for example, the appointment of colonial governors was a matter of Crown prerogative in Britain, whether the colony concerned had a statutory or a prerogative constitution.

The historical fact is that, for a long period of time after 1688, the British Parliament did not choose to intervene in the governmental arrangements for overseas colonies, either in the initial provisions of the colonial governmental institutions or in the continuing supervision of them from London. In these respects matters were largely left in the hands of the King and his Privy Council, and the department of the Privy Council primarily concerned was known as the Board of Trade and Plantations.

The Quebec Act of the Imperial Parliament in 1774 was the first major and comprehensive intervention by the Parliament in the field of colonial government, and from then on, in the period after the American Revolution, the provision of governmental institutions for the remaining British North American colonies became a mixture of Parliamentary and Royal Prerogative provisions emanating from London. Newfoundland constitutes an exception to this dependence on the royal prerogative powers. Government and law in Newfoundland, such as they were, came under the auspices of statutes of the Imperial Parliament all the way, starting in 1698. The resulting essential and anomalous historical points in these respects about Newfoundland will be given later.

To continue now with the general picture, provision of colonial governors, councils, legislative assemblies and courts does not explain everything. The further question remains—how did these colonial areas acquire their respective general systems of private and public law? To have been given English colonial governmental institutions necessarily implied that the relevant rules and principles of English public law that were essential context for those institutions had been extended to the colonies, and were in force there. But beyond this there were the specific laws of property, contract, tort and crime for a colony—whence came these bodies of law in the first place? The constitutional position was that a new colonial legislature did not start from zero. It did not operate in a vacuum so far as such local laws were concerned.

In the case of a colony acquired by settlement, the settlers from Britain were considered to have brought with them to the new territory so much of the total existing body of English common law and statute law as was suitable to conditions in the new place. This included the ordinary domestic English laws of contract, property, tort and crime. It also included an important public law principle, the right of citizens to participate in the legislative process through a representative assembly. Translated to a colony acquired by settlement, this was to the effect that the colonists were entitled to participate, through a local representative assembly, in the local enactment of laws in and for the colony, including local laws of taxation. The crown in Council, as we have seen, could provide a settled colony with governor, council, assembly and courts without reference to the British Parliament. But the Crown in Council could not otherwise make new laws binding the local inhabitants. The new colonial assembly could make such local laws (within wide limits), and so at all times could the British Parliament, but not the King in Council. Thus the total body of law of a colony acquired by settlement, but which had *not* been given a local legislature, was the automatically received English law brought in, so to speak, in the pockets of settlers, plus any specially applicable statutes of the British Parliament.

In the case of a colony acquired by conquest and cession, the position was somewhat different. The point about receiving the English public law that was necessary context for the British colonial governmental institutions established there is the same as for a colony acquired by settlement. But, in the area of the regular private law of contract, property and tort, and the ordinary criminal law, the rule was that the pre-conquest laws of the conquered colony remained in effect and continued in force, unless and until altered by the appropriate British authorities in London, the appropriate authorities in this case being either the Crown in Council or the British Parliament. For the inhabitants of a conquered colony, there was no received common law right to a representative colonial assembly, and the King in Council as well as the British Parliament could make ordinary local laws for the colony. But there is a final point of constitutional law about this. Once the King in Council had granted a representative assembly to a conquered colony, or had even promised to do so, thereafter the King in Council could not alter the ordinary local laws of that colony by order-in-council. The position then became the same in this respect as that of a colony acquired by settlement.

This last point gives a constitutional reason why it was necessary for the British Government to obtain the Quebec Act of 1774 from the British Parliament to make the changes in the colonial government of Quebec upon which they had decided by that time. In 1763, by royal proclamation alone in the usual manner, the King granted to his new colony of Quebec a representative assembly, and he further decreed at the same time that English law was in all respects to replace French law. The assembly was never summoned. By 1774, the British Government had decided to restore to the French-Canadians the pre-conquest French law of property and civil rights. This was only one of the changes they contemplated, but now this step at least could only be taken by a statute of the British Parliament. The royal promise of an assembly in 1763 precluded purely prerogative action on this point. Since a British statute was necessary in any event for this part of the new plan for the colonial government of Quebec, apparently the British government decided to put the whole of the new governmental arrangements into the statute. Once this was done, the commitment to British statutes was irrevocable. There was no going back to the use of the British royal prerogative powers alone for later constitutional changes respecting the government of Quebec. From this point on, as we shall see presently, the form of basic constitutional change for Quebec and Ontario was always by Imperial statute. The relationship of Crown and Parliament in Britain herself after 1688 meant that no statute of Parliament could be amended or altered by the King in Council.[1]

The inclusion of "Ontario" along with what has just been said about Quebec should be explained at this point. The boundaries of the new British colony of Quebec were clearly specified in the Royal Proclamation of 1763, and comprised little more than the settled part of the valley of the St. Lawrence River. The western boundary of the new colony ran from the south eastern corner of Lake Nipissing to the point of intersection between the St. Lawrence River and the 45th parallel of north latitude, which is the site of the present city of Cornwell, just a short distance west of Montreal. Clearly then, the area west of this line, including nearly all of what is now southern and eastern Ontario, did not receive the general grant of English law made to Quebec in the Royal Proclamation of 1763. This western area was part of New France and had indeed become British territory by conquest and cession in 1763, but the Royal Proclamation described it as Indian territory outside the boundaries of any colony, and expressly forbade settlement there. Presumably the pre-conquest law, whatever it was, continued in the Indian territory.

In any event, the Quebec Act of the British Parliament of 1774 changed the situation dramatically. The western boundary of the royal colony of Quebec was moved westward to the junction of the Ohio and Mississippi rivers, and northward to the southern limits of Hudson Bay Company territory. Thus the royal colony of Quebec did come to include in 1774 all of what is now southern and eastern Ontario within its boundaries. Accordingly, the provisions of the Quebec Act to the effect that the French law of property and civil rights and the English criminal law, should henceforth be the law of the colony, were applicable to the newly included area. For the latter area, this was the first enactment by the British authorities establishing a local legal system—the Quebec Act of the British Parliament, which took effect on May 20th, 1774. The rest of the constitutional history of Quebec and Ontario will be traced later, involving as it does subsequent changes by Imperial statutes.

By contrast, however, the constitutional establishment and development of the British North American colonies in the area we now know as the Maritimes was carried out by the King in Council alone, acting through the issuance of the usual prerogative instruments. This refers to Nova Scotia, New Brunswick, Prince Edward Island and Cape Breton Island, in the years before The British North America Act of 1867. If a colony possessed a purely prerogative constitution, that colony could be divided, added to, or merged with another colony by

---

[1]Authorities for these propositions about colonial government are: *Campbell v. Hall*, 98 E.R. 1045 (1774, King's Bench); *In re Cape Breton*, 13 E.R. 489 (1846, Privy Council); *Kielley v. Carson*, 13 E.R. 225 (1842, Privy Council).

royal prerogative acts alone, subject to the rights to a local representative assembly explained earlier, within whatever territory was embraced by the new boundaries. For example, upon cession by France to Britain in 1763, Cape Breton Island was merged with Nova Scotia by the Royal Proclamation of 1763. In 1784, Cape Breton Island was given a separate Lieutenant-Governor and promised its own Council and Assembly. The Assembly never met. In 1820, Cape Breton was once again merged with Nova Scotia for all purposes. After the Royal Proclamation of 1763, the later changes described were legally accomplished by Royal Instructions to that effect given in the various Commissions and Instructions issued by the King in Council to the Governor-in-Chief of Nova Scotia and the Lieutenant Governor of Cape Breton in these years.

A further matter of general principle remains to be explained relating to the ordinary body of English private law and English criminal law, which the inhabitants of a colony possessed by settlement were deemed to have brought with them to the new territory, so far as it was suitable to conditions in the new world. For some purposes at least, colony by colony, this reception must be given an effective date. The actual date on which the first settlers landed is not used for this purpose, if indeed it could be determined. Usually some significant date in the early history of the colony is selected and designated as the effective date for the automatic reception of ordinary English law. In fact these designations have been made by judicial decisions or by statutes. Where the matter rests with judicial decision, the satisfactory general criterion seems to be that given by Chief Justice Forbes of Newfoundland in 1822 and by Chief Justice Haliburton of Nova Scotia in 1848. Chief Justice Forbes said:

> An opinion of Mr. Fane, the law adviser to the Board of Trade, is cited in Reeve's History, p. 111, wherein it is said that the laws of the parent country cease to apply to the new country when it becomes a settlement; and, if so, adds Mr. Reeves, it may be important to ascertain from what time Newfoundland may be considered as a settlement.
>
> But with every respect for the opinions of such very eminent men, it has fallen within my experience to learn that the colonial courts date the discontinuance of English statute laws, not from the time of the colony being settled, but from the institution of a local legislature in the colony; and the reason of the rule is, I think, with the interpretation given it by the colonial lawyers.[2]

Chief Justice Haliburton said:

> In the early settlement of a colony, when the local legislature has just been called into existence, and has its attention engrossed by the immediate wants of the infant community in their new situation, the courts of judicature would naturally look for guidance, in deciding upon the claims of litigants, to the general laws of the mother country, and would exercise greater latitude in the adoption of them than they would be entitled to do as their local legislature, in the gradual development of its powers, assumed its proper position. Every year should render the courts more cautious in the adoption of laws that had never been previously introduced into the colony, for prudent judges would remember that it is province of the courts to declare what is the law, and of the legislature to decide what it shall be.[3]

---

[2]*Young v. Blaikie* (1822), 1 Nfld. L.R. 277, 283.
[3]*Uniacke v. Dickson* (1848) James R. 287.

In the case of Nova Scotia, the Assembly first met in 1758. The corresponding date for Newfoundland, as we shall see, is 1833. This seems to be the principle applicable *on this point* to the British North American colonies of the Atlantic region including Newfoundland. By contrast, from Ontario westward, the dates of reception were set by statute.

It was obviously critical to fix a date of reception as the date upon which the automatic importation of ordinary English statutes stopped. Statutes are of course precisely dated. For example, Nova Scotia received the English Statute of Uses of 1536[4] and the English Statute of Frauds of 1677[5], but not the English Divorce and Matrimonial Causes Act of 1857[6]. On the other hand, Manitoba, Saskatchewan and Alberta did receive the English Divorce Act (of 1857) because the date of reception in the former Hudson's Bay Company territory was fixed by statute at July 15, 1870. This English Divorce Act remained their divorce law until 1968, when the Parliament of Canada finally used its powers for the first time to enact a new divorce law for all the Provinces.

By contrast, the date of reception had virtually no significance respecting the automatic importation of the English common law into a settled colony. In effect, the importation went on continuously, for two reasons. First, there was the conception of the nature of the common law prevailing in the 18th and 19th centuries. In Britain and overseas, the common law was considered to be a superior and complete body of principles with virtually the status of natural law. When an English judge decided a new case by a principle that had not been stated before, he considered that he was merely discovering a principle that had always been there in the common law awaiting the moment of the need to use it. If one conceives of the English common law as having this character, then reception is an all-or-nothing proposition. The *fact* of reception then matters, not the date.

The second reason for the insignificance of the date of reception of the common law was the continuing constitutional authority of the decisions of the highest courts in England as precedents for the courts of the colonies. Even if we admit we are dealing in judge-made law, the authority of English judicial precedents tended to make reception of the English common law continuous. As we shall see in Chapter 3, until December 23rd, 1949, appeal lay from the final courts in Canada to the Judicial Committee of the Privy Council in London. As late is 1927, in the course of giving judgment on an appeal from Ontario, Viscount Dunedin for the Judicial Committee said:

> [W]hen an appellate Court in a colony which is regulated by English law differs from an appellate Court in England, it is not right to assume that the Colonial Court is wrong. It is otherwise if the authority in England is that of the House of Lords. That is the supreme tribunal to settle English law, and that being settled, the Colonial Court, which is bound by English law, is bound to follow it. Equally, of course the point of difference may be settled so far as the Colonial Court is concerned by a judgment of this board.[7]

---

[4]27 Henry VIII, c. 10.
[5]29 Charles II, c. 3.
[6]20 & 21 Victoria, c. 85.
[7]*Robins v. National Trust,* [1927] A.C. 515, 519.

The judicial House of Lords was of course virtually the same body—the same judges—as the Judicial Committee of the Privy Council. The point is then that if you are following the precedents afforded by the highest English courts on common law points anyway, the date of reception of the common law does not matter. In any event, English judicial precedents since 1949 do not have any constitutional authority in Canada. They still enjoy persuasive value on the merits of their reasoning.

One other general point about the automatic reception of ordinary English common law and statute law should be briefly explained. The rule was that both categories of English law were received in a colony so far as they were suitable to conditions in that overseas territory. The issue of suitability (or ''applicability'') was often raised and argued in the colonial courts of British North America. At times, decisions went against the reception of English statutes or even the reception of certain rules of the common law, though the latter exclusions were rare. Usually it was an English statute that was excluded as unsuited to conditions in the New World, though the date of the statute was before the date of reception. As we have seen, if an ordinary English statute was passed after the date of reception for a colony, it was not received there, no matter how suitable it might be for overseas conditions.

These general rules for the extension and reception of English law overseas obtained in the American colonies before 1776. Thus, English law continued in the American States after the Revolution, subject to change by the newly independent American courts and legislatures. This of course explains why the legal systems of Canada and the United States have much in common. Hence American judicial precedents, especially in the common law area, may have valuable persuasive merit for the Common Law Provinces of Canada. The same can be said of Australia, New Zealand and the other common law countries of the British Commonwealth.

In the balance of this Chapter, and in Chapter 3, by a brief review of highlights, we may see the continuity of Canadian constitutional development to the independence of the present day.

II. HISTORICAL HIGHLIGHTS OF THE EXTENSION OF BRITISH GOVERNMENTAL INSTITUTIONS AND LEGAL SYSTEMS TO BRITISH NORTH AMERICA IN THE 18TH AND 19TH CENTURIES

(a) Nova Scotia, New Brunswick, Cape Breton Island and Prince Edward Island

We have already seen that these were the colonies with Prerogative constitutions, embodied in Royal Proclamations and Royal Commissions and Instructions to colonial Governors. The typical constitution included the Governor, an appointed Council, an elected Assembly, and local courts constituted by the Governor, though the Chief Justice of a colony was usually appointed directly by the Imperial authorities in London.

For Nova Scotia, this essential scheme is contained in the Commission and

Instructions to Lord Cornwallis in 1749. The first session of the Legislative Assembly of Nova Scotia was in 1758, hence, as we have seen, this is the date of the reception of ordinary English Law for Nova Scotia.

In 1763, Cape Breton Island and Prince Edward Island were ceded to Britain by France and were merged with Nova Scotia by the Royal Proclamation of 1763.

In 1769 Prince Edward Island was separated by the appointment of its own Governor, and in 1773 the first assembly met. The latter date then is the date for the reception of ordinary English law in Prince Edward Island.

In 1784 New Brunswick and Cape Breton Island were separated from Nova Scotia, each with its own Governor. The New Brunswick Legislative Assembly met in 1784, and so this is the date of the reception of ordinary English law there. The Cape Breton Assembly was never called, and Cape Breton Island was merged again with Nova Scotia in 1820.

In spite of the historical facts about much fighting in these areas between Britain and France in the 17th and 18th centuries, for the legal and constitutional purposes of the times, these were considered to have been colonies possessed by settlement rather than by conquest.

(b) The Special Case of Newfoundland

In 1497, John Cabot discovered Newfoundland and claimed it for Henry VII of England. Very soon, the rich fishing areas of Newfoundland waters and the adjacent Grand Banks were under exploitation by England, France, Spain and Portugal. To make a long story short, the policy of the British Government until the early 19th century was to forbid settlement and the development of a colony in Newfoundland. So, none of the usual rules applied, except the supremacy of the British Parliament. The reason for this was that the British Government wished the commercial exploitation of the rich fisheries to be confined to ships based on the western and southern ports of Britain herself, ships that would make only a temporary summer-time use of ports and shore areas of the island of Newfoundland. The British naval authorities also favoured this policy as a way of training seamen who would become available in Britain for the Royal Navy. Various statutes of the British Parliament, starting in 1698, made laws prohibiting permanent settlement. Nevertheless, settlers did start to stay through the winter in defiance of these statutes, and gradually a Newfoundland based fishery came into existence. So far as local law was concerned, the situation was chaotic for centuries. In 1792 the British Parliament did pass a statute[8] providing a court for Newfoundland, but only for the fishing season. The courts provided were largely ineffective, but the same British statute did specify that both the civil and criminal law of England applied in Newfoundland, and was to be the law administered by the new courts. This of course was subject to the prohibitions in other British statutes specifically applying to Newfoundland, making permanent settlement there illegal.

It was not until the second decade of the 19th century that British policy

---

[8]C. 46, 32 George III.

changed and the Newfoundland settlers were accorded the normal status of a self-governing colony by statutes of the British Parliament. In 1817 the Governor was instructed for the first time to stay through the winter. In 1824 an Imperial Statute reformed the judicature and made normal City Corporation Government possible for St. John's.[9] Finally, in 1832, another British statute authorized the calling of an elected Assembly and, accordingly, Royal Instructions were issued to the Governor to do so. Thus this was a statutory and not a prerogative colonial constitution. The Assembly met for the first time on January 1st, 1833.[10] This then is the cut-off date for the reception in Newfoundland of ordinary English statute law, some 335 years after John Cabot's discovery of the island.[11]

(c) Quebec Retains the French Civil Law
The Royal Colony of Quebec, 1760-1791
Upper and Lower Canada, 1791-1841
The Province of Canada, 1841-1867

We have already carried the story of what is now Quebec and Ontario to the enactment by the British Parliament of the Quebec Act of 1774. We saw that the Quebec Act revoked the Royal Proclamation of 1763 for the enlarged Royal Province of Quebec, restored the pre-conquest French law of property and civil rights, and continued the English criminal law. Also, as explained earlier, these changes respecting French civil law and English criminal law have to be dated from the Quebec Act itself (1774) for nearly all of what is now Ontario, since the latter area was made part of the Royal Colony of Quebec for the first time by the Quebec Act.

Government and law under the Quebec Act continued until 1791, when the British Parliament, by the Constitutional Act of that year, provided that the Royal Province of Quebec was to be divided into two new Royal Provinces, Upper and Lower Canada respectively. The actual boundary between the two Canadas was delineated by an Imperial Order-in-Council dated August 24th, 1791. This is still the boundary between Ontario and Quebec today, having been confirmed as such by section 6 of The Imperial British North America Act of 1867.

The Imperial Constitutional Act of 1791 also assured elective legislative assemblies to both Upper and Lower Canada. (From 1774 to 1791 there had been no elected Assembly in Quebec, the Quebec Act having provided a legislature that consisted of the Governor and an appointed Council only.) Hence, in 1791, both Upper and Lower Canada became entitled to the full system of local colonial self-government characteristic of the period. Section 33 of the Imperial Act of 1791 provided, among other things, that all existing civil and criminal laws were to remain in force as specified in the Quebec Act of 1774, subject to being repealed or varied by the new colonial parliaments of Upper and Lower Canada respectively. Lower Canada was of course content with the position under the

---

[9] 4 & 5 George IV, c. 67.
[10] 2 & 3 William IV, c. 78.
[11] Generally, on Newfoundland, see: A. H. McLintock, *The Establishment of Constitutional Government in Newfoundland, 1783-1832* (London, 1941).

Quebec Act of 1774 and made no change. It was otherwise in Upper Canada, which by this time had been populated largely by English American loyalists expelled from the United States. The first Parliament of Upper Canada convened on September 17, 1792 at Niagara. As it had been authorized to do by the Imperial Statute of 1791, it enacted "That from and after the passing of this Act, in all matters of controversy relative to property and civil rights, resort shall be had to the Laws of England as the rule for the decision of the same." The effective date—the date "of the passing of this Act"—was October 15, 1792. This then is the effective date of reception of English law in Ontario in the realm of property and civil rights.

As for the ordinary English criminal law, as we have seen the effective date of reception for the area now Ontario was the date of the Quebec Act, May 20, 1774. However, the legislators of Upper Canada eventually decided that they wished to have the benefit of the criminal law of England as it stood on the date the first Parliament of Upper Canada met, that is, September 17, 1792. The reason stated for this was that various improvements were made in the criminal law of England by English statutes in the period 1774-1792. Accordingly, the first act of the session of the Parliament of Upper Canada in 1800 provided that the criminal law of England as it stood on September 17th, 1792 was the criminal law of the Province. As already explained, the real significance of the "date of reception" is as the cut-off date for the automatic reception in the overseas territory concerned of the ordinary domestic English Statutes suitable for conditions in the territory.

In 1841 Upper and Lower Canada were united under a single Parliament as the Province of Canada (extending from the Gaspé to Windsor), by virtue of the Union Act of 1840 of the Imperial Parliament in London. This arrangement lasted until 1867, but for many purposes in this period the distinction between Upper and Lower Canada was legally and officially maintained. Section 46 of the Imperial Act of 1840 provided that the existing laws of Upper and Lower Canada respectively were to continue as they were before the union, subject only to later change by proper legislative authority. When Confederation came in 1867 by virtue of The Imperial B.N.A. Act of that year section 6 of the Act provided:

> The parts of the Province of Canada (as it exists at the passing of this Act) which formerly constituted respectively the Provinces of Upper Canada and Lower Canada, shall be deemed to be severed, and shall form two separate Provinces. The part which formerly constituted the Province of Upper Canada shall constitute the Province of Ontario; and the part which formerly constituted the Province of Lower Canada shall constitute the Province of Quebec.

So, it is fair to say that Upper and Lower Canada re-emerged as original partners in the formation of the Dominion of Canada in 1867, along with Nova Scotia and New Brunswick.

(d) Hudson's Bay Company Territory

The territory of the Hudson's Bay Company included the whole of the drainage basin of Hudson's Straits and Hudson's Bay. It was granted by a Royal Charter of Charles II in 1670 to ''the Governor and Company of Adventurers of England trading into Hudson's Bay'', a purely prerogative act of the King without reference to the British Parliament. The royal grant comprised ownership of the land, monopoly of trade, and local powers of government. The charter specified that civil and criminal justice was to be administered according to the laws of England, and that the principal officers of the company at its ports and factories had judicial powers in this respect. Accordingly, the reception of English law started in 1670 in this territory, which came to be known as Rupert's Land. Reception was presumably continuous thereafter, as there was no regular colonial status or local legislature. The acquisition of this vast territory was one of the principal objects of Confederation in 1867, and the further constitutional developments in the area will be reviewed presently in connection with the growth of Canada after Confederation.

(e) Vancouver's Island and British Columbia

Vancouver's Island and British Columbia were originally separate colonies that were given their respective colonial constitutions by the specific authority of a series of statutes of the British Parliament. The starting point is two Imperial Statutes of 1803 and 1821 which, generally speaking made arrangements for courts having jurisdiction in all the territories west of Upper Canada and north of the United States.[12] This included Vancouver's Island and New Caledonia (as mainland British Columbia was then called). These two Imperial statutes provided for local judicial officers in these territories, but also provided the serious civil and criminal cases were to be removed to and tried in the courts of Upper Canada, according to the civil and criminal laws in force in Upper Canada. Thus, as we have already seen in the cases of Quebec and Newfoundland, once the statutory route had been taken, further British statutes were necessary to authorize further changes and developments in the colonial constitutions of the area.

The principles involved were all explained earlier, so the various steps will simply be listed here in the order of their occurrence.

(1) By Imperial statute in 1849,[13] Vancouver's Island was constituted a separate colony and withdrawn from the operation of the Imperial judicature statutes of 1803 and 1821. Parliament also authorized Her Majesty in Council to provide the usual type of colonial constitution by Royal Prerogative Instruments. Governor Blanshard was commissioned in 1849, and the first elected assembly was called in 1856.

(2) By Imperial statute in 1858[14] New Caledonia was re-named British Columbia, was withdrawn from the operation of the Statutes of 1803 and 1821, and was constituted a separate colony, consisting of the mainland of what is now British Columbia. The governor alone was authorized by the statute to make local laws for British Columbia. A Proclamation of the Governor made November 19th, 1858, enacted that the civil and criminal laws of England as they were on that date were in force in British Colum-

---

[12] 1803, 43 George III, c. 138; 1821, 1 & 2 George IV, c. 66.
[13] C. 48, 12 & 13 Victoria.
[14] C. 98 of 21 & 22 Victoria.

bia, "so far as they are not, from local circumstances, inapplicable to the Colony of British Columbia."

(3) By Imperial statute in 1866,[15] Vancouver's Island and British Columbia were united into a single colony, called British Columbia, under a Governor and Council with local legislative powers. Only a minority of the Council were elected persons. The majority were appointed.

(4) The Governor and Council of the newly united colony of British Columbia enacted "The English Law Ordinance, 1867", on March 6, 1867. This ordinance provided that the civil and criminal laws of England as they existed on November 19th, 1858, were in force in all parts of the colony, subject to any specific legislation of the colonies of Vancouver's Island or British Columbia in force in 1867.

● ● ● ●

We have now completed the account of the extension of governmental institutions and legal systems to British North America, colony by colony, up to the time of Confederation—the formation of "one Dominion under the name of Canada" in 1867. Certain general points about the British colonial system as a whole need now to be explained briefly to conclude this treatment of the Pre-Confederation period.

(f) Paramount British Statutes

In relation to the automatic reception of the ordinary English common law in the British North American colonies on various dates including the received domestic English statutes, the local colonial legislatures were free to make variations and changes for the respective colonies by local statutes, and they did so frequently. But there was a distinct class of British statutes that were applicable to the colonial territories expressly or by the necessary implication of their terms, regardless of the dates on which they were passed. We have already mentioned many of them, for example the Quebec Act of 1774 and the various Imperial statutes specifically applicable to Newfoundland and British Columbia. British statutes regulating such matters as merchant shipping, British citizenship, status of aliens, and rights of appeal to the Judicial Committee of the Privy Council were also in this paramount class of Imperial statutes. These were said to be in force overseas *ex proprio vigore*. British statutes of this class were in force in every colony and could not be abrogated or amended in any way by any colonial legislature. The British Parliament remained supreme overseas as well as at home, if it chose to be specific about the application of its statutes overseas.

But, except for this class of British statutes, a colonial legislature could alter or repeal locally applicable English laws. A declaration to this effect for the legislature of the Parliament of Canada was made in the Imperial Union Act of 1840, and this declaration was repeated generally for all self-governing colonies in the Imperial Colonial Laws Validity Act of 1865.

The special class of paramount British statutes is obviously important in our constitutional development. The British North America Act itself, in 1867, was

---

[15]C. 67 of 29 & 30 Victoria.

one of these paramount British statutes. Accordingly, the development of the legislative independence of Canada in later years, and related issues concerning the amendment of the Canadian constitution, are concerned with what happened to this doctrine of the legislative paramountcy of the British Parliament in relation to the self-governing colonies. This is the necessary background for understanding the significance of the British Statute of Westminster of 1931.

(g) Royal Powers for the Reservation or Disallowance of Colonial Legislation by Imperial Order-In-Council

(i) Reservation or Disallowance of Provincial Legislation in Canada After Confederation

One other measure of Imperial control over colonial legislation should be briefly explained. The Governor of a colony could assent to colonial legislation, withhold assent and thereby veto the legislation, or he could reserve it for the signification of Her Majesty's pleasure in London. With respect to colonial legislation assented to by the Governor, nevertheless it could be disallowed by Imperial Order-in-Council in London after having been reported there. With respect to colonial legislation reserved for London's approval, it did not become law unless and until that approval was given by Imperial Order in Council.

These Imperial veto powers of Her Majesty in Council in London were very much alive in 1867, and indeed are specifically declared to obtain with respect to statutes of the Parliament of Canada, in sections 55, 56 and 57 of The B.N.A. Act of 1867. Very quickly, however, as between London and Ottawa, these powers fell into disuse. One Canadian statute of 1867 was reserved by the Governor-General and assent withheld in London. Another Canadian statute, to which the Governor-General had assented in 1872, was disallowed by Imperial Order-in-Council. That was the end of it, and these powers lapsed by desuetude.[16]

But also, section 90 of The B.N.A. Act of 1867 vested in the Governor General in Council in Ottawa the same powers of disallowance respecting provincial statutes assented to or reserved by a provincial Lieutenant Governor subject to a one-year time limit. This power has not lapsed. The Supreme Court of Canada held in 1938 that it was, and is, a fully subsisting power.[17] The power has been used many times since 1867, especially in the earlier years of Confederation.[18]

(h) The Durham Report and Responsible Government

The full story of the achievement of responsible government in British North America in the 1830's and the 1840's cannot be given here. Suffice it to say that the chief dilemma of the Old Empire was that the Governor of a colony frequently found his two masters in conflict, and that he could not serve both of them. Too often he was caught between his colonial assembly on the one hand

---

[16]A. L. Burt, *The Evolution of The British Empire and Commonwealth From the American Revolution* (Boston, 1956), 635.

[17]*Disallowance and Reservation Case,* [1938] S.C.R. 71.

[18]See Dawson: *The Government of Canada* (5th ed., by Norman Ward, Toronto, 1970, 213-217.

and the British Government in London on the other. In his famous Report of 1837, Lord Durham proposed the solution. He proposed that the colonial Governor should be required to select his executive advisers—his cabinet—from the majority party in the elected assembly, to change them when the majority party changed, and to take their advice on all matters, except certain reserved subjects. The reservations were few: "The constitution of the form of government—the regulation of foreign relations, and of trade with the mother country, the other British colonies, and foreign nations—and the disposal of the public lands. . . ."[19] Except for these matters, the Colonial Governor, Durham recommended, should be instructed and required to assent to colonial statutes and policies sponsored by his "responsible" colonial government. Ten years after the Durham Report, instructions along these lines were issued to colonial governors by the British Government. Early in 1848 responsible government on these terms came to Nova Scotia, and later the same year to the Province of Canada. Soon it was in effect in all the British North American colonies east of the Great Lakes.

But what became of the reserved subjects? In the middle years of the 19th century, and before 1867, control of public lands in the colonies was conceded to the respective colonial governments, where necessary by Imperial statutes to that effect.[20] The fate of the other two reservations—the constitution of the form of government in a colony and the conduct of foreign relations—is another part of the story of the development of full Canadian independence after Confederation and is discussed in Chapter 3, *infra*.

(i) The Development of the Independence of The Colonial Judiciary

The final general point of constitutional significance about pre-Confederation British North America concerns the independence of the colonial judiciary. If we go back to the revolutionary settlement after 1688 in Britain herself, we find that the royal judges of the Common Law Courts were guaranteed life tenure in office during good behaviour. Formerly, their tenure had been at the pleasure of the King. This guarantee of life tenure is found in section 3 of the British Act of Settlement, 1701.[21] But this security of tenure was not considered to be applicable to overseas territories, so the judges of colonial courts continued to be appointed with tenure at the pleasure of the Crown. This made them vulnerable to pressure from the Governor, or the King in London. Also, because of a shortage of trained professionals in the colonies, senior colonial judges participated in colonial politics as members of colonial councils or even as elected members of colonial assemblies. Frequently the Chief Justice of a colony acted also as Attorney General of the colony. In Upper and Lower Canada, in Nova Scotia and the other eastern colonies, this was changed in the 1830's and the 1840's by colonial statutes conferring life tenure on colonial judges, and by Royal Instructions from London to the Chief Justices to keep out of politics.[22]

---

[19]Dawson, *op. cit*, 14.
[20]See: G. V. La Forest, *Natural Resources and Public Property under The Canadian Constitution* (1969, Toronto), 12-14.
[21]C. 2 of 12 and 13 William III.
[22]W. R. Lederman, "The Independence of the Judiciary" (1956), 34 Can. Bar Rev. 1151-1156.

In this way the model for the superior courts afforded by section 3 of the British Act of Settlement of 1701 was put into effect in British North America before 1867. This judicial system then found expression in sections 96 to 101 of The B.N.A. Act of 1867, dealing with the judicature of the new Dominion of Canada.

Also, through the whole of the colonial period, appeal to the Privy Council in London from decisions of the final court in a colony was provided for by the colonial constitutions, whether they were statutory or prerogative. Moreover, the Imperial Judicial Committee Acts of 1833 and 1844 made a professional court of the Judicial Committee and confirmed the rights of appeal to it from the colonies. The abolition of appeals to the Judicial Committee of the Privy Council did not come for Canada until 1949.

III. CONFEDERATION AND THE GROWTH OF CANADA AFTER 1867

(a) Federal Union in 1867

The federal union of Nova Scotia, New Brunswick, Quebec and Ontario took place on July 1st, 1867, by virtue of The Imperial British North America Act of that year.

It is beyond the scope of this account to give the details of the growth of Canada by the addition of new Provinces and Territories after 1867. The purpose of the account to this point has been largely fulfilled—to give the background of The B.N.A. Act of 1867, so that those who take the trouble to read the Act in its entirety may understand the extent to which it embodies the continuity of our governmental institutions and legal systems in Canada over a period of hundreds of years.

(b) The Addition of Provinces and Territories to Canada after 1867

The essential constitutional picture of this development has been succinctly given by Mr. Elmer A. Driedger Q.C. in his notes to The B.N.A. Act, *A Consolidation of The British North America Acts 1867 to 1965* (1967, Ottawa), 2-3, as follows:

> Canada now consists of ten provinces (Ontario, Quebec, Nova Scotia, New Brunswick, Manitoba, British Columbia, Prince Edward Island, Alberta, Saskatchewan and Newfoundland) and two territories (the Yukon Territory and the Northwest Territories).
>
> The first territories added to the Union were Rupert's Land and the North-Western Territory, (subsequently designated the Northwest Territories), which were admitted pursuant to s. 146 of The British North America Act, 1867 and the Rupert's Land Act, 1868, 31-32 Vict., c. 105 (U.K.), by Order in Council of June 23, 1870, effective July 15, 1870. Prior to the admission of these territories the Parliament of Canada enacted the Act for the temporary Government of Rupert's Land and the North-Western Territory when united with Canada (32-33 Vict., c. 3), and the Manitoba Act (33 Vict., c. 3), which provided for the formation of the Province of Manitoba.

British Columbia was admitted into the Union pursuant to s. 146 of The British North America Act, 1867, by Order in Council of May 16, 1871, effective July 20, 1871.

Prince Edward Island was admitted pursuant to s. 146 of The British North America Act, 1867, by Order in Council of June 26, 1873, effective July 1, 1873.

On June 29, 1871, the United Kingdom Parliament enacted The British North America Act, 1871 (34-35 Vict., c. 28) authorizing the creation of additional provinces out of territories not included in any province. Pursuant to this statute, the Parliament of Canada enacted The Alberta Act, (July 20, 1905, 4-5 Edw. VII, c. 3) and The Saskatchewan Act, (July 20, 1905, 4-5 Edw. VII, c. 42), providing for the creation of the provinces of Alberta and Saskatchewan respectively. Both these Acts came into force on Sept. 1, 1905.

Meanwhile, all remaining British possessions and territories in North America and the islands adjacent thereto, except the colony of Newfoundland and its dependencies, were admitted into the Canadian Confederation by Order in Council dated July 31, 1880.

The Parliament of Canada added portions of the Northwest Territories to the adjoining provinces in 1912 by The Ontario Boundaries Extension Act, 2 Geo. V, c. 40, The Quebec Boundaries Extension Act, 1912, 2 Geo. V, c. 45 and The Manitoba Boundaries Extension Act, 1912, 2 Geo. V, c. 32, and further additions were made to Manitoba by The Manitoba Boundaries Extension Act, 1930, 20-21 Geo. V, c. 28.

The Yukon Territory was created out of the Northwest Territories in 1898 by The Yukon Territory Act, 61 Vict., c. 6, (Canada).

Newfoundland was added on March 31, 1949, by The British North America Act, 1949, (U.K.), 12-13 Geo. VI, c. 22, which ratified the Terms of Union between Canada and Newfoundland.

(c) The Determination of the Date for the Reception of English Civil and Criminal Law in Manitoba, Saskatchewan, Alberta, The North West Territories and The Yukon Territory

The Imperial Order in Council under the British Rupert's Land Act of 1868, transferred Rupert's Land and the North-Western Territory to the new Dominion of Canada with effect July 15, 1870. By both federal and provincial statutes, the date for the reception of English civil and criminal law for all these provinces and Territories was soon fixed at July 15, 1870. Thus, in these areas, ordinary English statutes suitable to their conditions have been received as part of the local law if they were dated before July 16, 1870. The relevant statutory references are as follows.

For Manitoba:

Queen's Bench Act, c. 12, S.M. 1874, s. 5. (Also in c. 36, R.S.M. 1891, s. 8).

Manitoba Supplementary Provision Act, c. 53, S.C. 1888, s. 4.

For the North-West Territories (including what later became Saskatchewan, Alberta, and the Yukon Territory):

North-West Territories Amendment Act, c. 25, S.C. 1886, s. 3.

A NOTE: ON THE DEVELOPMENT OF CANADIAN INDEPENDENCE SUBSEQUENT TO 1867

Most of the essential changes altering the original colonial position will only be sketched here, very briefly indeed, to provide a minimum of background for the independence issues that remain current and urgent. Argument and detail concerning the latter are the subject of the next two essays.

So far as executive government is concerned, we have seen that independence was achieved in domestic affairs with the advent of responsible government in the principal British North American colonies almost twenty years before Confederation. But the conduct of foreign affairs for Canada, largely an executive or royal prerogative function, remained in the hands of the British Cabinet for many decades after 1867. Nevertheless, by a series of precedents and conventions over many years, culminating in 1939, it became established that the Canadian Cabinet alone controlled the exercise of royal prerogative powers concerning all of Canada's foreign and external relations. In other words, in these matters as in domestic matters, the Queen became bound by the advice of her Canadian ministers.

Coming now to judicial independence we find that appeals to the Judicial Committee of the Privy Council in London were fully and finally abolished in 1949, making the Supreme Court of Canada truly the final and ultimate Court of Appeal for Canada. The Judicial Committee itself upheld as valid amendments to the Supreme Court Act by the Parliament of Canada which had this effect.

Finally, in the areas of legislative power and constitutional amendment, we find that, with one exception, the paramountcy of British statutes specially applicable overseas was abolished. The abolition was formalized when, in 1931, the British Parliament, with the agreement of Canada and the other Dominions, enacted the Statute of Westminster. Henceforth, the Parliament of Canada could freely amend or repeal for Canada any British statutes concerned with the national subjects of primary legislative power, and the respective Provincial Legislatures could do the same with British statutes concerned with provincial subjects of legislative power. But, the essentials of the Canadian federal union itself, including the *division* of primary legislative powers just referred to, are provided in the British North America Act, passed by the British Parliament in 1867, and in certain amendments of it by that Parliament since 1867. So, at Canada's request, the Statute of Westminster of 1931 made an exception of the British North America Act so far as the latter contained essentials of the Canadian federal constitution. In these respects, in effect the British North America Act as amended remains paramount and thus remains beyond the reach of change by ordinary statutes from Canada, whether of the Parliament of Canada or one of the Provincial Legislatures. Accordingly, action by the British Parliament is still at least formally necessary to amend the British North America Act, insofar as the latter lays down essentials of Canada's constitution as a federal union.

This gives rise to the major remaining constitutional issue of Canadian independence, namely, can Canadians agree on a purely domestic amending procedure, and, on the basis of such agreement, bring the constitution home from

Britain? In other words, can we bring about patriation of the constitution with respect to its future amendment? Moreover, the answer has important present implications concerning the forms and methods of negotiation in Canada that are appropriate to bring about substantial and substantive constitutional reforms, something that is urgent here and now (Spring, 1980). These are the questions considered at length in Chapters 5 and 6.

Chapter 5

The Process of Constitutional Amendment for Canada

Reprinted with permission from (1966-67),
12 McGill Law Journal 371

I. INTRODUCTION

In 1967, Canada completes her first century as a federal country under the British North America Act. Also, at this particular time, Canadians find themselves urgently considering and discussing whether or not important changes should now be made in our federal constitution, that constitution having served us so far almost without substantial amendment. The main pressure for change comes from claims for better constitutional recognition of the French fact in Canadian life, both within and beyond the boundaries of the Province of Quebec. Among other things, this raises questions of the methods of constitutional change in a federal country which accordingly now require our attention in Canada more than ever before. This paper expresses personal comment, opinion and analysis of the author concerning the central issues of method in constitutional change as they now confront us. Do we now bring the federal constitution home to Canada and, if so, on what terms as to domestic control of change or amendment?

It appeared quite recently that this question was settled. A complete set of domestic constitutional amending procedures was agreed upon at a Federal-Provincial Conference of the Prime Minister of Canada and the Premiers of the Provinces on October 14, 1964, as embodied in the text of a bill entitled ''An Act to provide for the amendment in Canada of the Constitution of Canada.'' This was popularly known as the Fulton-Favreau Formula, being named for the two Federal Ministers of Justice primarily responsible for negotiating its final form. In February, 1965, a White Paper on ''The Amendment of the Constitution of Canada'' was issued under the auspices of the Honourable Guy Favreau, then Federal Minister of Justice.[1] This document set forth the history and present position respecting amendment, the story of the development of the Fulton-Favreau Formula and an analysis of the meaning of the Formula. Nevertheless second thoughts set in, primarily, but not only, in the Province of Quebec, and

---

[1](1965) Queen's Printer, Ottawa, hereinafter cited as the White Paper. The full text of the Fulton-Favreau Bill or Formula is given in Appendix 3 starting at page 110.

the final agreement of the Lesage Government and the Legislature of Quebec was not forthcoming as expected. Then in June of 1966 the Lesage Government was defeated by the National Union Party of Daniel Johnson, which had been explicitly opposing the Fulton-Favreau Formula. With the Johnson Government in power in Quebec, it is now clear that the whole problem of patriation and amendment of the Canadian Constitution is open for review once more.

In any event, the White Paper of 1965 is a full and careful historical document the text of which was accepted as accurate by the Federal and Provincial Governments before it was published. There is no point in recapitulating here what has been well covered in the White Paper. Accordingly, in what follows I assume a knowledge of the main elements of the White Paper and of the chief features of the proposed set of procedures for amendment known as the Fulton-Favreau Formula.

II. THE CONSTITUTION AND THE TECHNICAL SYSTEM OF THE FULTON-FAVREAU FORMULA

About the first thing to be done if one is to consider methods of amending the constitution is simply to define the meaning of the category 'constitution' or 'constitutional law'. All law flows from or is part of the constitution, so that there is a sense in which all laws are constitutional laws, finding their legitimate ancestry proximately or remotely in what Professor Hans Kelsen called the Basic Norm.[2] Obviously one cannot subject all legal change to special amending procedures, so that more precise and discriminating definitions of the content of the 'constitution' are necessary. An excellent short definition is that of Sir Ivor Jennings,[3] who said that the word 'constitution' in its more precise sense "means the document in which are set out the rules governing the composition, powers and methods of operation of the main institutions of government, and the general principles applicable to their relations to the citizens." His example was the Constitution of the Irish Republic. In Canada, we have to think in terms of many statutory documents and as well of appropriate parts of the historically received English common law concerning the Crown. Nevertheless, I suggest that the sort of things we consider to be peculiarly constitutional, whatever their respective forms, are those described by Sir Ivor Jennings. And, of course, not all these things need to be subjected to special legislative procedures.

The Fulton-Favreau Formula has to face this many-sided problem of definition, and does it very well. It employs the general phrase 'the Constitution of Canada', and then proceeds to give this further definition in two ways: by examples in section 11 and by spelling out sub-divisions of constitutional matters in sections 2 to 8. Section 11 reads as follows:

> Without limiting the meaning of the expression "Constitution of Canada", in this Part that expression includes the following enactments and any order, rule or regulation thereunder, namely,
> (a) the British North America Acts, 1867 to 1964;

[2] Hans Kelsen, General Theory of Law and State (1949) chapter X.
[3] Sir W. Ivor Jennings, The Law and the Constitution, 5th edition (1959), 33.

(b) the Manitoba Act, 1870;

(c) the Parliament of Canada Act, 1875;

(d) the Canadian Speaker (Appointment of Deputy) Act, 1895, Session 2;

(e) the Alberta Act;

(f) the Saskatchewan Act;

(g) the Statute of Westminter, 1931, in so far as it is part of the law of Canada; and

(h) this Act.

This seems to suggest the Jennings concept of the word 'constitution', the examples giving some precision of definition without restriction to the sort of thing exemplified.

In addition, as indicated, sections 2 to 8 of the Formula spell out more precisely defined sub-divisions of things constitutional, including, it should be noted, the separate constitutions of the respective provinces. In this way different types of constitutional change are assigned to different amending procedures, as deemed appropriate. For example, amendments affecting "the powers of a province to make laws" would require a statute of the Parliament of Canada and the concurrence of the legislatures of all the provinces.[4] Thus a requirement for unanimity would be imposed respecting the whole of the federal distribution of legislative powers. On the other hand, a statute of the Parliament of Canada having the concurrence of "the legislatures of at least two-thirds of the provinces representing at least fifty per cent of the population of Canada" was thought to be enough to effect change in "the principles of proportionate representation of the provinces in the House of Commons prescribed by the Constitution of Canada."[5] Then, as a final example, when it came to amending the constitution of a province, "except as regards the office of Lieutenant-Governor", the Formula provides that a simple statute of the provincial legislature concerned would be effective (as indeed it has been since 1867).[6] Thus, for different sub-divisions of constitutional matters we go all the way from extraordinary and rigid to ordinary and flexible processes of change in the proposals made.

● ● ●

III. THE PRESENT POSITION RESPECTING AMENDMENT OF THE CONSTITUTION OF CANADA: HOW TO BRING THE CONSTITUTION HOME

The important part of our constitution respecting current issues of amendment and patriation is given in certain critical sections of the B.N.A. Acts.[7] The problems involved may be adequately considered if discussion here is confined to two types of constitutional matters; (1) the distribution of legislative powers between the Parliament of Canada and the legislatures of the provinces, and (2) some elements of the structure or composition of the Parliament of Canada. In these re-

---

[4]Sections 1 and 2 of the Fulton-Favreau Formula.

[5]Sections 1, 5 and 6 (g) of the Fulton-Favreau Formula.

[6]Section 7 of the Fulton-Favreau Formula.

[7]See the White Paper, Appendix 1, starting at page 54 for "A Consolidation of The British North America Acts, 1867 to 1964".

spects the old supremacy of the Imperial Parliament at Westminster has been formally preserved by section 7 of the Statute of Westminster, 1931,[8] though the same statute declared the abolition of that supremacy in all other respects for Canada. And even regarding the reserved matters of amendment, the preamble to the Statute of Westminster and the declarations by Imperial Conferences to which it refers plainly imply that complete autonomy was to be Canada's for the asking, if and when the various governments of federated Canada could agree among themselves on the necessary domestic procedures for such amendments. There has not yet been agreement, so we must ask—What is the present position?

After reviewing the procedures leading to amendments of the B.N.A. Act in the period 1867-1964, the White Paper summarizes the basic constitutional position in four propositions which may be briefly expressed as follows.[9]

(1) Although an Act of the United Kingdom Parliament is necessary to amend the B.N.A. Act, "such action is taken only upon formal request from Canada. No Act of the United Kingdom Parliament affecting Canada is therefore passed unless it is requested and consented to by Canada. Conversely, every amendment requested by Canada in the past has been enacted."

(2) The request must take the form of a joint address of the Canadian House of Commons and Senate to the Crown praying that the appropriate measure be laid before the Parliament of the United Kingdom.

(3) "[T]he Canadian Parliament will not request an amendment directly affecting federal-provincial relationships without prior consultation and agreement with the provinces."

(4) "[N]o amendment to Canada's Constitution will be made by the British Parliament merely upon the request of a Canadian province." The British Government will not move the British Parliament to act except on a request originating with the Federal Government of Canada.

Such is the existing method of constitutional amendment for matters still specially entrenched in the B.N.A. Acts. Thus we see that our present basic law of amendment has been made by longstanding official precedent, custom and practice modifying the constitutional law of the old British Empire in the manner just indicated. Anyone who doubts the validity and force of such custom, convention and practice should read again the preamble to the Statute of Westminster, 1931, which makes it clear that even that statute purports to be declaratory of a basic 'constitutional position' already 'established' by other means than statute—e.g. the agreed declarations or conventions of Imperial Conferences.

In any event, the result is that, in critical respects, amendment of the Canadian Constitution in the matters indicated consists in some steps that must be taken in Canada followed by others that must be taken in the United Kingdom. While the latter are purely formal now, nevertheless they represent a respect in which the Canadian Constitution is not now and never has been at home. Bring-

---

[8]22 George V, Chapter 4 (U.K.).
[9]The White Paper, 15-16.

ing it home then means to make into law a set of amending procedures that can be carried out in Canada entirely by Canadian governments, legislative bodies, or electorates, acting severally or in combinations of some kind. If we are to have legitimate as distinct from revolutionary change, then the present method of amendment focussed on London should be followed one last time to institute a new domestic method for amendment focussed on Canada. Rules made by custom and convention seem already to have done as much as they can do to bring the Canadian Constitution home to Canada. What we now need is to acquire at one stroke a complete and precise set of domestic procedures for amending the Canadian Constitution. The slow and piece-meal development characteristic of custom and precedent as law-making processes is not now appropriate for this task. The only proper and legitimate way to obtain the complex scheme needed in one operation at the moment of our own choosing is by a statute of the United Kingdom Parliament enacted in response to the existing request and consent rules as the last statute for Canada of that Parliament. This would in effect repeal section 7 of the Statute of Westminster and make Canadian legislative autonomy formally complete in the last area where up to this point it has been formally reserved. This is what successive Federal Governments at Ottawa have attempted to do by agreement with the provinces. This is what the Pearson Government has attempted to do with the Fulton-Favreau Formula. It should be noted that section 10 of the Formula, the so-called renunciation clause (from the point of view of the Parliament of the United Kingdom), would terminate for all purposes the request and consent procedure as a means of putting British statutes into force in Canada.

This brings me to my basic point about the merit of the Fulton-Favreau Formula *as a means of bringing the constitution home*. It is true that the Formula is rigid in that it applies the rule of unanimity to the whole range of the distribution of legislative powers between Parliament and the provincial legislatures. Nevertheless, we are under the rule of unanimity now in this respect by virtue of the existing request and consent rules. All we have to do to bring the constitution home is to substitute a domestic rule of unanimity for one focussed on London. If we are stuck with the rule of unanimity anyway for the present, and apparently we are, why not do this? It is embarrassing for the British and humiliating for Canadians to maintain any longer these obsolete and incongruous formal steps of requesting the British Parliament to act for us. Accordingly, my view is that we should use the Fulton-Favreau Formula as a means of bringing the constitution home. Then later, under the Formula, if we can get unanimous agreement, we can modify the scope of the Formula's rule of unanimity and place more matters under the rule permitting change by the concurrence with Parliament of at least two-thirds of the provinces comprising at least fifty per cent of the country's population.

The opponents of the Fulton-Favreau Formula as a means of bringing the constitution home make strange companions. On the one hand is a group who favour stronger powers at the centre for Parliament and who fear that the rule of unanimity would prevent this being brought about by amendment now or in the future even though the need for it was very great. On the other hand is a group, particularly strong in the Province of Quebec, who want greater powers assigned to the provinces, or at least to the Province of Quebec, and who fear that the rule of unanimity would prevent such changes by amendment now or in the future. But, the point is that we are under the rule of unanimity anyway, and neither of these groups is worse off if the requirement is embodied in a domestic procedure rather than in one that takes us to London.

With all due respect to both groups of opponents of the Fulton-Favreau Formula, it does seem that some of them must be harbouring the hope that there might be circumstances in which they could persuade the British Government and Parliament to amend the Constitution of Canada respecting the distribution of legislative powers in disregard of the convention requiring unanimous consent of the provinces before the Canadian Parliament requests such an amendment. I do not think the present convention permits the British Government and British Parliament to override any provincial dissent in this type of constitutional matter. In the face of any provincial dissent, I think the present convention requires that the British Government and Parliament do nothing, simply regarding the request from the Canadian Parliament in these circumstances as improper, that is as unconstitutional or illegal. It would be an intolerable reversion to colonial status to suggest that the British Government or Parliament could be or should be involved in any substantial way in decision-making as to whether or not to modify the federal distribution of legislative powers in Canada. If they were asked to override provincial dissents in this type of matter, they would be substantially involved. To repeat, we should use the Fulton-Favreau Formula *as the means to bring the constitution home.* Once we have it home on these terms, the Formula itself contains the procedures whereby its own undue rigidity could be modified if Canadians themselves could reach the point where the Parliament of Canada and the legislatures of the provinces were agreed about how to do it. If we cannot reach that point, we are going to have to rest upon the status quo anyway.

We may turn now to another point that should be made concerning the merit of the Fulton-Favreau Formula. So far, the argument has proceeded in relation to amendments or proposed amendments to the federal distribution of legislative powers. But there is another important type of amendment that has figured in federal-provincial relations. I refer to the composition of Parliament as an institution—as our central legislative body. For example an amendment of the B.N.A. Act was required to re-adjust representation in the House of Commons, that is to change the system whereby each province was given its quota of members in proportion to its population.[10] Between 1867 and 1949, such amendments were secured by an act of the British Parliament in response to a joint address from the Canadian Parliament. As the convention developed in this class of matter, provincial consents were not necessary and the provinces were not consulted. In effect, then, a Federal Government at Ottawa could obtain this type of amendment by its own decisions alone. In 1949, without consulting the provinces, the Federal Government moved the Parliament of Canada to request an amendment of

---

[10]The White Paper, 13, items (8) and (9).

the B.N.A. Act which provided in effect that, in all cases appropriate for use of the joint address procedure without provincial consent, changes in the Constitution of Canada could be made by an ordinary statute of the Parliament of Canada. The British Parliament passed the amendment as requested,[11] and a new class (1) of section 91 of the B.N.A. Act was thereby enacted. It states that the legislative authority of the Parliament of Canada includes:

> The amendment from time to time of the Constitution of Canada, except as regards matters coming within the classes of subjects by this Act assigned exclusively to the Legislatures of the provinces, or as regards rights or privileges by this or any other Constitutional Act granted or secured to the Legislature or the Government of a province, or to any class of persons with respect to schools or as regards the use of the English or the French language or as regards the requirements that there shall be a session of the Parliament of Canada at least once each year, and that no House of Commons shall continue for more than five years from the day of the return of the Writs for choosing the House: provided, however, that a House of Commons may in time of real or apprehended war, invasion or insurrection be continued by the Parliament of Canada if such continuation is not opposed by the votes of more than one-third of the members of such House.

An example of the use of this new power occurred in 1952 when the Parliament of Canada enacted a statute providing a new section 51 of the B.N.A. Act respecting the provincial quotas by population for members in the House of Commons.[12] More than one provincial government had protested that the 1949 amendment went too far and that the provinces did have a real interest in the composition of the House of Commons and matters of like nature. Hence the provinces contended that the power of change should not rest with the Canadian Parliament alone. Prime Minister St. Laurent promised that, if the federal and provincial governments could agree on over-all domestic amending procedures, federal powers in this respect could be re-written somewhat in an effort to meet the objections.[13] This was actually accomplished some years later in the Fulton-Favreau Formula produced by the Federal-Provincial Conferences of 1964. Section 12 of Part II of the Formula would repeal class (1) of section 91 of the B.N.A. Act, as enacted in 1949, and substitute for it section 6 of Part I of the Formula. The latter section waters down very considerably the powers given the Parliament of Canada in 1949. For example, a change in "the principles of proportionate representation of the provinces in the House of Commons" would require under the Formula a statute of the Parliament of Canada followed by the concurrence of at least two-thirds of the provinces having at least fifty per cent of the population of the country. As stated earlier, the 1949 statutory powers of the Canadian Parliament were essentially the same as those the Canadian Parliament had between 1867 and 1949 by virtue of joint addresses not requiring consultation with the provinces. The substance of power and decision-making did not change in 1949, only the form of its exercise. Hence section 6 of the 1964 For-

---

[11]See footnote (7).
[12]The B.N.A. Act, 1952, R.S.C. 1952, c. 304.
[13]The White Paper, 25.

mula does embody a reduction of federal power in relation to 1867 and 1949. It represents a major concession by the Federal Government to the provinces, no doubt in an effort to win their agreement to the over-all Formula. The Federal Government gets little credit for this from anyone, when in fact it deserves a great deal of credit for seeking to meet provincial complaints in this reasonable way.

Strangely enough though, section 9 of Part I of the 1964 Formula seems designed to obscure what is really happening in this respect. Section 9 says:

> Nothing in this Part diminishes any power of the Parliament of Canada or of the legislature of a province, existing at the coming into force of this Act, to make laws in relation to any matter.

This is technically true of Part I of the Formula, but is not true of the over-all effect of the Formula as soon as one reads section 12, the first section of Part II. (Section 12 repeals class (1) of section 91 of the B.N.A. Act as enacted in 1949). The White Paper carefully refrains from explaining that the combined effect of sections 6 and 12 of the Formula is to negate section 9 of the Formula in this respect. Perhaps section 9 of the Formula is an attempt to placate the more extreme partisans of strong central power. If so, it doesn't quite come off. Anyway, section 9 should simply be dropped from the Formula and section 12 should be included in Part I where it belongs.

To recapitulate then, I am in favour of enactment of the Fulton-Favreau Formula now as the best means to bring the Constitution of Canada home. I am not opposed to considerable change in the substance of the Formula either now or later, as I have indicated, provided the necessary unanimous consent can be obtained now or later. Nevertheless, there is no prejudice to anyone in using the Formula as it stands as the means to bring the constitution home. This is clearly the best way, but it is not perhaps the only way in theory. Theoretically the device of a special constituent assembly could be used to bring the constitution home, and this will now be briefly examined.

A constituent assembly, as I understand it, would be an extraordinary representative body set up by the constitution and itself authorized to change the constitution by meeting prescribed conditions as to procedure and voting. Those who advocate such an assembly usually have in mind re-writing the Constitution of Canada in a major way. No doubt such a body could in theory be instituted for Canada if it were authorized by a statute of the British Parliament passed in response to a joint address of the Parliament of Canada in which all the provinces had concurred. This would be the only legitimate or constitutional way such an extraordinary body could be set up in Canada. If this were to be done, there would have to be prior federal-provincial agreement on a wide range of things. A number of questions would have to be answered about membership of the proposed constituent assembly, about how it was to proceed and what it could do. The following list of such questions is suggestive.

(1) Who would select and accredit delegates?

(2) Who would instruct delegates—what discretion would they have?

(3) What kind of a majority would be required to pass or adopt a proposed new constitutional clause at the assembly?

(4) Who would be bound by the passing of a clause in the assembly sessions?

(5) What ratifications, if any, would be required for clauses passed in the assembly sessions?

(6) Would a dissenting minority be bound by majority votes or majority ratifications?

Simply listing these problems means to me that a constituent assembly is simply not a practical possibility at this time. Nor would it be desirable if it were practical. We do not need a major re-writing of the Canadian Constitution at all. The existing constitution, as developed by judicial precedent and official practice, has served Canadians well for one hundred years and does not need wholesale change to continue to serve us well. On the other hand we must always be ready to study the need for certain particular changes by amendment here and there to meet the needs of new conditions. If a proper case for such change can be made in some specific respect, then we should give that change effect through the operation of a permanent and completely Canadian amending procedure like the Fulton-Favreau Formula—a procedure that arises naturally out of our history and traditions, and which uses our existing legislative and executive institutions of government. Public debate and discussion can take place in legislative and parliamentary sessions, before parliamentary committees, and in other ways congenial to our great inheritance of English parliamentary institutions and responsible government. There are for instance many types of conferences that could be held on constitutional issues. *These would not of course be constituent assemblies*, but rather gatherings designed to inform, to educate, to advise or to make recommendations. They would be concerned with helping to form public opinion and to reach significant consensus among officials and citizens about specific items of desirable constitutional change. I agree with what the Prime Minister of Ontario, the Honourable Mr. Robarts, said recently on this subject in a public address to a group of business men in Montreal:[14]

> It also is time in our country that we sat down and examined, apart from the fiscal problems which have dominated discussions in recent years, some of the constitutional difficulties that arise from time to time. I have suggested a series of conferences at which we could meet together to discover and discuss areas of agreement and disagreement, of accommodation and of compromise, Province to Province. We would discuss not only constitutional questions but would explore the cultural and social problems of our changing world. I believe that much can be done to relieve the stresses and strains which have affected Canada without necessarily changing the *British North America Act*. If it is found that some sections should be changed, then let us change them; where no change is either desirable or necessary, let us leave it unaltered. I see no need for a new Constitution, only the possibility of some adjustments to a Constitution that can readily be amended to serve us well in the future.

I believe this pragmatic approach is the right one, and indeed the only practical one. This is the way to maintain a proper balance from time to time between con-

---

[14]"Remarks by The Honourable John Robarts, Prime Minister of Ontario, To The Advertising And Sales Executives' Club of Montreal, Montreal, Wednesday, November 23rd, 1966." (Mimeographed text as released by the office of the Prime Minister of Ontario).

stitutional stability and constitutional change, taking due account of the need for central power on the one hand and provincial autonomy on the other. So far as these adjustments call for specific constitutional amendments from time to time, we should be able to look to purely Canadian procedures appropriate for the purpose.

A NOTE ON THE VICTORIA CHARTER OF 1971

As indicated in the previous chapter the Fulton-Favreau Formula proved unacceptable in Quebec and did not go into effect. In 1971, at a Federal-Provincial Conference in Victoria, among other things, the Government of Prime Minister Trudeau proposed a new formula for the amendment of the specially entrenched parts of the B.N.A. Act entirely within Canada, adoption of which would have accomplished patriation.

This proposal was to the following effect: Amendments of the specially entrenched parts of the Constitution could be made when so authorized by resolutions of the Senate and House of Commons of the Parliament of Canada, and also by resolutions of the legislative assemblies of at least a majority of the provinces that included:

(1) Ontario,

(2) Quebec,

(3) At least two of the four Atlantic Provinces,

(4) At least two of the Western Provinces with combined populations of at least 50 per cent of the four Western Provinces.

The Victoria Charter also failed to go into effect because it was unacceptable to Quebec. After this, constitutional reform activity became reduced to a low level, until the need for it was abruptly revived by the victory of the Parti Quebecois in the Quebec Provincial election of November 1976. There is now (Spring 1980) urgent need for a major renovation of Canada's federal constitution if the separation of Quebec is to be avoided and the Canadian federal union continued with Quebec included. This is the situation addressed in Chapter 6.

Chapter 6

Constitutional Amendment and Canadian Unity

Reprinted with permission from *Special Lectures of the Law Society of Upper Canada 1978: The Constitution and the Future of Canada* (Toronto: Richard De Boo Ltd., 1978)

I. INTRODUCTION

In Canada our special distinction in the constitutional sense is that we have combined democratic parliamentary government on the British model with a federal system; essentially a federal division of legislative powers by subjects between the Parliament of Canada on the one hand, and the respective parliaments of the ten provinces on the other. It is true that we have had our troubles as a country in the past, but, on the whole, for about 110 years the Canadian federal constitution has been one of the most successful and stable systems of government in the modern world. Nevertheless, we now find ourselves facing fundamental questions about the nature and future of our country, questions raised by the current political movement among some French Canadians for the independence of Quebec.

I do not believe there has been a comparable period of need in our history to face up to fundamentals since the Canadian Confederation was first put together in the earlier part of the decade of the 1860's. The issues are indeed basic ones that concern the primary elements of our national community from sea to sea. These basics are not exclusively constitutional or political or legal or cultural or economic or linguistic or religious. They are not confined in their character by any one of these limiting adjectives; rather they are factors that are in some measure all these things and more. This all-pervasiveness means that no one specialist or group of specialists has all the answers for the issues involved. So, as a constitutional lawyer, I do not see myself as a purist of some sort who thinks that things legal and constitutional can somehow be neatly separated and given over-riding effect in relation to the primary facts and factors or our national community life. Nevertheless, I do consider that the study of constitutional law, which is necessarily a broadly conceived approach to these things, does provide valuable insights that may permit basic problems to be given more definition and to be made more manageable. In any event, this is the spirit in which I approach my mandate here today. For me, constitutional law arises out of our whole history and tradition as a people, and one must constantly relate these rules and principles of law and government to the organic ongoing life of our national community, from which they derive their validity.

Be that as it may, my immediate task is to attempt to delineate the limited but important extent to which basic constitutional procedures and changes may contribute to the solution of current issues. The starting point is to remember Dr. Corry's warning: one must not expect either too much or too little of the basic federal constitution. On the one hand it must speak succinctly in rather abstract terms that lend themselves to somewhat flexible judicial interpretations designed to meet changing social conditions over time. But, on the other hand, these same constitutional terms must not be so abstract that they are in effect all things to all people. By virtue of their inherent core of meaning and authoritative interpretation, the terms must be and become precise enough so that they provide meaningful definitions and guidelines for the everyday processes of democratic parliamentary government at both the provincial and national levels. The power-conferring words relevant to these different levels of government are in considerable competition with one another, and so continuing political and judicial efforts at balance and equilibrium are required.[1] In any event, having provided definitions that are meaningful but general, the constitution then leaves further and detailed law-making to the regular majoritarian democratic processes in the parliaments of Canada and the provinces respectively. But of course the basic elements of the constitution that define the primary provincial and federal institutions and determine their respective powers are not themselves subject to change by ordinary majorities and ordinary statutes. Rather, as should be the case, they are subject to change only by extraordinary amending procedures which are difficult enough that, politically, they cannot be invoked either easily or often. One of the important puzzles of our present situation is the bearing this has on the present crisis of Canadian unity. That problem is precisely the subject of this paper.

I propose to give the specifics of the present extraordinary amending procedures of the Canadian constitution, the procedures, that is, that are applicable to the specially entrenched parts of that constitution. It is essential to try to get this straight if we are in the years immediately ahead to accomplish certain basic changes in the federal constitution, changes, that is, that may be both necessary and effective to keep Canada united. But, should it be that that cannot in the end be done in spite of every effort, then, even though the event is at present unlikely, we should now also face squarely this question: What is the amending procedure necessary to permit the legitimate secession of Quebec from the Canadian federal union?

For most people, our special constitutional amending procedures are a highly technical and mysterious subject, and we have heard little about them in the current debates on the crisis of Canadian unity. This is strange because the

---

[1]See my essay entitled "Unity and Diversity in Canadian Federalism: Ideals and Methods of Moderation" (1975), 53 Can. Bar Rev. 597.

subject is of critical importance here and now, and not just later, a few years down the road. There are two main reasons for this current importance.

First, the special amending procedure tells us when some or all of the provinces, acting through their governments and parliaments, must agree with the federal government and parliament if certain basic changes are to be made. To meet these rules for a well-distributed democratic consensus in the country is to accomplish legitimate constitutional change. Basic change brought about by *other* means would be in some measure at least revolutionary change, though such other means might also be peaceful ones. I consider it obvious that the legal constitutional methods of change must be preferred, since they exist and are reasonable. This being so, the legal constitutional methods have direct and immediate implications for the ongoing political processes of the country. The constitutional rules tell us what the goals of the political efforts for basic change should be in this sense—they tell us the nature and range of the consents that need to be obtained by political persuasion, in Canada as a whole and in the provinces, in order legitimately to accomplish (or to defeat or modify) the basic changes that some groups are seeking. The amendment rules also tell us a great deal about the form intergovernmental negotiations should take in the country, as we start down the road to possible basic changes.

There is in addition a second reason for the importance of the legal amending procedures. To follow established constitutional methods of change, to keep to the ways marked out by precedent, custom, history and tradition, is to honour the methods that have been recognized and accepted by our democratic parliaments and our responsible governments over a long period. This reassures people amid the uncertainties of change. Moreover, most people are likely to be satisfied that basic changes which come by such careful means have come fairly, and so should be recognized and accepted willingly. Even strong dissenters will have some feeling, albeit reluctant, that they should make the best of the new situation. These are the virtues of our established forms of democracy and due process of law. We would be foolish indeed not to rely on them in our present time of troubles.

II. THE PRESENT PROCESS FOR CONSTITUTIONAL AMENDMENT

There are many issues that affect the constitution and the legal system generally, but I can only speak here of the most fundamental and urgent constitutional matters relevant to our present discontent. I refer to three basic elements of the B.N.A. Act for which special amending procedures are required, if there is to be change.

(a) The Federal Union itself

The Preamble and Chapter II of the B.N.A. Act explicitly establish a federal union of Ontario, Quebec, Nova Scotia and New Brunswick under the name of Canada. Further, there is provision in other sections, and in the B.N.A. Act of 1871, for procedures to accomplish "the eventual admission into the Union of other Parts of British North America''. Nothing at all is said about any province of Canada leaving the Union after it has once been included or admitted, but, in my view, the power of special amendment is total and does cover this possibility as well.

(b) The Federal Division of Legislative Powers

In the B.N.A. Act, the ordinary primary legislative powers are listed by subjects and divided, some being allotted to the federal parliament and the others to the respective provincial legislatures. These are the guidelines for compromise between unity and diversity that make Canada a federal country.

(c) Guaranteed Human Rights and Freedoms

The B.N.A. Act does not contain a general Bill of Rights. Nevertheless, it does have some specially entrenched guarantees for the religious character of separate schools in Ontario and Quebec, and for the use of the English and French languages in the federal parliament and the federal courts of Canada, and the parliament and the courts of Quebec. We may need some further guarantees of this type.

The movement for national independence in the Province of Quebec, and the election there of the Parti Québécois provincial government on November 15, 1976, raise issues in all three of the basic constitutional areas mentioned. If we are to hold Canada together, and I fully expect and believe that we can do so, then some accommodations and revisions would be needed in the system for the division of legislative powers and probably also in the areas of specially guaranteed human rights and freedoms, both for individuals and groups. Such changes could only be made by special constitutional amendment; they could not be made by ordinary statute either in the parliament of Canada or the legislature of a province. At present this means the consent of all the provinces and the government and parliament of Canada.

But what about the integrity of the Canadian federal union itself? In the years immediately ahead, in spite of all efforts to avoid this result, it might become clear as a matter of political fact that there was a large and urgent majority in Quebec favouring secession of Quebec from Canada. This is certainly not the position at the moment, quite the contrary. The possibility is remote, but even so, its potential implications should be faced. As stated earlier, they are all-pervasive in character, and my mandate is to speak of only one important dimension of them, the implications arising from the constitution. What are they? My statement of them is this. To permit or authorize the secession of a province from the Canadian federal union as a legitimate constitutional development, all the steps of our current special amending process would have to be followed. So, again we see that no ordinary federal or provincial statute could accomplish this result. At present the special process means the consent of all the provinces, the consent of the Parliament of Canada, and the obtaining of a statute to this effect from the British Parliament in London. As indicated earlier, this is also the position respecting the accommodations and revisions mentioned with respect to the division of powers and special guarantees of human rights, on the assumption that the Canadian federal union itself continues.

The rules for amending the specially entrenched basic elements of the B.N.A. Act are not found in that statute itself or in any other single formal constitutional document. Rather they have been established step by step over a long period of years by official precedent, custom, practice and convention among the governments and parliaments concerned. These are the government and parliament of Canada, the governments and legislatures of the Canadian provinces, and the government and parliament of Great Britain. The resulting rules for amendment have been gathered together and given their best expression in a White Paper of the Government of Canada on the subject, published and tabled in the House of Commons in February 1965, under the name of the Honourable Guy Favreau, then Minister of Justice.[2]

So far as they concern the issues mentioned, these rules may be briefly stated as follows:

(1) While a statute of the British Parliament is necessary for amendment of the B.N.A. Act, the British Parliament does nothing on its own initiative. It acts only in response to and in accordance with a formal request from Canada.

(2) The proper form for a request from Canada is a joint address of the House of Commons and the Senate of the Parliament of Canada to the Crown. The British Government and Parliament will not amend the B.N.A. Act on the direct request of a Canadian province only.

(3) "[T]he Canadian Parliament will not request an amendment directly affecting federal-provincial relationships without prior consultation and agreement with the provinces." Where only one, or some but not all, of the provinces are directly affected, then prior consultation is necessary only to secure the agreement of the province or the provinces affected.

Two questions now arise at this point. What is the status of these rules, and what is their bearing on determination of current issues, including the possible secession of Quebec? A number of points need to be made in these respects.

There may be some doubts about the status of these rules. Are they full-fledged constitutional laws or are they something less? Are they merely political conventions of the constitution that do not have the force of law and which can, to some extent at least, be varied or disregarded?[3] In my view these rules are basic constitutional laws in every sense and should be recognized as such by the governments and parliaments concerned, including the British. It is well established in the British Commonwealth of Nations that full-fledged laws of this basic character can be and are made by precedent, custom, practice and convention. There are judicial statements to this effect in the Supreme Court of Canada

---

[2] *The Amendment of the Constitution of Canada,* Honourable Guy Favreau, Minister of Justice, February 1965 (Queen's Printer, Ottawa).

[3] Professor Peter Hogg takes this view. See: Peter W. Hogg, *Constitutional Law of Canada* (Toronto: Carswell, 1977), 7-11 and 18-21.

and the Judicial Committee of the Privy Council.[4] The Statute of Westminster of

---

[4](a) Supreme Court of Canada, per Sir Lyman P. Duff, C.J.C., *Reference re Weekly Rest in Industrial Undertakings Act*, [1936] 3 D.L.R. 673, 678-9:

"The argument on behalf of some of the Provinces (while conceding equality of status between the Dominions and Great Britain in respect of such matters, and the political responsibility of the Dominion government in respect of all treaties or agreements to which the Dominion is a party) denies the authority of the Governor-General, acting on the advice of the Canadian Government, to conclude a treaty or an agreement with a foreign state. The prerogative, it is said, resides in the Crown and it is most earnestly contended that the power to exercise this prerogative has never been delegated to the Governor-General of Canada or to any Canadian authority.

"With reference to the Report of the Conference of 1926, which in explicit terms recognizes treaties in the form of agreements between governments (to which His Majesty is not, in form, a party), it is said that since an Imperial Conference possesses no legislative power, its declarations do not operate to effect changes in the law, and it is emphatically affirmed that, in point of strict law, neither the Governor-General nor any other Canadian authority has received from the Crown power to exercise the prerogative.

"The argument is founded on the distinction it draws between constitutional convention and legal rule; and it is necessary to examine the contention that, in point of legal rule, as distinct from constitutional convention, the Governor-General in Council had no authority to become party by ratification to the convention with which we are concerned.

"There are various points of view from which this contention may be considered. First of all, constitutional law consists very largely of established constitutional usages recognized by the Courts as embodying a rule of law. An Imperial Conference, it is true, possesses no legislative authority. But there could hardly be more authoritative evidence as to constitutional usage than the declarations of such a Conference. The Conference of 1926 categorically recognizes treaties in the form of agreements between Governments in which His Majesty does not formally appear, and in respect of which there has been no Royal intervention. It is the practice of the Dominion to conclude with foreign countries agreements in such form, and agreements even of a still more informal character—merely by an exchange of notes. Conventions under the auspices of the Labour Organization of the League of Nations invariably are ratified by the Government of the Dominion concerned. As a rule, *the crystallization of constitutional usage into a rule of constitutional law* to which the Courts will give effect is a slow process extending over a long period of time; but the Great War accelerated the pace of development in the region with which we are concerned, and it would seem that the usages to which I have referred, the practice, that is to say, under which Great Britain and the Dominions enter into agreements with foreign countries in the form of agreements between Governments and of a still more informal character, must be recognized by the Courts as having the force of law." (My emphasis.)

Notice that Chief Justice Duff is here dealing with the power of the Canadian Governor-General in Council to bind Canada *as a matter of law* to the obligations contained in international treaties or agreements as described. He was not overruled on this point in the Judicial Committee of the Privy Council, though the latter court did overrule him on the other point in the case; the competence of the Canadian Parliament to implement the Labour Conventions by legislation as domestic law in Canada.

(b) Judicial Committee of the Privy Council, per Lord Jowitt, L.C., *Privy Council Appeals Case (Attorney-General for Ontario v. Attorney-General for Canada)*, [1947] A.C. 127, 153-4:

"It is possible to regard this matter from a somewhat wider point of view, as, indeed, it is regarded in the judgment of Sir Lyman Duff. Giving full weight to the circumstances of the Union and to the determination shown by the provinces as late as the Imperial Conferences, which led to the Statute of Westminster, that their rights should be unimpaired, nevertheless, it appears to their Lordships that it is not consistent with the political conception which is embodied in the British Commonwealth of Nations that one member of that Commonwealth should be precluded from setting up, if it so desires, a Supreme Court of Appeal having a jurisdiction both ultimate and exclusive of any other member. The regulation of appeals is, to use the words of Lord Sankey in the *British Coal Corporation* case a "prime element in Canadian sovereignty," which would be impaired if at the will of its citizens recourse would be had to a tribunal, in the constitution of which it had no voice. It is, as their Lordships think,

1931 itself purports to be declaratory of constitutional principles already established by custom and convention.[5] Also, the draft of the Statute of Westminster was modified by a special section for Canada (section 7) to meet the wishes of the Canadian provinces, who were consulted about this by the Government of Canada. Finally, we might note that the Government of Canada consulted the provinces about the text of the Favreau White Paper of 1965, and they agreed that it was historically accurate.[6]

So, we do have in Canadian constitutional law a full-fledged amending process for the specially entrenched parts of the Canadian constitution, and we may now note that this includes the amending process itself. No doubt we may need a new amending process that is somewhat more flexible than the present one, probably along the lines of the proposals at the Victoria Conference of 1971.[7] But, in order to accomplish that, we would have to follow the existing amendment procedure one last time to institute the new procedure, and then, for the next amendments after that the new procedure would govern. This formula ensures the constitutionality of change, even in the amending formula itself.

But some persons may argue that the present rules for amendment do not touch secession by a province at all and that there is no way in which this could be made constitutional. As indicated earlier, I think this view is wrong. My reason is historical. The original power of the British Parliament to change the B.N.A. Act, one of its own statutes, was plenary and unlimited. With respect to the B.N.A. Act, all that has changed is that this plenary power is now exercised by the British Parliament only in response to and in accordance with a proper request from Canada, and not on its own initiative. What *is* a proper request from Canada is controlled by the principles for the joint address given us by custom, practice and convention over the years, as explained.

I have also said that I consider that the consents of all the provinces (including the one wishing to secede) and the consent of the federal parliament are necessary under those rules to permit the constitutionally legitimate secession of a province from the Canadian federal union. This is because to my mind it is obvious that such secession would directly involve and affect vital interests of all the other provinces as well as of the country as a whole. But some constitutional scholars are taking a different position. They say that the present rules for

---

irrelevant that the question is one that might have seemed unreal at the date of the British North America Act. To such an organic statute the flexible interpretation must be given which changing circumstances require, and it would be alien to the spirit, with which the preamble to the Statute of the Westminster is instinct, to concede anything less than the widest amplitude of power to the Dominion legislature under s. 101 of the Act.''

[5] 22 Geo. V, chapter 4. In part, the Preamble reads as follows:

"And whereas it is in accord with the established constitutional position that no law hereafter made by the Parliament of the United Kingdom shall extend to any of the said Dominions as part of the law of that Dominion otherwise than at the request and with the consent of that Dominion.''

[6] Statement in Parliament by the Right Honourable L. B. Pearson, Prime Minister, House of Commons Debates, Second Session, 26th Parliament, volume XI (1965) 11574-5.

[7] A ready source for the text of the Victoria Charter of 1971 is as follows: Final Report, The Special Joint Committee of the Senate and the House of Commons on the Constitution of Canada, Fourth Session, 28th Parliament (1972), Appendix B.

amendment permit secession with the consent only of the province wishing to secede and the federal parliament. This bilateral consent, they say, is enough because the relations of the other nine provinces to the federal parliament would remain unchanged. Hence, it is argued, only the federal parliament and the province wishing to secede are directly concerned.[8] As I have said, I think this view is wrong. It is simply not sensitive enough to the true extent of regionalism in our Canadian federal union, as manifested by the very existence of the provinces and the distinct geographical groupings into which they fall. It takes a very narrow appreciation indeed of provincial interests and modern federalism to permit one to say that other provinces are not directly and vitally affected as provinces when one province wishes to secede. To make this point, one may refer, for example, to section 121 of the B.N.A. Act, which declares that trade shall be free among the provinces of Canada. The secession of Quebec would put an end to that, to the direct prejudice of every other province as well as Quebec. Such secession would also mean that Ontario would become so much the dominating influence in the central parliament of what was left of Canada that the whole balance of power between the centre, the Atlantic and the West would be drastically altered and would probably be unacceptable to the Atlantic Provinces and the Western Provinces. And so one could go on.

Essential words of wisdom on this subject were published in December of 1977 by Mr. Dominique Clift, a leading Canadian and Quebec journalist and commentator. He said:[9]

> Some theorists maintain that present trends in constitutional law favor the view that what is not expressly forbidden is therefore permitted. Hence, if Quebec unequivocally expressed a desire to become independent, secession could be sanctioned by a simple act of the British Parliament amending the B.N.A. Act according to the recommendations of the Canadian government.
>
> Obviously, such a simple scenario is not realistic. It does not take into account the complex manner in which the federal system actually works in Canada. It also ignores the political reactions which such a momentous change would certainly provoke.

---

[8]Professor Jacques Brossard, *L'Accession à la souveraineté et le cas du Québec* (Les Presse de l'Université de Montréal, 1976), p. 264.

Professors John Whyte and John Claydon, "Legal Aspects of Quebec's Claim for Independence" in *Must Canada Fail?*, ed. Richard Simeon (Montreal: McGill-Queen's Press, 1977), pp. 271-80, especially at p. 277, where the following statements are made:

> "Under the present regime for constitutional amendment . . . the British Parliament ought to enact amendments to the B.N.A. Act which would recognize special status or separation for Quebec if the request to do so comes from Quebec and from the central government, and it is the product of negotiated agreement between the governments of those two political units. The federal government, in making a special status or a secession agreement, may want to consult with the provinces or with Canadians generally through a national referendum. But it is not obliged, under constitutional law, to do the former and may not be obliged to do the latter. More important, the interests of the provinces in the Quebec settlement do not imply a requirement for obtaining unanimous provincial consent. They are represented, according to our perception of the constitutional mandates, through the promotion of Canadian or national interests by the federal government."

(Regarding the significance of a referendum, see footnote 11 and the text associated with it.)

[9]*Report on Confederation*, vol. 1, No. 2, Montreal, December 1977, "Working on a Mandate to Negotiate", 7.

There is no way the federal government, acting alone, could give its consent to Quebec's secession. It might have the legal power to do so, but it is missing the moral authority. If past amendments to the B.N.A. Act are any guide, and if the protracted discussions that have been going on for years on proposed changes constitute a sort of political precedent, then there would have to be thorough consultations with other provincial governments before responding to the problem of Quebec independence.

But the likeliest outcome of the Parti Québecois referendum is that it will demonstrate a desire for change that falls short of actual independence. Faced with such an expression of popular will, the federal government would find it even more difficult to act alone and unilaterally. The changes demanded by Quebec would inevitably have a direct impact on the status of the other provinces, thus making it imperative that they be brought into the whole process of discussion and negotiation.

The burden of my analysis is of course that Mr. Clift should not worry about the constitutional law of amendment being unrealistic. It does in my view require the consents of the provinces as well as of the federal government and parliament in these circumstances, and hence implies precisely that there should be the process of negotiation Mr. Clift describes, whether we are talking of the independence of Quebec or of basic changes falling short of the grant of such independence.

Accordingly, I say again that political processes and activities should respect the rules for amendment, and should aim to achieve the consents they require, if basic changes are to be implemented. Furthermore, I would emphasize that the rules for amendment are themselves of a fundamental kind quite directly dependent for their efficacy on enduring acceptance and willing compliance by ministries, parliaments and the people themselves. In my view, the only enforcement measures that are applicable at this basic level are the peaceful pressures that come to bear on all concerned by virtue of these general and enduring factors of recognition and acceptance. What I mean by that is this. I spoke earlier of the level of political reality as well as of the level of constitutional law and of the interaction between them. If, in spite of our best political efforts to avoid the result, it became obvious in the years immediately ahead that there was a large and persistent majority in Quebec in favour of secession and independence for the province, then the rest of us should at that point give the constitutional consents required, though this would be done with great sorrow and regret. The possibility of reaching this point is still remote, and we must work at the level of political persuasion to ensure that it remains remote and never becomes reality.

Let us return now to some necessary further consideration of the nature and the implications of the special amending process. While I stand by what I have been saying about this, I owe to the constitutional authorities who differ from me somewhat fuller reasons for my position. They will say to me that surely I do not mean that a veto by Prince Edward Island as the lone dissenter among the provinces could stop a constitutional amendment. I agree this would not make much sense, with all due respect to the Islanders. Politically, it would be very unlikely to happen, but I admit that is not a sufficient answer to the objection. To answer properly, I go back to the enduring political and social facts that the special amendment rules are of a very fundamental kind, made directly by custom, precedent and practice over significantly long periods. Underlying custom, precedent and practice are of course the established expectations of the people about the process, and these expectations are not unchanging. There is such a thing as the development of new elements in customary laws. Such laws may change incrementally, step by step, in response to developing appreciation by the people of changes in the conditions obtaining in our society. I believe the Canadian people would accept as legitimate what I would call substantial compliance with the requirements for provincial consents in special constitutional amendment. My inference about this is that if all the larger provinces and most of the smaller ones agreed with the federal government and parliament, then, given the urgencies of today and tomorrow, this would be generally accepted by our people as a legitimate mandate for basic constitutional change. Constitutionally, this would be a substantial compliance situation. But the dissent of any one of the larger provinces would frustrate substantial compliance. I refer to the dissent of Quebec or Ontario or Alberta or British Columbia. Likewise, I would infer that the dissent of three of the Atlantic Provinces, or of both Manitoba and Saskatchewan, would block substantial compliance. In other words, I am suggesting that the enduring basis of public acceptance underlying our customary law of amendment has probably moved to the position I have just described, which you may note is very close to the Victoria formula proposed in 1971, though it does not correspond exactly with that scheme.

Moreover, I would emphasize that the processes thus established are democratic processes following our established British parliamentary traditions. They rest on the consent of the elected federal parliament and the elected provincial legislatures, either directly or through the ministers of governments responsible to those parliamentary bodies. Notice that the special amendment process does accordingly require a high degree of democratically mandated consent, well-distributed across the regions of this broad and somewhat loose-jointed country. A simple majority of votes or provinces in the country does *not* suffice; but, for fundamental changes, this is as it should be.

I said earlier that the nature of the amending process has important implications for the form that political negotiations in Canada should take as we work our way toward the definition of possibly acceptable constitutional changes, and the remarks of Dominique Clift quoted earlier reinforce the point. The negotiating process should reflect rather faithfully the special amending process which the negotiations seek to use. This makes federal-provincial conferences of ministers the normal way for these inter-governmental negotiations, remembering that these ministers are accountable to their respective parliaments and so to the people of Canada and the provinces. But here we come upon a dilemma. Concerning the negotiating framework, Quebec would probably insist on one-to-one negotiations between the Quebec Government on the one hand, and the rest of Canada on the other hand, the latter being represented by the governments of Canada and the other nine provinces. This is the opinion of Professor Léon Dion of Laval University. In a public lecture at Queen's University in February 1978 he said:[10]

---

[10]"Canada and Quebec: The Significance of Nationalism", Walter L. Gordon Lecture Series, Queen's University, February 9, 1978.

Above all there must be agreement on the framework within which the negotiations will take place. Many participants in the current debate seem to imply that the ten provincial governments will sit down at the conference table with the federal government as initiator and referee. But Quebec will never agree to negotiate under such conditions, even if the number is reduced to five or even three. It has long been known—or it should have been known—that Quebec will insist on one precondition: namely, that it be allowed to negotiate with its partners one to one and in complete equality. . . .

So, even with the exception of the Liberal Party of Quebec, which as yet has no policy on this point, it is already clear that the parties representing the majority of the electorate [of Quebec] will not agree to Quebec's taking part in any negotiations until the federal and other provincial governments have accepted the principle of bilateral negotiation. Nor should this be surprising, because that principle is part of the nationalistic heritage that every political party in Quebec must draw on if it wants to survive.

Professor Dion is probably the senior political scientist in Quebec today. He maintains an impartial position and enjoys great prestige. He does not consider that the Quebec nationalism of which he speaks is incompatible with the continuance of Quebec as part of the Canadian federal union, and he is personally in favour of a somewhat revised Canadian federalism that would ensure the continuance of Quebec in the union. But he does believe that, for any Quebec government, Quebec nationalism does have these one-to-one implications for the negotiating process that lies ahead. He is not very optimistic that English Canada would be able, or if able would be willing, to negotiate in this way. He sees a long period of indecision and confusion ahead.

Perhaps I am too sanguine, but I am more hopeful than Professor Dion about the negotiating process. On issues agreed to be vital to the French language and culture in Quebec and Canada, a satisfactory way might be worked out to accord to the Quebec Government this one-to-one status, at federal-provincial conferences where all the provincial governments and the federal government were present. There would in effect have to be a conference within a conference—a caucus of the nine Anglophone provinces and the federal government to prepare a single position to be negotiated with the Quebec Government. Sophisticated leadership by the federal government would be essential to the success of such a negotiating arrangement, but some such negotiating system could well be workable. If this resulted in agreement on certain revisions of the terms of the Canadian federal union sufficient to keep Quebec in the union, then the full-fledged amending procedure I have explained would have to be followed to implement the new terms. Thereafter, Quebec would continue in Canada with its status as a province defined by the new terms. If we should find that the unlikely happens and that, unfortunately, we have to negotiate terms for the secession of Quebec, then certainly I would expect the conference within a conference technique to be followed. In any event, wherever the negotiation leads, there would be this necessity for the federal government and the nine provincial governments other than Quebec to act in concert. Moreover, I do not see the technique of a conference within a conference in the manner described as inconsistent with the implications for the negotiating process that arise from the rules of the special amending procedure as I have given them.

Neither would it be inconsistent with the negotiating process implied by the nature of our system for special constitutional amendment for the governments engaged in such negotiations to resort from time to time to referenda (provincial or federal) on constitutional issues, or to hold elections (provincial or federal) on constitutional issues. Such appeals to the people of course would be consistent with all I have been saying about the democracy of the special amending process, provided one remembers that the special amending process requires consents that are well distributed across the whole country. Popular mandates secured in referenda or elections, to be significant for purposes of basic constitutional change, would have to produce several majorities in the various provincial regions, as well as in the country as a whole, corresponding to the requirements of the special amending process described earlier. These electoral techniques would not permit us to escape from the essential regional pluralism of Canada for purposes of basic constitutional change. Moreover, in our democratic parliamentary system, a referendum is simply an officially sponsored public opinion poll that is not self-executing as to basic political or legal change. It is advice to the parliament or parliaments concerned and no more.[11]

This leaves me with one final issue concerning our system for special constitutional amendment, namely, the patriation of the Canadian constitution from Britain. You will recall that our present system of special amendment ends up with the formal need for a statute of the British Parliament. This is not a central issue here for the moment because all the substantial steps in the amending process have to be taken in Canada, and if Canadians can arrive at an agreed position, the British would be glad to implement it without question. It is our fault and not theirs that they retain even this residual formal responsibility, and they would be glad to rid themselves of it by one last British statute that, among other things, sanctioned an entirely domestic constitutional amending process for Canada. Patriation in this latter sense would, ideally, be desirable as a separate operation. Prime Minister Trudeau has urged upon the provinces that this should be done, and I have supported the idea in previous public addresses on the subject.[12] But I have concluded reluctantly that such a separate act of patriation is not now politically feasible in this country. The present Government of Quebec would not agree to it; perhaps no government of Quebec would. Other provinces might drag their feet at this point as well. So what do we do?

Our task in Canada as I see it is this. We must attempt to negotiate our way to a complete and agreed package of amendments designed to revise Canadian federalism so as to hold the country together. The complete package would contain some changes in the federal division of powers, some changes in the structure of central institutions (for example the Senate and the Supreme Court of

---

[11]*In re The Initiative and Referendum Act*, [1919] A.C. 935; *R. v. Nat Bell Liquors Ltd.*, [1922] 2 A.C. 128.

[12]March 19, 1977 to a Joint Seminar of the Canadian Bar Association and the Dalhousie Law School in Halifax; and August 31, 1977 to a plenary session of the Canadian Bar Association at its annual meeting in Ottawa.

Canada), some new specially entrenched human rights and freedoms, and an entirely domestic basic constitutional amending procedure. With a complete package like that we could then properly approach the British and ask them to say goodbye with one last British statute, which they would be delighted to do.

In any event, we should not approach the British for basic changes concerning which there were substantial provincial dissents in Canada. In my view, not only would this be improper, it would be unconstitutional, it would be illegal. This would be contrary to our special constitutional law of amendment as established over the years by custom and precedent. This is not a popular view of the constitutional position in Ottawa, and perhaps not in London either, but I think it is the position. If the Ottawa Government doubts this, they could refer it to the Supreme Court of Canada for an advisory opinion. If the British Government in London doubts it, they have power to refer it to the Judicial Committee of the Privy Council for an advisory opinion.

III. THE VALUES AND OBJECTIVES OF CANADIAN FEDERALISM

So far I have spoken mainly of constitutional and political methods and procedures, and certainly the importance of these is very great. But, in the end, they are the servants of the positive and substantive human values of Canadian federalism. What are some of these values?

First, a personal note. The national unity of Canada has always been very real to me, because I grew up in Saskatchewan in the 1930's. I lived through the double disaster there of drought and Depression. When trouble came there was no crop insurance, no unemployment insurance, no health or hospital insurance, no welfare income schemes. Yet help came. The rest of the country stood by and essential finance and supplies came in through the agency of the federal government in Ottawa. That was an extreme situation, but it convinced me that there was such a thing as Canadian national unity, which co-existed with the proper distinctiveness of the various provinces.

Since the Depression and World War II, we have put in place the income security schemes and the health and hospital insurance that I mentioned as having been missing in the 1930's. The leadership of the federal government and parliament was essential to this, and so was the collaboration of the provincial governments and parliaments. We accept taxation for this, and the richer regions help the poorer regions to maintain standards of personal well-being. It has been and is the federal union of Canada that has made this sort of reciprocal and mutual help possible on a meaningful scale. Regardless of things that may divide us, we have had this recognition in Canada that we are our brothers' keepers. That is not the whole story of the basis of our national unity of course, but it is proper, among our present discontents, to point to what we have accomplished as a country in this respect.

Further, in the modern world, I suggest it is dangerous for a country to be too small. Bigness is necessary to cope with world-wide interdependence and technology. It is also needed as a sufficiently broad base on which to maintain personal and group security in conditions of human dignity and economic well-being. In Canada's federal constitution, we have a system for a unique combination of unity for the whole and diversity for the provincial parts, over the northern half of the rich North American continent. We should count our blessings. We will have to change the equilibrium point between national unity and provincial diversity from time to time, as circumstances change, but the Canadian federal union itself should continue.

Among the blessings we have to count in Canadian life is the French Fact in our country. This is one of our chief claims to distinction as a country. I know that our French-speaking fellow citizens have suffered certain injustices in the past concerning their language and culture. I do not condone these injustices, but they *are* in the past, and major steps to remedy them have been and are being taken. Also part of our good fortune in Canada is that we include in our midst many other ethnic and linguistic groups in addition to the historic English and French groups. We would do well to remember that ethnically there is now no majority group in Canada—we are a country of minorities. It is not just idle rhetoric to speak of the many strands that make up the Canadian mosaic.

Finally, we do not just count our own blessings here at home. We must look to our position in the world. If we do that, we see a world in which there are some 2,500 different languages and dialects, but only about 140 nation-states to accommodate these linguistic groups. The world is full of bilingual and multilingual countries, many if not most of them with much more serious problems and differences than those which occur in Canada. Surely we can continue to offer to the world an example of how major linguistic and ethnic groups can live together under a federal constitution that maintains both unity and diversity in proper measure.

Of course we must concern ourselves with what French-speaking Canadians have a right to expect, and with what English-speaking Canadians have a right to expect. But there is an overriding question: What does the rest of the world have a right to expect from Canada?

FURTHER DEVELOPMENTS AND REFERENCES

The essay on "Constitutional Amendment and Canadian Unity" was delivered as a public lecture in March 1978. In June of 1978, the Trudeau Government proposed several measures of constitutional reform, one of which was the abolition of the present Senate and its replacement by a very different sort of second chamber for the Parliament of Canada, to be called the House of the Federation. The proposals were introduced into Parliament as Bill C-60, which also expressed the claim by the government that the changes proposed respecting the second chamber could constitutionally be implemented by a simple statute of the Parliament of Canada. This claim was made by virtue of the terms of section 91(1) of the B.N.A. Act of 1949. It will be recalled that this provision empowered the Parliament of Canada to amend "the Constitution of Canada" by ordinary statute, subject to a number of explicit exceptions, the first two of which were "matters coming within the classes of subjects by this Act assigned exclusively to the Legislatures of the provinces, or as regards rights or privileges by this or any other Constitutional Act granted or secured to the Legislature or the Government of a Province, . . .". No exception was expressly stipulated concerning the structure of the Parliament of Canada itself.

Nevertheless, it was my view that section 91(1) did not have so broad a meaning. In the March lecture I had said (00):

> But of course the basic elements of the constitution that define the primary provincial and federal institutions and determine their respective powers are not themselves subject to change by ordinary majorities and ordinary statutes. Rather, as should be the case, they are subject to change only by extraordinary amending procedures which are difficult enough that, politically they cannot be invoked either easily or often.

I did not develop the point further respecting the basics of the composition of the Parliament of Canada at that time, because the specific and official Senate reform proposals were still in the future. However, a few weeks later, they were on the table in Bill C-60. To make a long story short, Bill C-60 was referred to two Special Parliamentary Committees on the Constitution, one a Senate Committee and the other a Joint Committee of the Senate and House of Commons. I was invited to appear as an expert witness before both Committees, and, particularly before the Joint Committee, I challenged the Government's view concerning the legitimate method of constitutional amendment for basic second-chamber reform of the Parliament of Canada. I argued that the phrase "Constitution of Canada" in section 91(1) of the B.N.A. Act had to be given a quite restricted meaning in the first place, that it did not extend to basic changes in the composition or powers of the present Senate or House of Commons, and that, accordingly, such changes required action by the British Parliament in response to a joint address from the Canadian Parliament to which the respective provinces had consented. (An alternative way to reach the same result was to argue that the second express exception in section 91(1) could and should be given a very broad meaning.)

But other expert witnesses before the Joint Committee supported the Government's view of what was proper, and, faced with this confusing diversity of expert opinion, and at the urging of the Joint Committee, the Government referred the issue to the Supreme Court of Canada for an opinion. The Court, with eight of the nine judges sitting, answered in a unanimous judgment issued on December 21, 1979.

The main thrust of the judgment, for present purposes, can be given in three propositions:

(1) Constitutional history is relevant and admissible in aid of the proper interpretation of the B.N.A. Act, and to establish the nature of critical and operative constitutional customs, precedents and conventions about amendment that are outside the B.N.A. Act.

(2) The four principles about amendment explained and expressed in the Favreau White Paper of 1965 remain valid, in particular the fourth prin-

ciple "that the Canadian Parliament will not request an amendment directly affecting federal-provincial relationships without prior consultation and agreement with the provinces". (The four principles were quoted with approval by the Court.)

(3) Accordingly, the phrase "Constitution of Canada" in section 91(1) of the B.N.A. Act is strictly limited in scope, being confined to what may be described as "housekeeping matters" respecting the central Government and Parliament of Canada. The phrase does not extend to elements of the structure of the central Government or Parliament of Canada that are basic to Canada's constitution as a federal union. The changes in the Senate proposed in Bill C-60 of June, 1978, are fundamental in this latter sense and thus cannot be implemented by a statute of the Parliament of Canada. Rather, the fourth of the Favreau White Paper principles is applicable.

It seems then that the positions taken about the nature of the processes of constitutional amendment in the essay "Constitutional Amendment and Canadian Unity" are in the main the same as those taken by the Supreme Court of Canada in the *Senate Reference Case: Re B.N.A. Act and the Federal Senate* (1979), 30 N.R. 271, 102 D.L.R. (3d) 1. See also: Minutes of proceedings and Evidence of the Special Joint Committee of the Senate and of the House of Commons on the Constitution of Canada. *Issue No. 5,* Third Session of the Thirtieth Parliament, 1977-78, Wednesday, August 23, 1978, Evidence of Professor W. R. Lederman and *Issue No. 12,* Tuesday, September 12, 1978, Evidence of Professor W. R. Lederman.

Part III
The Canadian Judicial System

Chapter 7

The Independence of the Judiciary

Reprinted with permission from (1956), 34 Canadian Bar Review
769-809, 1139-1179

I. INTRODUCTION

It has been widely accepted legal doctrine that the English constitution begins
and ends with the one principle that Parliament is supreme—that there is nothing a particular parliament cannot do by an appropriately worded statute. This
is said by many authorities to be the result of the revolutionary settlement
worked out in 1688 and the years immediately following. Yet there are both
historical and theoretical reasons to doubt whether the completely unlimited supremacy of Parliament in this sense was established at that time or at any time.
Indeed history rather indicates that other principles also assumed very great importance constitutionally at the end of the seventeenth century, and these other
principles—then reaffirmed or established—could operate only as limitations in
some degree at least on the supremacy of a particular parliament.[1]

   We have the recent testimony of Dr. A. L. Goodhart that the English are
not as much without a constitution as they profess to be. He gives four principles which he maintains are equally basic as first or original principles of the
English constitution. They are briefly as follows: (1) "That no man is above
the law" (among other things, this means that all official persons, the Queen,
the judges and members of Parliament included, must look to the law for the
definition of their respective positions and powers). (2) "that those who govern
Great Britain do so in a representative capacity and are subject to change. . . .
The free election of the members of the House of Commons is a basic principle
of English constitutional law." (3) That there shall be freedom of speech, of
thought and of assembly. (4) That there shall be an independent judiciary.
"The fourth and final principle which is a basic part of the English constitution
is the independence of the judiciary. It would be inconceivable that Parliament
should to-day regard itself as free to abolish the principle which has been accepted as a corner-stone of freedom ever since the Act of Settlement in 1701. It
has been recognised as axiomatic that if the judiciary were placed under the authority of either the legislative or the executive branches of the Government

---

[1] A. L. Goodhart, English Law and the Moral Law (Stevens & Sons Limited, London, 1953) 55.

then the administration of the law might no longer have that impartiality which is essential if justice is to prevail.''[2] Sir William Holdsworth expressed a very similar view on the status of the judiciary. He said.[3]

> The judges hold an office to which is annexed the function of guarding the supremacy of the law. It is because they are the holders of an office to which the guardianship of this fundamental constitutional principle is entrusted, that the judiciary forms one of the three great divisions into which the power of the State is divided. The Judiciary has separate and autonomous powers just as truly as the King or Parliament; and in the exercise of those powers, its members are no more in the position of servants than the King or Parliament in the exercise of their powers. . . . it is quite beside the mark to say that modern legislation often bestows undivided executive, legislative and judicial powers or the same person or body of persons. The separation of powers in the British Constitution has never been complete. But some of the powers in the constitution were, and still are, so separated that their holders have autonomous powers, that is, powers which they can exercise independently, subject only to the law enacted or unenacted. The judges have powers of this nature because, being entrusted with the maintenance of the supremacy of the law, they are and always have been regarded as a separate and independent part of the constitution. It is true that this view of the law was contested by the Stuart kings but the result of the Great Rebellion and the Revolution was to alter it.

The purpose of this essay is to examine judicial independence in Canada, but here is in other respects England is the source of our inheritance, and Dr. Goodhart's remarks at least emphasize the great and continuing importance of autonomous courts. It will be necessary to return to the general issues he has raised in the last part of this essay, because they are basic for Canada as well as Britain. Indeed, in the context of a federal constitution judicial independence has special significance. Meanwhile, other connected matters require review. First, the elements of judicial independence as developed in England will be examined historically, a movement culminating in certain provisions of the Act of Settlement of 1701. Then the delay in the extension of these principles to British North America until after the American Revolution will be explained, leading to an exposition of the position under Imperial constitutional law in British North America on the eve of Confederation. Next an attempt will be made to expound the present constitutional position in Canada affecting the independence of the judiciary under the relevant federal statutes and the pertinent sections of the British North America Act, 1867. There are certain problems for Canada of current importance the understanding and solution of which depend in part on English judicial history and development, for instance: (i) What is a superior court within the meaning of section 96 of the B.N.A. Act? (ii) May the salary of the superior-court judge be reduced or stopped by authority of a federal statute while his commission continues in effect? (iii) May a retiring age be imposed on superior-court judges by federal statute? (iv) In constituting

---

[2]*Ibid.*, 56-60.
[3]Sir W. S. Holdsworth, His Majesty's Judges (1932), 173 Law Times 336, 336-377.

federal courts under section 101 of the B.N.A. Act, is the federal parliament limited by sections 99 and 100 of that act on the tenure and salary of superior-court judges? Finally, there will be some theoretical analysis and assessment of the nature of the judicial function and the modern importance of judicial autonomy, with a view to bringing certain substantial considerations, in addition to the historical ones, to bear on problems of the Canadian judicial system.

II. THE ELEMENTS OF JUDICIAL INDEPENDENCE HISTORICALLY CONSIDERED

A brief examination of some high points in the development of the principal English courts is needed for appreciation of judicial independence as we have come to know it in the Anglo-Canadian legal world. As usual, history and constitutional exposition go hand in hand.

(a) The emergence of central royal courts and of a judiciary

There was no professional judiciary in the localized communal courts of Saxon England or in the private courts held by feudal lords for their tenants. Centralization of the judicial function in the hands of a special class of officials awaited the strong government of the Norman kings in the centuries immediately following the Norman Conquest. At this time great power was successfully asserted for the central government and was concentrated in the king and his immediate entourage of magnates, chosen counsellors and officials. This group constituted the *Curia Regis*. At first the *Curia Regis* was undifferentiated in functions, acting as a unit in all types of political decisions and governmental acts. The king personally presided at many of its sessions, including those involving a judicial function, and it followed him in his extensive travels about his country.

But soon some significant specialization did occur under Henry II (1154-1189). Sir William Holdsworth tells us that "The legislation of Henry II added enormously to the jurisdiction of the Curia Regis. . . . the king's court acquired a wide civil and criminal jurisdiction, and wide powers of supervision over the conduct of all the local courts and officials."[4] It did not take long to find that the *Curia Regis* could not directly handle this great press of new business, and so some delegation and division of labour became necessary. Henry's predecessors had made some desultory use of royal commissioners, travelling apart from the *Curia Regis* but as delegates of it, to supervise local government and dispense royal justice. Henry extended and regularized this practice with his system of itinerant royal justices, who were invested by their commissions with wide governmental powers, very prominent among which were powers to hear and determine pleas concerning possession of land and pleas of the Crown. In 1176 eighteen justices were assigned to six circuits, and from this year there

---

[4]Sir W. S. Holdsworth, A History of English Law (Little, Brown, and Company, Boston, 3rd ed., 1922), 47. Henceforth this work will be referred to as Holdsworth, followed by the volume and page numbers.

were always some itinerant justices functioning. Here we have the direct pre-cursors of the judges of assize and the beginning of a separate judiciary.

Nevertheless there was some dissatisfaction with the itinerant justices—certain of them no doubt were rather arbitrary—so that in 1178 Henry decided to supplement the itinerant-justice system with an alternative for litigants in the form of a regular central body. A contemporary account quoted by Holdsworth records that "He selected five men only, two clerks and three laymen, who were all of his own household. And he ordained that those five should hear all the suits of the realm, and adjudicate upon them, and that they should not de-part from the Curia Regis, but should remain there to hear men's suits; pro-vided that if any question arose among them which they could not solve; it should be reserved for the king's hearing, and should be settled as it should seem good to him and the wiser men of the realm."[5] This was the beginning of the Court of Common Bench or Common Pleas. Within a century this tribunal was clearly established as a separate body sitting apart from the king under its own chief justice. Moreover, it had become specialized in jurisdiction to com-mon pleas (these being roughly private-law matters between citizen and citizen as distinct from public-law issues touching the person or powers of the king or touching the central government). Originally the new court was to remain with the king and the *Curia Regis* and hence to follow them in their travels, but by 1215 this was altered, Magna Carta providing that "Common pleas shall not follow our courts but shall be held in some certain place". Even in early times this "certain place" was usually Westminster, and before long it was perma-nently fixed there. Later the other central royal courts were also located there.[6]

In the story of the Court of Common Pleas we see the pattern for the emer-gence of the other common-law courts and later of the Court of Chancery; hence the historical origins of these other bodies will not be pursued here in any detail. The Court of King's Bench split off from the *Curia Regis* by a gradual process terminating about the end of the fourteenth century. It exercised impor-tant criminal jurisdiction, extensive civil jurisdiction (for example, trespass *vi et armis*, the fertile mother of actions) and "a general superintendence of the due observance of the law by officials and others".[7] Then also the Court of Ex-chequer emerged about this time. The Exchequer itself as a distinct government department of revenue and finance had developed in the twelfth century, and by the early fourteenth century the separation from this department of a Court of Exchequer had occurred. This court was composed of a bench of "Barons of the Exchequer" with power originally to determine revenue and taxation cases.[8] By the fourteenth century then, except for the Court of Chancery, the shape of the modern central judicature is apparent in England.

But the original status of the king and his council as the source of justice still

---

[5]Holdsworth, Vol. I, p. 51; T. F. T. Plucknett, A Concise History of the Common Law (Butter-worth and Co., London, 3rd ed., 1940) 136. Henceforth this work will be referred to as Plucknett, followed by the page number.
[6]Holdsworth, Vol. I, 196-197.
[7]*Ibid.*, 212.
[8]*Ibid.*, 231-235.

had much force, and in the latter part of the fourteenth century special petitions to the king for justice multiplied. In large measure this came about because the procedure and remedies of the common-law courts were becoming settled and not a little complex, so that they were no longer flexible enough to be able to cope with all grievances. Where these special petitions concerned issues of private law between citizen and citizen, an overworked King and Council soon delegated disposal of them to the Chancellor. He was a logical choice for the purpose because he was a principal royal official constantly in attendance at court and moreover was in charge of the royal writ system and the necessary secretarial staff.[9] Thus, soon there was a Court of Chancery. But when the special petitions concerned grave issues of criminal justice or public law, involving for example complaint of injustice or oppression at the hands of local magnates, they were not passed on to the Chancellor but reserved to the King and his Council. By the time of Henry VIII the King's Council in this aspect became the Court of Star Chamber.[10]

Having thus cursorily surveyed the history of the central courts, our interest now lies in the selection of judges and the appearance of a legal profession.

(b) The selection of judges

"With the establishment of the Court of Common Pleas, the decisive step was taken: the future of the common law was put into the hands of judges. Everything will therefore depend on the mode of selection of these judges and the position assigned to them."[11] In the late twelfth century and early thirteenth century, when the central royal courts were appearing, judges were drawn from the nascent civil service of the day. Governmental servants or officials were in the main clerics of the minor orders, for to hold the status of clerk was at this time the key to advancement in diplomacy, finance and the royal civil service, as well as in purely ecclesiastical pursuits. For a time, "in the great tradition of Norman administration", these civil-servant judges did their work well, but this state of affairs did not last. Henry II was succeeded by Richard I, who was absent from England for most of his reign, and then came King John, whose administration was, if anything, too vigorous. He fell into serious contention with the barons and smaller land owners, and eventually they wrung Magna Carta from him. Under Henry III the struggle with the greater and lesser magnates continued, culminating in the Baron's War of the third quarter of the thirteenth century.

In these circumstances the royal civil services deteriorated badly. Royal incompetence, financial mismanagement and neglect of administration were largely to blame. Holdsworth tells the story in the following passages.[12]

> During the reign of Henry III the absence of a vigorous ruler had made itself felt in the growing and widespread corruption of the constantly increasing tribe of royal officials. Bracton . . . bears witness to the deterioration of the bench; and the political songs of the times are full of similar complaints. The cause is not far to seek.

---

[9]Plucknett, 162.
[10]*Ibid.*, 163-164.
[11]*Ibid.*, 210.
[12]Holdsworth, Vol. II, 294-295.

The royal officials, even the judges, were both poorly and irregularly paid. Generally the other officials of the courts had no salaries, but were paid either from the damages recovered, or for the services which they performed for litigants. . . . Such being the case, the Crown cannot be altogether acquitted of blame. 'That the king's servants were miserably underpaid', says Mr. Hall, 'was admitted even then, and yet it was notorious that in most cases they were able to amass considerable fortunes'.

Finally complaints became so vehement that in 1289 Edward I appointed a commission of inquiry with all necessary powers.

The result was disgraceful to all branches of the civil service, and especially to the bench. It constitutes, to use Maitland's words, 'our one great judicial scandal'. Of the judges of the Court of King's Bench two out of three were removed; of the judges of the Court of Common Pleas four out of five. . . . Five of the itinerant justices . . . were found guilty of various crimes.

Thus we have here our first encounter with the bearing of salary and finance on the integrity and competence of the judiciary, a subject to which we shall return. In any event, Edward I and his advisers had a crisis in the courts on their hands and necessarily considered reforms and changes for the judiciary. Where were persons suitable for judicial office to be found? Almost inevitably the royal civil-service had at first supplied the judges, but by the end of the thirteenth century an alternative source was at hand. By this time a separate and autonomous legal profession had emerged, having developed in response to the needs of litigants resorting to the new central royal courts.

It is trite to say that the origins of the legal profession are somewhat obscure, but the point for our purposes is that one had arisen by the thirteenth century. At first the profession was a group of pleaders and advocates before the royal courts, which Plucknett describes as "small, active, learned and (like the court itself) centralised".[13] And Dean Pound tells us, "All through the thirteenth century we find reference to pleaders. The Year Books of the time show a small group of them doing all the work of framing the pleadings in a colloquy with the judges. Also the opinions of these pleaders are cited or reported in the earlier Year Books on a par with those of the judges."[14] This seems to have been a natural development parallel to the rise of separate courts with increasingly complex procedure. Accordingly we find that Edward I and his immediate successors turned from the civil service to the legal profession for judges. Except for the Court of Exchequer, where the change occurred later,[15] the displacement of

---

[13]Plucknett, 211.

[14]Roscoe Pound, The Lawyer from Antiquity to Modern Times (West Publishing Co., St. Paul, 1953), 81.

[15]From the emergence of the Court of Exchequer in the early fourteenth century, the Chief Baron was usually a lawyer, but this was not usually true at first of the other barons. Until the sixteenth century the latter were usually civil servants raised to the Exchequer Bench because of their practical knowledge of the revenue acquired in lesser offices connected with it. But, as the jurisdiction of the Exchequer expanded to include some "common pleas", it became desirable that the barons should all be legally qualified as were the other judges; hence in 1579 the definite practice of appointing them from the serjeants-at-law was instituted. Holdsworth, Vol. I, 235-237.

royal clerks (civil servants) by lawyers was complete early in the fourteenth century.[16] Perhaps the king was influenced in making the change by the example of the Pope, who at this time was appointing judge-delegates *ad hoc* from among eminent practitioners of the canon law, to hear and determine particular ecclesiastical causes. But whereas the Pope was appointing judge-delegates for certain controversies only, it had become accepted in England, no doubt *because* the royal courts were at first part of the civil service, that they should be manned by full-time judges with some continuity of tenure. Moreover, anything less would reverse the current trend away from the direct personal influence of the king. So, though the king now took his judges from the legal profession, they were full-time judges as had been their civil-servant predecessors. The distinguished legal historian, Professor Plucknett, testifies to the very great importance for the future of this new policy of appointment from the legal profession:[17]

> If the old system had persisted, and if the judges had continued to be members of the civil service, with different careers from the bar, we should have had in England (and probably in America too) something like the system prevailing in several continental countries to-day. According to this system, the young lawyer has to decide very early in his career whether he will go to the bar or to the bench. Naturally these two careers attract different types of men. At the bar the competition is severe, progress slow, but success brings considerable wealth and great social and political influence. Brilliant and adventurous men are attracted by a career at the bar. A candidate who elects for the bench has very different prospects. He has a salary instead of prospective profits, certainty instead of a gamble. His first post is in a petty court in the provinces; like other functionaries, satisfactory service will bring him advancement from lower to higher courts, from distant towns to the metropolis. The mentality which such a career attracts is very different from that of the advocate, and the result is that bench and bar are divided by differences of interest and training.

> .   .   .   .   .

> . . . the way of combining the permanent courts with the legal profession was to choose the permanent judges from among the serjeants (who for the moment were the branch of the profession that mattered most). The system has persisted, with very little modification, to the present day both in England and in all jurisdictions where the common law prevails. Its great characteristic is the intimate connection between bench and bar. In the middle ages this was emphasized by the fact that the serjeants during term time lived together in their inns and discussed their cases in-

---

[16]"We shall see that by 1316 the order of serjeants at law had been formed. This order consisted of the leading practitioners who were promoted to be members of the order by the crown; and, when the judges ceased to be chosen from the royal clerks, they naturally came to be chosen from this order of serjeants, and soon came to be chosen solely from its members. Probably this rule began with the court of Common Pleas. In the course of the fourteenth century, it was extended to the King's Bench; but it was not till the latter part of the sixteenth century that the same rule was applied to the court of Exchequer. By that time, however, the rule that only a serjeant could be made a judge had become somewhat of a form. From the middle of the sixteenth century onwards it became the custom to make any lawyer, whom it was desired to raise to the bench, a serjeant at law, merely that he might be made a judge. But the rule that no one could be made a judge unless he was a serjeant was not altered until the Judicature Act of 1873." Holdsworth, Vol. I; 197.
[17]Plucknett, 212-213.

formally together simply as serjeants, without distinction between those on the bench and those at the bar. Even with the rise of newer branches of the profession, the decline of the serjeants and the rise of the attorney and solicitor general, the same fundamental situation remained. . . . The judges were men who had passed a large portion of their life in the world of practical affairs and had won success there. And finally, the common experience and training unite bench and bar in an under-standing of each other which is difficult to attain when their professional lives are spent in different careers. This cooperation between bench and bar is of the utmost importance for the working of the common law system.

Henceforth judicial competence and integrity would depend in a large measure on the quality of the legal profession—upon its training, learning and experience. Here then is one of the important elements of judicial independence as we know it. But, although the judges were no longer civil servants or controllable as such, the royal power over them was originally considerable.

(c) **Royal power to instruct judges and to preside in the royal courts**

In the early days of the common-law courts the influence of the king was often direct and great. Either he might himself be present and presiding over the jus-tices or, if not, they might have had a specific directive from him what to do in a particular case or type of case. By about the end of the fifteenth century both these forms of personal royal participation in the judicial function had decayed. Concerning the first, Holdsworth says, "In early days the king actually decided cases; and there are instances of this practice in Henry III, Edward I and Edward II's reigns. But, when Fortescue wrote at the end of the fifteenth century, it had ceased to be usual; and Coke merely stated the existing practice in answer to James I's claim to decide cases for himself."[18] It is true that James I did, on oc-casions, preside over the Court of Star Chamber and give judgment there.[19] But this no doubt helped to cause the abolition of that tribunal by Parliament within a few years. Concerning royal power to issue instructions to the judges, Plucknett (when speaking of the growing independence of the courts) has this to say: "A great step in this development was the solemn enactment of the Statute of North-ampton in 1328 which declared that no royal command under the Great or Smaller Seal shall disturb the course of the common law, and that if such a com-mand is issued, the judges shall ignore it. Slowly but steadily the judges ventured to enforce the plain words of this important act, and so to assume the detached position which is typical of most modern judiciaries."[20] Thus, while the king was and is still in theory the fountain of justice, this came to be true only in the sense which Blackstone has explained in a much-quoted passage from his *Com-mentaries:*[21]

But at present, by the long and uniform usage of many ages, our kings have dele-gated their whole judicial power to the judges of their several courts, which are the

---

[18]Holdsworth, Vol. I, 194.
[19]Holdsworth, Vol. I, 500; Plucknett, 162.
[20]Plucknett, 145.
[21]Sir William Blackstone, Commentaries on the Laws of England (Lewis Edition, Philadelphia, 1898) Book I, 267.

grand depositories of the fundamental laws of the kingdom, and have gained a known and stated jurisdiction, regulated by certain established rules, which the Crown itself cannot now alter but by act of parliament.

Although these developments represent further progress toward judicial independence, nevertheless all was not yet safe or settled. The power to appoint to judicial office and to determine conditions of removal from office remained with the king, and any real abuse of his powers could subvert judicial autonomy. It was this type of pressure that played so large a part in the turbulent relations of the Stuart kings with the judiciary in the critical seventeenth century.

(d) Tenure of judges (their appointment and removal)

The judges were able to develop the principles of private law with impartiality and free of royal or executive interference from the early days of the common-law courts. But until the eighteenth century, on public-law issues of moment touching the royal power or position, great pressure was at times applied by the king to the judges through the royal power of dismissal from office. As a rule, before the seventeenth century, judges had been granted their offices during the king's good pleasure *(durante bene placito)* and thus could be dismissed by him at any time without cause. The Chief Baron and other Barons of the Exchequer were exceptions, their royal commissions being granted to endure during good behaviour *(quamdiu se bene gesserint)*. Such grants of office were conceived to be in much the same category legally as grants of estates in land. The relatively modern notion of contract simply did not exist in these earlier times and thus played no part in the legal conception that was developed of the nature of judicial office. As we shall see, the grantee during good behaviour could be removed from office at the instance of the grantor (the king) for breach of the condition of the grant, that is, for failure to conduct himself well in the office.

So far as appointees at pleasure were concerned, although there had been some arbitrary dismissals of judges in the disturbed conditions of the fourteenth century, in practice their security of tenure then improved somewhat. "In the fifteenth century the atmosphere was very different, and the judges (with the sole exception of Fortescue) kept resolutely apart from the wars of the roses. Under the Tudors the judges were scarcely any more disturbed by political changes: the chief justices were dismissed at the accession of Mary, whose accession they had tried to impede, and Elizabeth is suspected of dismissing a judge from political motives, but beside these facts we must place others showing how the judges could take an independent stand against both queen and council."[22] Thus there had been in practice a real measure of judicial independence and security of tenure in Tudor times, though appointments were at pleasure. Moreover the quality of the bench at this period was high, for the sixteenth century was the golden age of legal education at the Inns of Court and Chancery, and many lawyers and judges had first attended the Universities of Oxford or Cambridge. Holdsworth testifies to the beneficial effects for the legal system and the country. "On the

---

[22]Taswell-Langmead's Constitutional History (10th ed. by T. F. T. Plucknett, Sweet and Maxwell, London, 1946) 519.

whole the distinguished lawyers and judges of this period were better educated men than their predecessors in the fourteenth and fifteenth centuries; and this was, no doubt one of the main reasons why the common law showed so many signs of improvement and so marked a capacity for expansion. Those who administered it were not wholly untouched by the new learning. They could therefore in some degree emancipate their minds from barren technicalities, and appreciate the large changes which were taking place in all spheres of the national life.''[23]

But, with the advent of the Stuart kings early in the seventeenth century, a change for the worse set in which was not reversed until very late in the century. A great constitutional struggle was joined over the scope of the royal prerogative powers as against both the common law and Parliament. To what extent did the king have discretionary powers unfettered either by the ''ancient common-law rights'' of Englishmen or the need for parliamentary sanction by statute? The strict legal position was not so clear and a rather good case could be made on the basis of Tudor and mediaeval precedents for a very considerable and independent prerogative power. The Stuart kings lost in the end, but what they did, so to speak, was badly to overplay a rather good hand.[24] Frequently, and no doubt inevitably, the basic issue of the extent of the royal prerogative power was forced before the courts in legal form and the judiciary became involved in a partisan way.

It is not surprising that the Stuart kings used their undoubted royal powers to dismiss judges at pleasure, and appoint others, to secure so far as they could a bench of royalist sympathies. For instance, Sir Edward Coke's opinion against the Crown in a constitutional case in 1616 brought his immediate dismissal.[25] This use of the power of dismissal was of course regarded as improper by the parliamentary party and many of the common lawyers, and so we find that, during the period of the Commonwealth (1649-1660), the Exchequer practice became the general rule and all judicial appointments were made during good behaviour. Unfortunately this new policy did not long survive the Restoration, for soon Charles II reverted to appointments during pleasure. Both he and James II turned once more to the power of dismissal as a means of securing judicial decisions favouring the Crown in every litigation or prosecution that in any way touched the extent of the royal power or position. Such an assault on the integrity of the central royal courts was all the more necessary for the restored Stuarts because the Courts of Star Chamber and High Commission, which had served James I and Charles I so well, had been abolished by the Long Parliament.[26] The position steadily worsened for the courts, and so far indeed did James II carry dismissals that virtually all judges of ability and integrity were driven from the bench.

Their replacements in judicial office were incompetent or corrupt, or both, for only the incompetent or corrupt would take up the posture of extreme subser-

---

[23]Holdsworth, Vol. V, 346.
[24]*Ibid.*, Vol. VI, 30.
[25]Plucknett, 52.
[26]Holdsworth, Vol. X, 416.

vience the king was demanding.[27] Typical of this sorry group were the notorious Chief Justices Scroggs and Jeffreys. We are told, for example, that Jeffreys made large sums of money out of those accused of complicity in Monmouth's rebellion—one bribe alone being £ 4,000. As a contemporary report puts it, "Ye poor and miserable were hanged, but ye more substantiall escaped".[28] Thus, by the eve of the Revolution of 1688, the courts had been brought very low indeed in public and professional esteem. All the decent legal talent of the day (including several ex-judges) was in practice at the bar, none of it was on the bench. "Westminster Hall was indeed standing on its head."[29] When James II fled England, Jeffreys (by now Lord Chancellor) was nearly killed by a mob in the streets. He took refuge in the Tower of London, where he died within a few weeks.[30]

It is no surprise then to find that reform of the tenure of judicial office took some priority in the revolution settlement. William III quickly dismissed the judicial lackeys of James II and restored the Commonwealth practice of issuing all judicial commissions during good behaviour. His new judges were of course chosen from lawyers who had supported the revolution settlement, but as they were the bulk of the bar good candidates were not lacking. Still, no statute yet required that the king *must* appoint judges during good behaviour, though apparently it was by inadvertence only that such a provision had been omitted from the hastily-drawn Bill of Rights.[31] Parliament sought to repair the omission in a bill passed in 1692 to ascertain the commission and salaries of judges, but William III vetoed the bill (by refusing royal assent) because he had not been consulted beforehand about its financial provisions: that judges' salaries were to be charged on the hereditary revenues of the Crown.[32] But, almost ten years later, William did give his assent to the Act of Settlement,[33] which provided in paragraph seven of its third section that, from the accession of the House of Hanover, *"judges commissions be made* quamdiu se bene gesserint, *and their salaries ascertained and established; but upon the address of both houses of parliament it may be lawful to remove them"*. With the accession of George I in 1714 this provision took effect.

It should be explained at this point that when the Act of Settlement spoke of "judges" it meant the judges of the central courts of common law, so far at least as the English judicature was concerned. The Court of Chancery, owing to its peculiar history, was in a unique situation and was not included. Until the nineteenth century, the only Chancery "judges" were the Lord Chancellor and the Master of the Rolls. The Lord Chancellor, who remained a principal privy councillor and later became a principal cabinet officer, always had held and still holds

---

[27]For the full story, see Holdsworth, Vol. VI, 501-512.

[28]Holdsworth, Vol. VI, 508.

[29]*Ibid.*, 511.

[30]"By Jeffrey's own request he was taken, in a frenzy of terror, to the Tower, guarded by two regiments of militia, whose strongest efforts could scarcely keep off the thousands who pressed around the cavalcade with execrations and threats of vengeance." Edward Foss, The Judges of England 1066-1870 (John Murray, London, 1870) 373.

[31]Taswell-Langmead, *ante,* footnote 22, 518.

[32]Holdsworth, Vol. VI, 234 (footnote).

[33]12 and 13 William III (1701), c. 2.

his office at the pleasure of the Crown. This was a mark of the primary status of the Lord Chancellor in early times in the *Curia Regis* or King's Council, and no doubt the same can be said of the original tenure at royal pleasure of the judges of the Common Pleas and King's Bench. This marked their high origin as members of the *Curia Regis* close to the king himself. Presumably this tenure has persisted for the Lord Chancellor because, in addition to judicial duties, he has retained other primary official functions at the center of government, whereas the judges of the Common Pleas and King's Bench became separated from the *Curia Regis* and wholly specialized in the judicial function. In this respect, then, the modern position of the Lord Chancellor as a judge is anomalous.

The Master of the Rolls provides an illuminating contrast in the matter of tenure. He never enjoyed primary status as a member of the *Curia Regis*; rather he was originally just what his title suggests: chief of the clerks or masters in the Chancery and principal custodian of its records. The usual feudal or mediaeval system to provide for the discharge of such lesser governmental offices was to grant a life estate (or even an estate of inheritance) in the office, as if it were a parcel of land. The grantee was given the duty and power of performing the func-tions of the office and was rewarded by exclusive personal entitlement for the term of the grant to collect fees from members of the public who desired him to act officially. Such a grantee of office could not be dispossessed of his functions or fee-income so long as the term of his grant was running and he observed its conditions. This was certainly the mediaeval position of the members of the offi-cial staffs of the Chancery and the central courts of common law; indeed it con-tinued to be their situation until the judicial reforms of the nineteenth century. Now, though appointed by the Crown, the Master of the Rolls originally be-longed to this lower level of government, and hence it seems that he enjoyed the life estate in office usual to this category of official.[34] One may also conjecture that the same considerations explain the customary life tenure, already men-tioned, of the Barons of the Court of Exchequer, that court having developed out of the Exchequer as a government department and not directly from the *Curia Regis*. Initially then we have feudal property-conceptions to thank for the idea of life tenure in office, though of course the generalizing of this tenure for judges occurred long after the mediaeval period for reasons relevant to later times and not dependent on feudal conceptions.

Though the Master of the Rolls' grant of office did not refer to judicial duties, nevertheless he accumulated them by delegation from the hard-pressed Lord Chancellor and by custom. The Master of the Rolls first appears with some judicial functions in the fifteenth century, and from the seventeenth century he was invariably a lawyer.[35] His independent position as a judge of first instance with customary chancery jurisdiction was confirmed by statute in 1730,[36] to dis-

---

[34]Holdsworth, Vol. I, 246-252, and 416-428, and see the biographies referred to in footnote 35 *post*.

[35]These things appear from a perusal of biographies of the earlier Masters of the Rolls in Foss's work cited in footnote 30.

[36]3 Geo. III, c. 30.

pose of a controversy then current that in status the Master of the Rolls was a mere delegate of the Chancellor. Finally, just to complete the story of the judges of chancery jurisdiction, the Lord Chancellor and the Master of the Rolls were eventually reinforced. In 1813, by statute, a Vice-Chancellor was provided for the Court of Chancery who was to be a barrister of fifteen years standing and to enjoy tenure during good behaviour, subject to removal by joint parliamentary address as in the Act of Settlement.[37] In 1841 a further statute provided for two more Vice-Chancellors on the same terms.[38]

It may now be emphasized that to make judges commissions *quamdiu se bene gesserint* was a grant of their offices *for life*, subject to observance of the condition of good behaviour. This was made clear in the case of *Harcourt v. Fox* in the King's Bench in 1692-3.[39] A statute of 1689 had provided that the appointment of the clerk of the peace for a county (an important official) must be "for so long time only as such clerk of the peace shall well demean himself in his said office", that is, *quamdiu se bene gesserit*. The power of appointment rested with the keeper of the county records *(Custos Rotularum)* but was henceforth to be on these terms only.

> *Gregory Justice:* I conceive that by this Act the clerk of the peace has his office for his life, by these words, 'to have and enjoy so long as he shall well demean himself in the office'. If these words had been annexed to a grant of any other office in Westminster Hall, without all question the grantee had been an officer for life.[40]

> *Holt Chief Justice:* I knew the temper and inclination of the Parliament, at the time when this Act was made; their design was, that men should have places not to hold precariously or determinable on will and pleasure, but having a certain durable estate, that they might act in them without fear of losing them; we all know it, and our places as Judges are so settled, only determinable upon misbehaviour. . . . Now I think since the making of this last statute in the first of this King and Queen, he [the clerk of the peace] has absolutely an estate for life in his office . . . determinable only upon misbehaviour.[41]

Appeal was taken by writ of error to Parliament and the judgments of the justices of the King's Bench were there affirmed. The Attorney-General, presumably before the House of Lords, is reported to have given his opinion as follows:

> When an office is granted *quamdiu se bene gesserit*, it is a freehold, and to last during the parties' life. It is so even in the case of the King, whose grant shall be taken most strictly against himself. If the king grant an office *quamdiu se bene gesserit*, it is a freehold for life.[42]

---

[37] 53 Geo. III, c. 24.

[38] 5 Vict., c. 5.

[39] 1 Show. 426, 506 and 556; 89 E.R. 680, 720 and 750.

[40] 89 E.R. at 728.

[41] *Ibid.*, 734.

[42] *Ibid.*, 750. Apparently Coke took the view that the king could not change the customary tenure during pleasure of the judges of the Common Pleas and King's Bench, and that hence he could *only* make such appointments on these terms. In this view, *a statute was essential* to authorize as well as to require that judges' tenure be for life during good behaviour. *Harcourt v. Fox* is to the contrary, and it is a King's Bench case confirmed in the House of Lords. But this was apparently an issue before the Act of Settlement. See Joseph Chitty, Jun., Prerogatives of the Crown (Butterworth, London, 1820) 76.

The authoritative passages just quoted make very clear the proprietary conception of the legal nature of these offices. It will be noted also that the historical definition of this tenure is inconsistent with any requirement for an automatic or compulsory retirement age. Compulsory retirement of judges for age alone could only be imposed by specific statutory modification of the historical and established legal meaning of tenure during good behaviour. The appropriate legislative or constitution-amending body in this respect for the country concerned would have to act. We shall return later to this problem in considering the position of the Canadian judiciary.

Now, to complete the story of the establishment of judicial security of tenure in office, only one weakness remained: the peculiar effect of a demise of the Crown. The rule was that on the death of the king all royal appointees, judges included, vacated their offices whatever their tenure. An act of 1760 altered this so far as judges were concerned by providing:[43]

> That the commissions of judges for the time being, shall be, continue and remain, in full force, during their good behaviour, notwithstanding the demise of His Majesty (whom God long preserve) or of any of his heirs or successors; any law, usage, or practice, to the contrary thereof in any wise notwithstanding.

Thus we reach the modern position in England on security of judicial tenure, though strictly speaking the relevant provisions of the Act of Settlement and the Act of 1760 are now superseded by later provisions to the same effect in the modern statutes governing the English judicature.[44]

We must now turn to a detailed examination of the means of removing judges from office that obtain in England, the modern position not necessarily being as clear as one might expect. To effect removal of a judge appointed for life during good behaviour there are apparently four methods other than a parliamentary joint address under the modern statutory equivalents of the seventh paragraph of the third section of the Act of Settlement. When appearing as counsel for the Irish judge, Sir Jonah Barrington, before Parliament in 1830, Mr. Denman (afterwards Lord Chief Justice) is reported by Todd to have said that "independently of a parliamentary address or impeachment for the removal of a judge, there were two other courses open for such a purpose. These were (1) a writ of *scire facias* to repeal the patent by which the office had been conferred; and (2) a criminal information (in the court of King's Bench) at the suit of the attorney-general".[45] In addition, a judge might in some circumstances be removed by a special statute of Parliament which, for instance, simply abolished his office in a judicial reorganization.

As a fourth method, impeachment for corruption in office before the House of Lords presumably is still possible for judges, but the removal procedure of the Act of Settlement by joint address would no doubt always be used now. As a matter of parliamentary procedure, it involves a careful and fair parliamentary

---

[43] 1 Geo. III, c. 23. The Demise of the Crown Act of 1901 is the corresponding modern provision.
[44] Supreme Court of Judicature (Consolidation) Act, 1925 (15 and 16 Geo. 5, c. 49), s. 12(1).
[45] Alpheus Todd, Parliamentary Government in England (Longmans, Green, and Co., London, 1887) Vol. II. 858-859.

hearing upon which the old impeachment procedure would not improve. As for proceedings at the instance of the Crown in the Court of Queen's Bench by writ of *scire facias* or criminal information, Todd has this to say:[46]

> The legal effect of the grant of an office during good behaviour is the creation of an estate for life in the office. Such an estate is terminable only by the grantee's incapacity from mental or bodily infirmity, or by his breach of good behaviour. But like any other conditional estate, it may be forfeited by a breach of the condition annexed to it; that is to say, by misbehaviour. Behaviour means behaviour in the grantee's official capacity. Misbehaviour includes, firstly, the improper exercise of judicial functions; secondly, wilful neglect of duty, or non-attendance; and, thirdly, a conviction for any infamous offence, by which, although it be not connected with the duties of his office, the offender is rendered unfit to exercise any office or public franchise. In the case of official misconduct, the decision of the question whether there be misbehaviour rests with the grantor, subject, of course, to any proceedings on the part of the removed officer. In the case of misconduct outside the duties of his office, the misbehaviour must be established by a previous conviction by a jury. When the office is granted for life, by letters patent, the forfeiture must be enforced by a *scire facias*. These principles apply to all offices, judicial or ministerial, that are held during good behaviour.

It is noteworthy that a grantee can fail in "good behaviour", that is to say, can fail to "well demean himself in his office", by "incapacity from mental or bodily infirmity" as well as by the wilful means mentioned.

Several authorities on the English constitution agree with Todd that these proceedings in the Queen's Bench, without any reference whatever to Parliament, are still available for the removal of superior-court judges,[47] but Sir Ivor Jennings is more doubtful: he says, "They can be removed—and this perhaps means they can be removed only—on an address from both Houses of Parliament".[48] If the statutory provision for joint parliamentary address originating with the Act of Settlement is to be construed as exhaustive on means for the removal of judges, then Jennings' conjecture is correct. Likely the older methods do survive, but probably would not be used only in painfully obvious cases. As we shall see later, their survival may have a bearing on the validity of certain provisions of the Canadian Judges Act.

In any event, it seems that the scope of the statutory power of removal by joint parliamentary address is wider than the older possibility of forfeiture in the

---

[46]*Ibid.*, 857-858. The writ of *scire facias* is still available for this purpose and was not abolished by the Crown Proceedings Act of 1947. See Halsbury's Laws of England (3rd ed.) Vol. 11, 154. The opinion of Professors Cowen and Derham to the contrary is therefore doubtful. Otherwise, they support what Todd has said. See their article, The Independence of the Judges (1953), 26 Aust. L.J. 463.

[47]Sir W. Anson, Law and Custom of the Constitution (Keith, 4th ed.) Vol. II, Part I, 234-235; Chalmers and Hood Phillips' Constitutional Law (6th ed. by Hood Phillips, Sweet and Maxwell, London, 1946) 391-392; A. B. Keith, Constitution of England from Queen Victoria to George VI (Macmillan and Co., London, 1940) Vol. II, 327; E. C. S. Wade and G. G. Phillips, Constitutional Law (Longmans, Green and Co., London, 1946) 215; Viscount Sankey, Parliamentary Debates (House of Lords) Vol. 90 (1933) 76-77.

[48]Sir Ivor Jennings, The Law and the Constitution (University of London Press, London, 4th ed., 1952) 227.

Queen's Bench for misconduct. Todd tells us: "This power is not, in a strict sense, judicial, it may be invoked upon occasions when the misbehaviour complained of would not constitute a legal breach of the conditions on which the office is held. The liability to this kind of removal is, in fact, a qualification of or exception from, the words creating a tenure during good behaviour, and not an incident or legal consequence thereof."[49] Parliament of course would be unlikely to act except on imputation and proof of grave misconduct, but the point is that the parliamentary concept of misconduct is potentially wider and more various than that the Court of Queen's Bench would take notice of under the common law. It was Anson's opinion that misbehaviour, so far as Parliament is concerned, might cover "any form of misconduct which would destroy public confidence in the holder of the office".[50] Finally, there is no reserve royal discretion when a parliamentary address for removal has been made. By constitutional convention, the sovereign must act as requested.[51]

There is not much to say about removal of judges by special statute. If the British Parliament *may* do anything by statute, no United Kingdom judge is out of reach. In fact, no judge is beyond reach of the House of Commons, for concurrence of the House of Lords now can be dispensed with soon enough. Todd does mention one case in 1867, when the Court of Admiralty in Ireland was being invested with a new common-law jurisdiction, for the exercise of which the incumbent judge was not considered competent by training or experience. The parliamentary bill proposed in one clause to alter his status from "good behaviour" to "pleasure of the Crown", obviously so that he might be compulsorily retired. "The judge protested strongly against this proceeding, and his friends took the sense of the House upon the clause. But as it was provided in another part of the Bill that the judge should be entitled, on his retirement, to receive an annuity equal to his full salary, the proposed clause was agreed to by a large majority."[52] This seems reasonable. Parliament could hardly be denied the power to make a bona-fide re-arrangement of a part of the judicature for such reasons and on such terms as in this case. I doubt if Dr. Goodhart would consider this an attack on the general principle of tenure during good behaviour for superior-court judges.

(e) Parliamentary debate concerning judicial conduct

Apart from debates on judicature statutes, parliamentary rules impose much restraint on debate concerning judicial conduct. "By the theory of our constitution, those to whom the administration of justice is entrusted are not responsible to Parliament, except for actual misconduct in office."[53] And even then parliamentary consideration of allegations of misconduct against a judge is not to proceed unless (1) preliminary investigation has revealed a prima-facie case of miscon-

---

[49] Todd, *ante,* footnote 45, Vol. II, 860. Note the punctuation, and the disjunctive "but", in the relevant passage from the Act of Settlement, quoted earlier.

[50] Quoted by Chalmers and Hood Phillips, *ante,* footnote 47, 391-392.

[51] *Ibid.,* 392.

[52] Todd, *ante,* footnote 45, Vol. II, 877-878.

[53] *Ibid.,* Vol. I, 571.

duct that would, if fully proven, warrant the judge's removal, and (2) a definite motion to proceed with the determination of the issue is made. Obviously the cabinet has responsibility to take a position in such an extreme case. But, saving extreme cases, constitutional usage forbids either House of Parliament to consider or debate any matter civil or criminal which is before the courts for determination or is about to be submitted to them. As Todd puts it, quoting Mr. Gladstone:[54]

> But nothing could be more injurious to the administration of justice than that the House of Commons should take upon itself the duties of a court of review of the proceedings of an ordinary court of law; or of the decisions of a competent legal tribunal,—or that it should tamper with the question whether judges are on this or that particular assailable and endeavour to inflict upon them a minor punishment by subjecting their official conduct to hostile criticism.

Nor can debate arise over the parliamentary provision of judicial salaries, for they are now permanently charged by statute on the consolidated revenue fund and hence do not come up for review and possible debate every year as do annual supply items. It seems that a judge also is not liable to proceedings for contempt of Parliament for what he says or does in the execution of his judicial office, even though adverse criticism of Parliament is involved.[55]

(f) Payment of judges

The detailed history of the payment of judges in England need not concern us. Holdsworth says that "From the first they were paid salaries by the crown which in the course of years were gradually and continuously increased".[56] Further, until the judicial reforms of the nineteenth century, their salaries were not the only source of income allowed to judges. They were entitled in various ways to share in the fees which litigants paid, and the chief justices in particular enjoyed very valuable patronage, in that they had the disposal of the non-judicial offices of their courts. In other words they were entitled to grant the offices for a price and the grantee was then deemed to have a freehold in the office just as if it were a parcel of land.[57] Certain legislative reforms of the judicature in the earlier years of the nineteenth century put an end to this situation and provided for generous salaries which were to be the sole income of the judges. But, until these changes, interests in fees and patronage were important elements in the financial independence of the judges. Indeed, particularly for the chief justices, the royal or parliamentary salary was at times quite a secondary source of income. Furthermore, this judicial right to patronage had been successfully defended against the king.[58]

In any event, the seventh paragraph of the third section of the Act of Settlement dealt with payment as well as tenure of judges, providing that their salaries

---

[54]*Ibid.*, Vol. I, 574.
[55]*Stockdale v. Hansard* (1839), 112 E.R. 1112, *per* Coleridge J. 1203; Hugo Fischer, Civil and Criminal Aspects of Contempt of Court (1956), 34 Can. Bar Rev. 121, 133.
[56]Holdsworth, Vol. I, 252.
[57]*Ibid.*, 248.
[58]*Bridgman v. Holt* (1693). See Holdsworth, Vol. I, 261.

were to be "ascertained and established". It does not appear that financial pressure in the form of the withholding or reduction of salary had hitherto been used as a means of controlling judges, though, as we have seen, inadequate salaries contributed to the judicial scandals of the later thirteenth century. There were times also when the royal treasury was badly in arrears in paying judicial salaries, though not by design to put pressure on the judges. But apparently those who framed the constitutional settlement at the end of the seventeenth century foresaw the possibility of pressure and attempted to foreclose it. The possibility might have been in their minds because Parliament itself had been successfully using the power of the purse against the king for some time. It is worth recalling that the bill William III vetoed in 1692 attempted to "ascertain and establish" judicial salaries by making them a permanent charge against the royal hereditary revenues.

In the course of the eighteenth century, Parliament did make definite statutory provision for judicial salaries. Moreover the modern position in England seems to be that, unless and until Parliament has provided or in effect has promised a salary, no judicial vacancy exists to which the sovereign may appoint anyone. A dispute arose in the last years of the nineteenth century in New Zealand concerning this point, and the Judicial Committee of the Privy Council took the position that the English and New Zealand law was the same. Hence the Judicial Committee, which included on this occasion Lord Halsbury, Lord Watson, Lord Herschell and Lord MacNaghten, expressed itself on the English position:[59]

> It appears certain that since the reign of James I, with two possible exceptions, the latest of which dates back as far as 1714, no addition has been made to the number of judges without express parliamentary sanction. In the Act of Settlement it was provided that the judges' commissions should be made quamdiu se bene gesserint, 'and that their salaries should be ascertained and established'. The latter provision was not completely carried into effect until a subsequent period. The remuneration was in former times derived partly from fees and partly from the civil list of the Sovereign. By several Acts passed prior to the reign of George III, the salaries of the judges were in part provided by certain sums charged upon the duties granted by those Acts.

Then came a statute of great importance, chapter 23 of the first year of George III (1760), entitled "An act for rendering more effectual the provisions in [the Act of Settlement] relating to the commissions and salaries of judges". It is worth rather full quotation. The preamble is, in part, as follows:

> Whereas your Majesty has been graciously pleased to declare from the throne to both houses of parliament, that you look upon the independence and uprightness of judges, as essential to the impartial administration of justice, as one of the best securities to the rights and liberties of your loving subjects, and as most conductive to the honour of your crown; and in consequence thereof, your Majesty has recommended it to the consideration of your parliament, to make further provision for continuing judges in the enjoyment of their offices during their good behaviour,

---

[59]*Buckley v. Edwards*, [1892] A.C. 387, 392-393.

notwithstanding the demise of your Majesty, or any of your heirs and successors; and your Majesty has also desired your faithful commons, that you may be enabled to secure the salaries of judges, during the continuance of their commissions; and whereas in return for this paternal goodness, and in the justest sense of your tender concern for the religion, laws, and liberties, of your people, we have taken this important work into our consideration, and have resolved to enable your Majesty to effectuate the wise, just, and generous purposes of your royal heart:

Section one of this act (on the continuance of judicial commissions in spite of a demise of the sovereign) has already been quoted. Section two merely reiterated the royal power to remove a judge on a joint address from Parliament requesting removal. Section three is as follows:

And be it enacted by the authority aforesaid, That such salaries as are settled upon judges for the time being, or any of them, by act of parliament, and also such salaries as have been or shall be granted by his Majesty, his heirs, and successors, to any judge or judges, shall, in all time coming, be paid and payable to every such judge and judges for the time being, so long as the patent or commissions of them, or any of them respectively, shall continue and remain in force.

Section four in effect reinforced section three by providing that, to the extent that judges were dependent upon salaries granted by George III, those salaries were to remain a charge upon the duties and revenues supporting the royal civil list of George III's successors after his death. The further story of the mode of paying judges out of public moneys is complex, but the trend was consistent and the result clear. In 1787 the consolidated fund was created by statute and some of the payments due to judges charged against it. The process of statutorily charging all salary moneys payable to the judges on the consolidated fund was substantially complete by about 1799, but not finally complete in every detail until 1875. It has already been mentioned that the result of this development is to prevent any routine or frivolous discussion of the conduct of judges by Parliament in financial debate.[60]

Speaking of the significance of the statute of 1760, Lord Herschell for the Privy Council had this to say:[61]

Their Lordships think that the Act of 1 Geo. 3, c. 23, would render it difficult to contend that the Crown could after that date appoint additional judges for the payment of salary to whom Parliament had given no sanction. For the salaries of the judges were then, by the authority of Parliament, secured to them during the continuance of their commissions, and after the demise of the Sovereign were charged upon the revenues granted by Parliament for the civil government of the realm. The recital which precedes this legislation shews that, with a view to their independence, it must have been intended that all the judges should be in this position, and it certainly cannot have been the intention of Parliament to enable the Sovereign to increase without its sanction the charges which after the demise of the Sovereign were to be imposed on the revenues of the realm.

---

[60]See The Parliamentary Debates (fifth series) Vol. 90 (1933-34) The House of Lords, *per* Lord Rankeillour, 63 and Viscount Sankey L.C. 77-80.
[61][1892] A.C. 393.

Two significant conclusions seem warranted, then, on the English position: (i) parliamentary provision for a salary is necessary for the creation of a judicial vacancy to which the sovereign may appoint, and (ii) once there has been an appointment, the judge is entitled to have his salary continue so long as his commission is in effect, that is, for life during good behaviour. In both the Act of Settlement and the later Act of 1760 for rendering the Act of Settlement more effective, tenure during good behaviour was coupled with what was in effect a prescription that judicial salaries were to be assured for the same period. Sir William Blackstone was in no doubt that this was the intention, purport and effect of the two enactments, and, on the Act of 1760, he is a contemporary authority. In his *Commentaries*, published in 1765, he says:[62]

> And now, by the noble improvements of that law [the Act of Settlement], in the statute of 1 Geo. III c. 23, enacted at the earnest recommendation of the king himself from the throne, the judges are continued in their offices during their good behaviour, . . . *and their full salaries are absolutely secured to them during the continuance of their commissions*. . . .

Finally, it is of interest to find that, as late as 1931, the question whether a judge's salary might be reduced during the currency, of his commission became a point of controversy in Great Britain. One of the measures taken to meet the financial emergency of the period was the National Economy Act of 1931, which authorized the remuneration "of persons in His Majesty's Service" to be reduced by order in council, even where the amount of the salary for the office had been specified by statute. The Government ordered reduction of judicial salaries by one fifth, along with a great many others, but the constitutional propriety of this action was widely doubted. Sir William Holdsworth argued that judges were not "in the service of His Majesty" within the meaning of the National Economy Act. Only public officers who could be instructed in the name of the Crown how to perform their functions (he said) could be described as "servants of" or "in the service of" His Majesty.[63] As we have seen, royal power to instruct the judges in this sense was on its way out by 1328.

Professor E. C. S. Wade took issue with Holdsworth,[64] arguing that judges were properly described as "in the service of His Majesty", and that, as a matter of statutory construction, the words in issue were intended to include the judges. Government spokesmen took the same line, and the cuts were put in effect. But the most significant development was that the judges themselves sent a confidential memorandum on the subject to the Prime Minister on December 4th, 1931, which became public when it was read into the record of the House of Lords on July 24th, 1933, by the Lord Chancellor at the request of the Lord Chief Justice and the Master of the Rolls.[65] It is clear from this unique document that the judges themselves fully agreed with Sir William Holdsworth:

---

[62]Blackstone, *ante*, footnote 21, Book I, 267-268 (italics mine).

[63]Holdsworth, The Constitutional Position of Judges (1932), 48 L.Q. Rev. 25.

[64]E. C. S. Wade, His Majesty's Judges (1932), 173 Law Times 246 and 267. A reply by Holdsworth is printed in the same volume 336.

[65]Reproduced starting at 103 of (1933), 176 Law Times. The quotation is not quite the whole of this memorandum.

The judges of His Majesty's Supreme Court of Judicature think it their duty to submit certain considerations in regard to the recent reductions of the salary payable to judges which seem to have escaped notice.

It is, we think, beyond question that the judges are not in the position occupied by civil servants. They are appointed to hold particular offices of dignity and exceptional importance. They occupy a vital place in the constitution of this country. They stand equally between the Crown and the Executive, and between the Executive and the subject. They have to discharge the gravest and most responsible duties. It has for over two centuries been considered essential that their security and independence should be maintained inviolate.

The Act of Settlement made clear provision for this in the following terms: 'That after the said limitation shall take effect as aforesaid, judges' commissions be made *quamdiu se bene gesserint*, and their salaries ascertained and established; but upon the Address of both Houses of Parliament, it may be lawful to remove them'. . . . Further by sect. 12 of the Act of 2 and 3 Will. 4, c. 116, judges were exempted from taxes.

It was long ago said that there can be no true liberty in a country where the judges are not entirely independent of the Government; and the soundness of the remark has never been questioned. Art. III of the Constitution of the United States runs as follows: 'The judicial power of the United States shall be vested in one Supreme Court, and in such inferior courts as the Congress may from time to time ordain and establish. The judges, both of the supreme and inferior courts, shall hold their offices during good behaviour, and shall, at stated times, receive for their services, a compensation, which shall not be diminished during their continuance in office'.

In this matter our country has set an example to the world, and we believe that the respect felt by the people for an English judge has been partly due to his unique position, a feeling which will survive with difficulty of his salary can be reduced as if he were an ordinary salaried servant of the Crown.

It was owing to the general acceptance of these views that on the one hand the salaries of High Court judges have never been the subject of a House of Commons vote, but have been charged on the Consolidated Fund, and that on the other hand the judges hold their office as expressed above during good behaviour and are removable only on an Address to the Crown by both Houses of Parliament.

If the salaries of the judges can be reduced almost *sub silentio* by the methods recently employed, the independence of the Judicature is seriously impaired. It cannot be wise to expose judges of the High Court to the suggestion, however malevolent and ill-founded, that if their decisions are favourable to the Crown in revenue and other cases, their salaries may be raised and if unfavourable may be diminished.

We must express our deep regret that no opportunity was given to the judges of offering a voluntary reduction of salaries for an appropriate period; but we recognize that the Government was in a grave difficulty and that the time for consideration was very short. . . .

Late in 1933, Viscount Buckmaster gave notice of a motion in the House of Lords that, among other things, in the opinion of the house judges' salaries should not be diminished during their continuance in office. In the debate that followed, Viscount Sankey, the Lord Chancellor, defending the Government's action in 1931, pointed out that there had been several adjustments by statute of judicial salaries since the Act of Settlement, some he said, being increases and some decreases. He then continued:[66]

> On constitutional grounds the action then taken is not open to challenge on the ground that it strikes at the constitutional position of the judge. But then it is said: 'If you cut off twenty percent of the Judges' salaries you can cut off eighty percent or one hundred, and what then becomes of the Judges' independence?' You can do these things of course. But grave measures taken in grave political emergencies are not to be measured and criticised by such a reductio ad absurdum. They must be looked at in common sense and with due sense of proportion. When anyone makes an attempt so to deal with the Judges' salaries that their position is really threatened, these arguments will be open to those who oppose so ill advised and, I make bold to say, so wicked a proposal. They do not touch the action taken by this Government or their predecessors.

At least the Lord Chancellor admitted that salary reductions could be carried to the point where they would threaten judicial independence and thus raise a grave constitutional issue. Moreover it is not clear that there *were* other statutory salary reductions in the period since the Act of Settlement. The changes to which Holdsworth refers in his *History* all seem to be increases,[67] though it is difficult to be sure what the net effect was when the mode of payment was being slowly changed from charges on special taxes and royal revenues to charges on the consolidated fund, and when judicial income from patronage and fees was being progressively eliminated. Many statutes and many years are involved. In any event, it seems that the balance of authority definitely favours the view that it is unconstitutional in Britain to cut the salary of an individual judge of a superior court during the currency of his commission. It would seem to be unconstitutional also for Parliament to attempt a general reduction of the judicial salary scale to an extent that threatens the independence of the judiciary—as I have shown, even Viscount Sankey left this question open. Subject to these two limitations, Parliament has power to adjust the level of judicial salaries.

Further, there is the problem of the liability of the judges to income tax, a question that has arisen in Canada, Australia and South Africa, as well as in Britain. In their memorandum just quoted, the English judges referred to the plenary tax exemption granted them in a statute of 1832. The exemption did not remain for long. In the Income Tax Act of 1842[68] the judges were specifically mentioned as liable along with all others. In the Canadian case, the Judicial Committee of the Privy Council asked itself whether "judicial emoluments are in a class apart, protected by some paramount principle making inapplicable to that form of income a tax imposed by statute in terms wide enough to include it". Their answer was "Neither the independence nor any other attribute of the judiciary can be affected by a general income-tax which charges their official incomes on the same footing as the incomes of other citizens".[69] This seems to be the accepted

---

[66] Parliamentary Debates (House of Lords) Vol. 90, 80.
[67] See Holdsworth, Vol. I, 252-254 and 262.
[68] 5 and 6 Vict., c. 35, Schedule (E), third paragraph.
[69] *The Judges v. Attorney-General for Saskatchewan* (1937), 53 T.L.R. 464, 466.

position then in Commonwealth countries including Britain. It is here perhaps that the British government of the day should have rested its case for the cuts effected under the National Economy Act of 1931. That reduction was non-discriminatory in the sense that all salaried public offices of whatever nature were affected on the same terms, and those relying on private incomes also were suffering, under the impact of the economic depression. The principles of general applicability and non-discrimination are essential to keep in mind.

(g) Disqualification of judges for interest

Possible pressures from the executive or parliament are not the only threats to the independence or impartiality of judges. There are more subtle pressures to guard against. During the British controversy on the National Economy Act, it was mentioned by Sir William Holdsworth and by the judges themselves that no normal judicial determination of the applicability of the statute to the judges was possible, for, one and all, they were disqualified by interest from deciding such an issue. This points to a very old principle favouring the impartiality of the royal courts—that no man should be judge in his own cause. In 1701, Chief Justice Holt went so far as to say "That if an act of Parliament should ordain that the same person should be party and judge, or which is the same thing, judge in his own cause, it would be a void act of parliament; . . . it cannot make one who lives under a government judge and party".[70] Chief Justice Hobart had said the same thing almost a hundred years earlier, stating that the principle was one of immutable natural law.[71] The modern position no doubt is that a statute of this kind would prevail, though the courts would construe against making a person judge in his own cause if any alternative meaning could be fastened upon the statutory words. The importance of the principle in any event is demonstrated by the fact that it was discussed in terms of natural law. Interested judges are expected to disqualify themselves by declining to adjudicate, but if, inadvertently or for other reasons, they do not do so, what then?

The leading case is *Dimes v. Grand Junction Canal Company* in 1852 in the House of Lords,[72] involving a dispute over valuable rights in land. A decree had been made in the Court of Chancery by the Vice-Chancellor and then appealed to and affirmed by the Lord Chancellor. But the Lord Chancellor had a large interest as shareholder in the canal company. Appeal was taken to the House of Lords and the judges were summoned to advise on the position created by the Lord Chancellor's interest. The result was that the Lord Chancellor was ruled to have had a disqualifying interest, his affirmation of the decree was therefore voidable, and the House considered the Vice-Chancellor's decree on its merits as if under direct appeal. The house accepted the unanimous opinion of the judges delivered by Baron Parke: "We think that the order of the Chancellor is not void; but we are of opinion, that as he had such an interest which would have disqualified a

---

[70]*City of London v. Wood* (1701), 12 Mod. 669.

[71]*Day v. Savadge* (1615), Hobart 85. This case and *City of London v. Wood* are referred to in J. W. Gough, Fundamental Law in English Constitutional History (Oxford, 1955) 38-39 and 145, respectively.

[72]3 H.L.C. 758; 10 E.R. 301.

witness under the old law, he was disqualified as a Judge; that it was a voidable order, and might be questioned and set aside by appeal or some application to the Court of Chancery, if a prohibition would not lie."[73]

If interest is alleged against the judge of an inferior court or tribunal, disqualification is tried and if necessary enforced in the appropriate superior court by one of the prerogative writs. But these writs do not lie against one of the central royal courts, so apparently the procedure then is to apply to the other judges of the court for the avoidance of the voidable order of their interested colleague, or to take the same step by way of appeal, if there is a regular channel of appeal open to a disinterested tribunal. Baron Parke did concede that cases of necessity might exist where the decree or order of an interested judge would stand. Presumably such an order might have to be made in a court of first instance to lay the foundation for appeal to a disinterested tribunal, where the latter had only appellate jurisdiction. The words of Baron Parke were that in "a case of necessity . . . the objection of interest cannot prevail. Of this the case in the Year Book . . . [1430] . . . is an instance, where it was held that it was no objection to the jurisdiction of the Common Pleas that an action was brought against all the Judges of the Common Pleas, in a case in doubt which could only be brought in that court."[74] In 1936 the Saskatchewan Court of Appeal was confronted with the problem of the liability of all the provincial judges to provincial income tax following a direct reference of the question to it by the provincial cabinet under the constitutional Questions Act of the province. The interested judges took the view that they were in a position of necessity within the meaning of the *Dimes* case,[75] and they were affirmed in this view by the Judicial Committee of the Privy Council.[76] The Privy Council judges of course were disinterested, and the necessity here may be said to have consisted in laying a basis for appeal to that tribunal. In any event, the Saskatchewan justices of appeal had to answer by an opinion because the statute said so, regardless of the bearing of common-law necessity.

But now the question arises, Why could not the appropriate branch of the Supreme Court of Judicature in England have determined the applicability of the National Economy Act in 1931 to the English judges as a matter of common-law necessity? This issue figured in the exchanges between Professors Wade and Holdsworth at the time, with the latter taking the view (in which the judges' memorandum supported him) that the objection of interest was insurmountable. He said: "The case of *Dimes v. Grand Junction Canal* . . . shows that the slightest suspicion of a particular and personal interest will debar a judge from sitting in judgment. Sect. 17 of the Judicature Act 1925 shows how wide this principle is. A statutory permission to adjudicate was needed to get rid of the objection, even when the judge's interest was a general interest as one of a class of persons affected by a tax. The statutory permission would clearly not apply when the in-

---

[73] 10 E.R. 312. This is an interesting example of "lifting the corporate veil" to identify the shareholder with the company, something usually done only to advance some high public purpose.
[74] *Ibid.*, at 313.
[75] *Re The Income Tax Act*, [1936] 4 D.L.R. 134, 135.
[76] (1937), 53 T.L.R. 465.

terest was particular and personal.''[77] Professors Wade and Holdsworth did agree at least that a disinterested board of the Judicial Committee of the Privy Council might have been composed and the question referred there by the Crown under Section 4 of the Judicial Committee Act of 1833.

In concluding this topic, I might note briefly further detail on the nature of disqualifying interest for judges of any rank. "A distinction must be drawn between pecuniary interest and prejudice. The smallest pecuniary interest is, subject to any statutory authority to the contrary, a bar to the justice acting, but where the interest is not pecuniary the question arises whether the interest is of such a substantial character as to make it likely that he has a real bias in the matter. That which then has to be considered is the effect likely to be produced upon the minds of the public as to the fairness of the administration of justice, and this is a question of degree to be decided in every case.''[78] It is a sign of their primary constitutional status that the superior-court judges must be trusted to apply to themselves the rules they have a duty to enforce for inferior tribunals.

(h) Other powers and privileges contributing to the autonomy of the courts

As has been shown, the central royal courts developed to the point where they could hold the king at arm's length (and later the cabinet as well, when that body came to control the king). The final position was as Blackstone described it, that the king had irrevocably delegated the whole of his judicial power to his judges, and that he could not instruct them beforehand, or remove them (during good behaviour), or stop their salaries. But, on the other hand, precisely because they were royal delegates, albeit singularly autonomous ones, the judges did benefit in power and position in ways that furthered their constitutional independence. They had attributed to them certain powers and privileges originally characteristic of the king himself when, in the early years after 1066, he did *personally* perform substantial judicial functions. They include the power to punish for contempt of court, the infallibility of court records, and the personal legal immunity of judges from liability to aggrieved litigants complaining of absence of jurisdiction, misconception of law or fact, bias or corruption. As the matter of appeals is closely related to the last two of these topics, it will also be briefly considered.

(i) Powers to punish for contempt

Quite aside from history, the necessity is obvious for extensive judicial power to deal punitively with contempt of court, that is, with disobedience to court orders or processes and other forms of serious interference with or obstruction of the due administration of justice. One simply could not speak of the independence of courts not somehow armed with reasonable means of defending themselves in this way. The early Norman kings enjoyed such powers as a feature of their plenary personal governmental jurisdiction, particularly over disobedience to royal writs and misconduct by court officials. Originally, then, contempt of court

---

[77](1932), 173 Law Times, 337.
[78]Halsbury's Laws of England (2nd ed.) Vol. 21, 536-537.

"consisted of an offence against the sovereign as the fountain of justice, or against his royal palace, where justice was said to have been dispensed by the king in person. Contempt was considered as an offence because it imputed to him a breach of the coronation oath to 'administer justice to his people'."[79] In due course these powers were transmitted to the judges of the central royal courts and elaborated by them in their precedents. In large measure definition of the nature and extent of the powers is still a matter for the common law in both Britain and Canada,[80] though from early times some statutory provisions have occasionally entered the picture.[81] A succinct description of what is involved has been given by Professor Hood Phillips:[82]

> Contempt of Court may be either civil or criminal. Civil contempt of Court consists of disobedience to an order of the Court made in civil proceedings. Though punishable by fine or imprisonment, this is merely a form of civil process. Criminal contempt of Court is a common law misdemeanour, and may take such forms as: (i) contempt committed in face of the Court such as directly insulting the judge; (ii) interference with juries, parties or witnesses, or the publications of comments on a pending case which are calculated to prejudice a fair trial and so to interfere with the course of justice; (iii) the publication of matter scandalizing the court, e.g., scurrilous abuse of a Judge with reference to remarks made by him in a judicial proceeding.

For present purposes there is no point in a detailed consideration of the complexities of contempt-of-court jurisdiction. It is enough to say that, so successfully did the central royal courts develop their own powers in this regard, there are modern misgivings that they go too far. Particularly is this so about the power of a superior court summarily to punish by fine or imprisonment a contempt committed outside the court by a stranger to the criminal or civil proceedings concerned.[83] In any event, it is clear that contempt powers adequate to maintain judicial autonomy have been assured to the courts themselves.

(ii) The infallibility of court records

The creation and status of records have been of great importance in the development of the separate status of the central royal courts, and here again we must start with the early Norman kings as personal dispensers of justice. Originally there was no systematic keeping of written records, and the personal memory of the king about what he had previously done in his court was taken to be infallible and conclusive when any question arose. The royal judges were soon invested with like infallibility of memory, so that their personal recollections about previous decisions of their courts also became incontrovertible. Soon the judges, when called upon, would cause a written record to be made of their recollections, and from that point it was a natural transition to the contemporaneous keeping of

---

[79]Fischer, Civil and Criminal Aspects of Contempt of Court (1956), 34 Can. Bar Rev. 121.
[80]See, The Criminal Code, 1953-54 (Can.) c. 51, s. 8.
[81]See, The Criminal Code, 1953-54, c. 51, ss. 108, 457, 514(2), 610 and 612.
[82]Chalmers and Hood Phillips, *ante,* footnote 47, 398-399.
[83]See article by Fischer, *ante* footnote 79 (1956), 34 Can. Bar Rev. 121; also Holdsworth, Vol. III, 391-394.

records of judicial proceedings.[84] Pollock and Maitland say that "In England at an early time the proceedings of the royal court were committed to writing. Thenceforward the appeal to its record tended to become a reference to a roll, but it was long before the theory was forgotten that the rolls of the court were mere aids for the memories of the justices; and, as duplicate and triplicate rolls were kept, there was always a chance of disagreement among them."[85] The plea rolls date from about 1194 and form (in the words of these same historians) "a magnificent series of judicial records".[86] The final step was soon taken, and in a way that was to be expected: the infallibility of the royal memory was transferred to the written record itself, which thus acquired an independent status. Sir Edward Coke describes the result in these words: "It is called a record, for that it recordeth or beareth witness of the truth. . . . it hath this sovereign privilege that it is proved by no other but by itself".[87] Our modern terminology, which does not improve on Coke's way of putting it, is that court records are entitled to be judicially noticed.

Coke also gives us the reasons of substance which justify this privilege for judicial records. He said: "In this point the law is founded upon great reason; for if the judicial matters of record should be drawn in question, by partial and sinister supposals and averments of offenders, or any on their behalf, there will never be an end of a cause, but controversies will be infinite".[88] There are thus sensible roots of governmental necessity here. Some official person or tribunal at some point must have the last word if issues of public or private law are ever to be settled and the legal system maintained as a going concern. It has been characteristic of the central royal courts that, within their wide and important jurisdictions, they have had the last word—subject to occasional appeals to Parliament as a court. This is another clear sign of their primary constitutional status.

The central courts of common law, the Common Pleas, King's Bench and Exchequer, were for obvious reasons the first tribunals to acquire records of the sanctity described, and hence they were the first courts of record. As time went on and they had to contend for jurisdiction and status with the Chancery, the Star Chamber, the ecclesiastical courts and others, the judges of the central courts of common law went so far as to maintain that their courts were the *only* courts of record, that the records of these other bodies, if any, did not have the same quality of finality as those of the common-law courts. This was clearly just a way of asserting the constitutional superiority of the common-law courts and the common law against other tribunals and the law they administered. Accordingly much was made in the sixteenth and seventeenth centuries of the differences between courts of record and courts not of record, and this has left some residue of unhistorical and unmeritorious distinctions.[89] Anyway, the Court of Chancery

---

[84]See Holdsworth, Vol. V, 156-159.
[85]Sir F. Pollock and F. W. Maitland, The History of English Law (Cambridge University Press, 2nd ed., 1898), Vol. II, 670.
[86]*Ibid.*, Vol. I, 169.
[87]Quoted by Holdsworth, Vol. V, 158, footnote 6.
[88]Quoted by Holdsworth, Vol. VI, 237.
[89]See *ibid.*, Vol. V, 157-161.

more than held its own, but, except to note this, further details need not concern us.

In any event, the original and correct idea persisted that the infallible official record was a mark of highly-placed and powerful courts of direct royal ancestry. This infallibility of record had important implications that were soon to be worked out. The only way of going behind the record of a court of record to question its decision by way of appeal was by a writ of error, whereas the decisions of lesser courts could be more easily attacked. The writ of error, as will be seen later, was about the only means of appeal available from the central royal courts until the nineteenth century. The infallibility of the formal record of the courts of common law also had a definite bearing on the development of the total personal legal immunity of the judges of those courts for anything done by them in their judicial capacity, a subject now to be examined.

(iii) The personal legal immunity of judges

The development of the complete immunity of judges for their judicial acts is historically connected with the idea of the superiority of a court of record and the earlier and imperfect types of appeal from or review of original judicial decisions. The mediaeval conception was that to complain of a judgment one must attack the judge himself. For instance, a writ of false judgment could be brought in the king's court against the decision of a local communal or feudal court and, if the complaint succeeded, not only would the decision be altered, but the erring judge would be fined and perhaps subjected also to a suit for damages at the instance of the aggrieved litigant. But, after an initial period of some uncertainty in the thirteenth century, it became established that a writ of false judgment would not lie against a royal judge. "In the case of courts of record, . . . it was held, certainly as early as Edward III's reign, that a litigant could not go behind the record, in order to make a judge civilly or criminally liable for an abuse of his jurisdiction."[90] With the writ of error came the idea that the record of an original judicial decision could be removed from one royal court to another and reviewed in the latter for error on the record. Correction then followed if need be, without rendering the erring judge in any way personally liable either to pay a fine or to compensate an aggrieved litigant. Thus, by the writ of error procedure, review and possible correction of the decision of a royal judge was separated from any question of his personal legal liability. One exception to this was made by statute in favour of the liberty of the subject. "Judges of the Supreme Court are liable to a penalty of 500 pounds for wrongfully refusing to issue a writ of habeas corpus in vacation in the case of a person in custody on a criminal charge."[91] Saving this, by the eighteenth century we find judges of the central royal courts enjoying total personal immunity for judicial acts.

In theory, even superior-court judges would be liable if they acted completely without jurisdiction, for then their purported judicial acts would not be judicial acts but private ones only. A hypothetical example of this given by the

---

[90]Holdsworth, Vol. VI, 235; and see Pollock and Maitland, *ante*, footnote 85, Vol. II, 666.
[91]Chalmers and Hood Phillips, *ante*, footnote 47, 396.

older writers is the Court of Common Pleas assuming to hear and decide a charge of felony. But alleged lack of jurisdiction came to mean little or nothing in the case of the judges of the central royal courts, for they had power finally to hear and determine issues on the extent of their own jurisdiction. Hence, if such a judge purported to act judicially, the worst that could be said of him, even if he did go quite outside his jurisdiction, would be that he was mistaken in deciding something he had undoubted power to decide—the nature and extent of his own jurisdiction.[92] Thus, though acting in error, he would still be acting judicially. And so the modern position is reached, as expressed by Lord Esher in 1895 in *Anderson v. Gorrie.*[93]

> . . . the question arises whether there can be an action against a judge of a Court of Record for doing something within his jurisdiction, but doing it maliciously and contrary to good faith. By the common law of England it is the law that no such action will lie. The ground alleged from the earliest times as that on which this rule rests is that, if such an action would lie the judges would lose their independence, and that the absolute freedom and independence of the judges is necessary for the administration of justice.

The result is that superior-court judges may proceed with their judicial duties secure in the knowledge that they cannot personally be harassed by disappointed litigants, however vexed or powerful. The only recourse against such a judge personally, if he abuses his position, is to effect his removal from office by parliamentary address or possibly one of the other extraordinary means considered earlier. Even after removal, liability would not attach personally to the ex-judge for harm done by the abusive judicial acts that were the reason for his removal. The superior-court judge then is in a different position from all other official persons in government. Generally speaking, if any *other* official person acts quite beyond his jurisdiction, his actions are private and not official though he purports to act officially, and if he thereby does harm, in the sense of the normal law of property or tort, he is personally liable in damages as a private person.[94] Judges of inferior courts are in this position, because an inferior judge does not have the last word on the nature and extent of his own jurisdiction; in his case lack of jurisdiction can be established before a superior court by use of one of the prerogative writs.[95]

This is not to say that there are no basic rules of jurisdiction for superior courts that their judges are obliged to observe, for there are of course. Once again we see, as a sign of their primary constitutional status, that superior-court judges must be trusted to apply to themselves the rules they have a duty to enforce against other officials and tribunals. In other words, while they have the legal

---

[92]See Holdsworth, Vol. VI, 236-240.

[93][1895] 1 Q.B. 668, at 670.

[94]See: E. C. S. Wade, Comment on *Roncarelli v. Duplessis* (1951), 29 Can. Bar Rev. 665; Harry Street, The Law of Torts (Butterworth and Co., London, 1955) 97-102; Jennings, The Law and the Constitution (4th ed.) 204-211. (This is not of course to be confused with problems of the *vicarious* liability of the Crown as an employer.)

[95]Concerning the prerogative writs and judicial review see C. M. Schmitthoff, The Growing Ambit of the Common Law (1951), 29 Can. Bar Rev. 469; and also Holdsworth, Vol. I, 226-231.

duty and power to determine lack of jurisdiction in others, they are not themselves subject to a like determination at the hands of others. There is of course the safeguard of appeals within the hierarchy of the superior courts themselves, whereby the superior-court judges in effect check on one another, and the ultimate possibility of parliamentary removal of judges in extreme cases. Nevertheless, the clear implication is that superior-court judges participate in the original distribution of governmental powers effected by the first principles of the English constitution. Again this development is not merely fortuitous. The reason of substance already mentioned respecting the infallibility of the records of the central royal courts applies here also—that at some point there must be an end to disputation on the interpretation and application of statute law or common law (whether public or private). Hence the constitution necessarily designates certain officials or tribunals to speak the last word on these matters, and for the most part, in England, the superior courts have been so designated. (The House of Lords as a court has long been quite distinct from Parliament as a legislature.) If the House of Commons (led by the cabinet) is displeased with the judicial interpretation of a statute, then it can change the wording of the statute and try again.

(iv) Appeals[96]

The nature of the judicial system of appeals is clearly relevant to understanding the primary and separate status of superior courts. The writ of error has already been mentioned as the old form of appeal from the central courts of common law. Almost from the beginning some kind of appeal has been possible. As Pollock and Maitland say, ''The king's court cannot be charged with false judgment; but gradually as it breaks into segments and throws off wandering satellites, something like an appeal from one segment to another or from the satellite to the central nucleus becomes possible. . . . The idea of a complaint against a judgment which is not an accusation against a judge is not easily formed. But gradually in Edward I's day as the king's court assumed a triple form—Common Bench, King's Bench, King in Council— . . . men became familiar with the notion of a 'procedure in error' which does not call for a defence from the judges who are said to have made the mistake.''[97] Writs of error from the Common Pleas went to the King's Bench, and then could go on to Parliament. Writs of error from the King's Bench originally lay only to Parliament, but by a statute of 1585 a Court of Exchequer Chamber was composed of at least six judges of the Common Pleas and Barons of the Exchequer to hear most writs of error from the King's Bench, with a further appeal possible to Parliament as a court. Writs of error from the Exchequer went to another statutory Court of Exchequer Chamber composed of the Lord Chancellor and the Lord Treasurer. Finally, by statute in 1830, the King's Bench lost its power to deal with errors from the Common Pleas ''and the

---

[96]For an extensive treatment of the subject see O'Halloran, Right of Review and Appeal in Civil Cases before the Judicature Acts, 1875, and Development of the Right of Appeal in England in Criminal Cases (1949), 27 Can. Bar Rev. 46 and 153. A third article in the series by Mr. Justice O'Halloran, Problems in the Modern Appeal in Civil Cases, is to be found *ibid.* at 259.

[97]Pollock and Maitland, *ante* footnote 85, Vol. II, 668.

court of Exchequer Chamber was made a court of appeal intermediate between the three common law courts and Parliament. The court consisted of the judges of the two courts which had not given the decision against which the appeal was brought.''[98] Within each of the common-law courts there was also from early times review of original decisions by way of the motion for new trial. By this means the judgment of the original judge might be reviewed and corrected by his colleagues of the same court ''en banc''.

As for the Court of Chancery, originally only the Lord Chancellor could re-hear a case, if he chose to do so. By the late seventeenth century, however, the right of the House of Lords to hear and determine appeals from the Chancery was established. But for this, the only review would be re-hearing by the Lord Chancellor of some case originally decided by himself or the Master of the Rolls. In the nineteenth century, the Vice-Chancellors were added to the Master of the Rolls as in effect judges of first instance, and in 1851 a statutory Court of Appeal in Chancery was created. ''It consisted of two Lords Justices in Chancery and the Lord Chancellor if he liked to sit there. They could be assisted, on the request of the Lord Chancellor, by the Master of the Rolls, the Vice-Chancellors, or any of the judges.''[99]

As for the House of Lords itself, from the fourteenth century the whole house heard and voted on appeals. Usually the judges were summoned to advise on the issue concerned, and their advice was almost invariably followed. From 1844 it became the established convention that only lords learned in the law should vote upon appeals, and in 1883 the attempt of a lay peer to vote was ignored.[100] In 1876, by statute, provision was made for the appointment of Lords of Appeal in Ordinary, who must be barristers of fifteen years standing or persons who have held high judicial office for at least two years. They were afforded all the safeguards of the Act of Settlement. As is well known, the Judicature Act of 1875 consolidated the central royal courts and the old appeal systems under a general court of appeal, which became the intermediate court of appeal under the House of Lords as a court.

Enough has been said to make clear two things important for present purposes: (i) that some form of appellate jurisdiction has always been a feature of the powers of the central royal courts, along with their original jurisdiction; and (ii) that it was the judges of the central royal courts themselves, often re-grouped for the purpose, who exercised appellate jurisdiction over one another. Even before the House of Lords itself became a distinct professional superior court, the advice of the royal judges, summoned for the purpose, usually prevailed there when the house was functioning as a judicial appeal tribunal.[100]

(i) The holding of non-judicial office by judges

Originally the judges of the central courts of common law were primary members of the Norman *Curia Regis*, but soon they ceased to function in this way. Never-

---

[98]Holdsworth, Vol. I, 245.
[99]*Ibid.*, 443.
[100]See Holdsworth, Vol. I, 376-377.

theless they remained under a standing liability to be summoned to advise the King-in-Council, and the King-in-Council in this aspect turned into the House of Lords. This liability to attend the House of Lords, though only as advisers, rendered the common-law judges ineligible to sit in the House of Commons, just as the peers themselves were ineligible for the popular chamber.[101] But if a judge were a peer as well as being a judge, he was entitled to participate in the non-judicial business of the House of Lords, and there are many instances of his doing so. Indeed the Lord Chancellor normally presides over the House of Lords. The Master of the Rolls was also in an anomalous position. Until 1873, he was allowed to sit in the House of Commons, the last to do so being Sir George Jessel, who was Member of Parliament for Dover while he was Master of the Rolls.[102] By statute all superior-court judges in Britain, including the Master of the Rolls, are now declared incapable of sitting in the House of Commons.[103]

Another critical question in this regard is whether a superior-court judge may also be a member of the cabinet. In theory the king could summon whomsoever he pleased to advise him as a privy councillor and cabinet member, and we find that this was done with some judges in the earlier years of the cabinet system. Unknown either to Parliament or the public, Lord Chief Justice Mansfield of the King's Bench was a member of the cabinet from 1757 to 1765. When the fact became known later there was much adverse comment. In 1806 the issue became one of public controversy both in and out of Parliament when Lord Grenville insisted on appointing Lord Chief Justice Ellenborough of the King's Bench to his ministry. Again adverse criticism was sharp. Todd is of opinion that, since this last incident, it has become established that such appointments are unconstitutional:

> Such an appointment would now be regarded as open to grave constitutional objections . . . because, being an *independent* judicial office, it is incompatible, on true constitutional principles, with the position of a responsible adviser of the crown. For, however pure might be the conduct of one in such a situation, he would be sure to bring suspicion upon the administration of justice before him in all political cases.[104]

The position of the Lord Chancellor is anomalous, but he is the exception that proves the rule. In any event he observes conventional limits on partisanship.

Thus we find established in England the general principle that superior-court judges are to be judges only. They are not to participate in either legislative or executive government as members of the House of Commons or the ministry of the day.

This concludes the present survey of the development in England of the main elements of judicial independence. With respect to the status and function of the central royal courts and their judges, the survey supports Dr. Goodhart's view of judicial independence. One may insist that an autonomous judicature is a

[101]Todd, *ante,* footnote 45, Vol. II, 324.

[102]*Ibid.*, 325-326.

[103]Supreme Court of Judicature (Consolidation) Act, 1925, s. 12(2).

[104]Todd, *ante,* footnote 45, Vol. II, 198.

primary element in the English constitution without denying that Parliament is primary in law-making power. But parliamentary primacy, though it goes very far, does not extend to the point that Parliament could constitutionally overthrow the independent judicature as a co-ordinate institution of first importance in maintaining the rule of law. "The people as a whole, and Parliament itself, recognise that under the unwritten Constitution there are certain established principles which limit the scope of Parliament. It is true that the courts cannot enforce these principles as they can under the Federal system in the United States, but this does not mean that these principles are any the less binding and effective."[105] Now we must turn to the extension of the principle of judicial independence to North America, a process by no means automatic and moreover long delayed.

III. STATUS OF SUPERIOR COURT JUDGES IN COLONIAL NORTH AMERICA

(a) Before the American Revolution

The seventeenth and eighteenth centuries saw extensive settlement and development of the American colonies under British auspices. It was at the beginning of the eighteenth century, when principles of colonial government were already rather well defined, that the Act of Settlement in England provided that judges' commissions should be made *quamdiu se bene gesserint* and their salaries ascertained and established. Looking back, one rather expects to find that this statutory guarantee would have taken effect contemporaneously in overseas territories as well as in Britain. British settlers were deemed to take with them to colonies acquired by settlement most of the common law of England and so much of the total body of English statute law as was applicable in the early days of the colony concerned to conditions in the New World. In addition, there was always the over-riding legislative supremacy of the Imperial Parliament. That body could at any time legislate for the colonies by statutes made applicable to them expressly or by necessary intendment.[106]

Why would not one or the other of these principles of Imperial constitutional law transport the seventh paragraph of the third section of the Act of Settlement to the New World? Certainly the first two sections of the statute were expressly applicable in all British territories, determining as they did (and still do) the succession to the throne. The fourth and last section looks applicable overseas by necessary intendment, and the same comment seems appropriate concerning at least some of the paragraphs of the third section other than the one about the judges. Finally, the seventh paragraph itself is not limited in its terms: it speaks only of judges' commissions in general. Nevertheless, this guarantee of judicial independence was confined in its application to the judges of the central courts of common law in London, and was thus severed from most other parts of the Act of Settlement for purposes of extension overseas. As a matter of legal and

---

[105]Goodhart, *ante,* footnote 1, 55.
[106]See J. E. Read, The Early Provincial Constitutions (1948), 26 Can. Bar Rev. 621.

constitutional history, then, neither the rule of necessary intendment nor the rule of general suitability to early colonial conditions was considered to carry this paragraph of the Act of Settlement to the New World.

In retrospect this seems anomalous, but the reasons lie in the original English conceptions of the basis of colonial government, and partly also in conditions in these early days in the colonies themselves. In the first place, provision for governmental institutions in overseas territories, even after 1688, was almost exclusively a preserve of the royal prerogative. True enough, after 1688, the supremacy of the Imperial Parliament over the royal prerogative could have been asserted at any time, but it was in fact late in the eighteenth century before this happened. The Quebec Act of 1774 was the first important parliamentary intervention to determine the nature of a colonial government. Hence, before 1774, the accepted constitutional position was that full power and responsibility to prescribe the nature of colonial governmental institutions, including the judiciary, rested with the king. He proceeded with the advice and assistance of English ministers and appropriate committees of the Imperial Privy Council, and the critical legal instruments were orders in council, royal proclamations, instructions to colonial governors, or other prerogative acts not requiring the concurrence or even the notice of the English Parliament. It is true, though, that the representative assemblies in the colonies were permitted some influence. Frequently the Crown approved, or at least accepted, statutes of the American colonial assemblies establishing various courts for the colonies concerned. But the superiority of the royal prerogative remained and was asserted on several occasions by royal disallowance of colonial judicature statutes that were disapproved in London.[107] Thus it was natural for English law officers and privy councillors in the early eighteenth century to consider that the Parliament at Westminster was speaking only of English judges in the Act of Settlement and did not intend to take a hand in the details of colonial government. Parliament just did not concern itself with such details of colonial government at this period. Hence the original prerogative power to issue judicial commissions during pleasure simply continued for colo-

---

[107]L. W. Labaree, Royal Government in America (Yale University Press, New Haven, 1930) 380. And see generally chapter IX on the administration of Justice. Henceforth this work will be referred to as Labaree, followed by the page number.

Apparently, even today, the normal rule in British colonies that have not attained full self-government is that judges' commissions run during pleasure only. See *Terrell v. Colonial Secretary*, [1953] 2 All E.R. 490. Here, the claimant had been a judge of the Supreme Court of the Straits Settlements. He alleged that he had been prematurely retired, and that this was contrary to the tenure during good behaviour he enjoyed because the 7th paragraph of the 3rd section of the Act of Settlement applied in Malaya. Lord Justice Goddard seems right in his conclusion that this provision did not apply in Malaya, but, with respect, he is wrong to suggest this was because of the "repeal" of this part of the Act of Settlement by the English Statute Law Revision Act of 1881 (44 & 45 Vict., c. 59). If the life-tenure provision of the Act of Settlement had been carried to Malaya by the rule of necessary intendment, the exception in the Statute Law Revision Act found in section 4(b) would have continued the life-tenure provision after 1881 *in Malaya*. On the other hand, if the life-tenure provision had been extended to Malaya before 1881 by the rule of general suitability, a later repeal in England would not have changed the law of Malaya. There are many examples of this in Canada's legal history. (For the restricted effect of the Enlgish Statute Law Revision Acts, see Halsbury's Statutes of England (2nd ed.) Vol. 24, 451.)

nial judges, untouched by the Act of Settlement. Moreover, this power was jealously guarded in London, as we shall see, by royal disallowance of colonial statutes that were inconsistent with judicial tenure during pleasure for the colonies concerned.

Now we may turn briefly to a general picture of the judicial system that was established in the West Indies and colonial America by this uneasy collaboration between the Privy Council and the colonial governors, on the one hand, and the local assemblies, on the other:

> The Governor, with the consent of his Council, could create courts of justice to administer the common law. It was generally assumed in the eighteenth century that he could create courts of equity—though the legality of the exercise of this power was perhaps more doubtful. But the power to create courts was also claimed by the Assemblies; and Acts were passed to establish new courts. In some places the Governor, or the Governor and Council, acted as a court of Exchequer, as a court of probate, and as a court for matrimonial causes. In many colonies the Governor and Council were the highest court of appeal in the colony; and sometimes the Governor or the Governor and Council sat as a court of Chancery, and administered an equitable jurisdiction.[108]

Also, appeal lay in cases of sufficient importance from the Governor in Council to the Privy Council in London. The judges of these colonial courts were usually appointed by the governor and his executive council as agents under the governor's commission and instructions to exercise the royal appointing power in this respect. The chief justice of a colony was often an exception to this: frequently he was directly appointed at the instance of the Privy Council in London and also paid from London. In any event, with only a few anomalous exceptions, the tenure of office of all colonial judges, London-appointed or not, was during the royal pleasure only.

In addition to the colonial courts proper, there was another group of courts directly and entirely under the control of the British government. "By commission from the Lords of the Admiralty the Governor was given power to act as Vice-Admiral, and to appoint deputies to act as judges and officials of the vice-admiralty courts. In all, twelve such courts were established from New Hampshire and Massachusetts to Barbados."[109] These courts had the customary admiralty jurisdiction, which came to include enforcement of the hated Imperial Acts of Trade and revenue measures like the Stamp Act. Thus they became objects of intense hostility for the American colonists in the contest for power that marked this period. It is the implications of this contest for the judiciary that must now concern us.

The eighteenth century in colonial America witnessed a great constitutional struggle strikingly similar to that of the seventeenth century in England. In America, too, the climax was revolution. The British governments concerned tried to insist on the widest scope for the royal prerogative as a means of detailed control from London, but in opposition the colonists insisted on their ancient

---

[108]Holdsworth, Vol. XI, 59.
[109]*Ibid.*, 60.

common-law rights as Englishmen and on a major part of governmental control for their representative assemblies. It turned out that for the most part the assemblies had the better of the contest because of their financial power, which grew from the same roots as that of the House of Commons in England. One of the ancient common-law rights of an Englishman was that he might not be deprived of his property without his consent. The corollary of this in the field of taxation was "no taxation without representation", but the individual taxpayer was taken to have consented to be taxed through his representatives in the House of Commons if a majority of them agreed there to the tax. The law officers advising the Privy Council considered that this principle of common law had crossed the ocean with the settlers and that a colonial government could not levy taxes in the colony without the consent of a representative colonial assembly. Further, British governments of the day, under prevailing mercantilist theories, considered that colonies should tax themselves and pay their own way. When to these factors is added the financial strain of the French and Indian wars, it is not surprising that the result was to make the royal governors heavily dependent on their respective colonial assemblies for the revenue necessary to carry on.[110] With very few exceptions this included dependence on the assemblies for the salaries of the colonial judges. So it was that often, as a feature of the wider struggle, colonial judges were found to be either pawns or partisans of the governor, on the one hand, or of the "popular faction" in the assembly, on the other. The London authorities and the governors tried to assert their control of judges through the power of appointment and dismissal, whereas the assemblies exerted the pressure by stopping judicial salaries or by imposing conditions on the grant of them.

In these circumstances voices were raised in America asking why the security of tenure granted English judges in the Act of Settlement was not also appropriate for colonial judges. The Jamaica Assembly passed a statute in 1751 prescibing that all judges of the local supreme court were to hold office during good behaviour. The Board of Trade had its parent body, the Privy Council, disallow the legislation, and from 1754 the instructions to all royal governors directed that colonial judicial commissions were to be granted during pleasure only.[111] There was bitter opposition in several colonies, of which New York was typical. The assembly there, with the approval and support of the judges, introduced a bill requiring judicial tenure during good behaviour. Governor Colden indicated that he might work for the acceptance of the bill if the assembly would also make permanent and adequate provision for judicial salaries. But the assembly refused thus to ascertain and establish salaries and would promise only annual appropriations. The Board of Trade held out in the face of a prolonged stoppage of appropriations, and eventually had its way. Judicial tenure in the colony continued to be at pleasure. The reasons of the British government are summarized by Professor Keith as follows.[112]

---

[110]Labaree, 430-431.

[111]*Ibid.*, 390-391.

[112]A. B. Keith, Constitutional History of the First British Empire (Oxford, 1930) 260-261. Keith also points out that, in 1778, royal instructions to Lord Howe to treat with the revolutionaries offered, among other things, to permit the local election of judges, subject to approval of the choice by the Crown, such judges then to enjoy tenure during good behaviour under royal commissions. But it was too late (see 383-384).

The arguments of the Board [of Trade] were in effect that lack of adequate salaries compelled the appointment of men who used the office for their own advancement and often became partisans of a factious Assembly whose support had been regulated . . . by consideration of the measure in which they had served their ends. To give these men ignorant of law tenure during good behaviour, while dependent on the caprice of the Assembly, would be to destroy the interests of individuals and lessen the just dependence of the colony on the mother country. This was sound enough, but it was less convincing to say that, while the change of tenure in England had been due to errors of the Crown, there was no similar need for action in America, for the Assemblies were no doubt justified in regarding the judges as too subservient in many cases to the Governor, who could dismiss them at will, as Cosby had done in the case of Lewis Morris because he decided a salary claim against him. A better argument was based on the difficulty of filling posts satisfactorily and the advantage, when a good judge was available, to be able summarily to vacate an office held by a less fit person. The real solution of permanent tenure and adequate salary appealed to neither party, though neither was candid enough to say so, and the principle was admitted only by both sides in the stress of the revolutionary epoch.

Professor Labaree considers the basic trouble to have been that British officials in London did not appreciate that Englishmen in America would, quite properly, expect essentially the same constitutional rights as Englishmen in England. Particularly as the colonies became more mature and prosperous, the colonial Englishmen simply would not accept the London view that certain parts of the British constitution were not for export.[113]

The American concern with true judicial independence in the eighteenth century may well have been more genuine than Professor Keith concedes. The ninth specification of the Declaration of Independence in 1776 complained of George III that ''He has made the judges dependent on his will alone, for the tenure of their offices, and the amount and payment of their salaries''. Also, in the immediate post-revolutionary decades in the United States, most state constitutions and the federal constitution provided for tenure on the model of the Act of Settlement. ''Thus in the post-revolutionary period in America we find that in general judges were selected by the executive or legislature to serve in most instances during good behaviour.''[114] Indeed so far as the new federal courts were concerned, the complete English guarantees (just as Blackstone conceived them to be) are spelled out in the Constitution of 1789:

> The judicial Power of the United States shall be vested in one supreme Court, and in such inferior Courts as the Congress may from time to time ordain and establish. The Judges, both of the supreme and inferior Courts, shall hold their Offices during good Behaviour, and shall, at stated Times, receive for their Services a Compensation which shall not be diminished during their Continuance in Office.

It is true that the prevailing system today in the state courts of the United States is the election of judges for relatively short and fixed terms, but this was not a result of the American Revolution near the end of the eighteenth century. Rather it was

---

[113]Labaree, 394-395.

[114]Arthur T. Vanderbilt, Cases and Other Materials on Modern Procedure and Judicial Administration (Washington Square Publishing Corporation, New York, 1952) 1164.

a consequence of the surge of Jacksonian democracy in the second and third quarters of the nineteenth century. This movement was characterized, among other things, by the idea that any man could perform any office without special training or qualification, from which it followed that all important officers of government (including judges) should be popularly elected at regular intervals and thus be subject to frequent change. These later developments, and the escape of the federal courts from them, are succinctly described by Chief Justic Vanderbilt of New Jersey.[115]

> We will do well to remember that for the first three quarters of a century of our national history practically all of the judges were appointed. . . . It was the change in New York in 1846 to elected judges that set the pattern for the popular election of all judges for short terms. Within ten years, fifteen of the twenty-nine states existing in 1846 had by constitutional amendment provided for the popular election of judges; and in each of the states that have entered the Union since 1846 all or most of the judges are elected by the people for terms of years. Only the relative unimportance at that time of the federal trial courts, the appointment of new justices in succession to Marshall and his associates, and the difficulty of amending the Federal Constitution saved the United States from an elective judiciary.

Now we must turn our attention to what remained of British North America after the American Revolution.

(b) From the American Revolution to Confederation

The pre-revolutionary contest for power between governor and assembly in the Atlantic colonies was not immediately repeated in the Old Province of Quebec, for the obvious reason that, until 1791, there was no popular assembly in this colony. The Royal Proclamation of 1763 had directed the calling of an assembly, but this was never done, and the Quebec Act of 1774 provided only for an appointed council to act with the governor. This in effect confirmed what had been done since 1763, and an ordinance of the governor and council in 1764 had provided a system of courts for Quebec. This system was not altered by the Quebec Act, though the seventeenth section of that statute carefully reserved the primacy of the royal prerogative in the establishment of courts and the appointment of judges. Except for the assembly, the usual colonial pattern for a judiciary was soon evident. It was still Imperial policy that colonial judicial commissions should run during pleasure only. The royal instructions to Lord Dorchester in 1786 repeated the standard provision of 1754 that judges were to be granted commissions on these terms only.[116] Also, though a real attempt to find a lawyer was usually made, often lawyers were not available for judicial office, and, moreover, pluralism in office-holding was usual. The remarkable story of Adam Mabane, whose professional training had been in medicine at the University of Edinburgh, is an apt illustration. Dr. Hilda Neatby tells us.[117]

---

[115]*Ibid.*, 1165.

[116]A. Shortt and A. G. Doughty, Documents relating to the Constitutional History of Canada (King's Printer, Ottawa, 1918) 822.

[117]Hilda M. Neatby, The Administration of Justice under the Quebec Act (Minneapolis, The University of Minnesota Press, 1937) 55.

His career as a common pleas judge is only half understood unless it is remembered that he was simultaneously pursuing the careers of doctor, legislative councillor, leader and organizer of the French party, criminal court judge, judge in the court of appeals, and confidential adviser successively to the governors, Carleton and Haldimand, and Lieutenant Governor Hope. Governors might come and go, but Mabane stayed on, and the policy that governed Quebec for thiry years was his policy.

No doubt such pluralism was forced by the need to make diversified use of the talent of the few able people available in the early days of a colony, but also it caused the partisan involvement of colonial judges in local politics and made imperial insistence on their tenure at pleasure understandable.

But it is important to appreciate that tenure at the pleasure of the king was not tenure at the pleasure of the colonial governor and council, and the development of this distinction in post-revolutionary British North America brought a significant measure of secure tenure to colonial judges. Indeed, as early as 1670, the instructions to Governor Lynch of Jamaica forbade dismissal of judges or other officials ''without good and sufficient Cause, which you shall signify in the fullest and most distinct Manner to Us by one of Our Principal Secretaries of State and to the Lords of the Committee of Our Privy Council for Trade and Plantations for their Information''.[118] This provision also was standard and is found repeated in the instructions to Lord Dorchester in 1786. It does not seem to have meant too much before the American Revolution, but at least it called upon a governor to explain himself and implied an imperial power of review.

In any event, in 1782 the Westminster Parliament passed the Colonial Leave of Absence Act, which provided for review and confirmation by an appropriate committee of the Privy Council in London of any proposal by a colonial governor and council to dismiss colonial judges and certain other officials. This statute,[119] otherwise known as Burke's Act, was part of the British government's policy of reforming and tightening-up colonial administration in the years immediately following the loss of the American colonies. The effect of the act was that colonial officers appointed under patent from the Crown could not be removed by a colonial governor and council except for persistent absence from the colony without leave, neglect of duty or other misbehaviour in office. The officer to be suspended or removed was entitled to a fair hearing in the colony, and was given a right of appeal to London, ''whereupn such amotion shall be finally judged of and determined by his Majesty in council''. Todd considered that this gave some genuine security of tenure to colonial judges, for the real executive threat to their security lay with the local governor and council.[120] The prerogative power to dismiss appointees at pleasure without cause remained with the king, but after 1782 it could not be said that this royal power was delegated in any measure to colonial governors.

With the passing of the Constitutional Act of 1791,[121] the Old Province of

---

[118]Labaree, 388, and footnote 116.
[119]22 Geo. III (1782), c. 75.
[120]Todd, *ante*, footnote 45, Vol. II, 882.
[121]31 Geo. III, c. 31.

Quebec was split into Upper and Lower Canada. Each colony was to have its own government, including, for the first time in these territories, representative assemblies, and henceforth the superior and inferior courts of each colony were constituted by local legislation of assembly and council. To trace these details of judicature and jurisdiction is beyond the scope of this article, but it is relevant to note that the pre-revolutionary pattern of struggle for power in the American colonies soon became manifest in Upper and Lower Canada, with similar implications for the status of the judiciary. The judges were usually either pawns or partisans of the governor and were often leading members of the executive or legislative councils, or both. Judges were also eligible for seats in the assemblies of both Upper and Lower Canada, and several did hold assembly seats. Occasionally a judge would be found aligned with the popular or reform party of the assembly, and two of these exceptional cases in Upper Canada are of interest in connection with the executive power to dismiss a colonial judge.

In 1806, Robert Thorpe was sent by the Colonial Office to be a justice of the Court of King's Bench in Upper Canada. He is described by the historian Duncan McArthur as "a reckless and irresponsible political adventurer" who immediately took it upon himself to lead the opposition to the administration of the governor, Sir Francis Gore. "His favorite pastime, when on his judicial circuits, was to deliver cheap and ponderous political orations to the assembled populace . . . ".[122] Thorpe secured election to the assembly and continued his activities, whereupon Sir Francis Gore complained to the Colonial Secretary. It turned out that Thorpe had previously been a judge in Prince Edward Island, where he had been removed from his position for similar behaviour, and when Gore's complaint was received Thorpe was again deprived of judicial office. Apparently this was direct removal by the King on the advice of the Colonial Secretary in London, by virtue of the commission at pleasure. It is the only instance of direct prerogative removal the writer has been able to discover in British North America in this period. Thorpe apparently stayed in Upper Canada and continued his political activity.

The second case is that of John Walpole Willis,[123] who also was sent by the Colonial Office to Upper Canada as a judge of the Court of King's Bench, with the intention in this instance that he should become the Vice-Chancellor of the proposed new court of equity when uncertainty over the proper manner of constituting that court could be resolved. Willis was well qualified legally, and well connected politically and socially in England. To make a long story short, he soon found that Upper Canada had an ailing chief justice due for retirement, and that the only real contender to succeed to the post (other than himself) was John Beverley Robinson. Robinson was Attorney-General and a leading member of the local ruling oligarchy centered on the governor, and thus, naturally, was the governor's candidate for the office. Apparently Willis attached himself to and gained favour with the opposition party in the assembly, the reformers, as a

---

[122]*Canada and Its Provinces* (Toronto, 1913), Vol. III, 184-185.
[123]A. Dunham, *Political Unrest in Upper Canada, 1815-1836* (Longmans, Green and Co. Ltd., London, 1927) 111-115.

means of furthering his prospects for judicial advancement. Then followed much intrigue, both social and political. The climax came in 1829 when, in the face of practice and precedent to the contrary, Judge Willis insisted that the Court of King's Bench could not legally sit without a chief justice. He declined to hold court and the work of the King's Bench came to a halt. Governor Maitland thereupon removed him from office, and though Willis had a hearing before the Privy Council, that body confirmed the dismissal. Todd says that this was the first occasion upon which the procedure of Burke's Act was followed.[124]

Notwithstanding the cases of Thorpe and Willis, in Upper and Lower Canada the superior-court judges were usually themselves members of the ruling oligarchy centered in the executive and legislative councils and led by the governor. The familiar type of struggle with the popular party in the assembly ensued, particularly in Lower Canada. In part it took the form of trying to separate the judges from the executive and legislative organs of colonial government. In 1814 the French-Canadian party in the Assembly of Lower Canada tried to impeach Chief Justices Jonathan Sewell and James Monk and, in 1817, Judge Charles Foucher of the King's Bench. There was doubt of the power of the Legislative Council to try an impeachment presented by the Assembly, by analogy to the British House of Commons and House of Lords, and in fact all three cases ended up before the Prince Regent in Council in London and were decided there in favour of the judges.

The motives of the popular party were of course political: they were trying by every means to reduce the power of the governing colonial oligarcy and, as the judges were identified with that group, they were fair game. About 1812 a statute in Lower Canada made judges ineligible to sit in the House of Assembly and eventually, many years later, a similar statute was passed in Upper Canada. Whatever the motives, these were in fact first steps toward establishing the independence of the judiciary, and before the 1830's were out more progress was made, though principally in Upper Canada. This further progress is described by Professor McArthur as follows:[125]

> It was with greater difficulty that the connection between the judges and the executive and legislative councils could be broken. The appointment of judges was a prerogative of the crown, and the crown insisted, as in the case of Justice Kerr in 1832, that no judge should be suspended until it became satisfied that there was adequate cause. The assembly at first sought to obtain control over the judiciary by resort to impeachment. . . . The assembly then directed its energies to securing control over the funds from which the salaries of the judges were paid, in order that by withholding their salaries they might exercise an effective recall. The only choice of the judiciary seemed to be between dependence on one or other political party. Under these circumstances it is not surprising that there should have been but little popular confidence in the independence of the judges. In Upper Canada, where the situation was less acute, a compromise was reached by which the judges were declared to hold office during good behaviour, but were rendered liable to be

---

[124]Todd, *ante*, footnote 45, Vol. II, 883.
[125]Canada and Its Provinces, Vol. IV, 462-463.

removed by joint address of the legislative council and assembly, subject to appeal
to the king in council.

This statute on the King's Bench of Upper Canada in 1834, which was approved
and accepted by the imperial authorities, seems the first statutory requirement for
judicial tenure during good behaviour in British North America. Truly we have
come a long way from the imperial disallowance of a similar Jamaican statute in
1754. Also, about 1830, the imperial authorities made it clear that henceforth
they would not appoint judges to the executive or legislative councils. In Lower
Canada, there was promise of similar developments, but passions grew too hot
and we are told that ''The elevation of the judges to a position of dignity and independence was a task reserved for the statesmanship of the Union period''.[126]

In spite of these steps towards judicial independence, the main governmental problem of conflict between the popular assemblies, on the one hand, and the
councils and governors, on the other, remained, and in 1837 matters reached the
stage of rebellion in both Upper and Lower Canada. Close upon these events
Lord Durham was sent, as High Commissioner and Governor-General of British
North America, to investigate, report and make recommendations. This is no
place to dwell upon the details of Lord Durham's Report. Suffice it to say that, in
spite of certain defects, it was epoch-making in the statesmanlike solution it offered of the ''dilemma of the old empire''. It took the British government about
twelve years to realize this, but the eventual adoption of Durham's principal
recommendations made possible a newly-conceived Commonwealth under the
British Crown, and probably prevented a second American Revolution.

Briefly, Durham recommended that the colonial governor should be instructed to choose his executive from persons who enjoyed the confidence of the
assembly, by whose advice he should be bound, and that colonial legislation
should be permitted to prevail, except in both cases on a few matters of unques-
tioned concern to Britain such as foreign affairs, external trade, ''relations with
the mother country'' and ''the constitution of the form of government''.[127] Immediately after recommending this local application of the British cabinet system
in the colonies, Durham's Report says: ''The independence of the judges should
be secured, by giving them the same tenure of office and security of income as
exist in England''.[128] Upper and Lower Canada were united as Durham recommended, and the independence of the King's Bench judges already achieved in
Upper Canada was extended to Lower Canada.

The historian Edward Kylie describes the completion of the development as
follows:[129]

> In 1843 an act of the Canadian legislature declared it 'expedient to render the
> Judges of the Court of King's Bench in that part of this Province which heretofore
> constituted the Province of Lower Canada, independent of the Crown'. Such judges
> were hereafter to hold their offices during good behaviour, not during pleasure, and

---

[126]*Ibid.*, 463.
[127]The Earl of Durham, A Report on Canada (London, Methuen and Co. Ltd., 1922) 207.
[128]*Ibid.*, 241.
[129]Canada and Its Provinces, Vol. V, 157.

they could be removed only on a joint address of the legislative council and the legislative assembly. In 1849 the same principle was applied to the Court of Queen's Bench and the Superior Court newly constituted in Lower Canada, and to the Courts of Common Pleas and of Chancery in Upper Canada. . . . Meanwhile the removal of the judges from the executive and legislative bodies was being made complete. No justice in any of the courts established in Lower Canada was allowed to sit or vote in the executive council, or in the legislative council or assembly. . . . The judges in the . . . Upper Canadian courts were likewise restricted to the discharge of their peculiar duties.

The removal of judges during a period of ten or fifteen years from membership in the legislative councils, particularly the removal of the chief justices, caused the long-standing appellate jurisdiction of these bodies to lapse. Hence in 1849 we find statutes in the legislature of Canada constituting new and separate appeal courts for the two parts of the colony, perhaps influenced by the example afforded by the statutory court of Exchequer Chamber, mentioned earlier, that was set up in England in 1830. A new Court of Queen's Bench in Lower Canada made up of four judges was given appellate civil and criminal jurisdiction and jurisdiction in error. In Upper Canada a Court of Errors and Appeals was constituted, "formed by the judges of the Court of Queen's Bench, the judges of the Court of Common Pleas, and the judges of the Court of Chancery".[130] Of course, further and final appeal still lay to the Privy Council in London, and during this period the Judicial Committee of the Privy Council, as we have known it in modern times, was provided for in the Imperial Judicial Committee Acts of 1833 and 1844.

Similar steps toward judicial independence are discernible in the history of Nova Scotia—indeed the whole development proceeded more smoothly there than in the Canadas, and in some respects also more rapidly. The usual conflict between the representative assembly and the governor in council eventually reared its head in Nova Scotia, but it never became so violent an issue as in the other American colonies, where it led to revolution in 1776, or in Upper and Lower Canada, where it was marked by rebellion in 1837. The early picture in Nova Scotia (about 1760) was this:[131]

> With little immediate prospect of paying their own way, the Assembly had little incentive either to use or abuse the power of the purse by which the other powers of provincial Assemblies in America had so diligently been extorted. In Nova Scotia as in Georgia the deficits in the cost of civil government were met by the House of Commons, and the power of the purse in effect lay with the British Government. Much of the early prosperity of the province, moreover, was the result of lavish military and naval expenditures during the Seven Years' War. Fish and naval stores were the staple exports. The situation of the province on the threshold of New France gave it an importance out of all proportion to its population and revenues. A measure of accommodation could scarcely fail to result from these mutual interests.

---

[130]*Ibid.*, 158-159.
[131]Chester Martin, Empire and Commonwealth (Oxford, 1929) 71.

The loyalty of Nova Scotians was strengthened at a critical moment when in 1776, at their urging, the reactionary and arrogant Governor Legge was removed by the home government. From 1776 to 1783, also, about 35,000 loyalists came to Nova Scotia from the rebelling colonies to the south and provided an additional element strongly devoted to the British connection. In 1776 the Assembly, in a moderately worded address, did urge upon the British government certain reforms of colonial administration. These included a recommendation that judges of the Nova Scotia Supreme Court should have their commissions during good behaviour. But there was no question of severing the British connection over this or the larger issue dealt with in the address, that of taxation in America by the British Parliament.[132]

Much as in Upper and Lower Canada, complete statutory guarantees of independence for superior-court judges in Nova Scotia accompanied the grant of responsible government about the middle of the nineteenth century, but certain important elements of judicial security were realized by statute and in practice much earlier. In 1754 the Supreme Court of Nova Scotia was established under the royal commission issued in London appointing Jonathan Belcher to be Chief Justice of Nova Scotia and defining his authority.[133] This court has functioned continuously ever since. It consisted soon of a chief justice and two puisne justices. The chief justice was directly appointed in London by prerogative act to hold office during pleasure and was paid from the British treasury. The puisne judges received their commissions, also during pleasure, from the governor and were paid from the colonial revenues. The first chief justice, as had been mentioned, was Jonathan Belcher, a qualified lawyer from New England. He was also legal adviser to the governor and senior member ex officio of the council. Chief Justice Belcher urged that the governor and council could not legally make laws in the colony without the consent of a representative assembly. The Board of Trade accepted the validity of Belcher's representations and insisted that the reluctant governor call an assembly, which was done in 1758. Chief Justice Belcher apparently was the draftsman of much of the early Nova Scotian legislation passed by assembly, council and governor, and his position exemplifies once more the pluralism in office-holding characteristic of early days in a colony.

In any event, with an assembly in being, local statutes took over the regulation of the Supreme Court, and in 1789 we find a Nova Scotian statute[134] remarkable for the extent to which, at this early date, it approached the contemporary English guarantees of judicial independence. As the British government must have accepted it, it represents no doubt the limit to which they were prepared to go at this time in affording security to colonial judges. Clearly, also, the statute in question was drafted with one eye on the English act of 1760 for better effectuating the judicial provisions of the Act of Settlement, quoted earlier. This is the text of the Nova Scotian statute:

---

[132]*Ibid.*, 84.
[133]Charles J. Townsend, History of Courts of Judicature in Nova Scotia (1900), 19 Canadian Law Times, 92.
[134]29 Geo. III, c. 12.

Whereas the independence and uprightness of the Judges are essential to the impartial administration of justice, and has ever been considered as one of the best securities of the rights and liberties of the Subject, in order therefore to make a suitable provision for such appointments and establish the permanency thereof:

I. *Be it enacted*, by the Lieutenant-Governor, Council and Assembly, That there shall be paid annually to the two Puisne Judges of the Supreme Court, during their continuance in office and residence in the Province, the sum of four hundred pounds currency each, which said sum shall be paid out of the public moneys in the Treasury, by warrant from the Governor, Lieutenant-Governor, or Commander in Chief for the time being, on the Treasurer thereof.

II. *Provided always*, That nothing herein contained, shall extend, or be construed to extend, to change the nature of His Majesty's commissions to such Judges, but the Puisne Judges shall be removed at the pleasure of His Majesty, or upon the joint address of the Council and Assembly, to the Governor, Lieutenant-Governor, or Commander in Chief for the time being.

Presumably Burke's Act of 1782 would have ensured review by the Privy Council of any proposed dismissal by joint address of Assembly and Council, but, nevertheless, we do see here the popular assembly guaranteeing judicial salaries from colonial revenues and being accorded a regular and powerful place in the dismissal process. When one bears in mind the events that occurred in New York and other American colonies just a few years earlier, it appears that there was in truth a spirit of sympathy and accommodation between Halifax and London unique at this period.

As in Upper and Lower Canada, further developments belong to the nineteenth century. Except for council membership, statutes during the first twenty-five years of the century disqualified superior-court judges from holding offices other than their judicial ones.[135] About 1830, the British government's decision not to appoint judges to colonial councils in British North America had the effect in Nova Scotia of barring all judges except the Master of the Rolls and the Chief Justice. The Master of the Rolls was barred from the council by local statute in 1836, but the Chief Justice lingered on, and the story of his removal brings Joseph Howe on the scene.

In theory the council in Nova Scotia at this time had two parts, legislative and executive, but in fact it was a single interlocking oligarchy in the hands of a privileged group. Joseph Howe and his party in the Assembly induced that body to address the King asking for a separation of the Council into its two parts, and at the same time criticized the membership of the chief justice in the Council. The address said in part: "This Assembly is convinced that the presence of the Chief Justice at the council board has a tendency to lessen the respect which the people ought to feel for the courts over which he presides . . .". In the debates in the Nova Scotia Assembly that preceded the address, Joseph Howe spelled out his complaint about the chief justice with more colour and detail:[136]

---

[135]Beamish Murdoch, Epitome of the Laws of Nova Scotia (Halifax, Joseph Howe, 1833), Vol. III, 53-54 and footnotes.

[136]William Annand, The Speeches and Public Letters of the Honourable Joseph Howe (Boston, John P. Jewett and Company, 1858) Vol. I, 141 and 106.

Mr. Howe then referred to the influence which the Chief Justice wielded over the hopes, and fears, and prospects of some seventy or eighty lawyers, and several hundred students, spread over the country, who naturally imbibed his political opinions, and were apt to support him against the views and interests of the people. Such men as the learned member from Cape Breton . . . might, from the possession of wealth, or the force of talent, brave this influence; . . . but, nevertheless, over a large class of the less able and independent it was all powerful. For this reason, and many others equally sound, he was anxious to remove the Chief Justice from the Council. Let us, he said, act decisively on that truly British idea, that judges should be kept from the heats and contentions of politics. While we battle with each other in the open fields of political strife, while the conflicts of opinion rage without and within these walls, while we struggle and contend for the mastery, let us have some sacred tribunal to which when blinded and agitated by passion or interest, we can all with confidence appeal.

The Colonial Secretary, Lord Glenelg, agreed with these representations and gave the necessary instructions for their implementation in a despatch dated April 30th, 1837. He said in part, "The principle to be steadily borne in mind and practically observed is, that all the Judges, including the Chief Justice, should be entirely withdrawn from political discussions, and from all participation in the measures of the local government, or of any persons who may be acting in opposition to it".[137] Accordingly, the chief justice disappeared from the Council. One result of this was, as in the Canadas, that the appellate judicial function of that body lapsed. No special statutory provision for a new and distinct appeal court was made before confederation in Nova Scotia. The Supreme Court exercises appellate jurisdiction en banc somewhat on the model of the older procedure on a motion for new trial in the central courts of common law in London.

For present purposes the story in Nova Scotia is completed by a statute of the province in 1848 entitled "An Act to render the Judges of the Supreme Court, and the Master of the Rolls, independent of the Crown, and to provide for their removal".[138] It required that henceforth the judges mentioned should hold their offices during their good behaviour: "Provided always, That it may be lawful for the Governor to remove any Judge of the said Supreme Court, or the Master of the Rolls, upon the Address of the Legislative Council, and House of Assembly, and in case any judge so removed shall think himself aggrieved thereby, it shall be lawful for him, within Six Months, to appeal to Her Majesty, in her Privy Council, and such a motion shall not be final until determined by Her Majesty in Her Privy Council". Nova Scotian judges had not suffered any insecurity in practice, but now, like their brethren in Canada, they were given all the guarantees of the Act of Settlement, plus an appeal to the Privy Council if the local legislature should vote for their removal. Practically speaking, the more important development for their independence seems to have been their earlier removal from local politics.

A word remains to be said about the continuing effect of Burke's Act of

---

[137]*Ibid.*, Vol. II, 523-524.
[138]11 Vict., c. 21.

1782 in this immediate pre-Confederation period. It permitted removal of a colonial judge for misbehaviour by action of the local governor and council alone, subject to appeal to the Privy Council. Being an imperial statute expressly applicable overseas, Burke's Act was not affected by colonial statutes in Nova Scotia or the Canadas which provided for removal by joint address of the two houses of the colonial legislature. Nevertheless, as Todd shows, the accepted position was that, in colonies having such legislation and enjoying responsible government, removal by joint address of the colonial legislature would be the normal way of proceeding. But in painfully obvious cases of "legal misbehaviour" Burke's Act could still be used and a colonial judge suspended or removed without a joint address from the colonial legislature, subject to review in the Privy Council. Todd assimilates this latter type of removal to removal of an English superior-court judge at the instance of the Crown by writ of scire facias in the Queen's Bench to repeal his patent for misbehaviour.[139]

> . . . where the remedy by parliamentary address [in the colony] is open, a judge should only be proceeded against under the statute 22 Geo. III., in a case analogous to that which, in England, would warrant the issue of a writ of *scire facias* to repeal the patent of a judge for misdemeanour in office. If so, the institution of proceedings by a governor and council under the statute, against a delinquent judge, may be looked upon as a substitute for the more formal and less available method of applying for the repeal of a patent granted during 'good behaviour', upon an alleged breach of the condition thereof.

In any event, the writer has not been able to discover any case of removal by joint address or under Burke's Act in British North America after the grant of responsible government.

We have now reached the eve of Confederation in this study, but before going on (in part IV) to the present Canadian position, we may assess briefly the lessons for an independent judiciary of the history reviewed to this point. It seems a proper inference that judicial independence is a governmental virtue in its own right, and throughout the centuries under consideration in England and America there was always significant recognition of this fact. But, also, it is apparent that judicial independence is difficult to attain or maintain when there is a basic contest in the state for legislative and executive power that is being pressed by rival groups to or near the level of rebellion or revolution. England in the seventeenth century, America in the eighteenth century and, to a lesser degree, British North America in the nineteenth century illustrate this. But more significant in the three cases is the fact that each time the guaranteeing of judicial independence was a feature of the settlement of great constitutional conflicts. In England the issues of the seventeenth century were settled in favour of the primacy of parliamentary legislative power over that of the royal prerogative, and this new supremacy was quickly used to restore and guarantee security of judicial tenure and salary. The American colonies in the eighteenth century solved their power-conflict by fracturing the British connection and subjecting their new executives

---

[139]Todd, *ante*, footnote 45, Vol. II 889.

and legislatures to the popular control of common electorates. But their constitutional convention and their new state constitutions soon sanctioned an independent judiciary on the model of the Act of Settlement. In British North America in the nineteenth century the dilemma of the old empire was solved by the grant of responsible government on Durham's plan, and some of the final guarantees of judicial independence came at the same time.

But it is important not to conclude from these last developments that judicial independence in British North America was somehow a function or by-product of responsible government. Judicial independence came in England decades before the rise of the cabinet system. In the United States, judicial independence was achieved immediately after the Revolution in association with executives and legislatures that there separately and directly elected; certainly not with the cabinet system. And, in British North America, several important steps toward an independent judiciary were taken well before the grant of responsible government, indeed well before any conception of the possibility of colonial responsible government had dawned in London. To repeat, then, historical evidence suggests that judicial independence is a distinct governmental virtue of great importance worthy of cultivation in its own right.

IV. CANADIAN SUPERIOR COURTS UNDER THE BRITISH NORTH AMERICA ACT

(a) Introduction: Nature of the judicial plan of the B.N.A. Act

The judicial provisions of the confederation act of 1867[140] make it clear that the federating provinces and the new nation were to continue to follow the model afforded by the English judicature. Here, as in other respects, there was to be "a Constitution similar in Principle to that of the United Kingdom". The existing courts in each province were continued by section 129, subject to certain other provisions of the act that divided power and responsibility for the judicature between provincial and federal authorities. Section 92(14) gave the provinces "exclusive" legislative power over "The Administration of Justice in the Province, including the Constitution, Maintenance, and Organization of Provincial Courts, both of Civil and of Criminal Jurisdiction, and including Procedure in Civil Matters in those Courts".

This is a very wide power, but it is subject to certain important subtractions in favour of the federal authorities. Criminal procedure is an "exclusive" federal legislative category by section 91(27), and sections 96 to 100, inclusive, make collaboration of the federal executive and cabinet necessary to complete the establishment of provincial superior, district or county courts. Section 101 gives the federal parliament an over-riding power to establish certain federal courts. These sections require quotation in full:

> 96. The Governor General shall appoint the Judges of the Superior, District, and County Courts in each Province, except those of the Courts of Probate in Nova Scotia and New Brunswick.

---

[140]30-31 Vict., c. 3.

97. Until the Laws relative to Property and Civil Rights in Ontario, Nova Scotia, and New Brunswick, and the Procedure of the Courts in those Provinces, are made uniform, the Judges of the Courts of those Provinces appointed by the Governor General shall be selected from the respective Bars of those Provinces.

98. The Judges of the Courts of Quebec shall be selected from the Bar of that Province.

99. The Judges of the Superior Courts shall hold office during good Behaviour, but shall be removable by the Governor General on Address of the Senate and house of Commons.

100. The Salaries, Allowances, and Pensions of the Judges of the Superior, District, and County Courts (except the Courts of Probate in Nova Scotia and New Brunswick), and of the Admiralty Courts in Cases where the Judges thereof are for the Time being paid by Salary, shall be fixed and provided by the Parliament of Canada.

101. The Parliament of Canada may, notwithstanding anything in this Act, from Time to Time, provide for the Constitution, Maintenance, and Organization of a General Court of Appeal for Canada, and for the Establishment of any additional Courts for the better Administration of the Laws of Canada.

To summarize, the result is that minor courts in the provinces, such as those of magistrates or justices of the peace, are entirely within provincial control. District, county or superior courts of the provinces, including provincial appellate courts, require the collaboration of provincial and federal authorities for their establishment and maintenance. Then at the apex of the structure is the "General Court of Appeal for Canada", the Supreme Court of Canada, entirely constituted by the federal parliament and executive.

There is not, generally speaking, any division of jurisdiction in these courts corresponding to the division of legislative powers between the provincial legislatures and the federal parliament. In general they "administer justice" concerning all types of laws, whether such laws fall legislatively within the purview of provincial legislatures or the federal parliament. Indeed, the final appellate jurisdiction of the Supreme Court of Canada in this plenary sense cannot be impaired or excluded by provincial legislation.[141] It is true that the federal parliament could go a long way, perhaps all the way, in placing exclusive original jurisdiction to administer laws legislatively within its range in the hands of purely federal courts, under the closing words of section 101. To a quite limited degree this has happened in the case of the Exchequer Court of Canada, but, with this exception, there is no significant vertical division in the Canadian judicial system corresponding to the division between the separate systems of state and federal courts in the United States.

Keeping in mind that this article is confined to superior courts, two matters now await our attention. They are (i) the tenure and salaries of superior-court judges in Canada, and (ii) the existence of a separation of powers in Canada in the sense of a constitutionally guaranteed jurisdiction for superior courts. These two problems will be considered first in relation to provincial superior courts and then in relation to federal superior courts.

---

[141]*Crown Grain Co. Ltd. v. Day,* [1908] A.C. 504.

(b) Provincial superior-court judges: Federal powers and responsibilities

Even were there no other evidence, a mere reading of sections 96 to 100 of the B.N.A. act discloses the intention to reproduce superior courts in the image of the English central royal courts. By section 96 appointment of provincial superior-court judges remains a royal prerogative, now to be exercised by the Governor General under control of the federal cabinet. Also, by sections 97 and 98 such judges must be lawyers drawn from the bars of their respective provinces. Section 99 is obviously a close reproduction of the famous provisions for tenure during good behaviour and removal by joint parliamentary address of the Act of Settlement. Finally, section 100 requires that the salaries of superior-court judges "shall be fixed and provided by the Parliament of Canada". The Act of Settlement said salaries were to be "ascertained and established", but it seems obvious that "fixed and provided" was intended to convey the same meaning. It is a fair conclusion, then, that provincial superior-court judges are assimilated respecting appointment, tenure, removal and security of salaries to the position of the judges of the historic English superior courts after the Act of Settlement.

This is simple to say, but some of its implications need further development. In the first place, the cumulative effect of sections 96 to 100 inclusive is to assign by necessary implication to the federal parliament *legislative* power over the appointment, tenure and removal of provincial superior-court judges, *subject to the limitations contained in these sections themselves*. The assignment of legislative power over judicial salaries is express, subject to the same limitations. As shown in part II of this essay, the case of *Buckley v. Edwards* is authority that, in England, parliamentary provision for the necessary salary has to be assured by statute before a judicial vacancy can be said to exist. Likewise in Canada then it would seem that, unless and until the federal parliament has provided for the necessary salaries, judicial vacancies for provincial courts within section 96 do not exist, even though the provinces have done their part. In other words, both must act to create a superior-court judgeship. Accordingly, there is a specific constitutional basis for the position taken by Mr. St. Laurent in 1946 when, as Minister of Justice, he was speaking in debate on amendments to the federal Judges Act. He said of the provinces:[142]

> They are the ones who determine what courts they will have and how many judges constitute the bench of each court. Of course we have something to say in the matter. We do not admit that they can provide for any number of judges, a number that would be out of all proportion to the number required to handle the judicial business. But we try to meet the desires of the provincial authorities in providing sufficient judges for the courts which they organize as being the ones required for their local needs.

No doubt this necessity for collaboration means that either a perverse federal government or a perverse provincial one could impair or deadlock the administration of justice in the superior or county courts of a given province. But we are

---

[142]Debates, House of Commons, Dominion of Canada, Session 1946, Vol. IV, 3732.

here at the primary level of constitutional power and duty, where one must assume that the two authorities will collaborate willingly with a due sense of responsibility to establish and maintain necessary courts.

Coming now to the tenure during good behaviour prescribed in section 99, this also has the same meaning as in England. Accordingly, successive federal governments have taken the view that here is a constitutional guarantee of tenure for life that forbids any federal statutory provision for an automatic and compulsory retirement age for superior-court judges. Whether or not on other grounds one considers this regrettable, it seems the proper legal conclusion for the reasons given in part II of this article.

Also, as in England, it is probable that the provision for removal of superior-court judges by joint address in the federal Parliament is additional to, and thus not exclusive of, the older prerogative type of removal without reference to Parliament. This was fully discussed in part II of this essay in connection with the corresponding provision of the Act of Settlement. Indeed, there is a procedure for removal of a superior-court judge in the federal Judges Act[143] without reference to Parliament which, if it is justified at all, must rest upon this older prerogative. Section 31 reads as follows:

> A judge who is found by the Governor in Council, upon report of the Minister of Justice, to have become incapacitated or disabled from the due execution of his office by reason of age or infirmity shall, notwithstanding anything in this Act, cease to be paid or to receive or to be entitled to receive any further salary, if the facts respecting the incapacity or disability are first made the subject of inquiry and report as provided in section 33, and the judge is given reasonable notice of the time and place appointed for the inquiry and is afforded an opportunity by himself or his counsel of being heard thereat and of cross-examining witnesses and adducing evidence on his own behalf.

Section 33 provides that the commission of inquiry into the facts shall be composed of one or more judges of federal or provincial superior courts. Dr. R. MacGregor Dawson tells us that there has been considerable recent use of this procedure, in the sense that a threat to employ it has so far in each case brought in the desired resignation from the allegedly disabled judge.[144]

But it is very doubtful that this is a constitutionally permissible procedure. True enough, the Governor General in Council is now, in every respect concerning the federal range of subjects, in full possession of the royal prerogative powers for Canada. Probably these include the ancient right of the Crown to effect forfeiture of a grant of office during good behaviour for breach of the condition of the grant, that is, for failure by the grantee to conduct himself well in the office. Todd seems to have suggested that "incapacity from mental or bodily infirmity" might have constituted a sufficient breach of the condition for this type of removal in England, but there do not seem to have been any instances of it. Anyway, such a forfeiture, though moved by the Crown, required confirmation

---

[143]R.S.C., 1952, c. 159.
[144]R. MacGregor Dawson, The Government of Canada (Toronto, The University of Toronto Press, 2nd ed., 1954) 475.

by the Court of King's Bench in proceedings for a writ of *scire facias*. Perhaps sections 31 and 33 of the Judges Act can be regarded as laying down simpler procedure for the exercise of this crown right to forfeit a conditional grant of office for breach of the condition of the grant. But it seems that the inquiring superior-court judges only report on the facts, the critical determination of the existence of the fatal degree of incapacity being left to the federal cabinet. Hence this is no mere procedural regulation of the old crown right of forfeiture under which a superior court had the last word; it is the vesting of a new power in the federal executive. On both precedent and principle, if there is to be such non-parliamentary removal of a superior-court judge, the last word should rest with other superior-court judges and not with the political executive. In my view section 31 of the Judges Act is inconsistent with the meaning of tenure during good behaviour prescribed in section 99 of the B.N.A. Act.

But, it may be answered, section 31 is not "removal", it is merely stoppage of salary. This of course is a quibble. Complete stoppage of salary (and pension rights) is removal by subterfuge. And anyway, even at face value, the subterfuge is unconstitutional. Presumably the idea is that an adverse determination under section 31 for a particular judge completely stops his salary but leaves his commission running and in force. It will be recalled that Blackstone said of the English superior-court judges that "their full salaries are absolutely secured to them during the continuance of their commissions". The words "fix and provide" in section 100 of the B.N.A. Act put Canadian superior-court judges in this same position, which leads to the conclusion that section 31 of the Judges Act is ultra vires because repugnant to section 100 of the B.N.A. Act. Further, anyone who argues that the salary can be stopped while the commission continues must admit that this is no mere procedural streamlining of the old crown right to effect forfeiture. The result of the latter was to terminate the commission itself and ipso facto stop the salary.

Finally, Burke's Act of 1782 offers no foundation for section 31 of the Canadian Judges Act. Burke's Act probably was repealed by necessary implication from the passing of sections 96 to 101 of the B.N.A. Act in 1867, these being inconsistent provisions of a later imperial statute. But if it was not, then the Statute of Westminster of 1931, the Privy Council Appeals case of 1946, and the new letters patent of the Governor General of 1947, singly or in combination, are fatal to Burke's Act. Perhaps there is need for a speedy procedure to remove superior-court judges in extreme cases of disability resulting from age or infirmity, but salary-stoppage by the executive is no way to do it and is probably ultra vires, as the whole course of English and Coloninal judicial history indicates it should be. If there is to be a non-parliamentary procedure at all, the last word should rest with other superior-court judges.

In the matter of salary security, it is interesting that a federal government recently acted on the Blackstonian version of the meaning of security-of-salary provisions like section 100 of the B.N.A. Act, though not in connection with alleged judicial disability. In 1932 the problem of including judges in a general salary-cutting statute for the civil service was before the Canadian House of

Commons. As shown in part II of this essay, the same issue was a matter of controversy in England in 1931 and 1932. The Canadian government proposed a ten per cent statutory salary deduction for the civil service, but the judiciary were specifically exempted. Prime Minister Bennett said of this:[145]

> The judges are not included in this measure. It has been contended by legal authority, and an article in the last issue of the Law Quarterly Review goes into the matter rather fully, that it would be a breach of the statutory rights of judges to undertake to make a curtailment of their salaries in this way. There are, however, other methods by which the matter may be dealt with, and the government has not finally determined what action it may take in that regard.

Undoubtedly the article referred to was Sir William Holdsworth's, which has been explained and approved in part II of this essay. When in his turn the Minister of Justice, Mr. Hugh Guthrie, was pressed to explain the exemption of judges, he made it clear that he held the same view of the importance of the judiciary and of the security of their salaries as Holdsworth.[146] But there was much pressure to extend the deduction to judges, and eventually the cabinet gave in. The result was a special Income Tax Act to levy an additional tax of ten per cent for one year on judicial salaries. The Minister of Justice asserted that this action was justified by a Privy Council decision on the taxing power of the federal parliament. He must have been referring to *Caron v. The King* in 1924,[147] but on examination this case does not support the validity of a discriminatory tax of this character, only of a non-discriminatory tax. Also, as shown in part II of this essay, the Judicial Committee in 1937 reiterated this principle of non-discrimination respecting judges in upholding the validity of applying a general provincial income tax to them.[148] It looks as if the special taxing statute of 1932, as a taxing statute, was ultra vires the federal parliament. A general income tax of ten per cent on all public salaries might have been valid to effect the total object, including the judicial salaries.

Finally, in this regard, while Holdsworth argued for security of judicial salaries in England partly as a matter of statutory construction, the argument is stronger in Canada. The words "fixed and provided" are specially entrenched in the constitutional sense as part of section 100 of the B.N.A. Act and hence confer a guarantee of salary to superior-court judges that cannot be impaired by an ordinary federal statute. It might be contended that since 1949 this has ceased to be so, for in that year the new subsection (1) of section 91 of the B.N.A. Act gave the federal parliament new power to amend the Canadian Constitution.[149] But it is very doubtful if this new power reaches sections 96 to 101 inclusive of the B.N.A. Act, 1867. The new section 91(1) says that the federal Parliament may by ordinary statute provide for "The Amendment from time to time of the Constitution of Canada, except as regards matters coming within the classes of

---

[145]Debates, House of Commons, Dominion of Canada, Session 1932, Vol I, 562.
[146]*Ibid.*, pp. 829-831.
[147][1924] A.C. 999.
[148]*Ante,* p. 179?
[149]13 Geo. VI, c. 81 (Imperial).

subjects by this Act assigned exclusively to the Legislatures of the provinces, or as regards rights or privileges by this or any other Constitutional Act granted or secured to the Legislature or the Government of a Province . . .''. Under sections 96 to 100 of the B.N.A. Act, 1867, the legislatures or the governments of the provinces have been entitled to expect that, when they constituted necessary superior courts under section 92(14), there would be federal appointees to head these courts who would be superior-court judges as were the judges of the English central royal courts after the Act of Settlement. This is surely a right or privilege secured to the legislature or the government of a province as such from 1867. In other words, the provincial authorities are not merely forced to rely on federal collaboration to create and maintain necessary provincial superior courts, they are *entitled* to such collaboration. Also, so far as section 101 is concerned, the provincial interest in the "General Court of Appeal for Canada" is obvious. This body hears appeals on provincial laws and now rules finally on the distribution of legislative powers itself. The provincial authorities are entitled to expect that the Supreme Court of Canada shall be and shall continue to be in every respect a superior court, a point to be dealt with more fully later.

Thus the writer arrives at the view that sections 96 to 101 inclusive of the B.N.A. Act are still specially entrenched, that is to say, are subject to alteration only by a process of constitutional amendment involving the consent of the provinces as well as of the federal Parliament. Admittedly this leaves us with the problem of the judge who is unaware, or unwilling to concede, that incapacity has supervened due to age or infirmity, but some way should be found to deal with this that does not threaten judicial independence. An automatic retiring age enacted by proper constitutional amendment would solve much of the difficulty. More generous pension provisions, particularly for the wives of judges, would also help.

(c) Guaranteed jurisdiction of provincial superior courts respecting interpretation and application of laws within section 92 of the B.N.A. Act

Problems of tenure are not the only ones raised by the constitutional provisions under consideration. Sections 96 to 100 have been judicially construed to impose a separation of powers at the provincial level in favour of the provincial superior courts. So we must ask what is the test delineating the separation or defining the limits of the guarantee. It is here that most of the case law on the Canadian judicature is concentrated, and several leading essays in this journal have covered the field exhaustively. Mr. John Willis,[150] Dr. Morris Shumiatcher[151] and Professor Bora Laskin[152] all agree that interpretation has confirmed a substantial separation of powers, but Mr. Willis and Professor Laskin express doubts whether such a result should have been derived from the words of section 96, in particular, and

---

[150]John Willis, Section 96 of the British North America Act (1940), 18 Can. Bar Rev. 517.

[151]M. C. Shumiatcher, Section 96 of the British North America Act Re-examined (1949), 27 Can. Bar Rev. 131.

[152]Bora Laskin, Municipal Tax Assessment and Section 96 of the British North America Act (1955), 33 Can. Bar Rev. 993.

the other sections on the judicature. A further detailed review of the cases is not necessary or possible in this article, but, as I consider the guarantee of jurisdiction to provincial superior courts to be *necessarily* implied in sections 96 to 101 of the B.N.A. Act, some reasons for my position need to be given.

To clear the way for the right explanation of this necessary implication, one must first dispose of a false explanation frequently offered to justify such a separation of powers. We must reject the idea that natural law or legal science gives us a neat threefold material division of governmental functions into the legislative, the administrative and the judicial. If such a division were possible as a matter of substance, then a guaranteed separation of powers could be based upon it. One would merely need to insist that only courts could exercise the judicial function, only legislatures could legislate, and so on. But authorities like Sir Ivor Jennings[153] and Professor Hans Kelsen[154] have made it clear by reason and illustration that no such threefold division exists. At times, in the cases on section 96 of the B.N.A. Act and in those on the supervision of inferior tribunals by the prerogative writs, the judges have reached for this distinction. But the resulting confusion confirms that Jennings, Kelsen and others of like mind are right to insist that no functional test exists.

My analysis proceeds on the footing that the nature of governmental functions permits only a twofold material classification of powers or functions. The state is a legal animal, and there are only two functions to perform in relation to laws: either you make laws or you apply them to the persons and circumstances their terms contemplate. So, functionally, there is only the distinction between law-making and law-applying, and even between these two there is a twilight zone. The primary law-making or legislative power in Canada resides in representative legislatures, though they delegate some limited powers of this nature to subordinate tribunals and officials. The law-applying power is assigned to a great variety of persons variously described as administrative, executive or judicial officers or tribunals. Primarily the judicial tribunal or court merely offers one system or method of applying laws. Administrative or executive officers and tribunals offer other and different systems or methods of applying laws. The question of guaranteed jurisdiction for superior courts as against administrative tribunals comes then to this: Are there some laws which the legislature concerned must entrust for interpretation and application exclusively to superior courts?

Now to reason in this way is not to discount the status of the courts, particularly the superior courts. What we must seek is understanding of the real basis of their importance. The superior courts, because of their unique combination of institutional characteristics and procedural practices, occupy a primary and central place in the total law-applying process. The prototype for the superior court is supplied by the English central royal courts after the Act of Settlement. It is this history alone that defines for us the essential institutional and procedural charac-

---

[153]See, Sir W. Ivor Jennings, The Law and the Constitution (University of London Press, 4th ed., 1952), Appendix I starting 265.

[154]Hans Kelsen, General Theory of Law and State (Cambridge, Harvard University Press, 1949) *passim*.

teristics of these tribunals. There is no "judicial function" as such in legal or political theory that will perform this office of definition for us. Thus the "judicial function" with which this article is concerned is simply law-applying by superior courts on the English model. Of course, since he who would apply a law must interpret its meaning, interpretation is a part of law-applying.

We must consider the guarantee of jurisdiction to the provincial superior courts in Canada in these terms. What law-applying tasks should be a monopoly of the superior courts? What legislative schemes are by their nature such that they should be entrusted for interpretation and application to superior courts, to the exclusion of administrative tribunals or executive officials? This is a matter of substantive jurisdiction to interpret and apply particular types of laws, legislative schemes or statutes, and here also the English example has operated and is indispensable. In other words, the standard way to create a superior court has been and is to follow the English model in substantive jurisdiction as well as in the appointment, tenure and payment of judges. In this regard, both before and after 1867 in British North America, our judicature statutes have recited that the local superior court is to have in its territory jurisdiction equivalent to that enjoyed by the English central royal courts of common law and chancery. So there is typical superior-court jurisdiction just as there are typical superior-court institutional characteristics.

But Mr. Willis and Professor Laskin, if I understand them correctly, have argued that when a provincial legislature passes laws within section 92 of the B.N.A. Act, it should have a fully free choice as to the institutional arrangements to prevail for the administration of those laws. That is, they seem to say that a provincial legislature should be free to assign or re-assign the law-applying power and task concerning any law within the scope of section 92 to a provincial administrative tribunal or executive official, rather than to a provincial superior court. Moreover, they assert, there is nothing in the normal meaning of the words in sections 96 to 100 of the B.N.A. Act to dictate a different result, any contrary implication being an unwarranted judicial gloss on these "plain" words. Thus they argue in favour of a purely institutional test of the position of a superior court for purposes of these sections. If it were alleged that a provincial tribunal was not properly constituted because of sections 96 to 100, the only question would be whether the provincial legislation had given the tribunal the institutional characteristics of a superior court. If it was clear that the province had intended to create a superior court on the English model in this sense, then and only then would it be necessary to await federal appointment of a chief officer under section 96 on the terms of sections 97 to 100. On this view one would not look to the nature of the statute assigned to the provincial tribunal for administration and ask—Is this the sort of thing that only a superior court should do? One would ask only—Did the province intend that this tribunal should employ superior-court procedure and that it should be headed by a member of the legal profession on terms of tenure, payment, exclusion from other governmental office, and so on, characteristic of the English superior-court judge? If the answer to such questions were negative, then a provincial appointee could head the tribunal and to the tribunal could be assigned the administration of any law within the scope of section 92 of the B.N.A. Act. There would be no testing of the matter by typical superior-court jurisdiction in substance.

At the most, an exclusive institutional test like this would mean that the whole of the interpretation and application of laws within section 92 of the B.N.A. Act could be withdrawn from provincial superior courts and vested in provincial administrative (that is, non-curial) tribunals or provincial minor courts. Mr. Willis seems to think there are enough political and practical inhibitions to prevent this extreme result, but I do not share his faith. There have been several famous (or notorious) feuds between certain provincial governments and certain federal governments. Often different political parties are in control at Ottawa and in provincial capitals. I should fear that at times a provincial government, if it were free to do so, would commit at least some important laws within section 92 for administration to non-curial tribunals *just to place provincial appointees in control of the law-applying process*, regardless of how desirable curial administration in the superior-court sense might be for that type of law. Probably, for laws within the scope of section 92 of the B.N.A. Act, this would also have the effect of defeating the plenary appellate jurisdiction intended by section 101 of the B.N.A. Act for the "General Court of Appeal for Canada". To the extent that *non-curial* provincial tribunals had a monopoly of the law-applying process for laws within section 92, there would be no *court* of last resort in the province to which the appellate jurisdiction of the Supreme Court of Canada could attach. Since the purely institutional test is pregnant with these undesirable results, it is fortunate that a different line of interpretation has prevailed in the Canadian courts and the Judicial Committee of the Privy Council. Another test has been used, which we shall now examine.

This other test is based squarely on the typical jurisdiction in substance of superior courts rather than on the typical institutional characteristics of superior courts. It is the nature of the law-applying task in issue that is crucial. One focuses on the statute or legislative scheme to be applied and asks—Is this statute of such a nature that clearly it ought to have a superior-court administration rather than a non-curial administration? If the answer is affirmative, then the statute in question must be committed to a provincial superior court for authoritative interpretation and application to the persons and circumstances contemplated by it. If the answer is negative, only then may the province commit the law-applying task to a non-curial provincial tribunal.

My submission is that this is the basis and purport of the judgments in the leading cases on section 96 of the B.N.A. Act. In *Toronto v. York*[155] in 1938 it was decided that binding interpretation of a contract without limit and in the abstract was a typical superior-court task, and hence power to do this could not be given the Ontario Municipal Board, though the board could be given a price-fixing power, since that was not a legal task for which a superior court was appropriate or necessary. A power to fix or set prices is a delegated legislative

---

[155][1938] A.C. 415.

power in these circumstances. In the recent case of *Toronto v. Olympia*,[156] the ruling was that only a superior court was appropriate to interpret and apply with finality provincial laws defining the types of property respecting which the owners were to be liable to direct provincial property taxation, whereas tax assessors and provincial tribunals that were not superior courts could finally interpret and apply the laws by which valuation of items of property assumed or admitted to be taxable was to be accomplished. Thus the issue of taxability was separated from that of valuation, though both involved the interpretation and application of provincial laws. In the *John East* case,[157] it was held that the provincial statute there in question provided a new plan for the regulation of industrial labour relations by certification and collective bargaining—a scheme that was not by its nature appropriate for superior-court administration. Therefore it was intra vires the province to assign the administration of the statute to a purely provincial tribunal that was not a superior court. In short, the provincial superior courts do have an irreducible core of substantive jurisdiction assured to them, in that there are some law-applying tasks within the scope of section 92 that must be entrusted to them.

It has been objected that this fixes on provincial governments a separation of powers respecting the mode of administration of provincial laws that is rigidly determined by the dead hand of history—the state of typical superior-court jurisdiction in 1867. It is true of course that, just as we have to look to English legal history for typical superior-court institutional characteristics, so we must pay some attention to the same history to determine typical superior-court jurisdiction. But this test of jurisdictional substance is not necessarily either rigid or out of tune with modern times because it has historical elements, as a careful reading of the *John East* case shows. The test of the *John East* case is, quite simply, to ask whether the provincial legislative scheme concerned is the sort of thing a superior court ought to administer. Of course this question has to be asked in the light of (i) the sort of institution a superior court is, and (ii) the sort of substantial jurisdiction that has been historically typical of superior courts. History is not a series of accidents, and the historical reasons for a given type of superior-court jurisdiction might still be valid, or there might be new reasons why such superior-court jurisdiction would make modern sense. Historical analogy is certainly involved, but there is a lot of history, and analogy is itself a very flexible instrument. So, if historical analogy is employed with perception and imagination, there need not be any dead hand irrelevant to modern times resting on this guarantee of superior-court jurisdiction. In the *John East* case, Lord Simonds makes this very clear:[158]

> It is legitimate therefore to ask whether, if trade unions had in 1867 been recognized by the law, if collective bargaining had then been the accepted postulate of industrial peace, if, in a word, the economic outlook had been the same in 1867 as it became in 1944, it would not have been expedient to establish just such a

---

[156]*Toronto v. Olympia Edward Recreation Club Ltd.*, [1955] S.C.R. 454.
[157]*Labour Relations Board of Saskatchewan v. John East Iron Works Ltd.*, [1949] A.C. 134.
[158]*Ibid.*, 150-151.

specialized tribunal as is provided by sec. 4 of the Act. It is as good a test as another of 'analogy' to ask whether the subject-matter of the assumed justiciable issue makes it desirable that the judges should have the same qualifications as those which distinguish the judges of superior or other courts.

In other words, given the institutional virtues and limitations of a superior court on the English model, is administration of this statutory plan for labour relations a legal task peculiarly appropriate to a superior court or is it not? Analogy to past instances of superior-court jurisdiction in England and British North America before 1867 may be helpful and indeed, if analogy is very close, it may be decisive. But historical analogy is often quite tenuous, and moreover competing analogies frequently turn up and compel resort to non-historical criteria anyway. As Dr. Shumiatcher has made admirably clear, the *John East* case means that the emphasis is on the answer of the reasonable man in modern circumstances about the desirability of superior-court administration of the statute in question, with whatever subsidiary aid history may afford. In the *John East* case itself, this test favoured the provincial tribunal, but the same test is just as likely in other cases to confer new jurisdiction on the superior courts as to deny it to them. Thus it does not freeze either the provincial superior courts or the provincial non-curial tribunals to the actual or potential jurisdictional scope they respectively had in 1867. Rather, the *John East* case sanctions a test whereby new legislative schemes not contemplated in 1867 may be assigned either to superior courts or to provincial tribunals that are not superior courts, as appropriate. Indeed this test would permit some reassignment of old items of jurisdiction either way due to radical change in relevant circumstances and conditions.

There is no doubt then of this result as a matter of authoritative interpretation, but is it an unwarranted gloss on the "plain" words of sections 96 to 100 of the B.N.A. Act? A common view is that this implication of guaranteed jurisdiction arises from the significance of the federal appointing power in section 96, and surprise is expressed that a mere appointing power can mean so much. I do not think the implied guarantee of jurisdiction rests on so slender a foundation. It arises from the cumulative effect of all the judicature sections of the B.N.A. Act. These provisions collectively make it clear that the B.N.A. Act contemplates the continued existence and functioning of superior courts on the English model as basic institutions of our form of government. This and nothing less is what calls for the necessary implication of a substantive separation of powers in favour of provincial superior courts. It would be absurd to permit such courts to be denuded of all substantial jurisdiction so that they would continue, if at all, merely as empty institutional shells. The only peculiar thing that section 96 does is to provide a simple negative test of whether the provincial tribunal whose jurisdiction is being challenged is a superior court. If the provincial legislation did not leave it to be headed by a federal appointee, it cannot be a superior court, whatever else it may be, *and one gets straight on to the real question—whether the statutory provision it was to administer is appropriate in modern circumstances for exclusive superior-court administration.*

I should still find this necessary implication of a substantial separation of powers if the B.N.A. Act had provided that provincial superior-court judges were to be appointed by the provincial cabinets and their salaries fixed and provided by provincial statute, subject to sections 97 to 99 inclusive as they stand, and subject to the plenary appellate jurisdiction of the "General Court of Appeal for Canada" in section 101. The Privy Council seems to have proceeded on this wider basis of implication, as the following statement from *Toronto v. York* indicates:[159]

> While legislative power in relation to the constitution, maintenance and organization of Provincial Courts of Civil Jurisdiction . . . is confided to the Province, the independence of the judges is protected by provisions that the judges of the Superior, District, and County Courts shall be appointed by the Governor General (s. 96 . . .), that the judges of the superior courts shall hold office during good behaviour (s. 99), and that the salaries of the judges of the Superior, District, and County Courts shall be fixed and provided by the Parliament of Canada (s. 100). These are three principal pillars in the temple of justice, and they are not to be undermined.

Further support for this broad type of implication is found in the parallel afforded by the *Alberta Press* case.[160] There Chief Justice Duff said that the British North America Act presumed the continuance of the federal parliament as a representative and democratic legislature, and that hence the free public opinion necessary as a foundation could not be undermined by restrictions on the freedom of the press attempted by provincial legislation. Also, Viscount Haldane said in the reference on the Initiative and Referendum Act of Manitoba[161] that a provincial legislature can not efface itself or abolish itself. In other words, he said that section 92 of the B.N.A. Act presumes and prescribes the continuance of provincial legislatures with the primary legislative functions there given. The implication that the B.N.A. Act contemplates the continuance of provincial superior courts with a guaranteed core of substantive jurisdiction is of the same order.

Finally, this guaranteed core includes appellate as well as original jurisdiction. Professor Laskin makes a very valuable point in his article on the *Olympia* case when he explains the flexibility this could bring to arrangements for the administration of provincial laws. The point seems to have been neglected in cases on the subject. Yet, as shown in part II of this article, some form of appellate jurisdiction has always been a feature of the powers of the central royal courts, and it is typical superior-court jurisdiction past and present that concerns us. To find a measure of guaranteed appellate jurisdiction would mean that it would be within the powers of a province to commit certain provincial laws to provincial non-curial officials, tribunals or minor courts in the first instance, but beyond the powers of a province then to forbid appeal from them to a superior court.

Take for example the historic King's Bench function to determine by the prerogative writs whether an inferior tribunal or government official is acting

---

[159][1938] A.C. 426.
[160]*Reference re Alberta Statutes*, [1938] S.C.R. 100.
[161][1919] A.C. 935, 945.

within his powers under the statutes that confer them. This may be technically an original jurisdiction, but in reality it is the entertaining of an appeal from a non-curial or minor court determination. The inferior tribunal that is being charged with having acted ultra vires must in the first instance have acted on its own determination of what its own powers were. On this view, the disregard by superior courts of privative clauses in provincial statutes is constitutionally sound, for the clauses would deny their guaranteed reviewing or appellate jurisdiction. On this view, the provinces cannot deny to the superior courts power to review and determine finally the scope of statutory and common-law powers conferred on provincial government officials or on provincial minor courts or non-curial tribunals. As explained in part II of this essay, the Court of King's Bench exercised from early times ''a general superintendence of the due observance of law by officials and others''. I should think it remains a matter of governmental necessity that the last word on such distributions and divisions of powers is peculiarly appropriate to superior courts. Indeed, as shown in part II, it is historically characteristic of superior courts that they determine even the limits of their own powers under the relevant constitutional laws and statutes.

It has been suggested that judges, being human, will tend to enlarge unduly the area of their own guaranteed jurisdiction under the B.N.A. Act. But any governmental official or tribunal will feel this inflationary or imperialistic tendency to expand the area of power, and nevertheless someone must have the last word. As will be argued in part V, superior-court judges, on the whole, are the group of official persons least likely to seek unduly to expand their own powers. That is one purpose and effect of their unique independence and security. Hence it is no accident that historically the superior courts have been entrusted with determining finally, not only the limits of their own powers, but those of other governmental officials and bodies as well.[162] And, in a federal country, it is necessary to rely on the superior courts for determination of the original distribution of legislative powers itself.

(d) The federal superior courts

Section 101 of the B.N.A. Act contemplates the establishment of federal superior courts. This arises from the use of the word ''court'' in the section, and indeed the ''General Court of Appeal for Canada'' would necessarily and pre-eminently be a superior court on the English model. To consider that section 101 could mean anything else would be so incongruous as to be absurd. Also, the Exchequer Court of Canada has been created under this power with the characteristics of a superior court, both institutional and jurisdictional. The two questions considered about the provincial superior courts now arise again for the federal superior courts and their judges. Do sections 99 and 100 of the B.N.A. Act about tenure and salary limit the federal Parliament respecting such judges, and, in any event, do the federal courts have guaranteed jurisdiction that is specially entrenched in the sense already explained?

---

[162]See, Louis L. Jaffe and Edith G. Henderson, Judicial Review and the Rule of Law: Historical Origins (1956), 72 L.Q. Rev. 345. In particular, see the passages on pages 346 and 347.

(i) Guaranteed tenure and salaries for federal superior-court judges?

Successive federal governments have proceeded on the assumption that sections 99 and 100 of the B.N.A. Act do not apply to federal superior courts because section 101 confers federal judicial powers "notwithstanding anything in this Act". Hence it has been provided by ordinary federal statute that judges of the Supreme and Exchequer Courts of Canada must retire at seventy-five (in spite of section 99) and also, on this view, it could be said that federal judges are subject to the salary-stopping provisions of section 31 of the Judges Act, though it is offensive to section 100 of the B.N.A. Act. Nevertheless there are plausible reasons to consider that the proper meaning to be taken from the B.N.A. Act is that sections 99 and 100 are applicable to the federal superior courts. It may be argued with reason that the phrase "notwithstanding anything in this Act" in section 101 has the office of giving the balance of section 101 an effect overriding any other provision of the act inconsistent with it. Hence, section 101 over-rides the provincial administration of justice power in section 92(14), which otherwise would be almost unlimited. But there is no need to over-ride sections 99 and 100 in favour of section 101 because, in so far as section 101 contemplates the establishment of superior courts, sections 99 and 100 are not inconsistent, in fact quite the contrary. They prescribe certain of the essential characteristics that superior courts must exhibit to be superior courts. There is no need to stand them off. Likewise one can say that a binding implication arises from sections 97 and 98 that judges of federal superior courts must be selected from the legal profession.

In other words, my reasoning is that the "notwithstanding" clause in section 101 performs the same office there that it does earlier in the opening words of section 91, that is, it supports specific categories of federal power against any verbally inconsistent category of provincial power and, having done that, is *functus officio*. Hence my view that the term "superior court" in sections 99 and 100 includes any federal superior courts constituted under section 101. If this is correct, then the judges of federal superior courts are in the same position respecting salary, tenure, retirement and removal as judges of the provincial superior courts, and for the same constitutional reasons.

(ii) Guaranteed jurisdiction for federal superior courts?

When one realizes that the guaranteed jurisdiction of the provincial superior courts rests upon a wider basis of necessary implication than the "mere" federal appointing power in section 96, as explained earlier, then it follows that the same wider basis of implication is equally relevant to the federal superior courts and should confer on them a similarly guaranteed jurisdiction. This would mean that laws within section 91 of the B.N.A. Act appropriate only for superior-court administration on the test of the *John East* case must be assigned by the federal Parliament for administration to a superior court. This necessity could be satisfied by resort to a provincial superior court or to a federal superior court, but it would have to be to one or the other. If sections 97, 98, 99 and 100 of the

B.N.A. Act apply to the federal superior courts as suggested earlier, then the basis for the implication is as obvious as for the provincial courts in the field of provincial laws. Even if these sections do not apply, the fact that section 101 contemplates federal superior courts might be said to mean also that some guaranteed substantial jurisdiction is contemplated within the scope of section 91. This approach casts some doubt, as Professor Laskin suggests it would, on the propriety of the Income Tax Appeal Board as presently constituted.

But all these arguments are particularly strong with respect to the appellate jurisdiction of the Supreme Court of Canada, which covers the entire legal field of federal and provincial laws. Surely the B.N.A. Act necessarily implies that the ''General Court of Appeal for Canada'' must be a superior court in the fullest sense, and that it is guaranteed typical and appropriate superior-court appellate jurisdiction. At least so far as interpretation of the B.N.A. Act itself is concerned, there seems no doubt of a guaranteed separation of powers favouring both provincial and federal superior courts:

> . . . consideration of the legislative capacity of Parliament or of the Legislatures cannot be withdrawn from the Courts either by Parliament or Legislature. In my view this statement may rest upon the safe ground that by necessary implication from what has been said in the B.N.A. Act, the Superior Courts whose independence is thereby assured, are just as surely made the arbiters of the constitutional validity of statutory enactments as Parliament and the Legislatures are made law enacting bodies. If, as I think, it is not open to question that neither Parliament nor Legislature may provide as the concluding words of an enactment that it shall be deemed to be *intra vires* by all Courts in the country then neither the one nor the other of these legislative bodies can reach the same end by denying access to the Courts for the determination of constitutional questions.[163]

Since the end of appeals to the Judicial Committee of the Privy Council, these considerations have taken on a new urgency and importance, especially concerning final interpretation of the federal distribution of legislative powers. If the views expressed here are correct, then the Supreme Court of Canada is not at the mercy of ordinary federal statutes, but enjoys a specially entrenched position, in the constitutional sense explained earlier, in respect both of appropriate appellate jurisdiction and the appointment, payment, tenure, retirement and removal of its judges. My submission is that a reading of the B.N.A. Act not only permits but favours this result. In a federal country like Canada, it is essential that the final tribunal of constitutional interpretation should possess this status.

V. General Considerations and Conclusions

As shown in parts I and II of this essay, there is high authority to the effect that the basic independence of the English superior courts is a first principle of the constitution capable of withstanding even the legislative primacy of the United Kingdom Parliament itself. If it is reasonable to take this position in England, by so much the more is it reasonable to do so in a federal country like Canada. The

---

[163]*Per* McGillivray J.A. in *I.O.F. v. Lethbridge,* [1938] 3 D.L.R. 102-103.

necessities of federalism simply provide additional reasons to follow the model afforded by the English judicature. Hence we may concede the legislative primacy of the federal parliament and the provincial legislatures in their respective fields and nevertheless insist on the primary and specially-entrenched place of the superior courts of the country in the function of interpreting and applying law. Both directly and indirectly the superior courts promote impartial and objective application of laws to the persons and circumstances those laws contemplate by their terms, and it is important to remember that this includes the distributions and divisions of governmental powers, both primary and secondary, effected by constitutional laws. Furthermore, however trite, it needs to be said again that the interpretation and application of laws are no mere mechanical process. To find and apply the proper law in many critical instances is a most delicate and difficult operation, a process that involves discretions at times legislative in their scope.

Of course it is true that only a very small fraction indeed of the total of necessary legal decisions in both private and public law issues from superior courts, but this small fraction is very important. Superior-court decisions provide precedents for a multitude of more or less similar instances which can then be confidently and expeditiously settled at other levels. Moreover, the superior courts afford an example of the most careful fairness and impartiality in the administration of law, thus setting an ideal for other officials and tribunals.

But, it may be asked, how is it that all these fine results follow from the conditions of judicial independence studied in this article? Many of these conditions are negative ones, making the judge irresponsible, or non-accountable, in office and preventing his removal except in the most extreme circumstances. As Dr. R. MacGregor Dawson shows, the answer is that the conditions of judicial independence, negative though most of them are, will stimulate any person of moral integrity to do his best. Given learning and ability as well as a conscience, this will be a very effective best. Political irresponsibility in these circumstances generates moral responsibility and conscientious effort. And thus, if care has been taken with the appointment in the first place, the conditions of judicial independence will justify themselves:

> The judge must be made independent of most of the restraints, checks and punishments which are usually called into play against other public officials. . . . He is thus protected against some of the most potent weapons which a democracy has at its command: he receives almost complete protection against criticism; he is given civil and criminal immunity for acts committed in the discharge of his duties; he cannot be removed from office for any ordinary offence, but only for misbehaviour of a flagrant kind; and he can never be removed simply because his decisions happen to be disliked by the Cabinet, the Parliament, or the people. Such independence is unquestionably dangerous, and if this freedom and power were indiscriminately granted the results would certainly prove to be disastrous. The desired protection is found by picking with especial care the men who are to be entrusted with these responsibilities, and then paradoxically heaping more privileges upon them to stimulate their sense of moral responsibility, which is called in as a substitute for the political responsibility which has been removed. The judge is placed in a position where he has nothing to lose by doing what is right and little to gain by doing what

is wrong; and there is therefore every reason to hope that his best efforts will be devoted to the conscientious performance of his duty.[164]

It is quite clear then that the success of our system of judicial independence rests upon the appointment of well-qualified persons to judicial office, and the question of how best to ensure this arises. The writer considers that responsibility and power in this respect should remain with the federal Cabinet, in particular with the Prime Minister and the Minister of Justice. They must answer eventually to the national Parliament for the quality of judicial appointments, and this is the proper constitutional reflection of the vital interest all citizens have in the proper administration of justice. No doubt official or voluntary associations of the legal profession may play a valuable advisory rôle at times, but the real power of appointment should rest where it is now, at the highest level of political responsibility. Nevertheless, the professional contribution is a vital one, the impartiality and effectiveness of judges depending in important measure on the education, traditions, experience and autonomy of the legal profession from which they are drawn. Hence the main contribution that lawyers as a whole can make to the quality of the bench is to be true to their own standards as members of a learned profession.

FURTHER DEVELOPMENTS AND REFERENCES

The essay on "The Independence of the Judiciary" was published in 1956. The following subsequent developments should be noted.

(1) In 1960, in response to a joint address of the Canadian Parliament to which all the provinces had consented, the British Parliament amended section 99 of the B.N.A. Act to require superior court judges to retire at age seventy-five, if they attained that age while still in office. This is a sensible limitation on tenure for life that does not impair the independence of the judiciary. The new text of section 99 is quoted in Chapter 8.

(2) In 1971, the Canadian Judicial Council was established by amendments to the Judges Act of the Parliament of Canada. The Council consists of the Chief Justice of Canada (chairman) and also of the Chief Justice and Associate Chief Justices of each superior court, or branch or division thereof, in Canada: Judges Act, R.S.C. 1970, c. J-1, s. 40 (as amended by R.S.C. 1970, c. 16 (2nd Supp.), s. 10; 1974-75, c. 48, s. 17 and 1976-77, c. 25, ss. 15(1), 16. While the Council has an educational function, in that it may establish seminars for the continuing education of judges, our main concern here is with its powers of enquiry and recommendation concerning the conduct of judges.

Section 40 of the Judges Act provides in part as follows:

40(1) The Council shall, at the request of the Minister of Justice of Canada or

---

[164]The Government of Canada, *ante,* footnote 144, 486. Also see, R. MacGregor Dawson, The Principle of Official Independence (London, P. S. King and Son Ltd., 1922), chap. II. This is indispensable reading for anyone interested in the position of judges.

the attorney general of a province, commence an inquiry as to whether a judge of a superior, district or county court should be removed from office . . .

(2) The Council may investigate any complaint or allegation made in respect of a judge of a superior, district or county court.

(3) The Council may, for the purpose of conducting an inquiry or investigation under this section, designate one or more of its members who, together with such members, if any, of the bar of a province, having at least ten years standing, as may be designated by the Minister of Justice of Canada, shall constitute an Inquiry Committee.

After the inquiry, the Council reports its findings to the Minister of Justice and may recommend removal of the judge in question. This formalizes the necessary inquiry process in the given circumstances, leaning heavily on the judges themselves as a collective group. No doubt this is wise and proper, but the power of the Council or Committee of Inquiry stops with recommendations. So, the constitutional position about removal itself, as set forth in the 1956 essay (Chapter 7) is not changed.

Indeed, the revised statutory provisions of the Judges Act repeat the long-standing provisions of the Act that the Governor-in-Council, on a finding of disability, may stop a judge's salary before or apart from actual removal. As argued in the 1956 essay, I very much doubt the constitutional validity of such salary stoppage respecting superior court judges.

(3) Concerning the appointment of judges, I said at the end of the 1956 essay that I considered "that responsibility and power in this respect should remain with the federal Cabinet, in particular with the Prime Minister and the Minister of Justice". Since 1956 I have modified my views about this a great deal, and would now put heavy reliance on specially composed judicial appointing commissions. This idea is developed in detail in the essays in Chapters 10 and 11.

Chapter 8

The Supreme Court of Canada and the Canadian Judicial System

Reprinted with permission from *Transactions of the Royal Society of Canada*, Vol. 13, Series IV, 1975

I. THE CANADIAN JUDICIAL SYSTEM IN GENERAL

In this year 1975, we are marking the 100th anniversary of the foundation of the Supreme Court of Canada. It is fitting then to ask some basic questions about the nature of the Court and what it does and should be doing. In order to do this though, we must look briefly at the historical roots of our superior courts and at the Canadian system of judicature generally.

As usual, English constitutional history is the starting point. It is well known that the revolutionary settlement in Britain after 1688 established the supremacy of the parliamentary power to legislate over the power of the king to legislate by virtue of the royal prerogative. What is not so well known is that guarantees of the independence of the superior courts were an equally basic part of the revolutionary settlement. Previously, most superior court judges had been appointed to hold office at the royal pleasure, but the Stuart kings had used this power to subvert the independence of the judiciary by dismissing judges who were not outright royal partisans.

William of Orange agreed to change this by use of the royal appointing power—he granted judicial offices for life during good behaviour. William also gave royal assent to the Act of Settlement of 1701. Among other things, the Act of Settlement, by virtue of the newly established parliamentary supremacy, required that, from and after the accession of the House of Hanover, the king *must* appoint the superior court judges for life during good behaviour. Parliament required that "judges commissions be made quamdiu se bene gesserint, and their salaries ascertained and established; but upon the address of both houses of parliament it may be lawful to remove them." This took effect with the accession of George I in 1714.[1]

Speaking of the independence of the judiciary in Britain herself, Sir Arthur Goodhart had this to say of the principle: "It would be inconceivable that Parliament should today regard itself free to abolish the principle which has been

---

[1] 12 and 13 William III (1701), c. 2.

accepted as a corner-stone of freedom ever since the Act of Settlement in 1701. It has been recognised as axiomatic that if the judiciary were placed under the authority of either the legislative or the executive branches of the Government then the administration of the law would no longer have that impartiality which is essential if justice is to prevail."[2] There are, as we shall see later, other elements in the terms upon which judges hold office that support their independence, but security of tenure in office is the key to the matter.

While it took some time for the development to occur, superior courts on the full English model eventually became the core of the judicial systems in the colonies of British North America before Confederation. This developed at about the same time as the achievement of responsible government, but was distinct from it. The independence of the judiciary stands then on its own feet as a separate basic constitutional principle and virtue in our inheritance of English public law and institutions.[3]

Writing of this in an earlier essay, I said:

> By the middle of the nineteenth century at the latest, and in some cases earlier, the British North American colonies had established superior courts on the model of the historic English Central Courts of Justice, usually by appropriate colonial judicature statutes approved in London. This means that the English superior court as it was after the Act of Settlement (1701) became in due course a most important feature of our great English constitutional inheritance.
>
> The English judicial system is characterized by a separation of powers in favour of the independence of the judiciary—a separation of the courts from control or influence by either legislative or executive bodies. Sections 96 to 101 of the B.N.A. Act establish our Canadian superior courts, and a reading of these sections (quoted hereafter) reveals the hallmarks of several hundred years of English judicial development. The judges are to be appointed from the autonomous legal profession, they are not civil servants. They enjoy guaranteed salaries and permanent tenure until death or an advanced age (seventy-five years), whichever comes first. They can be removed earlier only by joint address of Senate and House of Commons for grave misbehaviour. The result is that our judges need only have regard to reason, conscience, and the evidence in their duty-bound endeavours to interpret laws according to the meaning and purpose expressed or implied in those laws. This is the essence of judicial independence.
>
> The interesting thing is that this separation of powers permitted the establish-ment of an essentially unified judicial system for Canada in 1867 without offence to the federal idea. The existing courts in each province were continued by section 129 of the B.N.A. Act, subject to certain other provisions of the act that divided power and responsibility for the judicature between provincial and federal authorities. Section 92(14) gave the provinces "exclusive" legislative power over "the Administration of Justice in the Province, including the Constitution, Maintenance, and Organization of Provincial Courts, both of Civil and of Criminal Jurisdiction, and including Procedure in Civil Matters in those Courts."
>
> This is a very wide power, but it is subject to certain important subtractions in

---

[2]A. L. Goodhart, *English Law and the Moral Law* (Stevens & Sons, London, 1953), 55, 60.
[3]W. R. Lederman, "The Independence of the Judiciary," *Canadian Bar Review,* 34 (1956), 770-809 and 1139-79 (1157-8).

favour of the federal authorities. Criminal procedure is an "exclusive" federal legislative category by section 91(27); and sections 96 to 100, inclusive, make collaboration of the federal executive and Parliament necessary to complete the establishment of provincial superior, district, or county courts. Section 101 gives the federal parliament an overriding power to establish certain federal courts. These sections require quotation in full:

96. The Governor General shall appoint the Judges of the Superior, District, and County Courts in each Province, except those of the Courts of Probate in Nova Scotia and New Brunswick.

97. Until the Laws relative to Property and Civil Rights in Ontario, Nova Scotia, and New Brunswick, and the Procedure of the Courts in those Provinces, are made uniform, the Judges of the Courts of those Provinces appointed by the Governor General shall be selected from the respective Bars of those Provinces.

98. The Judges of the Courts of Quebec shall be selected from the Bar of that Province.

99(1). Subject to subsection two of this section, the Judges of the Superior Courts shall hold office during good behaviour, but shall be removable by the Governor General on Address of the Senate and House of Commons.

(2). A Judge of a Superior Court, whether appointed before or after the coming into force of this section, shall cease to hold office upon attaining the age of seventy-five years, or upon the coming into force of this section if at that time he has already attained that age.

100. The Salaries, Allowances and Pensions of the Judges of the Superior, District, and County Courts (except the Courts of Probate in Nova Scotia and New Brunswick), and of the Admiralty Courts in Cases where the Judges thereof are for the Time being paid by Salary, shall be fixed and provided by the Parliament of Canada.

101. The Parliament of Canada may, notwithstanding anything in this Act, from Time to Time provide for the Constitution, Maintenance, and Organization of a General Court of Appeal for Canada, and for the Establishment of any additional Courts for the better Administration of the Laws of Canada.

To summarize, the result is that minor courts in the provinces, such as those of magistrates or justices of the peace, are entirely within provincial control. District, county, or superior courts of the provinces, including provincial appellate courts, require the collaboration of provincial and federal authorities for their establishment and maintenance. Then at the apex of the structure is the "General Court of Appeal for Canada," the Supreme Court of Canada, entirely constituted by the federal parliament and executive.

There is not, generally speaking, any division of jurisdiction in these courts corresponding to the division of legislative powers between the provincial legislatures and the federal parliament. In general they "administer justice" concerning all types of laws, whether such laws fall legislatively within the purview of provincial legislatures or the federal parliament.[4]

---

[4]W. R. Lederman, *The Courts and the Canadian Constitution* (Carleton Library no. 16; McClelland and Stewart, Toronto, 1964), 2-4.

The point in the last paragraph quoted needs further development. The unitary character of the Canadian judicial system, province by province, culminating in the Supreme Court of Canada as the "General Court of Appeal" for all of Canada on all subjects, is a great advantage to the individual citizen. For the most part, he need look only to one court system when he takes a case originally to a trial court or later on appeal to the higher levels of the system. Because the judiciary are independent of both cabinets and parliaments, this can be done without prejudice to the federal division of legislative powers by subjects. In any given case, the courts can administer the law in one operation whether federal statutes, provincial statutes, or a combination of the two are involved. Indeed, often a combination of federal and provincial laws is involved in the problem a citizen brings to the court, so that a merger of judicial power to deal with both is almost a matter of necessity. This is a point that has seldom been appreciated and is much misunderstood.

I believe good philosophical reasons can be given for this need to have courts of general or comprehensive jurisdiction in a federal state. Legislative power in a parliamentary body may move at a level of higher generality that contrasts with the specifics and particulars with which a court must deal. So, as a matter of legislation, we get general income tax laws from the federal parliament and general property laws from the legislatures of each of the provinces. But what of the citizen who goes to court to contest the assessment of income tax that has been put upon him? Now we are down from the legislative generalities to the specifics of everyday life, which is the level where people develop their particular problems. At this level we find that federal and provincial laws are interwoven and interpenetrating, and that frequently the citizen has a single or total problem that involves both. Federal tax liability for John Jones may turn not just on the application of a section of the federal Income Tax Act, but also on certain property law sections in the Civil Code of Quebec. A man charged with car theft under the federal Criminal Code may offer the defence that he was not a thief at all because he, not the complainant, was the owner of the car in question. Then the criminal court has a property issue to settle under provincial law before the criminal charge under federal law can be disposed of. These examples could be multiplied in the interpenetration of provincial family law with federal divorce law, provincial contract law with federal bankruptcy law, and so on.

But, some people point out that in the United States there are two separate systems of courts—a state court system in each state and a federal court system for the whole country, the latter culminating in the Supreme Court of the United States. This is true as far as it goes, but some people also think the dual court system in the United States corresponds to the division of legislative powers between Congress and the state legislatures. They think that issues under state laws are tried only in the state courts, and that issues under federal laws are tried only in the federal court system. This is simply not true. The respective state judicial systems and the federal judicial system each contain courts of general jurisdiction. As a matter of constitutional principle in the

United States, state courts are obliged to apply state laws of course, but also federal laws and the law of the constitution when they also prove to be applicable to the problem of the citizen before the court. As for the United States federal courts, at the trial level, half their cases involve state laws as a primary matter under their constitutional "diversity of citizenship" jurisdiction, and of course they must also apply federal law and the law of the constitution when the citizen before the court has a problem with these aspects.[5]

So there is no elegant federal dualism by subjects as between the two court systems of the United States; nor was it ever intended, by the Founding Fathers of the American Constitution that there should be. Had they intended this, it would have been impossible anyway, for the reasons of principle I have given. The current American situation recognizes the inevitable. Nevertheless, the dualism of the American judicial system taken as a whole brings with it many complications that are not present if you have only a single system of courts. In the United States, for instance, the question arises as to when you might stop proceedings in a federal court by another party because you have already raised the matter before a state court, and vice versa. The rules about all the procedural issues of moving back and forth between the two court systems in the United States are very complex, and run to hundreds of pages in the rule books. This may be a good system for the United States because it is a country with ten times the population of Canada and needs a great many more courts than we do. I very much doubt the need for such dualism in Canada.

The reason why I labour this point is twofold. In the first place, prominent scholars have argued that we should adopt a dual judicial system in Canada for reasons of federal theory. I have tried to show that there is no valid federal purpose to be served by doing this, and that all we would get would be great complications in judicial procedure without any compensatory benefits whatever. So, I consider that we should stay with our much simpler unitary judicial system in this country.

But, in the second place, we do have an issue of this sort looming on the horizon in Canada, and it concerns the Federal Court of Canada. You will recall that section 101 of the B.N.A. Act provided that the Parliament of Canada could establish additional courts for the better administration of the laws of Canada. It has been held that "laws of Canada" in this context means only federal laws and issues arising under them, that is, only laws within the purview of section 91 of the B.N.A. Act as a legislative matter.[6] For many years we had the Exchequer Court of Canada established under this power, with a very limited jurisdiction. Recently, the Exchequer Court has been replaced by the Federal Court of Canada, with Trial and Appellate Divisions having somewhat wider jurisdiction than the old Exchequer Court. Up to a limited point, the sep-

---

[5]H. M. Hart Jr. and H. Weschler, *The Federal Courts and the Federal System* (The Foundation Press, Inc., Brooklyn, 1953), 395-9. See also: Study of the Division of Jurisdiction between State and Federal Courts (as adopted and promulgated by the American Law Institute at Washington, D.C., 18 May 1965 and 21-22 May 1968), Appendix B, 465, 469-70.
[6]*Consolidated Distilleries Ltd. v. The King*, [1933] A.C. 508, [1933] 3 D.L.R. 1.

arate Federal Court can be justified, but certainly it should be carefully limited in jurisdiction, for otherwise it would encroach unduly on the general jurisdiction of the superior courts of the provinces. If this were to happen, we could get a serious and very damaging degree of judicial dualism in Canada. I will come back to this point later, but it is time now to turn more specifically to the Supreme Court of Canada itself. It is the apex of our Canadian judicial system, and constitutes the second and final level of appeal in our country. The Supreme Court of Canada entertains appeals on all subjects from the respective provincial courts of appeal and the Federal Court of Appeal. The precedents made by the decisions of the Supreme Court of Canada are binding throughout the whole of Canada.

II. THE STATUS AND FUNCTIONS OF THE SUPREME COURT OF CANADA

Where do appellate decisions such as those of the Supreme Court of Canada fit in the judicial scheme of things?

Speaking in very general terms, one may say that the usual judicial decision performs a twofold function. First, it gives the litigating parties a fair hearing, their day in court so to speak, and then authoritatively settles the issues of fact and law between them. Secondly, the terms on which the issues are settled may in some cases have a wider significance for others in essentially similar circumstances in the future. In the second situation, the exposition of the governing law by the judge or judges is frequently a precedent of some importance, or perhaps of very great importance, for a wider public. As Dean Roscoe Pound has put it:

> At least if he is an appellate judge, and to some extent in any court of general jurisdiction [the Anglo-American judge] . . . must so decide that his decision will enter into the body of the law as a precedent. He must so decide that his decision or the grounds thereof will serve, first, as a measure or pattern of decision of like cases for the future, and, second, as a basis of analogical reasoning in the future for cases for which no exact precedents are at hand.[7]

Relatively speaking, only a very few cases in trial courts have this precedent-setting value or potential, but, in any event, the first level of appeal is usually open to the losing litigant as a matter of right, at his option.

Thus, at the first level of appellate review, the interest of the particular litigant is still strong, as reflected in his right to have his day in the first appellate court, even after having had his day in the trial court. But it is usually considered that one level of appellate review is enough, as a matter of right, so far as the peculiar interest of particular litigants is concerned. If there is to be a second level of appellate review, then such review, it is thought, should take place only if the public interest is engaged by the case in a way that goes beyond the personal or private concerns of the particular parties to the case. To obtain a second appellate review in the highest appeal court, we find that,

---

[7]*Harvard Law Review* 36 (1923), 940-1.

usually, a litigant must petition that court for its consent to hear the appeal. The consideration of the petition for leave by the judges is then on the footing that the second level appeal hearing on the merits will be granted only if the wider public interest is engaged in some sufficiently important respect.

The point is that the function of the Supreme Court of Canada is to give leadership to all of Canada on issues of enduring public importance, as these issues manifest themselves in decisions in the lower courts and non-curial tribunals as well: decisions in prosecutions, actions, and other matters that one of the parties at least seeks to have reviewed in the Supreme Court of Canada itself by way of ultimate appeal. There is an important creative element in the judicial process of interpreting and applying laws, as Dean Pound explained. The quality of the output of the Supreme Court of Canada then is of great significance as a unifying influence for the whole of Canada.

Given that such judicial leadership is the function of the Court, we now encounter two groups of problems about the operating principles needed if the Court is successfully to pursue this objective, standing as it does at the second and final level of appellate review. I describe both groups of problems briefly, and then consider them in detail.

The first concerns the selection of the cases to be heard and decided by the Supreme Court of Canada. Not everyone who wishes to appeal from a lower court is permitted to do so, or, indeed, could or should be permitted to do so. But also, in the second place, one wants to be sure that all disputed legal questions or issues will at least be potentially eligible for appeal to the Supreme Court of Canada, though only a few important cases may be selected for such treatment each year. Cases that commence in some lower court potentially have this eligibility, but the difficulty here is that many legal decisions are originally made by officials, boards, or tribunals that are not courts at all. Unless the decisions of such officials, boards, or tribunals may be subjected to judicial review of some kind in one of the lower courts, usually a superior court of original jurisdiction, they do not enter the court system at all, and thus would not be eligible for possible appeal to the Supreme Court of Canada. The latter has only appellate jurisdiction and thus can only be approached through a lower court. We have a number of constitutional principles to ensure that non-curial decision-makers can be subjected to some form of judicial review in the lower courts at the instance of persons affected, so that such officials, boards, or tribunals do become potentially subject to the appellate jurisdiction of the Supreme Court of Canada.

Looking first at the problem of the selection of cases to be heard, we encounter the fact that the judicial function is personal, and this necessarily puts an upper limit on the number of cases that can be heard and decided in a single year. It is considered undesirable that more than a year should elapse between the acceptance of a case for hearing and the decision of it. The judges must themselves hear the cases and write their opinions. They have secretaries and research assistants, but no ghost writers. Experience in Britain, the United States, and Canada shows that a final tribunal such as the Supreme Court of

Canada can dispose of 120 to 150 cases a year, but no more. But hundreds if not thousands of cases are offered for appeal each year, so only a fraction of them can be heard. How do you select the relatively few that are to have this final review?[8]

We expect judicial leadership from the Supreme Court of Canada on the most important current issues in our legal and constitutional system, and the selection process reflects this. The judges themselves conduct brief preliminary hearings on applications for leave to appeal, and in their discretion they grant some applications and refuse others. The rationale here is that the judges, as knowledgeable men about the state of affairs in the country, are able, by this device, to keep their fingers on the pulse of the country. This is because the state of litigation in the lower courts, the types of cases that are being pressed there at any given moment, in a very genuine way reflects the pressure points in our social and political affairs. The judges themselves then select the cases that are most in need of a Supreme Court of Canada decision because of the element of public importance that they embody. The terms of the Supreme Court Act leave it to the judges themselves to determine and apply the criteria of public importance from time to time. Not everything of current public excitement is really matter of enduring public importance, but the judges, because of their permanent tenure in office, are in a position to take a long-range view of this which it is more difficult for others to take.

The Supreme Court of the United States has had this sort of control over its docket since 1925, and the same is true of the House of Lords as a court in Britain since 1934. But it was just on 28 January of this year, 1975, that the Canadian parliament put the Supreme Court of Canada in the same position.[9] In assessing the work of the Supreme Court of Canada then, we must remember that it has just been given one of the means necessary to proper performance of its function of judicial leadership, i.e. substantial control of the selection process whereby cases reach it for full hearing and decisions. Until this year, the Supreme Court was required to hear any civil case that involved $10,000 or more, if the losing litigant in the Court of Appeal below wished to go on. The Court had become badly overloaded and had fallen about two years behind in deciding cases, many of which were not worthy of its attention in the first place.

At last then, the Supreme Court of Canada is now in a position, for the most part, to exclude cases that a brief preliminary hearing indicates are not worthy of its attention. This preliminary hearing is conducted by three judges. Also, provincial courts of appeal and the Federal Court of Appeal in their discretion may give a litigant permission to go on to the Supreme Court of Canada, but these permissions are rare and are only given for cases of public importance. Further,

---

[8]*Report of The Special Committee of the Canadian Bar Association on the Caseload of the Supreme Court of Canada* (Canadian Bar Association, Ottawa, June 1973), which is reproduced as Annex A to *Proceedings of the Standing Senate Committee on Legal and Constitutional Affairs,* The Senate of Canada, Issue no. 1 for Tuesday, 12 November 1974.
[9]Statutes of Canada, 1974-75, c. 18.

the government of Canada may refer questions for decision directly to the Supreme Court of Canada by order in council and the Supreme Court must then take these cases. But these are very few in number and invariably have involved issues of public importance, such as the validity of federal or provincial statutes under the Constitution of Canada. There are also a very few serious types of criminal cases, for instance cases involving a death penalty, where appeal to the Supreme Court of Canada is a matter of right. Nevertheless, the over-all result of the recent amendments of the Supreme Court Act is that the Supreme Court itself is now substantially in control of the selection of the cases to be accorded full hearing and written opinions by it. As I have indicated, this is very important if it is to perform the function of judicial leadership that is its raison d'être.

The second question in this group about the Supreme Court refers to the range of cases eligible for appeal, because they can one way or another be commenced in or taken to courts of original jurisdiction. We have a number of constitutional principles which, in my view, ensure that all important legal issues in the country can, one way or another, be taken to the lower courts if the persons involved wish to do so. Once a case is in the court system, the possibility of appeal eventually to the Supreme Court of Canada is open, subject of course to discretionary control by that Court itself, as explained.

1. In the first place, many cases go normally as an original matter to the lower courts in the provinces. The constitutional rule is that no provincial statute can bar appeal to the Supreme Court of Canada from the court of last resort in the province for the case concerned. Provinces have attempted to do this, and the attempts have been ruled invalid.[10]

2. The second rule concerns constitutional cases under the specially entrenched clauses of the B.N.A. Act. Here the rule is that a constitutional issue under any of the specially entrenched clauses of the B.N.A. Act may always be taken to a superior court, at least by way of appeal if not as an original matter. There must be access to a superior court if any interested party wishes to take the issue there. Once in the court system, appeal to the Supreme Court of Canada becomes a normal matter of possibility within the system. No provincial or federal statute can bar this access to the courts on such constitutional issues. This too has been attempted, and ruled invalid.[11]

Constitutional issues of this kind are potentially all-pervasive because they usually involve the distribution of legislative powers between the federal parliament and the provincial legislatures, a distribution that covers virtually all subjects of legislation. Such cases may arise originally in many inferior or specialized tribunals that are not courts at all, or that at least are not superior courts. Family courts, provincial criminal courts, labour boards, municipal boards, and such bodies may rule on a constitutional challenge in the first place if it arises within the statutory definition of their respective jurisdictions. But then, appeal must lie by one means or another to a superior court. From then on, the normal possibilities of appeal to the Supreme Court of Canada are open. For ex-

---

[10]*Crown Grain Co. v. Day*, [1908] A.C. 504.
[11]*B.C. Power Corporation v. B.C. Electric Company and the A.G. of B.C.*, [1962] S.C.R. 642.

ample, a person charged with careless driving under the Provincial Motor Vehicles Act in a provincial criminal court is entitled to defend himself there by alleging that the provincial dangerous driving offence is ultra vires of the province. This is not a superior court, but the provincial court judge has both the right and the duty to rule on this defence, and to convict or acquit accordingly. But if the defence is rejected, then certainly the accused has the right of appeal to a superior court, and the possibility of appeal all the way to the Supreme Court of Canada. The same point can be made about the decisions of family court judges in purely provincial family courts.[12]

Recently, the Supreme Court of Canada has reinforced this principle of access by important decisions about the standing of a citizen of Canada, simply because he is a citizen, to raise before the courts the issue of the constitutional validity of any federal or provincial statute. In a situation where no one citizen or body of persons has a special interest and standing to challenge the constitutional validity of a provincial or federal statute, then *any* citizen may do so by bringing action for a declaratory judgment in one of the superior courts of original jurisdiction. A year ago the Supreme Court said that the Honourable Mr. Thorson, simply as a Canadian citizen, could bring an action in the Supreme Court of Ontario to have the federal Official Languages Act declared ultra vires of the Parliament of Canada. Likewise, a Mr. McNeil in Nova Scotia was told recently by the Supreme Court of Canada that he could challenge the Nova Scotian movie censorship statute in the Supreme Court of Nova Scotia.[13]

These are most important principles. They ensure that all official persons, elected or appointed, must obey the basic rules of the Constitution concerning the powers of the federal and provincial parliaments respectively. If they fail to do so, any citizen may take the matter to court in the last resort, should this be necessary. This recognizes that the constitution belongs to the people, not to the politicians. It recognizes, too, that all such cases are within the reach of the Supreme Court of Canada through the normal course of appeal in the court system.

3. The third rule in this group concerns a special doctrine that, so far, has been applied only to the provincial legislatures. It is to this effect: even though a statute has been enacted by a provincial legislature that is *within* provincial powers, nevertheless it may raise issues of interpretation and application that must be entrusted as an original matter to the provincial superior court, as constituted under section 96 of the B.N.A. Act. In other words, there is a guaranteed core of issues arising under valid provincial statutes that the province must assign to its provincial superior court as a matter of original jurisdiction. Title to land is one example, and unlimited jurisdiction to interpret contracts in general is another.[14] This doctrine has been much criticized, especially by administrative lawyers. Nevertheless, I think it is a proper and useful doctrine. Notice that it compels a province to set up the superior courts on the English model which are

---

[12]*Mann v. The Queen*, [1966] S.C.R. 238.
[13]*Thorson v. the A.G. of Canada (No. 2)* (1974), 43 D.L.R. (3d) 1.
[14]*Toronto v. York Township*, [1938] 1 D.L.R. 593.

contemplated by sections 96, 99, and 100 of the B.N.A. Act, and it compels the provinces to give them something to do. Our whole history points to this as a safeguard for the rule of law in our country. This also reinforces the constitutional point made earlier, in the first part of this paper, to the effect that the provincially constituted superior courts of general original jurisdiction, with their federally appointed judges, are intended to be the central tribunals of a unified Canadian system of courts. The federal parliament has no power to constitute superior courts of *general* original jurisdiction, or intermediate appellate courts of *general* jurisdiction. The federal parliament has power only to constitute courts of original or intermediate appellate jurisdiction that are limited to issues arising under federal laws alone in some respect, as explained earlier in connection with the Federal Court of Canada. Only the provinces have power to constitute courts of full general jurisdiction at these levels. The only court of full general jurisdiction that the federal parliament may constitute is the Supreme Court of Canada itself, at the second and final level of appeal for the whole country. Accordingly, we could not duplicate the American dual system of courts in Canada if we wanted to, without radical amendment of the B.N.A. Act. As explained earlier, both the federal and state court systems in the United States embody superior courts of general original and general appellate jurisdiction.

To return to the provincial superior courts in Canada, and their guaranteed core of jurisdiction in relation to provincial laws, we find that the courts themselves have determined what is typically a superior court matter within the meaning of this doctrine. Partly the definition comes from the history of what these courts have been doing in England and Canada. Also, the definition involves what a reasonable man would say was typical superior court jurisdiction in modern circumstances, given the type of tribunal that a superior court is. In any event there are many provincial matters that are not classified as within the guaranteed core. With respect to them, the provinces can set up what tribunals they please for interpretation and application of provincial laws.[15]

So far, I have explained the doctrine of the guaranteed core as applying to a province at the level of original jurisdiction, and the precedents are certainly to the effect that it does. But, logically, it seems that such a guarantee of judicial jurisdiction may in some matters be operative just at the appellate level of superior court jurisdiction. In other words, it may be constitutionally proper for a province to assign the *original* interpretation and application of a certain type of provincial law to a purely provincial tribunal of some sort, provided it also specifically allows a full appeal to a provincial superior court, for instance the provincial court of appeal. I do not know of any clear-cut judicial precedent to this effect, but it does seem logical and reasonable feature of the doctrine of the guaranteed core of superior court jurisdiction, so perhaps a precedent may be expected one of these days.

There is, however, one aspect of this doctrine that deserves some special attention. I refer to the so-called privative clauses that occur in some statutes, pur-

---

[15]*Labour Relations Board of Saskatchewan v. John East Iron Works, Ltd.*, [1949] A.C. 134; [1948] 4 D.L.R. 673.

porting to exclude certain traditional review functions of the superior courts. For example, it is proper constitutionally for a province to entrust the interpretation and administration of its labour relations law to a labour relations board that is not a court, the members of the board being provincial appointees.[16] But in the provincial statutes constituting such boards, you frequently find a clause to this effect: ''A decision, order or ruling of the labour board made under this Act is final and conclusive and is not open to question or review in any court, and no proceeding by or before the board shall be restrained by injunction, prohibition or any other proceeding in any court.'' We have already seen that such a privative or prohibitive clause is of no avail if the question before the provincial board involves a constitutional issue concerning breach of one of the specially entrenched clauses of the B.N.A. Act. The case we are now considering is a different one. We are now assuming that there is no such special constitutional issue. We are assuming that the provincial labour board, for example, is concerning itself with labour relations in an industry that is clearly within provincial legislative power under the B.N.A. Act, such as coal mining. Nevertheless, issues vital to the rule of law may still arise in two ways. It may be that the labour board has violated rules of natural justice in procedure, or it may be that the board has exceeded the powers actually conferred upon it by its provincial statute. Of course it is important to the on going rule of law in our country that officials, boards, and tribunals should stay within the limits of their respective statutory authorizations, and that even within those limits their decision-making should be carried out by basically fair procedures.

Historically, it was typically a primary function of the Court of King's Bench in England, one of the central superior courts, to exercise this supervisory review function over inferior courts and over officials, boards, and tribunals of all sorts. The Court of King's Bench could nullify decisions of these latter bodies for exceeding their statutory or common law powers, or for breaches of natural justice in procedure. The English superior courts and the superior courts of the provinces in Canada have consistently refused to obey privative clauses and have continued to review the proceedings of other tribunals for excess of jurisdiction or breach of natural justice in procedure. There are many precedents for this disregard, so it is reasonable to seek a proper constitutional explanation of it.[17] In the Canadian context—the system of courts provided by the B.N.A. Act—this disregard of privative clauses seems to be an example of the doctrine of the guaranteed core of jurisdiction for provincial superior courts that we have already considered at length. We want officials, boards, and tribunals to proceed fairly and in substance to stay within the limits of their respective statutory authorizations. Historically, and on the merits in the eyes of the reasonable man, supervision to this end is typically a superior court function, whether such review is to be characterized as original or appellate judicial jurisdiction.

Nevertheless, some of our legal scholars allege that successful privative

---

[16]See footnote 15.
[17]See footnote 15.

clauses have at last been devised, and they think this is a good thing.[18] I have looked at the basis of these claims and I consider them very doubtful. I stand by the assertion I have made that privative clauses are constitutionally invalid to the extent that I have explained. Note that this means that these important issues concerning the rule of law before non-curial provincial boards and tribunals can be drawn into the court system and thus be made available for ultimate review by the Supreme Court of Canada, should the parties seek to carry the appeal process that far. If this were not so, these issues would be beyond the reach of the Supreme Court of Canada, and all other courts for that matter. I do agree of course that the courts should practise restraint in exercising the review function. They should review only for fairness in procedure and for the outside limits of statutory jurisdiction. The courts should not use these powers as disguised means of substantially revising provincial board decisions that are really within the powers of decision-making the provincial legislature intended the board to have.

So far I have spoken of the guaranteed core of superior-court jurisdiction as against the provincial legislatures only, and in this respect there is little doubt about it. Does the doctrine also apply as against the federal parliament? Are there some matters legislatively within federal powers that must be entrusted to superior courts for interpretation and application as an original or appellate matter? I think there are. I think this constitutional guarantee for superior courts cuts both ways; that this is the logical result of our constitutional history and of the judicature sections of the B.N.A. Act. I first propounded this view in 1956, and it has been much criticized.[19] I may be a heretic among constitutional lawyers about this, but I still hold these views. I point out two things in support of my position. First, in the matter of divorce, which is a federal subject, it has been clearly held that divorce jurisdiction is in the core of guaranteed provincial superior-court jurisdiction.[20] Admittedly this applies to the days before there was a federal divorce law, that is before 1968, when for instance the right to divorce in the western provinces rested on historically received pre-confederation English statutes. Nevertheless, divorce is a federal subject under the B.N.A. Act, so my point re-

---

[18]"The Supreme Court of Canada has also made it clear that the various provincial Legislatures and the federal Parliament acting within their areas of competence can exclude completely the review powers of the courts in relation to particular decisions by an appropriately worded privative or exclusionary clause"; David J. Mullan, *Administrative Law* (Carswell, Toronto, 1973), 47. Professor Mullan cites as authority for this proposition *Woodward v. Minister of Justice,* [1972] 5 W.W.R. 581, a judgment of the Supreme Court of Canada. In question was a statute of the British Columbia Legislature concerning taxation of the Woodward estate. The statute in question was purely retroactive and in effect was particular to the Woodward estate. A general privative clause, such as concerns us here, is by its nature *prospective,* or it is nothing. I have read all the opinions in the case— those of the trial judge, the B.C. Court of Appeal, and the Supreme Court of Canada. With respect, I do not see that the case is authority for the proposition for which Professor Mullan cites it. No one doubts that a provincial legislature has the power to enact a purely retroactive and specific law, and that the enactment will be effective if the terms used are precise enough. In my view, this is all the *Woodward Case* really stands for. Thus it does not address the problem of general prospective privative clauses at all. I should add that Professor Mullan does not take a position on whether an effective general privative clause is desirable.

[19]Footnote 3, 1176-7.

[20]*Re Supreme Court Act Amendment Act 1964 (B.C.) A.G. of B.C. v. McKenzie,* [1965] S.C.R. 490; 51 D.L.R. (2d) 623.

mains. Then, secondly, it would be strange indeed if the elected members of the federal parliament could be reviewed by the superior courts to keep them within the limits of the B.N.A. Act, but the appointed members of the federal Labour Relations Board could not be reviewed by the same superior courts to keep them within the limits of a valid federal statute. And remember, if you cut out the superior courts of original or intermediate appellate jurisdiction in these matters, you also cut out the Supreme Court of Canada. So I maintain my heresy and am unrepentant.[21]

But there is one more question, and my attempt to answer it will bring this paper to an end. The question is this: given that the superior courts have the last word in reviewing the limits of authority of other officials and tribunals—even the parliaments themselves—to ensure that they stay within those limits, who then reviews the superior courts, including the Supreme Court of Canada, to see that they in their turn stay within their assigned powers? You will perhaps recognize here that very basic constitutional dilemma: Who watches the Watchman?

I think the answer is that, at this primary level of constitutional responsibility, the judges singly and collectively have to be trusted to obey the laws defining the function of superior courts and to check themselves. The two levels of appeal we have in our country are a safeguard here. A basic element of the rule of law is that doctrines, ideas, and principles are supreme, not persons, and superior court judges, believing in the law, must themselves scrupulously obey it. They must be all the more careful about this precisely because there is no one to review the limits of their powers as they review the limits of the powers of others. A parallel situation is that of the prime minister and cabinet ministers. No one can force them to obey the rules of cabinet government; rather, they must hold themselves to these rules because they know them, believe in them, and accept them as obligatory. At this primary level of constitutional responsibility, one must assume that the holders of the great primary offices of state, whether elected or appointed, will do their duty according to the law of the constitution—the basic accepted rules of organized society. Otherwise, at this level of first things, all arguments about "supremacy," "sovereignty," or "legitimacy" turn out to be circular. The fatal error of John Austin in his theory of sovereignty was that he looked for supreme persons rather than supreme ideas and principles. The judges look for supreme ideas and principles.

The late Robert MacGregor Dawson made this point more than fifty years ago. I close by quoting him.

> The judge must be made independent of most of the restraints, checks and punishments which are usually called into play against other public officials . . . He is

---

[21]There is one qualification to be made in asserting this principle in relation to legislation of the Parliament of Canada. The Federal Court of Canada is a superior court of original jurisdiction, so that a requirement for superior court interpretation and application could be satisfied by entrusting original jurisdiction respecting a federal statute to that court. Nevertheless, the extent to which this is done should be carefully limited in favour of the generally unitary Canadian system of courts based on the superior courts of the provinces. The latter, after all, have federally appointed judges, which should give the Parliament of Canada confidence in them.

thus protected against some of the most potent weapons which a democracy has at its command: he receives almost complete protection against criticism; he is given civil and criminal immunity for acts committed in the discharge of his duties; he cannot be removed from office for any ordinary offence, but only for misbehaviour of a flagrant kind; and he can never be removed simply because his decisions happen to be disliked by the Cabinet, the Parliament, or the people. Such independence is unquestionably dangerous, and if this freedom and power were indiscriminately granted the results would certainly prove to be disastrous. The desired protection is found by picking with especial care the men who are to be entrusted with these responsibilities, and then paradoxically heaping more privileges upon them to stimulate their sense of moral responsibility, which is called in as a substitute for the political responsibility which has been removed. The judge is placed in a position where he has nothing to lose by doing what is right and little to gain by doing what is wrong; and there is therefore every reason to hope that his best efforts will be devoted to the conscientious performance of his duty.[22]

FURTHER DEVELOPMENTS AND REFERENCES CONCERNING THE GUARANTEED JURISDICTION OF SECTION 96 COURTS

Though the doctrine itself is well established, important issues concerning the *extent* of the core of guaranteed exclusive jurisdiction for provincial superior courts or county courts continue to arise. Two recent examples are:

(1) *Polyglase v. Polyglase,* [1980] 2 W.W.R. 393: Custody of children as between competing parents was held by the British Columbia Supreme Court to be exclusively a matter for superior courts. (This case is under appeal to the Court of Appeal.)

(2) *Reference re Residential Tenancies Act* (1980), 26 O.R. (2d) 609 (Ont. C.A.): Certain decisions authorized for provincially appointed officials under the Residential Tenancies Act were held to be exclusively a matter for superior courts or county courts.

Also, the essential vitality of the historic inherent supervisory power of superior courts over inferior tribunals, in spite of provincially enacted privative clauses, seems to have been confirmed by the Supreme Court of Canada: *A.-G. Que. v. Farrah* (1978), 86 D.L.R. (3d) 161.

---

[22]MacGregor Dawson, *The Government of Canada,* 2nd ed. (University of Toronto Press, Toronto, 1954), 486. See also R. MacGregor Dawson, *The Principle of Official Independence* (P. S. King and Son, London, 1922), chapter II.

Chapter 9

Book Review of "Judicial Review of Legislation in Canada" B. L. Strayer

Reprinted with permission from (1970), 16 McGill Law Journal 723

In this treatise we have a comprehensive and systematic analysis of the process of judicial review in our federal country, that is, judicial review as the final word on the extent of the legislative competence of the Parliament of Canada on the one hand, and the legislatures of the Provinces on the other. This is the author's primary emphasis, though he does incidentally give some attention to related problems of delegation of powers to subordinate officials or tribunals. Dr. F. R. Scott wrote the foreword, and I agree fully with his general assessment. He says: "Professor Strayer is to be congratulated, not only for giving us the first thorough study of judicial review in Canadian legal literature, but for having done it with a masterful capacity to steer through the vast confusion of the case law that cannot but command the respect of theorists and practitioners alike" (p. vii). One can concur in this, as indeed I do, and yet question certain of Professor Strayer's theoretical points about the roots of the power of judicial review. I will indicate my doubts later, but in any event they are not major ones when we consider the great and overriding virtues of the book, which deserve the primary attention of reader and reviewer alike.

In the first place, the author provides a systematic and detailed analysis of how federal power-distribution issues have been raised, or may be raised, through regular forms of litigation initiated by persons with an interest in the authoritative determination of such issues by the courts. Thus the citizen has a considerable variety of ways in which he may seek to avoid the application of a statutory provision to himself, by alleging it to be *ultra vires* of the enacting parliamentary body, at *any level* in the judicial system. Public officials may also test statutes in some of these same ways. Professor Strayer does point to instances where judicial procedures to raise this type of issue are deficient or missing. Nevertheless, I am left with the impression that these procedural shortcomings are minor ones in the over-all picture of opportunities for judicial review.

In addition, in this connection, the book is particularly noteworthy for a comprehensive and balanced assessment of reference cases in our constitutional history and practice. The Supreme Court Act provides that the Government of Canada may put questions directly to the Supreme Court of Canada by order-in-council. After a proper hearing, the Court is required to answer these questions, with reasons. There are like provisions in the legislation of all the Provinces, conferring the same power on Provincial Governments in relation to their respective provincial superior courts. This power has often been used, by both Federal and Provincial Governments, to obtain important judgments from the courts on federal power-distribution issues. Professor Strayer tells us that in the period 1867 to 1966, a total of 197 federal power-distribution cases were dealt with finally by the Judicial Committee of the Privy Council or the Supreme Court of Canada. Of these, 68 were reference cases. Moreover, as a group, the 68 reference cases were definitely more important in their political, social and economic impact on Canadian society than were the 129 other cases, arising out of actual litigation between parties. Important powers for the Parliament of Canada and the Provincial Legislatures have been established or confirmed by reference cases. Professor Strayer's assessment implies that any politician, provincial or federal, who attacks the authority of the reference cases in our jurisprudence is swinging a double-edged sword.

But neither the Australians nor the Americans permit reference cases in their federal systems. Is Canada better or worse off to have them? The author discusses the arguments both ways, and concludes that, on balance, the reference by order-in-council is a useful and flexible way to raise federal power-distribution issues for judicial determination. He finds some of the adverse criticisms valid, but would correct these defects by reform of the reference system itself, not by its abolition. For example, he suggests that the questions to the courts should not be too abstract nor should they be put prematurely. Moreover, he argues that greater care should be taken with relevant factual evidence and argument in the hearing of reference cases. Personally I agree with these conclusions and would go a little further. It seems to me that the most satisfactory reference cases have been those in which the Court was questioned about the validity of a fully drafted bill, or a statute already enacted, so that the full text of a proposed or actual law was before it.

Mention of greater care concerning relevant evidence in reference cases leads us to consideration of some valuable general points the author makes about rules of practice and evidence for all federal power-distribution cases. He argues that there is a need for better judicial ascertainment of facts about the legislative effects of a challenged statute and the social context in which it operates. He shows that both the Judicial Committee of the Privy Council and the Supreme Court of Canada have at times in the past accepted certain rules of practice and evidence that, collectively, would permit improvement in this respect—rules concerning judicial notice, admissions, agreed statements of fact, direct evidence and opinion evidence of experts. His complaint is that the means at hand are not yet being used regularly enough, or systematically enough, by counsel or judges in constitutional cases, including reference cases. Professor Strayer's conclusion is: "A more general recourse to facts, particularly those pertaining to legislative effect, would diminish the importance of other elements in the adjudicative process and yield a more realistic jurisprudence'' (p. 181).

I agree with this, but would add a caution about a problem to which Professor Strayer did not address himself. It is all very well to say that the court should explore facts of legislative effects and social context, but where does this stop? The consequences of consequences could be pursued indefinitely. Clearly a court cannot proceed as if it were a Royal Commission with a large expert staff and years for research, hearings and reports. Here, as elsewhere in the law, the judges must stop with proximate consequences and exclude those that are remote. The judges are accustomed to making this distinction now in tracing the effects of a negligent act in tort, or the extent of damages flowing from a breach of contract, for which a defendant is to be held liable. The extent to which a court admits evidence of the effects of a statute in a federal power-distribution case, as an aid to functional interpretation of the federal distribution of powers, needs the same type of limitation. With this in mind, perhaps professor Strayer's point could be re-stated this way. The court should be more liberal and systematic with its concepts of what are the proximate, direct or obvious effects for society of putting the challenged statute into operation, evidence of such effects to be freely admitted. But still, as the evidence of this type offered slips off into areas of unduly remote consequences or other facts, where relevance is very indirect and tenuous, it should be excluded.

Let me turn now to the theoretical doubts I referred to earlier. I do not put these forward as serious adverse criticisms, but they should be mentioned as they do concern the roots of the special power of judicial review in our federal country, with which the book is primarily concerned. While, in the end, Professor Strayer accepts the specially entrenched power of judicial review as part of the basic constitutional law of Canada, he seems to do so with some doubts and reluctance. He thereby seems to imply that there is some element of judicial usurpation, albeit successful usurpation, in the establishment of this power. On the other hand, in an essay in the Canadian Bar Review in 1956, I argued that this power developed naturally by legitimate constitutional evolution for federal Canada, out of the long history of the common law jurisdiction of the English superior courts, which formed the model for the colonial superior courts. I pointed out as well that the inner logic of federalism pushed in the same direction, requiring as it did some institution for impartial determination of federal power-distribution issues as they arose, under the power-distributing lists of the B.N.A. Act, between the Federal Parliament and a Provincial Legislature. Under the influence of both history and logic, it was almost inevitable that the traditional courts should, with general consent, assume this basic interpretative task. It is true that the Provincial Legislatures control the constitution and procedure of provincial courts under section 92(14) of the B.N.A. Act, and that the Parliament of Canada has the same control over the Supreme Court of Canada under section 101 of the B.N.A. Act. It is also true that in Britain, no court can question the validity of a statute of the British Parliament. Professor Strayer seems to argue from this that I am wrong to say there has been legitimate historical continuity behind the specially entrenched power of Canadian courts to review statutes of the Federal Parliament or the Provincial Legislatures for competence, in relation to the primary distribution of legislative powers in the B.N.A. Act. In effect, he says Canadian superior courts cannot claim *by inheritance* a power to review parliamentary statutes for basic competence that their British counterparts never had in relation to the British Parliament, at least since 1688. The flaw in Professor Strayer's argument is that Canadian courts have never been faced by the full equivalent of the British Parliament in Canada or the Provinces, either before or after Confederation in 1867, or before or after the Statute of Westminster in 1931. At first, after 1867, the courts reviewed the validity of statutes of the Federal Parliament and the Provincial Legislatures because they were parliamentary bodies in the British Commonwealth *subordinate* to the British Parliament, and the B.N.A. Act was a statute of that Parliament, as well as being a federal constitution. In 1931, as I understand developments leading up to the Statute of Westminster, and the Statute of Westminster itself, the supremacy of the British Parliament was abolished, *but not the supremacy of the B.N.A. Act itself as the Canadian Constitution, distributing basic legislative powers between the parliaments of Canada and the Provinces.* The overriding power of judicial review for competence was already established in 1931 by history, custom, precedent and the needs of federalism in a British constitutional context. Legally and constitutionally it simply continued after 1931, and will continue, unless and until there is change by constitutional amendment. Such amendment is not within the power of the Parliament of Canada alone or the Legislature of a Province alone. In my view it would require the consent of the Parliament of Canada and all the Provinces. No such amendment is contemplated.

These are very complex questions on which no doubt reasonable men may reasonably differ. But the burden of my complaint against Professor Strayer here is that he chooses to raise the basic issue of the roots of the power of judicial review in a federal system—our system with our history—and then really does not deal with the problem in depth, that is at the level of the first things of our organized community life. It is not good enough to cast doubt on the specially entrenched character of the power of judicial review we are discussing by arguing that the Parliament of Canada, or a Provincial Legislature, could impair or destroy their respective court systems, for this purpose or for other purposes, in a number of procedural or substantive ways. No doubt the Parliament of Canada could repeal the Supreme Court Act, the Provinces could repeal their judicature statutes, or Governments could refuse to appoint any more judges. But all this amounts to saying is that there can be no built-in safeguards against these primary ways of committing constitutional suicide. At this level of first things constitutional, if Members of Parliament and Ministers do not understand the rules and principles of the system, believe in them, and do their duty accordingly, chaos and revolution set in. In the United States, in spite of their formal explicit constitutional special entrenchment, the United States Supreme Court could be abolished if the Presidents refused to appoint judges, or the Senate refused to ratify appointments, or the Congress simply repealed the law specifying the number of Supreme Court justices. One must assume that the holders of primary public offices will do their duty according to the basic accepted rules of their society. Otherwise, at this level of first things, all arguments about 'supremacy', 'sovereignty' or 'legitimacy' turn out to be circular.

Perhaps I have misunderstood Professor Strayer's views on the legitimacy of the power of judicial review under our federal constitution, and, if so, there is not really even this difference between us. In any event, in his last chapter, entitled 'The Future of Judicial Review', he does give the legitimate existence and the importance of the power his full and eloquent support. Among other things he says:

> Beyond this rather negative role of policing the federal system lies the broader role of constitutional development. In the process of keeping each legislative body within its own sphere, the courts should constantly re-examine the accepted definitions of legislative power. The need and the opportunity for dynamic constitutional interpretation are both apparent . . .
>
> It is axiomatic that the constitution, like all law, must adjust to changing conditions. Change by formal amendment being a practical impossibility, change by judicial redefinition becomes a necessity. (pp. 208-9).

I agree heartily with this, and recommend Professor Strayer's treatise most highly to all who seek better understanding of our federal constitution.

Chapter 10

Thoughts on Reform of the Supreme Court of Canada

Reprinted with permission from (1970), 8 Alberta Law Review 1

In this essay, Professor Lederman expresses some personal views on the reform of the Supreme Court of Canada. He would favour a more sociological approach by the Court to constitutional questions before it, rather than the literal or grammatical approach which has usually been followed, and in such cases would allow the Court to range more widely in the admission of expert and factual evidence. Also favoured is more flexibility in the use of precedent. Dealing with the composition and status of the Court, Professor Lederman disputes the contention that the Court's status gives an unfair advantage to the Federal Government, but nevertheless favours constitutional entrenchment of the Court's position. He opposes the use of the Court for constitutional questions only; rather he believes that it should remain a complete court of appeal for the country. He would slightly increase the number of judges, and alter the proportional regional make-up of the court to give more weight to the West and the Atlantic Provinces. Essentially apolitical nominating commissions are proposed for judicial appointments from the four main regions of Canada. Finally, Professor Lederman proposes some alteration in the rules governing cases to come before the Court, with the judges of the Supreme Court of Canada themselves determining, for the most part, which cases deserve their attention because they raise issues of national importance.

An important part of the current constitutional review in our country is consideration of the extent to which changes are needed in the status, structure and functions of the Supreme Court of Canada. This is a large and complex subject, and, in attempting within the limits of an essay of moderate length to survey the whole field, I can only identify and comment briefly on the main issues. In doing this, I write in the first person to emphasize that I am simply expressing my own views, as a student of things constitutional, for what they may be worth.

In the first place, I believe I can take it for granted that everyone accepts the proposition that a supreme interpretative tribunal—a judicial tribunal—is necessary to the working of a federal constitution. Such a tribunal must have the last word on whether provincial or federal statutes are within or beyond the powers listed in the constitution for the enacting legislative body. We are used to this in Canada in relation to distribution of legislative powers but now we are also talking of the possibility of a specially entrenched Bill of Rights like that of the

Americans. Such a Bill of Rights means that some undesirable types of laws are forbidden to legislative bodies, being things they cannot do by ordinary statute, and again a supreme judicial tribunal would be needed to make *this* work.

The main matters for comment seem to fall into two groups.

(1) What should be the principles and doctrines of interpretation that are the operating rules of the supreme interpretative tribunal for a federal country?

(2) What should be the composition, status and jurisdiction of this supreme tribunal? These two questions are interdependent to a degree, of course, because how an institution functions depends very considerably on how it is composed, on the background and training of its members and on the terms on which they hold their offices.

Let me speak first then of doctrines and methods of interpretation in the courts, with particular concern for interpretation of the distribution of legislative powers by the B.N.A. Act between the Federal Parliament on the one hand and the Provincial Legislatures on the other. To my mind there are principally two types of interpretation—literal or grammatical interpretation emphasizing the words found in statutes and constitutional documents—and, sociological interpretation which insists that constitutional words and statutory words must be carefully linked by judicially noticed knowledge and by evidence to the ongoing life of the country.

In my view, both the Judicial Committee of The Privy Council and later the Supreme Court of Canada have been too much devoted to literal or grammatical interpretation and have not employed sociological methods enough. I think this is the central issue concerning interpretation of our federal constitution and its development by interpretation. I am not much interested in the old controversy about whether the Judicial Committee of the Privy Council perverted the B.N.A. Act by giving too much power to the provinces at the expense of the Federal Parliament and Government. The O'Connor Report to the Senate maintained this was so,[1] but Mr. O'Connor made his points by arguments dependent on literal or grammatical interpretation. This type of interpretation gives an appearance of reliability and consistency, but this is only appearance.

As Hans Kelsen has said:[2]

> Since the law is formulated in words and words have frequently more than one meaning, interpretation of the law, that is determination of its meaning, becomes necessary. Traditional jurisprudence distinguishes various methods of interpretation: the historical, in contrast to the grammatical, an interpretation according to the "spirit," in opposition to a literal interpretation keeping to the words. None of these methods can claim preference unless the law itself prescribes the one or the other. The different methods of interpretation may establish different meanings of one and the same provision. Sometimes, even one and the same method, especially the so-called grammatical interpretation, leads to contradictory results. It is incumbent upon the law-maker to avoid as far as possible ambiguities in the text of the

---

[1] The Senate of Canada, Report on the B.N.A. Act, by W. F. O'Connor, Queen's Printer, Ottawa, 1939.
[2] *The Law of the United Nations* (1951) xiii.

law; but the nature of language makes the fulfilment of this task possible only to a certain degree.

A very interesting book has recently been published on the Privy Council's interpretation of the B.N.A. Act.[3] Its author is Professor G. P. Browne of Carleton University, and in my view Professor Browne has beaten Mr. O'Connor at his own game. Professor Browne, using methods of grammatical or literal interpretation, shows that one can find much justification *at this level* for the interpretations placed on the B.N.A. Act by the Judicial Committee. So, in my view, Browne and O'Connor simply cancel one another out. The truth is that the B.N.A. Act was simply ambiguous or incomplete in many respects as originally drafted and the answers just were not in the Act as to how these ambiguities were to be resolved and the gaps filled.

The much-abused Viscount Haldane knew this.[4]

> The draftsman had to work on the terms of a political agreement, terms which were mainly to be sought for in the resolutions passed at Quebec in October, 1864. To these resolutions and the sections founded on them the remark applies . . . that if there is at points obscurity in language, this may be taken to be due, not to uncertainty about general principle, but to that difficulty in obtaining ready agreement about phrases which attends the drafting of legislative measures by large assemblages. It may be added that the form in which provisions overlapping each other have been placed side by side shows that those who passed the Confederation Act intended to leave the working out and interpretation of these provisions to practice and to judicial decision.

To Viscount Haldane's political obscurities of language we should add the degree of obscurity that is inherent in language itself. This arises from the truth that words are not perfect vehicles of meaning, so that no matter how skilfully they are chosen and used, uncertainties about their meaning to some extent remain. This philosophically deeper type of obscurity is what Professor Kelsen was referring to as giving rise to the need for authoritative interpretation to choose between the alternatives that will frequently appear when even the most carefully drafted constitution, statute or legal document is to be applied to the institutions, persons and circumstances the words are alleged to contemplate. In any event, the Judicial Committee did resolve ambiguities and fill gaps, as indeed it was their constitutional duty to do. I am not happy with certain of their decisions on the merits, but nevertheless I do not think the Judicial Committee should now be disparaged for having failed to find answers in *the text* of the B.N.A. Act that just were not there to be found.

Also, to be fair to the Judicial Committee of the Privy Council they did not just employ grammatical interpretation in their cases from Canada. They knew that interpretation had to pay some attention to the social, political, cultural and economic facts of life in Canada. I remember listening to the argument concerning the Alberta Debt Adjustment Act before the Privy Council in 1943. The Hon-

---

[3]*The Judicial Committee and the B.N.A. Act,* (1967) University of Toronto Press.
[4]*John Deere Plow Co. Ltd. v. Wharton,* [1915] A.C. 330, 338.

ourable J. W. Estey, then Attorney-General of Saskatchewan, was arguing for the validity of the Alberta statute because his province had a similar statute that would fall if the Alberta Act fell. Before Mr. Estey started his legal argument, the Lord Chancellor asked him to explain why such drastic anti-creditor legislation was necessary at all. Mr. Estey then took some time to tell the story of the double disaster of drought and market collapse in the 1930's that had brought agriculture on the Canadian Prairies to its knees, so that some such measures as these were needed just to keep the farmers on the land so that they might try again. At this point, Lord MacMillan remarked, "Very well, Mr. Estey, the malady is admitted. Now, who is to be the physician?"

The Law Lords of the Privy Council then were often very astute about Canada, but, nevertheless, my complaint against them is that they did not seek often enough or systematically enough to relate interpretation to the facts of life in Canadian Society. Their interpretation was too much literal and not enough sociological. And also, since the judges of the Privy Council were not Canadians living under our federal constitution, there were a great many things they simply did not know as background knowledge of Canada. In more technical language, the scope of their relevant judicial notice was much narrower than that of Canadian judges. Many outstanding British judges sat on the Judicial Committee, but the handicap just mentioned is one that ability and integrity alone cannot overcome. Canadian judges also have been too literal and grammatical in their interpretations of the constitution, though operating as they did for so long in the shadow of the Judicial Committee, they had little choice about this. Nevertheless, I think Canadian judges should now combine the advantage of their superior native judicial notice of Canadian conditions with systematic and thorough sociological interpretation of the constitutional distribution of powers. The real prospect for improvement in interpretation lies in more intensive and extensive judicial appreciation of social, political, economic and cultural facts that give the various aspects of challenged statutes their relative importance in relation to the categories of federal and provincial legislative powers. The rules of evidence for constitutional cases should permit wide-ranging enquiry, expert opinion and gathering of facts to aid in the decisions to be taken. In my view, this is the only way to get meaningful, consistent interpretation of the federal distribution of legislative powers. It is an illusion to think that security and certainty in the interpretation of a federal constitution can be obtained by literal or grammatical methods of construing meaning. I am convinced that many of those who advocate extensive re-writing of the constitution for Canada do so because they have too much faith in what can be accomplished by words in documents, that is, too much faith in the value of literal interpretation.

But I do not want to press this point too far. Words are, within limits, reasonably objective means of communication and of thought, otherwise social organization and legal institutions would be impossible. The main thrust of my argument here is to emphasize that good constitutions are characteristically rather succinct documents that achieve a beneficial brevity by employing quite general and abstract phrases. For example, in the B.N.A. Act, the following are examples of such words and phrases used to distribute primary legislative powers and responsibilities: 'Trade and Commerce,' 'Property and Civil Rights,' 'Defence,' 'Municipal Institutions,' 'Criminal Law,' 'Banking' and so on. These phrases are clear enough in some of their implications and not so clear in others. In any event they often overlap one another and conflict to some extent in their logical relevance to particular legislative schemes to be found in federal or provincial statutes the validity of which is under challenge in the courts. It is between the alternatives thus arising that the judicial interpretative tribunal must choose. The nature of this task can perhaps best be explained by refining and expanding Lord MacMillan's question—Who is to be the physician? The full question the judges must put to themselves is—Who is the better physician, Federal Parliament or Provincial Legislature, given the type of legislative scheme under consideration and all the relevant circumstances? Issues of relative constitutional values are involved here for the judges, and such issues can best be assessed and decided in the light of all that can reasonably be ascertained of the effects of the challenged statute as operating law for the persons and social conditions contemplated by the terms of the statute.

Professor B. L. Strayer has shown that both the Judicial Committee in London and the Supreme Court of Canada have at times in the past accepted various rules of practice and evidence that collectively would permit the thorough ascertainment of crucial facts concerning the effects and social context of a challenged statute—rules concerning judicial notice, admissions, agreed statements of facts, direct evidence and opinion evidence from experts.[5] Professor Strayer complains that, though there are adequate procedures available as indicated, they are just not yet being used regularly enough or systematically enough by counsel or by judges in constitutional cases (including reference cases). Too often this is because the truly complex nature of federal power-distribution issues is simply not appreciated and accepted by Canadian lawyers and judges. Professor Strayer's conclusion is as follows:[6]

> It has been demonstrated that many elements, both factual and non-factual, enter into the determination of these questions. Once these elements are identified their relative importance can be better assessed. It submitted that the factual elements have yet to receive the attention they deserve, largely because of the confusion over the purpose of fact-introduction in constitutional cases. The importance of facts has been demonstrated, and the means of introduction suggested. A more general recourse to facts, particularly those pertaining to legislative effect, would diminish the importance of other elements in the adjudicative process and yield a more realistic jurisprudence.

Finally, in considering principles and doctrines of interpretation in the final court for federal power-distribution issues, there is the matter of adherence by the court to precedents embodied in its own previous decisions. The Judicial Committee of the Privy Council had the power to depart explicitly from its own pre-

---

[5] *Judicial Review of Legislation in Canada,* (1968) University of Toronto Press, chapter 6.
[6] *Supra,* n. 5, 181.

vious decisions, including those in Canadian constitutional cases. But no counsel ever persuaded it to do so, or at least to admit it was doing so, in Canadian constitutional cases. On the whole, the Judicial Committee was careful to follow its own previous decisions where they were found to be applicable because of sufficient similarity in the type of statute or issue concerned as between a previous case and a new one. We will return presently to the question of what is 'sufficient similarity' in federal power-distribution cases.

Meanwhile, it should be noted that the Supreme Court of Canada has taken the conservative and orthodox position that it is bound to follow its own previous decisions when sufficiently similar cases recur.[7] This contrasts with the position of the Supreme Court of the United States which explicitly claims and not infrequently exercises the power explicitly to depart from its own previous decisions. Until quite recently, the highest appellate court of the United Kingdom, the House of Lords, considered itself fully bound to follow its own previous decisions. But a short time ago, on behalf of the Law Lords composing the court, the Lord Chancellor announced that, while normally they would treat their own previous decisions as binding, they would henceforth "depart from a previous decision when it appears right to do so."[8]

It is not surprising then that we find the Government of Canada proposing to the Constitutional Conference of February, 1969, that "The Constitution should authorize the Supreme Court of Canada to depart from a previous decision when it appears right to do so."[9] It was made clear in the comment accompanying the proposal that this was to be a permissive provision leaving it entirely to the court itself to determine when it was 'right' to depart from precedent because 'circumstances demand it.'

I would offer three comments on this proposal. It is indeed wise and proper to ensure that the Supreme Court of Canada has this power and knows that it has it. But, in federal power-distribution cases, how is the court to determine, when it is 'right' to depart from precedent because 'circumstances demand it'? It can make this judgment rationally and with appropriate social sensitivity only if the relevant facts of legislative effects concerning the challenged statute are before it. This simply adds emphasis to the general points made earlier about the need for more socially sensitive interpretation—that the rules of practice and evidence for constitutional cases should permit wide-ranging enquiry, expert opinions, liberal judicial notice and direct evidence of critical facts, to aid and illuminate the value choices that have to be made. Perhaps the Constitution or the Supreme Court Act should contain a liberal permissive provision on *this* subject too, so that Supreme Court judges will not in future be able to say that they are bound by narrow exclusionary rules of practice or evidence in constitutional cases.

Nevertheless—and this is my second comment on precedent—even if the

---

[7]*See* Mark R. MacGuigan, *Precedent and Policy in The Supreme Court*, (1967) 45 Can. Bar Rev. 627-665.
[8][1966] 1 W.L.R. 1234.
[9]Right Honourable P. E. Trudeau, *The Constitution and The People of Canada*, 1969, Queen's Printer, Ottawa, 82.

Supreme Court is given power to depart from its own previous decisions and adopts more liberal rules of practice and evidence, adherence to precedents is the normal thing and indeed is the normal expectation of the people as a matter of justice. Reasonable consistency over time is one of the normal basic elements of justice. Certainly there should not be a slavish or mechanical following of precedents, though it should indeed be the normal thing in sufficiently similar circumstances. But this leads to the most fundamental of all questions about adherence to precedent—What is a precedent anyway? There are always some differences between past and present circumstances when one is comparing previous cases with a new case. When are the previous circumstances *sufficiently* similar to the new ones to make the previous case a precedent for the new one? When are the differences significant enough that the previous case can be dismissed as *not* amounting to a precedent?[10] This is the third matter for comment.

The philosophy and logic of precedent is the subject of an extensive literature that cannot be recapitulated here. Nevertheless, we can review briefly the special case of federal power-distribution issues in this respect. Typically, the final court is asked in this kind of case to decide whether a specific legislative scheme that has been passed as a statute by the Federal Parliament or a Provincial Legislature is within or beyond the powers of the enacting body. To do this the Court must assess the full meaning and main feature or features of the challenged statute, as manifest in the words of the statute and the effects it will have as operating law in the current social context. Its main theme or purpose then has to be classified in relation to the general categories of federal and provincial powers respectively, in the B.N.A. Act, to which reference was made earlier. So the basic subject of a federal power-distribution case is the challenged regulatory scheme designed to deal in a certain way with certain of society's problems and needs. As social problems and needs shift and develop, somewhat new statutory schemes are devised to deal with them. At times the new regulatory schemes in their social context will be sufficiently similar to those involved in previous power-distribution cases to be governed by the decisions in those previous cases as precedents. But when the social need for regulation and the regulatory scheme proposed are sufficiently new, then there is no precedent *just a matter of the logic and philosophy of the theory of precedent itself.* Then, without the aid of binding precedent, the Court must boldly face Lord MacMillan's question in the refined and expanded form I suggested for it. In the *John East Case,*[11] for example, the Privy Council did essentially ask themselves this question. They were, in 1944, considering a rather new scheme for the regulation of the relations of management and labour in industry, as enacted by a Provincial Legislature. They said in effect—If the Fathers of Confederation were in our position today and knew current social and industrial conditions as we know them, would they as reasonable men consider this scheme of regulation a proper one to be assigned to Provincial

---

[10]See "The Common Law System in Canada" by W. R. Lederman, in *Canadian Jurisprudence: The Civil Law and Common Law in Canada* (editor E. McWhinney) 1958, University of Toronto Press, 34-70.

[11][1948] 2 W.W.R. 1055.

Legislatures? They answered the question in the affirmative and held the provincial statute valid.

In other words, the doctrine of precedent itself is a realistically flexible instrument of adjustment, if controlled by imaginative use of history and full fact-finding about legislative effects and relevant social context. There is nothing in logic or philosophy, properly conceived, that precludes this flexibility. Indeed, logic frequently displays two or more alternatives for a final federal court but logic alone in such circumstances does not dictate the choice between them. We may conclude then that if the judges of the Supreme Court of Canada are moved by a flexible and imaginative conception of the doctrine of precedent, the need for them to use a power explicitly to depart from their own previous decisions would be rather rare.

I have expressed these views of the nature of precedent and federal power-distribution decisions in other places.[12] Some who disagree hold that this is too Olympian a view of the position of the final court interpreting a federal constitution. My answer is twofold. I have conceded that frequently the Court will find that there are sufficiently similar cases in the past, so that the doctrine of precedent should operate. But, not infrequently, the Court will also be confronted with a case where the elements of novelty are great enough to preclude the direct relevance of any precedents. Then indeed the judges inevitably find themselves high up on Mount Olympus, whether they like it or not, with a very broad discretion to be exercised about the proper situs of primary legislative power in our federal country. They must then proceed as wisely as they can by considering the original words of the constitutional distribution of powers in the B.N.A. Act, in relation to the new legislative scheme and all that can be reasonably ascertained of its effects and the circumstances in which it would be operative. We are back then to the importance of rules of practice and evidence for fact-introduction about legislative effects and social conditions. I conclude with what I said of the interpretative process in an earlier essay.[13]

> In summary then, we can now see that the classification process joins logic with social fact, value decisions and the authority of precedents, to define the distribution of law-making powers. The reasoning involved is not automatic or mechanical; rather it makes the highest demands on learning, intellect, and conscience. It permits expression to the real issues of public policy in the country, and indeed brings such issues into focus in many particular ways, thus facilitating their resolution. The point is that, so long as we have a federal constitution, we must be prepared to contend with the real complexity of the interpretative process. In other words, what has been described above is the inevitable operating jurisprudence of the federal form of social order. If we understand the process, we will expect neither too much nor too little of the constitutional distribution of legislative powers as it stands now, or as it may be if certain changes are made. There is much more room for reasonable differences of interpretation than most people realize. These differences then

---

[12]See W. R. Lederman, ''The Balanced Interpretation of the Federal Distribution of Legislative Powers in Canada'' in *The Future of Canadian Federalism* (editors Crepéau and Macpherson) 1965, University of Toronto Press 91-112.

[13]*Supra,* n. 12, 108-9.

should not be regarded as evidence of bad faith or ignorance; rather, they should be taken as a challenge calling for support of the working of our system of interpretation at its best level.

There we must leave the subject of doctrines of interpretation in federal power-distribution cases and move on to the second set of questions that should be discussed, namely those concerned with the composition, status and jurisdiction of the Supreme Court of Canada.

Concerning this second group of matters, let me first repudiate, for myself at least, a view that seems to have some currency at present. I do not accept the view that the Supreme Court of Canada judges are somehow under unfair or undue influence by the Federal Parliament and Government because the Federal Parliament enacted the Supreme Court Act and the Federal Cabinet appoints the judges. The Supreme Court of Canada is an impartial and objective judicial tribunal in the fullest sense. As such it is an important part of our great English constitutional inheritance—the typical English Superior Court as it stood after the Act of Settlement in 1701. It is a serious misunderstanding of the independence of our courts and judges to think of the judges of the Supreme Court of Canada as somehow delegates of the Federal Government. I reject this delegate theory. Nevertheless, I would agree that the Supreme Court of Canada should appear to be as impartial as in truth it has been and is. Justice must not only be done, it must be seen to be done. To this end, some changes could be made in the manner of appointing the judges and in the constitutional status of the court, changes that will be discussed presently.

Also, there is a very general proposal to alter the nature of our final federal court that should be carefully assessed at this point. It is proposed that the Supreme Court of Canada should be a final court for constitutional questions only, rather than what it is at present, namely a general court of appeal for Canada on the full range of justiciable issues under the laws of Canada and the Provinces—which includes, but is by no means confined to, federal power-distribution issues under the B.N.A. Act.[14]

I consider that the status of the Supreme Court of Canada should be maintained as a general court of appeal for Canada and as the final interpretative tribunal to determine the meaning of the federal constitution. In this connection the all-pervasive character of constitutional questions should be appreciated. A citizen may need to raise a constitutional issue at any time in connection with any type of matter at any level in our judicial system. The citizen charged with the provincial offence of careless driving should be able to plead in the Magistrates' court that the provincial statute concerned is *ultra vires* of the Province under the B.N.A. Act. Then the route of appeals should be open all the way to the Supreme Court of Canada if either party seeks to go that far. Moreover, the Supreme Court of Canada must be able itself to control what appeals are allowed to go through to it because they raise significant constitutional issues. The Court itself must have the final power to give leave for any appeal in the foregoing category.

---

[14]See Jacques-Yvan Morin, *A Constitutional Court for Canada* (1965), 43 Can. Bar Rev. 545-552.

Furthermore, constitutional issues arise in connection with other legal issues; they usually come as part of a complex package. The Supreme Court of Canada should then remain a general court of appeal on all legal issues. To appreciate and do justice concerning the constitutional issue itself, the Court must also be able to appreciate and do justice concerning the *other* legal issues that are inextricably a part of the complex in which the constitutional issue occurs. For example, the Quebec Padlock Law was challenged in connection with the breaking of a lease of an apartment in the City of Montreal. Did breach of this law justify the landlord in repudiating the lease?[15]

The complex and all pervasive nature of federal power-distribution issues may be better appreciated if we recall the nature of these issues. The federal constitution distributes law-making powers between the Federal Parliament on the one hand and the Provincial Legislatures on the other by two lists of classes or types of laws, one federal and the other provincial. These two lists together give a classification system for all the laws of Canada and the Provinces, laws disposing of the rights, duties, powers and liberties of Canadians. When some of these laws, existing or proposed, are challenged as beyond the powers of the Federal Parliament or a Provincial Legislature, judges who appreciate the whole system of law are needed to assess the theme, purpose and effects of the particular challenged law in its living context. There are competing issues of classification and competing precedents, so that any type of law may be challenged at one time or another in our history. This all-round appreciation of the total legal system then is necessary background and competence for the proper disposition of any federal power-distribution issues that may come up. Such a constitutional issue cannot be separated from the nature and effect of the statute the validity of which is being challenged. The plain implication here is that the more learned a judge is in all the main departments of the law—family law, criminal law, property law, commercial law and so on—the better qualified he is to decide wisely federal issues concerning the situs of the powers to pass these various types of laws.

It also follows that the best federal constitutional court is one that has a general as well as a constitutional appellate jurisdiction, because the appellate judges, in their non-constitutional cases, are ranging over many issues in all the principal departments of the total legal system. Thus they 'keep their hands in', so to speak, as reasonably expert and knowledgeable professional persons concerning all the main types of laws and current social problems. Moreover, as the French Civil Law obtains in many respects in Quebec and the English Common Law obtains in corresponding respects in the other Provinces, the judges of the Supreme Court of Canada have to educate one another in the essentials of these two systems, as often this will be necessary to full appreciation of the implications and merits of federal power-distribution decisions. The record of the Su-

---

[15]For an excellent exposition of the interdependence of laws and issues, with particular reference to the inter-action of Civil Law and Common Law concepts in Quebec cases, *see* Gerald E. Le Dain, Q.C. "Concerning the Proposed Constitutional and Civil Law Specialization at the Supreme Court Level", la Revue Juridique Thémis (1967), University of Montreal, 107-126. Dean Le Dain makes a very convincing case for maintaining the general appellate jurisdiction of the Supreme Court of Canada, covering non-constitutional as well as constitutional cases.

preme Court of Canada is good in the field of English-French comparative juris-prudence.[16]

Nor should we think only of constitutional issues in the Supreme Court of Canada, as has already been mentioned. If the constitution belongs to the people, then the citizen with a reason to do so is entitled to raise a constitutional issue of invalidity, to avoid the application of a law to himself, in any court of original jurisdiction in the land. Provincial courts of original jurisdiction and Provincial courts of appeal will frequently have to rule on such issues. At times the litigants will be satisfied with the answers they get in the Provincial courts, particularly in a Provincial court of appeal. Or, if they are not, the Supreme Court of Canada will have the assistance of the judgments in the lower courts. Also, if the sugges-tions made later in this essay are followed, the Supreme Court of Canada would be able to refuse to hear a further appeal to itself, if the disposition of the case in the Provincial court of appeal is deemed satisfactory by the Supreme Court of Canada judges who hear an application for leave to appeal. The Supreme Court of Canada is at present seriously over-loaded with work, and, as we shall see presently, there is a grave need for better screening of cases on appeal so that only those of true national importance are permitted to engage the attention of the final tribunal.

Let us now consider this and certain other changes in the composition, status and jurisdiction of the Supreme Court of Canada that would better enable the Court to discharge its vital functions in our society. First I list these proposed changes briefly and then discuss them in some detail in the order given.

(a) The number of judges might be modestly increased, to improve the na-tional character of the Court and its capacity to function in panels for its non-constitutional cases.

(b) The device of the official nominating commission might be used to sug-gest names of suitable prospective judicial appointees to the Federal Gov-ernment. The Provinces could be represented on these nominating com-missions and thus have some influence in the selection of judges for the Supreme Court of Canada.

(c) The essential provisions concerning the structure and powers of the Su-preme Court of Canada should be specially entrenched in the Constitution, thus avoiding even the appearance of the possibility of any undue influ-ence by the Federal Government or Federal Parliament on the Court.

(d) The rules governing appeals to the Supreme Court of Canada should be changed so as to limit the total work-load of the Court to cases, both con-stitutional and non-constitutional, that raise issues of true national impor-tance, the Supreme Court judges themselves having the last word on whether a nationally significant issue of this character is involved.

The questions of a modest increase in the number of Supreme Court judges and the use of official nominating commissions may be considered together. At present, the requirement that three of the nine judges should come from Quebec

---

[16]*Supra,* n. 15.

is statutory, but it is also just about as firmly established by convention that, of the remaining six, three should come from Ontario, one from the four Atlantic Provinces and two from the four Western Provinces. I believe the principal defect here to be the under-representation of the Atlantic region and the Western region. I would increase the Court to a total strength of eleven, giving an additional judge to the Atlantic region and the Western region. The result would then be as follows:

Atlantic Provinces	2
Quebec	3
Ontario	3
Western Provinces	3
	11

In this event, the quorum for a federal constitutional case could be nine of the eleven (instead of seven of the nine at present). Thus a collegiate approach of the court to federal power-distribution issues would be preserved. Non-constitutional cases could be dealt with by smaller panels, and the presence of more judges would facilitate this. Civil Law judges could be appointed ad hoc, as needed, from the superior courts of Quebec to ensure a majority of judges trained in the French Civil Law for non-constitutional cases from Quebec. In a panel of five, three or four could be Civil Law judges, or in a panel of seven, five could be Civil Law judges.

In any event, appropriate regional quotas for the membership of the Supreme Court of Canada might as well be expressed in the Constitution, as they seem to be permanent and necessary features of the structure of the Court. In this respect, though, it is important to remember a point emphasized by the Federal Government in its White Paper of February, 1969, entitled ''The Constitution and the People of Canada''. They stress that the Court must exercise a truly judicial and not merely an arbitral function.[17] The soundness of this statement deserves a rather full explanation. The judges of the Supreme Court are there to respond as men of learning, moral sensitivity and social knowledge to the legal issues and related social problems of Canada as a federal country. They are not on the Court as representatives or delegates. Rather they are there as highly placed official persons enjoying secure and permanent tenure in office, so that they need respond only to the call of reason and conscience.[18]

But, if this is so, why the regional quotas just suggested? The quotas are necessary and proper because Canada is a vast country differing in some critical ways region by region. There are common factors, but there are unique ones too. If we ensure that the judges are drawn from the various regions as indicated, we ensure that there is available within the Court collective experience and background knowledge of all parts of Canada. In judicial conferences and other contacts within the Court membership, the judges are able to inform and educate one another on essential facts and background from their respective parts of Canada.

---

[17]*Supra*, n. 9, 42.

[18]*See generally* on this subject: W. R. Lederman, *The Independence of the Judiciary* (1956), 34 Can. Bar Rev. 769 and 1139.

This is the vital factor of relevant native judicially-noticed knowledge that, as mentioned earlier, was missing in the judges of the Judicial Committee of the Privy Council. Here then is the rationale of regional quotas for the membership of the Supreme Court of Canada, and to observe the quotas *for this reason* does not turn the Court into an arbitral body of special pleaders or a miniature national parliament. The professional qualifications of the judges and their independence on the basis of secure tenure for life (or until age 75) means that they will behave judicially, and not as special pleaders or delegates, though they are systematically chosen from different parts of Canada. On this footing—the need for judicial notice of conditions in all parts of the country—it becomes obvious that the present Supreme Court of Canada has too few judges from the Atlantic Provinces and the Western Provinces; it has enough from each of Ontario and Quebec.

The Federal Government proposes to leave the membership of the Supreme Court at nine, with the regional quotas presumably remaining as they are. It also proposes to change the method of appointment so as to give the Provinces a share in the process of selecting Supreme Court judges. In the White Paper previously mentioned, this proposal is put as follows:[19]

> In considering the manner of selection of the members of the Court, the Government of Canada has been concerned that this body must exercise a judicial, not an arbitral, function. Judges should not be regarded as representatives of several different governments which could conceivably be allowed to appoint them. For this reason, a single system of appointment is to be preferred. It is recognized, however, that to ensure continued confidence in the Court it would be preferable that there be some form of participation on behalf of the provinces in the appointing process. It is therefore proposed that nominations of potential appointees be submitted by the federal government to the Senate for approval. If the proposals for the revision of the Senate are adopted, provincial viewpoints could be effectively expressed by this means. This system would not, of course, apply to those who were already members of the Court at such time as it might be reconstituted under the Constitution and with a new system of appointment.

The merit of this proposal, if any, depends entirely on what Senate reform would amount to, and that remains very obscure. Unfortunately the Canadian Senate has been and is the least successful of our governmental bodies. The main difficulty is that the Senators are appointed for life (or until age 75) by the Government of the day, and Governments have invariably used these appointments to reward faithful adherents of their own political party. The result has been a mediocre second chamber for the Federal Parliament that enjoys a poor reputation in the country, and on the whole it deserves this reputation, in spite of the best efforts of a small minority of able and dedicated Senators who, from time to time, do useful things. The only change the Federal Government is presently proposing for the Canadian Senate is to arrange that the Provincial Governments should appoint some of the Senators.[20] This could well mean that the new Senate would be more partisan and mediocre than is the present Senate. The necessity for ratifica-

---

[19]*Supra,* n. 9, 42.
[20]*Supra,* n. 9.

tion of judicial appointments by such a Senate could discourage good prospective candidates, even among adherents of the party in power, from coming forward.

This idea of Senate ratification seems to have been borrowed from the United States. There the federal judiciary, including the judges of the Supreme Court of the United States, are appointed by the President for life, subject to ratification by the Senate. The results of this in the United States have been of quite dubious merit, in spite of the fact that the United States Senate is an elected body of great prestige. The problem in the United States, as in Canada, is to seek out and appoint the best qualified persons as judges, regardless of political party affiliation. This may be done through the device of the official, non-partisan *nominating* commission. Partisan *ratification* requirements simply miss the whole point of what needs to be done.

I agree with what was said on this subject by Mr. Glenn R. Winters, Executive Director of the American Judicature Society, speaking in 1966 to the Association of Canadian Law Teachers. He said:[21]

> A governor is a political officer, and he gets to be governor by playing the game of politics and winning. The same is true of our national president. It is too much to expect of any human being in that position that he will always be able to resist the pressures of politics and keep his judicial appointments non-political.
>
> Statistics confirm what is common knowledge—that all federal judicial appointments are strongly influenced by partisan politics and in too many instances this results in appointments that are poor or mediocre. The highest percentage of appointments from the opposite party by any president has been eight per cent, and it has been as low as one or two percent.
>
> A sincere effort has been made over the past 15 or more years by the American Bar Association to make available the professional opinion of knowledgeable lawyers on the qualifications of candidates and to urge the appointment only of those who meet its standards. A great deal of good has been done on this by a very devoted and dedicated ABA committee, and I think there is no doubt that the federal judiciary today is of substantially higher quality than it would have been if the committee had not been at work. It is not, however, a complete or fully satisfactory answer to the problem, for several reasons. The judgment of the lawyers is not infallible, and their weakness is to place too great a value on legal proficiency, to favor what we speak of as the lawyers' lawyer. The bar committee has never affirmatively submitted names, but has limited itself to passing on names submitted to it, and this is undoubtedly right, for it would be too much power to put in the hands of a non-governmental agency if the bar were given the job of nominating the judges. In fact, some people feel that the present situation is going too far, in which a small, widely scattered committee which mostly depends upon the word of one of its members, has for most of the time and would like to have for all the time a virtual veto power over judicial appointments.
>
> Albert Kales' answer to this was the judicial nominating commission—the real heart of the merit plan. I will take just a minute to list briefly the important features of the nominating commission as envisioned by Kales and as actually adopted in a dozen or more of the states:

---

[21]*American Appointments, Proposals and Problems* (1967), 1 Canadian Legal Studies, 252, 253-4.

John M. Cuelenaere Public Library
05 OCT 99 06:02pm
FINE PAYMENT

23292200355507

Collected - overdues
  Mastering effective English /
  33292000218556 $0.40

  John M. Cuelenaere Public Library
       05 OCT 99 06:02pm
  ITEMS CHECKED OUT AND DUE DATES

       23292200355507

International Covenant on Economic,
33292000406151   Due: 26 OCT 99 *

Continuing Canadian constitutional
33292000124960   Due: 26 OCT 99 *

Amending Canada's constitution :
33292004985242   Due: 26 OCT 99 *

       Saturday and Sunday Matinees
     October 9 - Casper Meets Wendy
     October 16 - Quest for Camelot
        October 17 - THE MATRIX
All-Kids Craft Fair Registration-Oct.12
  SASKATCHEWAN LIBRARY WEEK-Oct. 17-23
Author Reading-Veronica E. Brock-Oct.19

1. It is a nominating rather than a confirming body, rendering affirmative assistance in going out and finding the right man rather than passively approving or disapproving of names submitted to it.
2. It contains lawyer members, in order that the vitally important viewpoint of the bar may have a voice in evaluating and choosing the nominees.
3. It contains at least one judge, in order that the interests of the bench itself may find appropriate expression.
4. It contains laymen, in order that technical legal qualifications may be kept in proper proportion to the equally or more important considerations of general education, integrity, and sensitivity to human problems.
5. The commission does not itself make the precise and final choice, but only makes a preliminary selection, leaving it to the governor or other appointing authority to make the final selection.
6. The governor is required to appoint from the commission's nominations, and may not accept them when they please him and disregard them when he feels like it.
7. In the membership of the commission, politics is minimized by making it either non-partisan or bi-partisan, and its nominations are non-partisan, with an effort to draw on the judicial talent of both parties.

It is desirable to learn from American experience and to adopt their procedures if and when they are better than our own. The American Senatorial ratification procedure has nothing to offer us by way of improvement, whereas the device of the judicial nominating commission has.

As applied to the Supreme Court of Canada, such commissions could improve the quality of judicial appointments and at the same time give the Provinces an effective part in the choice of judges. For instance, there might be a judicial nominating commission for each of the four Supreme Court quota regions mentioned earlier. Such a commission could be composed of both ex officio and appointed members, including ministers and senior officials of both the Federal and Provincial Governments, as well as the official provincial law societies, the judiciary and the lay public. Appointments of judges would still be made by the Governor General in Council (the Federal Government), but it would be mandatory for the appointees to be selected only from those persons listed as eligible by the appropriate judicial nominating commission. In these commissions, political party loyalties would be varied and would tend to cancel out, and some members would be genuinely non-partisan in this sense anyway. Such a commission would have no other rational way of proceeding except to seek to identify the persons in the region best qualified on the merits for high judicial office. This would continue the single system of appointment to the Supreme Court which the Federal Government is very properly concerned to preserve, but would at the same time give the Provinces an effective voice in the choice of the judges *and promote high quality appointments*. This is the way to improvement, both from the point of view of federalism and the quality of the judiciary. The sooner the proposals for ratification of judicial appointments by the Canadian Senate are completely abandoned and rejected, the better. They are both unwise and unfortunate.

This, however, is the only important respect in which I take strong exception to the Federal Government's proposals for reform concerning the Supreme Court of Canada. On the other points yet to be mentioned, the status of the court and its jurisdiction, I agree with the Federal proposals.

As to the status of the Court, the Federal proposals are in the following terms:[22]

> The first question that naturally arises relates to the means for providing the structure of the Court. At present the Constitution makes no provision for a Supreme Court other than to give to Parliament a power to establish one and to define its jurisdiction. The structure and jurisdiction of the Court are therefore provided by legislative act of the central government. The Government of Canada feels that it would now be more appropriate that the Constitution itself provide for the existence, the appointment and tenure of judges, and the major powers of the Supreme Court. This would be more consistent with the Court's role as the final interpreter of the Constitution of a federal state.

While it is now desirable to express the essential provisions concerning the structure and powers of the Supreme Court of Canada as superior constitutional law, it must be remembered that this would be a change in form and not in substance. The Supreme Court of Canada is truly independent now and always has been. Nevertheless, special entrenchment of its essential structure and powers in the Constitution would give it a better image in the eyes of those who do not understand, or who choose to ignore, the present truth about the substantial independence of the Court. I favour special entrenchment to the extent indicated in the Federal proposals for the sake of proper appearances, not because there is any truth in the allegations that the Supreme Court of Canada is now under undue influence by the Federal Government or Parliament or ever has been.

Finally, there is the problem of the total work-load of the Supreme Court of Canada, which is at present too great. The Federal White Paper deals with the problem of the total work-load only indirectly. It states:[23]

> If provision is to be made in the Constitution for the Court, it would also be necessary to consider how far its jurisdiction should be defined by that document. It is typical of several federal states that their final appellate tribunal has certain powers guaranteed to it by the Constitution, and the remainder are provided by enactment of the national legislature. We would propose a similar system for the Supreme Court of Canada. The Constitution could provide that the Court would enjoy ultimate appellate jurisdiction in any proceeding in which a constitutional issue is raised. This would preserve, free from legislative interference, the most essential function of a final court in a federal state—the power to review the validity of legislative or other acts of all governments. With this function preserved by the Constitution, the Court's other appellate and advisory jurisdiction could be defined by Parliament.

Except for federal power-distribution issues, this leaves open and unexamined many questions about what the rules for hearing appeals should actually

---

[22]*Supra*, n. 9, 40.
[23]*Supra*, n. 9, 42.

be. At present a great many non-constitutional cases engage the time of the Supreme Court because they are appeals as of right under a variety of out-dated and illogical rules, rules that favour to an undue extent the hearing of property, commercial or taxation issues involving large sums of money for wealthy litigants who are not willing to accept the results of their days in court at the provincial trial and appeal court levels. The position respecting appeals in criminal cases is not entirely satisfactory either. Professor Peter Russell has recently published an exhaustive and perceptive study of the jurisdiction of the Supreme Court which makes these and other points in very telling fashion.[24] He has illuminated an area for reform of the Supreme Court of Canada that has been hitherto much neglected. His main conclusion about the past is given in the following passage:[25]

> Finally, the most fundamental question of policy raised by both appeals as of right and appeals with leave is whether the present system represents the most appropriate mixture of the two modes of appeal. It is extremely difficult to discover any reasonable basis for the provisions which now give the litigant a right to appeal from the provincial appeal courts. The most striking result of the present system is that, in marked contrast to the highest courts of both Great Britain and the United States, the Supreme Court of Canada has relatively little control over its own docket: in its first fifteen years as Canada's ultimate court of appeals, [i.e. since 1949], fewer than one out of five of its reported decisions were in cases that the Court itself selected for review. Under this system the Court still functions in the main as a court of last resort for disgruntled but well-heeled litigants.

Professor Russell recommends that most appeals reaching the Supreme Court of Canada should do so because a reasonable quorum of Supreme Court judges have given leave to appeal on the footing that a preliminary examination by them of the case shows that an issue of national importance is involved, an issue that has not been or cannot be satisfactorily settled in the lower courts. Where federal power-distribution issues are involved, as identified by the Supreme Court itself, the presumption would certainly be in favour of leave to appeal and perhaps the appeal would be a matter of right.

Professor Russell would be stricter in excluding appeals on non-constitutional issues arising under provincial laws than I would. The point made early in this essay about the all-pervasive nature of constitutional issues has real force also in non-constitutional cases. Federal and provincial laws interact and interpenetrate in many and complex ways within a single province. To take a simple example, a mortgage transaction involves provincial land law, but the federal laws governing interest and bills of exchange are also involved. The complete judicial settlement of a disputed mortgage transaction may require decisions on several points, some arising under provincial laws and some under federal laws. Moreover, this interaction and interpenetration is growing as the Federal Parliament and the Provincial Legislatures pass more and more statutes to meet modern social problems like consumer protection, pollution control and urban renewal.

---

[24]Peter H. Russell. *The Jurisdiction of the Supreme Court of Canada: Present Policies and a Programme for Reform,* (1968) 6 Osgoode L.J. 1-8.
[25]*Supra*, n. 24, 28.

The point is valid for the areas of both private and public law. Because the Canadian Constitution provides us with a single system of courts with this comprehensive jurisdiction, it is much superior in this respect to the Constitution of the United States, with its separate systems of State and Federal courts. Canadians are thus saved and wasteful 'forum-shopping' that goes on in the United States between their two court systems.

At the apex of the single Canadian System is the Supreme Court of Canada. Obviously its jurisdiction should be as comprehensive respecting federal and provincial laws as is that of the lower courts, subject to the screening of cases for their national importance as indicated. Speaking of power-distribution cases in the Supreme Court, the Government of Canada has said:[26] ". . . a body of integral jurisdiction would be more in keeping with our traditions and with a sound appreciation of how our law works in practice. Artificial divisions in the interpretative process would not assist in the sound development of constitutional law". I agree and would generalize the argument to include non-constitutional cases in our federal country as well.[27]

---

[26]*Supra*, n. 9, 40.
[27]*Supra*, n. 15.

Chapter 11

Current Proposals for Reform of the Supreme Court of Canada

Reprinted with permission from (1979), 57 Canadian Bar Review 688

I. INTRODUCTION

Since its foundation in 1875, the Supreme Court of Canada has formed a vital part of our constitution. At least since 1949, when appeals to the Judicial Committee of the Privy Council were terminated, the Supreme Court has been our final and ultimate judicial appellate tribunal with comprehensive jurisdiction over the interpretation of the laws and the constitution of Canada as a whole, including the laws and constitutions of the several provinces. Needless to say, at this level, the power of judicial interpretation involves at times important choices and discretions that are virtually legislative in nature. So, when constitutional reform generally is in the air, inevitably the Supreme Court of Canada comes in for its share of attention.

This is true of the three sets of proposals for constitutional reform that will be considered here, for what they say about the Supreme Court. In order of appearance they are: The Constitutional Amendment Bill of the Trudeau Government, Bill C-60, in June of 1978,[1] the *Report* of the Committee on the Constitution of the Canadian Bar Association, entitled *"Towards a New Canada"*, in the August of 1978; and the *Report* of the Task Force on Canadian Unity entitled *"A Future Together"*, in February of 1979. Hereafter I will refer to them as the Trudeau Amendment Bill, the Bar Committee *Report* and the Pepin-Roberts *Report*, respectively. In referring to the Trudeau Amendment Bill, I include a Trudeau Government White Paper of August, 1978, giving reasons for the Bill's proposals respecting the Supreme Court of Canada. On the whole, the Bill and the two reports are to a high degree concerned to maintain and justify the *status quo*, and in my view quite properly so. Nevertheless, in certain respects, they do indeed propose significant changes, with some of which I also agree. The Bar Committee's *Report* is the most conservative, the Pepin-Roberts *Report* goes furthest in proposing change, and the Trudeau Amendment Bill is in the middle position. In assessing the Supreme Court of Canada, all three sets of proposals ad-

---

[1] Also Constitutional Reform—The Supreme Court of Canada, by the Hon. Otto E. Lang, Minister of Justice, August, 1978.

dress themselves to the topics of jurisdiction, size, regional quotas for membership, system for appointing judges to the court, and special constitutional status for the court. With this range, virtually every important issue that could be raised about the Supreme Court of Canada is raised one way or another. Let us proceed then to detailed consideration and analysis under these headings.

II. JURISDICTION

The two reports and the Trudeau Amendment Bill propose to continue the present final and comprehensive appellate jurisdiction of the Supreme Court for the whole of Canada. They are indeed right about this, for reasons which they give only in part, but which I now wish to restate and develop further. It is essential in some repsects, and at least very important and beneficial in others, that the Supreme Court of Canada should have this capacity to make final decisions that are binding precedents in all parts of Canada. Thus, in those vital respects, the court can bring consistency to the meaning and operation of the laws concerned for people in all parts of the country. And consistency in the sense of equal treatment by the law for all persons in essentially similar circumstances is a critical requirement of justice itself. What then are these matters of public and private law in our federal country respecting which this consistency is either necessary or highly desirable?

First and perhaps foremost in the "necessary" category is the positive constitutional division of primary legislative powers between the central Parliament on the one hand and the several provincial Parliaments on the other. These distributive provisions are specially entrenched, and are for the most part found in sections 91 and 92 of the British North America Act.[2] Also, a specially entrenched "Bill of Rights" may emerge from the present pressure for constitutional reform, and this also is a form of division of powers; technically a negative form, in defence of the positive human rights and freedoms specified for special protection. Such a "Bill of Rights" would protect certain basic human rights and freedoms across the whole country from undue impairment by ordinary statutes, either federal or provincial, even though the latter did satisfy the positive distribution rules for legislative powers. What amounts to undue impairment is essentially a judicial question, and a court would strike down an ordinary statute that it decided had such effect.

So, a central and final appellate court is necessary to referee the special constitutional issues just described, but this must not be taken to mean that the central court should be *just* a specialized constitutional court. In truth, the implication is the opposite, that these special constitutional decisions are best made by a final court of general jurisdiction. Such issues may and do arise in every department of the law and on virtually any subject. Moreover, before a court can decide on the constitutional validity of a challenged provincial or federal statute, it must first construe that statute for its ordinary meaning, if it were to be applied and enforced according to its terms. Only then can the further issue of constitutional va-

---

[2] 1867, 30 & 31 Vict., c. 3, as am. (U.K.).

lidity be addressed. Accordingly, judicial findings of validity or invalidity are each based on a particular and prior authoritative interpretation of the statute in question, and obviously that interpretation must then hold for all purposes. For example, at times alternative interpretations of a challenged statute are plausible, one narrower and one broader. If the court finds the statute valid on the narrower meaning only, then the broader meaning is thereafter excluded.[3] All this implies that judges making constitutional decisions should be generalists in the law, and not just experts in constitutional law. One can be assured of this if they have general jurisdiction as well as special constitutional jurisdiction. Fortunately, in Canada, our judicial system as a whole is for the most part designed to provide this single general jurisdiction, whether the issues arise under provincial laws or federal laws or (as is frequently the case) under both. This is true of the superior courts of original jurisdiction in the provinces and also of the provincial courts of appeal, the intermediate level of appeal. It is logical then that the Supreme Court of Canada should have the same single comprehensive power to settle all aspects of the case before it at the final level of appeal. Moreover, there are practical reasons, aside from the determination of special constitutional issues, for our unitary judicial system with its comprehensive jurisdiction, both original and appellate. Legal issues for ordinary citizens frequently come in single packages that involve matters arising under both federal and provincial laws. For example, bankruptcy under the federal statute may also involve issues under provincial property laws, and all the issues need to be settled if the citizen-litigant is to have justice. As indicated, our system provides for this to be done in one action before courts of general original and appellate jurisdiction in the provinces, so it makes sense that the Supreme Court of Canada should have the same powers.[4]

Moving on now from special constitutional issues, we find that there are other respects in which final judicial decisions with country-wide impact are essential or at least highly desirable. The case is obvious for such uniform and final interpretation of important issues arising from regular statutes of the central Parliament of Canada, for example the Criminal Code. At present about twenty-five per cent of appeals decided by the Supreme Court of Canada are criminal appeals. But what about provincial statutes on subjects assigned to the provincial legislatures, and the corresponding matters covered by the common law in the common law provinces and by the Civil Code in Quebec? One of the purposes of a federal constitution is to continue old diversities and to permit new ones, province by province, in *these* respects. Does it not follow then that the several provincial courts of appeal are the proper final tribunals for issues arising under valid provincial laws in their respective provinces? There is considerable force in this proposition up to a point, but only up to a point. Because many transactions and relations are inter-provincial, though based on provincial laws, relevant precedents from a final national appellate court are at least in the highly beneficial category.

---

[3] *McKay v. The Queen,* [1965] S.C.R. 798.
[4] *A.G. for Ontario v. A.G. For Canada,* [1947] A.C. 127, p. 151 (P.C.).

Among other things, we are now touching upon problems of private international law (alternatively known as the conflict of laws). For example, contract is generally a provincial legislative subject, but in a private commercial transaction between a resident of Ontario and a resident of Quebec, is Ontario law to be applied or Quebec Law, where the respective provincial contract laws differ critically in the result they would mandate for the two parties? The rules of conflict of laws have been developed, mainly by the courts, to resolve these complex and difficult problems. Thus, in the example given, if the transaction is more closely connected with Quebec than Ontario, Ontario courts as well as Quebec courts will apply Quebec contract law, and thus the results of action in court in either province would be the same. The converse proposition is true if the transaction were more closely connected with Ontario than with Quebec. But this beneficial reciprocity depends on a uniform definition in the conflict of laws rules of what constitutes ''closer connection'' for each province. To ensure this uniformity, interpretation needs in the end to be in the hands of a final national appellate court which can issue precedents binding for all the provinces in this respect.

We have just been speaking of an inter-provincial situation where the applicable provincial laws are different. But also there are other inter-provincial situations where the applicable provincial laws are the same. For example, in the areas of company law or insurance law, the statutes of different provinces frequently have common provisions. There are a great many inter-provincial relations and transactions between persons to which such uniform laws are relevant, and hence it is beneficial to those persons to have one consistent national interpretation of their meaning. In our system, the appropriate final appellate court for this is the Supreme Court of Canada.

Now we may look again at the proposition stated earlier that, up to a point, it is logical for the provincial court of appeal to be the final court for the province concerned on issues arising under provincial laws. Almost invariably this would seem to be proper when a given case raises issues *only* under provincial laws and the determination of them would have *no* wider significance beyond the boundaries of that province. To a large and growing extent, this is already the position, because such a case is most unlikely to be accepted for appeal by the Supreme Court of Canada. Since 1975, in most types of cases, a litigant must have the consent of the Supreme Court of Canada, or that of the provincial Court of Appeal involved, before being permitted an appeal to the Supreme Court of Canada. Usually this means the consent of the Supreme Court itself, after a brief hearing of the would-be appellant by three judges of the court. Unless the applicant for leave to appeal can show very quickly that some issue of genuine national importance is involved in his case, he is refused leave and the decision of the provincial Court of Appeal concerned stands as the final disposition of the case. So, referring to points made earlier, we find that leave to appeal is almost certain to be refused if (i) the issues in the case arise under the provincial law only, (ii) there is no basic constitutional question about the original validity of that law, and (iii) there are no inter-provincial dimensions to the case in terms either of private international law or uniformity with the provincial laws of other provinces. In such cases the provincial Court of Appeal concerned has increasingly, since 1975, become the final court of appeal for its own province. Speaking of Quebec, the Bar Committee's *Report* gives the figures for that province:[5]

> In 1975 the [Supreme Court of Canada] heard 31 predominantly civil law cases; in 1976, 16; in 1977, only 6. In 1975, it heard 8 cases on other Quebec statutes; in 1976, 5; in 1977, none.

Finally, one must remember that the Supreme Court of Canada is one court of nine judges which is able to hear and decide about 160 cases a year at the most. Moreover, the Supreme Court of Canada is the second level of appeal—the typical would-be appellant has already had his day in court twice, once at the trial court level and once at the provincial Court of Appeal level. In addition to the elements of national significance already mentioned, for an appeal to the Supreme Court of Canada, there must also be an element of overriding public and national importance in the case that takes it well beyond the particular interests of the litigants directly concerned. Unless this is so, there is no reason for the Supreme Court of Canada to give leave to appeal. While the categories of "public national importance" are never closed, all the same it is obvious that the Supreme Court of Canada judges must be strict about granting leave. The vast majority of cases in the court system, including for example criminal cases and private international law cases, will be finally decided in the trial courts or in intermediate appellate courts in the respective provinces. Those who see the general jurisdiction of the Supreme Court of Canada as a threat to the autonomy of the provinces in judicial matters should remember this. The Supreme Court of Canada has the task of giving judicial leadership on the crucial matters indicated, but it can only do this by being highly selective about hearing cases on the merits that are necessary or suitable for this purpose.

Now we must consider whether the Supreme Court of Canada as at present constituted is as well designed as it may be or should be to accomplish the above-mentioned task. In doing this we look first at questions of size and regional quotas for membership, then at the system for appointing judges to the court, and finally at the question of full constitutional status for the court.

III. SIZE OF THE SUPREME COURT OF CANADA AND REGIONAL QUOTAS FOR MEMBERSHIP

The starting point for consideration of these problems is the *status quo*. Briefly, it is as follows. The Supreme Court of Canada consists at present of nine justices, coming three from Quebec, one from the Atlantic Provinces, two from Ontario, and three from the Western Provinces. The Supreme Court Act[6] requires that three of the judges must come from the Bar of Quebec, but the other regional quotas are customary, with apparently an option as to whether there should be three from the Western Provinces and two from Ontario, or vice versa. The judges are appointed to permanent tenure for life or until age seventy-five by the

---

[5] *Towards a New Canada* (1978), 58.
[6] R.S.C. 1970, c. S-19, as am.

Governor General in Council, that is, by the Cabinet (the Federal Government of the day).

Respecting size and regional quotas, the three sets of reform proposals we are considering diverge somewhat. The Bar Association Committee proposes no change, though it has been ambiguous about customary regional quotas. The Pepin-Roberts *Report* proposes a court of eleven judges, six from the nine common law provinces and five from Quebec. It does not commit itself on the distribution of the six common law judges among the common law provinces. The Trudeau Amendment Bill also proposed a court of eleven judges, with four guaranteed to Quebec and seven coming from the other regions, at least one from each of the Atlantic Provinces, Ontario, the Prairie Provinces, and British Columbia. Note that under this proposal British Columbia would become a region separate from the Prairie Provinces for this purpose.

Clearly the matter of regional quotas is critical, and thus the reasons for them requires careful analysis. The Bar Committee's *Report* shows the greatest distrust of them, though it does say ". . . we do agree that an effort must always be made to ensure that the court as a whole has a deep understanding of all the regions in Canada".[7] This refers to the background knowledge which each of the several judges has of the major region of the country from which he comes, and so this statement does imply at least that no major region of the country should be without a judge on the Supreme Court. Thus the Bar Committee seems to agree that some attention in composing the court should be given to regional quotas. My expectation is that we will continue with the present customary quotas, that is, one from the Atlantic region, two from Ontario and three from the Western Provinces; or three from Ontario and two from the West. I find it difficult to believe that either Ontario or the West respectively would accept a Supreme Court with only one judge from Ontario or the West. Of course the Bar Committee would continue the quota for Quebec at three judges, as a matter of law. But the Committee does say that ". . . apart from Quebec, no province should have reason to expect representation at all times or by any particular number. What we should seek for the court are the best and most sensitive judicial minds the nation has to offer".[8] The last sentence quoted has a nice ring to it, but it does not quite stand up to analysis. Of course one wants the appointing authority to do the best it can about merit, but pure merit is seldom if ever as obvious as the Bar Committee's statement implies. With the best will in the world, how does the appointing authority identify the one laywer or judge in nine common law provinces who offers the best and most sensitive judicial mind for the single vacancy that has occurred? Perhaps I can make the point in this way. Take five cities where there are large concentrations of the legal profession—Halifax, Toronto, Winnipeg, Edmonton and Vancouver. Realistically, equivalent merit could be found among some eight to twelve or more lawyers and judges from these cities, at least one from each. But in my view that is as far as merit would take you. Rarely, if ever, could you deal in the superlative and say—Mr. X is *the best* of the lot. By all

---

[7]Towards a New Canada (1978), 58.
[8]*Op. cit., ibid.*

means let us emphasize merit, but this is not inconsistent with quotas for the major regions of the country. If the vacancy has occurred because the one judge from the Atlantic region has retired, then one of the several lawyers or judges from the Atlantic region who is the equal of the best of his counterparts in other regions should be appointed.

In my view then, regional quotas cannot be banished from the composition of the court, nor should they be. The country is diversified into four or five major regions, and recognition of this in composing the Supreme Court of Canada does not threaten to turn the court into a board of arbitration rather than a judicial tribunal. Such recognition does mean that background knowledge of all major parts of Canada will be brought to the conference table in the Supreme Court building in Ottawa when the justices meet to consider their judgments. It is most important that this should be so. Moreover, the judges are independent and impartial for reasons that have nothing to do with regional quotas. Once appointed, they hold office permanently for life or until age seventy-five and can be removed earlier only by Parliament for very serious misconduct. This is what accounts for their independence, as Professor Robert MacGregor Dawson made clear many years ago.[9]

> The judge must be made independent of most of the restraints, checks and punishments which are usually called into play against other public officials. . . . He is thus protected against some of the most potent weapons which a democracy has at its command: he receives almost complete protection against criticism; he is given civil and criminal immunity for acts committed in the discharge of his duties; he cannot be removed from office for any ordinary offence, but only for misbehaviour of a flagrant kind; and he can never be removed simply because his decisions happen to be disliked by the Cabinet, the Parliament, or the people. Such independence is unquestionably dangerous, and if this freedom and power were indiscriminately granted the results would certainly prove to be disastrous. The desired protection is found by picking with especial care the men who are to be entrusted with these responsibilities, and then paradoxically heaping more privileges upon them to stimulate their sense of moral responsibility, which is called in as a substitute for the political responsibility which has been removed. The judge is placed in a position where he has nothing to lose by doing what is right and little to gain by doing what is wrong; and there is therefore every reason to hope that his best efforts will be devoted to the conscientious performance of his duty.

So we find that the judges of the Supreme Court of Canada, once appointed, are not politically accountable to the regions from which they come. Also, for the same reasons, the judges are not accountable to any other branch of government, federal or provincial, for the manner in which they dispose of the cases that arise before them. They are accountable only to the law itself, including the law of the constitution. This is just as true of the judges from Quebec as it is of the judges from the other provinces. Regional quotas, including the mandatory quota from Quebec, have not up to now consistently produced patterns of regional uniformity of decision among the judges from a single region. So, as long as the constitu-

---

[9]The Government of Canada (2nd ed., 1954), 486.

tional principle of the independence of the judiciary holds, in my view the quotas will not have this effect, though no doubt the two or three judges from a single region will find themselves occasionally together and isolated on the same side of an issue. This does not happen very often. Furthermore, it should be noted that if the judges of the Supreme Court of Canada were not truly independent as just explained, then the mandatory quota for Quebec would alone be enough to turn the court into a board of arbitration staffed by accountable regional representatives. The difference between the Civil Code and the common law is certainly one of the reasons for a regional quota for Quebec, but not by any means the only reason. If Quebec were a province with the English common law, I would still argue for regional quotas, with Quebec one of the regions. These things having been said, of course every effort must be made within each of the major regions we are talking about to appoint one of the best persons available on the basis of merit, as vacancies occur in the respective regions. Quotas for the major regions of the country and appointment on the basis of merit are not inconsistent when it comes to composing the Supreme Court of Canada.

The Pepin-Robarts Task Force deals much more briefly with the composition of the Supreme Court of Canada than does the Bar Committee, and the Task Force makes quite a different proposal. They recommend that the court should be composed of eleven judges, six from the common law provinces and five from Quebec. This is one of the major respects in which the Task Force presses for recognition of the French-English duality in Canada. Though six to five is not quite literal duality, it certainly comes close. I do not think Quebeckers should expect this much, but, if it became necessary politically to agree to this as part of the price to keep Quebec in the Canadian federal union, then I would accept it. The Quebec judges, once appointed, would be truly independent for the reasons I have just given, and would not behave merely as a block of politically accountable representatives from the Quebec region. The Pepin-Robarts Task Force did not address the problem of regional quotas respecting the six judges from the common law provinces, but, as I have also just indicated, I do not think there is any escape from legitimate constitutional expectations in this regard.

As for the over-all size of the court, we have seen that the Bar Committee favours the present membership of nine justices, whereas the other two sets of reform proposals suggest a court of eleven justices. I favour the higher number for some very simple reasons. The present Supreme Court is hard-pressed, and the additional judges would make it easier to carry the heavy work-load. Also, appropriate quotas for membership from the major regions of Canada would be easier to set if the membership of the court were larger than at present. Nine is not a magic number. Indeed, I believe the court could function well as a single and unitary tribunal if the membership were as high as fifteen, with nine as the minimum quorum requirement for any sitting of the court. In these circumstances, there would be an overlapping of at least three judges between any two panels of nine. A higher quorum might be required for important constitutional cases.

What has been said to this point makes it clear that the system for appointing judges to the Supreme Court of Canada in the first place is of the highest importance. Does the present system on the whole do as well as can be done to select the best persons, or could it be improved? I emphasize that, in considering this question, I will be talking of systems and their implications. No disparagement of any Supreme Court justice past or present is intended. The Supreme Court of Canada has been and is a very distinguished judicial tribunal. The question is, could it be made even better and more effective by some well-calculated revisions in its constitution?

IV. THE SYSTEM FOR APPOINTING JUDGES TO THE SUPREME COURT OF CANADA

The *status quo* concerning the selection of Supreme Court of Canada judges is unilateral appointment by the federal government of the day, after a process of assessment and selection that can be characterized as necessarily confidential (if you approve of it) or as unduly secretive (if you disapprove of it). In any event, the Bar Association Committee, the Pepin-Roberts Task Force and the Trudeau Government in their Amendment Bill all propose to end the present unilaterialism one way or another.

The Bar Association Committee shows some sympathy for the Victoria Charter Formula of 1971 concerning appointments to the Supreme Court, which gave a major role to the provincial Attorneys General, but, in the end, the Committee said that:[10]

> The federal government should have the power under the Constitution to appoint judges to the Supreme Court with the consent of a Judiciary Committee of a reconstituted Upper House working in camera.

The Upper House the Committee proposes would be directly representative of provincial governments. The proposal of the Pepin-Roberts Task Force is the same, except that they would require the Federal Government to consult beforehand with the appropriate provincial Attorneys General. The Task Force contemplates the same kind of an Upper House as does the Bar Association Committee, but presumably the Task Force intends *public* proceedings for ratification before the appropriate committee of that House. The efficacy of both proposals thus depends on a total reform of the Senate, which is, to say the least, uncertain. In any event, neither the Committee nor the Task Force favours the present pure unilateralism.

The proposal in the Trudeau Government's Constitutional Amendment Bill of June, 1978, is more complex than the other two, but also borrows much from the amendments suggested at Victoria in 1971. What the former government proposed in 1978 was that, while only the federal government could nominate a candidate or candidates for appointment to the Supreme Court, the agreement of the appropriate provincial Attorney General must be sought. If the latter does not agree, then the differences between the provincial Attorney General and his federal counterpart are to be arbitrated by a so-called "nominating council". I say "so-called", because the council is confined to choosing between nominees of

---

[10]Towards a New Canada (1978), 55.

the federal Attorney General. The candidate approved by a majority of the nominating council then requires to be confirmed by the new second chamber proposed in 1978 by the former federal government, the House of the Federation. This would be very different from the present Senate, being composed of elected members, half of them being elected by the respective provincial legislatures on a complex formula.

The provisions for arbitration by a nominating council in the Constitutional Amendment Bill of 1978 are as follows:[11]

> S. 106.
>
> . . . (5) Within ten days of the day the Attorney General of Canada gives notice in writing to the Attorney General of the particular province that he proposes to convene a nominating council, the Attorney General of the particular province may inform the Attorney General of Canada by notice in writing that he selects either of the following types of nominating councils:
>
> (a) a nominating council consisting of the following members: the Attorney General of Canada or his nominee, and the Attorneys General of each of the provinces or their nominees;
>
> (b) a nominating council consisting of the following members: the Attorney General of Canada or his nominee, the Attorney General of the particular province or his nominee, and a chairman to be named by the two Attorneys General, and if within fourteen days from the expiration of the ten days herein referred to they cannot agree on a chairman, then the Chief Justice of the particular province or if he is unable to act, the next senior judge of his court, shall name a chairman;
>
> and if the Attorney General of the particular province fails to make a selection under this subsection within the ten days herein referred to, the Attorney General of Canada may select the person to be nominated.
>
> (6) Where a nominating council has been established under subsection (5), the Attorney General of Canada shall forthwith submit to it the names of not less than three persons qualified under this division to be appointed to fill the vacancy and about whom he has sought the agreement of the Attorney General of the particular province to their nomination for such appointment, and the nominating council shall not later than fourteen days after the submission to it of those names recommend therefrom a person for such nomination; a majority of the members of the council shall constitute a quorum thereof and a recommendation of a majority of its members at a meeting convened for the purpose shall constitute a recommendation of the council.

It is noteworthy that when you are all through with this elaborate procedure, nevertheless only nominees of the federal government have been considered.

I have three major comments to make on the foregoing sets of proposals. First, it is clear that no one wants the present unilateral process to continue, even though no doubt it does at times involve informal consultation with provincial Attorneys General as an act of grace and favour by the federal government of the day. So we are looking for some sort of significant change in the system of appointment. But, secondly, the three sets of proposals just explained each come

---

[11]Bill C-60, June 1978.

down heavily for ratification of a proposed appointee by the second chamber of the central Parliament. This is apparently seen as the best way to go to improve the system for appointment of Supreme Court judges. With respect, I doubt this, for the following reasons.

Everyone agrees that, in the words of the Bar Association Committee quoted earlier, ". . . we should seek for the court . . . the best and most sensitive judicial minds the nation has to offer". But, by the time you reach the point of ratifying or rejecting a single nomination, the "seeking" of which the Bar Committee speaks is over, and the single nominee will be confirmed unless something really bad can be marked up against him. As a system, such ratification provides only for the avoidance of downright poor nominations; it does not provide for positively seeking out the best available nominees in the first place. There has been a long experience with this in the United States, where Senate ratification of presidential appointments to the federal court system is required, including appointments to the Supreme Court of the United States. Students of the results in recent years say that, in spite of the requirement for Senate ratification, nevertheless, when the President is a Republican over ninety per cent of the judicial appointees are members of the Republican party, and when the President is a Democrat over ninety per cent of them are members of the Democratic Party.[12] So, to this extent at least, loyalty to the political party in power is given priority over merit pure and simple, and Senate ratification does nothing really to remedy this.

One can safely say that the same sort of party bias exists in Canada in our present system for judicial appointments by the federal government (whether that government is Liberal or Conservative).[13] Second chamber ratification would not change this in Canada any more than it has done so in the United States. Of course there is nothing wrong with active members of political parties being among those who are appointed to the Bench. It is wrong though that appointees should be mainly supporters of the government party, for this bespeaks an undue emphasis on loyalty and service to a particular party in the criteria for appointment. Of course the major political parties can and do each provide some persons of great merit for judicial appointment from among their own supporters. For this reason, we have a judiciary of very good quality in Canada in spite of the undue element of political party patronage in the system of appointment. Nevertheless, the over-all quality would surely be better if all members of the Bar were in fact equally eligible to be considered for judicial appointment on the basis of merit, whether they were supporters of the government party, one of the opposition parties, or no party at all. While this article is primarily concerned with the Supreme Court of Canada, it is necessary to speak of judicial appointments generally, because the general system is relevant to the Supreme Court of Canada. What makes sense as a reform measure generally makes sense also for appointments to

---

[12]Glenn R. Winters: American Appointments, Proposals and Problems (1967), 1 Can. Leg. Studies 253.

[13]A Symposium on the Appointment, Discipline and Removal of Judges (1973), 11 Alta. L. Rev. 279, remarks by G. M. Stirling, Q.C., pp. 285-287.

the Supreme Court of Canada, though no doubt it is true that successive federal governments have made some special efforts to emphasize merit when the court concerned was the Supreme Court of Canada.

This leads to my third major comment on this part of the three sets of reform proposals; they all neglect entirely the most promising measure that could be adopted to ensure appointment of the best qualified persons as judges. I refer to the use of appropriate official nominating commissions to provide short lists of the best qualified candidates for judicial office. The appointing authority is then obliged in law or virtually obliged in practice to appoint one of the persons listed. Such bodies function successfully in other countries, notably in the United States, where the so-called ''Missouri Plan'' is employed, at least to some extent, for the state court systems in almost half of the States. It is noteworthy that Chief Justice Bora Laskin has spoken with approval of this device. On August 23rd, 1977, speaking on judicial independence to the Meeting of Commonwealth Law Ministers in Winnipeg, he said:[14]

> Given that judicial independence is the touchstone and that professional competence and good character are the sought-after qualities, the guidance or recommendation of a qualified commission would certainly be an appropriate mechanism. This is not the time to examine such a mechanism in any detail. Some countries of the Commonwealth use it, and its effectiveness must depend on its membership and on the scope of the authority entrusted to it.

I do not have much space for detail either, but certain points should be made, however briefly. (1) These nominating commissions should be standing federal-provincial bodies with effective secretariats and full rules of procedure. They would be permanently in the business of maintaining lists of good prospects for judicial appointment. (2) The commission members should be almost entirely elected members of the federal Parliament and of the provincial legislature concerned. They should be drawn from both government and opposition benches at both the federal and provincial levels, on the nomination of the respective party leaders. They should include some lay persons as well as lawyers. Commissions composed in this way would operate in the mainstream of the public politics of the established political parties of our country. This is a high public political function that is to be performed, and it should not in my view be entrusted to a commission of non-elected persons, however eminent. (3) A two thirds majority in the commission should be enough to put a name on the short list for a given appointment, and the appointing authority should be required to appoint from the two or three names submitted. Perhaps a requirement that the appointing authority consult the commission would be enough, as the former would have a lot of explaining to do if it failed to appoint one of the persons thus recommended. (4) The commission should observe a high degree of confidentiality in its operations, though perhaps the short list submitted to the appointing authority should be published when the appointment is made.

Many more features of such a plan would have to be settled to make it oper-

---

[14]Multigraphed version.

ational, but there is now extensive experience and much literature on the subject in other countries to draw upon for guidance.[15] Finally, it should be obvious that federal-provincial appointing commissions such as those proposed are singularly appropriate to Canada's unitary judicial system under which judges possess general jurisdiction to try issues arising under federal laws or provincial laws or both. Moreover, with such commissions in place, the provinces would not be shut out from real influence on the choice of judges for the higher courts, including the Supreme Court of Canada.

V. THE CONSTITUTIONAL STATUS OF THE SUPREME COURT OF CANADA

Finally, we come to consider the rather anomalous fact that the essential structure and functions of the Supreme Court of Canada are not specially entrenched in the constitution, and so theoretically are subject to change by ordinary statute of the federal Parliament alone. This is incongruous for a central institution of the federal union itself. It is of course true that our constitutional usages and traditions of judicial independence are so strong that Parliament has never intervened in any way that would impair the true independence of the court. Just the same, all three sets of reform proposals we are considering favour special entrenchment of the basics of the structure and functions of the Supreme Court of Canada, so that there will not even be the appearance of any shortfall respecting its independence in relation to the central Parliament and Government of Canada.

The Supreme Court of Canada has been and is a very distinguished judicial tribunal. Nevertheless, as with all human institutions, there is at times need for some change and room for some improvement. The present seems to be one of those times.

FURTHER DEVELOPMENTS AND REFERENCES

Early in 1980, after the essay on current proposals for the Supreme Court of Canada had been published, the Liberal Party of Quebec published its "Beige Paper" on "A New Canadian Federation". The major change it proposed with respect to the Supreme Court of Canada was that, in constitutional matters, the central government, a provincial government or an individual litigant should have the option of requiring that a dualist constitutional bench should be composed for the case in question. Such a bench was to consist of equal numbers of judges from Quebec and from the other provinces, to which would be added the Chief Justice of Canada as presiding judge. It was also proposed that the office of Chief Justice of Canada should alternate for fixed terms between Quebec jurists and jurists from the other provinces.

This dualist proposal is very much like that in the Pepin-Robarts Report. Comments made in Chapter 11 about the latter in this respect are therefore relevant to the "Beige Paper".

---

[15]*E.g.:* A. Ashman and J. J. Alfini, The Key to Judicial Merit Selection, The Nominating Process (The American Judicature Society, August, 1974).

Part IV
The Federal Distribution of Legislative Powers and Co-operative Federalism

Chapter 12

Classification of Laws and the British North America Act

Reprinted with permission from *Legal Essays in Honour of Arthur Moxon*, J. A. Corry, F. C. Cronkite and E. F. Whitmore, eds. (Toronto: University of Toronto Press, 1953), 183

The heart of Canada's federal constitution is the distribution of legislative powers that is made by the British North America Act[1] between the central Parliament on the one hand and the provincial legislatures on the other. Laws, both actual and potential, have been separated into certain classes and those classes respectively assigned either to the central or to the provincial authority. Thus the law-making powers of Parliament are confined to the classes of laws allotted to it, and likewise with the various provincial legislatures. Accordingly, when a provision of the pre-Confederation law is to be altered or when a new law of some kind is proposed, the law or proposed law in question must be classified to determine which authority has power to alter it, in the former instance, or to enact it, in the latter. If our federal constitution is to endure and to work tolerably, this task of interpretation is plainly an exclusive judicial function and requires the services of independent tribunals of the first rank. "It is of the essence of the Canadian constitution that the determination of the legislative powers of the Dominion and of provinces respectively shall not be withdrawn from the judiciary."[2]

It is clear then that this task rests upon our courts, in particular now upon the Supreme Court of Canada, but it is not quite so clear that the task is as difficult as it is important. Indeed, the thesis of this essay is that the processes of classification concerned involve inevitable complexities which too often are only vaguely appreciated even in professional circles. First then, the nature of the process of classification in general will be examined. It will be found, for instance, that a basic distinction must be made between the classification of facts on the one hand, and the classification of laws on the other. Then the attempt will be made in the light of this general analysis to criticize and restate the accepted doctrine for interpretation of the B.N.A. Act.

---

[1]The British North America Act. 1867, 30 Vict., c. 3.
[2]*Ottawa Valley Power Co. v. A.G. for Ontario*, [1936] 4 D.L.R. 594, 603.

I. GENERAL CONSIDERATIONS ON CLASSIFICATION

Since we are to be concerned with divisions of the power to make or alter rules of law in the country, our first step must be to analyse carefully the nature of an ordinary rule of law. We have to examine the relation of a given particular rule to concrete facts on the one hand, and the grouping of such rules by systems for classification of them on the other. Certain basic considerations of analytical jurisprudence must be our first concern, and their nature is well described by Sir Frederick Pollock in a passage in which he clearly differentiates classification of laws from classification of facts:

> It is not possible to make any clear-cut division of the subject-matter of legal rules. The same facts are often the subject of two or more distinct rules, and give rise at the same time to distinct and different sets of duties and rights. The divisions of law, as we are in the habit of elliptically naming them, are in truth divisions not of facts but of rules; or, if we like to say so, of the legal aspect of facts. Legal rules are the lawyer's measures for reducing the world of human action to manageable items, and singling out what has to be dealt with for the time being, in the same way as number and numerical standards enable us to reduce the continuous and ever-changing world of matter and motion to portions which can be considered apart.[3]

By enlarging upon the last sentence of this quotation for the moment, more light can be shed on the nature of the legal classifications of facts. Rules of law as we know them are precepts of human conduct employed as a means of social control in a politically mature community. They must deal with such non-legal realities or facts as persons, things, conduct, and states of mind. They operate by discriminating between different kinds of persons and things, different kinds of conduct and states of mind, for purposes of defining the entitlement of the persons concerned to certain legal rights, privileges, powers, or immunities. Laws then must contain notional categories of facts, and must prescribe the criteria to be used in differentiating facts in order to define or establish these classes of them for legal purposes. For example, it is a natural fact that John Smith has passed his twenty-first birthday anniversary, but it is our law of contract which prescribes that before he does so he has no capacity to bind himself by a contract of loan and that afterwards this power does attach to him. It is the law which invests the attaining of age 21 with this significance; the fact of reaching that age is in itself legally quite neutral.

The process of applying law to facts then is the process of deciding which of these neutral and non-legal facts are appropriate to the legal categories or classes of facts defined in advance in our rules of law. The ability to do this depends upon the reasoning faculty in conjunction with one's general and legal training and experience. It depends upon perception of the prescribed elements of uniformity between certain real facts which exist or have occurred and the notional classes of facts or type-fact situations defined by and contained in our rules of law. This process is frequently called the subsumption of real facts

---

[3]Sir F. Pollock, *A First Book of Jurisprudence* (2nd ed., London, 1904).

under laws. Since rules of law are expressed in words, what we are really concerned with here is the problem of language itself, that of the meaning of words in relation to non-verbal realities. This question is always with us in any use of words for any purpose whatever. As Dr. Glanville Williams puts it, "Law is only a special department of language and . . ., whereas the application of law is limited, language is all-pervasive."[4] Thus classification of facts is not peculiar to legal problems; rather such problems are one manifestation of the universal question of the meaning or definition of words in relation to real non-verbal facts.

We are here in the realm of semantics, and even at the risk of seeming to labour the obvious, the basic postulates upon which this analysis proceeds in this respect had best be stated. One of the chief functions of words is to describe reality—things which exist or which have occurred. It is assumed here that in this regard the following propositions are true:

1. There is a real non-verbal world crowded with persons and things which men are capable of perceiving and differentiating.

2. Human beings have intentions, desires, and emotions. Such mental states are real things.

3. Language is a system of conventional verbal and written symbols called words which has been invented and built up by men over thousands of years wherewith to denote and differentiate (i.e. classify) the various items of the external world and also such mental realities as desires and intentions. Thus words are a man's tools of thought and his means of communication with others.[5]

4. Words, by usage or convention, are capable of a high degree of fixity of meaning, so that to an important extent they will have the same significance for different persons. It is this fixity of meaning which makes communication and hence all rational social organization and action possible, including the development and operation of legal systems. Nevertheless, we cannot achieve absolute precision with words as symbols. To quote Dr. Glanville Williams again: "The upshot is that the words we use, though they have a central core of meaning that is relatively fixed, are of doubtful application to a number of marginal cases."[6] The "marginal cases" are always with us, which should be no news to lawyers.

It follows that words are meaningful in this descriptive sense if there is a reality behind them. Thus, to assess the meaning of descriptive words one must seek to identify the real thing being symbolized. However, this is not the whole story by any means. Words are used also to express value-judgments, and here we encounter a different order of things. The problem here is not description at all, but rather decision respecting what it is politic, just, or right to do. As

---

[4]Dr. Glanville Williams, "Language and the Law: I" in (1945), 61 *Law Quarterly Review* 71.

[5]R. A. Wilson, *The Miraculous Birth of Language* (Guild Book ed., London, 1946), especially pp. 79 and 147; Z. Chafee, Jr., "The Disorderly Conduct of Words" in (1941), 41 *Columbia Law Review* 381.

[6]Dr. Glanville Williams, "Language and the Law: II" in (1945), 61 *Law Quarterly Review* 179, 191.

some jurists put it, we must separate the realm of the "is" from the realm of the "ought." This distinction is crucial for purposes of legal analysis because every rule of law has essential elements both of the "is" and of the "ought." Rules of law are reducible to this formula: "If so and so is the fact, then John ought to act in this way." The words expressing the first part of this formula comprise the fact-category and must be appropriate to designate things which exist or have happened in the sense developed above. The second part of the formula is the value-judgment setting forth what ought to be the behaviour of the person or persons designated, given the existence or occurrence of the facts described. There is much more to an ordinary rule of law, then, than simple description of facts, and hence the necessity for distinguishing the classification of facts from the classification of laws—a point to be more fully developed later. At the moment a further analysis of the classification of facts is in order.

What we have called the legal classification of facts then is simply the question of the meaning of certain words used in laws in relation to concrete non-legal and non-verbal facts, and to some extent a special legal terminology has necessarily been developed, which means a further refinement of this problem of language for lawyers and judges. Words used in their popular sense by clients and witnesses to describe their experience have to be translated into legal terms so that the legal significance of what has happened may be assessed. On the other hand, we know also that a feature of attempts to advance in law, as in other fields of systematic learning, is the increase of precision in the definition of words, for instance, by awareness of the use of the same word to denote things which are really different.

Further, it is clear that the legal classification of facts is an essential element in all legal processes of solution, though often a largely instinctive one. This may be further elucidated. A rule of law is a norm or standard which prescribes particular results which should obtain in terms of personal rights and duties on the footing of a hypothetical fact-situation which it defines. These fact-categories may be quite detailed or very general, but in any event they are conceptual or notional, and as such must be distinguished from real facts— things which exist or have happened. Accordingly, when a client comes to a lawyer with his story and his problem the lawyer's first step in the process of legal decision is in effect to put himself this question: "Of which classes or categories of facts in the law do these concrete facts constitute a particular instance?" The accurate answer to this question brings about the selection of the legal rules finally appropriate to the case, whereupon the prescriptions of legal result they contain will usually take effect. For example, X agrees in writing to buy Y's land for $1,000. Here we have concrete facts relevant to the fact-categories of consensus and consideration in the English law of contract, and by virtue of this subsumption it is prescribed in this instance that X and Y must as a matter of law keep their respective promises.

This process of matching facts with fact-categories is often far from easy. As Austin reminds us in his *Jurisprudence*, "The difficulty is in determining not what the law is or what the fact is, but whether the given law is applicable to the given fact."[7] Indeed, the central problem of relevance in the domestic law of evidence is nothing but the process of legal classification of facts here being described. Further, as Thayer states in his classic work on evidence: "The law furnishes no test of relevancy. For this it tacitly refers to logic and general experience, assuming that the principles of reasoning are known to its judges and ministers, just as a vast multitude of other things are assumed as already sufficiently known to them."[8] Examples of the necessity to rely upon the distinction between concrete facts and legal fact-categories occur in the law of evidence. They include the determination of the "facts in issue," the decision on what is inadmissible as opinion evidence, and most striking of all, the difference between a question of law for the judge and a question of fact for the jury. It is his knowledge of the substantive law relevant that enables the judge to tell the jury which facts require to be proven in the particular case. It is then for the jury to say whether they *are* proven.

But, the question may be asked, "If the legal system in question is embodied in a politically living and valid constitution, are not rights under it just as much real facts as anything else? Do we not state a *fact* in these circumstances when we say that X owns Blackacre?" The answer would be "yes," without qualification, if laws automatically applied themselves to non-legal facts in order to produce legal rights and duties. The truth, of course, is that this does not happen. Laws as ascertained by men must be applied to non-legal facts as perceived by men, in order to determine what rights and duties do obtain under a living legal system. No doubt in many cases this is a simple and obvious process, but in many others it is difficult, and it is these difficulties with special reference to constitutional law that we are attempting to explore here. Once a doubtful legal question *has been solved* by the person constitutionally authorized to do so, it is doubtless legitimate to speak of the *resultant* rights and duties as being and having been real facts. However, when our concern is with the processes whereby lawyers, judges, or officials arrive at a determination of legal rights and duties in a given concrete situation, the end result cannot be used as an element in the explanation of its own production. Thus, for our purposes here, finally confirmed rights and duties are not included in the "facts" of which we speak. We are necessarily confined to the facts of the non-legal world already described.

It is then non-legal and concrete facts which constitute the undifferentiated mass of data to be subsumed in our categories for the legal classification of facts, and as a final point we need to notice certain characteristics of such concrete facts. Real facts, things which exist or have occurred, are in themselves legally neutral. They have no inherent legal attributes whatever to give a clue to their legal significance, if any. Their only legal attributes are acquired ones, those which men ascribe to them by subsuming them in the manner explained under the rules of law deemed appropriate. The importance of remembering

---

[7]John Austin, *Jurisprudence* (5th ed., London, 1885), I, p. 230. See also G. W. Paton, *A Text-Book of Jurisprudence* (Oxford, 1946), 155-8.

[8]J. B. Thayer, *A Preliminary Treatise on Evidence at the Common Law* (Boston, 1898), 265.

this will appear later. However, though facts are in themselves legally neutral, they are also indefinitely impressionable. In other words, concrete facts are capable of simultaneous subsumption under several different rules of law. As Sir Frederick Pollock reminded us in the passage already quoted: "The same facts are often the subject of two or more distinct rules, and give rise at the same time to distinct and different sets of duties and rights." A moment's reflection on the historic dualism of Common Law and Equity in England will bring several illustrations of this to mind. Good examples also occur in a different field, that of the constitutional law of a federal state, such as Canada, where it has to be appreciated that a single set of concrete facts may be relevant simultaneously to valid federal and provincial laws. Clearly, it is important to remember this indefinite impressionability of concrete facts when dealing with the laws of the various legislatures of a federal country.

Let us turn now by way of contrast to a general consideration of the classification of rules of law. Of course, classification itself as a basic procedure does not alter. It is simply the arrangement into distinct classes of an undifferentiated mass of data by criteria which take account of various attributes inherent in the things concerned. However, as rules of law and concrete facts are different orders of things, obviously the criteria of classification are different depending on whether facts or laws are the subject-matter being classified. Rules of law attach prescribed rights and duties to some hypothetical condition or state of facts (here called a fact-category) and are thus norms, principles, or standards. They are concerned with the "ought" of human conduct, with what *should be* and not merely what *is*. The fact-categories they contain, while no doubt suggested by certain real-life situations, past, present, or anticipated, are nevertheless independent of actual facts. The legal fact-category is thus notional, and can exist even though concrete facts relevant to it have never occurred but are merely anticipated. There must be many examples of this in the statutes, in the dicta of judges, and in the speculations of jurists. This being so, it is proper and essential to distinguish the classification of laws as a different process from that of the classification of facts.[9]

Legal rules, then, considered in isolation from concrete facts, may be grouped in various classes by criteria which select uniform features of the concepts they contain, including the rights and duties they prescribe. As Dr. Martin Wolff puts it, "Classification may be compared with the mathematical process of placing a factor common to several numbers outside the bracket."[10] Thus rules of law may be classified (1) on the basis of some uniform feature of their fact-categories (that is the classes of persons, things, conduct, or intentions they contain); or (2) on the basis of some uniform features of the legal results they prescribe (that is the rights and duties they specify). For example, for purposes of the Canadian constitution we find that the class "criminal law" is

---

[9] "In value judgments there are always some individual words that are referential, but the statement as a whole does not purport to state past, present, or future reality." Dr. Glanville Williams, "Language and the Law: IV" in (1945) 61 *Law Quarterly Review* 384, 395. By "referential" is meant "descriptive of fact."

[10] M. Wolff, *Private International Law* (Oxford, 1945), 148.

defined as including all rules which in pith and substance *forbid* any conduct in the public interest.[11] Hence the criterion of this class is the prohibitive features common to the legal prescriptions of the rules so grouped. The type of conduct thus prohibited might be any sin of omission or commission. However, more often than not the grouping of rules in classes depends cumulatively on several criteria. For instance, certain rules are grouped as rules for the sale of goods because (i) their fact-categories are limited to tangible movable things, and (ii) their legal prescriptions concern only the transfer for money of the bundle of legal rights and privileges which make up "ownership" of such things.

Clearly, then, legal rules can be classified by a great number of criteria for any number of purposes. There is no one universal system of classification of laws valid for all purposes, though there have been several attempts by jurists to outline systems for which this claim is made. (The schemes of Professor Holland and Albert Kocourek might be cited as examples.) However, the true view is that systems of classification will be as various as the purposes which classification may be used to serve. In the words of Dean Roscoe Pound: "Classification is not an end. Legal precepts are classified in order to make the materials of the legal system effective for the ends of law."[12] The history of the categories "realty" and "personalty" in English law provides an interesting illustration of classification as a tool of policy. "Realty" is a class comprising those legal rules which confer proprietary rights over land to endure for an uncertain period. Thus, there are three criteria which form the basis of this particular class of rules of law: (i) they must be rules concerning rights over land; (ii) these rights must be rights in rem, i.e. they must avail against all comers, or nearly all; and (iii) these rights must be uncertain in the length of time for which they are to endure. (This third requirement refers to the well-known common law doctrine of estates.) It will be noted that rules concerning leasehold rights over land are excluded from the above class because the duration of the rights concerned is certain, being fixed between definite dates. Hence, they are characterized as rules of personalty; a class which came to include all rules conferring proprietary rights over things (including land) not classifiable as rules of realty. As Pollock and Maitland point out, the classing of rules conferring leasehold rights as rules of personalty served a very definite economic purpose in the thirteenth and fourteenth centuries. In medieval England land was the principal form of wealth and "real" rights over land were not freely transferable, being fettered by all the rigidities of the feudal system. For instance, prior to 1540, they were not freely alienable by will. On the other hand, proprietary rights over chattels could be freely disposed of by will, and thus by classifying leasehold rights over land as personalty, a valuable and freely bequeathable form of investment in land was made available. This peculiar legal dichotomy of "realty" and "personalty," then, enabled the law to satisfy a genuine economic need in medieval England.[13]

[11]*A.G. for British Columbia v. A.G. for Canada*, [1937] A.C. 368, 375.
[12]R. Pound, "Classification of Law" in (1924), 37 *Harvard Law Review* 933, 944.
[13]Sir F. Pollock and F. W. Maitland, *History of English Law* (2nd ed., Cambridge, 1898), II, 116, 117.

Perhaps it will have been noticed that we have just been speaking of the classification of legal rights as well as of rules of law. This should not be confusing if it is remembered that only laws can confer legal rights and hence a classification of rights is *ipso facto* a classification of laws, whether the laws concerned are being considered in relation to concrete or hypothetical facts. Again Sir Frederick Pollock's words are apt: "The divisions of law . . . are in truth divisions not of facts but of rules; or, if we like to say so, of the legal aspect of facts."

Usually systems for the classification of laws result from the meditations of jurists and derive what authority they have from the prestige of their respective authors. But it is otherwise with a federal constitution which of necessity contains a complete and authoritative system for the classification of laws as the basis of its allocation of law-making powers between the different legislatures concerned. In the B.N.A. Act such rules are found primarily in the well-known sections 91 and 92. These contain respectively enumerations of federal and provincial law-making powers. It is important to realize that these enumerated "subjects" or "matters" are classes of laws, not classes of facts. It is impossible for instance to look at a set of economic facts and say that the activity is trade and commerce within section 91(2) and therefore any law concerning it must be federal law. Rather, one must take a specific law (either actual or proposed) which is relevant to those facts and then ask if that rule is classifiable as a trade or commercial law. The Act very wisely recognizes this necessity in the wording of section 91(2). It does not say just "trade and commerce," it says rather "the regulation of trade and commerce," meaning of course "laws regulating trade and commerce."

The same can be said of all the enumerated classes in both sections 91 and 92. Some of them are obviously classes of laws on their face for they speak of rights, institutions, relations, or operations which have necessarily to be created or provided for by appropriate laws, e.g. taxation, legal tender, patents of invention and discovery, copyrights, marriage and divorce, criminal law, incorporation, municipal institutions, solemnization of marriage, and property and civil rights. The wording used for certain other classes makes them seem classes of fact, but these they cannot be. They must be read as the "trade and commerce" clause is worded: thus "seacoast and inland fisheries" truly means "laws regulating seacoast and inland fisheries." Similarly with such classes or categories as postal service, defence, banking, insolvency, and local works and undertakings. The late Chief Justice Harvey of Alberta seems to have put his finger on the point here being made when he said, in a recent case concerned with "banking" in section 91(15), "The word is used as the Statute [The B.N.A. Act] says as describing a subject for legislation, not a definite object."[14] We do not look just for banking as a matter of economic fact, we must look for regulation of banking as a matter of law.

It is important to insist that these enumerated classes are categories of legal rules and not of facts for the implications of this are too frequently forgot-

---

[14]*Reference Re Alberta Bill of Rights Act,* [1946] 3 W.W.R. 772, 778.

ten. Thus concrete facts alone cannot provide the mass of data appropriate for grouping under these categories, since facts as such are legally neutral. Or, to put it the other way around, facts alone cannot be characterized by subsumption within these classes as they are not classes of fact. They are classes of laws depending on normative or prescriptive criteria, and hence concrete facts alone are simply not relevant data, because they have no such attributes. For instance, facts alone cannot be characterized as criminal or proprietary or procedural, though particular legal rules appropriate to concrete facts may be one or the other. It is the country's ordinary rules of law, disposing of the rights, duties, liberties, capacities, and immunities of its citizens, that are the raw materials—the undifferentiated mass of data—relevant to the scheme of distribution of powers in the B.N.A. Act. You must talk in terms of such specific laws, actual or proposed, if you would determine whether the relevant legislative power is federal or provincial under the B.N.A. Act.

It follows that it is quite feasible to refer a challenged law (whether a bill or a statute) to our highest courts for a decision on where the power to enact it lies in the absence of any concrete litigious fact-situation involving adverse parties. Indeed, this is frequently done. Nevertheless the separate problems of the classification of facts cannot be entirely dismissed even from this picture. In order to classify the challenged rule, the court must first reach a conclusion regarding its true meaning—the full significance of the words in which it is expressed. Only thus are the various features by which it may be classified revealed. This decision will include the meaning of the words expressing that part of the rule which is its fact-category, which can best be assessed by testing its applicability to particular situations of fact, hypothetical or real. It is a recognized part of the reasoning process to gain additional insight concerning the meaning of a principle of conduct by making test applications of it to particular fact-situations to which it is deemed relevant, in order to determine what the effects of its observance would be. In this way all the problems of the classification of facts certainly enter the picture. No doubt this is why judges seem happier when a challenged law comes before them as a result of specific litigation, rather than by government reference. It is then easier to construe what the law means. Nevertheless, the classification of facts is still not our crucial problem in interpreting sections 91 and 92. We can admit that that process bears on the true meaning of the challenged law, but classification of that law cannot begin anyway until its true meaning is established, whether the issue of validity arises out of specific litigation or by government reference. The classification of facts is important, but anterior to the problem of whether a law is intra or ultra vires.

II. THE APPLICATION OF SECTIONS 91 AND 92 OF THE B.N.A. ACT

Certain of the essential principles for the interpretation of the B.N.A. Act now require consideration in detail in light of the foregoing analysis. In the first place the categories of laws enumerated in sections 91 and 92 are not in the logical sense mutually exclusive; they overlap or encroach upon one another in many more respects than is usually realized. To put it another way, many rules of law have one feature that renders them relevant to a provincial class of laws and another feature which renders them equally relevant logically to a federal class of laws. It is inherent in the nature of classification as a process that this should be so, and hence the concluding words of section 91 represent aspiration for the unattainable. It will be recalled that they read as follows: "And any Matter coming within any of the classes of subjects enumerated in this Section shall not be deemed to come within the Class of Matters of a local or private Nature comprised in the Enumeration of the Classes of Subjects by this Act assigned exclusively to the Legislatures of the Provinces." Over eighty years of judicial interpretation have demonstrated conclusively the impossibility of such mutual exclusion. "The language of [sections 91 and 92] and of the various heads which they contain obviously cannot be construed as having been intended to embody the exact disjunctions of a perfect logical scheme."[15]

For a simple illustration, take the well-know rule that a will made by an unmarried person becomes void if and when he marries. Is this a rule of "marriage" (s. 91(26)) or of "property and civil rights" (s. 92(13))? In England and the common law provinces of Canada it occurs in the respective "Wills Acts," and its validity in Canada as provincial law has not been challenged. This would suggest it is deemed a rule of "property and civil rights" for constitutional purposes. Yet if we turn to Private International Law (which has similar problems of classification) we find English and Canadian courts in agreement that this provision about marriage voiding a pre-nuptial will is to be deemed a matrimonial law for purposes of Private International Law.[16] Obviously, this rule could in addition be classed as testamentary or successive. In truth it is logically quite correct to classify it as matrimonial or successive or testamentary or as concerning property and civil rights. It is any or all of these things. The decision as to which classification is to be used for a given purpose has to be made on non-logical grounds of policy and justice by the legal authority with the duty and power of decision in that respect. The criteria of relative importance involved in such a decision cannot be logical ones, for logic merely displays to us as of equivalent logical value all the possible classifications. There are as many possible classifications of a rule of law as that rule has distinct characteristics or attributes which may be isolated as criteria of classification. Dr. Glanville Williams expresses this point very well in the following passage: "The above view as to definition . . . involves a rejection of Aristotle's doctrine of essences. Aristotle taught that essences are fixed in nature and that a definition is a phrase signifying this essence. On this view it is possible to dispute about 'true' definitions as though they are matters of fact. We now know that 'essence' simply means 'important feature,' and that what is important is a subjective or emotional matter. No definition ever states the sum total of the qualities that seem to go to the being of a thing; it always involves a selection

---

[15]*John Deere Plow Co., Ltd. v. Wharton*, [1915] A.C. 330, 338.

[16]*Re Martin*, [1900] P. 211; *Seifert v. Seifert*, [1915] 23 D.L.R. 440. See also W. R. Lederman, "Classification in Private International Law" in (1951), 29 *Canadian Bar Review* 3 and 168.

from those qualities, and the exact selection made depends very much on the purpose of the definition."[17] By "definition" Dr. Williams means the same thing as "classification." Definition is a process of classification. Thus there is not just one universally valid classification of a given rule of law good for all purposes. As has been said, several classifications are always possible, and which is best for a given purpose is a matter of judgment on higher grounds than logical ones.

How then do we determine the several features of a law by any one of which or by any combination of which it may be classified? This question takes us back to the question of the true meaning of the challenged law. In many of the cases we are told that it all depends on what is determined to be the "subject-matter" of the rule. Presumably this phraseology coupling "subject" and "matter" comes from the wording of the opening parts of sections 91 and 92, which speak of "exclusive Legislative Authority" extending "to all Matters coming within the Classes of Subjects next hereinafter enumerated" (s. 91), and "Laws in relation to Matters coming within the Classes of Subjects next hereinafter enumerated (s. 92). As has been pointed out, what is really being dealt with is power to enact *laws coming within the classes of laws next hereinafter enumerated*, and the B.N.A. Act could well be more concisely and clearly phrased in that way. "Subjects" and "matters" simply refer to meaning. Everything in a rule of law is "subject-matter" of it. "Subject-matter" can only refer to all features of its fact-category and the rights and duties prescribed. You must construe meaning before you can talk of subject-matter, and you only know what is subject-matter when you have settled meaning.

Further, in other cases a false antithesis is set up between the subject-matter of a rule on the one hand and its object or purpose on the other. For instance, Dr. MacRae states: "The Court, having regard to the language used in sections 91 and 92, has to find what the 'matter' is which is being legislated in relation to: and in doing this it must look, not merely at the subject-matter of the legislation (in the sense of the thing legislated about), but also at the object or purpose of the legislation. In other words, it has to look not merely at the thing legislated *about*, but the object or purpose legislated *for*."[18] This sounds plausible, but is not as helpful as it seems. In addition to speaking of the object or purpose of a rule, we may also speak of its intention and of its effects or consequences. But all these words lead us back to the one primary problem, the full or total meaning of the rule. There is an essential unity here that defies these grammatical attempts at separation. A rule of law expresses what should be human action or conduct in a given factual situation. We assume enforcement and observance of the rule and hence judge its meaning in terms of the consequences of the action called for. It is the effects of observance of the rule that constitute at least in part its intent, object, or purpose. Certainly the total meaning of the rule cannot be assessed apart from these effects. We must seek the full meaning of the challenged law because

---

[17] 61 *Law Quarterly Review*, 388-9.
[18] D. A. MacRae, *Constitutional Law* (mimeo.), 118.

the classes of laws in sections 91 and 92 depend on criteria which touch on all possible phases of the meaning of a law.

It should be noted that the problem of the colourable statement cannot be dealt with except in accordance with the foregoing analysis of total meaning. A colourable law is one which really means something more than or different from what its words seem at first glance to say. A law may have been so worded as to make it seem that it has only provincially classifiable features of meaning, and only when the effects of it (if enforced) are assessed can one ascertain a fuller or different meaning which supplies federally classifiable features. The Alberta Bill of Rights Act of 1946 is a classic example; it did not say "banks" or "banking" once, but it was classified as banking legislation none the less.[19]

The matter of intention also causes some confusion at this point. It is virtually impossible to find determinate human intenders behind most statutes. The examination of Hansard would not be nearly as helpful as many jurists suggest, though it might have some value. On the whole, the position is as the Privy Council itself has stated it: "The question is, not what may be supposed to have been intended, *but what has been said.*"[20] Here, as in other departments of the law, it has to be taken that ordinary consequences are intended consequences. Ordinary consequences are those reasonably informed men would expect as effects of the course of conduct the rule prescribes. The word intention, with or without adjectives such as "real," "true," or "essential," could well be completely dispensed with. It is superfluous, and at best represents a pseudo-subjective approach to meaning. Rules of law are for all manner of people, and hence the meaning ascribed to the words expressing them should be objectively and not subjectively determined.

Nevertheless, while all the effects of a particular rule are features of its meaning, it by no means follows that all are equally important. Let us suppose that the federal Government proposes to enact a heavy tax on the consumers of liquor. It can be seen that enforcement of the law will *(a)* bring in some revenue and *(b)* reduce consumption of liquor, which in turn will gladden the hearts of members of the W.C.T.U., facilitate the diversion of more alcohol to the manufacture of explosives, and put some marginal distillers out of business. These are all effects of the law and features of its meaning by which, severally or in combination, it may be classified in different ways. Which of the logically possible classifications is to prevail? As this law would put certain distillers in the provinces out of business it is a law concerning "Property and Civil Rights in the Provinces." But in a time of national peril there would be little difficulty in deciding that country-wide diversion of alcohol to the manufacture of explosives was its most important object, purpose, effect, or feature of meaning. Thus this circumstance would be the crucial feature of meaning for purposes of the division of legislative powers, and the law would be deemed a law of the national emergency class allotted to the central Parliament.

---

[19]*Reference Re Alberta Bill of Rights Act,* [1947] 4 D.L.R. 1 (P.C.).
[20]*Brophy v. A.G. for Manitoba,* [1895] A.C. 202, 216.

This suggests the main thesis of this essay: *That a rule of law for purposes of the distribution of legislative powers is to be classified by that feature of its meaning which is judged the most important one in that respect.* The thesis so stated points to the heart of the problem of interpretation, i.e. whence come the criteria of relative importance necessary for such a decision? In this inquiry, the judges are beyond the aid of logic, because logic merely displays the many possible classifications, it does not assist in a choice between them. If we assume that the purpose of the constitution is to promote the well-being of the people, then some of the necessary criteria will start to emerge. When a particular rule has features of meaning relevant to both federal and provincial classes of laws, then the question must be asked, Is it better for the people that this thing be done on a national level, or on a provincial level? In other words is the feature of the challenged law which falls within the federal class more important to the well-being of the country than that which falls within the provincial class of laws? Such considerations as the relative value of uniformity and regional diversity, the relative merits of local *versus* central administration, and the justice of minority claims, would have to be weighed. Inevitably, widely prevailing beliefs in the country about these issues will be influential and presumably the judges should strive to implement such beliefs. Inevitably there will be some tendency for them to identify their own convictions as those which generally prevail or which at least are the right ones. On some matters there will not be an ascertainable general belief anyway. In the making of these very difficult relative-value decisions, all that can rightly be required of judges is straight thinking, industry, good faith, and a capacity to discount their own prejudices. No doubt it is also fair to ask that they be men of high professional attainment, and that they be representative in their thinking of the better standards of their times and their countrymen.

Furthermore, our judges need all the assistance they can be afforded by the provision of data relevant for their constitutional decisions. What is wanted is emphasis on the approach pioneered in the United States by Mr. Justice Brandeis when at the Bar. In the so-called "Brandeis Brief," he would gather and place before the Supreme Court of that country an account of the *contemporary* economic and social factors which underlay the challenged law, to assist the judges there with the value-decisions confronting them. It might be said that the problem of ultra vires in the United States often differs too much from that in Canada for a parallel to be drawn, since the Americans have "Bill of Rights" clauses written into their Constitution defining things none of their legislatures can do by ordinary statute. Consider, for instance, a minimum wage law. The American courts have had to ask themselves whether such a law is urgent enough in the public interest to justify the limitation on freedom of contract that is involved, such freedom being deemed guaranteed in the Constitution except to the extent that it conflicts with some vital public interest. True enough, Canadian judges do not have to consider the substantive merit of a challenged law in this sense; indeed they are accustomed to labour the point that they are not concerned with whether such a law is good or bad, necessary or unnecessary. They say in effect that the malady and its proper cure are not their concern, rather that they have to ask only, Who is to be the physician? Yet does not the choice of physician depend to an important degree on the nature of the malady and of the proposed remedy? Admittedly if the challenged law is logically classifiable in only one way there is no problem, but the main thesis here is that such a situation will be rare, and that often so far as logic is concerned the challenged law will have features of meaning relevant to both federal and provincial classes of laws. Then our judges cannot be content simply to ask, Who is to be the physician? They must rather ask, Who is the better physician to prescribe in this way for this malady? To give a meritorious answer to this second question they need to consider as many factors as their American brothers. As was indicated earlier, widely accepted standards and beliefs are vital considerations in choosing the better alternative in this type of decision, but at least the principles of relative value should be ascertained and applied in the light of everything important that can be known about the need for the challenged law and what it would involve if observed and enforced.

Lest a false impression of complete uncertainty and fluidity be conveyed by the foregoing, the importance of the rules of precedent that obtain in our courts should be remembered. However open logically the classification of a given type of law may have been when first it was considered by the highest court, that decision will in all probability foreclose the question of the correct classification should the same type of law come up again. For instance it was argued that the federal Industrial Disputes Investigation Act of 1907 was within the power of the Canadian Parliament because its provisions regulating the settlement of industrial disputes were classifiable as "regulation of trade and commerce," "criminal law," and rules for "peace, order, and good government." Nevertheless the Judicial Committee pointed out that these provisions were also classifiable as laws concerning "property and civil rights in the province" and in effect ruled that such was *the* important or significant classification for constitutional purposes.[21] Hence the Act was declared ultra vires of the Canadian Parliament. Incidentally, in his argument for the validity of the Act, Sir John Simon had pointed to the absence of economic division in Canada on provincial lines; in other words many industries and labour organizations were national or at least interprovincial in scope and hence national regulation of industrial relations was desirable. But the Judicial Committee was not impressed. Tacitly but effectively they decided that provincial autonomy and diversity in the regulation of employer-employee relations were more important when they ruled that the challenged statute "in its pith and substance" interfered with civil rights. Thus the classification of this type of industrial regulation critical for constitutional purposes has been settled by precedent, and in like manner many other classifications are authoritatively settled. It is not clear yet whether the Supreme Court of Canada, supreme now in law as well as name, will assert a right to depart in exceptional circumstances from particular decisions in the accumulation of Privy Council precedents. Certainly it would seem that explicit departures, if any, will be rare. Nevertheless, some new and different scheme of industrial regulation, for example, might well be deemed

---

[21]*Toronto Electric Commissioners v. Snider*, [1925] A.C. 396.

outside the scope of the precedent just discussed, and then its classification in turn would have to be considered as a matter of first impression with all the problems here explained once more in full bloom.

Moreover, frequently there will be new laws, both federal and provincial, which the precedents on classification will not touch decisively or concerning which indeed there may be conflicting analogies. Thus in spite of the principles of precedent the full-blown problem of classification described earlier is often with us. Therefore, it is not merely those who would make or amend the federal constitution who must ask themselves and each other, What is truly of national concern and what is truly of provincial concern for purposes of law? Within the limits set by the terms of particular laws being challenged before them from time to time, the judges frequently confront this question *just as starkly as did the original constitution-makers themselves*. Further, as conditions change with the years, the relative importance of various classifiable features of particular laws may change as well. For instance the motor vehicle has brought to highway traffic today an interprovincial and international character undreamed of forty years ago; hence regulation of highway-using enterprises is now to be regarded to some extent in a new light.[22] Another way to put this point is to say that changed economic and social conditions and a different moral climate will give to present or proposed laws new features of meaning by which they may be classified and may also alter judgments on the relative importance of their several classifiable features. As their Lordships of the Privy Council have said: "It is . . . irrelevant that the question is one that might have seemed unreal at the date of the B.N.A. Act. To such an organic statute the flexibile interpretation must be given that changing circumstances require."[23] The authority of appropriate precedents then will remove much of the uncertainty just described as implicit in the process of classification but inevitably much unpredictability will remain. The principles of stare decisis are important in our courts, but the degree of certainty and predictability their operation can provide is often much overestimated or misconceived.

Having explored the main problem of interpretation regarding our constitutional division of legislative powers, we may now attend in detail to the particular doctrines developed by the judges to facilitate the making of the necessary decisions. In the case of many, if not most, particular laws, the overlapping of federal and provincial categories of laws logically relevant is inevitable, no matter how often the B.N.A. Act cries "exclusive." The courts have dealt with this overlapping in a number of ways. For one thing, they have limited the generality of the classes of laws in sections 91 and 92 by the so-called principle of "mutual modification," and have thus eliminated some of the encroachment of one upon the other. For example, consider the relation of the federal class, "regulation of trade and commerce," with the provincial class, "property and civil rights." Trade and commerce is carried on in articles in which persons have property and in respect of which they have civil rights. Obviously, in the logical sense there is

---

[22]*Winner v. S.M.T. (Eastern), Ltd.*, [1951] S.C.R. 887.
[23]*Privy Council Appeals Case*, [1947] 1 D.L.R. 801, 814.

here a wide overlapping. However, speaking generally, the courts have said that "regulation of trade and commerce" is to be reduced in generality and read as "regulation of interprovincial and international trade and commerce." Likewise, "property and civil rights" is to be rendered "property and civil rights except those involved in interprovincial and international trade and commerce." By these operations the overlapping of the literal words of the statute is reduced and some additional degree of exclusiveness is imparted to federal and provincial classes of laws. The reading of sections 91 and 92 as a whole certainly makes it clear that some of this rewording is necessary.

Nevertheless, in spite of all that can or should be done by mutual modification, some overlapping inevitably remains. Where this occurs, either one of two things has then been done. First, the feature of the challenged law relevant to a provincial class of powers has been completely ignored as only an "incidental affectation" of the provincial sphere, and the law concerned has been classed only by that feature of it relevant to a federal class of laws. Thus, in spite of the logical overlap the decision is made that only the federal Parliament has power to enact the challenged law. Obviously this decision involves a judgment that the provincial feature of the law is quite unimportant relative to its federal feature. On the other hand if the federal feature be deemed quite unimportant relative to the provincial feature, then the converse decision would be made.

But if the contrast between the relative importance of the two features is not so sharp, what then? Here we come upon the double-aspect theory of interpretation, which constitutes the second way in which the courts have dealt with inevitably overlapping categories. When the court considers that the federal and provincial features of the challenged rule are of roughly equivalent importance so that neither should be ignored respecting the division of legislative powers, the decision is made that the challenged rule could be enacted by either the federal Parliament or a provincial legislature. In the language of the Privy Council, "subjects which in one aspect and for one purpose fall within section 92, may in another aspect and for another purpose fall within section 91."[24] Clearly this decision raises some further problems. Under such principles of interpretation there may well be both a valid federal law and a valid provincial law directed to the same persons concerning the same things, but requiring from them different courses of conduct and thus having certain differing effects. Now if these different courses of conduct and effects are merely cumulative and not conflicting, then both rules may operate. But, if the two rules call for inconsistent behaviour from the same people, they are in conflict or collision and both cannot be obeyed. In these circumstances the courts have laid it down that the federal rule is to prevail and the provincial one is inoperative and need not be observed. The suspension of the provincial law continues so long as there is a federal law inconsistent in the sense explained. This is known as the doctrine of "Dominion paramountcy." Thus, it is a principle of our constitution that in the event of collision between a federal law and a provincial law each valid under the double-aspect theory, the federal features of the former law are considered in the last analysis

---

[24]*Hodge v. The Queen* (1883), 9 App. Cas. 117.

more important than the provincial features of the latter. At this ultimate point of conflict, presumably the federal classes and features relevant to them are deemed the more important simply because they have a national as opposed to a sectional reference. At any rate, "Dominion paramountcy" is said to be called for by the concluding words of section 91, quoted earlier.

It is clear then that in dealing with the overlapping of federal and provincial classes of laws, the courts must make the types of value-decisions described about the relative importance of the federal and provincial features of the challenged law. Some examples may now be examined. The Vacant Property Act of Quebec (1939) provided, to put it briefly, that all financial deposits in credit institutions unclaimed for thirty years became the property of the Crown in right of the Province of Quebec. The validity of this law was challenged. It was a question of the federal "banking" clause *versus* the provincial "property and civil rights" clause. The law was declared beyond the powers of a province, and in the course of judgment in the Privy Council the following passages occur:

> If that be the *main object and effect* of the provincial Act it does in their Lordships' view invade the field of banking. It comes in *pith and substance* within that class and the fact that it may *incidentally affect* certain other institutions cannot take away its *primary object and effect*.
>
> *In their* [Lordships'] view a provincial legislature enters upon the field of banking when it interferes with the right of depositors to receive payment of their deposits, as in their view it would if it confiscated loans made by a bank to its customers. Both are *in a sense* matters of property and civil rights, but *in essence* they are included within the category "banking."[25]

Further, in the *Alberta Bill of Rights Case* (1947) where there was the same type of problem concerning banking and property and civil rights, the Judicial Committee said:

> It is true of course, that in one aspect provincial legislation on this subject *affects* property and civil rights, but if, as their Lordships hold to be the case, the *pith and substance* of the legislation is "Banking" . . . this is *the aspect that matters* and Part II is beyond the powers of the Alberta Legislature to enact.[26]

In these two cases the property and civil rights features of the challenged laws were deemed relatively so unimportant in contrast to their banking features that classification for the purpose of determining legislative power was by the latter features only. The former were ignored. This may look like just another way of describing the result arrived at by the principle of mutual modification. For instance the decision in these banking cases could perhaps be put as a decision that "property and civil rights" should be read "property and civil rights except those of banking." Even so, one still has to decide whether the *non-banking* property and civil rights features or the banking features of a challenged statute are the more important, where such a statute logically has both aspects, as it did in the Quebec and Alberta cases.

---

[25]*A.G. for Canada v. A.G. for Quebec*, [1947] 1 D.L.R. 81, 87-8 (author's italics).
[26][1947] 4 D.L.R. 1, 10 (author's italics).

The quoted passages display the language which has become standard for expressing this judgment on value. The feature of the meaning of the rule deemed of outstanding importance is said to be "the pith and substance," "the essence," or "the aspect that matters." The feature deemed relatively unimportant is dismissed as merely "incidental." Other adjectives might be used to express the same contrast—the feature deemed of outstanding importance could be designated as "vital," "principal," or "capital," whereas the feature deemed unimportant could be called "secondary," "subordinate," "inferior," and so on. Also, some courts have put it this way, that what a rule is "in relation to" is primary, whereas that which it merely "affects" is secondary. In ordinary usage, there is no such contrast between "in relation to" and "affects." There is in fact no special magic in any of these incantations. Plainly, *whatever the form of expression adopted there is only one thing to be expressed: judgment on the relative importance of the federal and provincial features respectively of the meaning of the challenged law, for purposes of the distribution of legislative powers.* All the foregoing verbiage could be dispensed with and the words "important" and "unimportant" (or "more important" and "less important") substituted. Indeed, words like "pith and substance" or "essence" should be dropped entirely because they suggest that as a matter of final truth in philosophy or logic there is only one correct classification of a challenged rule. As we have already seen, this is a fallacy. Nevertheless, at times judges do so concentrate their gaze upon the feature of the challenged law they deem most important that they are found asserting that such law does not have other features relevant to the classes of the B.N.A. Act at all. In effect, the inevitable value-judgment is made, but its nature as a necessary choice between logically equal alternatives is unfortunately obscured for all concerned.

Finally we may examine an example of the application of the double-aspect theory. A good one is explained in the case of *Provincial Secretary of P.E.I. v. Egan* (1941) in the Supreme Court of Canada.[27] The Criminal Code of Canada provided that it was an offence to drive a motor vehicle while intoxicated and that in addition to any other punishment the court might on conviction make an order prohibiting the convict from driving a motor vehicle anywhere in Canada for a period not exceeding three years. On the other hand the Highway Traffic Act of Prince Edward Island provided for the licensing of drivers on the Island and that on a first conviction for driving while intoxicated the licence of such driver would be automatically and irrevocably suspended for twelve months. Suspension was to be for twenty-four months on a second conviction and for life on a third one. The Court found that the federal rule was valid as criminal law, and that the provincial rule was valid, inter alia, as licensing law and as a law defining provincial civil rights. It was further found that these laws were not inconsistent and that both were operative, presumably because the respective suspensions of the right to drive could be regarded as concurrent and cumulative rather than as conflicting. Thus, at the back of this decision must be at least the tacit judgment that the provincial features of the challenged part of the Highway Act were

[27][1941] 3 D.L.R. 305.

of equivalent importance with the federal features of the very similar provisions of the federal Criminal Code. In the words of Sir Lyman Duff: "It is important to remember that matters which, from one point of view and for one purpose, fall exclusively within the Dominion authority, may, nevertheless, be proper subjects for legislation by the Province from a different point of view, although this is a principle that must be 'applied only with great caution.' "[28]

One other allegedly separate principle of interpretation remains to be noticed, that known as the "ancillary doctrine." According to an eminent authority, the purport of this doctrine is as follows: "Provisions of a Dominion Statute which directly intrude upon provincial classes of jurisdiction and which, standing alone, would be incompetent to the Dominion, may nevertheless be valid as being necessarily incidental to full-rounded legislation upon a Dominion subject-matter, or to the effective exercise of an enumerated Dominion power, or to prevent the scheme of an otherwise valid Act from being defeated."[29] It is sometimes put alternatively that, in these circumstances, the Dominion can *trench upon* provincial jurisdiction. An example of this approach is found in the judgment of the Privy Council in the *Voluntary Assignments Case*: "Their Lordships would observe that a system of bankruptcy legislation may frequently require various ancillary provisions for the purpose of preventing the scheme of the Act from being defeated. It may be necessary for this purpose to deal with the effect of executions and other matters which would otherwise be within the legislative competence of the provincial legislature."[30] It should be apparent that this talk of the "necessarily incidental," or the "ancillary" is just another way of describing a dual-aspect situation and thus does not represent a separate problem in or approach to interpretation at all. We are not interested in what some part of a Dominion statute would have meant standing alone, because it does not stand alone. It takes some features of meaning from its context which it would not have if isolated. In its context it has both federal and provincial features deemed of equivalent importance and hence we have nothing more nor less than the double-aspect situation already considered.

Nevertheless, such talk does suggest one angle of the interpretation or classification problem not yet explored. So far the argument in this paper has proceeded largely on the footing of assessing certain simple and concise rules of law. This was necessary for clarity of exposition, but of course constitutional issues do nto always arise in such simple forms. A given statute is frequently a complex of particular rules, all facets of a single plan or scheme. Such a statute will stand or fall as a whole when its validity is questioned. On the other hand, the single plan or scheme or pattern concerned may be expressed in two or three statutes all of which have to be read together. By contrast, it may be that a single statute will fall into parts which can be taken as separate units for purposes of determining which authority has power to enact them. This would be a case where

---

[28]*Ibid.*, 309.
[29]Vincent C. MacDonald, "Judicial Interpretation of the Canadian Constitution" in (1935), 1 *University of Toronto Law Journal* 260, 273-4.
[30][1894] A.C. 189, 200.

"severance" is said to be appropriate. Clearly, because of the influence of context on meaning, it is going to be important what group of particular legal provisions the court selects as the unit for classification within federal or provincial classes of laws. It seems impossible to lay down any standard tests for grouping rules into a single pattern for this purpose, though presumably well-drafted statutes have only one principal theme. It seems a matter for the reasoning power and common sense of judges in each particular case. Judicial pronouncements, it is submitted, do make it plain that this question of the unit to be classified is a real one. For instance, in one of the cases concerning interest on Alberta bonds, Mr. Justice Ewing said, "A composite Act may be declared ultra vires in its entirety but it does not follow that each of its component parts if enacted separately would necessarily be declared to be ultra vires."[31] Likewise, in the *Alberta Bill of Rights Case* already referred to, Viscount Simon said:

> This sort of question arises not infrequently and is often raised (as in the present instance) by asking whether the legislation is ultra vires "either in whole or in part," but this does not mean that when Part II is declared invalid what remains of the Act is to be examined bit by bit in order to determine whether the Legislature would be acting within its powers if it passed what remains. The real question is whether what remains is so inextricably bound up with the part declared invalid that what remains cannot independently survive or, as it has sometimes been put, whether on a fair review of the whole matter it can be assumed that the Legislature would have enacted what survives without enacting the part that is ultra vires at all.[32]

The Supreme Court of Alberta had held that Part I of the Act was intra vires and Part II ultra vires. The Privy Council held that the two parts were not severable and that the whole was ultra vires.

By way of conclusion, the main points of the foregoing analysis may be summarized:

1. Basically, in applying sections 91 and 92 of the B.N.A. Act, we are concerned with a classification problem, which is really the problem of language itself. There are certain difficulties inherent in all processes of classification.

2. In legal analysis, classification of facts must be distinguished from classification of laws, since facts and laws are different orders of things.

3. When the constitutional validity of a law is challenged, we must seek to ascertain its full or total meaning. In part, this involves the process of classifying facts, and in part it calls for determining the effects of doing what the law requires.

4. Logically, a given law may be classified by any one or by any combination of the distinct features of meaning which it has. Thus, a given law can be classified in many different ways. The idea that there is only one true classification is a fallacy.

5. The application of sections 91 and 92 of the B.N.A. Act is a process of classification of laws, but inevitably the categories there specified are largely overlapping. Therefore a challenged law with features of meaning relevant to

---

[31]*I.O.O.F. v. Trustees of Ljthbridge Northern Irrigation District*, [1937] 4 D.L.R. 398, 400.
[32][1947] 4 D.L.R. 1, 11.

both federal and provincial categories of laws has to be classified by that feature of it deemed most important for purposes of the division of legislative powers in the country. The heart of the interpretative process thus often lies in the criteria of relative importance employed by the judges in making this type of choice.

6. Precedents on classification are important, but the degree of certainty they can afford is usually much overestimated.[33]

7. The task of the judges in this regard is as difficult as it is important. Criticism of what the courts have done, if it is to be constructive, should acknowledge with some humility that this is a field in which honest and able men may differ.

---

[33]For an exhaustive analysis relevant to this point, see F. E. LaBrie, "Constitutional Interpretation and Legislative Review" in (1950), 8 *University of Toronto Law Journal* 298.

Chapter 13

The Concurrent Operation of Federal and Provincial Laws in Canada

Reprinted with permission from (1962-63), 9 McGill Law Journal, 185

I. DEFINITION OF CONCURRENT FIELDS

The federal distribution of legislative powers and responsibilities in Canada is one of the facts of life when we concern ourselves with the many important social, political, economic or cultural problems of our country. Over the whole range of actual and potential law-making, our constitution distributes powers and responsibilities by two lists of categories or classes—one list for the federal parliament (primarily section 91 of the B.N.A. Act,[1] the other for each of the provincial legislatures (primarily section 92 of the B.N.A. Act). For instance, the federal list includes regulation of trade and commerce, criminal law, and a general power to make laws in all matters not assigned to the provinces. Examples from the provincial list are property and civil rights in the province, local works and undertakings, and all matters of a merely local or private nature in the province.

These federal and provincial categories of power are expressed, and indeed have to be expressed, in quite general terms. This permits considerable flexibility in constitutional interpretation, but also it brings much overlapping and potential conflict between the various definitions of powers and responsibilities. To put the same point in another way, our community life—social, economic, political, and cultural—is very complex and will not fit neatly into any scheme of categories or classes without considerable overlap and ambiguity occurring.[2] There are inevitable difficulties arising from this that we must live with so long as we have a federal constitution.

Accordingly the courts must continually assess the competing federal and provincial lists of powers against one another in the judicial task of interpreting the constitution. In the course of judicial decision on the B.N.A. Act, the judges have basically done one of two things. First, they have attempted to de-

---

[1] 30 & 31 Victoria (U.K.), c. 3.

[2] ". . . It is necessary to realize the relation to each other of ss. 91 and 92 and the character of the expressions used in them. The language of these sections and of the various heads which they contain obviously cannot be construed as having been intended to embody the exact disjunctions of a perfect logical scheme."—Viscount Haldane in *John Deere Plow Company Ltd. v. Wharton* [1915] A.C. 330, 338.

fine mutually exclusive spheres for federal and provincial powers, with partial success. But, where mutual exclusion did not seem feasible or proper, the courts have implied the existence of concurrent federal and provincial powers in the overlapping area, with the result that either or both authorities have been permitted to legislate provided their statutes did not in some way conflict one with the other in the common area. It is the problems arising from such concurrency that are the primary concern of this article.

But, before proceeding specifically to the problems that arise after concurrency has been found, it is necessary to examine carefully the interpretative process whereby the courts strive first to establish mutually exclusive spheres of federal and provincial law-making powers. The words 'exclusive' or 'exclusively' occur in section 91 of the B.N.A. Act respecting federal powers and in section 92 respecting provincial powers, hence the priority for the attempt at mutual exclusion. Only if this attempt fails do the judges then proceed to define by necessary implication certain spheres of common powers to regulate the same matter.

Here we encounter important considerations that go under the name of 'the aspect theory'. As Lord Fitzgerald said long ago in *Hodge v. The Queen*, ''subjects which in one aspect and for one purpose fall within section 92, may in another aspect and for another purpose fall within section 91.''[3] For instance, a law providing for suspension or revocation of the right to drive a car upon a highway because the driver was drunk has the provincial aspects of control of highways as local works and of the right to drive as a civil right in the province, these things reflecting the provincial responsibility for safe and efficient circulation of traffic. The law mentioned has also the federal aspect of criminal law, reflecting the federal responsibility to forbid and punish such dangerous anti-social conduct.[4] Where does the power to suspend and revoke drivers' licences reside, or do both parties have it? Such laws with double aspects in the logical sense are the usual and not the exceptional case.

In other words, simply as a rational or logical matter, the challenged law displays several features of meaning some one of which at least falls within a federal class of laws, and another one of which falls within a provincial class of laws. Rationally the challenged law is classified both ways—how then do we determine whether power to pass such a law is exclusively federal or exclusively provincial or is something both legislative authorities have? The basic solution here comes by decisions on the relative importance of the federal features and the provincial features respectively of the challenged law in contrast to one another. Respecting the detailed aspects raised by the challenged law, one must ask—when does the need for a national standard by federal law outweigh the need for provincial autonomy and possible variety as developed by the laws of the several provinces, or vice versa? The criteria of relative importance here arise from the social, economic, political, and cultural conditions of the country and its various regions and parts, and of course involve the sys-

---

[3](1883-84), 9 A.C. 117, 130.
[4]See: *Provincial Secretary of P.E.I. v. Egan and A.G. of P.E.I.*, [1941] S.C.R. 396, [1941] 3 D.L.R. 305.

tems of value that obtain in our society. The answers must be guided by and related to the categories and concepts of the British North America Act, and so at this point we find that the two interpretative situations mentioned earlier emerge.

(a) Mutual Modification and Exclusive Powers

If the federal features of the challenged law are deemed clearly to be more important than the provincial features of it, then the power to pass that law is exclusively federal. In other words, for this purpose the challenged law is classified by its leading feature, by its more important characteristic, by its pith and substance. And if, on the other hand, the provincial features are deemed clearly more important than the federal ones, then power to pass the law in question is exclusively provincial.[5]

In some instances, the solution to this dilemma of competing classifications may be grammatically obvious if one simply reads sections 91 and 92 together. For example, the provincial power 'Solemnization of Marriage' (92(12)) is obviously to be read as an exception to the federal power 'Marriage and Divorce' (91(26)). As a matter of construction the former is a particular sub-class completely comprehended by and carved out of the latter as a more general class or category. Only the provincial legislatures then can make law for marriage ceremonies, but only the federal parliament can make divorce law. Another example is afforded by 'Patents' and 'Copyrights' (91(22) and (23)) as small subdivisions of the general category of 'Property' (92(13)). In these cases the B.N.A. Act seems explicit enough on the priorities between competing classifications, and to the extent that the words of the Act are clear on such issues they are conclusive.

Nevertheless, most of the problems of competing classifications that arise are not so easily soluble. Take for instance the competition between 'Trade and Commerce' (91(2)) and 'Property and Civil Rights' (92(13)) considered in the *Parsons* case.[6] Neither of these classes of laws is gramatically or logically an all-inclusive general category of which the other is obviously a sub-division. As a matter of construction it can properly be said that each is to be read subject to the other, that neither should be permitted to push the other out of the picture completely, but the question remains: where is the line to be drawn? There is no answer to this to be found by a simple reading of the statutory words. The answer is not grammatically internal to the Act. These are simply two wide or general categories that overlap a large common area—all property or civil rights laws that are also trading or commercial laws fall both ways as a matter of simple logic. From the legal point of view, most trade and commerce is the transfer of property rights by contract, or the provision of services by contract. In the *Parsons* case, the judgment of relative importance called for at this point was a compromise. The general line of distinction between section 91(2) and section 92(13) was drawn as follows: given that the challenged law is both

---

[5]See: *Union Colliery Company of B.C. v. Bryden,* [1899] A.C. 580, 587.
[6]*Citizens Insurance Company v. Parsons* (1881-82), 7 A.C. 96.

property or contract law and trading or commercial law, if the trade or commerce is internal to a single province, then the property and civil rights aspect is the more important and provincial power is exclusive. But, if the challenged law is property or contract law about interprovincial or international trade or commerce, then its trading or commercial aspect is the more important and the federal power is exclusive. In this way an issue of relative importance originally open so far as the words of the Act are concerned becomes settled as a matter of judicial precedent.

Accordingly, if there is sufficient contrast in relative importance between the competing federal and provincial features of the challenged law, then in spite of extensive overlap the interpretative tribunal can still allot exclusive legislative power one way or the other. Once exclusive power has been determined to exist for either legislature, then the so-called doctrine of abstinence simply expresses the implication of this negatively. If the federal parliament does not choose to use its power of regulation in a particular *exclusive* federal field, nevertheless a province cannot enter the field with provincial legislation. The activity concerned simply remains unregulated.

But what if the federal and provincial aspects of the challenged law seem to be of equivalent importance? What if there is no real contrast in this respect? This leads to the second main interpretative situation.

(b) The Double-Aspect Doctrine and Concurrent Powers

If reasoning (a) has been attempted, but it develops that the federal and provincial aspects of the challenged law are of equivalent importance—that they are on the same level of significance—then the allocation of *exclusive* power one way or the other is not possible. For example, in the *Voluntary Assignments* case,[7] the Court pointed out that the federal parliament must be able to deal with priority among the execution creditors of an insolvent debtor from the point of view of effective bankruptcy legislation, but that, equally, provincial legislatures had to deal with priorities among such execution creditors from the point of view of the provincial responsibility for civil procedure and civil rights. Hence the provincial legislation was valid, there being no federal bankruptcy statute at the time.

Accordingly the idea of mutual exclusion if practical, but concurrency if necessary, explains much of Canadian constitutional law. For instance, one may ask, if Quebec was to be denied power to pass the Padlock Law because this invaded the exclusive federal criminal law sphere,[8] how is it that other provinces were permitted their provincial offences of simple careless driving, these not being considered to be such an invasion?[9] The judicial answers take

---

[7]*A.G. of Ontario v. A.G. of Canada*, [1894] A.C. 189.

[8]*Act Respecting Communistic Propaganda* (Province of Quebec) R.S.Q. 1941, c. 52. Generally speaking, the Act provided that any house or building used by the tenant or owner as a place from which communistic propaganda was distributed could be padlocked on order of the Attorney General for a year and thus withdrawn from any use whatsoever for that period. It was held to be *ultra vires* of the Province. See: *Switzman v. Elbling and A.G. of Quebec*, [1957] S.C.R. 285.

[9]See: *The Queen v. Yolles* (1959), 19 D.L.R. (2d) 19; *O'Grady v. Sparling*, [1960] S.C.R. 804.

the lines already suggested. True, the Padlock Law was in a sense property legislation as well as treason legislation, but its treason aspect was much more important than its property aspect, the latter being really a subterfuge. Hence, treason was the 'pith and substance' and federal power was found to be exclusive. But, where the offence of simple careless driving was concerned, the provincial aspect of responsibility for safe and efficient circulation of traffic on highways was real and was deemed equivalent in importance to the federal aspect of responsibility to forbid and punish grave and dangerous anti-social conduct of all kinds. Hence the finding was made that dangerous driving offences are a concurrent matter or field.

There seems a definite increase in the number and importance of concurrent fields being presently established by the courts. Of course, agriculture and immigration are expressly concurrent fields by section 95 of the B.N.A. Act, while temperance and insolvency have been with us by judicial implication since the nineteenth century.[10] Recent cases have added concurrency concerning conduct on highways, sale of securities, validity of trading stamps in retail stores, and aspects of Sunday observance.[11] This list is by no means exhaustive. So, precisely what concurrency means requires and deserves careful analysis. In 1907 in the Judicial Committee of the Privy Council, Lord Dunedin said that two propositions were established:[12]

> First, that there can be a domain in which provincial and Dominion legislation
> may overlap, in which case neither legislation will be ultra vires, if the field is
> clear; and secondly, that if the field is not clear, and in such a domain the two
> legislations meet, then the Dominion legislation must prevail.

The word 'meet' is used here in the sense of collision, but there may be joint occupation of a concurrent field without collision necessarily occurring. The different conditions of joint legislative tenancy will be discussed in Part II under the headings *conflict, supplement* and *duplication*.

II. CONFLICT, SUPPLEMENT AND DUPLICATION RESPECTING FEDERAL AND PROVINCIAL LAWS IN CONCURRENT FIELDS

Given that a concurrent sphere or field has been established, what if both the federal parliament and a provincial legislature have entered the field with statutes? What if 'the two legislations meet'?

If the meeting is a collision, *i.e.* if conflict or inconsistency or repugnancy is the result, the federal statute prevails and the provincial one is displaced and inoperative. But it is far from obvious what amounts to sufficient conflict or inconsistency or repugnance to effect this result.

---

[10]See: *A.G. of Ontario v. A.G. of Canada*, [1896] A.C. 348, and footnote 7.

[11]Highways—*P.E.I. v. Egan, supra,* footnote 4; *The Queen v. Yolles, supra,* footnote 9; *O'Grady v. Sparling, supra,* footnote 9. Securities—*Smith v. The Queen,* [1960] S.C.R. 776. Trading stamps—*The Queen v. Fleming* (1962), 35 D.L.R. (2d) 483. Sunday observance—*Lord's Day Alliance of Canada v. A.G. of B.C.,* [1959] S.C.R. 497.

[12]*G. T. Rlwy Company of Canada v. A.G. of Canada,* [1907] A.C. 65, 68.

We start with two statutes that are somehow concerned with the same matter, that matter being the respect in which a concurrent field has been found to exist. The two statutes may differ in what they prescribe about the concurrent matter, or they may be the same in what they prescribe about it. This can soon be discovered by construing and comparing their respective terms, remembering that the search is for substantial differences or substantial identities. As in other constitutional matters, one must not be put off by merely verbal differences or identities. Does the provincial statute differ from the federal one or does it duplicate the federal one? That is the first question, because the reasoning appropriate to difference is not the same as that appropriate to duplication.

And even difference has its variations. The provincial statute may differ from the federal one in either one of two ways—it may be inconsistent with the federal one or it may be merely supplemental to the federal one, adding something to what the federal statute does but not contradicting it. So, in considering the relation of a provincial statute to a federal one in a concurrent field, there are three basic states: (a) conflict, (b) supplement, and (c) duplication. For the sake of developing the analysis clearly, it is assumed to start with that we have provincial statutes that are pure examples of each of these states, *i.e.* first a provincial statute that is purely conflicting, second a provincial statute that is purely supplemental and finally a provincial statute that is purely duplicative. The problems presented by a mixed provincial statute—one that combines any two or all three of these types of provisions—can be disposed of if we know what is appropriate for the pure cases.

(a) Conflict

The situation envisaged here is actual conflict between the comparable terms of the provincial statute and the federal one. One finds that the same citizens are being told to do inconsistent things. One statute blows hot and the other cold. For example, a provincial statute says that a certain creditor is a secured creditor, but the federal Bankruptcy Act says he is an unsecured creditor. There can only be one scheme for priority among creditors in the event of bankruptcy of the debtor, hence the federal statute prevails and the provincial one is inoperative for repugnancy.[13] Another example is found in the *Local Prohibition* case of 1896.[14] There, Lord Watson compared the details of the Ontario statutory liquor prohibition scheme with the details of the federal liquor prohibition scheme of the Canada Temperance Act and found that the two differed sufficiently and that it would be impossible for both to be in force in the same county or town at the same time. Had it not been for its local option voting provisions, the Canada Temperance Act would automatically have displaced the provincial statutory scheme.

> It thus appears that, in their local application within the province of Ontario, there would be considerable difference between the two laws; but it is obvious that their

---

[13]*Royal Bank of Canada v. La Rue*, [1926] S.C.R. 218; [1928] A.C. 187.
[14]*A.G. of Ontario v. A.G. of Canada*, [1896] A.C. 343.

provisions could not be in force within the same district or province at one and the same time.[15]

Thus, Lord Watson made it clear that if any district voted the Canada Temperance Act into force, the provincial statutory scheme would be precluded or superseded in that district.

Thus the pure case of express conflict is clear on the authorities—the federal statute prevails. At least the doctrine of Dominion paramountcy must go this far, but there has been some suggestion recently that it goes no further—that this is *all* it means. In the recent case of *Smith v. The Queen* (1960),[16] which concerned federal and provincial offences of knowingly issuing a false prospectus to induce the sale of company shares, Mr. Justice Martland of the Supreme Court of Canada said that, unless the federal and provincial provisions in question conflict *"in the sense that compliance with one law involves breach of the other,"* they can operate concurrently.[17] If only such patent and positive conflict of comparable terms can invoke the doctrine of Dominion paramountcy, then that doctrine is indeed confined to the narrowest significance it could possibly be given. On this view, any supplemental or duplicative provincial legislation could operate concurrently with the federal legislation it supplemented or duplicated, and our enquiry into the scope of the doctrine of Dominion paramountcy could end right here. But, as we shall see, this does not seem to be the state of the authorities.

In addition to the patent and positive conflict of terms just considered, there is another type of conflict or inconsistency to be examined. The federal legislation in a concurrent field may carry the express or tacit implication that there shall not be any other legislation on the concurrent subject by a province. If this negative implication is present, any supplemental provincial statute would be in conflict with it, though there is no conflict between comparable terms of the two statutes. It would be normal to find this implication in a federal statute that could properly be construed as a complete code for the concurrent subject. To revert to the matter of priority among various kinds of creditors in a bankruptcy, the federal code of priorities would clearly have this negative implication, even if there were gaps in it here or there where something might be added or even if there were room for further refinements. It should be noted at this point that Mr. Justice Cartwright of the Supreme Court of Canada has carried this idea of conflict by negative implication to its ultimate limit. In *O'Grady v. Sparling* (1960),[18] the Supreme Court was considering the relation of two different dangerous driving offences. The Criminal Code of Canada at this time made it an offence to drive a car with "wanton or reckless disregard

---

[15][1896] A.C. 343, 368; see also 369-70.

[16]*Supra,* footnote 11.

[17][1960] S.C.R. 776, 800; (italics added). In the context of the *Smith* case it may not be right to fix Mr. Justice Martland with the full implications of these words. Nevertheless, their full implications do mark out the narrowest possible meaning of Dominion paramountcy, and perhaps this *is* what Mr. Justice Martland intended.

[18]*Supra,* footnote 11.

for the lives or safety of other persons.''[19] The Highway Traffic Act of Manitoba made it an offence to drive a car on a highway 'without due care and attention or without reasonable consideration for other persons using the highway.''[20] The provincial offence is much wider than the federal one, but overlaps and includes it. Mr. Justice Cartwright (dissenting) said:[21]

> In my opinion when Parliament has expressed in an Act its decision that a certain kind or degree of negligence in the operation of a motor vehicle shall be punishable as a crime against the state it follows that it has decided that no less culpable kind or degree of negligence in such operation shall be so punishable. By necessary implication the Act says not only what kinds or degrees of negligence shall be punishable but also what kinds or degrees shall not.

In other words, he is saying that if there is a federal statute of any kind in a concurrent field, this alone necessarily and invariably implies that there shall be no other legal regulation by a province of the concurrent subject. To carry negative implication this far would ban all supplemental or duplicative provincial legislation. To use the metaphor of the 'field', the effect of this view is that any federal statute touching a concurrent field constitutes total excluding occupation of that field by the federal parliament. This is the opposite extreme from the view of Mr. Justice Martland and thus represents the broadest sweep that could possibly be given the doctrine of Dominion paramountcy. Mr. Justice Cartwright's view is not the law, but, as stated, it does mark out one of the two extreme positions possible and so aids this attempt at analysis.

As suggested earlier, the negative implication discussed here is legitimate and realistic in some circumstances, and when it is present, the rule of Dominion paramountcy operates to cause the exclusion or suspension of any provincial legislation on the subject in hand. But this is by no means automatically the case for every federal statute in a concurrent field.

Finally, if one has a provincial statute that mixes repugnant provisions with supplemental or duplicative ones, it may be that the repugnant provisions can be severed. This depends on the normal tests for severance in a constitutional case—does the provincial statute still constitute a viable and sensible legislative scheme without the obnoxious section or sections?[22] If severance is not proper, then the whole provincial statute becomes inoperative. If severance is possible, then one goes on to the question whether the supplemental or duplicative provisions are respectively valid in their own right. The case of pure supplement is then next.

(b) Supplement

The situation envisaged here is that of a provincial statute which simply adds something to regulation of the concurrent matter without contradicting the fed-

---

[19]*Criminal Code*, 2-3 Eliz. II, S.C. 1953-54 c. 51, ss. 191(1), 221(1).

[20]R.S.M. 1954, c. 112, s. 55(1).

[21][1960] S.C.R. 804, 820-21.

[22]See: *Toronto Corporation v. York Corporation*, [1938] A.C. 415, 427; *A.G. for B.C. v. A.G. for Canada*, [1937] A.C. 377, 388-89.

eral statute in the field in either the positive or the negative sense explained in (a) A. H. F. Lefroy gives a good example of this[23]

> Thus, where the Dominion Companies Act provided a method for serving summonses, notices, and other documents on a company incorporated under that Act, this was held not to prevent provincial, or rather North-West Territorial, legislation, providing that such companies must file a power of attorney to some person in the Territories upon whom process might be served, before they could be registered and enabled to carry on their business in the Territories, thus providing another and more convenient method for the service of process upon such company.

Accordingly, provincial supplemental legislation in these circumstances is valid and operates concurrently with the relevant federal legislation. A refinement of this position was approved by the Supreme Court of Canada in the case of *Lord's Day Alliance of Canada v. Attorney-General of British Columbia.*[24] The federal statute in question was the Lord's Day Act,[25] section 6(1) of which is as follows:

> 6(1) It is not lawful for any person, on the Lord's Day, except as provided in any provincial Act or law now or hereafter in force, to engage in any public game or contest for gain, or for any prize or reward, or to be present thereat, or to provide, engage in, or be present at any performance or public meeting, elsewhere than in a church, at which any fee is charged, directly or indirectly, either for admission to such performance or meeting, or to any place within which the same is provided, or for any service or privilege thereat.

If it were not for the words *except as provided in any provincial law now or hereafter in force*, the field of regulation of Sunday commercial sports and movies would be completely occupied by the federal prohibition by virtue of the federal criminal law power. The Supreme Court considered that permissive Sunday observance legislation would also be proper for a province as a matter of civil rights in the province or as a matter of merely a local nature in the province, and that the federal parliament had deliberately and effectively made room for such permissive provincial legislation by the statutory words just quoted. Here then we have the federal parliament explicity drawing back from full occupation of the concurrent field to allow a different provincial provision on the subject to operate without conflict. It is the strongest possible case for the validity of non-repugnant and supplemental provincial legislation because, on the facts, a prohibition was withdrawn to make room for a permission to operate. The extreme view of the scope of negative implication explained earlier under (a), is inconsistent with the *Lord's Day Alliance* case of 1959.

The Saskatchewan *Breathalyser* case of 1957[26] is also a decision of the Supreme Court of Canada upholding the validity of a non-repugnant supplemental provincial statute. The matter involved was the legal status and effect of the re-

---

[23]A. H. F. Lefroy, *Canada's Federal System* (Toronto, 1913), 126.
[24]*Supra*, footnote 11.
[25]R.S.C. 1952, c. 171.
[26]*Reference Re Section 92(4) of The Vehicles Act*, 1957 *(Sask.)*, c. 93, [1958] S.C.R. 608.

sult of tests by the breathalyser machine to determine whether a driver on the highway was drunk. The federal Criminal Code, addressing itself to the evidentiary problem only, stated that

> No person is required to give a sample of blood, urine, breath or other bodily substance of chemical analysis for the purpose of this section.[27]

but also provided in effect that, if such sample was in fact given, the result of the chemical analysis was admissible evidence in the trial of a relevant charge under the Criminal Code.

The Saskatchewan statute provided that a driver suspected of being drunk who refused to take the breathalyser test at the request of a policeman was liable to have his licence to drive suspended or revoked. The Supreme Court of Canada held that the provincial legislation was not inconsistent with the federal legislation and was therefore fully operative, and moreover that breathalyser evidence obtained in Saskatchewan was admissible in the trial of the relevant federal offence.

The writer agrees with Mr. Justice Cartwright in this case that the finding of 'no conflict' here is wrong. As the learned judge put it.[28]

> . . . I am of opinion that a statute declaring that a person who refuses to do an act shall be liable to suffer a serious and permanent economic disadvantage does 're-quire' the doing of the act. With deference to those who hold a contrary view, it appears to me to be playing with words to say that a person who is made liable to a penalty (whether economic, pecuniary, corporal or, I suppose, capital) if he fails to do an act is not required to do the act because he is free to choose to suffer the penalty instead.

There is at least partial repugnance here, and the better decision would have been that the Saskatchewan requirement could not operate to create evidence admissible in the trial of the relevant federal offences but could operate as the evidentiary basis for a decision by the Saskatchewan Motor Vehicle Board to suspend or revoke a driver's licence. Nevertheless, given the majority finding that there was no conflict between the provincial and federal statutory provisions concerned, the case is authority, as stated earlier, for the proposition that supplemental provincial legislation remains operative. Now, only the final case of pure duplication remains to be examined.

(c) Duplication

The situation envisaged here is that of a provincial statute that literally or in substance duplicates the provisions of the federal statute in the field. (It does not matter which statute was passed first once both are in the field.) The authorities establish one of the implications of Dominion paramountcy to be that provincial duplicative legislation is suspended and inoperative. Simple duplication by a

---

[27]*Supra*, footnote 19, section 224(4).
[28][1958] S.C.R. 608, 622.

province is not permitted.[29] But, given that this *is* the state of the precedents, why *should* it be so? My submission is that there are proper reasons for this result, but they are not explained in the opinions of the judges in Canadian constitutional cases.

Where the provincial statute differs from the federal one, we have seen that the provincial provisions are suspended if they are directly or indirectly repugnant to the federal ones (a), but the provincial provisions are operative if they merely supplement the federal ones (b). Necessity born of repugnance accounts for the former result (a) and the logic of being different for the latter (b). But in the case of simple duplication we have neither repugnance nor difference. *In fact what one now finds by comparing the provincial and federal statutes in question is the ultimate in harmony.* Obviously this is what substantial duplication means. Yet at times the judges persist in saying that there is 'conflict' here, and that such 'conflict' somehow calls for the suspension of the provincial duplicative legislation. For instance, in *Smith v. The Queen*, Mr. Justice Ritchie (dissenting), after concluding that the provincial and federal offences there in question were the same, said: "I am of opinion . . . that there is a direct conflict between the impugned provisions of the provincial statute and those of the *Criminal Code* and that it is not within the competence of the Legislature of Ontario to create the offences here in question."[30] Likewise, Chief Justice Kerwin, giving one of the majority judgments in the same case, said there was *"no repugnancy"* between the provincial and federal offences because it was *not* the same conduct that was being dealt with by the two legislative bodies.[31] Obviously he implies that there would be repugnancy if the offences had been exactly the same.

Nevertheless, though it is not proper at all to speak of conflict or repugnance of terms when a provincial statute simply duplicates a federal one, is there a conflict in some other sense when this happens? Is it somehow an affront to the federal parliament that a provincial legislature should repeat the terms of a federal statute? No doubt the doctrine of Dominion paramountcy means that in a concurrent field the federal parliament is the senior partner, but what is repugnant about the junior partner merely repeating the senior one? In truth there is no conflict or repugnance of any kind in this situation. As seen in Part I, the provincial legislature and the federal parliament are properly making laws in the concurrent field in pursuance of legislative responsibilities and powers conferred by their respective aspects of interest. These aspects are equivalent as a matter of authority stemming from the constitution, so there is no clash of authority in the absence of actual inconsistency of statutory terms as explained earlier. Why then is duplica-

---

[29]See: *Home Insurance Co. v. Lindal & Beattie*, [1934] S.C.R. 33, *per* Lamont, J., 40; *Lymburn v. Mayland*, [1932] A.C. 318, *per* Lord Atkin, 326-27. Also, in the *Yolles, O'Grady* and *Smith* cases most of the judges (whether of the majority or dissenting) assumed that if the federal and provincial offences being compared were substantially the same, the provincial offence was suspended and inoperative.

In an excellent note on this subject, Professor Bora Laskin points out that simple duplication of federal legislation by a state is forbidden in both the United States and Australia. See Bora Laskin, *Canadian Constitutional Law* (Toronto, 1960), 98.

[30][1960] S.C.R. 776, 804.

[31][1960] S.C.R. 776, 780-81. Italics added.

tive provincial legislation suspended? The reason seems a very simple one—economy. It is wasteful of legislative and administrative resources to allow simple duplication, besides being confusing for all concerned. Since the province in effect admits that the federal legislation is in exactly the terms it wants, the federal legislation is serving the provincial interest just as the provincial legislature wishes it to be served. But still the provincial spokesman may ask, why not suspend the federal legislation then and avoid duplication that way? The answer in favour of the federal legislation would seem to be twofold: (a) the federal parliament is in the better position to effect economy and avoid confusion because of its wider territorial jurisdiction, hence the provincial duplicative legislation should be suspended, and, anyway, (b) the nation is greater than its parts, hence when the scales are evenly balanced, as here, the national parliament should be preferred over the provincial legislatures. So, the normal rule is that a provincial statutory provision is suspended and inoperative if it simply duplicates a federal one.

But what if the provincial provision in question is a mixed one in the sense that it both duplicates and supplements the corresponding federal one? This was the position in both *Yolles v. The Queen* and *O'Grady v. Sparling*.[32] In both these cases, the provincial offence was to drive a car on a highway "without due care and attention or without reasonable consideration for other persons using the highway", while the corresponding federal law made it an offence to drive a car with "wanton or reckless disregard for the lives or safety of other persons." Mr. Justice Roach pointed out in the *Yolles* case that the provincial offence as expressed cannot really be severed into its duplicative and its supplemental parts so as to suspend the former and save the latter. "Section 29(1) does not confine the lack of 'due care and attention' or the absence of 'reasonable consideration for others' to an attitude that is less than wanton or reckless. The Court cannot unscramble section 29(1) or rewrite it. The Legislature alone can do that."[33] Mr. Justice Roach was right to consider this not a proper case for severance, but was he right to conclude that therefore the whole provincial section was suspended? In the latter conclusion he was dissenting, the majority decisions in both the *Yolles* and *O'Grady* cases being to the contrary.

The majority decisions seem correct and justifiable. A provincial section that combines inseverably duplicative and supplemental elements does not necessarily require the same treatment as one that combines inseverably repugnant and supplemental elements. Logically, economy permits exceptions that inconsistency must deny, and in the cases mentioned the majority judges took advantage of this. Here is the importance of elucidating the different reasons for susperseding duplicative provisions on the one hand and repugnant ones on the other. The normal rule is that duplicative provincial provisions are inoperative, but, by way of exception, when a provincial provision is an inseverable combination of duplicative and supplemental elements, the whole provincial provision stands and operates concurrently with the federal provision in both duplicates and supple-

---

[32]*Supra*, footnote 11.
[33](1959) 19 D.L.R. (2d) 19, 44.

ments. This is the proper rationale of the *Yolles, O'Grady, Stephens* and *Smith* cases.[34] This exception to the general rule is important but quite limited, and it contrasts of course sharply with the position that obtains when a provincial provision inseverably combines *repugnant* and supplemental elements—the whole of such a provision is necessarily superseded by the federal one. In other words, when the duplicative is in combination with the supplemental, the former is operative because of its combination with the latter, but when the repugnant is combined with the supplemental, the latter goes into suspension with the former.[35]

Unfortunately the reasons for the exception just explained and the limited nature of the exception do not come out too clearly in the majority opinions of the four leading cases just mentioned. There is a tendency among some of the learned judges to deny the existence of the duplicative or overlapping element, and to say that because there is *some* difference between the provincial and federal offences as to the mental state required, this makes them *totally* different, so that the provincial offence is merely supplemental after all. But it does not really make sense to deny the genuine though partial duplicative element in these cases. Also, in the same cases, there is a tendency among some of the learned judges to argue that, because the concurrent matter in issue has a provincial aspect and a different federal aspect, partially overlapping provincial and federal laws enacted respectively under these aspects of authority are themselves entirely different laws because the two aspects of authority involved are different. This does not stand up either. As we saw in Part I, it is the existence of two equivalent but different aspects of authority that establishes a concurrent field in the first place. The double-aspect theory opens two gates to the same field, but there it leaves us. It does not resolve any of the *subsequent* difficulties of conflict, duplication, or supplement being analyzed here.

There has been a new development since the decision of *O'Grady v. Sparling* the implications of which serve to illustrate the effect of this group of cases. In the session of 1960-61, the Parliament of Canada added to the Criminal Code a new provision making it an offence to drive a motor vehicle "in a manner that is dangerous to the public, having regard to all the circumstances."[36] This is in addition to the federal offence of driving with "wanton or reckless disregard" that was the sole federal provision at the time of the *Yolles* and *O'Grady* decisions. There is really no difference between driving in a manner dangerous to the public, and driving with lack of due care and attention (simple negligence). Negligence is defined by whether a reasonable man would foresee the likelihood of causing harm to others by his conduct, *i.e.* by whether his conduct was *dangerous* to the public. In *O'Grady v. Sparling* the Supreme Court of Canada expressly adopted the twofold distinction of these offences into advertent negligence and inadvertent negligence, pointing out that inadvertent negligence was the respect in which the provincial offence was wider than the federal one of

---

[34]*Supra*, footnote 11. *Stephens v. The Queen*, [1960] S.C.R. 823.

[35]Of course, a provincial statute may combine provisions exclusively within provincial powers with others in a concurrent field of one or more of the three types discussed here—conflicting, supplemental or duplicative. This was true of both the Ontario and Manitoba Highway Traffic Acts. The argument made here is not affected by this circumstance, though the application of the rules for severance might become rather complex in some situations.

[36]9-10 Eliz. II, S.C. 1960-61, c. 43, s. 3.

showing wanton and reckless disregard. It follows that the provincial 'lack of due care' offence now merely duplicates the new federal offence of simple dangerous driving. Hence provincial careless driving offences like those of Ontario and Manitoba are now suspended and inoperative, and any charge laid under such a provincial section should be quashed.[37] This is the effect of the general rule that a provincial provision that is severable and merely duplicative is to be severed and superseded by the federal provisions duplicated. Authority for this proposition has already been quoted.

Subject then to the limited exception explained, the general rule requiring the suspension of provincial duplicative legislation is a salutary one. If the possibility of effective provincial duplicative legislation was wide open, then, for example, a provincial legislature could duplicate the whole of the federal law of theft as legislation to protect property rights in the province. Crown attorneys could take their choice of whether to prosecute under the federal theft sections or the provincial onces, and the provincial Attorneys General could control this choice. Awkward questions about double jeopardy or the right to trial by jury could arise. Fortunately, under the present rules, there are two reasons why a province could not duplicate the federal law of theft in the Criminal Code. In the first place the federal theft sections are by their nature comprehensive, constituting what purports to be a complete code on the subject of theft. Hence the negative implication discussed under (a) earlier is genuinely present and precludes any provincial theft legislation operating. Even if this were not so, simple duplication is not allowed anyway, as we have seen in the analysis just concluded under (c).

The position of provincial legislation in a concurrent field then may be summarized as follows. Provincial legislation may operate if there is no federal legislation in the field or if the provincial legislation is merely supplemental to federal legislation that is in the field. Duplicative provincial legislation may operate concurrently only when inseverably connected with supplemental provincial legislation, otherwise duplicative provincial legislation is suspended and inoperative. Repugnant provincial legislation is always suspended and inoperative. These are the implications of the doctrine of Dominion paramountcy developed by the courts.[38]

---

[37]It is true that some authorities consider there are three grades of negligence for these purposes. See the judgment of LeBel, J.A. in the *Yolles* case, (1959) 19 D.L.R. (2d), 19, 49-50. Mr. Justice LeBel referred to *McLean v. Pettigrew* [1945] S.C.R. 62, as supporting this view. *McLean v. Pettigrew* is a conflict of laws case in tort and such a threefold distinction was unnecessary to the decision. In any event, the Supreme Court of Canada in the *O'Grady* case has adopted two grades of negligence as the governing distinction for purposes of the issues touching Dominion paramountcy—the distinction being that between advertent negligence and inadvertent negligence.

There has also been some suggestion that Lord Atkin sanctioned a threefold distinction in the case of *Andrews v. Director of Public Prosecutions*, [1937] A.C. 576, when discussing parallel sections in the English Road Traffic Act of 1930. I cannot find any such threefold distinction in Lord Atkin's judgment. See [1937] A.C. 576, 584.

[38]It should be noted that in one respect, old age pensions, we have a doctrine of provincial paramountcy, by virtue of section 94A of the B.N.A. Act added in 1951 by 14-15 Geo. VI (U.K.), c. 32:

94A. It is hereby declared that the Parliament of Canada may from time to time make laws in relation to old age pensions in Canada, but no law made by the Parliament of Canada in relation to old age pensions shall affect the operation of any law present or future of a Provincial Legislature in relation to old age pensions.

In conclusion, it should be noted that the existence of a concurrent field means that there is room for political agreement between provincial and federal governments about whether the federal parliament or a provincnial legislature undertakes the regulation of this or that phase of a concurrent matter. The precise equilibrium point in practice then would become a matter for political and administrative decision. As governmental activities continue to expand in our modern urban and industrial society, we can expect much more concurrent operation of federal and provincial laws in the old areas of joint occupation and in new areas as well. The adjustments involved will continue to call for both judicial and political decisions of a high order.[39]

FURTHER DEVELOPMENTS AND REFERENCES

The essay on concurrency was published in 1963. The following significant subsequent developments may be noted.

(1) In determining when there was duplication of provincial and federal offences concerning dangerous driving on highways, I followed the reasoning of the *O'Grady* case[1] that two basically different offences could be identified: advertent dangerous driving and inadvertent dangerous driving. Only the first was a federal offence at the time of *O'Grady*. Shortly thereafter, Parliament amended the Criminal Code of Canada to create a new federal dangerous driving offence. Then came the case of *Mann v. The Queen*,[2] in which the Supreme Court of Canada identified three basically different dangerous driving offences rather than two. These might be described as follows: (i) Driving with wanton or reckless disregard for the safety of others; (ii) Driving in a seriously dangerous manner; and (iii) Driving in an ordinary inadvertently careless manner. The new federal offence of 1961 was characterized as (ii) above but not (iii). Thus it was held that there was still not duplication of the provincial offence (iii) by the federal offences (i) and (ii). The provincial offence covered (iii), and a *fortiori* (i) and (ii) as well. Thus the specific example of complete duplication I used in the 1963 essay was rejected, but not the general reasoning given there to the effect that, when provincial legislation inseverably supplements as well as duplicates federal

---

[39]As Dr. J. A. Corry has pointed out, our country is increasingly moving away from the older classical federalism of 'watertight compartments' with provincinal legislatures and federal parliament carefully keeping clear of one another. We seem to be moving towards a co-operative federalism. "The co-ordinate governments no longer work in splendid isolation from one another but are increasingly engaged in cooperative ventures in which each relies heavily on the other." See J. A. Corry, "Constitutional Trends and Federalism," in the volume of essays *Evolving Canadian Federalism* (Durham, N.C., U.S.A., 1958), 96. The multiplication of concurrent fields is one of the facets of this trend. Even if the precise equilibrium point in a concurrent field is reached by political decision or agreement, nevertheless the bargaining position of federal and provincial governments is defined by the judicial decisions about concurrency and the doctrine of Dominion paramountcy.

[1][1960] S.C.R. 804.

[2][1966] S.C.R. 238.

legislation, the provincial legislation remains fully operative. My submission then is that this latter reasoning explains the result in *Mann* as well as the result in *O'Grady*.

(2) The reasoning of the 1963 essay on concurrency was specifically discussed in the case of: *Multiple Access Ltd. v. McCutcheon et al.*[3] Mr. Justice Morden gave the judgment of the Ontario Divisional Court and spoke with approval of the reasoning of the 1963 essay. He found the case to be one of simple duplication and ruled that the provincial legislation was thereby rendered inoperative. His reasons were adopted by the Ontario Court of Appeal.

(3) In spite of the foregoing, considerable uncertainty remains about what amounts to full occupation of a concurrent field by federal legislation so as to render provincial legislation inoperative, particularly with respect to the notion of federal legislation apparently intended to provide a complete code for the matter in hand, an issue discussed in the 1963 essay.

See majority and dissenting opinions in the Supreme Court of Canada in the following cases: *Ross v. Registrar of Motor Vehicles*,[4] *Bell v. A.-G. P.E.I.*,[5] concerning the suspension of drivers' licences and *Robinson v. Countrywide Factors Ltd.*,[6] concerning fraudulent preferences and bankruptcy.

---

[3](1977), 78 D.L.R. (3d) 701, 710 (Ont.Div.Ct.); affd 86 D.L.R. (3d) 160*n* (C.A.); revg Henry J., Ontario High Court, 65 D.L.R. (3d) 477.
[4](1973), 42 D.L.R. (3d) 69.
[5](1973), 42 D.L.R. (3d) 82.
[6](1977), 72 D.L.R. (3d) 500.

Chapter 14

The Balanced Interpretation of the Federal Distribution of Legislative Powers in Canada

(The Integrity of the Process of Interpretation)
Reprinted with permission from *The Future of Canadian Federalism*
P. A. Crepeau and C. B. Macpherson, eds. (Toronto and Montreal:
University of Toronto Press, 1965), 91

As Canada approaches the centennial of her formation under a federal constitution, the times call for thoughtful consideration of both the past and the future. For almost one hundred years now the distribution of law-making powers made by the BNA Act between the parliament of Canada and the legislatures of the provinces has been under interpretation in the courts. For much the greater part of the period, the final interpretative tribunal was the Judicial Committee of the Privy Council in London, but since 1949 the Supreme Court of Canada has taken the place of the Judicial committee.[1]

While respecting the previous course of interpretation, the Supreme Court of Canada has also shown in some instances that it can and will move along new lines as the basic needs of the country change with changing times.[2] This suggests that it would be profitable to examine closely the system of interpretation itself, if we would discern something of the shape of the future. What are the essential elements of the system of interpretation of the distribution of powers? Where is it flexible and where rigid? What is the nature of its appeal to both reason and authority? Is the traditional superior court essential to the process?

Certainly the system of interpretation has its purely technical side, but that is not all by any means. Though one starts by looking at a technique or procedure, soon, by travelling this route, one uncovers the detailed and substantive working conceptions of Canadian federalism. In other words, study of the process of interpretation soon reveals essential elements that must be respected if we are to have a balanced federal constitution—one that maintains and develops reasonable equilibrium between centralization and provincial autonomy in sub-

---

[1]*A.G. for Ontario v. A.G. for Canada,* [1947] A.C. 127 (Privy Council Appeals Case).
[2]For example, respecting the trade and commerce power, see *Murphy v. C.P.R. and A.G. for Canada,* [1958] S.C.R. 626.

ject after subject of public concern. In a brief and preliminary way, I described the process as follows in an earlier essay.[3]

> The federal distribution of legislative powers and responsibilities in Canada is one of the facts of life when we concern ourselves with the many important social, political, economic or cultural problems of our country. Over the whole range of actual and potential law-making, our constitution distributes powers and responsibilities by two lists of categories or classes—one list for the federal parliament (primarily section 91 of the BNA Act), the other for each of the provincial legislatures (primarily section 92 of the BNA Act). For instance, the federal list includes regulation of trade and commerce, criminal law, and a general power to make laws in all matters not assigned to the provinces. Examples from the provincial list are property and civil rights in the province, local works and undertakings, and all matters of a merely local or private nature in the province.
>
> These federal and provincial categories of power are expressed, and indeed have to be expressed, in quite general terms. This permits considerable flexibility in constitutional interpretation, but also it brings much overlapping and potential conflict between the various definitions of powers and responsibilities. To put the same point in another way, our community life—social, economic, political, and cultural—is very complex and will not fit neatly into any scheme of categories or classes without considerable overlap and ambiguity occurring. There are inevitable difficulties arising from this that we must live with so long as we have a federal constitution.
>
> Accordingly the courts must continually assess the competing federal and provincial lists of powers against one another in the judicial task of interpreting the constitution. In the course of judicial decisions on the BNA Act, the judges have basically done one of two things. First, they have attempted to define mutually exclusive spheres for federal and provincial powers, with partial success. But, where mutual exclusion did not seem feasible or proper, the courts have implied the existence of concurrent federal and provincial powers in the overlapping area, with the result that either or both authorities have been permitted to legislate provided their statutes did not in some way conflict one with the other in the common area.

The two lists just mentioned, federal and provincial, are collectively complete (or nearly so) in their enumeration of governmental powers.[4] Accordingly they comprise a classification system for these powers. But, any such classification system brings with it inevitable philosophic dilemmas in logic and valuation for those charged with applying the system to the life of the country. Often our courts have faced these dilemmas in terms of what they call the aspect theory,[5] which is an all-pervasive idea helpful in the solution of such problems. What follows in the balance of this essay is principally an attempt to explain and illustrate the total process of interpretation of the BNA Act on the basis of the aspect theory.

---

[3]W. R. Lederman, "The Concurrent Operation of Federal and Provincial Laws in Canada" (1962-63), 9 *McGill L.J.*, 185.

[4]A very few powers are withheld from both legislative bodies. See for examples sections 91(1), 93, 121, and 133 of the BNA Act, 30 & 31 Victoria, C. 3 (UK) as amended to date.

[5]"Subjects which in one aspect and for one purpose fall within Sect. 92, may in another aspect and for another purpose fall within Sec. 91." Lord Fitzgerald, in *Hodge v. The Queen*, (1883-84), 9 A.C. 117, 130.

I. CLASSIFICATION OF LAWS AND THE ASPECT THEORY

Our legal system consists of a great multitude of rules defining the rights, duties, privileges, powers, and immunities of the people over the whole range of human affairs. Legal relations are specified in everything from crimes to contracts, from torts to taxes, from wills to welfare. It is to this body of the ordinary laws of the land, and to proposed new laws, that the classification system of our federal constitution must be applied.

It seems labouring the obvious to say that only classes or categories of laws can be used to distribute law-making powers, or, putting it the other way around, that only particular laws are appropriate data for the various categories of a system of classification of laws. Nevertheless, there is considerable importance in the point. With respect to both the federal and provincial lists, the BNA Act speaks of power "to make laws in relation to matters coming within the classes of subjects hereinafter enumerated." This is all right provided one realizes that "subjects" and "matters" simply refer to different *aspects* or features of the laws to be classified. It would have been a better and simpler description of the true position if the BNA Act had spoke only of power "to make laws coming within the classes of laws hereafter enumerated," for, as a matter of reason, that is inevitably the position anyway.[6] As Dr. Martin Wolf has put it,[7] "Classification may be compared with the mathematical process of placing a factor common to several numbers outside the bracket." For instance, the federal category "criminal law" has been defined as including all rules that forbid a specified type of conduct with penal consequences for breach. The prohibitive and penal features are the common denominators here, the aspects that count in this definition of criminal law.

To repeat then, sections 91 and 92 of the BNA Act contain categories of laws, not categories of facts. As Sir Frederick Pollock has said,[8] "The divisions of law, as we are in the habit of elliptically naming them, are in truth not divisions of facts but of rules; or, if we like to say so, of the legal aspect of facts." In other words, when classifying to distribute legislative powers, we approach the facts of life only through their legal aspects, that is, only to the extent that such facts have been incorporated in rules of law as the typical fact-situations contemplated by those rules. For example, one cannot simply look at a particular financial transaction and say, "That is banking within the meaning of section 91(15) of the BNA Act, and hence the federal Parliament and only the federal Parliament can make laws to regulate or affect that transaction in any way." Rather, one must frame the terms of the law whereby one proposes to do something to regulate that type of financial transaction, and then look at that law to see if it is a banking law. What one proposes to *do* by a law about a certain type of fact situation may well have as much bearing on classification of that law as does the nature of the facts alone. Law is normative, not merely descriptive.

---

[6]The writer developed this theme in detail in an earlier essay entitled "Classification of Laws and the British North America Act," in *Legal Essays in Honour of Arthur Moxon* (Toronto, 1953), 183-207.

[7]M. Wolff, *Private International Law* (London, 1945), 148.

[8]Sir F. Pollock, *A First Book of Jurisprudence* (2nd ed., London, 1904).

The important lesson from this is that, if we would reason our way to precise and meaningful conclusions about the significance for the future of our distribution of law-making powers in Canada, we must be prepared to be specific about the terms of the proposed laws that we hope to have passed in the federal Parliament or the provincial legislatures. On the whole, vague general questions about legislative jurisdiction cannot be answered with any real clarity or precision. The truth of this point can be illustrated from the so-called "reference cases," that is, cases where the judgments are in response to questions put directly to the court by a government. For instance, the federal cabinet is empowered to put questions to the Supreme Court of Canada by order-in-council and the Court is required to answer.[9] If these direct questions take the form of asking the judges to assess the validity of laws that have been enacted, or at least fully drafted, then the judges can and do answer fully and with precision on the issue of legislative powers. Reference cases of this type command as much influence in the realm of precedent as do cases originating in actual litigation, in spite of occasional judicial protestations to the contrary.[10] In both types of cases the actual texts of the laws at issue are available. The *Privy Council Appeals Reference* of 1947,[11] which concerned new draft sections for the Supreme Court Act,[12] is as influential as the case of *British Coal Corporation v. The King*,[13] which was decided in 1935 as the result of actual litigation. The former case expands and adds to the reasoning of the latter, and both are precise and meaningful.

By contrast, nothing much but confusion and talk of competing alternatives comes out of the *Reference respecting Waters and Water Powers*[14] considered by the Supreme Court of Canada in 1929. The questions from the cabinet in that case were very general ones about legislative competence to regulate the use or exploitation of rivers, lakes, and canals. Relevant draft laws were not either suggested or quoted. The reporter for the Canada Law Reports gave up on the headnote. He says plaintively at the start of the report:[15] "In view of the difficulties which the court found in dealing with the questions before it and of the impossibility of giving precise and categorical answers, it was thought best, in order to avoid misleading as to what was decided, to put as a headnote the text of the formal judgment." At one point in the formal judgment, their lordships said of two of the questions, "These questions cannot be answered categorically either in the affirmative or in the negative."[16] The authority to make a reference to the courts is useful, then, only if these questions are properly framed in the light of the process of decision that is involved.

But, even if the Court does have an actual legal text before it, there may still

---

[9] The Supreme Court Act, R.S.C. 1952, c. 259, 55.
[10] See Gerald Rubin, "The Nature, Use and Effect of Reference Cases in Canadian Constitutional Law," (1959-60) 6 *McGill LJ*, 168, esp. 177.
[11] See footnote 1.
[12] See footnote (9), 54.
[13] [1935] A.C. 500.
[14] [1929] S.C.R. 200.
[15] *Ibid*.
[16] *Ibid.*, 201.

be difficulty similar to that just considered. As Mr. Justice Rand pointed out in the *Saumur Case* in 1953,[17] the law at issue may be so vague and general in its terms that it fails because, given its full meaning, it would exceed the specified powers of either the federal parliament or a provincial legislature. It will be recalled that the Quebec City by-law in that case was as follows: "It is . . . forbidden to distribute in the streets of the City of Quebec any book, pamphlet, booklet, circular, tract whatever, without having previously obtained for so doing the written permission of the Chief of Police." In commenting on this, Mr. Justice Rand points out that the laws of a federal country must be specific and detailed enough that they make sense in relation to the categories of the system for the distribution of law-making powers.[18]

> Conceding . . . that aspects of the activities of religion and free speech may be affected by provincial legislation, such legislation, as in all other fields, must be sufficiently definite and precise to indicate its subject matter. In our political organization, as in federal structures generally, that is the condition of legislation by any authority within it: the courts must be able from its language and its relevant circumstances, to attribute an enactment to a matter in relation to which the Legislature acting has been empowered to make laws. That principle inheres in the nature of federalism; otherwise, authority, in broad and general terms, could be conferred which would end the division of powers. Where the language is sufficiently specific and can fairly be interpreted as applying only to matter within the enacting jurisdiction, that attribution will be made; and where the requisite elements are present, there is the rule of severability. But to authorize action which may be related indifferently to a variety of incompatible matters by means of the device of a discretionary licence cannot be brought within either of these mechanisms; and the Court is powerless, under general language that overlaps exclusive jurisdictions, to delineate and preserve valid power in a segregated form.

The lesson mentioned earlier may perhaps now be repeated and restated. The most fruitful constitutional discussions are likely to be those that start with specific legal remedies and measures conceived to be useful or necessary to meet our various national and regional problems. With such proposed legal measures in mind, it is then feasible to go on to the special federal issues of whether power to enact this or that measure lies at present with the federal parliament or the provincial legislatures. Also, this approach will raise in specific and useful ways issues of whether power is presently misplaced and needs to be relocated or reformed by amendment of the system for distribution of powers itself.

Nevertheless, even if one does have a specific and simple legal rule to assess for validity, critical dilemmas of classification still arise. Take, for example, the simple proposition, "Marriage revokes a pre-nuptial will of either spouse." Marriage is a federal category of jurisdiction under section 91(26) of the BNA Act while property is a provincial category under section 92(13). Obviously the rule quoted is both marriage law and property law. It has both its matrimonial aspect and its proprietary aspect. Logically it falls within both the federal and provincial lists. When the item being classified points both ways in this

---

[17]*Saumur v. Quebec and A.G. for Quebec,* [1953] 2 S.C.R. 299.
[18]*Ibid.,* 333.

manner, is it to be characterized as proprietary or matrimonial for purposes of assigning power to enact it?

Consider another example suggested by the recent decision of the Supreme Court of Canada upholding the validity of the Ontario statute, the Unconscionable Transactions Relief Act.[19] In that case the law provided that, in respect of money lent, if in all the circumstances the cost of the loan was excessive and the transaction harsh and unconscionable, the judge could reform the contract so as to make its terms fair and reasonable, and order the necessary adjustments at the expense of the lender. Certainly this law has its contractual aspect, and contract is a classic example of civil rights within the provincial category of property and civil rights. But also the same law concerns interest charges, and thus has an aspect or feature pointing logically to the federal category of interest in section 91(19) of the BNA Act. Again one must ask—which aspect is to prevail for purposes of the division of legislative powers?

The point to appreciate is that these simple examples are not exceptional; indeed, they illustrate the usual position. Nearly all laws or legislative schemes have a multiplicity of features, characteristics, or aspects by which they may be classified in a number of different ways, and hence potentialities of cross-classification are ever present. The more complex the statute, the greater the number of logical possibilities in this regard. So, in the case of a particular law challenged for validity, one aspect of it points to a federal category of power with logical plausibility, but, with equal logical plausibility, another aspect points to a provincial category of power. Or, looking at the other side of the coin, one can say the same thing another way. The respective federal and provincial classes of laws often overlap one another as general concepts in many important respects, and thus compete, so to speak, through this partial coincidence of categories, for the allegiance of the statutes to be classified. When one says that the rule, "marriage revokes a pre-nuptial will," is both matrimonial and proprietary, one is necessarily saying that logically the concept of marriage law and the concept of property law overlap one another respecting rules of matrimonial property law. Similarly, in the other example given earlier, the concept of contract law (included in civil rights) and the concept of interest law overlap one another respecting rules regulating unconscionable interest charges. To repeat, this partial but multiple coincidence of categories is the usual and not the exceptional situation for a classification system such as that embodied in the BNA Act. Those who make a federal constitution must generalize in some degree the concepts to be used to distribute law-making powers. But, once such lists have been made, those who must interpret the constitution encounter the broad extensions of meaning and the overlapping of concepts that generalized thought makes inevitable. At this point it is clear that such generalized concepts must be used with care if we would preserve the balance of our federal constitution—preserve, that is, a proper equilibrium between significant provincial autonomy and adequate central power.

---

[19]*A.G. for Ontario v. Barfried Enterprises Ltd.* (1964), 42 D.L.R. (2d) 137. *Unconscionable Transactions Relief Act,* R.S.O. 1960, c. 410.

The danger is this, that some of the categories of federal power and some of those of provincial power are capable of very broadly extended ranges of meaning. If one of these concepts of federal power should be given such a broadly extended meaning, *and also priority over any competing provincial concept*, then federal power would come close to eliminating provincial power. The converse could happen just as easily, with the federal power suffering virtual eclipse. Take for example the federal category of criminal law. If all that is necessary for valid legislation under this head is that the federal Parliament should prohibit something with penal consequences for breach, then Parliament can enact any legislative scheme it pleases provided it sprinkles the statute concerned with a few prohibitions and penalties. There would be very little left of independent provincial power if the federal Parliament could really get away with this. And the attempt has been made. In the Board of Commerce Act and the Combines and Fair Prices Act of 1919,[20] the federal Parliament, among other things, enacted a most elaborate and detailed scheme for the positive control by the Board of Commerce of supplies and sales of consumer goods at every level, with penalties for breaches of the regulations. The courts rejected the argument that this could be sustained under the federal criminal law power at the expense of provincial powers over local industry and commerce within the province. In the *Margarine Case*[21] the courts reached the same result in much the same circumstances concerning attempted federal prohibition of the local manufacture and sale of that one commodity.

In the *Padlock Law Case*,[22] by contrast, the shoe was on the other foot. Briefly, the Quebec legislature had enacted a prohibition on the dissemination of communistic propaganda from any house or building in the province, the penalty being the padlocking of a house so used against any use whatever for up to one year. Counsel for the province argued that this was valid provincial property legislation under section 92(13) because, under this heading, any use whatever of land or buildings could be regulated by a province. The Court rejected the argument, pointing out that there would be no real limit to what a province could do at the expense of federal powers if such an extended conception of the scope of property law were to prevail. In such circumstances, the federal writ would run only in remote air space.

An example of an extreme extension of meaning that has prevailed is afforded by judicial interpretation of the commerce power in the United States. There the Congress was given power by the constitution ". . . to regulate Com-

---

[20]*In re: The Board of Commerce Act, 1919, and The Combines & Fair Prices Act, 1919* (1921), 1 A.C. 191.

[21]*Reference re Validity of Section 5(a) of the Dairy Industry Act*, [1949] S.C.R. 1. Mr. Justice Rand made it clear in the following words that the definition of "criminal law" for purposes of the BNA Act was not just a matter of prohibition and penalty only. At pages 50-51 he said: "Is the prohibition then enacted with a view to a public purpose which can support it as being in relation to criminal law? Public peace, order, security, health, morality: these are the ordinary though not exclusive ends served by that law, but they do not appear to be the object of the parliamentary action here. . . . [T]here is nothing of a general or injurious nature to be abolished or removed: it is a matter of preferring certain local trade to others."

[22]*Switzman v. Elbling and A.G. for Quebec*, [1957] S.C.R. 285.

merce with foreign Nations, and among the several States. . . ."[23] In the modern period at least, the Supreme Court of the United States has extended the meaning of the commerce power to the furthest limits of which it is capable, so that now there is little or nothing left of the independent power of the respective American states over any economic activities local to a state. For example, the American Supreme Court has held that the commerce power of the Congress extends to regulation of the labour standards of the maintenance employees of the owner of a building (janitors, electricians, window washers, and so on) where the owner has rented the building to a tenant who is principally engaged in the production of goods for inter-state commerce.[24] Now, if a "house-that-Jack-built" chain of relevance like that is to be permitted to extend the meaning of "commerce among the several states," all limits are indeed off. No wonder Professor Alexander Smith, in his recent treatise on the subject, has stated: "[I]t is not extravagant to say that the federal system in the United States exists only on Congressional sufferance."[25]

The Americans may like this sort of result, and indeed it may suit their needs very well. It would never do for Canada. But, if we would maintain a balanced federal system here, there are two dilemmas of classification for the distribution of legislative powers that one must solve. They have been revealed in the foregoing analysis and may be briefly recapitulated as follows.

1. *The categories of legislative power.* No one of the general concepts by which power is given should be allowed to prevail to the extreme limits of its potential meaning, regardless of the competing scope of other concepts. There must be some mutual limitations of definition, and even then much overlapping will remain.

2. *The laws to be classified.* The laws challenged for validity, the particular items to be classified, are almost invariably ambivalent in the logical sense, in that they exhibit both federal and provincial aspects or characteristics. Different aspects of the same particular law point to categories in both the federal and provincial lists respectively, even though no one category in those lists is allowed an extremely extended meaning. So, on this account alone, there must be some further step in the classification process whereby the federal aspect is made to prevail over the provincial one, or *vice versa*, for purposes of decisive classification.

Let us now consider the solutions of these problems.

II. SOLUTIONS OF THE DILEMMAS OF THE DISTRIBUTION OF LEGISLATIVE POWERS

Their lordships of the Privy Council were not long in discovering that they faced the problems of interpretation just outlined. It soon became clear to them that the solutions had to be based on appreciation of the many aspects of meaning involved in the classification process—the range of aspects covered by the defini-

---

[23]Article 1, s. 8(3).
[24]*Kirschbaum Co. v. Walling* (1942), 316 U.S. 517.
[25]Alexander Smith, *The Commerce Power in Canada and the United States* (Toronto, 1963), 371.

tion of a category of laws on the one hand, and the multiplicity of classifiable aspects that a single statutory scheme could exhibit on the other. The process or system is by no means automatic or productive of just one set of "right" answers. It is largely a matter of framing the right questions in the right order, and there are judicial choices to be made about the proper answers at each stage.

In the first place, the courts have indeed tended to avoid extremely extended meanings for categories of federal power at the expense of those of provincial power, and *vice versa*. Definitions have tended to be mutually restrained where the context seems to call for this. Many examples of such mutual modification could be given,[26] but perhaps one of the best (and most difficult) is afforded by interpretation of the federal power. The opening words of section 91 give the federal parliament power ". . . to make Laws for the Peace, Order and good Government of Canada, in relation to all Matters not coming within the Classes of Subjects by this Act assigned exclusively to the Legislatures of the Provinces; . . ." Classes assigned to the provinces, however, include "Property and Civil Rights in the Province," and "Generally all Matters of a merely local or private Nature in the Province." Obviously there is much logical overlapping of concepts here with the consequent competition explained earlier. The danger to the balance of the constitution of overextending the definition of the federal general power was expressed in 1896 by Lord Watson in the *Local Prohibition Case*.[27]

> . . . [T]he exercise of legislative power by the Parliament of Canada, in regard to all matters not enumerated in s. 91, ought to be strictly confined to such matters as are unquestionably of Canadian interest and importance, and ought not to trench upon provincial legislation with respect to any of the classes of subjects enumerated in s. 92. To attach any other construction to the general power which, in supplement of its enumerated powers, is conferred upon the Parliament of Canada by s. 91, would, in their Lordships opinion, not only be contrary to the intendment of the Act, but would practically destroy the autonomy of the provinces. . . .
>
> . . . Their Lordships do not doubt that some matters, in their origin local and provincial, might attain such dimensions as to affect the body politic of the Dominion, and to justify the Canadian Parliament in passing laws for their regulation or abolition in the interest of the Dominion. But great caution must be observed in distinguishing between that which is local and provincial . . . and that which has ceased to be merely local or provincial, and has become a matter of national concern. . . .

Lord Watson did leave some permanent scope for a federal general power of permanent significance, particularly as he fully recognized that there might be some concurrency between that power and competing heads of section 92. But, restriction of definition no doubt went too far with Viscount Haldane when, in 1925 in the *Snider Case*,[28] he construed the federal general power as an emergency

---

[26]See *Citizens Insurance Co. of Canada v. Parsons* (1881-82), 7 A.C. 96, 106-7.
[27]*A.G. for Ontario v. A.G. for Canada*, [1896] A.C. 348, 360-61.
[28]*Toronto Electric Commissions v. Snider*, [1925] A.C. 396.

power only in any respect in which it competed logically with one or more of the categories of section 92. As we have seen, this could be just about every respect that mattered.

In any event a more reasonable scope for the federal general power was established by Viscount Simon in the *Canada Temperance Federation Case* of 1946.[29] After rejecting "emergency" as the test, his Lordship said:

> . . . [T]he true test must be found in the real subject matter of the legislation: if it is such that it goes beyond local or provincial concern or interests and must from its inherent nature be the concern of the Dominion as a whole (as for example in the *Aeronautics case . . .* and the *Radio case . . .*) then it will fall within the competence of the Dominion Parliament as a matter affecting the peace, order and good government of Canada, though it may in another aspect touch upon matters specially reserved to the Provincial Legislatures. . . . Nor is the validity of the legislation, when due to its inherent nature, affected because there may still be room for enactments by a Provincial Legislature dealing with an aspect of the same subject in so far as it specially affects that Province.

In other words, if a federal statute is challenged and the federal general power is invoked to support it, in competition with the usual provincial powers, then, if the challenged statute proposes to do something that needs to be done at the nation-wide level if it is to be done effectively, or done at all, then this element of necessity causes the statute to fall within the federal general power. It is not enough if one shows that there is some mere convenience or advantage to be obtained by federal legislative action of the type at issue. But, on the other hand, one no longer has to go beyond genuine necessity and establish emergency to invoke the federal general power. So a balanced definition results—some real necessity that is more than just convenience or advantage but less than outright emergency.

Nevertheless, in spite of mutual modification of definitions because of the whole context of the BNA Act, much overlapping of concepts inevitably remains. In other words, the ambivalent character of particular laws or statutes persists. This constitutes the second dilemma of classification. The first step towards solution is to construe the challenged statute itself carefully to be sure of having determined its full meaning, that is, the full range of features by any one of which or by any combination of which it may be classified. A rule of law expresses what should be human action or conduct in a specified factual situation, hence the consequences of observing and enforcing the rule are among its vital aspects of meaning. As Lord Maugham said in the *Alberta Bank Taxation Case* of 1939,[30] in a case of difficulty one must look at the effects of the legislation: "For that purpose the Court must take into account any public general knowledge of which the Court would take judicial notice, and may in a proper case require to be informed by evidence as to what the effect of the legislation will be." Unless this is done, the classification process might well be purely formal or grammatical.

---

[29]*A.G. for Ontario v. Canada Temperance Federation*, [1946] A.C. 193, 205-6.
[30]*A.G. for Alberta v. A.G. for Canada*, [1939] A.C. 117, 130.

In any event, having thus determined the full range of features of the challenged statute, we find the usual situation, that federal aspects and provincial aspects are both present and compete to control characterization of the statute for purposes of determining the power to enact it. To resolve this competition, the courts must now assess the relative importance of the respective federal and provincial features of the statute in contrast with the other. Accordingly, criteria of relative value enter the picture. If the judges find a clear contrast, if for instance they deem the federal aspects clearly more important than the provincial ones, then the conclusion is that power to pass the statute is exclusively federal. For the purpose of distributing legislative power then, the challenged statute is decisively classified by its leading feature, by its more important characteristic, by its primary aspects, by its pith and substance. These are synonymous phrases. And if, on the other hand, the provincial features are deemed clearly more important than the federal ones, the power to pass the law in question is exclusively provincial. In this way exclusive power can be assigned to federal parliament or provincial legislature in spite of the purely logical ambivalence of the challenged statute because of its different aspects.

For example, the Vacant Property Act of Quebec (1939)[31] provided, to put it briefly, that all financial deposits in credit institutions unclaimed for thirty years became the property of the Crown in right of the Province of Quebec. This would have the sensible effect and object of permitting savings institutions to clear their books of great numbers of small accounts long since forgotten by depositors who could not be traced. But the statute was held *ultra vires* of the province because the Privy Council concluded that this was primarily banking legislation and only secondarily was it property and civil rights legislation.

> If that be the main object and effect of the provincial Act it does in their Lordships' view invade the field of banking. It comes in pith and substance within that class and the fact that it may incidentally affect certain other institutions cannot take away its primary object and effect.
>
> In their [Lordships'] view a provincial legislature enters upon the field of banking when it interferes with the right of depositors to receive payment of their deposits, as in their view it would if it confiscated loans made by a bank to its customers. Both are in a sense matters of property and civil rights, but in essence they are included within the category "banking."[32]

Further, in the *Alberta Bill of Rights Case* (1947) where there was the same type of problem concerning banking and property and civil rights, the Judicial Committee said: "It is true, of course, that in one aspect provincial legislation on this subject affects property and civil rights, but if, as their Lordships hold to be the case, the pith and substance of the legislation is "Banking" . . . this is the aspect that matters and Part II is beyond the power of the Alberta Legislature to enact."[33]

But, what if the contrast between the federal and provincial features respec-

---

[31]Statutes of Quebec, 3 George 6 (1939) c. 28.
[32]*A.G. for Canada v. A.G. for Quebec*, [1947] A.C. 33, 44 and 46.
[33]*A.G. for Alberta v. A.G. for Canada*, [1947] A.C. 503, 518.

tively of the challenged law is not so sharp that one can be selected as the leading feature? What if both seem to be leading features? Take, for example, a law making dangerous driving of automobiles an offence with penalties. Because of its power over the civil right to drive and over highways as local works, it is important that a provincial legislature be able to pass such a law in aid of its responsibility for the safe and efficient circulation of traffic on the highways. But likewise it is important that the federal parliament under its general criminal law power should be able to pass such a law in aid of its responsibility to forbid and punish grave and dangerous anti-social conduct of all kinds.

In these circumstances, federal and provincial laws are permitted to operate concurrently, provided they do not conflict in what they prescribe for the persons subject to them. In the words of Lord Dunedin, two propositions are established[34]: "First, that there can be a domain in which provincial and Dominion legislation may overlap, in which case neither legislation will be *ultra vires*, if the field is clear; and secondly, that if the field is not clear, and in such domain the two legislations meet, then the Dominion legislation must prevail."

To sum up, for a concurrent field to be found by interpretation, the following conditions must obtain: (1) the provincial and federal categories of power concerned must overlap logically in their definitions; (2) the challenged law must be caught by the overlap, that is, it must exhibit both provincial and federal aspects of meaning; and (3) the provincial and federal aspects of the challenged law thus manifest must be deemed of equivalent importance or value.

In recent years there seems to be a liberal trend respecting concurrency developing in the Supreme Court of Canada. In the first place, the number of concurrent fields recognized or created by judicial interpretation is increasing. One of the latest examples of this in the Supreme Court of Canada is afforded by the decision there upholding the Ontario Unconscionable Transactions Relief Act as valid provincial legislation.[35] This means that laws restraining or reforming interest charges that are harsh or unconscionable fall both ways in our federal system. They may be enacted by a province as a modification of the contract law of undue influence, this being a species of civil rights in the province. Or, they may be enacted by the federal Parliament under the specific federal power conferred by the word "interest" in section 91(19).

In the second place, given that a concurrent field has been found, the court

---

[34]*G.T. Rlwy. Co. of Canada v. A.G. for Canada*, [1907] A.C. 65, 68.

[35]See footnote 19. Other examples are:

Highways
    P.E.I. v. Egan, [1941] S.C.R. 396; *The Queen v. Yolles* (1959), 19 D.L.R. (2d) 19; *O'Grady v. Sparling*, [1960] S.C.R. 804.

Sale of Securities
    Smith v. The Queen, [1960] S.C.R. 776.

Trading Stamps
    The Queen v. Fleming (1962), 35 D.L.R. (2d) 483.

Sunday Observance
    Lord Day Alliance of Canada v. A.G. for B.C., [1959] S.C.R. 497.

Federal Election Propaganda
    Regina v. McKay & McKay (1964) 43 D.L.R. (2d) 401.

is becoming quite liberal about permitting federal and provincial statutes to live together in that field. In other words the judges seem reluctant to find conflict fatal to the provincial statute if they can avoid this result. This seems particularly true of concurrent fields created by the overlap of the federal and provincial criminal law powers, being sections 91(27) and 92(15) respectively of the BNA Act. Nevertheless, if there is conflict between federal and provincial statutes in a concurrent field, the doctrine of dominion paramountcy is to the effect that the federal statute prevails and the provincial one is thereby displaced and suspended. So, in the end, federal power is over-riding in a concurrent field. One authority must be paramount in the event of conflict in a concurrent field, for the citizen cannot be subjected to two laws that contradict one another.

New and specifically defined areas of concurrency no doubt and useful flexibility to the constitution, and often permit the provinces to legislate in joint fields where the federal Parliament coult act but has not done so. Also, there may be political agreements about what each legislative body will or will not do in the concurrent area, thus making possible one form of co-operative federalism. Examples are the federal-provincial taxation agreements and Sunday observance legislation.[36] Nevertheless, there is still need to avoid over-extension of the definition of the scope of federal categories of power if balance is to be maintained in our constitution. Complete concurrency of federal powers with provincial ones, coupled with the doctrine of dominion paramountcy, would mean the end of a balanced federal system in Canada. The trend to increased concurrency then may have its dangers for the autonomy of the provinces, though so far the main effect of the trend has been to uphold provincial statutes.

Accordingly, federal constitutional interpretation in Canada might be said to call for mutual exclusion of powers if practical, but concurrency if necessary. Moreover, whether one finds mutual exclusion or concurrency, the process requires decisions about the relative values represented by the competing federal and provincial aspects of the challenged statute. Often these are difficult decisions indeed, but they are inescapable. So the question becomes: Is the statutory scheme at issue something that is better done province by province on the basis of provincial autonomy, or is it something better done uniformly over the whole country on a nation-wide basis? What criteria of value move the judges in this respect? In an earlier essay, the writer attempted the following answer to this.[37]

> In this inquiry, the judges are beyond the aid of logic, because logic merely displays the many possible classifications; it does not assist in a choice between them. If we assume that the purpose of the constitution is to promote the well-being of the people then some of the necessary criteria will start to emerge. When a particular rule has features of meaning relevant to both federal and provincial classes of laws, then the question must be asked, Is it better for the people that this thing be done on a national level, or on a provincial level? In other words, is the feature of the challenged law which falls within the federal class more important to the well-being of the country than that which falls within the provincial class of laws? Such consider-

---

[36]See *ibid.*
[37]*Legal Essays in Honour of Arthur Moxon*, 197-8.

ations as the relative value of uniformity and regional diversity, the relative merit of local *versus* central administration, and the justice of minority claims, would have to be weighed. Inevitably, widely prevailing beliefs in the country about these issues will be influential and presumably the judges should strive to implement such beliefs. Inevitably there will be some tendency for them to identify their own convictions as those which generally prevail or which at least are the right ones. On some matters there will not be an ascertainable general belief anyway. In the making of these very difficult relative-value decisions, all that can rightly be required of judges is straight thinking, industry, good faith, and a capacity to discount their own prejudices. No doubt it is also fair to ask that they be men of high professional attainment, and that they be representative in their thinking of the better standards of their times and their countrymen.

Once again, the importance is apparent of exploring all aspects of the challenged law as a matter of meaning and evidence. A legal system must in general be related to the social, economic, and cultural realities, and to the accepted values and beliefs, of the country concerned. Indeed a legal system exists to take account of these realities in a way that advances those values and beliefs as far as laws can do so. In a federal country like Canada this applies to the special issues concerning which legislative body—the central or the provincial—should be responsible for this or that statutory scheme. Professor Bora Laskin seems to have all this in mind when he speaks of "constitutional values" in a special sense. He says[38]:

> What the process of constitutional adjudication involves is a distillation of the "constitutional value" represented by challenged legislation (the "matter" in relation to which it is enacted) and its attribution to a head of power (or class of subject). This is not to say that the process is mechanical or that there are logically-discoverable essences which go to make up a class of subject. The distribution of legislative power must surely be envisaged as an instrumental or operating scheme, ample enough to embrace any subject or object of legislation. The classes of subjects must hence be conceived as vehicles through which social or economic or political policy is expressed, and these considerations (however they may be inarticulate or concealed in precedent or logic) cannot be ignored when the courts give content to the classes of subjects and measure the validity of legislation accordingly.

At this point one may well ask: Why all the emphasis on the analytical logic of classification that characterizes the present essay, if in the end logic alone is indecisive? The answer is that such analytical reasoning is necessary to prepare the way for and to reveal the need of the value judgments that *are* in the end decisive. Good analytical jurisprudence isolates issues of form and reveals issues of substance in their true colours. If you can frame the right questions and put them in the right order, you are half way to the answers. In other words, by proper questions and analysis, the issues requiring value decisions are rendered specific and brought into focus one by one in particular terms, so that ordinary mortals of limited wisdom and moral insight can cope with them. This is the reason for in-

---

[38]Bora Laskin, Canadian Constitutional Law (2nd ed., Toronto, 1960), 76-7.

sisting that if you would distribute law-making powers you must classify laws, and that if you would classify laws you must at least draft the terms of the statute you are talking about and then ascertain all its aspects of meaning as a rule for social action of some kind.

In any event, it ought to be clear that a judge interpreting a federal constitution is no mere automaton—that, on the contrary, he has critical choices to make at different stages of the process. Nevertheless, authoritative precedent does enter the picture in a very important way, and by this factor the guide lines of the distribution of legislative powers are given considerable stability and even rigidity. Writing of this factor elsewhere, I said:[39]

> Lest a false impression of complete uncertainty and fluidity be conveyed by the foregoing, the importance of the rules of precedent that obtain in our courts should be remembered. However open logically the classification of a given type of law may have been when first it was considered by the highest court, that decision will in all probability foreclose the question of the correct classification should the same type of law come up again. For instance it was argued that the federal Industrial Disputes Investigation Act of 1907 was within the power of the Canadian Parliament because its provisions regulating the settlement of industrial disputes were classifiable as "regulation of trade and commerce", "criminal law", and rules for "peace, order and good government". Nevertheless the Judicial Committee pointed out that these provisions were also classifiable as laws concerning "property and civil rights in the province" and in effect ruled that such was the important or significant classification for constitutional purposes. Hence the Act was declared *ultra vires* of the Canadian Parliament. Incidentally, in his argument for the validity of the Act, Sir John Simon had pointed to the absence of economic division in Canada on provincial lines; in other words many industries and labour organizations were national or at least inter-provincial in scope and hence national regulation of industrial relations was desirable. But the Judicial Committee was not impressed. Tacitly but effectively they decided that provincial autonomy and diversity in the regulation of employer-employee relations were more important when they ruled that the challenged statute "in its pith and substance" interfered with civil rights. Thus the classification of this type of industrial regulation critical for constitutional purposes has been settled by precedent, and in like manner many other classifications are authoritatively settled. It is not clear yet whether the Supreme Court of Canada, supreme now in law as well as name, will asset a right to depart in exceptional circumstances from particular decisions in the accumulation of Privy Council precedents. Certainly it would seem that explicit departures, if any, will be rare. Nevertheless, some new and different scheme of industrial regulation, for example, might well be deemed outside the scope of its precedent just discussed, and then its classification in turn would have to be considered as a matter of first impression with all the problems here explained once more in full bloom.
>
> Moreover, frequently there will be new laws, both federal and provincial, which the precedents on classification will not touch decisively or concerning which indeed there may be conflicting analogies. Thus in spite of the principles of precedent the full-blown problem of classification described earlier is often with us.

In summary then, we can now see that the classification process joins logic

---

[39] *Legal Essays in Honour of Arthur Moxon,* 199-200.

with social fact, value decisions and the authority of precedents, to define the distribution of law-making powers. The reasoning involved is not automatic or mechanical; rather it makes the highest demands on learning, intellect, and conscience. It permits expression to the real issues of public policy in the country, and indeed brings such issues into focus in many particular ways, thus facilitating their resolution. The point is that, so long as we have a federal constitution, we must be prepared to contend with the real complexity of the interpretative process. In other words, what has been described above is the inevitable operating jurisprudence of the federal form of social order. If we understand the process, we will expect neither too much nor too little of the constitutional distribution of legislative powers as it stands now, or as it may be if certain changes are made. There is much more room for reasonable differences of interpretation than most people realize. These differences then should not be regarded as evidence of bad faith or ignorance; rather, they should be taken as a challenge calling for support of the working of our system of interpretation at its best level. Up to this point, we have assumed that the superior court on the English model is the proper type of tribunal to have the last word on interpretation by the process described. This assumption is correct, but now needs further explanation.

III. THE NECESSITY FOR INDEPENDENT JUDICIAL REVIEW OF THE FEDERAL DISTRIBUTION OF POWERS

The need for final judicial review of the federal distribution of legislative powers has roots in the necessities of a federal system. Neither the federal Parliament nor the provincial legislatures could be permitted to act as judges of the extent of their own respective grants of power under the BNA Act. If they were, soon we would have either ten separate countries or a unitary state. Nor are such issues of interpretation suitable for determination by voting in some kind of a special body composed of numerous delegates or representatives assembled for the purpose. In the end this would simply mean majority rule or deadlock through minority veto. Rather, the interpretative process is best carried out in one of our traditional superior courts where, by submission and argument, appeal can be made to the reason, understanding, and sense of values of impartial judges who enjoy secure and permanent tenure during good behaviour.

This is the present position in Canada. Final review of the distribution of legislative powers by superior courts is a principle specially entrenched in the Canadian constitution by necessary implication. As Mr. Justice McGillivray has expressed it, speaking in the Alberta Court of Appeal[40]:

> . . . consideration of the legislative capacity of Parliament or of the Legislatures cannot be withdrawn from the Courts either by Parliament or Legislature. In my view this statement may rest upon the safe ground that by necessary implication from what has been said in the BNA Act, the Superior Courts whose independence is thereby assured, are just as surely made the arbiters of the constitutional validity of statutory enactments as Parliament and the Legislatures are made law enacting bodies. If, as I think, it is not open to question that neither Parliament nor Legisla-

---

[40]*I.O.F. v. Lethbridge*, [1938] 3 D.L.R., 102-3, affirmed in the Privy Council, [1940] A.C. 513.

ture may provide as the concluding words of an enactment that it shall be deemed to be *intra vires* by all Courts in the country then neither the one nor the other of these legislative bodies can reach the same end by denying access to the Courts for the determination of constitutional questions.

As the learned justice suggests, certain principles are necessary to ensure the integrity of the interpretative process in the hands of our superior courts, particularly the Supreme Court of Canada. Neither the federal nor provincial legislative bodies can deny access to the courts on constitutional questions, nor can either of them instruct the courts how to determine such issues of validity.[41] The legislative bodies cannot, by statutory recitals, settle the classification of their own statutes for purposes of the distribution of powers. That is, they cannot tell the judges which aspect of the challenged statute is to be considered its leading feature. Selection of the aspect that matters is the exclusive prerogative of the court, and the so-called doctrine of colourability is simply an instance of this rule, meaning that, for example, so far as the court is concerned, a statute cast in the form of a tax law may nevertheless be found to have banking as its leading aspect.[42] Likewise, a statute cast in the form of land law may nevertheless be found to have the crime of sedition as its primary characteristic.[43] Furthermore in this regard, no legislative body is permitted finally to settle the truth of jurisdictional facts by statutory recitals. In the *Fort Frances Case*,[44] Viscount Haldane made it clear that, even on the issue of the existence or continuance of emergency conditions sufficient to invoke the federal emergency power, the court reserved ultimate decision to itself, though normally it would take the word of the federal Parliament or government for this.

The interpretation of a federal distribution of legislative powers and responsibilities is then a complex process of reasoning, balancing, and deciding that calls for the special qualities of the superior court as that institution was developed in England after the *Act of Settlement* of 1701.[45] This type of tribunal is one of the most important features of our great inheritance in Canada of English public law and institutions. This is not to say that every official working decision about what the federal constitution means should be made in court, for instance in the Supreme Court of Canada. Great numbers of working decisions must, of course, be made at every important level of government by a great variety of officials and their legal advisers. Nevertheless, the relatively few issues taken to the Supreme Court of Canada are critical because this is the final resort in a showdown, and in any event, Supreme Court decisions, being final, are controlling in the field of interpretation, laying down the principles and guide lines to be respected at the other levels of government.

It is necessary that the Supreme Court of Canada should be our final interpretative tribunal rather than the Judicial Committee of the Privy Council in London, though the latter body often served Canada well in earlier times. The point

---

[41]See also note by Laskin, *Canadian Constitutional Law*, 192-3.
[42]See footnote 32.
[43]See footnote 22.
[44]*Fort Frances Pulp & Power Co. Ltd. v. Manitoba Free Press Co. Ltd.*, [1923] A.C. 695, 706.
[45]12 & 13 William III (1701), U.K. c. 2, s. 3.

is simply that the judges of the Supreme Court of Canada are Canadians who live all their lives in Canada with the problems and conditions that obtain here under our federal constitution. Because of the discretions inevitably inherent in the process of interpretation, this should bring more wisdom and realism to the process than could be expected of an outside tribunal.

At present the Supreme Court of Canada is constituted by ordinary federal statute, and the judges are appointed by the Governor-General in Council, that is by the federal cabinet. This leads some persons to have misgivings to the effect that the Supreme Court of Canada may not be as truly independent of the Parliament and Government of Canada as it should be in a federal country. In this respect the Supreme Court of Canada may seem to compare unfavourably with the Judicial Committee of the Privy Council.

In my view these misgivings are unfounded. The Supreme Court of Canada is pre-eminently a superior court in every sense, and our whole constitutional tradition means that the Canadian Parliament would never change the Supreme Court Act in any way prejudicial to the true independence of the Court or its judges. Nevertheless, if it were thought useful to do so, the Statute of the Court could be specially and formally entrenched in appropriate clauses of the Canadian constitution.

As for the power of appointing Supreme Court judges, I consider this should remain with the prime minister of Canada and his cabinet, responsible as they are to the Parliament of Canada representing all parts of the country. The main point is that, once a highly qualified person has been appointed to the security and independence of the Supreme Court Bench, he must simply be trusted to rise to the challenge of the office with integrity and intelligence. This applies both to constitutional interpretation and to the disposal of ordinary appeals. The presence of judges learned in the French civil law of Quebec is ensured by the provision of the present statute of the court that requires one-third of the judges to be selected from the bar of Quebec. In the result, the two great legal traditions of the Western world come together in the Supreme Court of Canada. The French civil law of Quebec traces its roots back two thousand years to the finest period of the Roman law. The English common law tradition of the other provinces is the distinguished inheritance of one thousand years of English history. Drawing as it does on these two sources, the Supreme Court of Canada should be able to serve the country well. Judges and lawyers of the civil law and the common law have found that they can communicate sympathetically with one another—that they can understand one another. I believe this is because the appeals to reason and justice in both systems of law are basically the same.

My position is then that the Supreme Court of Canada should be continued in its present function and power of final interpretation of the distribution of legislative powers. No institution is perfect, but an independent superior court manned by Canadian judges provides the best tribunal available for balanced interpretation of law-making powers of Canada and the provinces in relation to one another.

FURTHER THOUGHTS

In the foregoing essay, in 1965, I spoke with approval in general terms of the "national dimensions" test of the scope of the federal general power in section 91 of the B.N.A. Act, given by Viscount Simon in the *Canada Temperance Act* case of 1946. Since 1965, I have considerably refined and somewhat modified my views of the meaning of "permanent national dimension" in this respect. These later views are explained in the essay reproduced in the next chapter, which was published in 1975.

The doctrine of "colourability" is mentioned in the essay in the previous part of this chapter, and I have learned over many years of teaching that some students get too broad a notion of what it means. In the essay I stated:

> Selection of the aspect that matters is the exclusive prerogative of the court, and the so-called doctrine of colourability is simply an instance of this rule, meaning that, for example so far as the court is concerned, a statute cast in the form of a tax law may nevertheless be found to have banking as its leading aspect. Likewise a statute cast in the form of land law may nevertheless be found to have the crime of sedition as its primary characteristic.

In other words, a parliamentary draftsman is not allowed to play games, so to speak, with the form of a statute in order to conceal some non-formal aspect of that statute which is really its main thrust or pith and substance. Nevertheless, when statutes are challenged for constitutional validity, in many if not most instances, form is simply neutral or ambivalent and the competing aspects are plainly out in the open, and so may be openly weighed and contrasted.

Chapter 15

Unity and Diversity in Canadian Federalism: Ideals and Methods of Moderation

Reprinted with permission from (1975), 53 Canadian Bar Review 597

Canada is a federal country of great extent and variety in which we respect both unity and diversity. This is difficult to do, but we *have* now been doing it with a large measure of success for well over 100 years. The total process of governing Canada revolves about a division and distribution of primary legislative capacities or powers by two lists of subjects, one list for the federal Parliament (primarily section 91 of the British North America Act)[1] and the other for each of the provincial legislatures (primarily section 92 of the British North America Act). Instead of subjects, one might speak of categories or classes. For the most part, sections 91 and 92 taken together comprise a complete system for the distribution of primary legislative powers and responsibilities in Canada over virtually the whole range of actual and potential law-making. The courts have held the distribution is complete, with some very few exceptions that prove the rule. The exceptions are concerned with certain specific rights to use of the French or English languages, certain specific rights to denominational schools, and free trade across provincial borders. Without disparaging the importance of these exceptions, it is fair to point out that nearly all of our constitutional jurisprudence in the courts for 100 years has concentrated on issues of the distribution of powers.

My concern in this article is to offer some thoughts on the nature and quality of the judicial interpretation of sections 91 and 92 of the British North America Act over the years. Until the end of 1949, of course, the dominant court was the Judicial Committee of the Privy Council in London. Only since 1949 has the Supreme Court of Canada emerged from the shadow of the Judicial Committee and become supreme in law as well as in name. So, while we are celebrating this year the hundredth anniversary of the creation of the Supreme Court of Canada, we are only celebrating the twenty-fifth anniversary of the supremacy of the Supreme Court of Canada as the final tribunal of appeal for Canadians.

The definitive study of the Privy Council period in constitutional interpretation was published in 1971 by Professor Alan C. Cairns. This is an essay of about

---

[1] 1867, 30 & 31 Vict., c. 3, as am. (U.K.).

forty-five pages in the "Canadian Journal of Political Science," entitled "The Judicial Committee and Its Critics". I agree with Professor Cairn's conclusions, so I give them rather fully in his own words:[2]

> In brief, if the performance of the Privy Council was as its critics suggested, replete with inconsistencies and insensitivity, the confused outpourings of the critics displayed an incoherence completely inadequate to guide judges in decision-making. To contrast the performance of the Judicial Committee with the performance of its opponents is to ignore the dissimilarity of function between artist and critic. It is however clear that the Judicial Committee was much more sensitive to the federal nature of Canadian society than were the critics. From this perspective at least the policy output of British judges was far more harmonious with the underlying pluralism of Canada than were the confused prescriptive statements of her opponents. For those critics, particularly on the left, who wished to transform society, this qualified defence of the Judicial Committee will lack conviction. However, such critics have an obligation not only to justify their objectives but also the role they advocated for a non-elected court in helping to attain them.
>
> Whether the decline in the problem-solving capacity of governments in the federal system was real or serious enough to support the criticism which the Privy Council encountered involves a range of value judgments and empirical observations of a very complex nature. The purpose of this paper has been only to provide documentation for the minimum statement that a strong case can be made for the Judicial Committee, and to act as a reminder that the basic question was jurisprudential, a realm of discussion in which neither the Privy Council, its critics, nor its supporters proved particularly illuminating.

Note that Professor Cairns deplores the general confusion that has reigned concerning a positive philosophical jurisprudence of constitutional judicial review in Canada. Secondly, note that in any event he thinks the record of their Lordships of the Privy Council is a lot better in this regard than that of their critics. Note finally that he says the basic question was and is jurisprudential.

Accordingly, writing as a critic who has been both chastened and challenged by what Professor Cairns has said, I now offer some thoughts on the essential operating jurisprudence of Canadian federalism. I assume in so doing that judicial review at all levels, and especially at the highest level, is essential to the process of interpreting a federal distribution of primary legislative powers. I have made the case for this proposition several times in earlier published essays,[3] and I will return to it near the end of this article. What I now do is to select two points to develop about the essential operating jurisprudence of our federal distribution of legislative powers, and in the course of discussing them, I will offer some opinions on the quality of what judges have said they were doing, and on what other critics have said the judges should have been doing.

In the first place, I address the nature of the Canadian system for the distribution of legislative powers. This then leads in the second place to a consider-

---

[2](1971), 4 Can. J. Pol. Sc. 301, 343-344.

[3]The Independence of the Judiciary (1956), 34 Can. Bar Rev. 769 and 1139; The Balanced Interpretation of the Federal Distribution of Legislative Powers in Canada, in MacPherson and Crépeau (eds), The Future of Canadian Federalism (1965), 91.

ation of the significance of what I prefer to call the federal general power, but which often is called the federal peace, order and good government power.

Starting then with the nature of the Canadian federal system, we find that our way of distributing legislative powers has been to set up two rather detailed lists of federal and provincial legislative capacities. In an earlier essay, I described the two lists and the methods of interpreting them in these terms:[4]

> The federal distribution of legislative powers and responsibilities in Canada is one of the facts of life when we concern ourselves with the many important social, political, economic or cultural problems of our country. Over the whole range of actual and potential law-making, our constitution distributes powers and responsibilities by two lists of categories or classes—one list for the federal parliament (primarily section 91 of the *B.N.A. Act*), the other for each of the provincial legislatures (primarily section 92 of the *B.N.A. Act*). For instance, the federal list includes regulation of trade and commerce, criminal law, and a general power to make laws in all matters not assigned to the provinces. Examples from the provincial list are property and civil rights in the province, local works and undertakings, and all matters of a merely local or private nature in the province.
>
> These federal and provincial categories of power are expressed, and indeed have to be expressed, in quite general terms. This permits considerable flexibility in constitutional interpretation, but also it brings much over-lapping and potential conflict between the various definitions of powers and responsibilities. To put the same point in another way, our community life—social, economic, political, and cultural—is very complex and will not fit neatly into any scheme of categories or classes without considerable overlap and ambiguity occurring. There are inevitable difficulties arising from this that we must live with so long as we have a federal constitution.
>
> Accordingly the courts must continually assess the competing federal and provincial lists of powers against one another in the judicial task of interpreting the constitution. In the course of judicial decisions on the *B.N.A. Act*, the judges have basically done one of two things. First, they have attempted to define mutually exclusive spheres for federal and provincial powers, with partial success. But, where mutual exclusion did not seem feasible or proper, the courts have implied the existence of concurrent federal and provincial powers in the overlapping area, with the result that either or both authorities have been permitted to legislate provided their statutes did not in some way conflict one with the other in the common area.

The words quoted imply the point I now wish to develop more explicitly. We have here two lists of powers that are in total competition one with the other in all their parts, total competition, that is, to embrace challenged provincial or federal statutes and to stamp them with legitimacy as exercises of provincial or federal legislative power respectively. The federal general power competes with the provincial general power, the federal criminal law power competes with the provincial property power, and so on. Proper use of words—good grammar and syntax—is essential as a starting point for the expression of a scheme of division of powers. But it is only the starting point, and it is a mistake to think that the

---

[4]The Concurrent Operation of Federal and Provincial Laws in Canada (1962-63), 9 McGill L.J. 185.

task of interpretation is grammatical and syntactical only, treating the constitutional document in isolation from the economic, social and cultural facts of life of the society to which the constitutional document relates, both historically and currently. Yet this has frequently been done in Canada. The famous O'Connor Report of 1939[5] castigates the Judicial Committee because it perversely contradicted the so-called "plain words" of section 91 of the British North America Act. Many years later, Professor G. P. Browne, in his book on the Privy Council period,[6] discovered full justification for the Judicial Committee's results in the grammar and syntax of the same so-called "plain words" of sections 91 and 92. So, O'Connor and Browne simply cancel one another out, and in so doing demonstrate the truth of the following remarks by Professor Hans Kelsen who said (speaking of the constitution of the United Nations):[7]

> Since the law is formulated in words and words have frequently more than one meaning, interpretation of the law, that is determination of its meaning, becomes necessary. Traditional jurisprudence distinguishes various methods of interpretation: the historical, in contrast to the grammatical, an interpretation according to the "spirit", in opposition to a literal interpretation keeping to the words. None of these methods can claim preference unless the law itself prescribes the one or the other. The different methods of interpretation may establish different meanings of one and the same provision. Sometimes, even one and the same method, especially the so-called grammatical interpretation, leads to contradictory results. It is incumbent upon the law-maker to avoid as far as possible ambiguities in the text of the law; but the nature of language makes the fulfilment of this task possible only to a certain degree.

So I say one needs to insist that the power-conferring words and phrases of sections 91 and 92 must be related to the cultural, social and economic realities of the society for which they were and are intended, both historically and currently, if they are to make sense as basic guide lines for government at both the provincial and federal levels.

To illustrate what I mean, I wish to take up a neglected historical point. I refer to the historically established meaning of the phrase "Property and Civil Rights" in central British North America from 1774 to 1867. The phrase comes from the Quebec Act of 1774 of the Imperial Parliament,[8] which provided that French law and custom were to obtain respecting property and civil rights in the royal colony of Quebec. This covered all the law except English criminal law, and except the English public law that came to Quebec as necessary context for English colonial governmental institutions. In her recent book on the subject, Dr. Hilda Neatby, a distinguished Canadian historian, has demonstrated from the official documents of the time that the phrase property and civil rights in the Que-

---

[5]Report by W. F. O'Connor, The Parliamentary Counsel to The Honourable the Speaker of the Senate relating to "The enactment of the *B.N.A. Act*, 1867, any lack of consonance between its terms and judicial construction of them and cognate matters" (1939).
[6]The Judicial Committee and the British North America Act (1967).
[7]The Law of the United Nations (1951), xiii-xv.
[8]14 Geo. III, c. 83 (U.K.).

bec Act had and was intended to have this very broad significance.[9] Moreover, these words retained this very broad significance in Upper and Lower Canada between 1791 and 1841, and in the United Province of Canada, 1841-1867. The Fathers of Confederation knew all about this—they lived with it every day—and naturally they took the broad scope of the phrase for granted. Accordingly they realized that, in setting up a central Parliament in their new federal system, a considerable list of particular central powers would have to be specified in some detail as subtractions from the historically established meaning of the phrase property and civil rights. Otherwise the use of that phrase in the provincial list would leave very little for the new central Parliament. Because of this, I reiterate, the Fathers of Confederation knew that a general grant of power to the central Parliament in all matters not assigned to the provinces would in and by itself *not* be enough to give the central Parliament all the powers they wished it to have, for example over banking, or marriage and divorce or bills of exchange. I am not just speculating at large when I say this. One can see it in the text of both the Quebec and London Resolutions:[10]

Quebec Resolutions
43 (15) Property and civil rights, excepting those portions thereof assigned to the General Parliament.
   (18) And generally all matters of a private or local nature, not assigned to the General Parliament.
London Resolutions
41 (15) Property and civil rights (including the solemnization of marriage) excepting portions thereof assigned to the General Parliament.
   (18) And generally all matters of a Private or Local Nature not assigned to the General Parliament

The same point also emerges from a comparison of the penultimate draft of the British North America Act with the final draft that was enacted.[11] I infer from the comparison that the ''notwithstanding'' clause in the opening words of section 91 and the ''deeming'' clause in the closing words were designed to ensure that the twenty-nine specific categories in the original federal list were to be taken as withdrawn from the historic scope of the provincial property and civil rights clause, and withdrawn also from the new provincial category of things generally of a local and private nature in the province.

In other words, the implication is plain that this double-listing was done because the Fathers of Confederation, the Colonial Secretary and the parliamentary draftsmen were all satisfied that it was necessary; that the rather long and particular federal list, supported by the ''notwithstanding'' clause and the ''deeming'' clause, was essential if items like banking, marriage and divorce, copyright, connecting railways, and so on were to be within the power of the new federal Parliament, where they wanted them to be.

---

[9] Quebec, 1769-1791 (1966), *passim*.
[10] Joseph Pope, Confederation (1895), 47 and 106.
[11] *Op. cit., ibid.*, 233-236.

Accordingly, it follows that the twenty-nine specific categories of federal parliamentary power originally listed in section 91 are not merely illustrations of what would have been embraced anyway by the federal general power to make laws in all matters not assigned to the provinces. For the reasons of historical fact that I have given about the phrase property and civil rights, the federal list was not just superfluous grammatical prudence, it was compelled by historical necessity and has independent standing. Many if not most of the twenty-nine enumerated heads in section 91 confer powers on the federal Parliament that would not have been attracted to that Parliament by the federal general power alone in single-handed competition with the historic provincial property and civil rights clause.

The result of this reasoning about the nature of section 91 may be recapitulated as follows. The twenty-nine more particular powers, the so-called enumerated powers, add greatly to the competence that would have been invested in the federal Parliament by the federal general power alone, though no doubt there is a modest amount of overlapping. On the other hand, the federal general power is no mere appendage to the twenty-nine enumerated powers, an appendage labelled "for emergencies only". It covers considerable ground that the enumerated powers do not cover. What then do we see when we look at the complete picture afforded by sections 91 and 92? I say we see a total system of power-distribution wherein thirty heads of federal power, including a national general and residuary power, compete with sixteen heads of provincial power, one of which is a local general and residuary power. The grammar and syntax of sections 91 and 92 are as consistent with this result as with any other, and the history of central British North America from 1774 to 1867 confirms this alternative as the correct picture of the system. This is why I describe Canadian power-distribution as the total competition of thirty federal heads of power with sixteen provincial heads of power. Because of amendments since 1867 we should now speak of thirty-two and sixteen. So potentially the logical extent of this competition is all the permutations and combinations of thirty-two versus sixteen. The picture is indeed a complex one, but anything less is surely oversimplification.

When the time came to compose a federal constitution for Canada, we can count ourselves fortunate that the history of property and civil rights in the royal colony of Quebec and the successor colonies compelled the use of two rather long lists of federal and provincial powers. The many power-conferring phrases used were all equal in status as parts of a single system and thus had each to be read in a context that included all the others. As a result, there had to be restraint, moderation and mutual modification in the scope that was to be given any one of them.[12] The federal trade and commerce clause could not be allowed to destroy all commercial significance for the provincial property and civil rights clause, or *vice versa*. The provincial property power could not be extended indefinitely at the expense of the federal criminal law power, or *vice versa*, and so on.

As Canada expanded westward geographically and accepted heavy immigration, the country became more and not less diverse. The kind of a federal doc-

---

[12]*Citizens' Insurance Company v. Parsons* (1881-82), 7 A.C. 94, 106-110.

ument that history gave us facilitated the development of a carefully balanced federalism that accommodated old and new diversities as well as ensuring essential unities. Unique flexibility for Canada comes from having *many* power-conferring phrases in competition with one another, and the equilibrium points established between them portray the critical detail of Canadian federalism. The power-conferring phrases themselves are given by the British North America Act, but the equilibrium points are not to be found there. They have necessarily been worked out painstakingly by judicial interpretation and precedent over many years. Furthermore, particular equilibrium points are not fixed for all time. As conditions in the country genuinely change and truly new statutory schemes are enacted, judicial interpretation can adjust and refine the equilibrium of the division of legislative powers to meet the new needs. So the high importance of sophisticated judicial interpretation as an ongoing process is obvious.

Let me now turn in the second place to one particular aspect of that interpretation—the proper scope to be given to the general power of the federal Parliament—the power to make laws for Canada in all matters not assigned to the legislatures of the provinces. There is also a provincial general power to make laws in all matters of a merely local or private nature in the province, and, theoretically, it raises the same interpretative problems as does the federal general power. But the cases have concentrated on the federal general power, so this analysis does likewise.

The basic interpretative problem here may be explained as follows. Leaving the two general powers out of the count, there are thirty-one specific grants of powers to the federal Parliament and fifteen specific ones to the provincial legislatures. Let us assume that a new statute has been passed by the federal Parliament and that its validity has been challenged. The federal government now claims that the statute is valid because its primary concern is a *new* subject entitled to be treated as within the residuary reach of the federal general power, and thus in effect to be added to the existing list of thirty-one specific federal subjects. Accordingly our question becomes this: when is such a claim allowed for a subject not specifically listed in either section 91 or 92, and when is it disallowed? In other words, when is it proper to enfranchise a new category to be added to the thirty-one existing specific federal categories by virtue of the residuary significance of the federal general power?

Well, look at some examples of what the courts have done about unlisted subjects. Aviation, atomic energy and the incorporation of Dominion companies have each been enfranchised as additions to the list of federal subjects by virtue of the residuary reach of the federal general power.[13] But labour relations, and pollution are also completely unlisted subjects. They too are real enough as subjects of concern in our society and they have not been enfranchised as new federal subjects by virtue of the federal general power.[14] Rather, each of these sub-

---

[13]*In re Regulation and Control of Aeronautics in Canada*, [1932] A.C. 54; *Johannesson v. West St. Paul*, [1952] 1 S.C.R. 292; *Pronto Uranium Mines Ltd. v. O.L.R.B.* (1956), 5 D.L.R. (2d) 342 (Ont. H.C.).

[14]*Toronto Electric Commissioners v. Snider*, [1925] A.C. 396. *Reference re Industrial Relations and Disputes Investigation Act*, [1955] S.C.R. 529.

jects has been itself subdivided into several parts that could be reclassified piecemeal according to some of the already established specific categories of thirty-one federal and fifteen provincial subjects. The parts are thus distributed accordingly, some to the federal Parliament and others to the provincial legislatures. Take the example of labour relations. If you have a business or industry that is under federal jurisdiction, like banks or inter-provincial railways, power to regulate their labour relations is federal. If you have a business or industry under provincial jurisdiction, like a retail store or a coal mine, power to regulate their labour relations is provincial. The same sort of point can be made about the various powers to regulate the abatement of pollution of our air, land or water. Why is the regulation of aviation made a new federal category, a unit in its own right, while labour relations is broken up and parcelled out piecemeal by the operation of several of the specific categories—the thirty-one federal ones and the fifteen provincial ones? What tests does the subject "aviation" meet that the subject "labour relations" fails to meet to warrant such radical differences in treatment? This is no frivolous question; it is a fundamental one about the positive operating jurisprudence of our federal system.

To answer this question, we must first take account of the many possibilities of multiple classification or cross-classification that exist by virtue of the philosophy of the classification process itself as it relates to the distribution of legislative powers. A prohibition against emitting noxious chemicals from an industrial plant into a river, for example, may be logically classified as property law, criminal law, fisheries law, pollution law, environmental law, recreational law, public health law, and so on. Logically the prohibition may be properly characterized as any or all of these things. But which classification is to dominate for the purpose of our federal distribution of powers? Clearly, as a first step, the significant classification of a challenged law for this purpose should be sought among the specific categories listed in the British North America Act. There are forty-six of them—thirty-one in the federal list and fifteen in the provincial list. If this first search among the forty-six categories does not result in a dominant classification of the challenged law satisfactory in terms of the social needs and facts of the country, then as a second step you consider invoking the federal general power. I suggest that you can take the second step and successfully invoke the federal general power if two conditions are met. First, the new subject must, as a matter of evidence, arise out of the needs of our society as something that necessarily requires country-wide regulation at the national level. Secondly, and leaving aside true emergencies, the new subject should also have an identity and unity that is quite limited and particular in its extent.

Note that whether we are assessing the impact of the forty-six specific subjects listed in the British North America Act, or considering the possibility of adding a new subject to the federal list, we are not simply engaging in philosophical speculation at large about the many dozens or indeed hundreds of logically possible classifications for the challenged law.

Yet this latter range of logically possible classifications cannot be entirely ruled out of the process. Counsel seeking to invoke the federal general power in order to support a challenged federal statute on a new basis will search the whole range of dozens or hundreds of philosophically relevant classifications in order to find the one unlisted class that may serve their purpose—the one which they can then propose as a new subject for the federal list by virtue of allegedly sufficient evidence of social fact and social need for this type of regulation at the national level. If we now shift from counsel to judges, we have an alternative statement of the basic problem. By what tests do the judges determine the success or the failure of such propositions from counsel about a new subject?

Perhaps I can clarify this with the example of aviation. Both the Judicial Committee and the Supreme Court of Canada have held that aviation was a subject that deserved to be added as a new specific category to the federal list by virtue of the federal general power. Why did they do this? Because technologically and industrially aviation has a factual unity as a transportation system and implications for transportation as a force in the life and development of Canada that make provincial boundaries frustrating or irrelevant, in relation to the legal regulation necessary. Read the judgment of Lord Sankey in the *Aeronautics* case of 1932[15] and that of Mr. Justice Locke in the *Johanneson* case of 1952,[16] and you will see this reasoning well expressed, especially in the words of Mr. Justice Locke. This illustrates the way in which new subjects win entitlement to be added to the federal list.

It is interesting to note that this is the way Viscount Haldane thought of the national emergency power. Speaking of it in the *Board of Commerce* case, in 1922, he located the subject of national emergency under the federal general power because it involved "conditions so exceptional that they require legislation of a character in reality beyond anything provided for by the enumerated heads in either section 91 or section 92 . . .".[17] That is exactly the right reasoning, in accordance with my analysis. Nevertheless, as we know, Viscount Haldane went too far when he also said, in effect, that national emergency of some sort was the *only* subject that could qualify for status as a new subject under the federal general power. That is not in accordance with the analysis I am offering here. My analysis leads to the conclusion that the possibilities of enfranchising new specific subjects as within the federal general power are always open. They are never closed. But getting a new specific subject added to the federal list in this way has never been easy, and this is as it should be. It should in principle be very difficult to add a subject in this way, either to the federal list by virtue of the federal general power or to the provincial list by virtue of the provincial general power, which speaks of unlisted matters local in character.

Why should it be very difficult in principle to invoke the federal general power? Because it is essential in our federal country that the balance between federal and provincial subjects of primary legislative powers should remain stable—reasonably constant—subject only to a process of gradual changes when

---

[15]*Supra*, footnote 13.
[16]*Ibid.*
[17]*In re The Board of Commerce Act, 1919, and the Combines and Fair Prices Act, 1919*, [1922] 1 A.C. 191, 200.

these are rendered truly necessary by the demands of new conditions in our society from time to time. This applies not only to the federal general power, but of course also to the whole scheme of division of powers. Nevertheless, the cases concerned with the scope of the federal general power are the cases that raise most clearly issues of the over-all nature of our federal system, hence my concentration on those cases in this article. The balancing and adjusting necessary is typically a task for sophisticated judicial interpretation—it is basically jurisprudential in the sense that it is an appeal to law as reason.

For the most part, I think the judges of the Judicial Committee and the Supreme Court of Canada, in their cases on the federal general power, have understood this necessity well, and have decided issues and given reasons accordingly. For me, the primary words of wisdom on the subject are those of Lord Watson, whom I consider the greatest of the Privy Council judges concerned with the Canadian constitution. In the *Local Prohibition* case of 1896, he said:[18]

> There may, therefore, be matters not included in the enumeration, upon which the Parliament of Canada has power to legislate, because they concern the peace, order, and good government of the Dominion. But to those matters which are not specified among the enumerated subjects of legislation, the exception from s. 92, which is enacted by the concluding words of s. 91, has no application; and, in legislating with regard to such matters, the Dominion Parliament has no authority to encroach upon any class of subjects which is exclusively assigned to provincial legislatures by s. 92. These enactments appear to their Lordships to indicate that the exercise of legislative power by the Parliament of Canada, in regard to all matters not enumerated in s. 91, ought to be strictly confined to such matters as are unquestionably of Canadian interest and importance, and ought not to trench upon provincial legislation with respect to any of the classes of subjects enumerated in s. 92. To attach any other construction to the general power which, in supplement of its enumerated powers, is conferred upon the Parliament of Canada by s. 91, would, in their Lordships' opinion, not only be contrary to the intendment of the Act, but would practically destroy the autonomy of the provinces. If it were once conceded that the Parliament of Canada has authority to make laws applicable to the whole Dominion, in relation to matters which in each province are substantially of local or private interest, upon the assumption that these matters also concern the peace, order, and good government of the Dominion, there is hardly a subject enumerated in s. 92 upon which it might not legislate, to the exclusion of the provincial legislatures. . . .
>
> Their Lordships do not doubt that some matters, in their origin local and provincial, might attain such dimensions as to affect the body politic of the Dominion, and to justify the Canadian Parliament in passing laws for their regulation or abolition in the interest of the Dominion. But great caution must be observed in distinguishing between that which is local and provincial, and therefore within the jurisdiction of the provincial legislatures, and that which has ceased to be merely local or provincial, and has become matter of national concern, in such sense as to bring it within the jurisdiction of the Parliament of Canada.

Then, after Viscount Haldane's aberration about emergency, we come back on

---

[18]*Attorney General for Ontario v. Attorney General for the Dominion and the Distillers and Brewers Association of Ontario*, [1896] A.C. 348, 360-361.

track with the judgment of Viscount Simon in the *Canada Temperance Act* case of 1946.[19] He cited the *Local Prohibition* case with approval, and proceeded to re-state the test of the scope of the federal general power in words that are in substance the same as those of Lord Watson:[20]

> In their Lordships' opinion, the true test must be found in the real subject matter of the legislation: if it is such that it goes beyond local or provincial concern or interests and must from its inherent nature be the concern of the Dominion as a whole (as, for example, in the *Aeronautics* case and the *Radio*[21] case), then it will fall within the competence of the Dominion Parliament as a matter affecting the peace, order and good government of Canada, though it may in another aspect touch on matters specially reserved to the provincial legislatures. War and pestilence, no doubt, are instances; so, too, may be the drink or drug traffic, or the carrying of arms. In *Russell v. The Queen*,[22] Sir Montague Smith gave as an instance of valid Dominion legislation, a law which prohibited or restricted the sale or exposure of cattle having a contagious disease. Nor is the validity of the legislation, when due to its inherent nature, affected because there may still be room for enactments by a provincial legislature dealing with an aspect of the same subject in so far as it specially affects that province.

In the period since 1949, the Supreme Court of Canada has consistently followed and upheld what I would call the Watson-Simon conception of the scope of the federal general power; the Supreme Court justices have exhibited the caution and restraint that the Watson-Simon view embodies.

But this does not entirely answer the dilemma I put earlier; why was aviation treated as a new federal subject while labour relations was denied the benefit of the federal general power, divided into several parts, and distributed piecemeal in accordance with the more particular relevance of the parts to some of the original specific federal and provincial powers? In his recent distinguished essay on "Sir Lyman Duff and the Constitution", Professor Gerald Le Dain has expressed the dilemma in these terms:[23]

> Many matters within provincial jurisdiction can be transformed by being treated as part of a larger subject or concept for which no place can be found within that jurisdiction. This perspective has a close affinity to the notion that there must be a single, plenary power to deal effectively and completely with any problem. The future of the general power, in the absence of emergency, will depend very much on the approach that the courts adopt to this issue of characterization.

What I am trying to explain and illustrate in this analysis is what Professor Le Dain has perceptively pin-pointed as "this issue of characterization". In other words, am I able to answer my own question about the different treatment of aviation and labour relations as unlisted legislative subjects? I said earlier that, in normal circumstances, leaving aside true emergencies, to qualify under the fed-

---

[19]*Attorney General for Ontario and Others v. Canada Temperance Federation and Others*, [1946] A.C. 193.

[20]*Ibid.*, at p. 205.

[21]*In re Regulation and Control of Radio Communications in Canada*, [1932] A.C. 304.

[22](1882), 7 App. Cas. 829.

[23](1974), 12 Osgoode Hall L.J. 261, 293.

eral general power a new subject should genuinely need regulation at the national level, and should also have a natural unity that is quite limited and specific in its extent—a natural unity that can be given quite particular definition philosophically. Aviation meets this test. It was a new form of transportation with a natural industrial and technological unity necessarily nation-wide in scope so far as need for legislative action was concerned. Also, as a subject, aviation is quite limited and specific in extent, relatively speaking. It is just one of many forms of transportation, and as a legislative subject it does not imply large scale trespass upon major areas of existing provincial powers. Aviation is an important subject of course, but in its legislative implications it does not take over great portions of the laws of property and civil rights or municipal institutions.

But contrast with this labour relations as a unitary legislative subject. This is no limited subject or theme, this is a sweeping subject or theme virtually all-pervasive in its legislative implications. Every employer in every business or industry there is has labour relations, from the corner store to General Motors. If "labour relations" were to be enfranchised as a new subject of federal power by virtue of the federal general power, then provincial power and autonomy would be on the way out over the whole range of local business, industry and commerce as established to date under the existing heads of provincial power. The same point can be made about environmental pollution or economic growth or language requirements as unitary legislative subjects.

Notice too that this reasoning cuts both ways, it is a double-edged sword. If it were claimed that something called "culture" is, in all its aspects and as a unit, a subject that falls entirely within provincial jurisdiction because of the provincial general power over all matters of a local or private nature in the province, this would be equally contrary to the spirit and philosophy of our Canadian system for the division of legislative powers. Let me illustrate this point by a quotation from an editorial in the newspaper *La Presse*, for Friday, November 9th, 1973. The editorial writer, M. Guy Cormier, is asking for some definition of the phrase "cultural sovereignty". He says:[24]

> The word "culture" is a catch-all besides being a trap. One of the major weaknesses of the famous Laurendeau-Dunton Commission was that its work started under the terms of a mandate which gave no definition of the word "culture". So, why repeat the same foolish mistakes?
>
> Nowadays, everything is cultural. A book is certainly a cultural product, as is a film, a record, or a song. But is not a song factory, or a word factory, like the C.B.C. also a cultural reality? In a way oil is also "cultural", since oil is automobiles, home comforts, a whole manner of existence and a life style.
>
> Nowadays, therefore, everything is cultural. A notion which used to be reserved for delicate, manual or mental exercise, for literature, music, painting, or needlework, is today extended to tools and computers. In this perspective, the "Boeing 747" is a modern cultural phenomenon.

In general, what we see here is the need to keep the power-conferring

---

[24]Translation by the translation service, Ministry of Treasury, Economics and Intergovernmental Affairs, Government of Ontario (multigraphed).

phrases of our federal-provincial division of powers at meaningful levels of specifics and particulars. And from this it follows that federal and provincial statutes should be drafted with sufficient detail and particularity that they take due account of those characteristics of our division of primary legislative powers. These are two sides of the same coin. No one has expressed this better than Mr. Justice Rand of the Supreme Court of Canada. In the *Saumur case* in 1953 he said:[25]

> Conceding, as in *Re Alberta Legislation*,[26] that aspects of the activities of religion and free speech may be affected by provincial legislation, such legislation, as in all other fields, must be sufficiently definite and precise to indicate its subject-matter. In our political organization, as in federal structures generally, that is the condition of legislation by any authority within it: the courts must be able from its language and its relevant circumstances, to attribute an enactment to a matter *in relation to which* the legislature acting has been empowered to make laws. That principle inheres in the nature of federalism; otherwise, authority, in broad and general terms, could be conferred which would end the division of powers. Where the language is sufficiently specific and can fairly be interpreted as applying only to matter within the enacting jurisdiction, that attribution will be made; and where the requisite elements are present, there is the rule of severability. But to authorize action which may be related indifferently to a variety of incompatible matters by means of the device of discretionary licence cannot be brought within either of these mechanisms; and the court is powerless, under general language that overlaps exclusive jurisdictions, to delineate and preserve valid power in a segregated form. If the purpose is street regulation, taxation, registration or other local object, the language must, with sufficient precision, define the matter and mode of administration; and by no expedient which ignores that requirement can constitutional limitations be circumvented.

It is true as stated earlier that all legislative powers are distributed in Canada, but that does not mean that there is a single power, either federal or provincial, to embrace any problem or subject that can be philosophically identified as such, out of the thousands of logically possible identifications. All problems or subjects can be fitted into the total of forty-eight categories in sections 91 and 92 of the British North America Act one way or another, and Mr. Justice Rand's point is that this must be done if federal or provincial statutes are to have validity—that they must be drafted with a particularity that has this requirement in mind. So I claim that the words of Mr. Justice Rand which I have quoted support the main thrust of my reasoning on the Canadian division of legislative powers.

A vital point about my main thesis here should now be made. As a student of Canadian federalism, I have complained by way of example of the sweeping character of "labour relations" as a single category and have said that it should in effect be treated as outside the distribution-of-powers system and broken down into several more particular parts. These parts are then each allotted, some one way and some the other, according to their particular relevance to some of the

---

[25]*Saumur v. City of Quebec and the A.G. for Quebec,* [1953] 2 S.C.R. 299, 333.
[26]*In the Reference re the Accurate News and Information Act of Alberta,* [1938] S.C.R. 100.

thirty-one specific federal categories and the fifteen specific provincial ones. But in breaking down one of these all-pervasive classes or subjects, we may find one or more of the resulting parts left over, so to speak. We may find that we have one or more of the several parts that do not have relevance to one of the thirty-one specific federal categories or the fifteen specific provincial categories. Now, with respect to these left-over parts, we are down to interpretative competition between the two residuary clauses. In these circumstances, the federal general power then embraces the left-over part or parts of inherent national significance or importance. The provincial residuary power in section 92(16) would likewise embrace any left-over part or parts of a merely local or private nature in the provinces.

Another example of one of these sweeping or all-pervasive categories is language—language requirements or options. Virtually all communication, thought and social organization depend on the use of language. In the case of *Jones v. Attorney General of Canada et al.* last year,[27] the full Supreme Court gave judgment on the constitutional validity of the federal Official Languages Act.[28] Chief Justice Laskin gave the unanimous judgment of the court upholding the validity of the statute as within the powers of the federal Parliament. I believe that the extent to which he used the federal general power to uphold the validity of the statute is in harmony with the general analysis I am offering here. He said:[29]

> Apart from the effect of s. 133 and s. 91(1), to be considered later in these reasons, I am in no doubt that it was open to the Parliament of Canada to enact the *Official Languages Act* (limited as it is to the purposes of the Parliament and Government of Canada and to the institutions of that Parliament and Government) as being a law "for the peace, order and good Government of Canada in relation to [a matter] not coming within the Classes of Subject . . . assigned exclusively to the Legislatures of the Provinces". The quoted words are in the opening paragraph of s. 91 of the *British North America Act, 1867*; and, in relying on them as constitutional support for the *Official Languages Act,* I do so on the basis of the purely residuary character of the legislative power thereby conferred. No authority need be cited for the exclusive power of the Parliament of Canada to legislate in relation to the operation and administration of the institutions and agencies of the Parliament and Government of Canada. Those institutions and agencies are clearly beyond provincial reach.

Chief Justice Laskin then goes on to point out that the federal general power likewise supports the validity of the provisions of the federal Official Languages Act concerning the use of the English or French languages in courts properly established by federal statute, and in all criminal courts and proceedings in Canada. He adds that these are *also* matters respectively within the power of the federal Parliament under section 101 of the British North America Act, concerning the establishment of courts for the better administration of the federal laws of Canada, and the federal criminal law and procedure power in section 91(27) of the British North America Act. Criminal law and procedure generally are not of

---

[27](1974), 45 D.L.R. (3d) 583 (S.C.C.).
[28]R.S.C., 1970, c. O-2.
[29]*Supra,* footnote 27, 588-589.

course in the list of provincial powers, and so here is one very important respect in which the federal general power is indeed illustrated and re-affirmed by one of the later enumerated powers in section 91. As I said earlier in this analysis of our power-distribution system, there is some overlapping of this kind in section 91 of the British North America Act. This does not impair my main thesis that the overlapping is far from complete in the whole area of property and civil rights, in the broad historical extent of that phrase in British North America from 1774 to 1867. In any event, as I read Chief Justice Laskin, he is not saying and did not intend to say that all mandatory languages requirements and options form a single subject for purposes of the power-distribution system, a subject that would be embraced by the federal general power. I believe he is saying in effect that the subject requires considerable sub-division into several parts, which is in accordance with my analysis in this article.

Pollution affords a further example of a sweeping category or theme that needs this piecemeal treatment for purposes of our power-distribution system. Recently the Supreme Court of Canada faced an example of this issue also, in the case of *Interprovincial Co-operatives Limited v. The Queen in Right of the Province of Manitoba*.[30] They gave judgment on March 26th of this year. The majority opinion was given by Mr. Justice Pigeon. The problem concerned interprovincial rivers flowing into Lake Winnipeg, and mercury pollution of the rivers originating at points on the rivers in Saskatchewan and Ontario that allegedly ruined the fisheries in Lake Winnipeg. Mr. Justice Pigeon held that certain Manitoba legislation on the subject was beyond provincial powers, and was exclusively within federal power by virtue of the federal general power in its residuary character. But he carefully confined what he said to the pollution of *interprovincial* rivers bringing residents of different provinces into legal conflict with one another as to their respective legal rights and duties. This was not property and civil rights *in the Province of Manitoba*. This is just one of many parts or aspects into which the general subject of pollution may be sub-divided. Note that Mr. Justice Pigeon did not say or suggest in any way that pollution was a single subject for purposes of power-distribution, embraced in all its aspects by the federal general power.

Returning now for a moment to the proposition that Professor Le Dain correctly isolated as having some currency in our constitutional jurisprudence—"the notion that there must be a single plenary power to deal effectively and completely with any problem"—I claim that this is a dangerous fallacy. To me, it is a dangerous oversimplification that could lead to constitutional chaos or to the end of federalism. I infer that Professor Le Dain does not like the proposition any more than I do, though he does not commit himself explicitly on the point. In any event, this danger deserves some further explanation.

The philosophy of classification systems is such that any doctrinaire group that wants to push its special cause to the limit can find a subject-label for that cause that is new, so far as the established lists in the British North America Act

---

[30](1975), 53 D.L.R. (3d) 321.

are concerned. Then the group proceeds to urge that the great importance of this new subject means that the federal Parliament can and should give them the legislation that they want under the federal general power. Special interest groups of all kinds can be expected to urge legislative salvation for themselves in this way, and, up to a point, this may be legitimate advocacy, but it is only advocacy and should be critically evaluated as such.

As Professor Cairns has remarked.[31] "A necessary consequence of a federal system is that each organized interest will seek to transform the most sympathetic level of government into the main decision-maker in matters which concern it." One should also add that the same dangerous misuse could be made of the provincial general power in section 92(16) of the British North America Act. Our society is full of a great variety of groups that in many respects have conflicting interests. These considerations emphasize why we must have the caution and restraint that I have tried to spell out as the full meaning of the Watson-Simon view of the federal general power. These same considerations emphasize why it is that the superior courts, as impartial and independent interpretative tribunals, must be the umpires of the federal system of division of legislative powers. To use a figure of speech from the gambling world, if you want federalism at all, this is the only game in town, like it or not.

Having said all that, I must now add that I do not deny the reality and importance of social problems grouped under headings such as pollution, economic growth, culture, quality of life, and the like. Of course these are important generalized concepts with social reality in our country. My point is rather that categories as all-pervasive as these ones are, cannot be allowed to dominate our distribution-of-powers system from within, so to speak. They must be treated as outside the system, which means they should each be subdivided into appropriate parts so that necessary legislative action can be taken by some combination of both federal and provincial statutes. Co-ordination of these legislative efforts should come through co-operative federalism—that is, by complementary federal and provincial statutes co-ordinated by virtue of custom, practice or intergovernmental agreements of some sort. This is a large subject in itself which I cannot develop further here.[32] Suffice it to say that *before* you can successfully practice co-operative federalism, you must have in place a fundamental distribution of legislative powers and resources between the central government and the provinces. The essence of co-operative federalism is federal-provincial agreement, whether tacit or explicit, about complementary uses of federal and provincial powers and resources. Hence unless the constitutional definitions of such powers and resources remain reasonably stable as the basis of the autonomy of the parties, subject only to the process of gradual adjustment I have already described, the respective bargaining positions of the two levels of government will be too uncertain for federal-provincial agreements to be reached.

---

[31]*Op. cit.,* footnote 1, 315.

[32]Cooperative Federalism: Constitutional Revision and Parliamentary Government in Canada (1971), 78 Queen's Q. 7; Some Forms and Limitations of Co-operative Federalism (1967), 45 Can. Bar Rev. 409.

Recently, the conception of the necessary operating jurisprudence of Canadian federalism that I have given at some length in this article has come under almost total attack by Professor Paul C. Weiler, a distinguished Canadian legal scholar with long experience in the field of labour relations and collective bargaining.[33] Much as I respect Professor Weiler, I must say that, on this subject, I thoroughly disagree with nearly all of what he has said.

Professor Weiler has said that the words and phrases by which our federal constitution distributes legislative powers were relevant to society and full of meaning when the constitution was first drawn up in 1867, but that, as society changed over the years in our country, these words and phrases became increasingly unreal and irrelevant to prevailing social conditions. Hence, he tells us that, 100 years later, the Supreme Court justices can really get no guidance from the original text of the British North America Act, no guidance from the concepts denoted by the original words and phrases. Thus he alleges that, in making interpretative decisions today, the Supreme Court is really making up a new constitution piecemeal as it goes along, and not doing it very well at that. Now I would agree that a final judicial interpretative tribunal has important degrees of discretion here, as in other parts of the law, but Professor Weiler goes much too far in what he has said.

I think Professor Weiler has got his history backwards. I consider the true history of the development of the British North America Act by judicial interpretation to be almost the complete reverse of what Professor Weiler says it is. As I said early in this article, the greatest uncertainty about the meaning of the power-conferring words and phrases of the constitution, in relation to one another, occurred at the beginning. As time went on and precedents accumulated, many years of judicial interpretation greatly reduced this uncertainty and made the distribution-of-powers system much more meaningful. In other words, after 100 years of judicial interpretation, the British North America Act has become much more meaningful than it was in 1867, and of course it was by no means devoid of meaning in 1867. We are talking of matters of degree and of the main trends, positive or negative, in the development of the meaning and utility of the constitution. Moreover, judicial interpretation over the years has shaped the original power-conferring words and phrases, in relation to one another, so that they have been capable of affording guide-lines for new problems of legislative power-distribution arising from social change. This parallels the function and operation of judicial precedent in other branches of the law, so there should be nothing surprising about it.

Now in saying this, I am definitely not saying that the British North America Act is complete and all-sufficient in the sense that it contains in its text detailed principles and concepts that automatically embody easy solutions for every problem in the division of legislative powers that may arise. If this were so, reading the Act would be all that was involved in constitutional interpretation. I know that this extremely simplistic view of interpretation and meaning is

---

[33]Law and Social Change, in Ziegel (ed.), Osgoode Hall Lecture Series (1973), Ch. 3, with critical comment by W. R. Lederman.

not valid. But Professor Weiler has gone to the opposite extreme. He says that the federal constitution has become virtually meaningless, so that the Supreme Court is really making up new constitutional rules as it goes along under the guise of interpreting the text of the British North America Act. This extreme is just as invalid as the other. It does not properly describe our true operating federal jurisprudence either. As usual, the truth lies at some middle position between these opposed extremes. I think Professor Weiler has gravely oversimplified the nature of constitutions and constitutional history.

Logically enough as a result of his views, however, Professor Weiler considers that we would be better off if the courts in general, and the Supreme Court of Canada in particular, were out of the business of judicial review of the federal constitution altogether. He would look instead to the model afforded by collective bargaining in labour relations for the operational jurisprudence of our federal system—he would put the main issues of the federal constitution into rather constant negotiation at federal-provincial conferences of our elected political leaders of government. For my part, I think these latter gentlemen already have quite enough to do operating *within* the guide-lines afforded by judicial review of the constituion.

In the latest version of his views, published last year, Professor Weiler does concede a marginal role for the courts.[34] If some unfortunate citizen is caught by actual conflict of federal and provincial statutes applicable to him, Professor Weiler would allow him to go to court. But, to me, this latest qualification simply makes Mr. Weiler's main position less credible than ever. Conflict or inconsistency is a complex and flexible idea. There are thousands of pages in the federal statute books, and tens of thousands of pages in the provincial statute books, to say nothing of subordinate legislation. A good counsel could nearly always find enough conflict or inconsistency of some kind to get into court, and you would be back to full-fledged judicial review.

In any event, I do not find the model afforded by labour relations jurisprudence in Canada to be satisfactory as a type of system for control of the operating fundamentals of our federal constitution. I repudiate the labour relations model as a substitute for sophisticated judicial review at the highest levels in these fundamental matters. It is to the latter that we must look for a satisfactory operating jurisprudence of Canadian federalism, and, while this is centred on the courts, it does not involve the courts alone. To quote Professor Cairns again:[35]

> A strong and effective court requires a variety of supporters. It must be part of a larger system which includes first class law schools, quality legal journals, and an able and sensitive legal fraternity—both teaching and practicing. These are the minimum necessary conditions for a sophisticated jurisprudence without which a distinguished judicial performance is impossible. Unless judges can be made aware of the complexities of their role as judicial policy-makers, and sensitively cognizant of the societal effects of their decisions, a first-rate judicial performance will only occur intermittently and fortuitously.

---

[34]In the Last Resort (1974), Ch. 6.
[35]*Op. cit.*, footnote 2, 331.

I say "Amen" to that, but again I feel both chastened and challenged. I have not yet said anything about my own views on this thing called policy-making, and to leave that out these days is to risk being characterized as a mere technician.

I do maintain that respectable beliefs in the realm of values lie behind the views I have expressed here. In the first place, a good federal division of legislative powers honours the values of pluralism—of the diversities in our society—as well as the need for a certain amount of unity. This assumes sophisticated and socially sensitive interpretation of the power-conferring words and phrases by impartial courts, especially the Supreme Court of Canada. The jurisprudential problem then is to achieve a balance between carefully defined unities and carefully defined diversities, the definitions collectively being comprehensive or potentially so. I have argued that it is a necessary part of our system to hold the definitions of federal and provincial categories of powers to a meaningful level of specific identity and particularity. The value of this is that, when we analyse our legislative needs, the issues requiring value decisions are rendered specific and brought into focus one by one in particular terms, so that ordinary mortals of limited wisdom and moral insight can cope with them. We are all ordinary mortals, so it is no use setting up a system that only God could operate. Moreover, I prefer federal systems to unitary ones because I believe in countervailing power among human institutions. I like to see our federal government having to compromise with provincial governments, and *vice versa*. I feel more secure as a citizen when the system requires this.

In the second place, it is necessary that impartial superior courts should act as umpires of the essential guide-lines for the respective federal and provincial responsibilities given by the federal constitution. Of course the value assumptions of the judges will enter into their decisions. We would complain if this were not so. They must weigh such matters as the relative values of nation-wide uniformity *versus* regional diversity, the relative merit of local *versus* central administration, and the justice of minority claims, when provincial or federal statutes are challenged for validity under the established division of powers. Inevitably, widely prevailing beliefs in the country about these issues will be influential and presumably the judges should strive to implement such beliefs. Inevitably there will be some tendency for them to identify their own convictions as those which generally prevail or which at least are the right ones. On some matters there will not be an ascertainable general belief anyway. In the making of these very difficult decisions of relative values, policy decisions if one prefers that word, all that can rightly be demanded of judges is straight thinking, industry, good faith, and a capacity to discount their own prejudices with due humility. No doubt it is also fair to ask that they be men or women of high professional attainment, and that they be somewhat representative in their thinking of the better standards of their times and their fellow citizens.

FURTHER DEVELOPMENTS AND REFERENCES

The essay reproduced in the previous part was delivered as a public lecture in June of 1975 and published in December of 1975. In October of 1975, the Federal Parliament passed the Anti-Inflation Act, the Government claiming that Parliament had power to enact sweeping economic controls for the country by virtue of the federal general power in section 91 of the B.N.A. Act. This was challenged and there was a prompt reference to the Supreme Court of Canada, which gave judgment on July 12, 1976: *Reference re Anti-Inflation Act.*[1]

Counsel for the Government of Canada argued for the validity of the Act on the basis of both branches of the federal general power; the emergency branch and the permanent national dimension branch. The court of nine upheld the validity of the Act on the emergency ground, seven to two. But also, four justices concurred with Mr. Justice Beetz that the Act could not be upheld as valid on the ground that it concerned something of "permanent national dimension." This was a majority of the court. The other four justices were not committed on the point.

On the "permanent national dimension" point, Mr. Justice Beetz referred favourably to the essay reproduced in the previous part of this chapter and adopted much of its reasoning. This is noted by Professor Peter Hogg in his recent treatise entitled *Constitutional Law of Canada.*[2]

---

[1](1976), 68 D.L.R. (3d) 452-536.
[2](Toronto: The Carswell Co. Ltd., 1977), 263-64.

Chapter 16

Continuing Constitutional Dilemmas: The Supreme Court and the Federal Anti-Inflation Act of 1975

Reprinted from (1977), 84 Queen's Quarterly 90

Toward the end of 1975, the Parliament of Canada passed the Anti-Inflation Act,[1] with effect from 14 October of that year. In securing passage of the Act, the Federal Government was responding to what it judged to be an urgent economic crisis in Canada, marked by unacceptably high levels of inflation and unemployment across the country. The long title of the statute is "An Act to provide for the restraint of profit margins, prices, dividends and compensation in Canada." The preamble stated that "the Parliament of Canada recognizes that inflation in Canada at current levels is contrary to the interests of all Canadians and that the containment and reduction of inflation has become a matter of serious national concern"; and further that "to accomplish such containment and reduction of inflation it is necessary to restrain profit margins, prices, dividends and compensation." The Act itself is long and elaborate in its restraining provisions, as are the guidelines made under it; but these details need not concern us here, as the main scope and purpose of the statute is clear enough, as just indicated.

In effect, the Act asserted that the Parliament of Canada had the legislative authority under the BNA Act to impose total controls in the form of ceilings on all profit margins, prices and forms of income for everyone in Canada, whether in private or public sectors of life. Though the Act and the guidelines it authorized did not literally reach everyone, they did cover enough critical groups and persons in all sectors of economic life that the measures could properly be described as an attempt at total economic control. This raised two controversial issues. First, could such measures succeed in containing and reducing inflation? Second, and in any event, did the Parliament of Canada possess the legislative power to enact such total measures, whatever their economic merit? The second issue is the one that concerns us here, though the purely economic data and opinion relevant to the first issue may have some constitutional significance.

For the constitutional issue, we start with the proposition that legislative

---

[1] *Statutes of Canada*, 1974-75, Chapter 75.

powers are divided between the federal parliament on the one hand and the respective provincial legislatures on the other. It is also true that, in this legislative division, all powers are distributed one way or the other. But, except for grave emergency situations, this totality of powers remains divided and the divisions must be respected. Among other matters, the total control of things economic is normally divided, so that among consitutional experts there was grave doubt whether the Parliament of Canada had power to go as far as it did go with the control measures of the Anti-Inflation Act. Thus it was to be expected that interests opposed to the Anti-Inflation Act would soon challenge its constitutional validity, alleging that it was null and void for trespass on exclusive areas of provincial power. When this did in fact occur, the Government of Canada acted quickly to refer the constitutional issues directly to the Supreme Court of Canada for decision, as prolonged uncertainty would not have been tolerable. The federal order in council referring the issues to the Supreme Court was dated 11 March 1976. The Court then authorized the Government of Canada, interested provincial governments, and certain labor and professional organizations to present documentary materials and oral arguments to the Court.

The hearing was held during the first week of June 1976, and the Court rendered judgment at a special session convened for the purpose on 12 July 1976.[2] (This must be something of a record for speed in such matters.) By a majority of seven to two, the Court upheld the validity of the Anti-Inflation Act as emergency or crisis legislation of temporary duration. In addition, five of the nine judges also held that there was no *permanent* basis of national dimension on which the Anti-Inflation Act could have been supported. On this latter point, the Chief Justice was uncommitted, as were three other judges who concurred with him. This latter group of four confined themselves to a positive finding under the emergency reasons only, which were sufficient on the evidence, as they assessed it, to dispose of the issues.

The authors of the written opinions were Chief Justice Laskin, Mr. Justice Ritchie and Mr. Justice Beetz, their reasons extending to almost eighty pages in the law reports. The remaining six judges concurred with one or other of those who wrote opinions, in varying combinations depending on the issues. By their majority reasons as indicated, the judges have moved definition and understanding of our federal constitution forward quite significantly respecting the nature of the federal emergency power and the nature of the federal residual power, the latter being based on a finding of sufficient permanent national dimension for some subjects of limited scope. Also, in the course of doing this, important precedents were set concuring the admission of extrinsic evidence, in this case economic facts and opinions, in aid of claims to valid exercise of federal emergency powers.

The *Anti-Inflation Reference Case* is almost certainly one of the most important constitutional decisions since Confederation in 1867. Nevertheless, we should not be too sanguine about what it has accomplished. Though it has indeed advanced definition and understanding, nevertheless continuing constitutional

---

[2]*Reference Re Anti-Inflation Act* (1976), 68 D.L.R. (3d) 452-536.

dilemmas remain that are always present in some form when it becomes necessary to apply a given federal division of original legislative powers to changing times and new circumstances in the country. While valuable improvements in definition and understanding of the power-conferring phrases in the constitition are accomplished from time to time, they are incremental in character and do not go to the extent that they make the future completely predictable. With this caution in mind, let us now look at the advances accomplished in this case. We shall do so under two main headings: problems of definition and problems of evidence.

The basic problems of definition of our divided legislative powers arise from the fact that the constitution confers federal and provincial powers by words usually having considerable generality of meaning. The competing phrases overlap one another in their significance, hence each must be read in context with all the others and there must accordingly be some mutual modification of meanings. In this process, authoritative and sophisticated judicial interpretation is necessary. In a previous essay some years ago, I described this interpretative process as follows:

> The federal distribution of legislative powers and responsibilities in Canada is one of the facts of life when we concern ourselves with the many important social, political, economic, or cultural problems of our country. Over the whole range of actual and potential law-making, our constitution distributes powers and responsibilities by two lists of categories or classes—one list for the federal parliament (primary section 91 of the B.N.A. Act), the other for each of the provincial legislatures (primarily section 92 of the B.N.A. Act). For instance, the federal list includes regulation of trade and commerce, criminal law, and *a general power to make laws in all matters not assigned to the provinces.* Examples from the provincial list are property and civil rights in the province, local works and undertakings, and *all matters of merely local or private nature in the province.*
>
> These federal and provincial categories of power are expressed, and indeed have to be expressed, in quite general terms. This permits considerable flexibility in constitutional interpretation, but also it brings much overlapping and potential conflict between the various definitions of powers and responsibilities. To put the same point in another way, our community life—social, economic, political and cultural—is very complex and will not fit neatly into any scheme of categories or classes without considerable overlap and ambiguity occurring. There are inevitable difficulties arising from this that we must live with so long as we have a federal constitution.
>
> Accordingly the courts must continually assess the competing federal and provincial lists of powers against one another in the judicial task of interpreting the constitution. In the course of judicial decisions on the B.N.A. Act, the judges have basically done one of two things. First, they have attempted to define mutually exclusive spheres for federal and provincial powers, with partial success. But, where mutual exclusion did not seem feasible or proper, the courts have implied the existence of concurrent federal and provincial powers in the overlapping area, with the result that either or both authorities have been permitted to legislate provided their statutes did not in some way conflict one with the other in the common area.[3]

---

[3]W. R. Lederman, ''The Concurrent Operation of Federal and Provincial Laws in Canada,'' *McGill Law Journal,* 9 (1962-63), 185.

Within this jurisprudential framework, what shape did the problems posed by the federal Anti-Inflation Act take? Recall that it was a statute that clearly and unequivocally set up a form of total economic control. The courts had previously sanctioned such total control only in wartime (World War I and World War II) under the federal general power described earlier. But there was no precedent for such a federal statute in peacetime on an emergency basis, or on any other basis for that matter. Now we do have a precedent to the effect that there may be peacetime economic emergencies that likewise would justify sweeping federal economic controls by means of federal statute, temporarily for the duration of the emergency. In the *Anti-Inflation Act Reference Case,* Chief Justice Laskin said:

> In my opinion, this Court would be unjustified in concluding, on the submissions in this case and on all the materials put before it, that the Parliament of Canada did not have a rational basis for regarding the *Anti-Inflation Act* as a measure which, in its judgment, was temporarily necessary to meet a situation of economic crisis imperilling the well-being of the people of Canada as a whole and requiring Parliament's stern intervention in the interests of the country as a whole.[4]

Speaking to the same effect, Justice Ritchie added: "The authority of Parliament in this regard is, in my opinion, limited to dealing with critical conditions and the necessity to which they give rise and must perforce be confined to legislation of a temporary character."[5]

In the absence of emergency, however, the usual divided economic powers of the constitution are in effect. Normally, the respective provincial legislatures have exclusive economic jurisdiction over most businesses and industries local to the province, local business transactions, the professions including teachers, and of course the remuneration of provincial and municipal public servants. The foregoing list is not exhaustive. In the presence of emergency, the provincial legislatures do not lose these powers, but their statutes in these matters cease to be exclusive and are subject to being overridden and thus rendered inoperative by inconsistent federal emergency legislation. At this point, Chief Justice Laskin rested his case, with the concurrence of Justices Judson, Spence and Dickson. They did not go on to consider the other argument put to the Court by the Government of Canada and the Government of Ontario in support of the Anti-Inflation Act. This was to the effect that the federal general power to make laws "for the Peace, Order and good Government of Canada" in all matters not assigned to the provinces[6] has a permanent residual operation in favor of federal legislative power, as well as the temporary emergency operation just discussed. The residual effect of the federal general power in favor of the Parliament of Canada depends in part on a finding of permanent national dimension or concern for the matter in hand, and the rules respecting this are also known as the "national dimension" or "national concern" doctrine.

Unlike the Chief Justice, Mr Justice Beetz did deal definitively with the doctrine of permanent national dimension. He found that the doctrine had strict

[4]*Reference Re Anti-Inflation Act* (1976), 68 D.L.R. (3d) 498.
[5]*Reference Re Anti-Inflation Act* (1976), 68 D.L.R. (3d) 507.
[6]*The British North America Act,* 1867, 30 & 31 Victoria (U.K.) Chapter 3, Section 91.

limitations and that it was not available as permanent support for sweeping economic measures such as those embodied in the federal Anti-Inflation Act of 1975. If allowed, this would in effect have been a major permanent amendment of the federal distribution of legislative powers. A review of the relevant judicial precedents illustrates the strict limitations. For example, on the positive side, aviation, radio, atomic energy, and the physical aspects and amenities of the national capital district have in effect been enfranchised as new, permanent and exclusive subjects of federal legislative power by the residual effect of the federal general power. Note that these are quite limited subjects in their potential scope. They are not all-pervasive themes like inflation or pollution or economic growth that would, as new federal subjects, amount to wholesale trespass on established provincial legislative fields. Mr Justice Beetz makes these points in the following words:

> In my view, the incorporation of companies for objects other than provincial, the regulation and control of aeronautics and of radio, the development, conservation and improvement of the National Capital Region are clear instances of distinct subject-matters which do not fall within any of the enumerated heads of s. 92 and which, by nature, are of national concern.
>
> I fail to see how the authorities which so decide lend support to the first submission. They had the effect of adding by judicial process new matters or new classes of matters to the federal list of powers. However, this was done only in cases where a new matter was not an aggregate but had a degree of unity that made it indivisible, an identity which made it distinct from provincial matters and a sufficient consistence to retain the bounds of form. The scale upon which these new matters enabled Parliament to touch on provincial matters had also to be taken into consideration before they were recognized as federal matters: if an enumerated federal power designated in broad terms such as the trade and commerce powers had to be construed so as not to embrace and smother provincial powers *(Parson's case)* and destroy the equilibrium of the Constitution, the Courts must be all the more careful not to add hitherto unnamed powers of a diffuse nature to the list of federal powers.
>
> The ''containment and reduction of inflation'' does not pass muster as a new subject matter. It is an aggregate of several subjects some of which form a substantial part of provincial jurisdiction. It is totally lacking in specificity. It is so pervasive that it knows no bounds. Its recognition as a federal head of power would render most provincial powers nugatory.
>
> I should add that inflation is a very ancient phenomenon, several thousand years old, as old probably as the history of currency. The Fathers of Confederation were quite aware of it.[7]

Notice that Justice Beetz says that aviation, radio and so on are subjects which by their nature are of national concern. New and limited subjects by their nature of purely local and provincial concern would be added to the *provincial* list of powers by operation of the *provincial* residual power in section 92(16) of the B.N.A. Act: ''Generally all matters of a merely local or private nature in the Province.'' The contrast between national and local nature is what separates the

---

[7]*Reference Re Anti-Inflation Act* (1976), 68 D.L.R. (3d) 524.

federal and provincial residual clauses. This accounts for the national dimension or national concern element in the definition of the federal residual power.

Furthermore, there are some important negative precedents supporting this part of the reasoning of Mr Justice Beetz. Permanent and all-pervasive measures of federal economic control were attempted in 1919, and were held to be beyond the powers of the Parliament of Canada in the *Board of Commerce Case* in 1922.[8] The same type of control was attempted again in the 1930s, in the last days of the Government of R. B. Bennett. His so-called "New Deal" statutes were all held to be beyond the powers of Parliament when they were referred to the courts.[9] The federal general power in its permanent aspect was argued unsuccessfully in all these cases.

In summary, to qualify for addition to the federal list of powers by virtue of the residual operation of the federal general power, a new subject must earn its way to a place on the federal list. This it may do if, as a matter of hard fact and evidence in our society as it has developed at the critical time, the subject is real, discrete and quite limited in scope, and is moreover of national dimension or significance as tested by the judgment that it makes good sense for the relevant and necessary legislation to be national legislation, rather than local legislation that may vary from province to province. Aviation, because of its implications as an interprovincial and international form of transportation, is an obvious example.

These requirements for new subjects that make it to the federal list are not easy to meet and should be strictly applied. As Mr Justice Beetz also pointed out, it is not permissible in this respect simply to play word games with alternative categories of classification. In the logical and linguistic sense, many alternative classifications for challenged statutes are always possible; alternative, that is, to the categories (power-conferring phrases) actually used in the B.N.A. Act. But the categories of the B.N.A. Act must be used, for it is the assured use of them that permits stability for governments and citizens, so that to a high degree governments know what powers and resources they possess and citizens know to which level of government to look on this or that subject.

To come back to the realm of economics, this means that, in the absence of emergency, powers remain divided; that neither the Parliament of Canada nor the respective provincial legislatures can deal with all prices or all incomes. For some businesses, industries and public servants, prices and incomes are exclusively subject to regulation by provincial statutes. For other businesses, industries and public servants, prices and incomes are exclusively subject to regulation by federal statutes. If any overall prices and incomes policy for the country is to be achieved across these lines of divided jurisdiction, cooperative federalism must be practiced. By virtue of federal-provincial intergovernmental agreements each level of government can pass laws for the groups for which it is responsible, laws that are harmonized in pursuit of the agreed objectives. In normal circumstances, this is the usual way to do things in a federal country. Indeed, in the ab-

---

[8][1922] 1 AC 191.
[9]For examples, see: *Reference Re The National Products Marketing Act,* [1936] SCR 398, [1937] AC 377; *Labour Conventions Case,* [1937] A.C. 655.

sence of emergency, such cooperative federalism is the only way to proceed. Sweeping new themes or aggregates, like "inflation" or "pollution," would bring the federal constitution to an end if they were allowed to dominate the division of legislative powers from within, so to speak, by virtue of the permanent operation of the federal general power. If this were allowed, the Parliament of Canada could be rendered all powerful by judicial interpretation, in which event Canada would cease to have a federal constitution.

Certainly, the current situation in Canada, in which the threat of secession by Quebec is a factor, calls for full respect for the established heads of provincial legislative power and responsibility. Such respect may be a factor in helping to maintain the unity of Canada as a federal state. The wisdom of the position taken on permanent national dimension by Mr Justice Beetz, with the concurrence of Justices Ritchie, Martland, Pigeon and de Grandpré, is thus apparent. It is perhaps noteworthy that in this group we have three judges from Quebec, one from Nova Scotia and one from Alberta.

There would also be danger to the integrity of the division of legislative powers (and therefore to national unity) if the Goverment and Parliament of Canada were allowed too easy a passage by the Court whenever they attempted to invoke the federal emergency power. Has this happened in the *Anti-Inflation Act Reference Case?* I do not think so, but, to assess the point properly we must now examine the rules of evidence of emergency that the court has sanctioned in the case.

Chief Justice Laskin in the *Anti-Inflation Case* has given us a distinguished analysis of the bearing of evidence on the determination of whether there is in fact an emergency in the constitutional sense. The question was whether there was a sufficiently urgent economic crisis to warrant some total type of economic control by federal statute. In matters of this kind, some relevant facts are so notorious that the judges are taken to know them without any formal submission of evidence by the parties. Such facts are said to be judicially noticed. For example, it is probable that evidence needed to establish a war emergency would be satisfied by facts entitled to judicial notice. But frequently more is needed. In the following passage from his judgment, the Chief Justice lists the documentary evidence authorized by the Court for the *Anti-Inflation Act Reference*.

The Attorney-General of Canada, having the carriage of the Reference, included in the case (1) the Order of Reference and the annexes thereto; (2) the federal Government's White Paper, entitled "Attack on Inflation," being the policy statement of the Minister of Finance tabled in the House of Commons on 14 October 1975, as a prelude to the introduction of the Bill, which became the *Anti-Inflation Act,* and to the Guidelines promulgated thereunder; and (3) the monthly bulletin of Statistics Canada for October 1975, containing, *inter alia,* various consumer price indices showing the index positions for certain periods up to and including September 1975. Leave was given in the order for directions of 6 April 1976, to other interested parties to file additional materials, and the Canadian Labour Congress included as an appendix to its factum an untitled study by Professor Richard G. Lipsey, now a professor of economics at Queen's University, Kingston, Ontario, in which he dealt with (1) the harm caused by inflation. (2) Canadian inflationary experience, (3) the State of the Canadian economy in 1975, and (4) various policy options in dealing with inflation, among them a prices and incomes policy. Telegrams from a large number of economists supporting the analysis made by Professor Lipsey were also submitted by the Canadian Labour Congress. The Attorney-General of Canada, following the filing of Professor Lipsey's study and as permitted by the order for directions, filed in answer a transcript of a speech delivered on 22 September 1975, by the Governor of the Bank of Canada, Mr Gerald Bouey. The Attorney-General of Ontario filed, after the permitted period for submitting answering material, a comment, prepared by the Ontario Office of Economic Policy, on the 1975 Economic Environment and the Anti-Inflation Program, designed to show the need for national action; and it also submitted a critique of Professor Lipsey's study, directed to the emphases of that study and to its interpretation of the historical context in which the federal anti-inflation program was instituted.[10]

The quotation makes it clear that there were conflicting economic factual materials and opinions before the Court. How does one get a decision out of this? If we examine carefully what the judges have said had to be proven, we will see that they also address the issues of who has the burden of proof, and how heavy that burden is for him who has it. Lord Wright, in the *Japanese Canadians' Case*[11] at the end of World War II said that those opposing the governmental judgment that there was an emergency had to provide very clear evidence that no emergency had arisen, or that emergency conditions that had once existed had come to an end. Chief Justice Laskin seems to have approved and restated this test. He has said that those alleging the governmental judgment of emergency to be wrong had to provide evidence showing that there was no rational basis for such a judgment. Plainly then, a very heavy evidentiary burden is placed on those who oppose the Government of Canada when it invokes emergency powers and secures from Parliament what it deems to be appropriate emergency legislation. Is the burden too heavy? My own view is this. If the Chief Justice means that the governmental decision for emergency must prevail unless it can be shown by evidence to be absurd—to have no rational basis in this sense—then the burden of proof on those who oppose the government's view would be well-nigh impossible to meet. The Government of Canada would then have too easy a passage for trespass on established areas of provincial legislative competence and responsibility. On the other hand if the Chief Justice's test of "no rational basis" is really a "reasonable man" test, that would be different. If the Chief Justice means that the opponents of the government view succeed if they can show by evidence that no reasonable man would conclude that emergency conditions existed, then the test strikes me as a proper one. The Government of Canada should have a presumption going for it on this point, but not one that is virtually irrebuttable. I believe that the second version of the presumption—the reasonable man test—is the view the Chief Justice takes. In support of this we should note that he is very careful to assert the reality of the final powers of judicial review by the Court concerning the factual basis of emergency.[12]

---

[10]*Reference Re Anti-Inflation Act* (1976), 68 D.L.R. (3d) 466-67.
[11][1947] A.C. 87.
[12]*Reference Re Anti-Inflation Act* (1976), 68 D.L.R. (3d) 499.

Thus we have seen that this landmark case has given us important advances in definition and understanding of critical constitutional issues. Nevertheless we have also seen that there are continuing dilemmas always present in the processes of decision. In any event the composite result of the *Anti-Inflation Act Reference Case* is a good one—no wide-ranging new powers for the Federal Parliament by judicial interpretation, except temporarily to meet outright emergencies. This strikes a good balance, and is a result to which all nine judges contributed, especially Chief Justice Laskin and Mr Justice Beetz. This vindicates the new Supreme Court practice of having the full bench sit to decide nearly all of the cases that come before the Court.

Chapter 17

Some Forms and Limitations of Co-Operative Federalism

Reprinted with permission From (1967), 45 Canadian Bar Review 409

In the world of today, any federal system needs in considerable measure to be a co-operative federalism. In Canada, for example, we have seen increasing necessity for agreements or understandings between the federal government and provincial governments concerning specified uses of their respective powers and resources on many matters. These agreements or understandings take many forms, operate in many ways and occur at every official level—specifically at the legislative, ministerial or civil service levels, or some combination of them. Such co-operation has been and is going on to a surprising degree.

But the success of these co-operative measures is not just a matter of a sufficient upsurge of good will in Ottawa and the provincial capitals. At times the life or death of particular ministries may be at stake, and in any event hard bargaining is frequently to be expected. Such bargaining necessarily takes place against the background of basic definition provided by the federal constitution. There must be initial definition of the powers and resources of each government in the federation before there can be bargains or agreements among them about what each government is to do or refrain from doing with its respective powers and resources. Co-operation and mutual good will we certainly need, but no amount of them will do away with the absolute necessity for a primary authoritative distribution of powers and resources in our federal constitutional document. At present this is the British North America Act, and, unless and until it is amended or replaced, its present scheme sets the basic framework within which co-operative measures between governments in Canada must be undertaken. So the text of the federal constitution is of continuing importance, but of course this point should not be pressed to extremes. Changing the wording of the constitution in this or that respect, for example, or even rewriting it wholesale, would not be a cure-all for everything that may be wrong in Canada. On the other hand, the opposite extreme should also be avoided—this is the idea that the text of the federal constitution, whatever it may be, really means little or nothing in the ongoing life and government of the country. Here the concept seems to be that the constitutional text is just a façade which can be made to give a legitimate front to any arrangements whatever arrived at among those in power for the moment in the political life of Canada and the Provinces.

As usual, the truth does not lie at either of these extremes. Much change and adjustment can be brought about by official agreement and practice, and it is essential to flexibility and efficiency of federal processes of government in the modern state that this should be so. Nevertheless, the text of the federal constitution as authoritatively interpreted in the courts remains very important.[1] It tells us who can act in any event. In other words, constitutionally it must always be possible in a federal country to ask and answer the question—What happens if the federal and provincial governments do not agree about a particular measure of co-operative action? Then which government and legislative body has power to do what? And even though federal-provincial agreement on some matter may come at the end of difficult negotiations, the question and answer just referred to will have influenced the result because the answer is a primary element in defining the bargaining power of the federal government on the one hand and the provincial governments on the other. Professor Peter H. Russell has made these points very well in the following passage from the introduction to his *Leading Constitutional Decisions*.[2]

> Politicians and administrators have certainly been more conspicuous than judges in the post-war evolution of Canadian federalism. This so-called "co-operative federalism" of the post-war period has been much less a litigious struggle between Ottawa and the provinces to defend and expand their own enclaves of power than a matter of political compromise and administrative pragmatism. While granting all this, we must still guard against dismissing too categorically the importance of the constitutional text and its application by the courts. In any of the issues that arise in federal-provincial relations, those who are responsible for working out the policies and strategies of the governments involved, no matter how pragmatic and flexible they may appear to be in dealing with the division of powers, must always operate on the basis of some assessment of the constitutional power which could be found to sustain the positions they wish to assume. In making these calculations, they will be guided by their awareness of previous constitutional cases and their anticipation of how alternative legislative and administrative schemes would fare if challenged in the courts. The number of major issues that are settled in court should not be regarded as the sole measure of the significance of judicial review. Just as important, but far more difficult to measure, is the extent to which judicial decisions, past, present, and future, enter into the considerations of the principal agents in the decision-making process.

Personally, I would emphasize the importance of authoritative judicial interpretation somewhat more than Professor Russell does, but essentially we seem to be in agreement.

One example of the relation of basic constitutional definition to bargaining power can be seen in the history of federal-provincial taxation agreements. There have been several federal-provincial conferences to settle these agreements from time to time, but on each occasion the federal government seems to have made

---

Concerning the importance of judicial interpretation, see W. R. Lederman, The Balanced Interpretation of the Federal Distribution of Legislative Powers in Cnaada (The Integrity of the Process of Interpretation) in Crépeau and MacPherson (eds), The Future of Canadian Federalism (1965), 91-112.

[2]The Carleton Library, No. 23 (Toronto, 1965), xxvi and xxvii.

the essential decisions and proposals, thus setting what the terms of the agreement were to be if there was to be agreement at all. The Provinces, particularly the economically weaker ones, have in the main found themselves in a "take-it-or-leave-it" position respecting the federal proposals. (I make no judgment at this point whether this is a good or bad thing; I am merely saying it has in fact been the pattern.) The question arises then—Why has the federal government been able to make its views prevail in these situations? No doubt many factors are at work, but the most important one is simily that, under the federal constitution, the federal taxing power is a much more potent instrument than is the taxing power of a Province. The latter must be direct and is confined territorially to a subject in the Province. The federal taxing power is not limited as to type and takes for its territorial base the whole of Canada, thus matching in jurisdiction the national or inter-provincial operations of many tax payers, particularly corporate ones. Thus, at least in the fields of personal and corporate income, the federal government is able to operate a taxation system that is both more effective and more fair than are the taxation systems of the respective Provinces operating independently. The federal and provincial taxpayers are the same persons or corporations, and they are very sensitive to considerations of effectiveness and fairness and also to the inconvenience and expense of multiple income tax returns.

A contrasting example with the same lesson is provided by the story of the Canada and Quebec pension plans. In 1951, for the first time and so far for the only time in Canadian constitutional jurisprudence, a principle of provincial paramountcy in a concurrent field was expressed when the British North America Act was amended to allow the federal Parliament to make laws relating to old age pensions. Section 94A (as later added to in a respect not relevant here) reads as follows:[3]

> The Parliament of Canada may make laws in relation to old age pensions and supplementary benefits, including survivors' and disability benefits irrespective of age, *but no such law shall affect the operation of any law present or future of a provincial legislature in relation to any such matter*.

The original Canada Pension Plan as proposed by the federal government differed in basic ways from the Quebec Pension Plan as proposed by the Quebec government. It will be recalled for instance that the latter was a fully-funded plan providing large sums for investment while the former was not. The Lesage government was able to insist on the scheme of the Quebec Pension Plan for Quebec to the exclusion of the Canada Pension Plan primarily because of the principle of provincial paramountcy in this respect, in section 94A of the British North America Act. Constitutionally this gave them the last word in any event for Quebec. Accordingly, to achieve the necessary degree of uniformity across the country, the federal government and the governments of the other Provinces accepted a revised Canada Pension Plan that was in harmony with the Quebec Pension Plan. I do not like section 94A, but I have no doubt about what it means or

---

[3]British North America Act, 1951, 14-15 Geo. VI, c. 32 (U.K.) as added to by British North America Act, 1964, 12-13 Eliz. II, c. 73 (U.K.).

what its influence has been. Anyway, this illustrates the delicacy and importance of paramountcy issues in our constitutional law, a subject to be analysed in more detail at a later point in this essay.

The text of our constitution then does set the basic terms that provide definition and context for the various forms of inter-governmental co-operation that have developed in the field of Canadian federal-provincial relations. But before going on to more detail concerning this, a few words may be useful about the nature of constitutions in general and of federal constitutions in particular. Woodrow Wilson said that "The State is a people organized for law within a definite territory." There are many types of such organization, but in any case one finds the primary organizational ideas of a particular modern state in its fundamental constitutional law. Here are the doctrines, principles and procedures that are the first things of community organization for the making and applying of laws. If one asks—Where is it that sovereignty or supremacy rests in the modern state?—the answer is that these primary doctrines, principles and procedures of the constitution *are themselves supreme*. It is fundamental to "The Rule of Law" that in the end such enduring ideas are supreme, and not particular official persons in office at particular times. All official persons are under the law; none are above it. It is these basic constitutional ideas that attract the long-run loyalty of citizens of the State. Now it is true that ideas must live in the minds of people, but the basic ideas of the constitution endure through generations because they are the focus of acceptance and loyalty over long periods of time. In this real sense they have objectivity and are not just subjective to particular persons at a particular time. The point has been made with great clarity by the Swedish jurist Olivecrona.[4]

> The machinery of the state is run by an ever changing multitude of persons, acting as monarchs, presidents, heads and members of the government, members of parliament, and so on. In general not one of these persons has even the faintest idea that the law should consist of his commands. Everyone of them finds in existence the rules which are called the law and are on the whole enforced. He can only bring about a change in some part of the law. The bulk of it existed before him and will continue to govern the life of the country when he is gone.
>
> Further it is to be noted that the law givers in general attain their positions and exercise their power by means of the rules of law. The monarch owes his place to the rules of the constitution concerning the succession to the throne, the head of the government has been appointed by the monarch, the members of parliament have been legally elected, and so on. It makes no sense to pretend that the rules which carry these people to their position are their own commands.

We may now ask—What is the characteristic first principle of a federal constitution? It is an original distribution by subjects of primary legislative powers between provincial or state governments on the one hand and a central government on the other. It means the territorial sub-division of the country to give a number of states or provinces, and also an original distribution by subjects of legislative powers between the central government in respect of the whole na-

---

[4]Law as Fact (1939), 32-33.

tional territory on the one hand and the several sub-regional governments for their respective fractions of the national territory on the other hand. This division of law-making powers by territorial sub-divisions and subjects means that the respective state governments and the central government develop in certain respects a peculiar involvement with the dependence on one another. In Canadian terms this leads to certain measures of inter-governmental co-operation in the field of federal-provincial relations. It is vital to realize that the conditions underlying these measures are in the main peculiar to a full-fledged federal system, so that we do not have here just another species of international relations.

To speak in more detail, the point is this. Independent countries like France and Britain can meet their needs for co-operation by international treaties or less formal agreements between their governments. But France and Britain are mutually exclusive as to territory and bodies of citizens, and each government for its own population and territory has the full range of legislative powers. This is not so between the federal government and the provincial governments of Canada. In the Canadian federation, Province by Province, the federal government and the respective provincial governments are responsible for the same territories and the same populations. The only separation is in the realm of ideas, the division of law-making powers by subjects between the federal government on the one hand and the provincial governments on the other. *Note that these conditions all differ from those obtaining between governments of independent countries in international relations.* The federal and provincial governments have joint responsibility for the same territories and populations, but each is limited to its own list of subjects of power for the purpose. Ideally the federal and provincial lists of powers should be crystal clear and mutually exclusive. But, as we shall see later, such perfection is not attainable in power-distribution systems and the exigencies of imperfection are the roots of many of the problems of federal-provincial relations.[5] In any event, it should be quite clear that federal governmental institutions in Canada are *not* just a sort of Canadian United Nations Organization (or United Provinces Organization) created by the Provinces and dependant for continued existence on the collective sufferance of the Provinces. Where federal subjects of power are concerned, provincial sub-division boundaries simply disappear and the federal government operates as a matter of original constitutional right in the whole of Canadian territory. Likewise the provincial governments operate concerning provincial subjects of power as a matter of original constitutional right in their respective sub-divisions of the national territory. In total operation this provides a system of government for the whole of the Canadian people and territory on all legislative subjects, a system that is vastly superior to anything possible by agreement between independent countries under the present régime of international law. Specifically, under the Canadian federal constitution, where intergovernmental co-operative measures are desirable in federal-provincial relations, both federal and provincial ministers and legislators are under the salutary political pressures of the need to respond to the wishes of the

---

[5] *Op. cit.*, footnote 1.

same electoral bodies of citizens in the same territory. Moreover, if an agreed solution for some problem situation in federal-provincial relations is not forthcoming, our federal constitution makes provision in several ways for a national solution by federal legislation in any event, if the need is sufficiently urgent.[6] Accordingly, a federal constitution like ours compared to the régime of international law provides much more effective pressure for governments to reach agreement in the first place, and in addition often provides an alternative of overall (national) legislative action in the absence of agreement, an alternative the like of which is altogether missing between governments of independent countries under the régime of international law. The proposal that the Province of Quebec should become an "Associate State" of the rest of Canada is nothing more nor less than a proposal to destroy the Canadian federal constitution in favour of the greatly inferior sort of thing that is possible in the way of intergovernmental arrangements between independent States under international law. There is no essential constitutional difference between the proposal for an Associate State and complete separation.

I have faith these things will not happen and that we can work out justice for all our people, including the French-Canadians, while preserving the essentials of a federal constitution. We simply cannot afford in the modern world, to revert to lower from higher forms of government. Indeed, so far as Canada is concerned, I would go further. Only by preserving the essentials of a federal constitution in Canada can we work out justice for all our people.

Earlier I said that the main separation between the federal government on the one hand and the provincial government on the other was in the realm of ideas—the division or distribution of law-making powers by subjects. If the federal and provincial lists of powers could be effectively clear, complete and mutually exclusive in all circumstances, each would tend to his own business and the need for federal-provincial co-operative measures would be at a minimum. But this is just not the situation in real life. Inevitably the lists of categories have conflicting and overlapping features, the reasons for which were well explained in 1940 in the *Rowell-Sirois Report*.[7]

> No amount of care in phrasing the division of powers in a federal scheme will prevent difficulty when the division comes to be applied to the variety and complexity of social relationships. The different aspects of life in a society are not insulated from one another in such a way as to make possible a mechanical application of the division of powers. There is nothing in human affairs which corresponds to the neat logical divisions found in the constitution. Therefore, attempts to exercise the powers allotted by the constitution frequently raise questions as to its meaning in relation to particular circumstances.

In more technical language, the point can be put this way. Nearly all laws or legislative schemes have a multiplicity of features, characteristics or aspects by

---

[6]For example, the federal general power in the opening words of section 91 of the British North America Act, and the doctrine of Dominion paramountcy in the event of conflict between federal and provincial statutes in a concurrent field.

[7]Report of The Royal Commission on Dominion-Provincial Relations (1940), Book I, p. 31.

which they may be classified in a number of different ways, and hence potentialities of cross-classification between the various categories of the federal and provincial lists are ever present. The more complex the statute, the greater the number of logical possibilities in this regard. So, in the case of a particular law challenged for validity, one aspect of it will point to a federal category of power with logical plausibility, but with equal logical plausibility another aspect points to a provincial category of power. Or, one can say the same thing another way. The respective federal and provincial classes of laws often overlap one another as general concepts in many important respects, and thus compete, so to speak, through his partial coincidence of categories to control the statutes to be classified. The courts have had to face these problems because of their final responsibility to interpret the federal distribution of powers, and have developed the all-pervasive aspect theory of interpretation to meet the situation. "Subjects which in one aspect and for one purpose fall within section 92, may in another aspect and for another purpose fall within section 91."[8]

In the course of judicial decisions on the British North America Act, the judges have basically done one of two things. First they have attempted to define mutually exclusive spheres for federal and provincial powers, and they have had considerable though partial success in doing this. But, where mutual exclusion did not seem feasible or proper, the courts have implied concurrency of federal and provincial power in the overlapping area, with the result that either or both authorities have been permitted to legislate, provided in the latter event that their statutes did not in some way conflict one with the other in the common area. In the event of conflict, the judicial doctrine of dominion paramountcy is to the effect that federal legislation prevails and provincial legislation is suspended or inoperative.[9] The interpretative course followed then might be summed up as follows—mutual exclusion if feasible but concurrency where necessary.

An example of the mutually exclusive result is offered by the *Inter-Provincial Bus Lines* case of 1954.[10] Here the Judicial Committee of the Privy Council held that the power to regulate inter-provincial or international motor vehicle enterprises carrying goods or persons across boundaries was exclusively federal, whereas the power to regulate such enterprises when they operated only within the boundaries of a single Province was exclusively provincial. The former were connecting undertakings (a federal responsibility), the latter were local undertakings (a provincial responsibility).

By contrast, the Unconscionable Transactions Relief Act of the Province of Ontario was upheld as valid by a judicial finding of concurrency in the field of interest charges.[11] This statute provides that, if in all the circumstances the cost of a loan is excessive and the transaction harsh and unconscionable, the court may order the contract reformed so as to make its terms fair and reasonable.

---

[8]*Hodge v. The Queen* (1883-84), 9 A.C. 117, 130.

[9]For a detailed analysis of what is involved in concurrency, conflict and paramountcy, see W. R. Lederman. The Concurrent Operation of Federal and Provincial Laws in Canada (1962-63), 9 McGill L.J. 185.

[10]*A.G. for Ontario v. Winner*, [1954] A.C. 541.

[11]R.S.O., 1960, c. 410, and *A.G. for Ontario v. Barfried Enterprises Ltd.*, [1963] S.C.R. 570.

Clearly this statute concerns the whole range of undue influence in contract (with excessive interest just one of several possible "undue" elements) and so logically falls within the provincial category of "Property and Civil Rights" under the British North America Act.[12] Also, it is equally obvious that insofar as it deals with interest charges it falls within the federal category of "Interest" under the British North America Act.[13] Thus the state in question has both its federal and its provincial aspects, and its validity depends, under the present system of interpretation, on determining whether one of these aspects is primary, or whether the two aspects are equivalent in their relative importance in accordance with the social and economic responsibilities of both levels of government. If the federal aspect of interest is primary, then only the federal Parliament can enact a law dealing with interest in this way, and the provincial statute falls because it deals with interest as well as other things. On the other hand, if the provincial aspect of interest, as part of the whole picture of undue influence in contract, is of equivalent importance to the federal concern with interest, then the provincial statute stands in its entirety, unless there is actually inconsistent federal legislation on interest—and the Supreme Court of Canada found this not to be so in the Ontario case. In other words, the Province is responsible for general undue influence laws in contract, and no such law is complete unless it includes remedies concerning undue interest rates as well as other facets of undue influence. Hence the judicial finding that, *in this context,* there is a provincial power to deal with interest concurrent with the federal power. Incidentially the decision on the Ontario Unconscionable Transactions Relief Act has very important implications— it has opened the way for the Provinces to enact comprehensive schemes for the protection of consumers generally, which some of them are now doing.

In any event, the point for present purposes is that the conditions governing federal-provincial co-operation differ to some extent, depending on whether one is talking of co-operation concerning mutually exclusive fields of power or concurrent fields of power. In either case, of course, there may simply be federal-provincial agreement that each will exercise its own powers for itself, but in a particular way that complements and does not frustrate the operation of legislation of the other. So far as form is concerned, this is no doubt the simplest type of federal-provincial co-operation in a concurrent field, but more of this later. In relation to exclusive fields of power, there is a further consideration, that of the delegation of legislative powers between the federal government on the one hand and provincial governments on the other.

The inter-governmental delegation that concerns the Canadian federal system has taken two forms which, for lack of better terms, might be designated as legislative and administrative. The legislative type involves the federal Parliament attempting to delegate directly to a provincial legislature power to make laws respecting some portion of an exclusive federal category of power, or vice versa. The administrative type of inter-governmental delegation involves the federal Parliament attempting to invest provincial officials with power and responsi-

---

[12] 1867, 30-31 Vict., c. 3 (U.K.).
[13] *Ibid.*

bility to apply federal laws, and this may at times include wide regulation-making powers for the provincial officials in part of an exclusive federal legislative field. As in the case of direct legislative delegation, administrative delegation may also be attempted between a provincial legislature and federal officials. The Supreme Court of Canada has ruled that legislative delegation is invalid and that administrative delegation is valid. This difference in result has its difficulties because, when wide regulation-making power is given, for example, by the federal Parliament to a provincial board or commission, it is difficult to see much distinction between legislative and administrative delegation. Nevertheless, it will be argued here that the distinction is a valuable one though it does have its gray areas.

First, as to legislative delegation, the leading authority is the *Nova Scotia Inter-delegation* case[14] in the Supreme Court of Canada in 1950. In this case the proposed Delegation of Legislative Jurisdiction Act of the Province of Nova Scotia had been referred as Bill 136 to the Supreme Court of Nova Scotia, which held it to be *ultra vires* of the Province. Appeal was taken to the Supreme Court of Canada which unanimously affirmed the decision of the Supreme Court of Nova Scotia *en banc*. Chief Justice Rinfret described the terms of Bill 136 as follows:[15]

> By virtue of this Bill, if it should come into force, by proclamation, as therein provided, the Lieutenant-Governor in Council, may from time to time delegate to and withdraw from the Parliament of Canada authority to make laws in relation to any matter relating to employment in any industry, work or undertaking in respect of which such matter is, by s. 92 of the *B.N.A. Act* exclusively within the jurisdiction of the Legislature of Nova Scotia. It provided that any laws so made by the Parliament of Canada shall, while such delegation is in force, have the same effect as if enacted by the Legislature.
>
> The Bill also provides that if and when the Parliament of Canada shall have delegated to the Legislature of the Province of Nova Scotia authority to make laws in relation to any matter relating to employment in any industry, work or undertaking in respect of which such matter is, under the provisions of the *B.N.A. Act,* exclusively within the legislative jurisdiction of such Parliament, the Lieutenant-Governor in Council, while such delegation is in force, may, by proclamation, from time to time apply any or all of the provisions of any Act in relation to a matter relating to employment in force in the Province of Nova Scotia to any such industry, work, or undertaking.
>
> Finally, the Bill enacts that if and when the Parliament of Canada shall have delegated to the Legislature of the Province of Nova Scotia authority to make laws in relation to the raising of a revenue for provincial purposes by the imposing of a retail sales tax of the nature of indirect taxation, the Lieutenant-Governor in Council, while such delegation is in force, may impose such a tax of such amount not exceeding 3% of the retail price as he deems necessary, in respect of any commodity to which such delegation extends and may make Regulations providing for the method of collecting any such tax.

---

[14]*A.G. of Nova Scotia v. A.G. of Canada,* [1950] 4 D.L.R. 369.
[15]*Ibid.,* 370-371.

This certainly raised the essential issues squarely, and the reasons of the judges for their negative decision are best given in their own words.

Chief Justice Rinfret:[16]

The constitution of Canada does not belong either to Parliament, or to the Legislatures; it belongs to the country and it is there that the citizens of the country will find the protection of the rights to which they are entitled. It is part of that protection that Parliament can legislate only on the subject-matters referred to it by s. 91 and that each Province can legislate exclusively on the subject-matters referred to it by s. 92. The country is entitled to insist that legislation adopted under s. 91 should be passed exclusively by the Parliament of Canada in the same way as the people of each Province are entitled to insist that legislation concerning the matters enumerated in s. 92 should come exclusively from their respective Legislatures. In each case the Members elected to Parliament or to the Legislatures are the only ones entrusted with the power and the duty to legislate concerning the subjects exclusively distributed by the constitutional Act to each of them.

Mr. Justice Taschereau:[17]

If the proposed legislation were held to be valid, the whole scheme of the Canadian Constitution would be entirely defeated. The framers of the *B.N.A. Act* thought wisely that Canada should not be a unitary state, but it would be converted into one, as Mr. Justice Hall says, if all the Provinces empowered Parliament to make the laws with respect to *all matters* exclusively assigned to them. Moreover, it is clear that the delegation of legislative powers by Parliament to the ten Provinces on matters enumerated in s. 91 of the *B.N.A. Act* could bring about different criminal laws, different banking and bankruptcy laws, different military laws, different postal laws, different currency laws, all subjects in relation to which it has been thought imperative that uniformity should prevail throughout Canada.

Mr. Justice Rand made the same points in a somewhat different way. The relationship of delegation involves subordination of the delegate to the delegating body, and so is simply not an appropriate relationship between the federal Parliament on the one hand and the provincial legislatures on the other. They are primary and coordinate legislative bodies under the constitution:[18]

Subordination implies duty: delegation is not made to be accepted or acted upon at the will of the delegate; it is ancillary to legislation which the appropriate Legislature thinks desirable; and a duty to act either by enacting or by exercising a conferred discretion not, at the particular time, to act, rests upon the delegate. No such duty could be imposed upon or accepted by a co-ordinate Legislature and the proposed Bill does no more than to proffer authority to be exercised by the delegate solely of its own volition and, for its own purposes, as a discretionary privilege. Even in the case of virtually unlimited delegation as under the Poor Act of England, assuming that degree to be open to Canadian Legislatures, the delegate is directly amenable to his principal for his execution of the authority.

---

[16]*Ibid.*, 371-372.
[17]*Ibid.*, 382.
[18]*Ibid.*, 386.

In other words, handing over a plenary and primary legislative discretion in this manner, even on a bilateral basis subject to revocation, is not really delegation at all, it is amendment of the federal constitution, however partial or temporary such amendment may be. And in any event, as Mr. Justice Rand further pointed out, the practical possibilities of revocation by the "delegating" body are severely limited:[19]

> The practical consequences of the proposed measure, a matter which the Courts may take into account, entail the danger, through continued exercise of delegated power, of prescriptive claims based on conditions and relations established in reliance on the delegation. Possession here as elsewhere would be nine points of law and disruptive controversy might easily result. The power of revocation might in fact become no more feasible, practically, then amendment of the Act of 1867 of its own volition by the British Parliament.

So much for legislative delegation—it is a necessary implication of our federal constitution that primary legislative powers cannot be traded or transferred, even with consent on both sides, between the federal Parliament and a Provincial legislature.[20]

In spite of this strong stand against inter-governmental delegation at the primary legislative level, the Supreme Court of Canada soon made it clear, in the *Prince Edward Island Potato Board* case of 1952,[21] that delegation to officials of the other government at the subordinate levels of the administration of laws and regulation-making was a different matter and was valid. The Legislature of Prince Edward Island had by statute provided for a Potato Marketing Board of provincially appointed persons empowered to make rules for the marketing within Price Edward Island of potatoes produced there, the board itself to be the sole marketing authority. This was valid legislation, being concerned with the intra-provincial marketing of local produce. Meanwhile, the *Federal Agricultural Products Marketing Act* of 1949,[22] dealing with the federal subject of inter-provincial and export marketing of agricultural products, provided as follows:

> 2(1) The Governor in Council may by order grant authority to any board or agency authorized under the law of any province to exercise powers of regulation in relation to the marketing of any agricultural product locally within the province, to regulate the marketing of such agricultural product outside the province in interprovincial and export trade and for such purposes to exercise all or any powers like the powers exercisable by such board or agency in relation to the marketing of such agricultural product locally within the province.
>
> (2) The Governor in Council may by order revoke any authority granted under subsection one.

---

[19]*Ibid.*, 387.

[20]This is subject to the exception to be found in section 94 of the British North America Act in favour of the federal Parliament at the expense of the legislatures of the common law provinces. Section 94 allows no revocation once the step has been taken of passing provincial powers to the federal Parliament—perhaps this is one reason why it has never been used. In any event, its presence in the British North America Act implies that there is to be *no other way* of transferring primary legislative powers by bilateral consent under the British North America Act. The Supreme Court of Canada in the *Nova Scotia* case noted and approved this implication.

[21]*P.E.I. Potato Marketing Board v. H. B. Willis Inc. and A.G. of Canada*, [1952] 4 D.L.R. 146.

[22]S.C. 1949, c. 16.

The Governor in Council made an order delegating this power respecting Prince Edward Island Potatoes to the provincial Board and the Supreme Court of Canada held the delegation to be valid and operative. As Mr. Justice Taschereau put it:[23]

> The Supreme Court of Prince Edward Island relied upon *A.-G. N.S. v. A.-G. Can.,* [1950] 4 D.L.R. 369, [1951]S.C.R. 31, to answer in the negative, but I do not think that that case supports the view that has been adopted. The judgment merely decided that neither Parliament nor the Legislatures can delegate powers to each other so as to change the distribution of powers provided for in ss. 91 and 92 of the *B.N.A. Act.* Here the issue is entirely different. The federal legislation does not confer any additional powers to the Legislature but vests in a group of persons certain powers to be exercised in the inter-provincial and export field. It is immaterial that the same persons be empowered by the Legislature to control and regulate the marketing of natural products within the Province. It is true that the Board is a creature of the Lieutenant-Governor in Council, but this does not prevent it from exercising duties imposed by the Parliament of Canada: *Valin v. Langlois,* 5 App. Cas. 115.

Thus, a means was found to combine in the hands of one regulatory body control over the whole marketing process of an agricultural product within and beyond the Province of production—a desirable result much sought after for years in constitutional practice.

Advantage was quickly taken of this new-found device in another field. The federal government, though it had vindicated its exclusive jurisdiction over inter-provincial and international commercial motor vehicle enterprises in the *Winner* case of 1954,[24] decided none the less that it was not prepared to undertake such regulation. Accordingly the federal Parliament passed the Motor Vehicle Transport Act of 1954,[25] which contained the following provisions:

Operation of Undertaking

3(1) Where in any province a licence is by the law of the province required for the operation of a local undertaking, no person shall operate an extra-provincial undertaking in that province unless he holds a licence issued under the authority of this Act.

(2) The provincial transport board in each province may in its discretion issue a licence to a person to operate an extra-provincial undertaking into or through the province upon the like terms and conditions and in the like manner as if the extra-provincial undertaking operated in the province were a local undertaking.

Tariffs and Tolls

4. Where in any provinces tariffs and tolls to be charged by a local carrier for local transport are determined or regulated by the provincial transport board, the tariffs and tolls to be charged by a federal carrier for extra-provincial transport in the province may in the discretion of the provincial transport board be determined and regulated by the provincial transport board in the like manner and subject to the like terms and conditions as if the extra-provincial transport in that province were local transport.

---

[23]*Supra,* footnote 21, 163.
[24]*Supra,* footnote 10.
[25]S.C., 1953-54, c. 59.

General

5. The Governor in Council may exempt any person or the whole or any part of an extra-provincial undertaking or any extra-provincial transport from all or any of the provisions of this Act.

All Provinces eventually took up this offer of delegation, most of them right away, so that effective control of interprovincial and international commercial motor vehicle carriers passed to the provincial Motor Vehicle Boards, Province by Province. It should be recalled that such a Board is composed of provincially-appointed and paid officials who get their policy instructions from the relevant provincial statutes and possibly from a provincial minister or the provincial cabinet, depending on the terms on which the particular Province has constituted its board. We came pretty close here to ten sets of laws for interprovincial and international commercial motor vehicle carriers, the very thing that Mr. Justice Taschereau pin-pointed as objectionable in the *Nova Scotia Interdelegation* case. Apparently the present federal government has doubts about the wisdom of what was done in 1954, because the new National Transportation Act of this year (1967)[26] provides machinery whereby a committee of the Canadian Transport Commission, called the Motor Vehicle Transport Committee, could take over the regulation of all extra-provincial commercial highway transportation enterprises, though the steps to do so have not been taken yet. No doubt the federal government intends to move in this direction. But no doubt also certain political and commercial vested interests have developed in the state of the several provincial sets of regulations under the delegation of the Federal Motor Vehicle Transport Act of 1954, and we will soon see how strong these are. Mr. Justice Rand's point about the difficult of revoking a delegated law-making power may soon be put to the test.

Yet, the delegation in the Federal Motor Vehicle Transport Act of 1954 was subject to some limitations. While a provincial board could withhold a licence to operate altogether from an extra-provincial motor vehicle carrier, if it did grant a licence it could not then discriminate against the extra-provincial carrier by comparison with intra-provincial carriers. Moreover, under section 5, an extra-provincial carrier could be exempted from control of the provincial board by a federal order in council. Note also that the regulation-making power delegated to the provincial board is confined to the one narrow subject of extra-provincial commercial motor vehicle enterprises, so that, all in all, it is characteristically subordinate and not primary law-making power. Nevertheless we are certainly here in the gray zone where just about as much harm to essential national powers can be done by a federal delegation of subordinate regulation-making powers to a body of provincial officials as by a federal delegation of primary legislative powers to a provincial legislature. One thing is clear from the terms of the British North America Act, that all integrated inter-provincial and internal forms of transportation and communication were to be exclusively subject to the jurisdiction of the federal Parliament.

---

[26]S.C., 1966-67. c. 69.

Yet, in spite of the foregoing considerations, the administrative type of inter-governmental delegation has been widely used in our constitutional practice and has brought valuable and indispensable elements of flexibility to our federal system. Indeed, some of it is called for by the very terms of the British North America Act itself. For example the federal Parliament is charged by section 91(27) with the making of criminal law, both substantive and procedural, whereas each provincial legislature is charged by section 92(14) with arranging for "The Administration of Justice in the Province". Accordingly, ever since 1867, provincial Attorneys-General and the permanent officials of their departments, including the Crown Attorneys, have administered the federal Criminal Code in their respective Provinces. Moreover, most of the criminal trials under the Criminal Code of Canada are conducted by provincially-appointed magistrates who are given their authority in this respect by the procedural section of the Criminal Code of Canada. Furthermore, while Ontario and Quebec provide their own police forces so that in these two provinces provincial police officers enforce the federal Criminal Code, the situation differs in the other eight Provinces. In them the provincial governments, by contract with the federal government, employ the Royal Canadian Mounted Police for enforcing provincial as well as federal offences in their respective territories. There are of course other examples of useful administrative delegations, but space does not permit their exposition here.

Before attempting an opinion on the merits of legislative or administrative delegation in our federal system, there is one further development to note. Part II of the Fulton-Favreau Bill for amendment of the Canadian constitution purported to establish a new procedure for direct inter-governmental delegation at the primary legislative level that would, if put into effect, reverse to an important extent the decision in the *Nova Scotia Inter-delegation* case. For one or two of the Provinces at least, this was apparently very important in inducing the agreement of 1964 on the formula as a whole. Briefly, the Fulton-Favreau Bill's draft delegation sections were to this effect.[27] The federal Parliament could enact a statute concerning the provincial subjects of prisons, local works and undertakings, property and civil rights and matters of a merely local or private nature in the Province, provided that:

(a) prior to the enactment thereof the legislatures of at least four of the provinces have consented to the operation of such a statute . . . or,

(b) it is declared by the Parliament of Canada that the Government of Canada has consulted with the governments of all the provinces, and that the enactment of the statute is of concern to fewer than four of the provinces and the provinces so declared to be concerned have under the authority of their legislatures consented to the enactment of such a statute.

---

[27] See The Amendment of the Constitution of Canada (Ottawa, 1965), a White Paper issued under the authority of the Honourable Guy Favreau, Minister of Justice. Appendix 3 contains the text of the so-called Fulton-Favreau Bill or Formula.

I am in favour of Part I of the Fulton-Favreau Bill as a means of bringing the constitution home. As indicated, though, I am opposed to the delegation proposals in Part II and think they should be dropped.

Likewise, a provincial legislature could enact a statute relating to any subject of Federal power provided that:

(a) prior to the enactment thereof the Parliament of Canada has consented to the enactment of such a statute by the legislature of that province, and

(b) a similar statute has . . . been enacted by the legislatures of at least three other provinces.

Revocation of these delegations at any time by the delegating legislative body was provided for. Thus the agreement of the federal parliament and four provincial legislatures would be necessary for a delegation either way under this scheme. The only exception was that there might be fewer than four provincial consents required concerning a provincial delegation to the federal Parliament if seven, eight or nine Provinces said they had no interest in the matter. But, so far as a delegation of federal power to the Provinces was concerned, it was to be mandatory that at least four Provinces should agree and enact "similar" statutes before any of those statutes could have effect.

It is now necessary to attempt some assessment of these various alternatives of inter-governmental delegation. My view is that the decision in the *Nova Scotia* case is correct and that direct bilateral trading or transfer of primary legislative powers between the federal Parliament and a provincial legislature should not be permitted. The substantial reasons for this were given by the judges in that case and typical extracts have already been quoted. It would be all too easy to engage frequently in such delegation under strong but temporary political pressures of the moment, thus creating a patch-work pattern of variations Province by Province in the relative powers and responsibilities of the federal Parliament and the provincial legislatures. This could seriously confuse the basic political responsibility and accountability of members of the federal Parliament and the federal Cabinet, and too much of this could destroy these federal institutions.[28] Not much more can be said for the delegation proposals of Part II of the Fulton-Favreau Bill. They seem to be either dangerous or useless. If the proposed delegation procedures could be worked readily, then the dangers to federal institutions just spoke of are present. If the procedure were to prove unworkable, and it *is* very complex, then it is a waste of time. Certainly it can have no attraction to those who desire to develop a particular status for Quebec, because the consent of four Provinces would be required for a delegation of federal powers, and where are Quebec's three companions in the circumstances?

The previous remarks refer to the passing of primary and plenary legislative discretions by inter-governmental delegation, but administrative delegation, as the term has been used here, forms quite a contrast. Here we are often concerned only with the application of laws the substance of which has already been determined in the proper legislative forum under the existing distribution of powers— Canadian Parliament or provincial legislature as the case may be. The administration of laws already formulated, that is their interpretation and application to

---

[28]Dr. Eugene Forsey has warned of this danger with great force and clarity. See his paper on The Legislatures and Executives of the Federation in Volume 1 of Background Papers and Reports of the Ontario Advisory Committee on Confederation (Toronto, 1967).

the persons and circumstances contemplated by their terms, still involves at times important discretions, but they are much lesser discretions than the primary legislative discretions exercised when laws are first formulated. Delegation at this administrative level is a proper and useful division of labour in government and does not threaten the situs of or the political accountability for primary legislative discretions in our federal system. Even when regulation-making power is involved for the subordinate delegate body, if that regulation-making power is properly limited, still there is no threat to responsibility for primary legislative discretions under our federal system. The courts have shown more disposition to control regulations of subordinate boards or commissions than to control statutes of Parliament or a provincial legislature.

While it is true, as we have seen in the case of the Motor Vehicle Boards, that a subordinate provincial board might be given a dangerous extent of regulation-making power by the federal Parliament, the courts could insist that this stop short of the sort of thing attempted in the proposed Delegation of Legislative Jurisdiction Act of Nova Scotia, described earlier. To take an extreme hypothetical example, if the federal Parliament proposed to delegate power to make criminal law generally to provincial Criminal Law Boards composed of provincially appointed officials, surely the courts would find this invalid as a colourable attempt to bring about the objectionable type of direct primary legislative delegation under the guise of administrative delegation. At least where inter-governmental administrative delegations are concerned, the courts should be strict about this and confine permissible regulation-making powers for the delegate body to developing the detail of the legislative scheme in the master statute concerned, which should in these circumstances contain the main standards or guidelines to be followed. Indeed, two master statutes are involved in these cases, one federal and one provincial. Neither should be a mere skeleton statute.

Mention of the two master statutes suggests another possibility that should be noticed as a final point in this consideration of inter-governmental delegation. The subordinate delegate body in such cases could be made up of federal and provincial officials. This seems to be quite within the scope of the precedent set by the *Potato Board* case. For example, in the field of the sale of company securities, given that part of the field is within exclusive provincial jurisdiction and part within exclusive federal jurisdiction, it would be constitutionally possible to compose a joint board of federal and provincial appointees with delegations of powers to the board that gave it a complete range of control over the sale of securities. Probably this would only work, as a matter of political accountability, if the federal and provincial governments were fully agreed in some detail on the nature of the controls to be exercised. If this were so and was sufficiently expressed in the master statutes, then the board members could no doubt get on harmoniously with the execution of their common tasks regardless of whether they were federal or provincial appointees. In any event, though it is highly speculative whether a joint board would work. It is clear that inter-governmental delegations of many kinds at the levels of administration of laws and subordinate regulation-making bring a very valuable element of flexibility to the Canadian federal system.

While delegation, as in the fields of agricultural marketing and motor vehicle enterprises, has given provincial governments some entry to exclusive federal fields of legislative jurisdiction, the federal government has in the main relied on other techniques to exert an influence in certain exclusive fields of provincial legislative jurisdiction. Conditional grants and federal crown corporations have been used to this end, and may properly be considered as distinct co-operative forms in the area of federal-provincial relations. What is here involved is the use of federal resources for undertakings that usually fall within provincial powers so far as legislative regulation of that type of undertaking is concerned. In the case of federal conditional grants, the offer of funds and the conditions attached, when accepted by the Province, amount to a federal presence and influence of some sort in a field legislatively provincial. For example, the federal government offered the provincial governments grants of federal money for the construction of the trans-Canada highway in the respective Provinces. Highways have always been considered local works under section 92(10) of the British North America Act. Nevertheless it was federal policy that there should be a trans-Canada highway and that it should measure up to certain standards and dimensions in construction. Accepting Provinces were required to meet these standards and to pay a relatively small porportion of the cost by matching grants from provincial funds. There have been many federal conditional grant programmes, and some are very complex. A detailed examination of them is beyond the scope of this essay, but certain general considerations concerning them require examination.

Professor G. V. LaForest in his recent treatise on *The Allocation of Taxing Power under the Canadian Constitution* gives the opinion that these grants-in-aid are constitutionally valid and permissible.[29]

> Federal statutes authorizing the grant of money to the provinces on condition that the provinces adopt legislation described in federal statutes, regulations or Dominion-provincial agreements constitute a well-worn route for implementing federal policies. Examples are blind and disabled persons allowances, hospital insurance and the trans-Canada highway arrangements. One of the usual condition is that the provinces should bear a definite proportion of the costs of the schemes. Since offers of money, especially for social service schemes, are difficult to refuse, the Dominion is thereby able not only to implement its policies by use of its own resources but also to divert the resources of the provinces to these ends as well.
>
> The validity of these schemes has never been tested; thus far neither the provinces nor the Dominion have demonstrated any inclination to refer the matter to the courts, and a private individual would seldom have the standing to question it. However they appear to be valid. Certainly payments to the provinces are constitutionally unobjectionable. Dominion subsidies to the provinces are provided by several constitutional provisions and (though these rest on no firmer foundation than an opinion of the Law Offices of the Crown) by several Dominion statutes. These, it is true, are given free of conditions, but in complying with the conditions attached to grants the provinces are merely exercising their own legislative powers. Whatever political implications these may have, therefore, it seems very doubtful if their constitutional validity could be successfully challenged.

---

[29](Toronto, 1967), 40-41.

It should be noted that the federal legislation concerned in these cases makes conditional offers of money, it does not contain compulsory regulations. For example the hospital insurance scheme mentioned is in the permissible category Professor LaForest describes because the compulsory features of it, so far as members of the public are concerned, are found in the provincial legislation of the accepting Provinces. This contrasts with the federal government's first attempt at an unemployment insurance scheme contained in the Employment and Social Insurance Act of 1935.[30] This federal statute set up a special unemployment insurance fund and purported to require regular contributions thereto from both employees and employers. The Act was held *ultra vires* of the federal Parliament by the Supreme Court of Canada and the Judicial Committee of the Privy Council. In the latter court, in striking down this statute, Lord Atkin made some general remarks about the nature of the federal spending power.[31]

> That the Dominion may impose taxation for the purpose of creating a fund for special purposes, and may apply that fund for making contributions in the public interest to individuals, corporations or public authorities, could not as a general proposition be denied. Whether in such an Act as the present compulsion applied to an employed person to make a contribution to an insurance fund out of which he will receive benefit for a period proportionate to the number of his contributions is in fact taxation it is not necessary finally to decide. It might seem difficult to discern how it differs from a form of compulsory insurance, or what the difference is between a statutory obligation to pay insurance premiums to the State or to an insurance company. But assuming that the Dominion has collected by means of taxation a fund, it by no means follows that any legislation which disposes of it is necessarily within Dominion competence.
>
> It may still be legislation affecting the classes of subjects enumerated in s. 92, and, if so, would be ultra vires. In other words, Dominion legislation, even though it deals with Dominion property, may yet be so framed as to invade civil rights within the Province, or encroach upon the classes of subjects which are reserved to Provincial competence. It is not necessary that it should be a colourable device, or a pretence. If on the true view of the legislation it is found that in reality in pith and substance the legislation invades civil rights within the Province, or in respect of other classes of subjects otherwise encroaches upon the provincial field, the legislation will be invalid. To hold otherwise would afford the Dominion an easy passage into the Provincial domain. In the present case, their Lordships agree with the majority of the Supreme Court in holding that in pith and substance this Act is an insurance Act affecting the civil rights of employers and employed in each Province, and as such is invalid.

The Tremblay Commission of Quebec on the constitution relied on this passage for its claim that federal conditional grants were contrary to the terms and intent of the British North America Act,[32] but most constitutional authorities are not in agreement. The *Unemployment Insurance* case was not dealing with the federal offer of a conditional grant-in-aid to a Province, it was dealing with a fed-

---

[30]S.C., 1935, c. 38.
[31]*A.G. for Canada v. A.G. for Ontario,* [1937] A.C. 355, 366-367.
[32]Report of the Royal Commission of Inquiry on Constitutional Problems (Quebec, 1956), Vol. II, 212-213.

eral statute that itself contained a compulsory all-inclusive public insurance scheme, and must be read subject to these limitations—hence the prevailing opinion that this decision does not invalidate Federal conditional-grant legislation.[33]

Nevertheless, the question should be asked whether conditional grants do not lead to different states of federal-provincial relations with different Provinces, if some accept certain grants while others do not? Does this not confuse political accountability and responsibility for members of the federal Parliament and cabinet? In this connection Professor Donald V. Smiley has made an important point in his treatise on *Conditional Grants and Canadian Federalism*. Federal conditional grants have not been primarily concerned with legislative regulation, they have been primarily concerned with providing resources for desirable social services, public works and the like. The emphasis is on the use and management of funds belonging to the federal government, and federal policies are thus pursued as a matter of managerial decisions and conditions set by the owner of the necessary funds, because he is the owner. For example, the federal government's Crown Corporation, Central Mortgage and Housing Corporation, cannot directly impose building codes on the construction industry in the Provinces; such legislative regulation is within provincial jurisdiction. But the corporation can say that it will not lend the federal government's money to home builders unless its specified construction standards are met. After all private lenders go this far. In any event, federal standards thus make themselves felt through the medium of contracts with builders. No builder can be told that he *must* meet the federal standards, but if he is not prepared to do so he does have to borrow his money elsewhere. Accordingly, dislocation of primary legislative power and confusion of the relevant political accountability is not much of an issue so far as conditional grants are concerned. But other matters of great importance to the Provinces are involved. To a considerable extent provincial priorities to the use of provincial revenues and resources are put under federeal influence through the need for matching provincial payments in some proportion to qualify for federal grants. Also, the matter of who gets credit for welfare schemes the public wants may well be vital to the political survival of particular provincial or federal governments. Nevertheless, I consider that the advantages of conditional grants greatly outweigh any disadvantages for the federal government and provincial governments. As Professor Smiley has said:[34]

> It is important not to exaggerate the possibility of the federal spending power as a device by which the influence of Ottawa can be extended. There are three limitations in this respect.
>
> First, federal action is nullified if the eligible recipient decides not to accept the conditions under which federal largesse is made available. Thus federal influence can be brought to bear only with the collaboration of others—in the case of the sub-

---

[33]See G. V. LaForest, *op. cit.*, footnote 29, ch. II. See also Donald V. Smiley, Conditional Grants and Canadian Federalism (Toronto, 1963).

Professors Smiley and LaForest upheld the validity of federal conditional grants and review the authorities.

[34]Smiley, *op. cit.*, *ibid.*, 26.

ject-matter of this essay, the provinces. To take a simple example, Ottawa might decree, although it does not, that federal grants are not to be paid on behalf of any hospital where the matron is not a Registered Nurse; it could not make it a federal offence to operate a hospital unless this condition was observed.

Second, the spending power holds few possibilities for extending the influence of the federal government in the regulatory field. One might conceive of an arrangement by which the federal authorities offered to pay a proportion of the costs incurred by provincial labour relations boards on the condition that provincial labour policies were carried out in a particular way; it is impossible to imagine the provinces being willing to accept any such grant. Thus in practice federal influence vis-a-vis the provinces can be enhanced only in those situations involving a service activity, and this influence can of course be most decisive where the function is a relatively costly one.

Third, in most circumstances, the federal government must accomplish its purposes through agencies other than its own administrative instrumentalities. The relation between Ottawa and these agencies is thus one of collaboration rather than of administrative superior and subordinates.

Federal initiative through conditional grants has brought great benefits to Canadians in every Province. Necessary welfare schemes have usually come more quickly, at better standards and in more places than would otherwise have been the case.

Accordingly, federal conditional grants have brought beneficial elements of flexibility to our federal system, elements that do not pose a threat to the essential basis of federal institutions or the autonomy of the Provinces. Each party has real bargaining power under the constitution, and so should be able to take care of itself in the inter-governmental negotiations about the terms of conditional-grant programmes. The federal government has superior revenue-raising and financial power for the reasons given at the beginning of this essay. The provincial governments and legislatures have the essential powers of compulsory legislative regulation that many of these programmes require at some point, as well as some of the revenues.

Furthermore, it seems that the federal government is always going to be in the position of having more revenue than it needs to carry out its direct responsibilities under the constitution. Federal taxing power is more effective and more fair than provincial power, in the types of taxes available and in the territorial extent of the power. Also, to a very significant degree, the federal Parliament needs to keep such taxes as those on corporation and personal income in its own hands as levers for managing the national economy in aid of full employment and prosperity. Finally, only the federal government can effect the net transfers of public funds to the Provinces located in the poorer regions of Canada to help them to improved conditions. And such improvement is one of the basic aims of Confederation. In the face of these considerations, it is no use to say that the revenue-raising capacities of the provincial legislatures and the federal Parliament should be precisely matched to the direct legislative responsibilities of each, by changes in the allocation of taxing powers under the constitution. This simplistic solution is impossible. My view is then that there will always be a surplus of funds in federal hands that should be dispensed to the Provinces in a mixture of conditional and unconditional grants. Conditional grants then, as a form of cooperative federalism, are with us indefinitely. It may be that we have reached a period when there should be more room for provincial influence on the nature of these schemes, and more sympathy at Ottawa for this. The inherent flexibility of this form of co-operative federalism means that new and different arrangements could be developed as the need or desire for them became clear. Better federal-provincial agreements concerning both conditional and unconditional federal grants-in-aid is one of the ways to real constitutional improvement.

So far we have been mainly concerned with forms of federal-provincial co-operation against the background of mutually exclusive federal and provincial powers. But, as indicated earlier, there are certain areas of concurrency in our constitutional law and jurisprudence. Of these some are given expressly in the terms of the British North America Act and others are implied through one of the applications of the aspect theory of interpretation. So far as express concurrency is concerned, Section 95 of the British North America Act provides as follows:

> In each Province the Legislature may make Laws in relation to Agriculture in the Province, and to Immigration into the province; and it is hereby declared that the Parliament of Canada may from Time to Time make Laws in relation to Agriculture in all or any of the Provinces, and to Immigration into all or any of the Provinces, and any Law of the Legislature of a Province relative to Agriculture or to Immigration shall have effect in and for the Province as long and as far only as it is not repugnant to any Act of the Parliament of Canada.

The issue of paramountcy in the event of conflicting statutes of Canada and a Province is one that must be faced since federal and provincial governments are dealing with the same citizens in the same territory, Province by Province. Section 95 does face the issue and resolves it in favour of the paramoutcy of the federal statute. Section 95 is an original section dated from 1867. Section 94A, dating from 1951 and dealing with old age pensions, establishes concurrency on this subject but with a principle of provincial paramountcy expressed for the first and only time in our constitutional law. An example of the implied type of concurrency was given earlier in this essay using the example of the Unconscionable Transactions Relief Act of Ontario and the question of interest charges. So far as implied concurrency is concerned, the doctrine of dominion paramountcy prevails in the event of conflicting federal and provincial statutes.

Our main concern with concurrency of legislative powers here is to see what kind of a background this affords for measures of federal-provincial co-operation. Obviously the principle of dominion paramountcy that obtains in all concurrent subjects except the old age pensions gives the federal government the greater bargaining power for federal-provincial agreements about the division of concurrent fields except for old age pensions. In any event, where powers are concurrent, one does not have to worry about delegations or conditions on grants-in-aid as means of entry to part of the jurisdiction of the other party. The appropriate form of co-operation is simply the straightforward inter-governmental agreement about how each is to use or refrain from using its existing powers in the same field. The most important examples of this are the federal-provincial taxation agreements. Both the federal Parliament and the provincial legislatures have full

powers of direct taxation. These have been authoritatively interpreted to be concurrent powers, so that both could tax simultaneously as long as the taxpayer has
capacity to pay.[35] So far as personal income is concerned, for example, the Provinces, except for Quebec, have agreed not to collect their own provincial income
taxes provided the federal Parliament will levy an income tax on a uniform basis
and hand over an agreed proportion of the harvest unconditionally to each par-
ticipating Province. In the case of Quebec taxpayers, special exemptions from
federal tax accomplish much the same result for Quebec. The terms of these
agreements are complex, but the form and basis of them are simple. As with all
agreements the bargaining power of the parties is important, and the bearing of
concurrency and paramountcy on this has already been discussed and exemplified.

    We have reviewed some of the more important forms of official federal-
provincial co-operation in Canada, and have assessed some of their implications
for our federal system. Inevitably and increasingly, federal and provincial governments are involved with one another and dependant on one another. Federal-
provincial conferences and major consultations of various kinds go on constantly
at all official levels. In 1966 there were almost as many formally scheduled
federal-provincial conferences of some kind or other as there were days in the
year. [36] On some days of any year there are no doubt more provincial cabinet
ministers in Ottawa than federal ministers. Such wide-ranging official co-operative activity is a sign of health and vitality in our federal system. Moreover such
co-operative federalism contains important elements of flexibility for meeting
some of the needs of change. It provides opportunities for innovation that may
help greatly to establish more satisfactory relations between the federal government on the one hand and the provincial governments on the other. In particular,
the legitimate forms of co-operative federalism have a continuing role of importance to play in developing a satisfactory relationship between the Parliament and
Government of Canada on the one hand, and the Legislature and Government of
the Province of Quebec on the other. Nevertheless, these co-operative measures
take place and can only take place against the background of basic definition provided by the first principles of our federal constitution. There are essentials here
at this fundamental level that must be honoured and preserved if Canada is to
continue and to progress as a federal country in her second century.

FURTHER THOUGHTS AND REFERENCES

In the 1967 essay just reproduced, I made a distinction between legislative delegation and administrative delegation. I argued that legislative delegation was the
sort of thing attempted in the *Nova Scotia Inter-Delegation* case, and that it was
not permissible. I also argued that there had to be a master statute that was not

---

[35]See G. V. LaForest, *op. cit.*, footnote 29, ch. II, where the authorities are reviewed.
[36]The Financial Post for May 21st, 1966, carried a listing of federal-provincial conferences of all
    types held or to be held in 1966. It covers almost two newsprint pages.

just a skeleton statute passed by the Parliament to which the B.N.A. Act had entrusted primary power in the matter concerned (e.g., the Parliament of Canada). Then there could be legitimate *administrative* delegation to officials of the other level of government (*e.g.*, a Provincial Government). I neglected to note that the master statute in question could be supplied by the device of legislation by adoption or reference in the parliamentary body primarily concerned under the federal division of powers. Thus, for the regulation of inter-provincial highway using enterprises, the Federal Parliament may get its master statute through adopting by reference the Ontario statute that regulates highway using enterprises that are local to that Province in their operations. The statute is sufficiently precise and detailed to be the basis then for a legitimate administrative delegation by the Federal Government to provincial officials, the Ontario Highway Transport Board. See *Coughlin v. Ontario Highway Transport Board*[1]

Nevertheless, I suspect that there is still vitality in the *Nova Scotia Inter-Delegation* case of 1951. I suspect it still remains true that if the adopting parliamentary body is too sweeping or indefinite in what it purports to adopt from the other parliamentary body, we have what may be characterized as attempted abdication or as attempted unilateral amendment of the federal division of powers by the former body.

I suspect that whenever the transaction can be so characterized, it will be held to be unconstitutional. There is support for this in a recent Supreme Court of Canada decision: *Re Manitoba Government Employees Association and Government of Manitoba et al.*[2]

---

[1] [1968] S.C.R. 569.
[2] (1977), 79 D.L.R. (3d) 1.

Chapter 18

The Creation of Corporate Bodies and the Functional Regulation of Legal Persons in the Canadian Federal System*

Reprinted with permission from *Telecommunications for Canada*. H. Edward English, ed. (Toronto, London, Sydney, Wellington: Methuen, 1973) 344

By way of introduction here it is necessary to explain with care some general principles relevant to the total legal position of all companies and industries in Canada including the telephone companies. The major general point is that, because our constitution is a federal one, legislative powers to provide for the incorporation of companies must be carefully distinguished from legislative powers to regulate specific types of businesses and industries as such. The constitution divides and distributes powers in both cases between the federal and provincial parliaments but it divides them along different lines. In other words, a federally incorporated company may carry on a type of business that, as such, has been placed by the constitution under the legislative power of the provinces. An example is the fire insurance business. The converse is also true. A provincially incorporated company may carry on radio broadcasting through the air, but only if it is licensed and permitted to do so under federal statutes and regulations. It is decidedly wrong to say that only the appropriate provincial legislature can regulate what its provincially incorporated companies do in any and every respect. It is likewise wrong to say that only the federal parliament can regulate what federally incorporated companies do in any and every respect. This is just too simple to fit the facts of life.[1]

---

*What is reproduced in this chapter is part of a larger essay entitled "Telecommunications and the Federal Constitution of Canada" (1973). The larger essay attempts to give in detail the total legal position of the various telephone companies in Canada, and, in the course of so doing, to deal with many constitutional issues in the field of electronic telecommunications. The part reprinted here, under the title given this chapter, is confined to the jurisprudential nature of corporate bodies generally and their relation to the functional division of primary legislative powers of the Canadian federal system. (The rest of the larger essay is not of the same systematic jurisprudential interest and, moreover, may be to some degree outdated by subsequent developments.)

[1]Relevant examples are the following.
(a) The Citizens Insurance Company, a federal company, was held liable to provincial regulation of its fire insurance contracts. *Citizens Insurance Company v. Parsons* (1881-82), 7 A.C., 96 (J.C. of P.C.).

Logically in this regard, there are not just two different constitutional situations, there are six of them.

1. A federal company engaged in a business subject to federal jurisdiction.
2. A federal company engaged in a business subject to provincial jurisdiction.
3. A federal company engaged in part in a federal business and in part in a provincial business.
4. A provincial company engaged in a business subject to provincial jurisdiction.
5. A provincial company engaged in a business subject to federal jurisdiction.
6. A provincial company engaged in part in a provincial business and in part in a federal business.

In case one, it is true enough that the company is under the federal parliament alone for both corporate existence and internal structure on the one hand and the doing of business as a going concern on the other hand. In case four, the provincial company is likewise under its provincial parliament only, in both respects. But, in case two, a federal company must respond to provincial laws for the doing of business as a going concern, though it remains subject to federal laws for its corporate existence and internal structure. In case three, a federal company must respond to both federal and provincial laws for the doing of business, though corporate existence and internal structure remain dependent upon federal laws. The corresponding statements can be made about a provincial company in cases five and six, likewise distinguishing corporate existence and internal structure on the one hand from the type of business being done by the provincial company on the other.

First then, we consider the nature of corporations as legal persons and the respective federal and provincial powers to create them. Secondly, we consider in detail the federal division of powers as it relates to control of corporate bodies engaged in the telecommunications industry, whatever the origin of the respective corporate bodies may have been. In both cases, without prejudice to the validity of the main distinction, we will find ourselves considering from time to time the relation between legislative powers to incorporate and powers to regulate, for, to some extent they do overlap. This may lead in some circumstances to

---

(b) The C.P.R. Company, a federal company, was held subject to provincial regulation of conditions of work for employees in its operation of the Empress Hotel in Victoria, B.C. *C.P.R. Company v. A.-G. for B.C.*, [1950] A.C. 122 (J.C. of P.C.).

(c) The Government of Ontario, conducting the Go Transit System on C.N.R. lines in and out of Toronto, was held to be subject to rate regulation under legislation of the Parliament of Canada. *The Queen in Right of Ontario v. The Board of Transport Commissioners for Canada* (1968), 65 D.L.R. (2d) 425 (S.C. of Canada). Likewise, the Government of British Columbia, importing whisky for its retail liquor stores, was held liable to pay the federally imposed import duties. *A.-G. for B.C. v. A.-G. for Canada*, [1924] A.C. 222 (J.C. of P.C.).

(d) In their brief on constitutional and legal problems to the study groups of the Department of Communications who prepared the report *Instant World* (footnote 3, Chapter I), The Canadian Association of Broadcasters state: "Radio and television stations have been established across the country in the vast majority of cases under provincial incorporation, but always subject to licencing and regulating by federal authorities." (11).

a conflict or apparent conflict between the federal power to incorporate, and the provincial power to regulate certain particular business in which federal corporations engage, or vice versa. Such conflict, if real, must be resolved by some constitutional rules for priorities or, if apparent only, must be properly explained away.

I. THE NATURE OF CORPORATE BODIES IN GENERAL, AND THOSE OF THE TELEPHONE INDUSTRY IN PARTICULAR

In order to sort out the federal power distribution problems in this field we must keep in mind certain very basic characteristics of legal systems. All laws are concerned in some way with relations of an obligatory nature between persons. So, the legal system must define the persons it will recognize as units capable of such relations, and then establish standards or rules that oblige one person to do or refrain from doing something for the benefit of another person.[2]

The total legal system is a network of a vast number of rules giving rise to duties, rights, powers, and immunities as between legal persons. The natural legal person is the human individual, and our law recognizes that each human individual is a full legal person in his own right. But also the law constructs other legal persons by recognizing certain organizations of human individuals as having separate and distinct legal personalities, apart from the human individuals who are concerned with them. In other words, the law in effect says to human individuals, "If some of you associate together in particular ways and meet certain conditions, you may secure for your organization recognition as a separate legal person." Hence, the corporation is an artificial legal person or unit distinct from the human individuals who are its officers, servants, directors, or shareholders. The word "artificial" here indicates that, unlike human individuals, corporations are constructed as legal units or persons by the law, not by nature. Nevertheless they can act only through the human individuals who are respectively their officers or employees.

Neither is the corporate organization "artificial" in the sense of being unreal; corporate bodies are very real indeed in their purposes, assets, human personnel and operations.[3] Moreover, being a legal person, the corporation itself can own things and make contracts under the regular law of ownership and contract. These abilities are essential to the conduct of business in a unified way as a going concern, and are among the main purposes and advantages of incorporation. The law of property gives wide discretion to an owner respecting control of the things owned. The main thrust of the law of contract is that legal persons may for the most part make whatever business agreements they please with one another, within broad limits they may write their own terms; but once they have

---

[2]For a general analysis, see: G. W. Paton, *A Textbook of Jurisprudence*, 3rd ed. (Oxford: O.U.P., 1968), Chapter XVI, "The Concept of Legal Personality."

[3]Martin Wolff, "On the Nature of Legal Persons" (1938), 54 L.Q.R. 494. Also, D. H. Bonham and D. A. Soberman, "The Nature of Corporate Personality," in *Studies in Canadian Company Law*, ed. by J. S. Ziegel (Toronto: Butterworth & Co., 1961), 3-32.

completed such an agreement, reciprocal obligations arise in law that each person shall do as he has promised. This is a necessary foundation for the whole of business, industry, and commerce. Furthermore, when a parliamentary body having jurisdiction decides to provide for some functional regulation of an industry or business, this frequently means review and control by a public board or commission of some of the terms of certain contracts made by the corporate bodies in that industry or business, particularly contracts with members of the public at large as customers or shareholders.

Another advantage of incorporation as a grant from the government is that a legal régime of internal organization and structure is provided for the corporate association whereby financial and industrial resources may be assembled on a large scale, and the talent and efforts of many human individuals hired, the whole complex being dedicated in law to the pursuit of the specified purposes of the association. Finally, the corporation or company may assemble resources and carry on as a going concern because the régime of internal organization and structure provided for it by the law gives the company unified internal decision-making procedures, involving its directors, shareholders, and managers. Whereas in the human individual as a legal person this capacity for decisions is provided by nature and can be taken for granted, when an association of human individuals is to be treated as a separate legal unit, as a distinct legal person capable of decisions, then legally sanctioned procedures for voting and giving authority to directors and managers are indispensable.

Accordingly, we find that there is a special body of corporation or company law that covers matters peculiar to the creation and functioning of corporations as legal persons. These include such things as obtaining the privilege of incorporation in the first place, the election of directors, the rights of minority shareholders, the raising of capital by the sale of securities, the authority of company officers to act for the company, and so on.[4]

Thus far it is apparent that I have been speaking of private investor-owned companies where the original financial assets are obtained by private sales of company shares to the public. A word of explanation is now necessary concerning the nature of a Crown corporation. The bare essentials of a corporate body are three-fold—legally specified corporate purposes, assets legally dedicated to those purposes, and human personnel for directing, managing, and operating the organization and who are under a legal duty to do so in pursuit of the corporate purposes. This includes of course their control and use of the assets. If a provincial legislature or the federal parliament is willing to put up the original financial assets out of public funds and to provide for government appointment of directors who can then proceed to hire the other personnel, no private shareholders or funds are in the picture. Nevertheless, such an organization can be created by statute with its own single and separate legal personality. Then it carries on like any other corporate person, but it must respond one way or another in the end to ultimate control by the incorporating government which takes the place of the

---

[4]J. S. Ziegel, "Constitutional Aspects of Canadian Companies," Chapter 5 in *Studies in Canadian Company Law, op. cit.*, 162.

shareholders in this respect. For example, the Canadian National Railways is a federal Crown corporation and its directors are appointed by the Government of Canada. Finally, it should be noted that the federal government and the provincial governments are themselves each distinct legal persons for purposes of direct operations by their respective governmental departments and agencies of all sorts. Historically this arises from the separate legal personality of the Crown and the later development in constitutional law of the divisibility of the Crown. Each provincial government and the federal government respectively have their own distinct legal personalities because of this historical inheritance and development of public law concerning the position of the Crown.[5]

These general considerations must now be set in the context of the Canadian federal constitution. I have already mentioned that both the federal parliament and the respective provincial legislatures may create or authorize the creation of corporate legal persons. What are these powers in detail?

The British North America Act[6] gives to the provincial legislature powers respecting "the incorporation of companies with provincial objects."[7] In my view, authoritative interpretation in the courts and general practice in the country have made it clear that the limitation "with provincial objects" has a territorial meaning only. A province may create a company with the full capacity enjoyed by the adult human individual as a legal person—the so-called common law corporation or company. In the economic field, this means a company with power to engage in any type of business or industrial activity. The phrase "with provincial objects" means only that the objects are intra-provincial in the sense that the provincial company can operate just within the territory of the incorporating province, as an original matter of entitlement by virtue of its provincial charter. Further, even in the territorial sense as a corporate entity, the provincial company can, so to speak, walk abroad and receive power to do business in another province, state, or country provided the governmental authority of that other province, state, or country, recognizes it and grants it the right to operate there. But, the provincial company cannot *demand* this recognition from other governments in other territories. Moreover, even if the provincial company confines its operations and facilities to the territory of the incorporating province, it may make interprovincial or international contracts of all kinds with legal persons of any sort in other provinces, states, or countries. Long-established principles of private international law permit this.[8] Here, for example, is the juridical basis for the intersystem contracts a provincial telephone company makes for interconnection at the provincial border with the facilities of another telephone company in another province of Canada or a state of the United States. In other words, a provincial

---

[5]See footnote 1, Chapter II.

[6]1867, 30 & 31 Victoria, C. 3 as amended (U.K.).

[7]B.N.A. Act, section 92(11).

[8]*C.P.R. Company v. The Western Union Telegraph Company* (1889) 17 S.C.R., 151, 158 (S.C. of Canada).

See also generally: G. C. Cheshire, *Private International Law*, 7th ed., (London: Butterworth & Co., 1965), Chapter VIII; and J. H. C. Morris, *Dicey and Morris on The Conflict of Laws* (London: Stevens & Sons Ltd., 1967), Chapter 27.

company can be authorized by the home province to engage in any type of business or industry and there is no limitation just to businesses or industries that, as such, are legislatively under provincial regulatory powers by virtue of section 92 of the B.N.A. Act. To repeat, the phrase "with provincial objects" as a limitation means only that a provincial company is necessarily limited to the territory of the incorporating province as its base of operations by virtue of its original charter.[9]

We come now to the power of the federal parliament to create corporate bodies. The only specific federal power of incorporation mentioned in the British North America Act is that to incorporate banks. But, the federal general power in section 91 of the B.N.A. Act is to the effect that the Parliament of Canada can legislate on all matters not by the B.N.A. Act assigned exclusively to the legislatures of the provinces. In other words, there is a full-fledged federal power to incorporate companies that are not necessarily to be confined to the territorial limits of a single province as their original territorial base. At its maximum, in this sense, the federal power of incorporation is power to make the original territorial base of a federal company the whole of the territory of Canada, and of course, using less than its maximum of power in this respect, the federal parliament may make the territorial base of a federal company any lesser part of the territory of Canada. As for the range of subjects that the Parliament of Canada

---

[9]*A.-G. for Ontario v. A.-G. for Canada*, [1916] 1 A.C. 598, 602.
Bonanza Creek Gold Mining Company v. The King, [1916] 1 A.C. 566.

Reading these two cases together, we find that Viscount Haldane made is clear that a province could create a common law corporation, and that the only limit contemplated by section 92(11) of the B.N.A. Act, the provincial incorporation of companies "with provincial objects," was a territorial limitation. Viscount Haldane of course knew full well that a common law corporation was not limited in its capacities by subject matters. The *Parsons case* (footnote 1, Chapter II) makes it clear that in this respect the federal power of incorporation is parallel. The federal parliament also could authorize the creation of a common law corporation. The only difference is in the original territorial base that could be granted provincial and federal companies respectively, as a matter of original right. This is distinct from the issue of such companies "walking abroad" and operating in other territories by permission of the governmental authorities of those other territories. Both federal and provincial companies may do so.

In view of this, I respectfully submit that Professors Ziegel and McNairn are wrong to suggest that the phrase "with provincial objects" may impose limitations by subject matters on provincial corporations. I have supported this view at length in an essay on the significance of the *B.C. Electric case* (1963).

See W. R. Lederman, "Legislative Power to Create Corporate Bodies and Public Monopolies in Canada," in *Contemporary Problems of Public Law in Canada*, ed. by O. E. Lang (Toronto: U. of T. Press, 1968), pp. 108-126. Professor Ziegel's views are given in "Constitutional Aspects of Canadian Companies," *op. cit.*, pp. 188-190. Professor C. H. McNairn's views are given in his essay: "Transportation, Communication and The Constitution, The Scope of Federal Jurisdiction," *Canadian Bar Review*, 47, 1969, 355, 360-65.

In answer to Professor McNairn, I hold the view that a Saskatchewan-incorporated railway company could obtain permission from the Alberta Government to operate in Alberta. Then, when in fact its railway works and operations were extended into Alberta, the whole enterprise would be a single connecting work and undertaking exclusively under federal regulatory jurisdiction, but operated by a Saskatchewan company. If you want a corporate body which, by virtue of its original statute or charter of incorporation could forthwith construct and operate connecting works and undertakings, without the need of any provincial permissions, then, true enough you must have a federal incorporation. But this simply recognizes the territorial limitation already adverted to respecting provincial companies as a matter of original right, nothing more.

may give a federal company for its corporate purposes, here, as in the case of the provincial power, the root meaning of incorporation is taken to extend to granting the full range of capacities that is characteristic of the adult human individual as a legal person. In other words, the Parliament of Canada too may create a common law corporation, and is not restricted to authorizing federal companies to engage only in businesses or industries that legislatively and functionally are exclusively under federal jurisdiction by virtue of section 91 of the British North America Act. Also, the federal company, operating from its Canadian territorial base, may reach out in the sense explained for a provincial company. It may make international contracts with legal persons in other countries and it may walk abroad and operate directly in the territory of another country, if the appropriate governmental authority of that other country will grant it recognition. To sum up, we may say that, except for the original territorial base that may be given their respective companies, the federal and provincial powers of incorporation are parallel powers.[10]

Finally in this regard, a charter of a federal or a provincial company need not go to the limit permissible and create a common law corporation. If it chooses, the incorporating government, federal or provincial, may limit the company to engaging only in certain specified business or industries. This occurs with *some* companies created by special statute, and with companies formed under the enabling provisions of a general company statute that imposes a limiting memorandum of association.[11] In such instances, the limitations are effective. The company is then incapable of engaging in other businesses or industries by virtue of its foundation document. An important example for present purposes is afforded by the special statute of the Bell Telephone Company (Bell Canada), which is an act of the Parliament of Canada passed in 1880 and amended several times since then. The modern statement of its main powers and purposes, as enacted by Parliament in an amendment of 1948, is as follows:[12]

> 5. (1) It is hereby declared that subject to the provisions of the Radio Act and of the Broadcasting Act and of any other statutes of Canada relating to telecommunications or broadcasting, and to regulations or orders made thereunder, the Company has the power to transmit, emit or receive and to provide services and facilities for the transmission, emission or reception of signs, signals, writing, images or sounds or intelligence of any nature by wire, radio, visual or other electromagnetic systems and in connection therewith to build, establish, maintain and operate, in Canada or elsewhere, alone or in conjunction with others, either on its own behalf

---

[10]"But . . . it is not necessary to rest the authority of the dominion parliament to incorporate companies on this specific and enumerated power [section 91(2) of the B.N.A. Act]. The authority would belong to it by its general power over all matters not coming within the classes of subjects assigned exclusively to the legislatures of the provinces, and the only subject on this head assigned to the provincial legislature being "the incorporation of companies with provincial objects," it follows that the incorporation of companies for objects other than provincial falls within the general powers of the parliament of Canada. The *Parsons case, op. cit.*, II, 116-17.

[11]The *Bonanza Creek case, op. cit.*, II, pp. 577-79.

[12]S.C. 1880, c. 67.
S.C. 1948, c. 81.
S.C. 1967-68, c. 48.

or as agents for others, all services and facilities expedient or useful for such purposes, using and adapting any improvement or invention or any other means of communicating.

(2) Notwithstanding subsection (1), the Company and its subsidiaries do not, however, directly or indirectly or by any other means, have the power to apply for or to be the holder of a broadcasting license as defined in the Broadcasting Act or of a licence to operate a commercial Community Antenna Television Service.

(3) The Company shall, in the exercise of its power under subsection (1), act solely as a common carrier, and shall neither control the contents nor influence the meaning or purpose of the message emitted, transmitted or received as aforesaid.

The positive grant of powers here in the field of telecommunications is a broad one. But also, both expressly and by implication, other powers are withheld. It is necessarily implied for example that Bell Canada cannot engage in the mining or oil businesses. It is expressly specified that it cannot engage in the business of radio or television broadcasting of programs to the public through the air. Subsection (3) seems also to prohibit the company from engaging in the operation of a general public utility computer facility offering full-fledged data processing services to the public. But, you may say, are not these negative prescriptions "regulation"? What then of the distinction insisted upon earlier between the power to incorporate and the power to regulate? We must return now to these considerations.

In the first place, why is it that we can distinguish the power to incorporate from the power to regulate? The basis of the answer was suggested earlier and now comes up for more careful explanation. The fundamental juristic truth is that all legal relations are interpersonal. So, the definitions of persons by the legal system logically can be distinguished from the regulatory control by the legal system of what those persons may or may not do as the operating units of the legal system. Thus, as stated earlier, incorporation and regulation can be distinguished for purposes of a federal distribution of powers. In other words, there is no legal or philosophical necessity for the division of powers in these two respects to follow the same lines. In the vast majority of cases, the present radio and television broadcasting companies have been provincially incorporated, but they cannot broadcast a sound or a picture without the licences required by the federal law, such broadcasting being exclusively under federal jurisdiction.[13] The functional federal power to regulate radio and television broadcasting is not embarrassed or inhibited because it has to be applied in many cases to provincial corporate persons. Likewise, the exclusive provincial legislative power to regulate the fire insurance business is not frustrated, inhibited, or confused in any way because provincial laws on this subject have to be applied to federally incorporated fire insurannce companies, along with all other types of legal persons engaged in the fire insurance business in the province—including provincial companies (of any province), British companies, and foreign companies.

But this distinction cannot always be made as clearly as in the examples just given. In a federal system there are some circumstances in which the power to incorporate in the hands of one level of government may, in a logical sense,

---

[13]See footnote 1(d), Chapter II.

overlap and conflict with the functional power to regulate a particular business in the hands of the other level of government. This may happen in four out of the six basic situations given earlier, when we first considered the relation of the power to incorporate and the power to regulate in our federal system. In the other two cases, that is, where the powers to incorporate and the powers to regulate are both federal, or both provincial, the occurrence of overlap and conflict are not a problem. There is in these latter two cases a merger of these powers in one pair of legislative hands anyway. When there is such a merger of powers, the main incorporating and the main regulating provisions for the particular type of business *may then be found together in the same statute*. An example is the federal Bank Act,[14] which both incorporates and regulates the general chartered banks of Canada.

Perhaps the other four cases of potential difficulty can best be explained in terms of an example. The business of automobile insurance is exclusively under the legislative jurisdiction of the respective provincial parliaments. Nevertheless, the federal parliament, as we have seen, may incorporate a company and as a feature of that incorporation give it the capacity (power) to engage in the auto insurance business anywhere in Canada. But this grant of capacity does not make the federal company invulnerable to any and all provincial regulation of its operations in the auto insurance business in the province. In other words, the federal grant of this capacity in these circumstances is no guarantee that the capacity can be used without limit, or indeed used at all. If the automobile insurance business in a province is in the hands of private enterprise, then the federal company can use its capacity, as may all other types of legal persons, and carry on in that business in that province. In doing so, the federal company would have to obey all provincial laws respecting compulsory terms in automobile insurance contracts, minimum reserves against potential liability to policy holders, and so on. In this regard there is one respect in which a federal company does enjoy some special protection ("special" in the sense that there is no corresponding protection for provincial companies in converse circumstances). The special protection is that provincial regulatory laws may not single out a federal company and discriminate against it in relation to the restrictions or requirements laid by provincial laws on other types of legal persons writing auto insurance in that province. For instance, a province could not require a federal company, in this example, to hold twice the reserves required of a provincial company against potential liability to policy holders, all other things being equal. Nor may a province single out a federal company and sterilize its corporate existence or internal structure as a person in the province, simply as a matter of company law only, that is, in a manner unrelated to some general policy of regulation for the whole auto insurance business in the province.[15]

But there are circumstances in which the exclusive provincial regulatory

---

[14]S.C. 1966-67, c. 87.

[15]This is the point of the reasons given by Chief Justice Sherwood Lett in: *B.C. Power Corporation Ltd. v. A.-G. of B.C. et al.* (1965), 47 D.L.R. (2d), 633, especially pp. 658-706. (The judgment was given in 1963, though not reported in the Dominion Law Reports until 1965.) See also: W. R. Lederman, "Legislative Power to Create Corporate Bodies and Public Monopolies in Canada," *op. cit.*

power, where it exists, may be broadly used in a way that would put the federal company out of business in that province. If the provincial legislature decides that the way to regulate automobile insurance in the public interest is to give a complete monopoly of the business to a provincial Crown corporation that it creates for this purpose, then it may do so. This does put all other legal persons in the field out of business in the province. The federal company is not being discriminated against in these circumstances. Provincial companies, British companies, foreign companies and unincorporated partnerships are all getting the same negative treatment. This is precisely what was done some years ago in Saskatchewan and recently in Manitoba in the field of automobile insurance. The constitutional law does not permit a federal company to hold out in these circumstances, *just because it is a federal company*. Likewise, in a field of business or industry exclusively within federal jurisdiction, the federal parliament may go all the way to a single public monopoly in the hands of a federal Crown corporation or a federal government department, and thus put some provincial corporations out of business. I should stress that I am not here assessing the economic or social merits of any particular public monopoly. Rather, I am making essential general points about the nature of federalism and federal constitutional law. I am simply saying now that one such general point is this; if one of the supreme democratic legislative bodies in a federal country decides some sort of public monopoly to be necessary, or desirable, in the public interest in a field of business or industry exclusively within the jurisdiction of that legislative body, then it has the power to institute these arrangements by appropriate legislation.[16] To illustrate this I used the extreme example of a single public monopoly in the hands of a Crown corporation or government department. Lesser examples may be given of valid overriding uses of functional regulatory power, that regulate by restricting rights or capacities of legal persons or by excluding some legal persons altogether. Monopoly may be granted to an investor-owned company in a given territorial area (a so-called ''chosen instrument''), usually subject to some regulation by a governmental public utilities board as to what the company may charge the public for its services. Or, at least at the federal level, a particular federal business may be divided up between two or more chosen instruments.[17] One example is the division of the aircraft transportation business between Air Canada, Canadian Pacific Airlines and several major regional airlines. Another example is afforded by the federal Bank Act, already mentioned, which restricts the grant of a general charter for banking to federal investor-owned corporate bodies, and then only to those of them that meet certain stringent conditions to the satisfaction of the Parliament of Canada, which will then amend the federal Bank Act to incorporate them. Thus functional regulation of a particular business may take the form of the regulatory governmental authority excluding all legal persons

---

[16]*Ibid.*

[17]My doubts about power at the provincial level here are these. In a field where functional regulation is itself not exclusively provincial but is partly federal and partly provincial, or where federal and provincial powers are concurrent with federal paramountcy, then I doubt that a provincial legislature could put a federal company out of business, even in aid of a non-discriminatory provincial scheme of public monopoly.

completely from that business, except for one corporation or a limited number of corporations that are approved by the regulatory governmental authority as the only operational legal persons to be allowed in the field.

The other general point to be made is this. However complex the foregoing may sound, the overriding constitutional priority described in favour of the efficacy of the functional power to regulate is absolutely essential if we are to have federalism at all. The B.N.A. Act divides powers functionally over various types of businesses and industries, without reference to the kinds of legal persons who may be involved. If this functional allocation of powers to regulate is to mean anything, it must override the power to incorporate in the event of conflict or apparent conflict. The alternative is impossible in the context of federalism, as shown by the following example. When a province incorporates a company and in the process specifies that it has capacity as a corporate body to broadcast radio programs through the air, then if we go on and say that the provincial company may therefore proceed to broadcast freely in defiance of federal laws that forbid this, or at least impose stringent conditions on broadcasting, *and all this because of the provincial incorporation*, then we have nullified the constitutional grant of functional power over radio broadcasting to the federal parliament. Likewise, any other functional federal regulatory field could be invaded as well by a province which simply recited appropriate capacities for one of its own companies. The converse is also true. If the federal government could invade the provincial functional power to regulate the mining industry in the province by simply incorporating a federal mining company which could then push aside provincial mining laws by virtue of its federal incorporation as a mining company, then the provincial powers over mining would be effectively nullified. It is obvious that such priority for the power of incorporation, or, in other words, such as extended meaning in constitutional law for the word "incorporation," would result in chaos and the end of federalism.[18]

Accordingly, the correct constitutional doctrine may be put in general terms as follows. When, as between the federal and provincial levels of government, one government incorporates a company with powers to engage in a particular type of business, but that type of business is functionally within the exclusive jurisdiction of the other level of government, then the grant of corporate capacity by the incorporating government is the grant of a contingent potential only. It is a

---

[18]There are other examples of this necessity to limit the power-conferring meaning of the competing general phrases in sections 91 and 92 of the B.N.A. Act. For instance, it has been held in the courts that the federal parliament cannot gain jurisdiction over provincial commercial matters by sprinkling a general federal commercial statute with a few offences and penalties, then on that account claiming the statute to be valid as federal criminal law. *In re The Board of Commerce Act and The Combines and Fair Prices Act, 1919* (1920) 54 D.L.R. 354 (S.C. of Canada.)

Likewise, to put the shoe on the other foot, the courts have held that a province cannot, in the name of its property power, control every activity that takes place on private or public land or in buildings affixed to the land. Such an extended meaning for "property" would entirely eliminate federal authority, except in remote air space. Hence, when the Quebec Government claimed that its *Padlock Act* was property legislation, the statute was held to be invalid because, in substance, its main feature was an attempt to enlarge the definitions of treason and sedition, matters properly and exclusively within the federal criminal law power as historic crimes. *Switzman v. Elbling and A.-G. of Quebec* (1957), 7 D.L.R. (2d) 337 (S.C. of Canada).

grant of a capacity that is always completely conditional on the extent to which the other government will permit it to be used by virtue of that other government's exclusive functional regulatory power over the type of business concerned. The other government may permit all legal persons of all types to operate, in which event the company could use its capacity. But the other government, as a functional matter, might forbid operations by some corporations or types of corporations, as we have seen, in which event the relevant capacities of these corporations would be completely non-operational no matter who incorporated them.

In terms of conventional constitutional doctrines for interpretation of the B.N.A. Act, what we have here is an example of the rule of mutual modification.[19] When essentially parallel powers of incorporation coexist in the same federal constitution with divided functional powers to regulate this or that business or industry, then the juridical concepts of "incorporation" and "functional regulation" should be mutually modified in their respective definitions so that, as far as possible, each can serve its purpose as a power-conferring concept without frustrating the power conferred by the other. These concepts occur expressly or by necessary implication in the same constitutional document, so they are context one for the other, and context always has a contribution to make to meaning. As we have seen, there is nothing in the juridical concept of incorporation that warrants giving the legislative power of incorporation priority over the legislative power of functional regulation of this or that type of business or industry as such, in a federal context. The power of incorporation can serve its function well enough if the incorporating government is limited to creating corporate legal persons with capacities that are contingent and conditional only in the face of the functional regulatory power of the other level of government in the federation. The natural legal person, the human adult individual, is in precisely this same position. Why should a corporate legal person be in any better position? Why should the artificial legal person do better than the natural legal person?

This is quite fundamental, and so perhaps will bear some restatement for the sake of further clarity and emphasis. As we have seen, it would be intolerable to extend the meaning of "incorporation" in the B.N.A. Act to embrace a power in the incorporating government to *guarantee* that any capacity given by it would be operational and could be used in any and all circumstances. This would permit nullification and destruction of functional regulatory powers in either the federal or the provincial lists of powers. Thus we find that the meaning of "incorporation" as a power-conferring phrase in the B.N.A. Act is confined to the creation of corporate bodies with capacities that are conditional or contingent only when, in matters to which the capacities relate, functional regulatory power rests exclusively with the other level of government in our federal system. The other side of this coin is that the government having the functional regulatory power over a particular type of business may indeed deal with the capacities of all types of legal persons in relation to engaging in that type of business. Otherwise, the power of functional regulation would be largely, if not entirely, ineffective. In

---

[19]The *Parsons case, op. cit.,* 108-110.

this way, interpretation safeguards the essentials of functional powers of regula-tion, since the British North America Act obviously manifests an intention that such powers should be meaningful and effective. Notice that the power of incor-poration does not suffer by this limitation of the meaning of "incorporation" to the conferring of conditional or contingent capacities in the sense explained. The incorporating government under this defintiion is able to put its corporation in as good a position as the natural legal person, the adult human individual, and this surely is the outside limit of what the concept of incorporation should mean so far as capacities or powers are concerned.

● ● ●

FURTHER REFERENCES

There is support for the position taken in the essay given in the previous part in a recent Supreme Court of Canada decision: *Canadian Indemnity Co. v. A.-G. B.C.*, [1976] 5 W.W.R. 748.

Chapter 19

Legislative Power to Implement Treaty Obligations in Canada

Reprinted with permission from *The Political Process in Canada*, J. A. Aitchison ed. (Toronto: University of Toronto Press, 1963) 171

Principally during the decades from 1920 to 1940, Canada achieved complete independence as an international juristic person. This came about by a legal process of conventional constitutional development which has been well described and documented by the late R. MacGregor Dawson:[1] But not long after Canada had thus taken her separate place in the community of nations, it became quite clear that this was a shrinking world where international obligations were growing rapidly and must continue to grow and multiply. The position now is, quite simply, that there must be a great flowering of international law with its attendant obligations, or the war of atomic fusion and fission will come when nothing much will matter anyway.

Assuming the better alternative, the essential growth of international obligations emphasizes sharply for Canada a problem always inherent in federal constitutions. To what extent, if at all, can a centralized power to perform treaty obligations be permitted to contradict the normal domestic division of legislative powers between the national Parliament on the one hand and the provincial legislatures on the other? In terms of a particular example, the dilemma is this: standards for maximum hours or minimum wages in factories are normally provincial matters within the provincial property and civil rights clause, but if the federal cabinet adheres to an international treaty or convention specifying basic standards in these matters, does the federal Parliament thereby acquire over-riding legislative competence to perform or implement these obligations? Certainly a strong central treaty-performing power seems necessary for proper participation in the life and progress of the international community; yet such power could threaten fields of jurisdiction that are unquestionably provincial ones under the constitutional division of legislative powers within the country. While one may disagree with Lord Atkin's *solution* of the problem, certainly he describes it accurately enough in the following passages from the Labour Conventions Case:[2]

---

[1] R. MacG. Dawson, *The Development of Dominion Status, 1900-1936* (Oxford, 1936).
[2] *A.-G. for Canada and A.-G. for Ontario and Others*, [1937] A.C., 326, 347-8.

It will be essential to keep in mind the distinction between (1.) the formation and (2.) the performance, of the obligations constituted by a treaty, using that word as comprising any agreement between two or more sovereign States. Within the British Empire there is a well-established rule that the making of a treaty is an executive act, while the performance of its obligations, if they entail alteration of the existing domestic law, requires legislative action. Unlike some other countries, the stipulations of a treaty duly ratified do not within the Empire, by virtue of the treaty alone, have the force of law. . . .

Once they are created, while they bind the State as against the other contracting parties, Parliament may refuse to perform them and so leave the State in default. In a unitary State whose Legislature possesses unlimited powers the problem is simple. . . .

But in a State where the Legislature does not possess absolute authority, in a federal State where legislative authority is limited by a constitutional document, or is divided up between different Legislatures in accordance with the classes of subject-matter submitted for legislation, the problem is complex. The obligations imposed by treaty may have to be performed, if at all, by several Legislatures; and the executive have the task of obtaining the legislative assent not of the one Parliament to whom they may be responsible, but possibly of several Parliaments to whom they stand in no direct relation.

The power to contract international obligations on all subjects now rests with the federal government, the Governor General in Council.[3] But the constitutional position in Canada as to legislative performance of treaty obligations thus assumed is uncertain. This obscurity is relatively new because the issue for the older type of Empire treaties is specifically settled by section 132 of the British North America Act.[4]

The Parliament and Government of Canada shall have all Powers necessary or proper for performing the obligations of Canada or of any Province thereof, as Part of the British Empire, towards Foreign Countries arising under Treaties between the Empire and such Foreign Countries.

Thus those who drafted the B.N.A. Act of 1867 did intend the Parliament of Canada to have plenary treaty-performing power respecting the only type of treaty in contemplation at the time, treaties affecting Canada concluded in the name of the Crown on the advice of the United Kingdom cabinet or ministers. But after the development of Canada's international independence, the courts construed section 132 strictly as reaching only the now obsolete Empire treaty, so that in this literal sense the section is largely spent. Nevertheless, it still has some indirect significance in the present situation. It does show that some sort of a central treaty-performing power was intended.

And what is the present situation? Uncertainty about the situs of power to

---

[3]There seems little doubt now that this is the position respecting the power of the federal executive. Though Lord Atkin did say in the Labour Conventions Case that he was not deciding the point, nevertheless he seemed to assume this result in favour of the federal executive. The case for the federal executive in this respect is made (in my view conclusively) by G. J. Szablowski, "Creation and Implementation of Treaties in Canada," (1956) 34 *Can. Bar Rev.*, 28, at 30-5.

[4]30 and 31 Victoria (Imp.), c. 3.

perform treaty obligations now obtains because two Privy Council judgments of equal authority contradict one another, taking respectively the two opposite and extreme positions that are possible in the circumstances. It is true that the Supreme Court of Canada now has the last word on the meaning to be given to the B.N.A. Act, but that tribunal has not yet been called upon to speak with clarity and finality on the treaty issue. The Supreme Court of Canada naturally strives to pay proper regard to Judicial Committee precedents, but when it does come to deal with the treaty-performing power the Court will face the contradictions mentioned, which we shall now examine.

On the one hand, the Radio Case of 1932,[5] speaking of the new Canadian independent international obligations, holds that the treaty-performing power of the Federal Parliament is still plenary. In other words, the decision was that assumption of an international obligation by the federal government thereby confers on the federal Parliament legislative power to perform that obligation so far as domestic legislation is necessary to that end. This is so even though the subject of the treaty obligation is one that, in the absence of a treaty, would be exclusively within provincial legislative jurisdiction under section 92 of the B.N.A. Act. On this view in the latter event the coming into existence of the treaty obligation in itself makes all the difference. The International Radiotelegraph Convention, 1927, was the international agreement in question in the Radio Case and had been separately concluded by Canada. After insisting that there was still a single treaty-performing power, Viscount Dunedin continued as follows.[6]

> Canada as a Dominion is one of the signatories to the convention. In a question with foreign powers the persons who might infringe some of the stipulations in the convention would not be the Dominion of Canada as a whole but would be individual persons residing in Canada. These persons must so to speak be kept in order by legislation and the only legislation that can deal with them all at once is Dominion legislation. This idea of Canada as a Dominion being bound by a convention equivalent to a treaty with foreign powers was quite unthought of in 1867. It is the outcome of the gradual development of the position of Canada vis-à-vis to the mother country, Great Britain, which is found in these later days expressed in the Statute of Westminster. It is not, therefore, to be expected that such a matter should be dealt with in explicit words in either s. 91 or s. 92. The only class of treaty which would bind Canada was thought of as a treaty by Great Britain, and that was provided for by s. 132. Being, therefore, not mentioned explicitly in either s. 91 or s. 92, such legislation falls within the general words at the opening of s. 91 which assign to the Government of the Dominion the power to make laws "for the peace order and good government of Canada in relation to all matters not coming within the classes of subjects by this Act assigned exclusively to the legislatures of the Provinces." In fine, though agreeing that the Convention was not such a treaty as is defined in s. 132, *their Lordships think that it comes to the same thing.*

In spite of this, the opposite position was taken in the Labour Conventions Case of 1937.[7] The conventions of the International Labour Organization in

---

[5] In re *Regulation and Control of Radio Communication in Canada*, [1932] A.C., 304.
[6] [1932] A.C., 312, (Italics added.)
[7] [1937] A.C., 326.

question were also of the new type of independently assumed Canadian international obligations. An attempt to implement them had been made by general maximum hour and minimum wage legislation of the federal Parliament. Lord Atkin in his reasons for judgment denied that, beyond the strict confines of section 132, there was a single treaty-performing power on all subjects to be found in the B.N.A. Act, and held the statutes in question to be *ultra vires* of the federal Parliament.[8]

> For the purposes of sections 91 and 92, i.e., the distribution of legislative powers between the Dominion and the Provinces, there is no such thing as treaty legislation as such. The distribution is based on classes of subjects; and as a treaty deals with a particular class of subjects so will the legislative power of performing it be ascertained. No one can doubt that this distribution is one of the most essential conditions, probably the most essential condition, in the inter-provincial compact to which the British North America Act gives effect.
>
> It follows from what has been said that no further legislative competence is obtained by the Dominion from its accession to inter-national status, and the consequent increase in the scope of its executive functions. It is true, as pointed out in the judgment of the Chief Justice, that as the executive is now clothed with the powers of making treaties so the Parliament of Canada, to which the executive is responsible, has imposed upon it responsibilities in connection with such treaties, for if it were to disapprove of them they would either not be made or the Ministers would meet their constitutional fate. But this is true of all executive functions in their relation to Parliament. There is no existing constitutional ground for stretching the competence of the Dominion Parliament so that it becomes enlarged to keep pace with enlarged functions of the Dominion executive. If the new functions affect the classes of subjects enumerated in s. 92 legislation to support the new functions is in the competence of the Provincial Legislatures only. If they do not, the competence of the Dominion Legislature is declared by s. 91 and existed ab origine. In other words, the Dominion cannot, merely by making promises to foreign countries, clothe itself with legislative authority inconsistent with the constitution which gave it birth.
>
> It must not be thought that the result of this decision is that Canada is incompetent to legislate in performance of treaty obligations. In totality of legislative powers, Dominion and Provincial together, she is fully equipped. But the legislative powers remain distributed, and if in the exercise of her new functions derived from her new international status Canada incurs obligations they must, so far as legislation be concerned, when they deal with Provincial classes of subjects, be dealt with by the totality of powers, in other words by co-operation between the Dominion and the Provinces. While the ship of state now sails on larger ventures and into foreign waters she still retains the water-tight compartments which are an essential part of her original structure.

The two extreme positions are then plain enough. In 1932 Viscount Dunedin said that the making of a treaty conferred in full the relevant legislative treaty-performing powers on the federal Parliament. In 1937 Lord Atkin said that the making of a treaty could add nothing at all to the legislative powers of the federal Parliament. It is true that Lord Atkin purported to distinguish the Radio

---

[8][1937] A.C., 351-4.

Case. He dismissed the remarks of Viscount Dunedin on the treaty-performing power as *obiter dicta* and said that the one true reason of that decision was the finding that regulation of radio communication was within the federal legislative powers anyway even if there were no treaty. But this is simply not a legitimate interpretation of Viscount Dunedin's reasons for judgment. If one reads what Viscount Dunedin said, obviously he was resting his decision on both grounds: *(a)* that the general power of section 91 gave full legislative jurisdiction to the federal Parliament to perform treaties on any subject; and *(b)* that radio communication was under federal jurisdiction anyway in the absence of a treaty because radio was a connecting undertaking under section 92(10) (a) of the B.N.A. Act. As Lord Chancellor Simonds remarked in a leading case in the House of Lords:[9]

> There is . . . no justification for regarding as obiter dictum a reason given by a judge for his decision, because he has given another reason also. If it were a proper test to ask whether the decision would have been the same apart from the proposition alleged to be obiter, then a case which ex facie decided two things would decide nothing. . . .
>
> If a judge states two grounds for his judgment and bases his decision on both, neither of those grounds is a dictum.

So the Radio Case cannot be dismissed as Lord Atkin purports to dismiss it. The Radio Case speaks for itself as a precedent to the Supreme Court of Canada in the words of Viscount Dunedin. As such it is in direct conflict with Lord Atkin's reasons for decision in the Labour Conventions Case. Two inconsistent propositions may both be wrong, but they cannot both be right. Meanwhile, neither of these cases stands ahead of or above the other as a precedent for the Supreme Court of Canada. In the circumstances, the Supreme Court is free as a matter of the principles of precedent to overrule one of these cases and follow the other, or, indeed, the Court is free to strike out on a new line that is not complete approval or disapproval of either of the extreme positions involved.

Certainly, it would seem that the extreme position of the Labour Conventions Case will have to be modified substantially if Canada is to be able to proceed with confidence in the international sphere. Fortunately, there are some signs that this will occur. Lord Wright, who was one of the five judges on the Privy Council Board for the Labour Conventions Case, has made it clear since that he dissented and in fact agrees with the doctrine of the Radio Case.[10] Also, in *Francis v. The Queen* in 1956,[11] Chief Justic Kerwin in the Supreme Court of Canada said that the Labour Conventions Case might well have to be reconsidered. But the most important development of recent years has been the case of *Johanneson v. Rural Municipality West Saint Paul* in the Supreme Court of Canada in 1952,[12] in which the matter of international obligations in aerial naviga-

---

[9]*Jacobs v. London County Council*, [1950] A.C., 361, 369-70.
[10]See Lord Wright's obituary tribute to Chief Justice Sir Lyman Diff (1955), 33 *Can. Bar Rev.*, 1123 at 1126-8.
[11][1956] S.C.R. 618, 621.
[12][1952] 1 S.C.R., 292.

tion came up for a second time. In the earlier Aeronautics Case of 1932,[13] Section 132 of the B.N.A. Act was decisive because an Empire treaty of 1919 was involved. But in the Johanneson Case the Chicago Convention on International Civil Aviation was the international agreement in issue, and of course to this convention Canada had adhered separately and independently. In the Johanneson Case the justices of the Supreme Court of Canada all agreed that aviation fell under the federal general power, treaty or no treaty, and hence there was no doubt of the power of the federal Parliament to perform the obligations of the convention. But also the statements of Lord Sankey in the first Aeronautics Case and of Viscount Dunedin in the Radio Case about the scope of the treaty-performing power gained some approval as alternate reasons for decision. Chief Justice Rinfret explicitly approved and followed the Radio Case:[14]

> [T]he convention on International Civil Aviation, signed at Chicago on December 7, 1944, has since become effective; and what was said in the *Radio Reference* by Viscount Dunedin . . . applies here, although the convention might not be looked upon as a treaty under s. 132 of the British North America Act, "it comes to the same thing."

Also, Justices Estey and Locke[15] approved the similar statement by Lord Sankey in the Aeronautics Case of 1932.

> Further, their Lordships are influenced by the facts that the subject of aerial navigation and fulfilment of Canadian obligations under s. 132 are matters of national interest and importance; and that aerial navigation is a class of subject which has attained such dimensions as to affect the body politic of the Dominion.

Mr. Justice Kerwin (now the Chief Justice) did not commit himself on the treaty-performing power as such, but he did uphold the jurisdiction of the federal Parliament over aviation by virtue of the general power in section 91, saying that aerial navigation was a matter of national dimensions and that *the terms of the Chicago Convention were evidence of this national character*.[16]

Now, in accepting as he does the terms and nature of an international agreement as some evidence of the national dimensions within Canada of the matter dealt with, Chief Justice Kerwin modified one of the worst features of the Labour Conventions Case—the part where Lord Atkin had made it painfully clear that he considered the existence of an international obligation to be completely irrelevant to issues of the distribution of legislative power within Canada. Lord Atkin said such power remains distributed in the presence of a treaty exactly as if there were no treaty at all. This plainly means that the distribution of legislative powers is to be determined by domestic considerations within the country, and that the existence or nature of a relevant international obligation means nothing even though the issue is how to perform that obligation within Canada.

At least Chief Justice Kerwin's remark suggests a new line of reasoning. If

---

[13]In *re The Regulation and Control of Aeronautics in Canada*, [1937] A.C., 54.
[14][1952] 1 S.C.R. at 303.
[15][1952]1 S.C.R. at 317 and 328.
[16][1952] 1 S.C.R. at 308.

the existence and nature of international obligations can be factors in invoking the federal general power, then we have indeed moved away from the extreme position taken by Lord Atkin. On this new line of reasoning, some international obligations of Canada could be of such character as to confer on the matters with which they were concerned national dimensions and national importance within Canada sufficient to invoke the federal general power. It is possible to maintain that some international obligations would have this effect without insisting with the Radio Case that all international obligations must have this effect. There are many types of international obligations, with endless variety of subject-matters. Moreover, power gained in this way by the federal Parliament would be concurrent with provincial power and not exclusive of it except in the event of inconsistency between the federal and provincial statutes concerned. The governing definition of the federal general power is now that of Viscount Simon in the Canada Temperance Act Case of 1946.[17]

> [T]he true test must be found in the real subject-matter of the legislation: if it is such that it goes beyond local or provincial concern or interests and must from its inherent nature be the concern of the Dominion as a whole . . . then it will fall within the competence of the Dominion Parliament as a matter affecting the peace, order and good government of Canada, though it may in another aspect touch on matters specially reserved to the provincial legislatures. . . .
>
> Nor is the validity of the legislation, when due to its inherent nature, affected because there may still be room for enactments by a provincial legislature dealing with an aspect of the same subject in so far as it specially affects that province.

No doubt this suggested use of the federal general power means going a long way towards the doctrine of the Radio Case, but it does not go all the way. To repeat, the latter doctrine was that the mere existence of an international obligation—any obligation on any subject—automatically invoked the federal general power in favour of the national Parliament. What I am now suggesting is that the federal general power is to be used somewhat selectively in this regard—that it would in many matters domestically provincial confer treaty-performing powers on the federal Parliament, but that this result would not follow in every case. It would not follow respecting certain matters of fundamental significance for provincial autonomy even though a relevant international obligation was in existence. The range and variety of international obligations is actually and potentially very great: why should all of them without discrimination be permitted the same impact on the federal constitution of Canada?

The need for some reservations in this regard can perhaps be demonstrated by reference to the Universal Declaration of Human Rights and Fundamental Freedoms of the United Nations.[18] Some jurists have complained that the present uncertainties about federal treaty-performing power have prevented Canada from supporting and adopting the Universal Declaration, and that this is a bad thing. But the thirty articles of the Declaration contain very general standards and re-

---

[17]*A.-G. for Ontario and Others and Canada Temperance Federation and Others*, [1946] A.C., 193, 205-6.

[18]A convenient source of the text is (1949), 27 *Can. Bar Rev.*, 203-10.

quirements that touch in one way or another every part of the total legal system of a modern country. If ratification of these thirty articles *ipso facto* conferred relevant and paramount legislative power on the federal Parliament, this would simply be the end of Canadian federalism. For instance, Article 26 speaks as follows of education:

> Everyone has the right to education. Education shall be free, at least in the elementary and fundamental stages. Elementary education shall be compulsory. Technical and professional education shall be made generally available and higher education shall be equally accessible to all on the basis of merit.

Here, the unlimited doctrine of the Radio Case coupled with Article 26 would mean that the federal Parliament could take over virtually the whole field of education. Similarly, Article 23 declares the right to work, the right to reasonable remuneration, and the right to form and join trade unions. An unlimited federal treaty-performing power for Article 23 would mean that the national Parliament could engage in regulation of local industries in the provinces and the regulation of the labour relations of local industries. And Article 21 calls for representative government, universal and equal suffrage, free voting procedures, and so on. Would satisfaction of this article mean that the federal Parliament could make the electoral laws for provincial legislatures? It would seem so. Hence the need for reservations respecting the scope of the federal treaty-performing power is apparent. If national federalsim is to continue, there must be certain fundamental matters in respect of which provincial autonomy is more important to Canada than is a national power to perform international obligations concerned with such matters.

The theme of this essay now emerges—that we should not accept the doctrine of the Labour Conventions Case or that of the Radio Case either. The former limits too severely our participation in the growing international community, but the latter could and quite possibly would eliminate the essential autonomy of the provinces and thus end the federal constitution. If we turn to the revived general power of the federal Parliament as defined by Viscount Simon in the passage quoted earlier, we have the means to test actual and prospective international obligations one by one on their respective merits for genuine and important national aspects in addition to the provincial aspects that would be the primary and exclusive ones in the absence of a treaty. In these circumstances, when a federal treaty-performing power was found in a particular matter, such federal power would not be exclusive but would be concurrent with the provincial power. The federal legislation thus authorized would be strictly limited to that necessary to implement the treaty obligation, and other aspects of the subject matter concerned would remain within provincial jurisdiction. The federal statute would override in the event of conflict with provincial legislation, but only in that event. This, of course, is the normal doctrine of Dominion paramountcy in a concurrent field.

One must admit that the distinction called for here between two classes of provincial matters, those that are fundamental and those that are less basic in character, is a difficult one to make. But at many other points in our federal system we have to make like distinctions and compromises, so this should not sur-prise us in the field of treaty performance. Anyway, under our system of judicial review, the Supreme Court of Canada can supply authoritative answers in re-sponse to appropriate references. Important international obligations, particu-larly multilateral treaties and conventions, take much time to negotiate, so that it would be quite practical to get specific opinions on prospective treaty terms from the Supreme Court. In most cases the Supreme Court would probably uphold federal treaty-performing power. After all, national states are jealous of the scope of their independent sovereign powers, and assumption of international ob-ligations means acceptance of limitations on those powers. Thus neither Canada nor any other state is likely to enter international agreements unless under the pressure of very real social, economic, political or military necessity for limita-tions on national sovereignty, such limitations taking the form of uniform inter-national rules in the matter concerned. These same real factors of pressure and necessity would usually establish the high degree of need for uniform action within Canada that would call for the operation of the federal general power. Nevertheless, it should not be automatically assumed that this would always be so, as in the doctrine of the Radio Case.

In summary then, what is the whole picture of the legislative treaty-per-forming power in Canada on the basis of the foregoing reasoning? First, if the subject matter of a treaty is something that falls exclusively or concurrently within federal jurisdiction under section 91[19] in any event—even in the absence of a treaty—there is no problem. The national Parliament then has full treaty-implementing power, and, indeed, is not confined to legislation strictly relevant to the treaty terms. The federal defence power and trade and commerce power are obviously of great importance here, to take but two examples. Secondly, if the subject matter of the treaty is something that falls exclusively within provin-cial jurisdiction in the absence of a treaty, then the creation of a treaty obligation on that subject likely would invest the matter with a federal aspect under the fed-eral general power concurrent with the original provincial aspect. In this event, the national Parliament would acquire relevant treaty-performing power, but power that could only be used to the extent specifically necessary to implement treaty terms. Other aspects of the matter would remain exclusively within provin-dial jurisdiction. In other words, in this situation, the extent of the federal treaty-performing power would be strictly limited by the scope of the treaty terms. Fi-nally, if the subject-matter of the treaty is something that falls exclusively within provincial jurisdiction in the absence of a treaty and, moreover, is something quite fundamental for provincial autonomy, then the conditions for invoking the federal general power are not met and, in Lord Atkin's phrase, legislative powers remain distributed. In this event—but only in this event—it would be essential to be assured of the necessary provincial legislation before making a treaty on such a subject matter.

---

[19]Or another section of the B.N.A. Act conferring relevant power on the federal Parliament, e.g., section 95.

Chapter 20

Comments on Co-operative Federalism and Financial Responsibility in Canada

Reprinted with permission from *Report of Proceedings of the Twenty-First Tax Conference* (Toronto: Canadian Tax Foundation, Toronto, 1969) 4

The problems of today in the realm of federal-provincial finance in Canada require one to examine both sides of the coin, the revenue side and the expenditure side. Obviously my remarks will be rather cursory, and also it is true that this session is primarily to be concentrated on governmental expenditures. But I have found it impossible to separate the two things in making some comments on significant points in the constitutional background. This is why I use the general term ''Financial Responsibility'' in the title of my paper, which is ''Comments on Co-operative Federalism and Financial Responsibility in Canada'', intending it to embrace both issues of the use governments make of their respective taxing powers and of the nature of the expenditures which they find it necessary or desirable to undertake.

The older nineteenth century conception of federalism was that, so far as powers and responsibilities were concerned, the respective lists of federal and provincial subjects could be mutually exclusive—in Lord Atkin's notorious phrase, that the compartments could be, and were on the whole, water-tight. Thus the federal government on the one hand and the provincial governments on the other could go their own respective ways, having little influence on or involvement with each other. True enough, it was recognized in the B.N.A. Act itself in 1867 that revenues could not be precisely matched to responsibilities, and that unconditional subsidies out of the revenues from federal taxation were necessary if the provinces, even then, were to meet their responsibilities. I will refer again to the significance of this shortly, but in 1867 it was thought that the simple system of subsidies then enacted would take care of the problem once and for all. I believe changes in dominion-provincial financial arrangements after that started in 1868 and have occurred regularly and with increasing frequency ever since. This has taken place, in this present century, under the pressure of the development in Canada of a modern, highly industrialized, highly urban, pluralistic welfare state. The positive state of today simply cannot be made to fit the old nineteenth century classical form. Professor R. L. Watts in his recent book on

New Federations[1] describes succinctly what has happened generally, and the words fit Canada very well. He remarks that it was considered traditional in the theory of true dual federalism to require

> that the general and regional governments be independent of each other, operating in separate and distinct spheres.

Then he continues:

> This conclusion rested on the assumption that the dependence of one level of government upon another would in effect mean subordination, and thus a violation of the federal principle. As long as the dependence of one government upon another is one-sided this presupposition is valid enough. If, however, both levels of government are dependent upon each other—interdependent—then dependence does not necessarily imply the subordination of one to the other. In such a case, where each level is to some degree dependent on the other, there would be a balance of power between general and regional governments. Thus, neither tier of government would be independent, but the authority of neither would be subordinate. This in fact is the contemporary situation in the older federations. The regional governments have become increasingly dependent upon the central governments for their finances, and the central governments have had to rely more and more on the administrative co-operation of the regional governments for the implementation of national policies. The activities of central governments have expanded dramatically, but so also have those of regional governments. The difference between the two versions of the federal concept is chiefly one of emphasis: "dual federalism" views the two sets of governments primarily as equal rivals, "co-operative federalism" views them as equal partners. What lies at the root of both theories is the premise that in a federation neither level of government is subordinate to the other.
>
> By the federal concept then I mean the principle of organization whereby a compromise is achieved between concurrent demands for union and for territorial diversity within a society, by the establishment of a single political system, within which, general and regional governments are assigned co-ordinate authority such that neither level of government is legally or politically subordinate to the other.

Partnership is the key word in the passage just quoted, and basically expresses what I mean by co-operative federalism. Each level of government, federal and provincial, has its own autonomous base of certain definite powers and resources; but what each does, or fails to do, with its respective powers and resources often vitally affects the other. Hence we have seen in Canada an ever-increasing necessity for agreements or understandings between the federal government and provincial governments concerning specified uses of their respective powers and resources on many matters. I believe in the future of Canada as a truly federal state, I believe our political leaders can ensure a great future for Canada as a federal state, but they will have to work at it in a spirit of partnership and co-operation—indeed, we will all have to work at it in this spirit. One of the things we must work at of course is better recognition of the historical "French Fact" in our politics, culture and institutions. Personally, I accept the principal

---

[1]R. L. Watts, *New Federations: Experiments in the Commonwealth.* Oxford: Oxford University Press (1966) 13.

recommendations of the first volume of the Report of the Royal Commission on Bilingualism and Biculturism in this regard. But, important though that is, this morning we are concerned with the economic aspect of the problems of Canadian federalism, so I wish to speak of two of the objects of Confederation in this field that are of very great importance and that bear upon the topic of the present session: "Government Expenditure: Planning and Control".

I. ECONOMIC OBJECTIVES OF CONFEDERATION

I would describe these two economic objectives as follows.

1. That Canada should form one free trading and commercial area where people, capital, services and commodities are free to move anywhere in the country without impediment or inhibition because of provincial boundaries.

2. That economic disparities between the different provinces and regions of Canada should be eliminated, or at least reduced, so that a decent basic minimum of income level, social services and welfare is available in all provinces and regions.

The first of these objects, the free trade area, might be described as an original object of Confederation. It was given some expression in section 121 of the B.N.A. Act.

All Articles of the Growth, Produce or Manufacture of any one of the Provinces shall, from and after the Union, be admitted free into each of the other Provinces.

This provision speaks only for commodities, and not of people, capital and services. Nevertheless its implications are clear.

The second object developed primarily in this century as a firm and growing expectation of the people. I refer to the idea that there should be, when needed, governmental action to ensure a basic and decent minimum of economic well-being in all parts of Canada, in other words that the state should concern itself positively with the measures necessary to bring this about. At the Confederation for Tomorrow Conference a year ago, and again at the federal-provincial conference in February of this year, the premiers of the Atlantic Provinces made it abundantly clear that the seriously unfavourable economic disparity suffered by the Atlantic Provinces is as great a threat to continuing Canadian federalism as would be any failure to afford proper recognition to the "French Fact" in Canadian federalism.

Now these two economic objectives of Confederation are still valid—the older one and the newer one. So, the question becomes, how are these objects served now by our present system of revenues and expenditures in Canada? Should there be, or can there be, changes that would improve matters?

Incidentally, you may have noticed that the two economic objects of Confederation are not necessarily in complete harmony—they do in fact conflict to some extent, so that our revenue and expenditure arrangements are always going to have to seek compromises or alternatives that serve one objective without at the same time seriously prejudicing the other.

II. TAXING AND SPENDING POWERS

I will now attempt to state my main position quite briefly, first negatively and then positively.

On the negative side, I point out that never in our history as a federation has it been considered possible to match exclusive possession of tax fields exactly to the respective lists of federal and provincial powers and spending responsibilities. This has never been deemed compatible with our objectives as a federation and moreover has never been the state of our constitutional law on the subject. If this was true on the merits and in law among the relative simplicities of the nineteenth century in British North America, how very much more true it is in the exceedingly complex society we have today. What I am saying is that the provinces can never be given exclusive possession and control of tax sources or tax fields the revenue from which would alone be sufficient to carry the full costs of their great and growing spending responsibilities, for example in such areas as education and urban renewal. Because of the need to serve the two overriding national economic objectives I have mentioned, federal taxation and federal revenues will always have to be sufficient to yield total revenues covering major transfer payments to the provinces as well as the direct cost of the specific federal responsibilities listed in the constitution.

This federal power is the positive side of the picture. The federal Parliament and government alone have the capacity to raise the necessary total revenues compatibly with the economic objectives of Confederation, and some of these revenues the federal authorities must share with the provinces in an appropriate mixture of unconditional and conditional grants to them. Of course the provinces can raise some of the money they need by their own independent taxes, but they can never raise all of it that way compatibly with the economic objectives of Confederation. Moreover, in this regard a modern government must now intervene to promote a stable economy and continuing prosperity with instruments of fiscal or financial control, which include the systems of taxation in force in the country as a whole. Here again, in Canada, the principal responsibility falls on the federal government. Only the federal Parliament and government are in a position to act effectively for all parts of the country in this respect. There should indeed be consultation with the provinces on a continuing basis, particularly as they are sharing in the revenues yielded by the federal taxation systems. Nevertheless, the primary responsibility is that of the federal authorities.

It is time now to ask just what is the constitutional position respecting taxation on the one hand and spending power on the other in the Canadian federation. Professor Frank R. Scott has outlined the position on taxation and borrowing very clearly[2] and I agree with what he says.

> Leaving aside minor variations, the principal ideas in the B.N.A. Act regarding the financial powers and the fiscal relations of the federal and provincial governments may be stated simply. The Parliament of Canada may adopt any mode or system of taxation it chooses, be it direct or indirect, progressive or regressive, fair or discri-

---

[2]F. R. Scott, "The Constitutional Background of Taxation Agreements", 2 *McGill Law Journal* (1955-56) 2.

minatory. The provinces are limited to direct taxation within the province in order to the raising of revenue for provincial purposes. Provinces may also gather the royalties and income from the sale and development of their natural resources (s. 109). All provinces were granted subsidies in 1867, at so much per head of population, calculated at an amount enabling provincial budgets to be balanced with the then existing provincial responsibilities. All provincial debts were assumed by Ottawa so that every provincial government started its federal life debt-free. But provinces were given power to borrow on the sole credit of the province (s. 92-3) and no restriction was placed upon the total amount that might be raised in this manner, nor upon the location of the lender. Hence provinces may incur international debts. It was not believed in 1867 that the needs of local government would be great, or that there was any danger of provincial fiscal policies endangering national economic plans. Jurisdiction over credit generally, through banks, currency and the issue of paper money, was in federal hands, along with control of interest. Both Parliament and the legislatures were prohibited from imposing any tax on Crown property (s. 125).

III. A NATIONAL FREE TRADING AREA

The limitation of the provinces to direct taxation is a necessary one in the interests of maintaining Canada as one free trading and commercial area. The point here relates mainly to the possible implications of indirect provincial taxes on commodities or services moving interprovincially. If each province were able to tax local manufacturers or middlemen, and not just final consumers in the province, you would in effect get varying export taxes at provincial boundaries, whereupon the reality of Canada as one free trading market area would go down the drain. On the other hand, federal transaction taxes on manufacturers or middlemen are uniform for the whole country and hence do not impair the reality of the free trading area in commodities. Essentially the same points can be made about interprovincial transactions in services. Moreover, the principle of the much-neglected section 121 of the B.N.A. Act is vital here as an overriding condition that both federal and provincial authorities must observe. Federal taxes of this type must indeed be uniform for the whole country, and provincial retail sales taxes must not discriminate between goods originating in the province concerned and goods coming from another province.

So far as direct taxation is concerned, there is only time to speak of the example afforded by personal and corporation income taxation. Here, too, the preservation of Canada as an effective free trading and commercial area in the sense explained depends on achieving a high degree of uniformity on a country-wide basis. This is a field of concurrent powers under the constitution, so that a great service has been performed for the country by the federal-provincial taxation agreements whereby the federal government operates a uniform system of income taxation over the whole country and shares the harvest or yield in a specified way with the provinces. I realize that the technique of harmonization is somewhat different for Quebec, but nevertheless I believe the main point here stands. In return, the provinces refrain from levying separate taxes of this type— or at least moderate their separate taxes within limits that do not threaten to "balkanize" the internal economy by causing large variations in the cost of doing business in the different provinces. There is some tolerance here for moderate differences. Nevertheless, a federal system of income taxation, having as its territorial base the whole country, can be more effective and more fair than separate provincial taxes. But the constitutional point is that we are dependent here on voluntary intergovernmental agreements—on the partnership principle of co-operative federalism, something we must make every effort to retain and advance.

It is instructive to compare what is happening in this type of matter in the Common Market countries of Western Europe—in the six countries of the European Economic Community. The six countries abolished all internal border tariffs between themselves over a year ago, but of course they discerned early that this would not be enough to ensure the reality of a free trading and commercial area. The six Common Market countries are now engaged in a major effort to accomplish harmonization of their separate taxation systems all along the line, including the taxes that support the level of critical social and welfare services. This is the subject of a remarkable report by experts within the Common Market, the Neumark *Report on Tax Harmonization in the Common Market*. I am not an expert on the European Common Market, but many who are consider that it is doubtful whether the E.E.C. can really succeed under the present institutions provided for it under the Treaty of Rome. The probability is that the E.E.C. can only finally succeed by going all the way to true and full federal institutions including a common democratic parliament for Western Europe with real legislative powers on the matters of common concern among the countries that are or may become members. Such a real parliament is lacking today as the overall political institution that would ensure success.

I find it very strange that Mr. René Lévesque should hold up the European Common Market as an example of the way in which Quebec could separate and yet, by a common market treaty with the rest of Canada, preserve the main economic benefits of Canadian federalism as it is now. To me, the lesson of what is happening in the European Economic Community is precisely the opposite. In the main, the present Canadian federal constitution is the example of what the European Economic Community must achieve if in the end it is to succeed. It cannot stand still, it must eventually move on to a true federalism like ours or slide back to the old European pattern of economic separatism in small units.

IV. REGIONAL ECONOMIC DISPARITIES

I come now to the second of the economic objectives of Confederation—the reduction or elimination of unfavourable economic disparities currently suffered by some of the provinces and regions of Canada. The problems here are very complex in many ways, and I can only comment briefly on one aspect, the provision of public funds to underwrite some of the solutions. In this respect we find that, among other things, we must rely on the federal Parliament and government for major transfer payments to the various provinces. There is in my view no real constitutional inhibition on transfer payments to the provinces, whether they be unconditional or conditional. As indicated earlier, it has been part of the terms of the B.N.A. Act from the beginning that transfer payments were to be made unconditionally out of the harvest of federal taxes to the provinces, to be spent for provincial purposes. So far as conditional grants are concerned, it is true that Lord Atkin vaguely suggested a constitutional limitation in the *Unempolyment Insurance* case, *Attorney-General of Canada v. Attorney-General of Ontario*, [1937] A.C. 355. Perhaps a federal grant to the provinces might have attached to it such detailed, numerous and rigorous conditions that the courts would regard it as an unconstitutional attempt to buy up, so to speak, some specific provincial regulatory power. But this has never been judicially tested, and I agree with Professors Donald Smiley and G. V. La Forest on this point. In excellent publications of the Canadian Tax Foundation[3] they have made it clear that they consider federal conditional grants as we have known them to be fully valid in the constitutional sense. Moreover, I point out that such grants have brought a very valuable element of flexibility to Canadian federalism, because of course there is wide flexibility about designing the terms of the federal-provincial agreements involved.

Finally, there is another reason now for sophisticated federal-provincial financial agreements defining which government is to bear the cost of particular responsibilities. Conditions of modern society are throwing up sweeping new areas of responsibility—vast new problem areas—that call for expensive measures of governmental control. Pollution of air, land and water is one example, urban renewal is another. Also, education is no longer a matter of a few years in primary school, and perhaps secondary school as well, as it was in 1867. In spite of provincial sensitivities, the federal interest in this area is obvious—one need only mention the retraining of workers, the promotion of research in the natural and social sciences and educational television to bring this point home. This is true under the present lists of the respective federal and provincial powers and responsibilities. It would remain true under any new lists we might succeed in drafting in the course of revision of the federal constitution. There will always be sweeping areas of need for integrated governmental action that will overlap the federal and provincial categories of powers and responsibilities. This too calls for federal-provincial agreements where each government agrees to take care of part of the problem, viewed as an integrated whole, and to bear a share of the cost of the total financial burden involved.

---

[3]Donald V. Smiley, *Conditional Grants and Canadian Federalism*. Toronto: Canadian Tax Foundation (1963).

G. V. La Forest, *The Allocation of Taxing Power Under the Canadian Constitution*. Toronto: The Canadian Tax Foundation (1967).

Chapter 21

The Constitution: A Basis for Bargaining

Reprinted with permission from *National Resource Revenues: A Test of Federalism*, Anthony Scott, ed. (Vancouver: University of British Columbia Press, 1976) 52

The right to the revenue from natural resources in Canada clearly involves the federal constitution (the B.N.A. Act) in several important ways. We are a federal country, and so the constitution does have terms that divide and distribute both legislative powers and the ownership of public lands between the provincial and federal levels of government. But automatic and detailed solutions do not emerge by easy logical deduction from the relevant sections of the constitution. Certainly there are several guidelines that do much to shape both the procedure for finding detailed solutions and the nature of the alternative solutions to be expected. In a brief and general way, this is what I shall attempt to explain in what follows.

I have recited the sections of the B.N.A. Act in the Appendix to this paper that deal with the distribution of the ownership of public lands, and the distribution of relevant legislative powers, such as the respective federal and provincial powers of taxation. I will also refer to these sections as part of the text of my discussion of the issues.

The basic point to remember is that any constitution, especially a federal one, is necessarily a complex document. In our federal constitution, each word or phrase used to distribute legislative powers and ownership of public lands to the respective provincial governments and the federal government is in a context of many other such words and phrases. These words are usually words of considerable generality of meaning and overlap one another in their significance. So each must be read in a context that includes the others, and there must be some mutual modification of meanings accordingly. Hence there is a need for sophisticated judicial interpretation of a federal constitution. Judicial review is very important.

I described this process in a previous essay some years ago as follows:

> The federal distribution of legislative powers and responsibilities in Canada is one of the facts of life when we concern ourselves with the many important social, political, economic, or cultural problems of our country. Over the whole range of actual and potential law-making, our constitution distributes powers and responsibilities by two lists of categories or classes—one list for the federal parliament (primarily section 91 of the B.N.A. Act), the other for each of the provincial legis-

latures (primarily section 92 of the B.N.A. Act). For instance, the federal list includes regulation of trade and commerce, criminal law, and a general power to make laws in all matters not assigned to the provinces. Examples from the provincial list are property and civil rights in the province, local works and undertakings, and all matters of a merely local or private nature in the province.

These federal and provincial categories of power are expressed, and indeed have to be expressed, in quite general terms. This permits considerable flexibility in constitutional interpretation, but also it brings much overlapping and potential conflict between the various definitions of powers and responsibilities. To put the same point in another way, our community life—social, economic, political, and cultural—is very complex and will not fit neatly into any scheme of categories or classes without considerable overlap and ambiguity occurring. There are inevitable difficulties arising from this that we must live with so long as we have a federal constitution.

Accordingly the courts must continually assess the competing federal and provincial lists of powers against one another in the judicial task of interpreting the constitution. In the course of judicial decisions on the B.N.A. Act, the judges have basically done one of two things. First, they have attempted to define mutually exclusive spheres for federal and provincial powers, with partial success. But, where mutual exclusion did not seem feasible or proper, the courts have implied the existence of concurrent federal and provincial powers in the overlapping area, with the result that either or both authorities have been permitted to legislate provided their statutes did not in some way conflict one with the other in the common area.[1]

So we have a situation of philosophical competition, so to speak, by the respective federal and provincial words or phrases, to embrace the challenged statute and stamp it as legitimate or valid as an exercise of federal or provincial powers, as the case may be. This means that the federal and provincial words and phrases must be authoritatively construed in relation to one another by the courts, so that there will be the authority of precedent for one of the rational alternatives for reconciling their respective meanings in relation to one another.

Consider, for example, one example of such competition that is very important to the subject of natural resources. I refer to the competition between the federal trade and commerce clause and the provincial property and civil rights clause. As a matter of legal history, a sale of goods is the transfer of property rights to certain commodities from a seller (the owner) to a buyer for a money consideration called the price. The transaction whereby this is accomplished in law is a contract. The right to make contracts and alienate property are classic examples in our legal history of property rights and civil rights. But the competing federal phrase is "trade and commerce." In commodity transactions—tangible movables—where does the one stop and the other start? If you give property and civil rights its fullest possible scope at the expense of the federal trade and commerce power, the latter means virtually nothing. The converse is also true. If every trading and commercial matter from the corner store to General Motors is embraced by the federal trade and commerce clause, there would be little left of the historical commercial meaning of property and civil rights.

---

[1]W. R. Lederman, "The Concurrent Operation of Federal and Provincial Laws in Canada," *McGill Law Journal* 9 (1962-63): 185.

In this respect, the courts reached the following compromise, which still stands as our essential constitutional law on the subject. This is a classic example of the mutual modification of definitions of which I have been speaking. The respective provinces have complete and exclusive jurisdiction over trading and commercial transactions that begin and end within a single province. But where tangible goods cross borders, either provincial or international, exclusive federal jurisdiction attaches to the trading and commercial transactions involved. While there are some qualifications to be added—there are some very limited areas of concurrent jurisdiction—the foregoing describes a main division between exclusive provincial legislative power and exclusive federal legislative power that still stands.

In particular, where marketing of products produced in a province is entirely local to that province, only the provincial legislature has power to enact a compulsory marketing scheme which includes, for example, compulsory price-fixing. On the other hand, where commodities that cross borders or are destined to cross borders are concerned, we are talking of interprovincial or international trade. In this latter event, only the federal parliament can enact mandatory marketing legislation that includes, for example, quotas and price-fixing. For the most part then, the federal parliament does have the power to enact into law national marketing schemes or policies—since most commodities involved do cross provincial or international borders, or would have to do so if their owners permitted them to enter into the marketing process. Nevertheless, I should think that complementary marketing legislation would be necessary, enacted by a province, for marketing that was entirely internal to that province from production to consumption.

I have mentioned the matter of ownership. The general scheme of the B.N.A. Act is that ownership of public lands is vested in the respective provincial governments. Insofar as resources from public lands are involved then, the owner is the province within the borders of which those lands are located. Sections 109 and 117 of the B.N.A. Act are generally to this effect. Until 1930, the situation was different in the provinces of Manitoba, Saskatchewan, and Alberta, and also in the Railway Belt and Peace River Block of British Columbia. But, in 1930, by agreements with these provinces, the federal government transferred the ownership of federal public lands generally to the provinces, so as to put them in the same position as that called for by sections 109 and 117 of the B.N.A. Act of 1867. The agreements were given full constitutional effect by amendments to the B.N.A. Act and other relevant British and Canadian statutes. There was an Act of the British Parliament in 1930 validating these agreements.

In the field of energy—certainly gas and oil, and possibly electricity as well—the ownership of the land is obviously important. Of course, all minerals are involved, and also forest products, in the ownership of land; section 92(5) of the B.N.A. Act makes it clear that the respective provinces have "the Management and Sale of the Public Lands belonging to the Province and of the Timber and Wood thereon." I should think that this means two things of significance for present purposes.

(1) As owner of minerals, for example, that are part of public lands, the province can, simply as owner, refuse to sell them for export out of the province. This would not apply to privately owned minerals.

(2) Under the property and civil rights clause, and under the general provincial power over matters of a local and private nature in the province, I consider that the province has the power to enact genuine conservation measures concerning the harvesting or extracting of natural resources from all provincial lands, not just the public lands.

These latter two propositions show that, in interpreting the B.N.A. Act, we not only have to reconcile the provincial property and civil rights clause with the federal trade and commerce clause, but also the provincial ownership of the resources in public lands, and the provincial power to enact conservation measures generally, with the federal trade and commerce power.

Let us now look at the taxing powers under the B.N.A. Act. Under section 91(3), the federal parliament may engage in "the raising of money by any mode or system of taxation." The corresponding provincial power is more limited. The provinces, by section 92(2), have power for "*direct* taxation *within the province* in order to the raising of a revenue for provincial purposes." The result of this is that only the federal parliament can levy import or export taxes because these are classically indirect taxes. Further, there are two special provisions of the B.N.A. Act that limit both provincial and federal taxing authorities. Section 121 forbids interprovincial tariffs. It states: "All Articles of the Growth, Produce or Manufacture of any one of the Provinces shall, from and after the Union, be admitted free into each of the other Provinces." Secondly, there are strict limits to whether the provinces may tax the federal government and vice versa. Section 125 of the B.N.A. Act states: "No Land or Property belonging to Canada or any Province shall be liable to Taxation."

A couple of relevant limitations follow from the foregoing. In the first place, mandatory marketing schemes, whether provincial or federal or some combination of the two, must respect the requirement that there shall be no financial provisions that are in effect interprovincial tariffs. This applies to the mandatory pricing provisions of such marketing schemes, or to provincial or federal taxation schemes such as sales taxes. When section 121 says that interprovincial trade shall be free, I take it to mean that neither taxing laws nor the financial provisions of commercial laws may breach this requirement. I emphasize this point because the pricing provisions of a compulsory marketing scheme are commercial law, not tax law. In other words, not every compulsory commercial-financial provision is a tax law, but section 121 catches them both anyway.

But what about straight taxation? Here we come across another problem that is current in this area of revenue from resources. When the Crown in right of the province—the provincial government—leases or grants mineral lands to private persons and reserves royalties, it is simply claiming one of the oldest forms of public revenue there is. Section 109 of the B.N.A. Act makes it clear that the provincial Crown is entitled to royalties respecting provincial lands. A royalty, in the sense in which I am using it here, is a payment to the lessor, in the case of mining leases, whereby the payment due is proportionate to the amount of the mineral that is worked from time to time in the leased land by the lessee. Now, where the lessor is the provincial Crown, the royalty revenues are provincial property. This property cannot be taxed by the federal parliament because of section 125 of the B.N.A. Act. But this means that the provincial government cannot be direclty taxed as such by the federal parliament under a federal taxing statute. When the federal parliament says that the *lessee* is not allowed to deduct from federal corporate income tax the royalty payments due to the provincial Crown, what then? Is this really the same thing as the federal parliament attempting to tax the provincial Crown itself for *its income* from royalties? If it is, it offends section 125 of the B.N.A. Act. If it is not, then the unfortunate lessee of the minerals has to pay the royalties to the provincial government, and also pay *income* tax to the federal government without the benefit of the royalties as deductions. I believe this is one of the issues between the province of Alberta and the federal government and Parliament at the present time. The courts have not yet been asked to resolve it, so we do not know whether the present federal disallowance of royalty deductions for federal revenue tax is really a disguised breach of section 125. Something depends too on whether the present royalty scheme of the Alberta government is to be truly characterized as a matter of "royalties" in the classic sense, and thus as within sections 109 and 125 of the B.N.A. Act. If "royalties" are put at an unreasonably high level, no room is left for the federal government to obtain revenues from income tax on resource development companies, if the royalties *must* be allowed as deductions. Conversely, federal income tax could be set so high that the companies had nothing left to pay royalties with, whether or not they were in theory deductible.

This prompts me to make two observations at this point. (1) Where federal and provincial authorities are collectively asking for too much money, it may well be that the federal authorities could insist on being paid in full first. (2) There is no constitutional prohibition against killing geese that lay golden eggs. Federal and provincial governments can be severally or collectively foolish about this—I fear it is true that the power to tax is the power to destroy. The federal and provincial tax collectors have to agree to some kind of a sharing that leaves natural resource enterprises viable and able to produce and flourish within reason. This brings me to my last topic, the necessity for co-operative federalism.

At this point we must realize that there are problems we must learn to live with if we are to have a federal constitution at all. One of these problems is illustrated by what I have just been saying. With respect to the total process of developing and exploiting a given natural resource like oil, there are certain problems of divided jurisdiction that we must learn to live with. Such problems are inevitable in federal countries. For example we have seen that the provinces own the resources in their public lands and can sit on them if they wish. But we have also seen that once natural resources have been severed from the land and have become commodities, then power to regulate the marketing of them is federal, if they are obviously destined (as most of them are) for export out of the province of production.

What is necessary then is that, if there is to be an effective *total* policy for the exploitation of a given natural resource, parts of that policy must be supplied by virtue of statutes of the province of production and other parts of that policy must be supplied by virtue of statutes of the federal parliament. This requires federal-provincial agreement about complementary uses of the respective federal and provincial legislative powers and powers of ownership. This is a political problem, a problem of federal and provincial bargaining. That is the process we are watching with respect to oil from Alberta and Saskatchewan at the present time. Notice that the constitutional provisions I have been outlining do not automatically eventuate in a total solution—a total sensible Canadian oil policy. But they do give an essential definition to the elements of the federal-provincial bargaining process that we call co-operative federalism. Divided jurisdiction, where there is a need for co-operation across the jurisdictional lines, has to be seen as an invitation to practise co-operative federalism—to agree on a properly complementary use of federal and provincial powers and resources.

There are a number of overall policy areas that cross the jurisdictional lines of our present division of legislative powers in our federal constitution. Another example is the abatement of pollution of air, land, and water. In this area, as one example, federal criminal law powers and provincial powers over torts and delicts have to be co-ordinated. Consumer protection is another area involving the provincial commercial powers (property and civil rights), the federal ones (trade and commerce), and the federal criminal law power. So, there is nothing unusual in the necessity for the co-ordinated co-operation of federal and provincial governments passing complementary statutes in order to accomplish a single national oil policy, if one wishes to stay with that example. This necessity and inevitability can be demonstrated philosophically—as a matter of the philosophy of classification systems and the multiple possibilities of cross-classification—but I have done that elsewhere and will refrain from doing it here.[2]

Federal-provincial agreements are therefore necessary, but the autonomy and the identity of the parties for the bargaining process is defined by the constitution itself. The purpose of the bargaining is to agree on wise complementary uses of the respective federal and provincial constitutional powers and resources.

APPENDIX

Excerpts from the B.N.A. Act

Powers of the [Federal] Parliament.

91. It shall be lawful for the Queen, by and with the Advice and Consent of the Senate and House of Commons to *make Laws*

Legislative Authority of Parliament of Canada

---

[2]W. R. Lederman, "Cooperative Federalism: Constitutional Revision and Parliamentary Government in Canada," *Queen's Quarterly* 78 (1971): 7, and "Some Forms and Limitations of Cooperative Federalism," *Canadian Bar Review* 45 (1967): 409.

for the Peace, Order, and Good Government of Canada, in rela-tion to all Matters not coming within the Classes of Subjects by the Act assigned exclusively to the Legislatures of the Provinces; and for great Certainty, but not so as to restrict the Generality of the foregoing Terms of this Section, it is hereby declared that (notwithstanding anything in this Act) the exclusive Legislative Authority of the Parliament of Canada extends to all Matters com-ing within the Classes of Subjects next hereinafter enumerated; that is to say,

1A   The Public Debt and Property
2.   The Regulation of Trade and Commerce
3.   The raising of Money by any Mode or System of Taxation.
29.   Such Classes of Subjects as are expressly excepted in the Enumeration of the Classes of Subjects by this Act assigned exclusively to the Legislatures of the Provinces.

And any Matter coming within any of the Classes of Subjects enumerated in this Section shall not be deemed to come within the Class of Matters of a local or private Nature comprised in the Enu-meration of the Classes of Subjects by this Act assigned exclu-sively to the Legislatures of the Provinces.

Exclusive Powers of Provincial Legislatures.

92.   In each Province the Legislature may exclusively make Laws in relation to Matters coming within the Classes of Subjects next hereinafter enumerated; that is to say, *Subjects of exclusive Provincial Legislation*

2.   Direct Taxation within the Province in order to the raising of a Revenue for Provincial Purposes.
5.   The Management and Sale of the Public Lands belonging to the Province and of the Timber and Wood thereon.
10.   Local Works and Undertakings other than such as are of the following Classes:
   a.   Lines of Steam or other Ships, Railways, Canals, Tele-graphs, and other Works and Undertakings connecting the Provinces, or extending beyond the Limits of the Province;
   b.   Lines of Steam Ships between the Province and any Brit-ish or Foreign Country;
   c.   Such Works as, although wholly situate within the Prov-ince, are before or after their Execution declared by the Parliament of Canada to be for the general Advantage of Canada or for the Advantage of Two or more of the Provinces.
13.   Property and Civil Rights in the Province.
16.   Generally all Matters of a merely local or private Nature in the Province.

109. All Lands, Mines, Minerals, and Royalties belonging to the several Provinces of Canada, Nova Scotia, and New Brunswick at the Union, and all Sums then due or payable for such Lands, Mines, Minerals, or Royalties, shall belong to the several Provinces of Ontario, Quebec, Nova Scotia, and New Brunswick in which the same are situate or arise, subject to any Trusts existing in respect thereof, and to any Interest other than that of the Province in the same.

Property in Lands, Mines, etc.

117. The several Provinces shall retain all their respective Public Property not otherwise disposed of in this Act, subject to the Right of Canada to assume any Lands or Public Property required for Fortifications or for the Defence of the Country.

Provincial Public Property

121. All Articles of the Growth, Produce or Manufacture of any one of the Provinces shall, from and after the Union, be admitted free into each of the other Provinces.

125. No Lands or Property belonging to Canada or any Province shall be liable to Taxation.

Chapter 22

Cooperative Federalism: Constitutional Revision and Parliamentary Government in Canada*

Reprinted from (1971), 78 Queen's Quarterly 7

In Canada, we have combined parliamentary government on the British model with a federal division of powers and responsibilities, between the Parliament of Canada on the one hand and the respective Parliaments of the ten provinces on the other. On this constitutional basis, we face the complexities of social control, through democratic government under the rule of law, in a pluralistic, industrialized, and highly urbanized society covering half a continent. We have learned that, in the world of today, any federal system must in considerable degree be a cooperative federalism. Thus, in Canada we experience increasing necessity for agreements or understandings between the federal Government and the provincial Governments concerning specific and complementary uses of their respective powers and resources, under the present constitution, on many particular matters.

If we consider carefully the reasons behind this necessity for federal-provincial agreements, a way seems to appear whereby, over time, we may coordinate the regular on-going processes of government in Canada and the provinces with steps to clarify or change the basic federal constitution, when the need for such steps to be taken has been specifically demonstrated. But, what we see at present is that, in the main, the issues of constitutional revision are being approached as a separate and extraordinary matter on the one hand, while, on the other hand, the regular processes of government go on, as they must, to cope with the pressing problems of today and tomorrow. Both involve federal-provincial meetings, conferences, and agreements of various kinds. Yet, for the most part, these two sets of federal-provincial activities are now running as separate operations.

My proposal is that we should simply consolidate these two processes into one process. In the federal-provincial meetings and conferences that would then constitute this one process, prime ministers, ministers, and senior officials, in their various meetings, should first consider what ought to be done by inter-

---

*A slightly revised version of a statement to the Special Joint Committee of the Senate and the House of Commons on the Constitution of Canada, given on 27 October 1970.

governmental agreements, under the existing constitution, to deal with urgent problems like inflation, unemployment, pollution, regional economic disparities, economic growth, urban development, and so on, that involve both levels of government. If satisfactory arrangements can be made for complementary action by the federal Government and provincial Governments on the basis of the respective existing powers and resources, this is agreed and they proceed. If not, and if it emerges that the trouble in one of these problem areas is that there are either uncertainties or deficiencies in the federal division of powers under the B.N.A. Act in this respect, then and only then does one consider a reference to the courts for clarification of the gray area, or outright amendment of the constitution *in the particular respect* where a defect has thus become apparent. This would be a step-by-step process for such amendments, but by no means an unsystematic process. I would expect it to lead to some changes in the federal distribution of powers, but by no means to a wholesale rewriting of that distribution. In any event, such amendments should be the last resort and not the first consideration.

Let me develop this theme briefly under two main headings: first, cooperative federalism and the division of legislative powers; second, cooperative federalism and parliamentary government.

I. COOPERATIVE FEDERALISM AND THE DIVISION OF LEGISLATIVE POWERS BETWEEN CANADA AND THE PROVINCES

I consider the present division of legislative powers in the B.N.A. Act to be at the heart of our federal constitution and thus the nature of this division is primary in assessing the relevance of that constitution to the solution of the urgent problems of modern Canada. I have also just said that there is positive necessity for federal-provincial inter-governmental agreements, whereby both levels of government must act in a complementary way, if they are to deal with urgent social problems that concern them both. Yet, if we read the respective lists of federal and provincial powers in the B.N.A. Act, they purport to be mutually exclusive, with the exceptions of agriculture, immigration and pensions. This raises a very basic question. Why would the country not be sufficiently well governed if the federal Government and the respective provincial Governments each simply went about its own business properly, within the ambit of its own written list of powers and responsibilities, without reference to the other level of government? The answer is that the country would decidedly not be well governed if this were attempted. Indeed, I question whether Canada could be held together and governed at all, today, by this approach.

The reasons for this were well explained in the Rowell-Sirois Report back in 1940.

> No amount of care in phrasing the division of powers in a federal scheme will prevent difficulty when the division comes to be applied to the variety and complexity of social relationships. The different aspects of life in a society are not insulated from one another in such a way as to make possible a mechanical application of the

division of powers. There is nothing in human affairs which corresponds to the neat logical divisions found in the constitution. Therefore, attempts to exercise the powers alloted by the constitution frequently raise questions as to its meaning in relation to particular circumstances.[1]

The superior courts have always recognized that, in wide measure, there is inevitable overlap of federal and provincial categories of powers, leading to much specific interpretation of federal and provincial laws, on the same subjects requiring social control through law. In the course of their judicial decisions on the B.N.A. Act, the judges have basically done one of two things. First they have attempted to define mutually exclusive spheres for federal and provincial powers, and they have had considerable though partial success in doing this. But, where mutual exclusion did not seem feasible or proper, the courts have implied concurrency of federal and provincial power in the overlapping area, with the result that either or both authorities have been permitted to legislate, provided that in the latter event their statutes did not in some way conflict one with the other in the common area. In the event of conflict, the judicial doctrine of dominion paramountcy is to the effect that federal legislation prevails and provincial legislation is suspended or inoperative. The interpretative course followed then might be summed up as follows—mutual exclusion if feasible but concurrency where necessary.

An example of the mutually exclusive result is offered by the Inter-Provincial Bus Lines case of 1954.[2] Here the Judicial Committee of the Privy Council held that the power to regulate interprovincial or international motor vehicle enterprises carrying goods or persons across boundaries was exclusively federal, whereas the power to regulate such enterprises when they operated only within the boundaries of a single province was exclusively provincial. The former were connecting undertakings (a federal responsibility), the latter were local undertakings (a provincial responsibility).

By contrast, the Unconscionable Transactions Relief Act of the Province of Ontario was upheld as valid by a judicial finding of concurrency in the field of interest charges.[3] This statute provides that if, in all the circumstances, the cost of a loan is excessive and the transaction harsh and unconscionable, the court may order the contract reformed so as to make its terms fair and reasonable. Clearly this statute concerns the whole range of undue influence in contract (with excessive interest just one of several possible "undue" elements) and so logically falls within the provincial category of "Property and Civil Rights" under the British North America Act. Also, it is equally obvious that insofar as it deals with interest charges it falls within the federal category of "Interest" under the British North America Act.

Thus the statute in question has both its federal and its provincial aspects, and its validity depends, under the present system of interpretation, on determin-

---

[1] Report of The Royal Commission on Dominion-Provincial Relations, 1940, Book I, 31.
[2] *A.G. for Ontario v. Winner* [1954] A.C. 541; [1954] 4 D.L.R. 657.
[3] R.S.O. 1960, c. 410. *A.G. for Ontario v. Barfried Enterprises Ltd.*, [1963] S.C.R. 570; 42 D.L.R. (2d) 137.

ing whether one of these aspects is primary, or whether the two aspects are equivalent in their relative importance in accordance with the social and economic responsibilities of both levels of government. If the federal aspect of interest is primary, then only the federal Parliament can enact a law dealing with interest as well as other things. On the other hand, if the provincial aspect of interest, as part of the whole picture of undue influence in contract, is of equivalent importance to the federal concern with interest, then the provincial statute stands in its entirety, unless there is actually inconsistent federal legislation on interest—and the Supreme Court of Canada found this not to be so in the Ontario case. In other words, the Province is responsible for general undue influence laws in contract, and no such law is complete unless it includes remedies concerning undue interest rates as well as other facets of undue influence. Hence the judicial finding that, *in this context*, there is a provincial power to deal with interest concurrent with the federal power.

Notice that this judicially implied type of concurrency is cautious, limited and specific. Nevertheless it is very effective. The provincial power to make general contract law is exclusive and complete, except for interest. So this particular implication of concurrency, in such circumstances, supplies the missing piece for complete provincial legislative schemes of consumer protection in the field of the law of contract. Some provinces are now taking advantage of this to enact such schemes. But if the provincial legislation does not have this comprehensive character and purpose, there is no concurrency.

In any event, the mention of consumer protection as an area where both levels of government have responsibilities under the existing constitution illustrates the main points I wish to make. The provincial aspects of consumer protection have just been mentioned. In addition to interest rates, the federal Parliament and Government are also in the picture, because of certain exclusive federal powers respecting bills of exchange, consumer credit from the chartered banks, criminally fraudulent advertising, monopolies in restraint of trade, and so on. What emerges clearly is that both federal and provincial laws are needed, yet the two levels of government can frustrate one another, unless laws from the two sources are harmonized. This can only be done by appropriate intergovernmental agreements about the uses to which each level of government will put its respective powers to provide consumer protection. Some powers are exclusive to the federal Government, others are exclusive to the provincial Governments, and still others are held in common because of the overlapping of power-distributing phrases in the B.N.A. Act, as just illustrated. The coordinated use of all these powers is necessary to obtaining a comprehensive and effective scheme of legislative protection for consumers.

This is only one example. The same sort of picture can be painted concerning other current and urgent social problem areas, like pollution of air, land and water, the quality of life in cities, all forms of communication and transportation, economic growth, and so on. In assessing the interpenetrating nature of federal and provincial powers in relation to broad problem areas, I would emphasize again that one important part of the picture is that many specific and limited instances of judicially implied concurrency will prove necessary to ensure effectively complementary federal and provincial statutes. Concurrency in the constitution is not confined to that explicitly and broadly recognized in agriculture, immigration and pensions.[4]

The conclusion I draw from all this is that, so long as we have a federal system at all, the problems of overlap and intrepenetration I have been illustrating are inevitably with us, socially, logically and philosophically. So long as there is a federal Parliament and Government with some kind of a list of powers appropriate for a central government over the national territory, and so long as there are provincial Parliaments and Governments, coordinate in status, each with a list of other powers deemed appropriate to them in their respective provincial regions, just so long will federal and provincial legislative responsibilities overlap and interpenetrate in wide measure respecting single broad social problem areas, one after the other, as life in our country throws up such problems for attention and solution from time to time.

Let me pursue the significance of this argument in another way. What would happen if you attempted to rewrite the federal division of powers so as to give all power over environmental pollution in every aspect to the federal Government? This would be so sweeping a grant of power that you would really thereby eliminate the autonomy of the provinces and abolish Canadian federalism. We would have a unitary state. Conversely, if you were to rewrite the federal division of powers so as to give all power to the respective provincial Governments over every aspect of urban development and the quality of life in cities, the federal Government would soon be finished and we would end up with ten countries and no Canada. If we are to have a federal system at all, then each level

---

[4]In approving the flexibility conferred by this type of judicially implied concurrency, which, as indicated, is cautious, limited and specific, I am definitely *not* agreeing with proposals of Judge Peter O'Hearn of Halifax. See his *Peace, Order and Good Government* (Toronto: Macmillan of Canada, 1964).

Judge O'Hearn proposed complete and general concurrency across the board on all subjects of legislative power for the federal and provincial parliaments. He would retain the federal and provincial lists of legislative subjects only to determine paramountcy in the event that both federal and provincial statutes had been enacted on the same subject *and* were in conflict or collision. If the subject were criminal law, the federal statute would override and, by contrast, if it were property law, the provincial statute would override. But, if only one statute were enacted, it would be valid whether federal or provincial, and whatever its subject.

In my view, in spite of its apparent simplicity, this is a panacea that just would not work and would threaten the end of federalism. I say this for the following reasons.

(a) Constitutional interpretation would not be simplified. Arguments about which legislature has the paramount power would be just as complex as those now current about which has the exclusive power.

(b) The problems of what amounts to conflict or collision between two statutes are themselves very complex. They do not arise where powers are mutually exclusive. Judge O'Hearn's proposals would multiply these problems of conflict wholesale, and each new issue would have to go to court.

(c) Legislatures and Governments would find it easy to "pass the buck" about unpopular legislation, alleging that the other fellow should do it. Conversely, they would rush to be first with popular types of statutes, whatever the subject. There would be no assurance that *responsibility* would be associated with paramountcy, in the way it is now with exclusive power.

(d) There would be a very strong tendency for the federal Parliament to win out on paramountcy issues, when they did go to court. Those who value provincial autonomy should beware.

of government, federal and provincial, must address itself to parts of the problems of environmental pollution and the problems of urban development. If we are to have a federal system at all, each level of government must be based on limited yet complementary lists of powers and resources so that, while each does have a significant autonomous base of powers and resources, it does not have so much of either that it can ignore the need to collaborate with the other level of government, in developing solutions for urgent modern social problems that are sweeping, if indeed not all-pervasive, in their nature.

This leads me to two major inferences about the federal constitution, one positive and one negative. My positive inference is that absolutely the first priority in constitutional development and reform is to establish better, more systematic, and more regular institutions and practices for federal-provincial consultations and collaborative actions. Such cooperation must take place against the basic background of the general constitutional division of powers and resources between the two levels of government. As indicated, the powers involved are both mutually exclusive and concurrent. My negative inference is that the basic background division of powers is the last thing you tamper with in seeking constitutional improvement, not the first thing. This arises from the fact that the essence of cooperative federalism is federal-provincial agreements about complementary uses of these basic powers and resources, and so presupposes their stability. That is, unless the definitions of them remain reasonably constant as the basis of the autonomy of the parties, subject only to a process of gradual adjustment step by step, cooperative federalism will be frustrated. Without this high degree of stability in the background, the respective bargaining positions of the federal and provincial governments will be too uncertain for federal-provincial agreements to be reached. I will first develop this negative point further, and then give attention to the positive one.

I have explained that, in our present constitutional division of powers and resources, we have a delicately poised balance which blends autonomy and interdependence in these things between the federal and provincial levels of government. This is achieved by two lists of power-distributing phrases in the British North America Act of 1867. For examples, "Trade and Commerce" and "Criminal Law" are two of the federal phrases, while "Municipal Institutions" and "Property and Civil Rights" are two of the provincial phrases. Admittedly such phrases are each capable logically of very broad meanings, but in over one hundred years of living federalism, they have been given properly restricted definitions, definitions which have preserved a truly balanced federalism in Canada. These necessary refinements of authoritative definitions have been given in hundreds of judicial decisions, and by many thousands of precedents established by custom and practice at the official level, concerning what each government should be doing. If you start interfering now in a wholesale way with these historic power-conferring phrases, you throw away over one hundred years of very effective definition and refinement of their meaning. You offer new and rather abstract phrases in their stead as power-conferring phrases, and so great uncertainty sets in about what would be the result. If the phrase "economic growth" were specified as a new field of federal power, who knows where federal powers would stop? If the phrase ''cultural affairs'' were specified as a new field of provincial power, who knows where provincial powers would stop? No one likes to face this much uncertainty unless it is absolutely necessary. In my view it is not necessary and is, indeed, positively dangerous. Our political leaders quite properly fear the uncertainties of this type of approach to constitutional change, they naturally draw back from it, and in the process the sound of dragging feet is loud in the land. I respectfully suggest that here is the basic reason why the federal-provincial constitutional revision conferences are largely stalled at the present time.

But still, some people seem to believe that if we could just get down on paper some new and better combination of abstract power-distributing phrases for the two levels of government, the new document would somehow be a panacea for all our ills. I repeat, this is a dangerous fallacy, and say that we cannot simply draft our way to a solution of our problems in this grossly over-simplified way. For the most part, the present division of powers in the B.N.A. Act, as developed by one hundred years of interpretation, does just about as much as any basic constitutional document can do with general phrases to establish the balance of powers and resources between the two levels of government necessary to make federalism to continuing reality in Canada. It does much more than any *new* basic constitutional document could do, for the reasons I have given.

This brings me to my first priority for constitutional development and reform, better and more systematic cooperative federalism. In my view our federal and provincial governments should concentrate their energies, separately and cooperatively, upon the most urgent social issues of our time—urban development, fair taxation, economic growth, and so on. Federal-provincial meetings of ministers, officials and experts should deal with the specifics of these real problems and the details of what the legislative solutions for them should be. Detailed federal-provincial agreements should be reached, for instance, concerning pollution control, about what each government is to do with its separate and concurrent powers in relation to the desired pollution control measures, and then each government gets on with the necessary legislation and administration as agreed, in accordance with the federal-provincial master plan.

If in the course of cooperative attempts to deal with an urgent social problem, it appears that there are uncertainties about basic constitutional powers of federal or provincial governments that inhibit attempts to cope properly with the problem, there should be a reference to the Supreme Court of Canada for an authoritative interpretation, to clear up the uncertainty. Such references are proper and useful if they are indeed specific and timely. One way to keep them specific would be to require that the statutory scheme to solve the social issue in question should be complete, and in the form at least of a fully-drafted bill. The reference of a fully-drafted bill, or a statute already enacted, would be well-calculated to elicit from the Supreme Court a good clarifying decision on the nature of the basic division of powers.

Finally, and as a last resort, if, in the attempts of governments to solve a specific social problem it appears that there is a deficiency or maladjustment in the basic division of powers, which judicial interpretation fails to solve, then and only then do the governments turn to amendment of the basic constitutional division of powers itself. This requires employment of the extraordinary constitution-amending process, which will be difficult to satisfy, if indeed we can ever make up our minds what it is to be.

Space does not permit further discussion of issues of judicial review and constitutional amendment here. Suffice it to say that I consider them highly important in any process of constitutional review, but second in priority after the development of better institutions and practices of federal-provincial cooperative federalism.

Let me turn then in the final part of these remarks to cooperative federalism and parliamentary government in Canada and the provinces.

II. COOPERATIVE FEDERALISM AND PARLIAMENTARY GOVERNMENT

Cooperative federalism is not a new development in Canada. It has been growing over the years in an unsystematic way. In 1966, for instance, there were well over one hundred federal-provincial meetings of first ministers, other ministers, and civil servants dealing with everything from comparative tax structures to poultry breeding. In early 1968, the special review of the constitution started with a federal-provincial conference of first ministers, and has been proceeding ever since with the well-articulated supporting organization that is now familiar. One of my main points has been that we should now merge these two streams of federal-provincial cooperative activities into one operation, to be carried on as a permanent and single federal-provincial consultative system, with plenty of freedom, of course, for the initiation of conferences of all kinds to deal with the urgent social problems of the country. Meetings of first ministers and other ministers are necessary to obtain the desired degree of coordination, as federal-provincial relations become increasingly complex. This is particularly true in the whole field of public finance, taxation, and budgets.

Developing the detail of these proposals for a single, permanent system is beyond the scope of this discussion, but I do wish to meet two obvious objections that might be made. The first is that the proposed single system for cooperative federalism would be a third level of government in Canada, and a secretive and undemocratic one at that. The second objection is that this proposal means abandoning as a failure the present efforts at constitutional revision, and in particular that it would mean the abandonment of any attempt to make special arrangements for Quebec as the home of the French Fact in Canada and North America. I deny that these objections are valid.

First, is there a threat to parliamentary and democratic government in the development of more regular and systematic intergovernmental cooperation for the coordinated use of existing federal and provincial powers, or at least for the use of federal and provincial powers that are not much changed from what they are now? This should not be viewed as an anti-democratic development, though some commentators and editors would have us believe that it is. Because of the cabinet system, the ministers who engage in intergovernmental consultations are responsible to their respective democratic parliamentary bodies for the policies they sponsor, the concessions they make and the agreements they sign. The policies and agreements can be considered and debated under many different procedural arrangements in the Parliament of Canada and the Legislatures of the provinces, to ensure the accountability of ministers and senior officials to their respective parliamentary bodies, and so to the people themselves. So far as constitutional change in Canada is concerned, I give a very high priority to improvements in the procedure of our parliamentary bodies themselves, both federal and provincial, so that elected members (including cabinet members) are better informed and more sensitive concerning the problems of our society and the needs of our people. Some reforms in parliamentary procedure have already been made, in Ottawa and in the provinces. It is most important that democratic controls should operate well on the processes of cooperative federalism. For example, I would like to see The Special Joint Committee of the Parliament of Canada on the Constitution become a permanent standing Joint Committee on federal-provincial intergovernmental cooperation, just to improve this process of democratic control.

Then there is the second objection to my emphasis on cooperative federalism, namely that it gives up on constitutional review and on any special arrangements for Quebec. This is not the case. I have pointed out that if specific cooperative attempts to solve urgent social problems do reveal deficiencies in the basic division of legislative powers, then we attempt to solve these deficiencies specifically, step by step, if and when they appear. I also favour careful attention to the status and functions of the Supreme Court of Canada, because of the importance of continuous and functional constitutional interpretation. I have conceded that we should continue to seek agreement on a domestic amending formula for the specifically entrenched parts of our federal constitution, though we can get by for a long time without formal amendment of this kind if we have to. But the most important point I would make here is simply this. To develop a new and sophisticated single system to coordinate the practice of federal-provincial cooperative federalism in every respect in Canada *would be in itself very great and very important and constitutional change.* It is no less important and no less constitutional merely because it does not require that formal extraordinary processes of amendment be followed. It need not even be done by ordinary statute. It could be done by federal-provincial agreement, which was the way we established the present special constitutional review machinery.

I would, however, ask that one new dimension should be developed. I suggest that federal-provincial consultation on many important issues should result in specific federal-provincial agreements that would be recorded in great detail as contracts or treaties. They would have time limits calling for periodic review and revision, and would perhaps need ratification in the federal Parliament and the provincial Legislatures. It is within this framework that I see special arrangements being developed for Quebec, and indeed for other provinces or regions of Canada, where appropriate. The special intergovernmental agreement harmonizing the Canada and Quebec Pension Plans is an example. We have many diversities to accommodate in Canada. I suggest that, in this type of cooperative "contract" or "treaty" federalism which I am proposing, there would be room for many special arrangements, provided a few overriding general conditions were written in, safeguarding the respects in which national uniformities should be assured. My hope, then, is that a viable, effective, and balanced cooperative federalism would result for Canada. I trust that this would mean a new spirit of equality in federal-provincial relations, reflecting the greatly increased importance the functions of the provinces have assumed in the twenty-five years since 1945. I hope that the Government of Canada will consider the provincial Governments to be partners and not subordinates, though, of course, primary leadership must often come from the Government of Canada. All of our governments collectively are concerned to satisfy one and the same set of persons: the citizens, taxpayers, and voters of every part of Canada.

FURTHER THOUGHTS

In 1980, as this volume of essays is being put together, I am no longer as complacent about the constitutional *status quo* as I was when, in 1971, I wrote the essay reproduced in the previous part of this chapter. Much has happened since then. See Part VI.

Nevertheless, there is still much truth in what was said in 1971.

Chapter 23

Mr. Justice Rand and Canada's Federal Constitution

Reprinted from (1979-80), 18 University of Western Ontario Law Review 31

"That law is reason is . . . as applicable to statutes as to the unwritten law."
Rand, J., *Johnson v. Attorney General of Alberta,* [1954] S.C.R. 127 at 138.

I. INTRODUCTION

In Canada, as in nearly all federal countries, a typical and essential task of the final court is to provide the rational and authoritative interpretations necessary to keep the federal parliament and the several provincial legislatures within their respective constitutional lists of legislative powers and responsibilities. Certainly this is one of the principal themes of Canadian constitutional law, and, during his sixteen years in the Supreme Court of Canada, from 1943 to 1959, Mr. Justice Rand consistently exerted an influence on such interpretation that was both rational and powerful. He possessed a very full understanding of the operating jurisprudence of a federal system such as ours, and took every opportunity to make it more sophisticated and realistic for the current case and for the future.

The purpose of this essay is to develop some particulars and specifics supporting these assertions; but, to do this, one must appreciate to start with that Rand's treatment of the federal division of legislative powers can seldom, if ever, be separated from certain other basic and related constitutional themes in which he believed. I refer to his concepts of the freedoms of expression and religion, of the rights of citizens, and indeed of the rule of law itself. For him these were foundation stones of our federal union, relying as it does on democratic parliamentary institutions following the model afforded by British parliamentary government, especially as it had developed in the nineteenth and twentieth centuries. Very often, though not always, questions of freedom of expression or religion, or the rights ot citizens, were raised and dealt with by Mr. Justice Rand as integral parts of cases that were concerned to settle issues of the division of legislative powers between provincial legislatures and the federal parliament. Accordingly, I propose to come to appropriate detail concerning human rights and freedoms later, in the context of the division-of-powers cases. But, before considering those cases (in Part II) some attention should first be given to Mr. Justice Rand's concept of the rule of law itself.

He conceived the recognition and acceptance of our whole body of laws to be a matter of a pervasive sense of objective obligation among the people. In other words, in Rand's view, the final focus of social acceptance and obligation in our country is on the ideas manifested in the first principles, procedures and doctrines of the constitution, and on the more particular rules of law derived from these first things by rational processes of enactment or interpretation or both. He knew that if such ideas, principles and processes with organic roots in the history and life of the community are themselves constitutionally supreme, then it follows that all official persons, whether elected or appointed, are under the law and none are above it. The vital thrust of this theory of obligation is that basic principles for society are formulated, become accepted, and endure over significantly long periods of time for an ever-changing population of citizens and officials. Thus there is a pervading sense of obligation toward the concepts involved that is objective, and not just subjective to particular persons at particular times. Nowhere does this view come through more clearly than in Mr. Justice Rand's judgment in the *Boucher Case*,[1] where he led the majority of the full Supreme Court in severely restricting the definition of seditious libel to a scope consistent with liberal parliamentary democracy. He said:

> The crime of seditious libel is well known to the Common Law. Its history has been thoroughly examined and traced by Stephen, Holdsworth and other eminent legal scholars and they are in agreement both in what it originally consisted and in the social assumptions underlying it. Up to the end of the 18th century it was, in essence, a contempt in words of political authority or the actions of authority. If we conceive of the governors of society as superior beings, exercising a divine mandate, by whom laws, institutions and administration are given to men to be obeyed, who are, in short, beyond criticism, reflection or censure upon them or what they do implies either an equality with them or an accountability by them, both equally offensive. In that lay sedition by words and the libel was its written form.
>
> But constitutional conceptions of a different order making rapid progress in the 19th century have necessitated a modification of the legal view of public criticism; and the administrators of what we call democratic government have come to be looked upon as servants, bound to carry out their duties accountably to the public. The basic nature of the Common Law lies in its flexible process of traditional reasoning upon significant social and political matter; and just as in the 17th century the crime of seditious libel was a deduction from fundamental conceptions of government, the substitution of new conceptions, under the same principle of reasoning, called for new jural conclusions.

Accordingly, the Court limited seditious libel to words amounting to actual incitement to violence or crime as a means of effecting governmental change.

To much the same effect is the equally famous case of *Roncarelli v. Duplessis*[2] in which Mr. Justice Rand also participated. Here the Premier of a Province was held liable in damages to a private citizen for acts wrongfully considered by the Premier to be official acts and justifiable as such. After his retirement

---

[1]*Boucher v. The King*, [1951] S.C.R. 265 at 285-6.
[2][1959] S.C.R. 121.

from the Court, and writing in the *Canadian Bar Review* in 1960, Rand himself commented on the case as follows:[3]

> The principle of the rule of law as an implication of a constitution "similar in principle to that of the United Kingdom", as the Act of 1867 puts it, was exemplified in an action brought against the Premier and the Attorney General of the Province of Quebec. He had arrogated to himself dictation to a liquor licensing Board to the extent of directing the cancellation of a licence held for many years by a well-known restaurateur on the ground that the licensee had furnished bail to a large number of Worshippers of Jehovah charged under city by-laws with peddling wares in the form of religious publications without permit. The revocation, as can be imagined, destroyed the business. The judgment found the authority of neither Premier nor Attorney General to extend to what had been done and that it was an act without legal justification, the cancellation of a privilege in the termination of which the Board itself would have been bound to act on reasonable grounds which were not present, and when brought about by a stranger to the Board was *a fortiori* wrongful.

Writing in the *Canadian Bar Review* in 1975, Mr. E. Marshall Pollock, Q.C., reached conclusions about Mr. Justice Rand's juridical thought and style similar to those set forth here. In this distinguished biographical essay, based in part on an assessment of all Rand's judgments on every subject, Pollock concluded:[4] "Rand's beliefs determined his conduct absolutely. As a result, his judicial pronouncements reflect more reliance upon original and imaginative thought and resort to first principles than they do upon precedent." Moreover, Pollock notes Rand's penetrating use of history in his judgments, remarking that ". . . he always took the trouble to find out where we had been." Constitutional law is necessarily a product of history and first principles, so the high intellectual qualities just identified are especially to be found in Rand's judgments concerning the federal division of legislative subjects between the Parliament of Canada and the Legislatures of the respective Provinces. There were about thirty of these judgments in his sixteen years on the court, and I now turn to what they reveal.

II. THE FEDERAL DIVISION OF LEGISLATIVE POWERS

My concern in this Part is with Mr. Justice Rand's contributions, both in process and substance, to the positive operating jurisprudence for judicial review of our constitutional division of primary legislative powers. Space does not permit a fully comprehensive and detailed treatment, so what follows is limited to certain points of main emphasis and some appropriate examples.

First, as a matter of process, I deal with Rand's explanations of the complex operating jurisprudence of legislative federalism; then as matters of substance, with his definition of the federal criminal law power, his concept of the relation of fundamental human freedoms to the division-of-powers system, and his view

---

[3]Ivan C. Rand, "Some Aspects of Canadian Constitutionalism" (1960), 38 Can. Bar Rev. 135 at 156.
[4]E. Marshall Pollock, "Mr. Justice Rand; A Triumph of Principle" (1975), 53 Can. Bar Rev. 519 at 526 and 529.

of the scope and future of the federal general power. Finally, in Part III, I come to Rand's views on the patriation of the Canadian Constitution from Britain.

Briefly, the basic problem of our constitutional interpretative process is this: the concepts expressed or implied by the power-conferring words of the respective federal and provincial lists in the B.N.A. Act overlap and conflict in many ways. As a matter of logic, philosophy, and the alternative values to be served, this competition raises many issues of the situs of legislative power to be resolved by judicial interpretation. Mr. Justice Rand appreciated all this to the full. His most systematic exposition of the process is found in his Oliver Wendell Holmes Lecture at the Harvard Law School in February, 1960, shortly after he had retired from the Supreme Court of Canada. Full quotation is warranted.[5]

> The internal distribution of legislative jurisdiction made by the Act of 1867 between Parliament and provincial legislatures is in the manner of a primary investment in Parliament of power to legislate generally for the Peace, Order and Good Government of Canada, subject to specific items as well as the generality of local matters conferred exclusively on the provinces, which in turn have withdrawn from them so far as breadth of language might be taken to include them within provincial competence, any of a number of specific items expressly declared to be paramount and exclusive, allocated to Parliament. From this endowment and distribution it can be seen that residual powers vest in the Dominion Parliament. The interlacing of this distribution clearly appears between such classes as Trade and Commerce, Navigation and Shipping, Interest, Promissory Notes and Bills of Exchange, Banking, Currency & Coinage, and Bankruptcy, within the Dominion field, and property and Civil Rights, Local Works and matters generally of a Local or Private nature, allocated to the provinces. Legislation may reflect different aspects of subject-matter, as for example the local law of the distribution of assets seized in execution of judgments against debtors as a matter of Property and Civil Rights, in contrast to a similar distribution under bankruptcy legislation. In the overlapping of this nature, Dominion legislation in its application supersedes the local law which is to that extent suspended from operation; the field is said to be "occupied" by the paramount law; in the absence of the latter, provincial law operates in *proprio vigore*.
>
> The test of the class of subject in which any statute or law affecting any matter lies becomes a question of the true nature of the statute or law: is it, as the Act of 1867 puts it, "in relation to" a matter within a class of subject allocated to the one or other jurisdiction? and that determination, when in doubt, is aided by seeking the aspect in which the matter is found to be dealt with, in which, ordinarily, its immediate purpose is most clearly indicated. As aids to the interpretation of the language of the Act of 1867 in its application to the realities of 1959, metaphors have been suggested such as a tree growing in organic expansion, a ship of water-tight compartments. The latter, if intended to do more than indicate the exclusiveness of jurisdiction, once the real nature of legislation is found, results from a preoccupation with the language of the statute, confining interpretation in substance to the unaided text, a somewhat arid and unrealistic conceptualism. Conditions and consequences have been taken into account, but that enlargement of considerations so significant to the interpretation of a fundamental instrument, does not seem as yet to have been pressed as it might have been.

---

[5] See, *supra*, note 3 at 151-52.

Further, as Rand pointed out in the *Saumur Case* in 1953,[6] statutes (whether national or provincial) in a federal system must always be drafted with a particularity that keeps in mind specifically the actual terms of the division-of-powers system. It is a fallacy to think that, whatever the terms of the statute or the nature and scope of the social problems with which it deals, the system must nevertheless somehow assign power to enact that very statute entirely one way or the other, to federal parliament or provincial legislature. Power to enact all its terms may well be divided on a mutually exclusive basis. Or the statute (or by-law) concerned may be in such broad terms that neither the central parliament nor a provincial legislature could authorize it. The latter was the situation in the *Saumur Case* itself, where the by-law purported to give to the Chief of Police of Quebec City power to prevent the circulation of any written or printed material whatever on the streets of the city. This is not merely labouring the obvious; the point is fundamental and is missed often enough. No doubt it is generally true that the federal parliament and the provincial legislatures between them possess the totality of legislative powers for the country, but, nevertheless, those powers are constitutionally distributed by a particular system of categories and this places its own limitations on how things may be done.[7]

Another aspect of interpretative process is the authority to be accorded to precedent in constitutional cases. Here we find Rand's attitude to be flexible and sophisticated. Appeals to the Judicial Committee of the Privy Council were abolished in 1949, during his term on the Supreme Court of Canada, so it was natural that he would have something to say about the significance of precedents from the Privy Council for the Supreme Court after 1949. In the *Ontario Farm Products Marketing Case* of 1957,[8] Rand pointed out that the Judicial Committee had not deemed itself bound invariably to follow its own previous decisions, and that it had engaged in restatements and revisions when judged necessary in the light of changing conditions in society. Rand claimed this same power of restatement and revision after 1949 for the Supreme Court of Canada.

In his Oliver Wendell Holmes Lecture at Harvard in 1960, Rand spoke even more clearly and plainly on this subject:[9]

> The Supreme Court has not, since 1949, faced directly the question of *stare decisis*. The Judicial Committee which set the law for Canada was not bound by that rule; and as the Supreme Court has succeeded in substance to the role and position vis-à-vis Canada of its predecessor, that court would seem to be equally free from such a constraint. Absoluteness in the rule is not, in any case, present; exceptions exist even in the House of Lords as the highest court of law for the United Kingdom, though they are specific and few. But English conditions do not face the Supreme Court. The interpretation of a written constitution limiting jurisdictions within a federal union, with more or less elaborate formalities for amendment, does not per-

---

[6]*Laurier Saumur v. The City of Quebec and The Attorney General for Quebec*, [1953] 2 S.C.R. 299 at 333.

[7]See W. R. Lederman, "Unity and Diversity in Canadian Federalism: Ideals and Methods of Moderation" (1975), 53 Can. Bar Rev. 597, 610-16.

[8]*Reference re The Farm Products Marketing Act*, [1957] S.C.R. 198 at 212-13.

[9]See, *supra*, note 3 at 160.

mit of the perpetuation of unsound judgments; constitutional amendments are of a different order from statutory amendments; as related to individual determinations, that is, whether specific matter is within the one or other jurisdiction, they are inappropriate and impracticable. In matters of private or ordinary public law the question is somewhat different; but however desirable certainty and uniformity undoubtedly are, the occasional resort to subtleties of distinction or bland disregard, in one form or other, of incompatible rulings, does not add to the stature of judicial process.

In spite of this impatience with narrow or rigid doctrines of *stare decisis*, no doubt Justice Rand was in the main loyal to the general lines laid down by previous decisions on the constitution. Presumably he knew he would not be influential with fellow judges if he got too far out of step. Nevertheless, more consistently than was the case with the others, he tended to look through and beyond the literal reasoning of previous cases to discover the broader principles of which those cases were but examples, and then to base *his* reasoning on those broader principles.

Consistent with this was his concern that constitutional decisions should be realistic in their relation to the conditions of Canadian society, both historical and current. Recall that, in the first passage quoted earlier from his Holmes Address at Harvard, in 1960, he protested about the "arid and unrealistic conceptualism" of confining interpretative conclusions to what could be gleaned from within the four corners of "the unaided text". In relation to a challenged statute and what it purported to do, he wanted both "conditions and consequences" to be "taken into account". He lamented that, in Canadian constitutional jurisprudence, "this does not yet seem to have been pressed as it might have been". Obviously he favoured more resort to judicial notice and more liberal admission of extrinsic evidence than he had experienced in his time on the Court.

We come now to certain of the matters of substance mentioned at the beginning of this Part. In my view, Mr. Justice Rand's greatest substantive contributions to our constitutional jurisprudence are his definition of the federal criminal law power, and his concept of the fundamental freedoms and of their relation to the division-of-powers system in general and to the federal criminal law power in particular.

When Rand joined the Supreme Court of Canada, substantive definitions of the federal criminal law power were in almost hopeless conflict and confusion. He certainly left the situation considerably better than he found it. In 1922, in *The Board of Commerce Case*,[10] Viscount Haldane had said that, for a challenged law to be included in the federal criminal law power, the subject-matter of it must be "one which by its very nature belongs to the domain of criminal jurisprudence". However, in 1931, in the *Proprietary Articles Trade Association Case*,[11] Lord Atkin took exception to this and insisted that the "criminal law"

---

[10]*In re The Board of Commerce Act, 1919, and The Combines and Fair Prices Act, 1919,* [1922] 1 A.C. 191 (J.C.P.C.).

[11]*Proprietary Articles Trade Association v. Attorney-General for Canada,* [1931] A.C. 310 (J.C.P.C.).

category of federal power was potentially an expanding one and that Parliament could create new crimes rather freely. He then expounded a purely formal test:

> Criminal law connotes only the quality of such acts or omissions as are prohibited under appropriate penal provisions by authority of the State. The criminal quality of an act cannot be discerned by intuition; nor can it be discovered by reference to any standard but one: Is the act prohibited with penal consequences?

Lord Atkin did then go on to admit that statutory provisions that were formally prohibitive and penal could nevertheless be colourable, which means that their criminal form would not correspond with their pith and substance, but rather that some *other* feature of them that was not criminal *was* their pith and substance— their leading feature. If this other feature was relevant to a head of provincial power, like property and civil rights, then the statutory provisions in question were not within the federal criminal law power, rather they were within the provincial property and civil rights clause. This was the actual result of the *Board of Commerce Case,* a result Lord Atkin accepted. But his acceptance of the result must mean logically that there are *two* tests to be met cumulatively, if a challenged law is to be classified as primarily "criminal" for purposes of the federal criminal law power;

(1) the law must be prohibitive and penal in form, and also
(2) the law must in pith and substance be of criminal character.

Lord Atkin tactitly admits this by allowing that the interpretative doctrine of colourability is potentially operative, but he leaves us completely in the dark as to what that substantive test of criminal character might be.

Mr. Justice Rand did not accept Viscount Haldane's fixed domain of criminal jurisprudence, but he did in effect agree with Haldane that the definition of criminal character must have its substantive branch as well as its formal one. Also, Rand agreed with Lord Atkin that "criminal law" for federal purposes was potentially an expanding field and that the Parliament of Canada could indeed create new crimes. Nevertheless, Rand held, form alone was not enough, and such laws must also exhibit certain substantive characteristics as primary characteristics, albeit these were rather general in nature. The critical passages from Rand's judgment in the *Margarine Case,* in 1948, are as follows:[12]

> Under a unitary legislature, all prohibitions may be viewed indifferently as of criminal law; but as the cases cited demonstrate, such a classification is inappropriate to the distribution of legislative power in Canada.
>
> Is the prohibition then enacted with a view to a public purpose which can support it as being in relation to criminal law? Public peace, order, security, health, morality: these are the ordinary though not exclusive ends served by the law, but they do not appear to be the object of the parliamentary action here. That object, as I must

---

[12]*Reference as to the Validity of Section 5(a) of the Dairy Industry Act,* [1949] S.C.R. 1 at 50-51. Mr. Justice Rand returned to this problem in *Goodyear Tire and Rubber Co. of Canada Ltd. v. The Queen,* [1956] S.C.R. 303 at 311-12 (The *Goodyear Case*), and in *Lord's Day Alliance of Canada v. Attorney-General of British Columbia,* [1959] S.C.R. 497 at 508-9 (the *B.C. Lord's Day Alliance Case*). As I read these passages, he did not alter the position he had taken in the *Margarine Case.*

find it, is economic and the legislative purpose, to give trade protection to the dairy industry in the production and sale of butter; to benefit one group of persons as against competitors in business in which, in the absence of the legislation, the latter would be free to engage in the provinces. To forbid manufacture and sale for such an end is prima facie to deal directly with the civil rights of individuals in relation to particular trade within the provinces . . .

The public interest in this regulation lies obviously in the trade effects: it is annexed to the legislative subject matter and follows the latter in its allocation to the one or other legislature. But to use it as a support for the legislation in the aspect of criminal law would mean that the Dominion under its authority in the field, by forbidding the manufacture or sale of particular products, could, in what it considered a sound trade policy, not only interdict a substantial part of the economic life of one section of Canada but do so for the benefit of that of another. Whatever the scope of the regulation of interprovincial trade, it is hard to conceive a more insidious form of encroachment on a complementary jurisdiction.

This conclusion is not in conflict with *Attorney-General of British Columbia* v. *Attorney-General of Canada*, (section 498a of the Criminal Code). There, the essential nature of the legislation was not the equalization of civil rights between competitors or promoting the interest of one trade as against another; it was the safeguarding of the public against the evil consequences of certain fetters upon free and equal competition. There is no like purpose here; there is nothing of a general or injurious nature to be abolished or removed: it is a matter of preferring certain local trade to other.

No doubt Mr. Justice Rand would agree that our inheritance in Canada of English criminal law and legal history aids to some extent the determination of what is of a substantively criminal nature. For example, he found anti-gambling legislation to have that character (the *Johnson Case*[13]); likewise with legislation compelling businesses to close on the specified holy days of a particular religion, including closure on Sundays (the *Birks Case*[14] and the *B.C. Lord's Day Alliance Case*[15]). In England through several centuries such prohibitions and their penalties were classified in substance as parts of the criminal law. The same might be said of laws against sedition and treason (the *Padlock Law Case*). In any event, we may note that it was typical of Mr. Justice Rand to perceive the philosophical and logical need for better definitions in this area and to move to meet the needs as he did.

By these tests Mr. Justice Rand found considerable exclusive territory for the federal criminal law, but also he recognized, in this as in other subject areas, that there was need for some judicially implied concurrent operation of federal and provincial laws, for example between federal criminal laws and provincial property laws. Nevertheless, when federal and provincial laws were thus found to be concurrent, Justice Rand was also alert to the need to protect the policy and effectiveness of the federal law from frustration by a concurrently operating but inconsistent provincial law. This is the purpose of the so-called doctrine of Do-

---

[13]*Johnson v. Attorney General of Alberta*, [1954] S.C.R. 127.
[14]*Birks v. City of Montreal and the Attorney General of Quebec*, [1955] S.C.R. 799.
[15]*Lord's Day Alliance of Canada v. Attorney General of British Columbia*, [1959] S.C.R. 497.

minion paramountcy in concurrent fields, which renders such inconsistent provincial laws inoperative. Implied concurrency brings valuable flexibility to constitutional interpretation, but there have to be some such limitations upon it. The big problem here, as Rand recognized, is that there may be and there are quite different concepts of what is "frustration" and what is "inconsistency". He leaned to definitions of these concepts that favoured the overriding operation of federal laws. As an example, for Rand, simple duplication amounted to inconsistency and was enough to render the provincial law in question inoperative. In other words, he considered that in these circumstances the federal law fully occupied the field. In the *Johnson Case*,[16] referring to the Criminal Code of Canada, he said:

> From this it is seen that the *Code* has dealt comprehensively with the subject matter of the provincial statute. An additional process of forfeiture by the province would both duplicate the sanctions of the *Code* and introduce an interference with the administration of its provisions. Criminality is primarily personal and sanctions are intended not only to serve as deterrents but to mark a personal delinquency. The enforcement of criminal law is vital to the peace and order of the community. The obvious conflict of administrative action in prosecutions under the *Code* and proceedings under the statute, considering the more direct and less complicated action of the latter, could lend itself to a virtual nullification of enforcement under the *Code* and in effect displace the *Code* so far by the statute. But the criminal law has been enacted to be carried into effect against violations, and any local legislation of a supplementary nature that would tend to weaken or confuse that enforcement would be an interference with the exclusive power of Parliament.

These issues of conflict and inconsistency in concurrent fields are possibly the most difficult in our federal constitutional jurisprudence. The point here is that Mr. Justice Rand's views about them remain very influential, though still controversial. For example, in a recent case concerning insider trading in corporate securities, the federal and provincial laws relevant simply duplicated one another.[17] Mr. Justice Morden in the Ontario Divisional Court, giving the majority judgment, referred with approval to Mr. Justice Rand's statement from the *Johnson Case*. Mr. Justice Morden's reasons were affirmed by the Ontario Court of Appeal, in this as in other respects.[18] Presumably the case is now on its way to the Supreme Court of Canada.

The foregoing analysis of Mr. Justice Rand's views concerning the federal criminal law power lead naturally to his conception of the nature of the freedoms of expression and religion, and their linkage to the legisgative division-of-power system. Let us look first at the critical passages from his judgment in the *Quebec Padlock Law Case* of 1957:[19]

---

[16]*Johnson v. Attorney General of Alberta*, [1954] S.C.R. 127, 138. See also: *In re: The Moratorium Act (Sask.)*, [1956] S.C.R. 31, 46-7.

[17]*Multiple Access Ltd. v. McCutcheon et al.* (1977), 78 D.L.R. (3d) 701 at 710; (1978) 86 D.L.R. (3d) 160 (Ont. C.A.). (Reversing Henry J., (1976), 65 D.L.R. (3d) 477 (Ont. H.C.).).

[18](1978), 86 D.L.R. (3d) 160. See also: *Ross v. Registrar of Motor Vehicles* (1973), 42 D.L.R. (3d) 68 (S.C.C.) and *Robinson v. Countrywide Factors Ltd.* (1977), 72 D.L.R. (3d) 500 (S.C.C.)

[19]*Switzman v. Elbling and Attorney-General of Quebec*, [1957] S.C.R. 285 at 306-7.

Indicated by the opening words of the preamble in the Act of 1867, reciting the desire of the four Provinces to be united in a federal union with a constitution ''similar in principle to that of the United Kingdom'', the political theory which the Act embodies is that of parliamentary government, with all its social implications, and the provisions of the statute elaborate that principle in the institutional apparatus which they create or contemplate. Whatever the deficiencies in its workings, Canadian government is in substance the will of the majority expressed directly or indirectly through popular assemblies. This means ultimately government by the free public opinion of an open society, the effectiveness of which, as events have not infrequently demonstrated, is undoubted.

But public opinion, in order to meet such a responsibility, demands the condition of a virtually unobstructed access to an diffusion of ideas. Parliamentary government postulates a capacity in men, acting freely and under self-restraints, to govern themselves; and that advance is best served in the degree achieved of individual liberation from subjective as well as objective shackles. Under that government, the freedom of discussion in Canada, as a subject-matter of legislation, has a unity of interest and significance extending equally to every part of the Dominion. With such dimensions it is *ipso facto* excluded from head 16 as a local matter.

This constitutional fact is the political expression of the primary condition of social life, thought and its communication by language. Liberty in this is little less vital to man's mind and spirit than breathing is to his physical existence. As such an inherence in the individual it is embodied in his status of citizenship. Outlawry, for example, divesting civil standing and destroying citizenship, is a matter of Dominion concern . . .

Prohibition of any part of this activity as an evil would be within the scope of criminal law, as ss. 60, 61 and 62 of the *Criminal Code* dealing with sedition exemplify. Bearing in mind that the endowment of parliamentary institutions is one and entire for the Dominion, that Legislatures and Parliament are permanent features of our constitutional structure, and that the body of discussion is indivisible, apart from the incidence of criminal law and civil rights, and incidental effects of legislation in relation to other matters, the degree and nature of its regulation must await future consideration; for the purposes here it is sufficient to say that it is not a matter within the regulation of a Province.

Mr. Justice Rand had said much the same thing about freedom of religion in the *Saumur Case* in 1953:[20]

That legislation ''in relation'' to religion and its profession is not a local or private matter would seem to me to be self-evident: the dimensions of this interest are nationwide; it is even today embodied in the highest level of the constitutionalism of Great Britain; it appertains to a boundless field of ideas, beliefs and faiths with the deepest roots and loyalties; a religious incident reverberates from one end of this country to the other, and there is nothing to which the ''body politic of the Dominion'' is more sensitive.

In passages such as those just quoted, there has been some suggestion that Rand was really saying that the freedoms of expression and religion were specially entrenched in the Canadian constitution by virtue of the preamble of the

---

[20]*Laurier Saumur v. The City of Quebec and The Attorney General for Quebec* [1953] S.C.R. 329.

B.N.A. Act of 1867, and that, therefore, there was an essential core area of these freedoms that could not be breached by ordinary legislation of either a provincial legislature or the federal parliament. I have concluded that Justice Rand did not intend to go that far and should not be read as having done so.[21] In this context he did accept, perhaps reluctantly, that all legislative powers were distributed. It seems to me that his statements in the *Padlock Law Case* (freedom of expression) and the *Birks Case* and the *B.C. Lord's Day Alliance Case* (freedom of religion)[22] concede this. He regarded the federal criminal law power as potentially fully effective to limit these freedoms, reinforced if necessary by the federal general power. He saw the provincial powers to restrict the freedoms mentioned as much lesser and incidental, confined to such things as civil actions for libel and slander.

Nevertheless, conceding all this, Mr. Justice Rand did move in the direction of special constitutional protection for these freedoms as much as our federal division-of-powers system permitted. He certainly did have in his mind as a matter of basic belief broad substantive conceptions of core areas for freedom of expression and religion that were essential for our society and our political system. We find him using this conceptual foundation in two ways. First, as a matter of construing challenged statutes, he presumed against legislative meanings that would breach the boundaries of the core area of freedom: recall that this was precisely what he did in the *Boucher Case* where he severely restricted the definition of sedition in the federal criminal law. Second, in the case of provincial statutes restrictive of essential freedoms, he could and would strike them down on the orthodox ground that they were attempting to invade exclusive fields of legislative jurisdiction belongong to the federal parliament, by virtue of the federal criminal law power and the federal general power. The *Birks* and *Switzman* Cases are examples of this.

Mr. Justice Rand retired for age from the Supreme Court of Canada in 1959. The next year, the Canadian Bill of Rights[23] became law as an ordinary statute of the Parliament of Canada, embracing all matters within the legislative authority of that Parliament. In section 1, the statute made a straightforward declaration of the constitutional existence of the freedoms of expression and religion, among others. In many ways, the interpretation of this statutory Bill of Rights has dominated the Canadian judicial scene in such matters during the decades of the 1960's and the 1970's. It is then a fair question to ask: How would Mr. Justice Rand have construed the Canadian Bill of Rights of 1960? Where, for example, would he have stood had he still been a member of the Supreme Court of Canada when it decided the cases of *Drybones* (1970)[24] and *Lavell* (1974)[25]? Fortunately we do not have to speculate. He told us in advance, plainly enough, in an essay

---

[21]Mr. E. M. Pollock, Q.C., came to the same conclusion in his essay in 1975 on Mr. Justice Rand. See, *supra*, note 4 at 541.
[22]See, *supra*, notes 14, 15 and 19.
[23]R.S.C. 1970, Appendix III.
[24]*Regina v. Drybones*, [1970] S.C.R. 282.
[25]*Attorney General of Canada v. Lavell*, [1974] S.C.R. 1349.

entitled "Except By Due Process of Law" which he published in 1961 in the Osgoode Hall Law Journal.[26] Speaking of the interpretation of the Canadian Bill of Rights, he said:

> Section 1 exhausts its force in the declaration which it makes; its terms are intended to define the recognized freedoms, not to furnish the means of enforcing them. In isolation the declaration would avail nothing against new legislation; as subsequent in time, conflicting provisions would in fact be in amendment or abrogation of it. Here we meet the difference between a written constitution as a political and legislative foundation agreed upon by the people of a state, and an enactment by the representative legislature of that people; the former is recognized as of a character of enactment capable of imposing restraints on statutory legislation and free from being affected by it. In the case before us, the Bill of Rights is enacted only as a statute and as no parliament can bind its own future legislative action, a declaration of rights with nothing more would be at the mercy of subsequent action by the same legislature.
>
> This difficulty is met by the provisions of section 2. There could be no question of ultra vires of parliamentary action in any former or subsequent legislation; the jurisdictional power enacting the Bill of Rights is precisely the same as that of any following enactment; the power is one and entire and its subsequent exercise affecting abrogation or abridgment of freedoms would be unchallengeable. To prevent this, the device provided by section 2 is that of an interpretative direction: all law of Canada is now placed under a condition that it is not to be deemed to violate the freedoms conferred; the condition is in the form of an obligation placed on courts to be observed in their interpretation of the law against the background of the Bill of Rights. They are to construe all such law as not infringing the rights; if the interpretation finds by the langauge used an infringement in fact then to the extent of that infringement the language or fact of the law must be disregarded as if the offending provision were omitted in the enactment of the law.
>
> If the language of the rule or principle or statement of law is ambiguous, or otherwise capable of it, obviously a non-infringing interpretation will be given; but if the language cannot fairly be so construed, it must, in effect, be treated as meaningless and as if struck out of the law. It might be that the entirety remaining would lead to results not within the contemplation of the statute and in such a case there might be a complete failure of effect. The courts cannot create new provisions which the statement of law is unable to support. But however this may be, the significant circumstance is the adoption of such means of giving force to the liberties proclaimed.

Clearly then, Rand would have been with the majority of the Supreme Court of Canada in *Drybones* when they gave overriding effect to the Canadian Bill of Rights in relation to other federal statutes. It seems equally safe to say that he would have been with the dissenting minority who upheld the stronger and substantive view of the Canadian Bill of Rights in *Lavell*. Moreover, Rand makes it clear in the same published essay of 1961 that he would have been forthright in learning from American Supreme Court jurisprudence concerning interpretation of parallel provisions of the American Bill of Rights. He agreed with the Ameri-

---

[26]Ivan C. Rand, "Except by Due Process of Law" (1961), 2 Osgoode Hall L.J. 171.

can view that "due process of law" requires judicial review of legislative enactments for compliance with basic and substantive standards of reasonableness. Accordingly, had he had the Canadian Bill of Rights in his armoury as a judge, it seems Mr. Justice Rand would have moved beyond presumptions of restrictive interpretation in favour of the freedoms. He would probably have moved virtually to special entrenchment of the recited freedoms against the Parliament of Canada. As for the Provinces, some of them now have comparable statutory Bills of Rights, and, anyway, as we have seen, Rand would have limited them severely in this area on orthodox division-of-powers grounds.

All this is not to say that Mr. Justice Rand's views went unchallenged even when he was on the Court. For example, not all of his brother judges agreed with him in the *Saumur Case* that legislative power concerning the original fundamental freedoms was primarily federal. Neither have his views gone unchallenged since he left the Court in 1959, or, indeed, since his death in 1969. As very recent cases concerning the Montreal Public Order By-law[27] and the Nova Scotia Board of Film Censors[28] show, the Supreme Court of Canada is still seriously divided on these issues, and one cannot predict when they will really be settled. To a degree, of course, such issues can never finally be settled. Interim solutions may be what we shall have to live with from time to time. In any event, there is a great deal that remains relevant and timely for this continuing controversy in what has been said by Rand the judge and Rand the juristic essay-writer.

In addition to what he said about the freedoms of expression and religion, Mr. Justice Rand also said important things about the substantive rights that go with Canadian citizenship. Typically, he took the opportunity to deal with this when it arose in a case on the division of legislative powers to regulate buses and trucks using provincial highways as part of interprovincial and international journeys.[29] Counsel for the Provinces had argued that, since the Provinces owned the highways, simply as a matter of their control of their own public lands, they could exclude any user or subject him to any conditions by provincial legislation, regardless of the fact that his highway-using enterprise was interprovincial or international. This prompted Mr. Justice Rand to give the most comprehensive and definitive statement concerning the significance of Canadian citizenship that we have in the Law Reports.

> The claim made for provincial controls is, in my opinion, excessive. The first and fundamental accomplishment of the constitutional Act was the creation of a single political organization of subjects of His Majesty within the geographical area of the Dominion, the basic postulate of which was the institution of a Canadian citizenship. Citizenship is membership in a state; and in the citizen inhere those rights and duties, the correlatives of allegiance and protection, which are basic to that status.
>
> The Act makes no express allocation of citizenship as the subject-matter of legislation to either the Dominion or the provinces; but as it lies at the foundation of the

---

[27]*Attorney General of Canada v. Dupond et al* (1978), 84 D.L.R. (3d) 420 (S.C.C.).
[28]*Re Nova Scotia Board of Censors et al and McNeil* (1978), 84 D.L.R. (3d) 1 (S.C.C.).
[29]*Winner v. S.M.T. (Eastern) Ltd.,* [1951] S.C.R. 887 at 918-20. The case went on to the Judicial Committee of the Privy Council, the last Canadian constitutional case to do so. The point about citizenship was not part of the reasons of the Judicial Committee, though they came down in favour of Mr. Winner. *Attorney-General for Ontario v. Israel Winner,* [1954] A.C. 541.

political organization, as its character is national, and by the implication of Head 25, section 91, "Naturalization and Aliens", it is to be found within the residual powers of the Dominion: *Canada Temperance* case (1), at p. 205. Whatever else might have been said prior to 1931, the Statute of Westminster, coupled with the declarations of constitutional relations of 1926 out of which it issued, creating, in substance, a sovereignty, concludes the question . . .

What this implies is that a province cannot, by depriving a Canadian of the means of working, force him to leave it: it cannot divest him of his right or capacity to remain and to engage in work there: that capacity inhering as a constituent element of his citizenship status is beyond nullification by provincial action . . . He may, of course, disable himself from exercising his capacity or he may be regulated in it by valid provincial law in other aspects. But that attribute of citizenship lies outside of those civil rights committed to the province, and is analogous to the capacity of a Dominion corporation which the province cannot sterilize.

It follows, *a fortiori*, that a province cannot prevent a Canadian from entering it except, conceivably, in temporary circumstances, for some local reason as, for example, health. With such a prohibitory power, the country could be converted into a number of enclaves and the "union" which the original provinces sought and obtained disrupted. In a like position is a subject of a friendly foreign country; for practical purposes he enjoys all the rights of the citizen.

Such, then, is the national status embodying certain inherent or constitutive characteristics, of members of the Canadian public, and it can be modified, defeated or destroyed, as for instance by outlawry, only by Parliament.

Highways are a condition of the existence of an organized state: without them its life could not be carried on. To deny their use is to destroy the fundamental liberty of action of the individual, to proscribe his participation in that life: under such a ban, the exercise of citizenship would be at an end.

Again we find that Rand has given us statements of principle to govern something of continuing importance, and, indeed, of direct current constitutional concern. For example, what has just been quoted about the rights of Canadian citizens is relevant to our concern today about the provincial language law of Quebec (Bill 101 of 1977) which, in its educational provisions, inhibits the immigration of anglophones to Quebec because their children would not be allowed to enter the historic English school system there.

Turning now to Mr. Justice Rand's view of the scope and nature of the federal general power (the power of Parliament to legislate on all subjects not assigned by the B.N.A. Act to the Provinces), much has already emerged about this in the earlier part of this essay. We have seen, for example, that he located there the power to create the status of citizenship, some of the main implications of which were beyond the reach of any exercise of provincial powers. The same is true of the freedoms of expression and religion: power to limit them, by legislation having that substantive purpose, was likewise embraced exclusively by the federal general power. To this, one may add that Rand indicates in his Harvard Lecture of 1960 that, had the opportunity occurred for him when he was on the Court, he would have located plenary power to implement international treaty obligations in the federal parliament by virtue of the opening words of section 91 of the B.N.A. Act.[30]

---

[30]See, *supra*, note 3 at 143.

Nevertheless, Rand was careful and disciplined in the reasoning he used to find new subjects of national character for the federal parliament in this way. Moreover, he recognized explicitly that section 92(16) of the B.N.A. Act "contains what may be called the residuary power of the Province"[31] which is, for unlisted subjects of an essentially local character, the full equivalent of the federal "Peace, Order and Good Government" power for national purposes. In his Harvard Lecture of 1960,[32] he uses with approval the "dimensions" langauge employed by Lord Watson concerning the federal general power in the *Local Prohibition Case* in 1896.[33] Presumably this means that Rand approves Watson's caution that too free a use of the federal general power would endanger essential provincial autonomy. Rand concluded in 1960 that there were some unreconciled divergencies in judicial definitions of the federal general power, and remarked that this "presents an opportunity for fresh consideration of residual resources".[34]

III. PATRIATION OF THE CANADIAN CONSTITUTION

Finally, in considering Mr. Justice Rand's contributions to Canadian constitutional jurisprudence, we come to the matters of the amendment and patriation of the Canadian constitution. The case law in the Supreme Court of Canada during his years there gave him little opportunity to address these problems, but they were on his mind. In 1950, he did say in the *Nova Scotia Interdelegation Case*[35] that it was no longer feasible or practical for the British Parliament, of its own volition, to amend the B.N.A. Act of 1867. He does however deal extensively with amendment and patriation of the Canadian constitution in his Harvard Lecture of 1960, just after he left the Court. For full detail, this source should be consulted; my concern here is to make one final point. Mr. Justice Rand was quite firm in his belief that developing custom, usage and convention in the British Commonwealth had removed irrevocably the former paramountcy of the British Parliament, both with respect to the B.N.A. Act itself and the Statute of Westminster of 1931. In saying this, clearly he rejects the theories of Austin and Dicey about the nature of law and of parliamentary sovereignty. One final quotation makes the point.[36]

> The question may be raised of the political and legal force of resolutions passed by Imperial Conferences and confirmed by legislation. It cannot, in my view, be less than this: that they are to be treated as creating constitutional commitments of a permanent nature, which once approved and entered upon become irrevocable as self-executing conventions, placed, by that fact, beyond repudiation. They have not become the subject of juridicial examination but that might happen. Should, for example, the British Parliament, of its own initiative, purport to repeal the Act of 1931 what would be the position of Canadian legislation and of Canadian courts?

---

[31]*Reference Re The Farm Products Marketing Act (Ontario)*, [1957] S.C.R. 198 at 212.
[32]See, *supra*, note 3 at 159.
[33]*Attorney General for Ontario v. Attorney General for Canada*, [1896] A.C. 348 (J.C.P.C.).
[34]See, *supra*, note 3 at 160.
[35]*Attorney General of Nova Scotia v. Attorney General of Canada*, [1951] S.C.R. 31 at 50.
[36]See, *supra*, note 3 at 148-49.

The answer must be that the purported repeal would not be recognized. Once such fundamental agreements have been reached, certainly when embodied in legislation, they become as executed treaties between peoples to be modified only by the agreement of the parties to them; and they bind equally discretionary action by the Sovereign. . . . The acceptance of the convention concludes resort to conflicting statutory power; if that were no so, the bonds of colonial relation embodied in statutes could never constitutionally be dissolved, there could be no termination of statutory enactment, a link of that nature would be perpetual; even express renunciation could be revoked. Actual or constructive revolution would then be the only means of establishing a status of independence.

Accordingly, we come back to where we started in this essay: the nature of law itself. We see again that Mr. Justice Rand believed law to be primarily a matter of the supremacy of principles, ideas and processes, rather than the supremacy of particular persons or groups of persons holding elective or appointive offices at a particular time. In any event, once again the relevance of Rand's opinions to our current constitutional problems is obvious. When he said "law is reason," he used the phrase in a very broad sense. For him it embraced the substantive principles served by due process. It is ten years now since the death of Mr. Justice Rand, but his ideas form a valuable legacy of guidance for today and tomorrow.

Part V
Guaranteed Human Rights and Freedoms in Canada

Chapter 24

The Canadian Constitution and the Protection of Human Rights

Reprinted from *The Practice of Freedom*, R. St. J. Macdonald and J.P. Humphrey, eds. (Toronto: Butterworths, 1979) 25

I. INTRODUCTION

When people speak of human rights in relation to the legal and constitutional system of a country, they raise broad and critical issues concerning social justice in that country. In a sense, the whole of the legal system is constitutional law, because it embodies and depends on the basics of the constitution as its first principles. In Canada, for example, these principles give us our democratic parliamentary bodies, responsible ministries, independent courts, and the federal division of legislative powers between Parliament on the one hand and the provincial legislatures on the other. Most detailed and specific laws then take the form of statutes passed by ordinary majorities in these legislative bodies over the years, of regulations made under statutory authority, and also of judge-made laws that arise from reasoned judicial decisions, a source of law with a long history that still has crucial current importance. The total result is a great mass of laws on every conceivable subject. But, however diverse the subjects, all laws have at least this common feature; directly or indirectly, they are concerned with the conduct of human individuals, separately or in groups. In Canada, the laws deal with the rights, duties, freedoms, and immunities of all persons who live in the country. In short, for certain given circumstances, and where there is some choice for the individuals concerned, laws specify what social conduct ought to be. So, using the word "rights" in a very wide sense, all law is human rights law.

If we were to stay with these broad definitions, the subject of "The Canadian Constitution and the Protection of Human Rights" would be almost limitless. At this point then, we must determine certain valid and usual, but quite limited, senses in which one may speak of constitutions and human rights. In both respects, in this chapter, we are to be concerned with certain basics only, not with the whole legal system.

Sir Ivor Jennings has proposed limiting the term "constitution" to mean "the rules governing the composition, powers and methods of operation of the main institutions of government, and the general principles applicable to their relations to the citizens.''[1] Given this definition, we will consider the proper function and interrelation of democratic parliaments and independent courts in the securing or safeguarding of certain personal rights and freedoms—these latter being selected for consideration because they have special importance and are fundamental. Paradoxically, their very importance lies in the fact that they have all-pervasive implications for public standards and the rule of law. At times we find that selected human rights and freedoms of this character are expressed in the authoritative form of a statutory or a constitutional ''Bill of Rights'' in highly abstract and succinct terms. Two examples may be given. The First Amendment of the United States Constitution is as follows: ''Congress shall make no law respecting an establishment of religion, or prohibiting the free exercise thereof; or abridging the freedom of speech, or of the press: or the right of the people peaceably to assemble, and to petition the Government for a redress of grievances.'' Notice that we have here what is called constitutional special entrenchment. Congress makes ordinary statute laws by simple majorities in the House of Representatives and the Senate (both democratically elected bodies) but, nevertheless, Congress may not by this means alter or infringe upon the First Amendment rights or freedoms in essential respects. Such changes would require the special majorities and the consents set out in the American rules for constitutional amendment, that is, a two-thirds majority in each of the Houses of Congress, followed by the consent (democratically ascertained) of three-quarters of the fifty states. These are difficult majorities to obtain, so that the fundamental human rights and freedoms thus specially entrenched are quite secure from any change that has not been long considered and widely approved.

In Canada, we have many of the same rights and freedoms expressed in our constitutional law, but they are for the most part, in the form of ordinary statutes of the Parliament of Canada or a provincial legislature. An example is the Canadian Bill of Rights, passed as an ordinary statute of the Parliament of Canada in 1960.[2] Section 1 is as follows:

> 1. It is hereby recognized and declared that in Canada there have existed and shall continue to exist without discrimination by reason of race, national origin, colour, religion or sex, the following human rights and fundamental freedoms, namely,
> (a) the right of the individual to life, liberty, security of the person and enjoyment of property, and the right not to be deprived thereof except by due process of law;
> (b) the right of the individual to equality before the law and the protection of the law;
> (c) freedom of religion;
> (d) freedom of speech;
> (e) freedom of assembly and association; and
> (f) freedom of the press.

In comparing the American and Canadian Bills of Rights, it is apparent that the

---

[1] Ivor Jennings, *The Law and The Constitution*, 5th ed. (Cambridge, England: Cambridge Univ. Press, 1961), 33.
[2] S.C. 1960, c. 44.

literary expression of certain human rights and freedoms is much the same; the difference is in the authoritative status of the two documents. Obviously, one cannot specially entrench the whole of a legal system, and of course the Americans do not purport to do this. There must be wide powers of legal change by the usual democratic majority processes, so that governments can meet the demands and expectations of their citizens. Nevertheless, we in Canada must consider whether or not there are a few basic human rights and freedoms that should be specially entrenched, on the American model. Which is the better way? Where do we attempt to strike a balance in human rights between these two methods of legal change, ordinary statute and special constitutional amendment? Where is the equilibrium point? What difference would it make for the power of the courts in relation to legislatures if we were to adopt some special entrenchment of certain human rights on the American model? These are the questions I will attempt to address in the two remaining parts of this chapter.

In the next section I consider the logical and philosophical relation of a bill of rights to the total legal system. One can do this fruitfully by way of rational analysis, setting aside for the moment questions about better authoritative form, special entrenchment, or ordinary statute. Nevertheless, the philosophical and logical analysis will reveal certain inevitable functional needs that impartial courts and democratic legislatures must attempt to satisfy by separate or complementary action. In the final section I consider these functional problems, principally the proper role of courts and legislatures, in the implementing of a bill of rights as a working set of standards for the country.

II PHILOSOPHICAL AND LOGICAL FEATURES OF A TYPICAL BILL OF RIGHTS

In considering the relation of a bill of rights to the actual ongoing structure and function of the total legal system as a matter of logic and philosophy, we must first emphasize the potentially ubiquitous character of such a set of general standards. Just about every expectation people have of the constitutional and legal system can be asserted in general terms as human rights—rights, that is, that should by some means or other be legally declared and made secure. This is manifested most plainly by a noble United Nations' document, "The Universal Declaration of Human Rights," endorsed by the world body in 1948.[3] Here we find expressed in succinct terms at a high level of abstraction a comprehensive set of standards reaching potentially to all parts of the legal system of a modern state. It speaks, for instance, of rights to vote and hold public office, rights to freedom of expression, rights to a fair trial, rights to organize and join trade unions, rights to work, rights to free public elementary education, rights to an adequate standard of living from birth to death, and so on. The United Nations Declaration is an idealistic document, but it is not easy to work with. The standards it recites are ubiquitous, and thus implementing them in relation

---

[3]A convenient source of the text of the Declaration is "A Canadian Charter of Human Rights," a White Paper published by the Government of Canada in 1968, Hon. P. E. Trudeau, Minister of Justice, Appendix III, 87-95.

to one another is a matter of facing complexities and conflicts that make heavy demands on our powers of reasonable thought, social research, and moral insight, as the basis for official decision. In any event, I propose now to attempt briefly to illustrate and discuss these problems under four headings: the distinction between rights and freedoms; conflicts between overlapping general principles and the need for compromise; the need for both generalities and particulars; and the relation between equality and discrimination as tests of justice.

(a) The Distinction between Rights and Freedoms

The concept of a general liberty or freedom as distinct from a specific right is critical to understanding that a liberal and democratic society needs enough law, but not too much law, and that keeping this balance is always a delicate and difficult task. In the McRuer Report on Civil Rights in 1969 this point was developed as follows:

Powers and rights are quite specific and detailed, properly speaking, and they are defined or given by common law or statute. For example, the power to vote is specifically conferred on citizens who meet certain qualifications under the terms of the appropriate statutes, and election officials have a specific duty to recognize qualified persons. The specific power is spelled out in the law, with corresponding specific duties resting on other persons to give effect to it. The so-called freedoms or liberties are much more general and indefinite in their nature.

It therefore is necessary to make some analysis of the distinction between rights and powers on the one hand and liberties, freedoms and privileges on the other.

Rights, duties and powers, because of their specific and definite obligatory content, belong together for the purpose of analyzing the implications of a Bill of Rights and for this purpose they must be contrasted with liberties, freedoms or privileges which, while they are essential concepts of a legal system, nevertheless lack the specific and detailed obligatory character of rights, duties and powers.

In the Canadian Bill of Rights we find declared as fundamental freedoms: freedom of religion, freedom of assembly, freedom of speech, and freedom of the press. (We use the term freedom of expression as comprehending the latter two.) What is the judicial nature of these freedoms, liberties or privileges, as they are variously called?

The concept of liberties or freedoms in a duly precise scheme of legal terminology is the concept of areas of option and opportunity for human activity that are residual in nature. These areas of conduct are free of specific legal regulation. In them the individual is free to act or do nothing without legal direction.

The principal object and purpose of a Bill of Rights in a democratic society is to safeguard the essential boundaries of these areas. The basic difference between a democracy and a dictatorship is that in a democracy the areas for the individual's freedom of action are open unless closed. That is, in a democratic society what is not forbidden is permitted, whereas in a totalitarian society what is not forbidden is compulsory.

But, if liberty is a matter of option and opportunity free of legal regulation, in what sense do liberties or freedoms touch and concern the law or depend on it? For example, why is a person's liberty to express a political opinion or worship as he pleases any concern of the legal system? Such options are not directly created or specifically defined by the law or the constitution, as is one's power to vote or one's right to collect a debt. Nevertheless, freedoms or liberties do depend on the legal system. Though they are not the specific creation or gift of the law they depend on the law for their enjoyment. Thus they have their legal features and hence are properly included in the scheme of working jural ideas.

Specific prohibitions found in the Criminal Code and in the law of torts ensure or are designated to ensure peaceful social conditions to which a meaningful choice can be made in the exercise of free options. The laws of crime and tort safeguard each man's areas of option and opportunity against coercion at the hands of others. The laws against trespass and violence safeguard the free enjoyment of the ownership of land, but such laws give no direction with respect to how the land is to be enjoyed. They just leave the owner in peace. Accordingly, peaceful human activity in areas of freedom depends on basic law and its enforcement. It is in this general sense of dependence on the portions of the legal system relevant to peace and order that it is proper to speak of freedom under the law, or as Lord Wright put it, "freedom governed by law."

In addition to furnishing safeguards to areas of freedom and liberty the law defines the boundaries of those areas. What is not forbidden is permitted, but certain things must be and are forbidden. In the words of Chief Justice Duff:

"The right of public discussion is, of course, subject to legal restrictions; those based upon considerations of decency and public order, and others conceived for the protection of various private and public interest with which, for example, the laws of defamation and sedition are concerned."

In other words, to delineate the unregulated area you must first define the regulated area. This is strictly a legal matter. Outside the regulated area the individual is free to choose. In this residual sense the extent of liberty or freedom in some given respect is a matter of legal definition and properly has its place in the working concepts of the laywer or jurist. For example, as Chief Justice Duff points out, when the law forbids the uttering of defamatory, seditious or obscene words, specific legal prohibition stops. At the boundary so marked freedom of expression starts, and now the law takes no hand at all except to stop riots or other breaches of the peace. Beyond this boundary the laws does not tell a man what to say, nor does it compel anyone else to listen to him or to assist him in being heard by publishing in some way what he has said. So far as the law is concerned, he is on his own, and the factors and pressures involved in his choices and efforts concerning self-expression are extra-legal ones.

The residual and unspecified character of liberties or freedoms in relation to specific legal obligations is critical when we come to consider the relation of public legislative power to liberties or freedoms. Freedom of expression, for example, is not a single simple thing that may be granted by some legislature in one operation. It is potentially as various, far-reaching and unpredictable as the capacity of the human mind. Freedom of expression is the residual area of natural liberty remaining after the makers of the common law and the statute law have encroached upon it by creating inconsistent duties with respect to the exercise of this freedom.[4]

On the basis of the foregoing reasoning, with freedom of expression as the ex-

---

[4]Royal Commission: Inquiry into Civil Rights, Honourable J. C. McRuer, Commissioner, Report No. 2, Volume 4, 1969, 1493-96. As a consultant to the Royal Commission, W. R. Lederman was joint author with the Honourable Mr. McRuer of the portions of the report from which this quotation and the quotation referred to in footnote 5 are taken.

ample, we see that the areas of option and opportunity for human activity free of specific legal direction (one way or the other) are of vital importance. The law does not regulate everything, and it would be intolerable if it even attempted to do so. But, even so, while the presumption is in favour of the areas of option and opportunity, freedom of expression and the other freedoms cannot be permitted to operate without limit. This leads to our second philosophical problem.

(b) Conflicts between Overlapping General Principles and the Need for Compromise

Staying with example of freedom of expression: while this embodies a basic value of our society, considerations of decency, public order, and private reputation nevertheless provide values of equivalent generality which conflict and compete with freedom of expression, and which deserve to be given some effect in spite of and at the expense of freedom of expression. This is the point of the words of Chief Justice Duff, just quoted. Hence, by way of exception to freedom of expression, the law specifically forbids the utterance of obscene or seditious words, or statements that falsely damage the good reputation of another person. The exceptions are a compromise between the values in competition, none of which can be allowed to go all the way at the expense of the others.

This need for compromise is general in relation to the full range of the accepted values and goals of our society. Another example can be given, this one from the area of labour relations. The United Nations Declaration of 1948 speaks of the right to work, but also of the right to organize and join trade unions, and of the right of unions to organize strikes. Our labour relations laws have the task of compromising the conflicting values involved here. If the labour laws provide—as they often do—for a legal strike by a recognized union after efforts at collective bargaining in good faith have broken down, then at that point the right to work gives way to the right to strike. Any attempts at strike-breaking by the owners of the industry, by hiring nonunion members, then raises issues of the right to work of the latter, and the right of the owners to hire them—issues that are very difficult and indeed, are unresolved in many labour relations codes. Nevertheless, the purpose of labour relations codes is to work out the necessary compromises between the values in conflict, and this involves much detailed law-making and interpretation by legislatures, courts, and labour relations boards. Note that compromise requires that the succinct and abstract assertions characteristic of a bill of rights must be supplemented by much more detailed law-making, if the necessary compromises between the general values in competition are to be effectively worked out. This general need for compromise and detail has been expressed in Article 29 of the United Nations Declaration of 1948 as follows:

1. Everyone has duties to the community in which alone the free and full development of his personality is possible.
2. In the exercise of his rights and freedoms, everyone shall be subject only to such limitations as are determined by law solely for the purpose of securing due recogni-

tion and respect for the rights and freedoms of others and of meeting the just requirements of morality, public order and the general welfare in a democratic society.

3. These rights and freedoms may in no case be exercised contrary to the purposes and principles of the United Nations.

But, jurisprudentially, there is another reason why such detail is needed, which brings us to the third philosophical problem.

(c) The Need for Both Generalities and Particulars

The jurisprudential truth we have to deal with here is that very general and abstract legal propositions are like semi-manufactured products. They are not finished off and fully ready for use by the consumer until there has been a further process of what Professor Hans Kelsen has called increasing individualization and concretization. This can be illustrated by other examples drawn from the United Nations Declaration of 1948.

The first example concerns the criminal law. The U.N. Declaration tells us simply that there shall be no arbitrary arrests, and that every person charged with a criminal offence is entitled to the presumption of innocence and to fair trial by an independent and impartial tribunal. That is about all its says. But to ensure justice in detail on these terms requires hundreds of pages of laws about the definition of offences and criminal procedure, and thousands of pages of judicial interpretation of them. The delivery of justice to the people also needs elaborate and expensive official institutions and systems, including police forces, departments of justice, courts, and penitentiaries. All this is necessary for the effective implementation of the general values expressed with such admirable abstraction and brevity in the U.N. Declaration. The process involves going through several stages from the abstract to the particular, from the general to the specific. Hundreds of different levels of generality merging into particularity, or vice versa, are theoretically possible, and many of them are involved in the realities of complete legal processes.

The other example from the U.N. Declaration concerns the very different subjects of income security and welfare. Article 25 of the U.N. Declaration states in part:

Everyone has the right to a standard of living adequate for the health and well-being of himself and of his family, including food, clothing, housing and medical care and necessary social services, and the right to security in the event of unemployment, sickness, disability, widowhood, old age or other lack of livelihood in circumstances beyond his control.

Obviously this illustrates the same truths as the first example. Involved is the whole system of the welfare state as it has developed over the past 100 years. Thousands of pages in our books of statutes and regulations manifest the particularization of the U.N.'s Article 25, to say nothing of the elaborate official organizations—like the unemployment insurance commission—that are necessary if justice is to be delivered to the consumer in the terms specified.

These two examples show that general principles mean little unless developed on a massive scale in meaningful detail; and yet they also show that we need to appreciate the general implications of what it is we are doing in detail. Particular detailed rules cannot be properly understood, or kept in their respective places as part of a reasonable and just system, unless we pursue the general implications of particulars as far as the mind can reach. In other words, general principles and their detailed implications are all necessary parts of the total constitutional and legal system. They are complementary one to the other, so that there is necessarily constant interaction between them in living legal processes.

If now we look again at the example afforded by Article 25 just quoted from the U.N. Declaration, we see clues that lead us to the final philosophical problem I have identified in this area. Article 25 requires that the law should engage in benign discrimination. The unemployed, the sick, and the aged are to be treated separately and given benefits to which the employed, the healthy, and the young are not entitled. Of course there are good reasons for this that appeal to one's sense of justice. But Article 7 of the U.N. Declaration tells us that, "All are equal before the law and are entitled without any discrimination to equal protection of the law."

(d) The Relation between Equality and Discrimination as Tests of Justice

One soon finds that the equal protection clause just quoted cannot be taken literally and without qualification, because persons and groups of persons differ in many of their interests, beliefs, and inherent characteristics, and in the interests of justice the law must take some account of this diversity. Nevertheless, human diversity is not unlimited; it rests on an essential foundation of common humanity. So, looked at from the point of view of its total treatment of human individuals and groups, the law is a mixture of equal treatment and discrimination between them. Accordingly, the dilemma of justice for legislators and judges is to determine when equal treatment for all is the fair and proper thing and when, on the other hand, some discriminations are necessary and fair.

Equal treatment is provided for (as it should be) by the laws of crime and tort forbidding the causing of physical harm to other persons: any and all persons. Of the same character are requirements for fair procedure in criminal cases and protection from arbitrary arrest or imprisonment. On the other hand, because of children's natural immaturity, the law provides that they do not have the contractual capacity of adults, and that young children are not capable of committing crimes. No one questions the justice of these distinctions, but they do not provide equal treatment for children and adults. Differences in relative legal positions between soldiers and civilians, citizens and aliens, and professional men and laymen afford other examples of discriminations having rational and just purposes. Also, we have already noticed the benign discriminations of the welfare state.

These examples illustrate why the equality clauses of bills of rights cannot be taken literally. They do not forbid justifiable or benign discriminations. What they forbid is *unjustifiable* discriminations. A bill of rights has its strongest impact when it lists certain criteria which it forbids as tests for legal discriminations. For example, Article 2 of the U.N. Declaration says: "Everyone is entitled to all the rights and freedoms set forth in this Declaration, without distinction of any kind, such as race, color, sex, language, religion, political or other opinion, national or social origin, property, birth or other status.'' Here we have identified certain criteria, the use of which for legal discriminations usually brings unjust and obnoxious distinctions between persons and groups and which, therefore, must be regarded strictly and with special suspicion as reasons for departing from equal treatment. But, even in these respects, there may occasionally be justifiable distinctions. For example, maternity leave for employed women in a labour code without loss of pay or status, is a sex discrimination as compared to treatment of men, but no one today argues that it is not justified. There is also discrimination on grounds of nationality: an alien is denied the citizen's right to vote. This is justifiable, provided there are reasonable means open by which aliens may become citizens in due course.

So we see once again in this analysis that abstractions such as the equality clause are semi-manufactured products that need to be completed in more detail before they can be made meaningful at the level of everyday life. With equality clauses, we must ask in what particular respects we should legislate equality, and in what particular respects we should legislate for discrimination, that is, for legally sanctioned diversity. If we make these specific decisions fairly in our courts and parliaments, we make progress towards justice, step by step.

It should now be apparent, in relation to the four philosophical and logical problems discussed, that, as a matter of ongoing governmental processes, a great deal of specific law making is necessary to make the changes that are required from time to time to keep the total legal and constitutional system functioning. The means of doing this in Canada are the concern of the final section of this chapter.

III. DEMOCRATIC PARLIAMENTS, INDEPENDENT COURTS, AND CONSTITUTIONAL SPECIAL ENTRENCHMENT

As outlined above in the proceding paragraphs, certain common themes emerged with functional implications for governmental institutions and processes. We want enough law, but not too much law. There should be wide areas of peaceful option and opportunity, but the extent of these freedoms cannot be unlimited; relatively modest but necessary limits must be spelled out by detailed and particular prohibitions. General principles such as those of the U.N. Declaration of Human Rights of 1948 overlap and conflict, and detailed law-making is necessary to set equilibrium points between them. Abstract general principles must be particularized by full and relevant detail in the laws, or they remain incomplete and ineffective in affording meaningful directions at the level of everyday affairs. Finally, in distinguishing between essential equalities and justifiable discriminations that are to be secured in some way by the legal system, one must deal specifically and in particular with the proper and just purposes to be served by equalities in some respects and discriminations in others.

Add to this the fact that we do not live in a static society; indeed the pace of change seems to be ever accelerating. In the social conditions of our country, while there is much that remains the same there is also much that changes, and these new social conditions raise up requirements for legal change. They cause people to have new and different needs and expectations in relation to what the law can and should do for them. In terms of the analysis offered in this chapter, abstract general standards to which we pay homage may well take on different specific implications in new social conditions, and different equilibrium points are sure to be needed between some of the abstract general principles of the system that overlap and conflict. How do we accomplish these many legal adjustments by our constitutional processes?

In our parliamentary system, democratic parliaments—both provincial and federal—are the primary law-making bodies. Most of the important social policy decisions for change are taken there and, in my view, *should* be taken there and expressed in statutes that are passed by an ordinary majority of the elected representatives of the people, under the leadership of the cabinet. Periodic elections give the members of democratic legislatures a unique and primary legitimacy for this purpose that appointed persons do not have.

Nevertheless, the independent courts, composed of judges appointed with secure tenure in office (for life or until an andvanced age) also have a very important part to play. Courts should not be seen as rivals of parliamentary bodies, but rather as partners with complementary functions to carry out that are likewise essential. They have to take the legal principles found in constitutions and ordinary statutes, which run at various levels of generality, and individualize them so as to give authoritative decisions at the particular level of everyday affairs for the persons contemplated by the terms of the laws. In this connection, courts have an authoritative fact-finding function that is crucial to the whole process of applying laws. It need hardly be emphasized that the historic independence of the judiciary, which we have inherited from Britain as part of our constitutional system, is essential to impartial and competent individualization of laws. I do not mean by this that all instances of the specific application of laws require judicial hearings and decisions; that would be impossible. The judges deal only with a very small number of critical cases, but, in so doing, and in giving reasons, they set standards for the whole range of the application of laws by other tribunals, by ministers, by civil servants, and by governmental officers of all kinds. But, while important discretions rest with the judges, the priority of ordinary statutes remains. Parliament can amend one of its statutes if it does not like the interpretation given to it by the courts.

There is, however, an exception to this in the case of laws that are specially entrenched in the constitution. In this respect, courts are placed in an especially powerful position. For example, the equality clause of the American Constitution is specially entrenched, because change in it can only be legislated by a two-thirds majority in both Houses of Congress, followed by the concurrence of three-quarters of the fifty states, democratically ascertained in each state. Such majorities are seldom politically feasible. This means that, most of the time, the superior courts have the last word about the meaning and the application to affairs in the country of specially entrenched laws.

These considerations raise the last question to be addressed in this chapter. Which laws should be specially entrenched, and which should be subject to ordinary processes of statutory change? This is a large question, and I consider it here primarily in relation to the typical principles of a bill of rights, several examples of which we have been discussing. I think the proper answer is essentially the one reached by the McRuer Royal Commission on Civil Rights in Ontario in 1969, that is to say, that special entrenchment should be limited to "the rights of the individual that are themselves the foundation of parliamentary democracy, as we have inherited it and as we know it." The Royal Commission spelled these rights out as follows:

We first list these rights as we see then in general language without regard to the precise literary forms they might take, and then comment on certain institutional requisites essential to their enjoyment.

(1) The right of every person to freedom of conscience and religion.

(2) The right of every person to freedom of thought, expression and communication.

(3) The right of every person to freedom of assembly and assocation.

(4) The right of every person to security of this physical person and freedom of movement.

(5) The right of every adult citizen to vote, to be a candidate for election to elective public office, and to fair opportunity for appointment to appointive public office on the basis of proper personal qualifications.

(6) The right of every person to fair, effective and authoritative procedures, in accordance with principles of natural justice, for the determination of his rights and obligations under the law, and his liability to imprisonment or other penalty.

(7) The right to have the ordinary courts presided over by an independent judiciary.

In these seven propositions, we have approached the fundamentals of government from the pont of view of the human individual. Involved in these propositions there are certain institutional requisites essential to their enjoyment or which at least have proven to be historically effective, for our system of government. The most important of these institutional requisites may now be briefly stated:

(1) That the only source and definition of power for elected or appointed official persons is the public or constitutional law itself, whether this takes the authoritative form of specially entrenched rules, ordinary parliamentary statutes, judicial precedent or basic established custom.

(2) Since Canada is a federal country with an original distribution of primary law-making powers by subjects between the Federal Parliament on the one hand and the Provincial Parliaments on the other, there must be an extraordinary amending procedure (special entrenchment) controlling the original distribution of powers and Provincial boundaries.

(3) That those who govern Canada at the primary legislative level in the Federal Parliament or the Provincial Parliaments do so in a representative capacity by virtue of their election as members of their respective parliamentary bodies, and are subject to change in periodic and free elections. Their usual method of law-making is, after due deliberation, to pass statutes by ordinary majorities under the leadership of their respective cabinets.

(4) That the final authoritative interpretation of judicial precedents, and, at critical points, the final authoritative interpretation of specially entrenched laws and ordinary statutes, rests with a well qualified, impartial and independent

judiciary enjoying appointment to permanent tenure in office during good bheaviour.[5]

In the Canada of today, more special entrenchment might be desirable or necessary concerning, for example, education and rights to the use of the English or French languages. Such rights might be regarded as necessarily implied, up to a point, in the requirement for freedom of expression. In any event, the main position taken in the quotations from the Royal Commission Report seems to be valid.

FURTHER THOUGHTS

Some care must be taken concerning the sense in which one uses the word "discriminate". In the foregoing essay I have obviously used it in a broad and neutral sense, which is one of the proper dictionary meanings. When I speak of the law discriminating, I refer to the law establishing differences—any differences—between one person and another, or one group of persons and other groups. In this sense of simple differentiation, I have argued that the law makes many discriminations in the name of justice. These are benign discriminations. But of course there are obnoxious discriminations that are unjust. This latter sense is the only sense in which many persons speak or write of discrimination. One must watch the context to avoid mistakes in the way the word is being used.

---

[5]*Ibid.*, 1570-72.

Chapter 25

A Comment on the Canadian Bill of Rights and the Judgment of the Supreme Court of Canada in the Case of: The Queen v. Joseph Drybones[1]

Reprinted in part from *Background Papers and Reports*, Vol. 2, 1970,
Ontario Advisory Committee on Confederation

In comments on interpretative alternatives concerning the Canadian Bill of Rights in 1967 I made the following statements:

> If the *Canadian Bill of Rights* is to be taken as providing rules for the interpretation of other federal statutes, effective only if there is ambiguity in those other statutes but not if their words are clear, then the *Canadian Bill of Rights* does not mean very much. On the other hand, if the *Canadian Bill of Rights* is to be construed as providing overriding principles amending or repealing any inconsistent federal statutory provision, whether the latter is in plain words or not, then the *Canadian Bill of Rights* will be much more effective. It must be said that the *Canadian Bill of Rights* is iteself poorly drafted, since it leaves the choice between these alternative meanings uncertain.
>
> ● ● ●
>
> Yet, politically, the *Canadian Bill of Rights* is not the sort of statute that any parliamentary body could easily change or repeal, though it takes the form of an ordinary statute. So long as it is in the statute book, it confers on Canadian judges important opportunities to strike down Canadian laws inconsistent with the liberties of the subject thus statutorily declared—opportunities that are very much like those possessed by American judges. Hence Canadian judges, if they choose to be bold about it, may now assert a good deal more influence and power in the field of civil liberties than English judges do. . . . As a compromise between English parliamentary supremacy and American judicial supremacy in this field the Canadian position may turn out to be better than either.

For the first time, the interpretative issue described in the above quotations was clearly raised late in 1969 before the Supreme Court of Canada. In the case of *The Queen v. Joseph Drybones*, the Court chose the bolder of the interpretative alternatives for the *Canadian Bill of Rights*, by a decisive majority of six to three.

---

[1](Judgment given November 20, 1969). Reported in (1970) 71 Western Weekly Reports, 161-181.

The facts of the case raised a clear conflict between an earlier statute of the Federal Parliament and the *Canadian Bill of Rights* of 1960, a conflict that could not be avoided by any rationally possible or sensible restrictive interpretation of the words of the earlier statute. Section 94 of the *Indian Act*, the earlier statute, made it an offence for an *Indian* to be intoxicated *off a reserve*. The Liquor Ordinance of the Northwest Territories made it an offence for *any person* to be intoxicated *in a public place*. The consequent discrimination arising from these two federal laws is described by Mr. Justice Ritchie in the following words.

> The result is that an Indian who is intoxicated in his home "off a reserve" is guilty of an offence and subject to a minimum fine of not less than $10 or a term of imprisonment not exceeding 3 months or both, whereas all other citizens in the Territories may, if they see fit, become intoxicated otherwise than in a public place without committing an offence at all. And even if any such other citizen is convicted of being intoxicated in a public place, the only penalty provided by the Ordinance is "a fine not exceeding $50 or . . . imprisonment for a term not exceeding 30 days or . . . both fine and imprisonment."

It was clear on the facts that Joseph Drybones had indeed been intoxicated in the Old Stope Hotel at Yellowknife in the Northwest Territories. He had been charged under Section 94 of the Indian Act.

Mr. Justice Ritchie then continued as follows:

> I think that the word "law" as used in sec. 1(b) of the *Bill of Rights* is to be construed as meaning "the law of Canada" as defined in sec. 5(2) (i.e., Acts of the parliament of Canada and any orders, rules or regulations thereunder) and without attempting any exhaustive definition of "equality before the law" I think that sec. 1(b) means at least that no individual or group of individuals is to be treated more harshly than another under that law, and I am therefore of opinion that an individual is denied equality before the law if it is made an offence punishable at law, on account of his race, for him to do something which his fellow Canadians are free to do without having committed any offence or having been made subject to any penalty.

> It is only necessary for the purpose of deciding this case for me to say that in my opinion sec. 94(b) of the *Indian Act* is a law of Canada which creates such an offence and that it can only be construed in such manner that its application would operate so as to abrogate, abridge or infringe one of the rights declared and recognized by the *Bill of Rights*. For the reasons which I have indicated, I am therefore of opinion that sec. 94(b) is inoperative.

> For the purpose of determining the issue raised by this appeal it is unnecessary to express any opinion respecting the operation of any other section of the *Indian Act*.

Quite clearly then, our final court has confirmed the view that the Canadian Bill of Rights is of overriding effect in the whole sphere of federal law in Canada. In particular, it is not just an aid to interpretation of earlier or later federal statutes should the wording of those other statutes be unclear. The idea of overriding effect is the one intended by the law officers of the Crown who advised Prime Minister Diefenbaker in 1960 concerning the Canadian Bill of Rights. One of these advisers was Mr. Elmer Driedger, Q.C., who, being Chief Parliamentary Draftsman at the time, drew the actual provisions of the Statute. Writing in 1968 on the subject, Mr. Driedger shows how complex a task it is to draft a general Bill of Rights. He considered that apt words had been used to give the Statute the desired overriding effect. He said:[2]

> The opening or general words of s. 2 read as follows:
>
> 2. Every law of Canada shall, unless it is expressly declared by an Act of the Parliament of Canada that it shall operate notwithstanding the *Canadian Bill of Rights*, be so construed and applied as not to abrogate, abridge or infringe or to authorize the abrogation, abridgement or infringement of any of the rights or freedoms herein recognized and declared, and in particular, no law of Canada shall be construed or applied so as to. . . .
>
> This provision is clearly a rule of interpretation. Granted that Parliament cannot bind itself and cannot bind future parliaments, it may nevertheless lay down the rules that are to govern the interpretation and application of its own statutes. The Interpretation Act is a long-standing example of this technique. The Bill of Rights applies to "every law of Canada," which is defined in subsection 2 of s. 5. The rule of interpretation prescribed by s. 2 is to apply to all laws of Canada, unless it is expressly declared by an act of the Parliament of Canada that any of those laws shall operate notwithstanding the Canadian Bill of Rights. The effect of this provision therefore would appear to be to abrogate the two rules of inconsistency, namely, that a particular statute overrides a general statute and that a later statute overrides an earlier one. Is such a provision effective? Parliament has not said that its own powers are any the less, nor that a future parliament must not enact a conflicting law. Parliament has said only that certain intentions shall not be imputed to it unless a special form of words is used. This does not differ from s. 16 of the Interpretation Act, which says that no provision or enactment in any act affects, in any manner whatsoever, the rights of Her Majesty, unless it is expressly stated therein that Her Majesty is bound thereby, and that Act also states that it applies to every act "now or hereafter passed."

In his reference to interpretation here, Mr. Driedger is speaking of the internal consistency of the whole body of federal laws. It has always been necessary to have interpretative rules of priority to maintain this consistency, when outright conflict occurs between the plain words of two different statutory provisions. Given two inconsistent federal laws, the interpretative rules for priority restore over-all consistency by prescribing full effect for one of them and suspending the operation of the other to the extent that it is inconsistent or repugnant. As Mr. Driedger points out, sections 2 and 5 of the Canadian Bill of Rights simply provide a special rule of priority when some other federal law is repugnant to a provision of the Canadian Bill of Rights. Such a conflict, Parliament has said, is to be resolved in favour of the Canadian Bill of Rights. Thus the priority rules for the particular over the general, or the later over the earlier, do not apply in this case. The supremacy of Parliament in the federal sphere of law is acknowledged, as it must be under our constitution, by the declaratory provision in the Canadian Bill of Rights that Parliament can give any other federal law priority over the

---

[2]E. A. Driedger, 'The Canadian Bill of Rights', in *Contemporary Problems of Public Law in Canada*, O. E. Lang (ed.), University of Toronto Press, Toronto, 1968, 37.

Canadian Bill of Rights if it enacts explicit words to that effect. Also, of course, Parliament could repeal the Canadian Bill of Rights itself. Nevertheless, the fact is that, politically, either of these last two steps would be quite difficult to take, so the Canadian Bill of Rights ends up with an unusually high degree of security as it now stands in the federal statute book. Yet this is not special entrenchment on the American model. In the ways indicated, an ordinary majority of the elected representatives of the people in Parliament may assert final power over the many important matters covered by the provisions of the Canadian Bill of Rights.

We seem to have here the formula for a very effective blending of judicial and parliamentary powers, a formula that stimulates appropriate judicial activism in favour of the specified rights and freedoms of the citizen, and yet still gives the last word to an ordinary majority in the democratically elected Parliament of Canada, if Parliament should choose to speak the last word by its normal legislative process. Mr. Driedger's essay on the subject convinces me that I was wrong to say, as I did in 1967, that the Canadian Bill of Rights is poorly drafted. The Statute will be very effective by virtue of the meaning intended by the draftsman and now confirmed by the Supreme Court of Canada. No doubt considerable problems lie ahead, but these will now centre upon questions of what is conflict or inconsistency between other federal laws and the provisions of the Canadian Bill of Rights. These are difficult questions, but on the whole it is a healthy development that the courts generally must now ask them and face them.

● ● ●

Chapter 26

Securing Human Rights in a Renewed Confederation

Reprinted with permission from *Must Canada Fail?*
Richard Simeon, ed. (Montreal and London: McGill-Queen's
University Press, 1977)

In December 1948 the General Assembly of the United Nations endorsed a noble document entitled "The Universal Declaration of Human Rights" which, in its first paragraph, speaks of "recognition of the inherent dignity and of the equal and inalienable rights of all members of the human family," and asserts this to be "the foundation of freedom, justice and peace in the world." This was not intended to deny that persons and groups differ in many of their interests, beliefs, and inherent characteristics; such denial would be hopelessly simplistic. Rather these opening words and the rest of the "Declaration" do affirm that human diversity in all its variety nevertheless rests on an essential foundation of common humanity for every person. This sense of common humanity should evoke mutual and reciprocal respect between persons and groups of persons in spite of the extent to which they differ one from another. The effective and just organization of society depends in the end on such sympathy and empathy between human individuals.

But we live in a world where there is a scarcity of good things, both tangible and intangible, including what may be described as opportunities for personal self-fulfilment. This scarcity means that every available person cannot simply do as he wishes or have what he wants without limit. We have to have processes our systems for sharing what is available, and this is the root of the need for constitutions, and for the government and legal systems that stem from constitutions. In the complex modern world we see that people must often look to governments and courts operating under the rule of law to create and maintain social conditions in which they may satisfy to a reasonable degree their basic needs and desires. Because of the relative scarcity of the good things of life, this is always a process of compromises between conflicting interests and claims, compromises that fall short of perfect satisfaction of those interests or claims. In terms of this analysis we come to a relative and pragmatic definition of justice. Practical justice means that the overall scarcity shortfall should be kept to the unavoidable minimum, and that the limited opportunities for self-fulfilment available should be distributed fairly among the people. One must add that what use people make of their opportunities is not the gift of a government or a law. What they may then accomplish is rather a matter of personal choice and effort. The last thing people want is that there should be a law telling them what to do or not to do at every turn. To be assured of reasonably broad areas of personal option and opportunity, our society needs enough law, but not too much law; always a delicate balance.

These are very lofty and general sentiments, but what is their bearing on present problems of Canadian unity? Simply this. Among the most important and fundamental of human rights are those concerning the use of language, and for the average person this mainly means rights, options, and opportunities to use one's mother tongue. I believe it is fair to say that the present crisis issues of Canadian unity are in the main language-related; and that the course of Canadian history has been such that these issues concern the assured use of the English language or the French language or both of them in education, in government, in business and industry, and in radio and television broadcasting. That list is not exhaustive, of course, as language is all-pervasive in significance and social impact. All communication between persons, and within and between groups of persons, depends on language. All organized activities of whatever kind can only go forward on the basis of the spoken and written word. A person's mother tongue is fundamental to his thinking and feeling, to his development and self-fulfilment, and to his relations with others. No wonder the area is so sensitive for both anglophones and francophones. And no wonder that, so far as law touches language use at all, it usually does so in terms of legally sanctioned rights and legally protected freedoms. Legal prohibitions are rare and should be carefully justified and limited when they are used.

The purpose of this paper is to bring to bear on present language-related issues critical to the unity of Canada the juristic learning and analysis that has been developed concerning fundamental human rights and freedoms generally. In so doing, I hope to make three points: these issues are very complex juristically, and over-simplification of them is foolish and dangerous; compromises of some sort between English and French language groups in Canada (and indeed in North America) on terms fair to both are inevitable and necessary, whatever the political or constitutional future of Canada may be; fresh linguistic compromises that should be appropriate and effective to keep Quebec within a genuinely revised and renewed Canadian federal union are indeed possible and available.

The starting point for juristic consideration of language rights is surely to examine the nature of freedom of expression itself, whatever the language or languages that may be the means of expression at a particular time or place. As a basic human liberty, freedom of expression is part of our historically inherited English public law. Moreover, it is declared in statutory form by the Parliament of Canada in the Canadian Bill of Rights of 1960, and declared also in statutory form by the National Assembly of Quebec in the Quebec Charter of Human Rights and Freedoms of 1975. Finally, this liberty or freedom is also proclaimed in the International Convention on Civil and Political Rights of the United Nations, which is binding on Canada, having been ratified as an international obligation by Canada in 1976, with the consent and approval of the provinces.

What then is the juridical nature of a freedom or liberty such as freedom of expression? In answer, I quote from what I said on this point when writing in the Canadian Bar Review in 1959 on the Canadian Bill of Rights.

> The concept of liberties or freedoms in a duly precise scheme of legal terminology is the concept of residual areas of option and opportunity for human activity *free of specific legal regulation.* In such areas of conduct there are neither affirmative legal prescriptions nor legal prohibitions—a man is at liberty to act or do nothing as he chooses, free of obligatory instruction by the law either way. Now to call these areas or classes of conduct residual is by no means to disparage them, far from it. Indeed, in a democratic country they are large and important areas, and one of the principal things a Bill of Rights attempts to do is to safeguard their essential boundaries. Only a relatively small portion of the total of actual or potential human activity is regulated in detail by specific legal duties, whether positive or negative, and life would be intolerable if this were not so. Indeed, just here lies one of the differences between democracy and dictatorship, for under a dictatorship there is in a sense too much law. The point is rather aptly made by the saying that, in a democratic country what is not forbidden is permitted, whereas in a totalitarian one what is not forbidden is compulsory. . . .
>
> To speak generally, this means that when you have defined the extent of specific legal regulation in terms of existing duties, *ipso facto* you have drawn the outside boundaries of the areas of liberty or freedom. To delineate the unregulated area you must first define the regulated area, to do which is stricly a legal matter. So, in this residual sense the extent of liberty or freedom in some given respect is a matter of legal definition and properly has its place in the working concepts of the lawyer or jurist. For example, . . . the law forbids the uttering of defamatory, seditious or obscene words, and there specific legal prohibition stops. At the boundary so marked freedom of expression starts, and now the law takes no hand at all except to stop riots or other breaches of the peace. Beyond this boundary the law does not tell a man what to say or what not to say, nor does it compel anyone else to listen to him or to assist him to be heard by publishing in some way what he has said. So far as the law is concerned, he is on his own, and the factors and pressures involved in his choices and efforts concerning self-expression are extra-legal ones.
>
> This residual and unspecified character of liberties or freedoms in relation to specific legal obligation is critical when we come to consider the relation of public legislative power to liberties or freedoms. Freedom of expression, for example, is not a single simple thing that may be granted by some legislature in one operation—it is potentially as various, far-reaching and unpredictable as the capacity of the human mind.

Nevertheless, as indicated, though very wide freedom of expression—freedom of language use—is a basic value of society, it cannot be allowed to operate without limit. Considerations of decency, public order, and private reputation also provide principles of equivalent generality that conflict and compete with freedom of expression, and which deserve to be given some effect in spite of and at the expense of the latter. So the law provides that, by way of exception, one is not free to utter obscene or seditious words, or words that falsely damage the good reputation of another person. Here we see the need for and the inevitability of compromise between competing and conflicting values of which I spoke earlier. Both legislators framing statutes and judges interpreting existing laws have to establish such compromises at reasonable equilibrium points between the values in competition. Nevertheless, the importance of freedom of expression means that the limitations on it should be few and as closely defined as possible. The presumption should run in favour of freedom of expression.

The need for compromise, however, is not peculiar to freedom of expression, it is general in relation to the whole range of proper values and goals of our society. For example, the United Nations declarations of rights speak of the right to work, but they also speak of the right to form and join trade unions and of the right of the latter to organize strikes. Our labour relations laws must somehow compromise the conflicting values involved here. If labour laws provide, as they often do, for a legal strike by a recognized union after efforts at bargaining in good faith have broken down, then, at that point, the right to work gives way to the right to strike. We find that this need for compromise is also generalized in the key United Nations documents on human rights and freedoms. For example, Article 29 of the United Nations Declaration of 1948 is as follows:

1. Everyone has duties to the community in which alone the free and full development of his personality is possible.

2. In the exercise of his rights and freedoms, everyone shall be subject only to such limitations as are determined by law solely for the purpose of securing due recognition and respect for the rights and freedoms of others and of meeting the just requirements of morality, public order and the general welfare in a democratic society.

3. These rights and freedoms may in no case be exercised contrary to the purposes and principles of the United Nations.

Compromise, then, as in the labour law example, itself requires much detailed law-making and interpretation by legislatures and courts or other tribunals. But jurisprudentially there is another reason why such detail is needed, which can be illustrated by another example from the United Nations Declaration. In general terms it tells us that there shall be no arbitrary arrest and that every person charged with a criminal offence is entitled to the presumption of innocence and to a fair trial by an independent and impartial tribunal. That is about all it says. That is fine, but actually to deliver justice in these terms to the citizens requires hundreds of pages of laws about detailed criminal procedure and thousands of pages of judicial interpretation of them. It requires also elaborate and expensive official institutions and systems, including police forces, departments of justice, courts, and penitentiaries. All these linkages are necessary for the effective implementation of general values expressed in very succinct and general terms. A failure in the linkages at any point may well result in denial of justice to the ultimate consumer, the human individual subject to charges or making claims. To quote from the McRuer Report of 1969 on Civil Rights:

Highly abstract principles do have great importance in themselves simply as directive principles concerning the goals and ideals of a society. Although it is true that general declarations of principles mean little unless worked out on a massive scale in precise detail, we must appreciate the general implications of what it is we are doing in precise detail. Particular detailed rules cannot be properly understood or applied as parts of a reasonable scheme or system unless we pursue as far as possible the general implications involved in them. Only then can we bring order and purpose to the mass of detail in our laws. . . .

. . . The point is that general principles and their detailed implications are all part of a legal or constitutional system. They are complementary one to the other. The general controls the mind in dealing with the particular. There is necessarily a constant interaction between the more general and the more particular in a living legal process, always conceding that it is beyond man's capacity to be ultimately general or finally particular in creating standards. The upper and lower limits of abstraction are relative, not absolute, for legal and constitutional purposes.

So far, in speaking of freedom of expression and language issues related thereto, I have said nothing of the problems posed by the fact that different communities and groups have different languages, and that relatively few persons are bilingual or multilingual. But of course this is frequently the situation, and here we encounter further conflicting values and interests in relation to freedom of expression; which means further need for compromises by appropriate and rather detailed laws. Nevertheless, I do maintain that these compromises should endeavour to accomplish their purposes with as little derogation from the master principle of freedom of expression as possible in the circumstances.

In any event, in Canada the course of our history has determined that our problems in this respect primarily concern the assured use of the English language or the French language or both of them, in education, parliamentary bodies, courts, government documents, public administration, business and industry, and so on. This is complicated by the fact that francophones are very much in the majority in the Province of Quebec, whereas anglophones are very much in the majority in the other provinces of Canada and in the United States. In these circumstances, the Bourassa government and the present Lévesque government of Quebec have felt compelled to take special legislative measures to protect the ongoing viability of the French language, culture, and way of life in Quebec. Moreover, the current movement for the political independence of Quebec has the same objective.

Consideration and analysis of these issues may usefully be undertaken at this point in relation to two sets of laws of the Province of Quebec, one actual and one proposed. In 1975 Quebec moved into the main stream of human rights legislation in the western world by enacting as a statute the Charter of Human Rights and Freedoms. On April 28 of this year (1977) the Charter of the French Language in Quebec was introduced into the current session of the Quebec National Assembly as Bill 1. Extensive hearings were held on the bill and on July 12 the Quebec government reintroduced the Language Charter as Bill 101. Bill 101 contains the amendments to Bill 1 that the Quebec government is willing to make as a result of the hearings, and so is very likely the form in which the Charter of the French Language will soon become law.

If Bill 101 is read in relation to the Quebec Charter of Human Rights and

Freedoms, my view is that the two may well be inconsistent in important respects. If so, which has priority and thus overriding effect? The Quebec Charter of Human Rights, in section 52, states that its essential provisions "prevail over any provision of any subsequent act which may be inconsistent therewith unless such act expressly states that it applies despite the Charter." Bill 1, the original proposed language law, did expressly state (in section 172) that it applied despite the Charter of Human Rights, but in this respect the Parti Québécois government has changed its position. It has dropped section 172 from Bill 101, thus leaving the Charter of Human Rights with priority over the forthcoming language law, in the event of inconsistency between them. It is encouraging at this juncture in Canadian affairs that the Quebec government has thus recognized the primacy of the essential values of a democratic society. Nevertheless, by way of contrast, we find that Bill 101 maintains the severe restrictions of the previous Bill 1 on rights of access to the minority anglophone school system of Quebec. No doubt the Quebec government considers there is no conflict between Bill 101 and the Quebec Charter of Human Rights and Freedoms, in this respect as well as in others. They may well be wrong about this. Let us consider the issue in relation to access to the historic anglophone school system, which is all that space permits in this short essay.

The Quebec Charter of Human Rights and Freedoms asserts in section 3 that every person possesses the fundamental right to freedom of expression, and in section 10 asserts further that every person should enjoy that right "without distinction, exclusion or preference based on race, colour, sex, civil status, religion, political convictions, language, ethnic or national origin or social condition." Articles 26 and 27 of the International Covenant on Civil and Political Rights of 1966 are to the same effect, though they are more explicit, and thus reinforce the Quebec Charter.

Article 26

All persons are equal before the law and are entitled without any discrimination to the equal protection of the law. In this respect, the law shall prohibit any discrimination and guarantee to all persons equal and effective protection against discrimination on any ground such as race, colour, sex, language, religion, political or other opinion, national or social origin, property, birth or other status.

Article 27

In those States in which ethnic, religious or linguistic minorities exist, persons belonging to such minorities shall not be denied the right, in community with the other members of their group, to enjoy their own culture, to profess and practise their own religion, or to use their own language.

As noted, Canada, with the concurrence of Quebec and the other provinces, has ratified this convention, article 50 of which specifies that it "shall extend to all parts of federal states without any limitations or exceptions." Our task now is to apply the foregoing general analysis concerning freedom of expression to the educational rights of linguistic minorities in Quebec and the other provinces of Canada. The issue may at some point be taken before the courts in these terms, so that, in exploring it here and giving my own views, I am looking at considerations the judges might well take into account in deciding such a case.

In the first place I feel full sympathy for the concept of the French language as the priority language in Quebec; that Quebec must be the homeland of French language and culture in North America. Nevertheless, the large anglophone minority in Quebec has historic rights to the use of the English language that should be allowed greater freedom and accorded greater recognition than we find in the proposed Charter of the French Language in Quebec. In the matter of education, leaving aside transitional provisions, parents will not be permitted to send their children to schools where the language of instruction is English unless one parent at least was himself or herself previously educated in Quebec in the anglophone school system of the province. In effect this gravely inhibits the immigration of anglophones to Quebec because it means, after the Charter of the French Language becomes law, that any anglophones who immigrate cannot send their children to a school system centred on their own language and culture, though historically that school system has existed and presently exists in Quebec. It seems to me, to adopt the words of Article 27 of the International Covenant on Civil Rights, that this does deny to anglophones who go to Quebec to live the fundamental right to enjoy their own culture and use their own language, whatever their reasons for immigration may be, and thus is in breach of Article 27.

In my view, the right to attend the anglophone school system in Quebec should obtain for any children whose mother-tongue is English, wherever the family comes from in the English-speaking world and whenever they come. At least Bill 22 of the Bourassa government did in effect allow this, though the statute had other shortcomings. I do not believe that there would be any threat to the full and effective priority of the French language in Quebec if the proposed Charter of the French Language were altered to accord rights of access to the English school system of Quebec in the terms I have just advocated. To do this would meet the standards in this respect of the Quebec Charter of Human Rights and Freedoms and of Article 27 of the International Covenant on Civil and Political Rights to which Quebec has subscribed as a part of Canada. In my view failure to make this change would be to fall seriously short of those standards. At the level of rights of immigration alone, to bar anglophone immigration to Quebec indirectly but effectively by restricting access to the historic anglophone school system would be obnoxious even if Quebec were politically a separate state. It is all the more obnoxious when Quebec is a province of Canada. It is not necessary to go this far to assure the priority of the French language and the security of the French culture in Quebec. The fundamental freedom that underlies my reasoning here is freedom of expression itself, and it is wrong to infringe on that freedom any further than is necessary for the reasonable protection of relevant competing interests and claims of the same order and level of importance.

On the other hand, since English-speaking persons are the minority linguistic group in Quebec, I think it is reasonable for the proposed Quebec Language Charter to require that children in the anglophone school system should, by virtue of instruction there, become fully proficient in French as their second language. This is a proper compromise between the competing requirements of the two linguistic groups for freedom of expression, in the circumstances that obtain in the Province of Quebec.

I am well aware that Canadian francophones in both Manitoba and Ontario were deprived of rights to education in French at the end of the last century and in the early years of this one. These denials of rights were wrong, and I do not defend or condone them, but they did occur generations ago. We should not now dwell unduly on past injustices, because things have changed. The situation is moving in favour of francophone minorities in most if not all of the nine anglophone Canadian provinces, especially in Ontario and New Brunswick. For example, in recent years in Ontario, a complete francophone school system, publicly financed, has become available to the French-speaking residents of the province, with two bilingual universities at the apex of the system. These francophone rights in Ontario are not yet expressed and assured in a straightforward way in legislation, as they should be. Ontario and other provinces of course have the same obligations to respect the historic minority educational rights of their francophone residents as those that I have asserted belong to the anglophone minority residents of Quebec. If the English-speaking provinces were to enact more and better legislation about this, and devote more resources to francophone school systems and also to teaching the French language to anglophone children, French Quebecers might well read such developments as assurance that they do not need to seek political independence for Quebec to protect the French language and culture. They might indeed conclude that they are better off within Canada in this respect. I acknowledge of course that the efforts of the federal Parliament and government under the Official Languages Act of Canada should likewise be persuasive and conducive to the same end, though it is beyond the scope of this paper to discuss them.

In conclusion, I return to the fundamental right of freedom of expression itself. As the root of opportunities for self-fulfilment this has both its individual aspects and its community or collective aspects. In both aspects, the standards involved need to be expressed in statutes, constitutions, judicial decisions, and international treaties. When conflicting claims and interests arise in the area, as they inevitably do, compromises must be established that keep infringement of the basic freedom itself to a minimum. Securing freedom of expression (and other basic human rights) in a renewed Canadian Confederation requires sophisticated efforts on the part of our parliaments, our governments, and our courts. If we can succeed with these efforts, the unity of Canada will endure. I am both very anxious and very hopeful.

FURTHER THOUGHTS AND REFERENCES

Current proposals for constitutional reform in Canada (1980) virtually all suggest new measures for special entrenchment of certain human rigts and freedoms. Examples are: the Trudeau Government in its Bill C-60 of 1978; The Report of the

Committee on the Constitution of the Canadian Bar Association, 1978; the Pepin-Robarts Report, 1979; The "Beige Paper" of the Quebec Liberal Party, 1980.

So, the continuing relevance of the issues and problems in Part V of this collection of essays is obvious.

Part VI
Addendum

Chapter 27

Continuing Relevance of Constitutional Jurisprudence

As these words are being written in August 1980, Canada is in the aftermath of the Quebec Referendum in which the people of that Province decisively rejected secession from Canada in favour of continued partnership in the Canadian federal union. This was in the expectation by Quebecers that there would be significant basic constitutional reform forthcoming reasonably soon, albeit reform that respected the essentials of federalism for all of Canada. The Western Provinces and the Atlantic Provinces likewise have expectations for some reform that respects the essentials of federalism, and Ontario as the largest province in population and industry has to be concerned if the other provinces are. And of course it is obvious that the essential country-wide national dimensions of Canadian federalism are the special concern of the Federal Government and the Parliament of Canada at Ottawa. Indeed, that Government and Parliament are specially responsible for the safe-keeping of those essential national dimensions, and for giving sophisticated and sensitive leadership to the constitutional reform process. A special effort to develop suitable and agreed reforms is currently being made, under the leadership of the Federal Government, which I hope will bring the needed changes. But the various proposals for change are too complex to be reviewed here—to do so would take another 500 pages. Rather, I propose to make some observations about constitutional change in general that are appropriate to the content of this collection of essays.

At this point in time, we do not know to what extent there will be basic constitutional reform in the near future. But, if significant reform does take place soon, would these essays thereby be rendered obsolete or would they have continuing relevance to the reformed constitution? I am not of course an unbiased commentator, but, for what it may be worth, my view is that the relevance of the essays would continue. I hope and indeed claim that these essays go some way toward explaining the inevitable and inherent problems of working a federal system like ours, involving as it does a division of ordinary legislative powers, democratic parliamentary institutions at both the provincial and central levels, certain specially entrenched rights and freedoms, and independent courts. These essential elements of the present Canadian constitutional system are going to continue, though there will probably be some specific changes in the division of powers and in specially entrenched rights and freedoms; and some specific reforms of the judicial and parliamentary systems.

I do then claim continuing relevance for these essays. In their coverage they concern the basic constitutional reform process itself (Part II), and also they seek to explain the full operating jurisprudence both of the federal division of legislative powers (Part IV) and of specially entrenched human rights and freedoms (Part V). In other words, considerations have been canvassed that are applicable generally to any significant division of legislative powers or entrenchment of rights. Moreover, essential to this operating jurisprudence is the function of the superior courts as final interpreters of basic constitutional provisions. Accordingly, both the quality and the independence of the judiciary are of critical importance and so have received much attention in these essays (Part III).

There is a further continuing relevance of some of these essays for law reform generally that should be noted. It is essential to appreciate that, in the grant total of legal change, only a very small proportion is change at the basic constitutional level. A vital distinction that runs through Parts IV and V is that between ordinary statutory change by simple majority in a single parliamentary body, and basic general guide-lines of the constitution which provide the overall framework within the limits of which ordinary statutory change may proceed. Change in these basic guide-lines themselves requires more than a simple majority in a single legislative body. It usually requires widely distributed consents or special majorities or both, especially in a federal country like ours. Accordingly, such basic changes cannot be made easily or often, which is as it should be.

Let us now look more closely at the relation between constitutional change and statutory change through the medium of the following example. Our constitutional law on division of powers tells us that criminal law is the responsibility of the Parliament of Canada, but it does not say anything, for example, about whether simple possession of marihuana is or is not a criminal offence. That is a question to be settled by a statutory change passed by a simple majority in the Parliament of Canada. The issue is not a basic constitutional one because the constitutional guide-lines are simply silent and neutral about it, as they are about the specifics of many things. In somewhat the same way, as explained in the essays in Part V, the general standards of a constitutional "Bill of Rights" are very heavily dependent on detailed implementation by ordinary statutes and regulations, and, at this latter ordinary level legitimate alternatives and exceptions may appear and require to be dealt with. This means that often, the specific reforms people want are available by ordinary statutory action at either the provincial or the federal level and are not basic constitutional issues at all. We should have a lively sense of the great extent to which we are and should be dependent for meaningful legal reform on ordinary statutes and political processes in our democratic parliamentary bodies. The point is that, if we characterize too many things as basically constitutional, we put too much of potential legal change to meet societal needs beyond the reach of the flexible statutory means of change. It is at times difficult enough to get an ordinary statute through in response to some urgent need for new legal measures. The problem of limiting the definition of what is properly to be considered "constitutional" is the subject of the first essay in this collection.

Related to what has just been said is the further fact that our constitution, typically, devotes itself in important measure to basic processes defining *how* to do things, rather than to specifying *what* should be done. So, we find that the democratic character of our parliamentary bodies, the independence of the courts, and the fairness of procedure in both are fundamental. And these things are not mere procedure. They have large implications. They mean respect for the people, individually and collectively, through appeals to rationality and justice in both parliaments and courts as a means of honouring positive and substantive human values.[1]

•

---

[1] I would add to these concluding remarks what I said in my essay on "Constitutional Amendment and Canadian Unity", under the sub-heading "The Values and Objectives of Canadian Federalism", to be found at pages 103 and 104 above.

Chapter 28

The Proposals of the Government of Canada for Basic Constitutional Change, October 1980

Prefatory Note

During the first week of October 1980, the Government of Canada introduced into the Canadian House of Commons a "Proposed Resolution for a Joint Address to Her Majesty the Queen respecting the Constitution of Canada", which included a fully drafted text of their proposals for certain basic constitutional changes, under the title of the Constitution Act, 1980. *As an invited commentator, I have published and signed two newspaper articles concerned with these changes. The first was in anticipation of them, in the* Toronto Star *for August 4, 1980. The issues expected did in fact arise in October when the firm proposals were made. After the specifics of them were known, I published further criticsm of them in the Kingston* Whig-Standard *for October 8, 1980.*

These articles are reprinted here in the order in which they appeared. In them I apply the principles and doctrines concerning basic constitutional change set out in Chapters 5 and 6 of these essays. Concerning the powers of Canadian courts related to some of these issues, the reader should also refer to the views of the late Mr. Justice Ivan C. Rand given at the end of Chapter 23.

W. R. L.

From the Toronto Star, August 4, 1980, p. A8.*

Problems of the proper method for amending the basic elements of Canada's constitution are naturally front and centre in the country's current constitutional debate. We are considering such changes as a new division of ordinary legislative powers in the field of electronic telecommunications, new specially entrenched language rights, and a new and different second chamber for the Parliament of Canada to replace the present Senate. Such changes cannot be made by a simple majority statute in a single legislative chamber, whether it is the

---

*This is the text of the original manuscript submitted by the author to the Star. What appeared in the newspaper was a slightly edited version of this to make it a little shorter. There were no changes in substance.

Parliament of Canada or a Provincial Legislature; rather, they require resort to an extraordinary legislative process for constitutional amendment which cannot be operated either easily or often. In this way the basic provisions of Canada's constitution are protected against frequent changes by simple majority. Such special procedures in constitutions, especially federal ones, typically require multiple consents or specially large majorities or both. Note also that these are democratic processes, based on existing elected legislatures and governments, which require a high degree of well-distributed consensus to authorize changes of a fundamental character. For example, basic constitutional amendment in the United States of America requires a two-thirds majority in both Houses of Congress, followed by the consents of three-quarters of the fifty States; the latter consents being ascertained by voting in the State Legislatures or in a State-wide referendum.

Canada has a similar special process that must be followed if any of the basics of her present federal and parliamentary constitution are to be changed. Indeed, we have had such a process for many years, but it is not to be found in the *British North America Act*, passed by the British Parliament in 1867. At that time the supremacy of the British Parliament for overseas territories was taken for granted; so that Canadians assumed that, as and when changes in the *B.N.A. Act* were needed, they would simply ask the British authorities to obtain the appropriate amendments from the Parliament at Westminster. Nevertheless, a Canadian law of amendment did grow up, after 1867, and outside the *B.N.A. Act*, about the conditions necessary to be met for a proper request of this kind to be sent to London. The rules concerned took form over a long period of years by virtue of official practice, custom, precedent and convention, which, for such a fundamental process, are regular sources of law and are recognized as such by the courts. The end result, our present special amending procedure, is this. When a basic amendment to Canada's federal constitution is proposed in Canada, it must have the approval of the federal parliament and the consent of all the provincial governments, whereupon a request is conveyed to the British Parliament in London that it should change the *B.N.A. Act* in the terms requested from Canada. Invariably the British Parliament has accepted and acted upon such a request, thus implementing the change desired.

There is no space here to trace the historical steps whereby the system was established. In any event, the resulting rules for amendment have been gathered together and given their best expression in a White Paper of the Government of Canada on the subject of amendment, tabled in the Canadian House of Commons on Feburary, 1965, under the name of the Honourable Guy Favreau, then Minister of Justice. The rules are stated as four principles, which are worth quotation in full.

> The first general principle that emerges in the foregoing resume is that although an enactment by the United Kingdom is necessary to amend the British North America Act, such action is taken only upon formal request from Canada. No Act of the United Kingdom Parliament affecting Canada is therefore passed unless it is requested and consented to by Canada. Conversely, every amendment requested by Canada in the past has been enacted.

The second general principle is that the sanction of Parliament is required for a request to the British Parliament for an amendment to the British North America Act. This principle was established early in the history of Canada's constitutional amendments, and has not been violated since 1895. The procedure invariably is to seek amendments by a joint Address of the Canadian House of Commons and Senate to the Crown.

The third general principle is that no amendment to Canada's Constitution will be made by the British Parliament merely upon the request of a Canadian province. A number of attempts to secure such amendments have been made, but none has been successful. The first such attempt was made as early as 1868, by a province which was at that time dissatisfied with the terms of Confederation. This was followed by other attempts in 1869, 1874 and 1887. The British Government refused in all cases to act on provincial government representations on the grounds that it should not intervene in the affairs of Canada except at the request of the federal government representing all of Canada.

The fourth general principle is that the Canadian Parliament will not request an amendment directly affecting federal-provincial relationships without prior consultation and agreement with the provinces. This principle did not emerge as early as others but since 1907, and particularly since 1930, has gained increasing recognition and acceptance. The nature and the degree of provincial participation in the amending process, however, have not lent themselves to easy definition.

We should note that the authority and legitimacy of these principles has been supported in two important ways. When the Favreau White Paper was tabled in the House of Commons, Prime Minister Pearson stated that his Government had consulted the Provinces about the text of it, and they all agreed that it was accurate. So, the Favreau White Paper is an agreed Federal-Provincial document. Secondly, the Supreme Court of Canada has recently quoted these principles with approval, and has used them, especially the fourth one, to assist it to reach the conclusion that the Senate of Canada could not be abolished or fundamentally altered simply by a statute of the Parliament of Canada. This judgment of the Court, given on December 21, 1979, was unanimous and is a landmark decision in our constitutional jurisprudence. Strange to say, little attention has been paid to its significance to date, so further comments are in order here.

In 1949, at the request of the Canadian Government and Parliament alone, the British Parliament had put a new Section 91(1) in the *B.N.A. Act* to the effect that the Canadian Parliament would henceforth, by one of its own statutes, have power to amend "the Constitution of Canada" except as regards the legislative powers assigned to the Provinces, or as regards rights or privileges of a constitutional character granted or secured to the Legislature or the Government of a Province. (There were certain other express exceptions as well, but the status of the Senate was not one of them). In 1978, the Government of Canada claimed that, by virtue of the new Section 91(1), it could, by securing the passage of a simple Canadian statute, abolish the Senate and replace it with a very different second chamber. There was doubt about this, and the question was referred to the Supreme Court of Canada. The Court held that the phrase "Constitution of Canada" in Section 91(1), given its context, referred merely to "housekeeping" changes concerning the central Government and Parliament of

Canada and nothing more. The Court further made it plain that compliance with the fourth general principle of the Favreau White Paper was necessary for an amendment abolishing the Senate. In the light of our constitutional history about the nature and function of the Senate, basic change in that body was a matter "directly affecting federal-provincial relationships". So, in effect, the Court has said that the fourth principle of the Favreau White Paper is still fully operative and controls matters directly concerned with the essentials of Canada's federal union. Such matters are simply not within the reach of Section 91(1) of the *B.N.A. Act*.

Now, in the light of what has been explained up to this point, we can reach certain critical conclusions about our current problems of patriation and amendment. As I see it, we have two things that currently we wish to do in these respects. First, we wish to eliminate the part the British Parliament still plays in the present Canadian process for special amendment, purely formal though that part now seems to be. Secondly, we wish to change the substantial requirements of the amending process so that it is somewhat less rigid than the present rule for unanimous consent of the Provinces, in addition to the approval of the Parliament of Canada, for all matters directly affecting federal-provincial relationships. A typical proposal having these objectives may be found in the "Beige Paper" of the Quebec Provincial Liberal Party concerning constitutional reform, published early in 1980. They proposed patriation and a less rigid amending procedure as follows:

> that proposed basic amendments must be adopted by the House of Commons of the Parliament of Canada, and also be approved by "all provinces which contain at least 25% of the Canadian population [Ontario and Quebec], by two of the four Atlantic Provinces and two of the four Western Provinces, including one of the two most populous provinces in each region".

(This is virtually the same as the Victoria Charter proposal on amendment in 1971).

In summary then, meaningful reform of our constitutional amending process for basic matters means bringing the process home so that all the steps it involves can be taken in Canada by Canadian governments and parliamentary bodies (patriation), and also relaxing somewhat the present requirements for unanimous consent of all the Provinces. The present necessity for the concurrent approval of the Parliament of Canada, or at least of the House of Commons, would of course be continued. It is not impossible to meet the present requirement for provincial unanimity, we have done so a few times int he past; but it is quite difficult and a less rigid formula seems preferable, given the need and pressure for change in the modern world. But now we encounter another fundamental constitutional principle; that the present formula for bringing about basic constitutional amendment must be complied with one last time to establish a new and different formula for this purpose. Then, for any basic amendments *after that*, compliance with the new formula is not only sufficient but is required. In other words, use of the old method one last time is necessary to put a new method in place. The element of continuity thereby ensured is a requirement of the rule of law itself. So our present situation is that one last request in accordance with the Favreau White Paper principles should go to London, if we would patriate the amending process and relax somewhat its requirements for provincial unanimity.

Now the question arises: If we request changes from London in these terms, are we asking for something that "directly affects federal-provincial relationships"? To my mind the answer is obviously yes, indeed we are. Surely nothing more directly affects basic federal-provincial relationships than a change in substance in the system whereby those very relationships may legitimately be altered. Accordingly I conclude that the Federal Government and Parliament cannot proceed unilaterally to accomplish patriation by means of a new and domestic amending formula obtained from the British Parliament by one last request to London. My opinion is that it would be unconstitutional for them to attempt to do so, and by "unconstitutional" I mean contrary to our present constitutional law. I am here referring to a change in the amending formula along the lines of the proposals of the Victoria Charter of 1971 or the Quebec Liberal Party's "Beige Paper" of 1980. I am saying that unilateralism would be constitutionally ineffectual for such change, and I expect Canadian Courts would say so, if and when the question was put to them, as it could be easily enough. In most Provinces, the question could be referred to the Provincial Court of Appeal by the respective Provincial Governments, whence a further appeal could be taken to the Supreme Court of Canada. Or, the Federal Government could refer the matter directly to the Supreme Court of Canada as it did in 1978 in the case concerning the Senate.

On the other hand, patriation by means of a new and domestic amending formula could be accomplished if the Provinces agreed and the Parliament of Canada approved one last request to London to this effect. This could be done in isolation, that is as a separate operation that asked for this and this alone, so far as strict constitutional law is concerned. But the present political situation in Canada seems to call for a different approach. Most of the Provinces apparently prefer that a considerable package of basic constitutional reforms should be fully agreed upon in Canada, including as just one item patriation by means of a new and domestic amending formula, and that then the complete package should be sent on its final trip to London. However difficult, I believe this is much the better way to proceed, and we should strive mightily for such agreement. So far as the constitutional law point is concerned, the inclusion in the last request to London of such other things as changes in the federal division of legislative powers, new specially entrenched human rights clauses, or a new second chamber for the central parliament, would simply confirm the constitutional need for the consent of all the Provinces, remembering always that the approval as well of the Parliament of Canada is also required.

There is now one final constitutional law question that should be asked. Is there a constitutional way to accomplish patriation of the *B.N.A. Act* at the request of the Government and Parliament of Canada only, that is, without the prior consent of the Provinces having been obtained? In my opinion there is one such way, involving a change in matters of form only, which might be described as simple patriation. For this, the last request from the Parliament of Canada to London should be confined to eliminating thereafter the need for a British statute in our amending process and nothing more. This could be done by providing a new procedure entirely local to Canada whereby all the formal steps necessary to implement later amendments could be completed in Canada. This would be a change in form only, because in substance this presumes that the rules about the *consents needed* remain the same as before. For example, if federal-provincial relationships were directly affected by a proposed amendment after simple patriation, the Parliament of Canada would still have to approve and all the Provinces would still have to agree. *If they did*, then the proposed amendment would take effect when these consents had been certified and proclaimed within Canada according to the new domestic formalities. It does seem to me that simple patriation on this plan does not directly affect federal-provincial relationships as a matter of substance, and that therefore consent of the Provinces would not be required. At least there would be a good case for this position. That is, I think there is a good chance that the Courts would accept this distinction between form and substance, with the result indicated. Throughout Canadian constitutional history, it has been legitimate to secure amendments to the *B.N.A. Act* at the request of the Canadian Parliament alone when federal-provincial relations were *not* directly affected. Our present need for a meaningful range of substantial constitutional change is very real, and simple patriation as an isolated measure would not do anything directly to meet this need. Nevertheless it might well be worth doing to prevent serious embarrassment for the British and for Canadians in the future.

Simple patriation, even by itself, would have one major virtue. So long as the British remain involved in our basic amending process, even formally, the danger exists that they may be put in the position of having to make substantive decisions about purely Canadian affairs, whether they like it or not. Suppose the worst situation from the British point of view. Suppose the Canadian Government and Parliament request an amendment from London that directly affects federal-provincial relationships, with one or more of the Provinces disagreeing and dissenting. What then does the British Parliament do? If it passes the amendment in spite of the Provincial dissents, it is backing the Canadian Government's position in the controversy. If it refuses to pass the amendment it would be approving the Provincial dissents and maintaining the status quo. The danger of this potential dilemma becoming reality is not remote, because it is by no means clear that either the present Canadian Government or the present British Government accepts the binding constitutional force of the fourth Favreau White Paper principle. Anyway, my view is now clear that both of them should accept it and act accordingly. Thus, I say that the Canadian Parliament should not send such a request to London in the first place, but that, if it does, the British Parliament should then ignore it as an improper request and do nothing. I consider the British as well as the Canadians are obliged to read and respect the fourth Favreau White Paper principle. Earlier I referred to the *Sen-*

ate Reference Case in the Supreme Court of Canada. The Supreme Court did not specifically address the point I am now dealing with, but it did approve the fourth Favreau White Paper principle. What I am now suggesting is that the reasoning I have just spelled out is a logical and reasonable implication of the fourth principle.

This leads to my final point, a combination of constitutional and political considerations. The last thing Canadians should ever do is to go to London for basic constitutional change against a background of constitutional disarray and dissent in Canada. This would be most unfair to the British and very embarrassing for them and for us. These are not their problems and they would have been glad to be rid of them long ago. That they still have them is our fault and not theirs. Moreover, for Canadians to go to London in these circumstances would be most humiliating. What would be left of our self-respect as citizens of an independent country in the modern world if we caused and promoted controversy in the British Parliament about these purely Canadian issues?

There is wisdom in the fourth principle of the Favreau White Paper. In seeking basic constitutional change, we should not go near London (as we must do one last time) unless and until we have first reached full agreement within Canada on these constitutional issues vital to the federal nature and the independence of our country. If such agreement is not forthcoming, then, as a last resort, I would favour simple patriation on the initiative of the Government and Parliament of Canada; this at least would keep our disagreements at home.

From the Kingston Whig-Standard, October 8 1980, p. 1.

The basic provisions of a country's constitution are first principles that develop out of the whole course of its history about the right way to do things. This is especially true of a country like Canada with a federal constitution resting on democratic parliamentary institutions and the cabinet system, at both the provincial and the national levels of government.

The present Government of Canada has just published its constitutional proposals in which it specifies certain fundamental changes that it wants in the nature of Canada's federal union and sets forth the methods whereby it proposes to accomplish these changes. The Federal Government and its legal advisers claim and believe that its proposed methods are in accord with Canada's basic and established constitutional principles, but, as a life-long scholar of these things, my position is that their proposed methods do not comply with those principles. There is no space here to argue fully the case for my position, but I shall give a brief outline of what it is and indicate some of the reasons that support it.

An extraordinary domestic amending procedure for the basic elements of Canada's constitution was not included in the *B.N.A. Act* passed by the British Parliament in 1867 because, in those colonial days, it was considered that it would be easy to get the British to make such amendments in the British Parliament itself, on request from Canada. This proved to be true enough, and quite a number of amendments were secured in this way. But also over the years, by usage, custom and precedent, rules grew up concerning the conditions necessary to be met for a proper request to be sent from the Canadian Parliament to London. These principles were best expressed in the Favreau White Paper on the history of constitutional amendment published by the Government of Canada in 1965. There were four of them and the fourth principle is the one that concerns us now. It provided "that the Canadian Parliament will not request an amendment directly affecting federal-provincial relationships without prior consultation and agreement with the provinces". So far, this principle has always been complied with, and the British Parliament concurrently developed the rule that they changed the *B.N.A. Act* only in response to a proper request from Canada.

This brings us to the present situation, as of Thursday last. The Trudeau Government now proposes two types of basic constitutional change—the special entrenchment of certain specified human rights and freedoms, and also new methods for amending the basic elements of our constitution in Canada. In my opinion, both changes directly affect federal-provincial relationships and so require not only the approval of the Parliament of Canada but as well the agreement of all the Provincial Governments. New specially entrenched rights reduce the powers of our parliamentary bodies, both Provincial and Federal, to make legal changes by ordinary statute. Special entrenchment makes the full and final definition of such rights dependent on judicial interpretation and thus increases the powers and responsibilities of the courts. This is certainly basic change in the nature of our federal union, and so falls under the fourth Favreau principle. Yet the Trudeau Government is requesting the British Parliament to make these changes without the consent of most of the Provinces.

Coming now to the amending process itself, the Trudeau Government is proposing that there should be new procedures for amendment starting two years after patriation. For the first two years, if their plan takes effect, they propose to retain the unanimity principle and to make basic changes only by the consent of all the Provincial Legislatures and the Parliament of Canada. If they stopped with that, their plan would be constitutional because in substance this would be compliance with the fourth Favreau principle. But they do not stop there. At the end of two years they propose that the amending process will change to a somewhat more flexible formula. At that point, we get either one of two formulae.

(1) The Victoria Formula of 1971, which calls for the consent of the Parliament of Canada, the consent of Ontario, the consent of Quebec, the consent of two of the four Atlantic Provinces and the consent of two of the four Western Provinces, provided that in the case of the Atlantic Provinces the two consenting Provinces comprise 50% of the population of the region, and the same for the two consenting Provinces in the West.

(2) An amending formula agreed upon by eight of the ten Provinces comprising 80% of the population of the country, provided this formula wins out in a national referendum in competition with the Victoria Formula.

But there is more. Separate from and in addition to the foregoing formula, there is an alternative method that definitely goes into effect. The Federal Government and Parliament will have the power to put any constitutional amendment they wish to a national referendum, and the amendment passes if it secures a majority over-all in Canada, and a majority in a combination of several of the Provinces, for example, assuming that the Victoria Formula has gone into effect, a majority in each of the Provinces whose consent would be required under that Formula, namely, Ontario, Quebec, two of the four Atlantic Provinces and two of the four Western Provinces, as explained earlier. Thus, the Federal Government and Parliament would be able to by-pass and disregard completely all the Provincial Governments and Provincial Legislatures.

I can now spell out the reasons why I consider these proposed changes to be contrary to constitutional law. The method of instituting them should comply with the fourth Favreau principle requiring unanimous consent of the Provinces as well as of the Parliament of Canada. To get new methods of amendment you have to employ the old method of amendment one last time. To my mind, the rule of law itself requires this element of continuity. Moreover, the present requirement for unanimity has been supported by high authority. The fourth Favreau White Paper principle was quoted with approval by the Supreme Court of Canada in the *Senate Reference Case*, December 21, 1979, though this case did not concern directly the situation that confronts us now, involving as it does the British Parliament as well as the Canadian Parliament.

So, whether I am right or wrong, there are good grounds for considering the proposed *Constitution Act, 1980* to be unconstitutional. I suspect that at some point the issue will have to go to court, because such uncertainty has to be cleared up and this is the only way to do it.

I regret having come to these conclusions. Provided legitimate methods of change are used, I am in favour of patriation, of a good Charter of Human Rights, and of the Victoria Charter for amendment. I have said so many times over the years. But do the ends justify the means? The methods the Trudeau Government is now proposing seem to me to be dangerous. The ongoing success of our Canadian Federal System depends on very extensive co-operative plans and measures at the federal-provincial inter-governmental level. This process is continuous and depends on mutual trust and goodwill. This means the Federal Government should treat the Provinces as partners and not as adversaries and should seek the widest possible consensus. It has not been doing either of these things lately.

Looking ahead to the next few weeks and months, it does not seem to me that compliance with the unanimity principle one last time is out of reach. Suitable opting-in provisions would establish such compliance concerning the proposed Charter of Rights, by limiting its impact to Provinces that consent. Also, the events of the summer suggest that a new and more flexible amending procedure might well be fully agreed upon in renewed negotiations among the First Ministers. Every effort should be made along these lines by responsible Ministers, and by Members of Parliament and of the Legislatures generally.

342.71 LED
Lederman, W. R. (William
Continuing Canadian
33292000124960   PA

APR   2012

T - - 2009

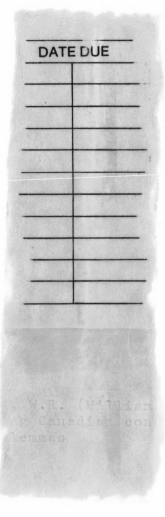

DATE DUE